SECTION 1983 LITIGATION: CLAIMS, DEFENSES, AND FEES

1989 Cumulative Supplement No. 1
Current to December 31, 1988

MARTIN A. SCHWARTZ
Professor of Law
Touro College–Jacob D. Fuchsberg Law Center
Member of the Bar of the State of New York

JOHN E. KIRKLIN
Director of Litigation
Civil Division
The Legal Aid Society of New York
Member of the Bar of the State of New York

Discard supplement labeled "1988 Cumulative Supplement" and replace with this softbound cumulative supplement.

AF675492

WILEY

Wiley Law Publications
JOHN WILEY & SONS
New York · Chichester · Brisbane · Toronto · Singapore

Copyright © 1987, 1988, 1989 by John Wiley & Sons, Inc.

All rights reserved. Published simultaneously in Canada.

Reproduction or translation of any part of this work beyond that permitted by Section 107 or 108 of the 1976 United States Copyright Act without the permission of the copyright owner is unlawful. Requests for permission or further information should be addressed to the Permissions Department, John Wiley & Sons, Inc.

This publication is designed to provide accurate and authoritative information in regard to the subject matter covered. It is sold with the understanding that the publisher is not engaged in rendering legal, accounting, or other professional service. If legal advice or other expert assistance is required, the services of a competent professional person should be sought. *From a Declaration of Principles jointly adopted by a Committee of the American Bar Association and a Committee of Publishers.*

ISBN 0-471-50940-X

Printed in the United States of America.

10 9 8 7 6 5 4 3 2 1

PREFACE

What we stated at the outset of the last supplement still holds true: the law of § 1983 litigation and § 1988 attorneys' fees continues to develop at a rapid pace. The courts are issuing large numbers of decisions, often involving important and difficult questions of law. Despite the already existing extensive body of law, there appears to be an unlimited number of nuances and new applications. One gets the sense that the resolution of each issue generates several others in need of solution. For these reasons, and because there are many important differences from circuit to circuit, in preparing this supplement we generally opted for inclusion rather than exclusion. In addition, because currency is so vital in this field, we have moved to a semiannual supplement schedule.

For its present (October 1988) term, the United States Supreme Court has compiled a staggering plenary docket of cases dealing with § 1983 litigation and § 1988 attorneys' fees. By the time this supplement was in its final stages of preparation (March 1989), the Supreme Court had already decided the following major cases, which are covered in the appropriate chapters:

Chapter 3: *De Shaney v. Winnebago County,* 57 U.S.L.W. 4218 (U.S. Feb. 22, 1989) (state does not have a constitutional obligation to protect child threatened with parental abuse).

Chapter 4: *City of Canton v. Harris,* 57 U.S.L.W. 4270 (U.S. Feb. 28, 1989) (municipal liability may be based upon deliberately indifferent training of police officers which is direct cause of violation of federal rights).

Chapter 5: *NCAA v. Tarkanian,* 109 S. Ct. 454 (1988) (NCAA's successful efforts to induce state university to suspend its basketball coach did not constitute state action).

Chapter 10: *Owens v. Okure,* 109 S. Ct. 573 (1989) (where state has more than one personal injury limitations period, federal court should select general personal injuries period or, if none exists, the residual period).

Chapter 21: *Blanchard v. Bergeron,* 57 U.S.L.W. 4191 (U.S. Feb. 21, 1989) (contingent fee agreement between plaintiff and counsel does not establish maximum fees recoverable under 42 U.S.C. § 1988).

In addition to these cases, the Supreme Court granted plenary review in the following cases involving § 1983 litigation and § 1988 attorneys' fees, which are expected to be decided by the end of the October 1988 term.

PREFACE

Chapter 3: *Kentucky v. Thompson,* below 833 F.2d 614 (6th Cir. 1987) – definition of liberty interests with respect to prison visitors.
Question presented: 56 U.S.L.W. 3874
Review granted: June 27, 1988

Brower v. Inyo County, below 817 F.2d 540 (9th Cir. 1987) – whether police use of blind roadblock resulting in death of fleeing motorist was a seizure within meaning of Fourth Amendment?
Question presented: 56 U.S.L.W. 3873
Review granted: June 27, 1988

Graham v. Connor, below 827 F.2d 945 (4th Cir. 1987) – constitutional standard for excessive force/arrest claims.
Question presented: 57 U.S.L.W. 3270
Review granted: October 3, 1988

Chapter 5: *Will v. Michigan Department of State Police,* below 428 Mich. 540, 410 N.W.2d 749 (1987) – is the state a § 1983 "person" which may be sued in state court?
Question presented: 56 U.S.L.W. 3711
Review granted: May 23, 1988

Chapter 6: *Gilhool v. Murth,* below 839 F.2d 113 (3d Cir. 1988) – whether the Education of the Handicapped Act operates to waive the Eleventh Amendment.
Question presented: 57 U.S.L.W. 3200
Review granted: October 3, 1988

Chapter 10: *Hardin v. Straub,* below 836 F.2d 549 (6th Cir. 1987) (following *Higley v. Michigan Department of Corrections,* 835 F.2d 623 (6th Cir. 1987)) – is state rule which tolls the limitations period for prisoners during incarceration inconsistent with § 1983?
Question presented: 57 U.S.L.W. 3277
Review granted: October 11, 1988

Chapter 15: *Texas State Teachers' Association v. Garland,* below 837 F.2d 190 (5th Cir. 1988) – validity of Fifth Circuit "central issue" prevailing party test.
Question presented: 57 U.S.L.W. 3198
Review granted: October 3, 1988

Chapter 16: *Independent Federation of Flight Attendants v. Zipes,* below 846 F.2d 434 (7th Cir. 1988) – propriety of Title VII fee award against intervenor union which unsuccessfully contested settlement agreement.
Question presented: 57 U.S.L.W. 3466
Review granted: January 17, 1989

Chapter 18: *Missouri v. Jenkins,* below 838 F.2d 260 (8th Cir. 1988) – whether Eleventh Amendment bars upward adjustment to fee award to compensate for the delay in payment; computation of fees for services performed by paralegals and law clerks.
Question presented: 57 U.S.L.W. 3249
Review granted: October 11, 1988

PREFACE

Other: *Neitske v. Williams,* below 827 F.2d 304 (7th Cir. 1988) – standard for sua sponte dismissal of pro se civil rights complaints.
Question presented: 57 U.S.L.W. 3198
Review granted: October 3, 1988

Coverage of this supplement includes cases decided by the United States Supreme Court as of March 3, 1989 and lower court decisions reported up to December 31, 1988.

The authors gratefully acknowledge the assistance of Paul Seres and Michael Sheinberg, students at Touro College – Jacob D. Fuchsberg Law Center, for their assistance in the preparation of this manuscript.

April 1989

MARTIN A. SCHWARTZ
New Rochelle, New York

JOHN E. KIRKLIN
Larchmont, New York

NEW IN THIS SUPPLEMENT

Note to the Reader: Materials which appear only in the cumulative supplement are listed below. Materials new to *this* supplement are indicated by an asterisk (*) in the left margin in the list and throughout the supplement.

CHAPTER 1

THE STATUTE: ORIGINS, FUNCTION, JURISDICTION, AND CHOICE OF FORUM

§ 1.1 The Statute

Page 4, add before first full paragraph:

In 1986, 20,842 prisoner civil rights suits were filed in the federal district courts. "Most of this litigation has very little merit." *Del Raine v. Carlson,* 826 F.2d 698, 702 (7th Cir. 1987).

§ 1.2 Historical Background

Page 7, add to footnote 29:

* After observing that "[n]othing divides this Court like a section 1983 case[,]" Judge Vance, dissenting, criticizes the law of § 1983 as "confused and misguided" and in "doctrinal turmoil" and laments that too many section 1983 cases in federal court do not belong there. Jones v. Preuit & Mauldin, 851 F.2d 1321, 1335, 1338-1341 (11th Cir. 1988) (en banc) (dissenting opinion). *See also* Stefan v. Laurenitis, 695 F. Supp. 1330, 1340 (D. Mass. 1988) (referring to "an explosion of unsupportable" § 1983 suits and "cases where counsel attempted to cloak a violation of state law in the robes of a federal civil rights violation in hopes of recoving fees"). *But see* Morgan v. District of Columbia, 824 F.2d 1049, 1056 (D.C. Cir.) ("While section 1988 has reaped its share of criticism for encouraging federal intervention in local affairs, it remains ... the workhorse of civil rights litigation"), *reh'g denied,* 824 F.2d 1240 (D.C. Cir. 1987).

§ 1.3 Functional Role

Page 8, add to footnote 39:

Some courts still erroneously refer to § 1983 as a statute that confers jurisdiction. Shah v. County of Los Angeles, 797 F.2d 743, 745 n.2 (9th Cir. 1986); Morell v. Stone, 638 F. Supp. 163, 164 (W.D. Va. 1986).

Page 9, add to first full paragraph:

When plaintiff has a constitutional claim under § 1983, this is the exclusive remedy
and a *Bivens*-type claim may not be stated directly under the Constitution. *Thomas v.*
* *Shipka,* 818 F.2d 496 (6th Cir.), *modified,* 829 F.2d 570 (6th Cir. 1987).

Page 9, add at end of section:

§ A 1983 claim "is fully assignable if it arises in connection with an injury to the plaintiff's business or property." *Bay Ridge Utility District v. 4M Laundry,* 717 S.W.2d 92, 96 (Tex. Ct. App. 1986), citing *Nelson v. Knox,* 230 F.2d 483, 484 (6th Cir. 1956).

§ 1.3A Pleading the Claim (New)

A § 1983 claimant must plead specific facts; conclusory allegations will not suffice.
* *Fonte v. Board of Managers,* 848 F.2d 24 (2d Cir. 1988); *Colburn v. Upper Darby Township,* 838 F.2d 663 (3d Cir. 1988); *Alfaro Motors v. Ward,* 814 F.2d 883, 887 (2d Cir. 1987); *Barr v. Abrams,* 810 F.2d 358, 363 (2d Cir. 1987); *Pace Resources v. Shrewsbury Township,* 808 F.2d 1023 (3d Cir.), *cert. denied,* 107 S. Ct. 2482 (1987); *Chapman v. Detroit,* 808 F.2d 459 (6th Cir. 1986); *Jacquez v. Procunier,* 801 F.2d 789 (5th Cir. 1986). *Jacquez* cites to *Hobson v. Wilson,* 737 F.2d 1, 30 (D.C. Cir. 1984) ("every . . . circuit has articulated a requirement of particularity of pleading for civil rights complaints"), *cert. denied,* 470 U.S. 1084 (1985). In *Colburn v. Upper Darby Township,* 838 F.2d at 666, the Court stated that the "heightened specificity" requirement for § 1983 claims requires allegations of "specific conduct" which violates plaintiff's federal rights. Plaintiff need not provide proof of the claim at the pleading stage. The Court observed that plaintiffs and their counsel may have difficulty meeting the heightened pleading standard and, at the same time, complying with the "sanction rule," Rule 11 of the Federal Rules of Civil Procedures.

Most courts take the position that the complaint need not specifically refer to § 1983
as long as the essential elements of the claim are pleaded. *Americans United for*
Separation of Church and State v. School District, 835 F.2d 627 (6th Cir. 1987);
* *Armstrong v. Fairmont Community Hospital Association,* 684 F. Supp. 1486 (D. Minn.
1987); *United States v. Washington,* 626 F. Supp. 1405, 1426-27, 1445 n.17 (W.D. Wash.
* 1985); *L.K. v. Gregg,* 425 N.W.2d 813 (Minn. 1988); *Massey v. Shepack,* 12 Kan. App.
2d 770, 757 P.2d 329 (1988); *Packard v. Gordon,* 148 Vt. 579, 537 A.2d 140, 144 (1987);
Guardianship of Hurley, 394 Mass. 554, 476 N.E.2d 941 (1985); *Bryant Avenue Tenants'*
Association v. Koch, 511 N.Y.S.2d 279 (1st Dep't 1987), *aff'd,* 71 N.Y.2d 856, ____
N.E.2d ____, 527 N.Y.S.2d 743 (1988); *Maldonado v. Department of Public Welfare,*
* 223 Neb. 485, 391 N.W.2d 105 (1986). *See also Albert v. Carovano,* 851 F.2d 561, 571
n.3 (2d Cir. 1988) (en banc) (claim under 42 U.S.C. § 1981). *See contra, Ball v. School*
District, 641 F. Supp. 1 (W.D. Mich. 1986). The issue frequently arises in conjunction
with a motion for attorney's fees under 42 U.S.C. § 1988. See **§ 15.1**.

§ 1.4 Federal Court Jurisdiction

Page 11, add at end of section:

Under the *Rooker-Feldman* principle, a federal district court has no jurisdiction to review a state court judgment, not only as to state law claims determined by the state court, but also as to constitutional claims presented to the federal court that are "inextricably intertwined" with the state court determination. *Hale v. Harney,* 786 F.2d 688 (5th Cir. 1986).

The *Rooker-Feldman* doctrine, while barring individual challenges to state bar disciplinary determinations, does not preclude attacks on the validity of state bar rules. *Hefner v. Alexander,* 779 F.2d 277 (5th Cir. 1985). While observing the difficulty of applying this distinction, the Fifth Circuit found that it had jurisdiction over "several 'general constitutional challenges' " mounted by the plaintiff. *Nordgreen v. Hafter,* 789 F.2d 334, 337 (5th Cir.), *cert. denied,* 107 S. Ct. 177 (1986). In determining whether the challenge was to an individual determination or to the validity of a legislative enactment, the Third Circuit looked to substance rather than form. "[A] close examination of Stern's case demonstrates that, despite his attempt to draft his complaint in the form of a general challenge to a state court rule, he in reality is seeking review of a state court judgment in his particular case. This does not pass
* muster under *Rooker-Feldman.*" *Stern v. Nix,* 840 F.2d 208, 213 (3d Cir.), *cert. denied,* 109 S. Ct. 77 (1988).

Rooker-Feldman does not apply when there has been no final state court judgment. *Delahunty v. Hawaii,* 677 F. Supp. 1052 (D. Haw. 1987). When there is federal court jurisdiction over a state bar disciplinary matter, res judicata may provide an alternative basis for dismissal. *Czura v. Supreme Court of South Carolina,* 632 F. Supp. 267 (D.S.C. 1986), *aff'd,* 813 F.2d 644 (4th Cir. 1987).

If a federal court plaintiff accepts and does not attack the state court judgment, *Rooker-Feldman* does not apply. *Lewis v. School Board,* 820 F.2d 143 (5th Cir. 1987). Nevertheless, the former teacher's § 1983 claim in *Lewis* was barred by res judicata.

§ 1.5 Pendent Jurisdiction

Page 13, add new paragraph before boldface subsection title:

The Supreme Court dealt with the interplay of pendent and removal jurisdiction in *Carnegie-Mellon University v. Cohill,* 108 S. Ct. 614 (1988). In that case, plaintiffs alleged federal and state law claims in their state court complaint. Following removal, the federal court granted plaintiffs' motion to amend the complaint to delete the federal claims, leaving only the pendent state claims. The Supreme Court determined that under these circumstances the district court has discretion to dismiss or remand the pendent state claims. "[A] remand generally will be preferable to a dismissal when the statute of limitations on the plaintiff's state law claims has expired before the federal court has determined that it should relinquish jurisdiction over the case." *Id.* at 619.

In the course of its discussion, the Court in *Carnegie-Mellon* reiterated the principles of pendent jurisdiction established by *United Mine Workers v. Gibbs,* 383 U.S. 715 (1966). The Court indicated that the statement in *Gibbs* that "if the federal claims are dismissed before trial . . . the state claims should be dismissed as well" (*id.* at 718), was not meant to establish a mandatory bar but only to indicate that this will normally be the appropriate outcome following the exercise of discretion. 108 S. Ct. at 619.

The Eleventh Circuit ruled that since state law may not restrict the scope of federal court pendent jurisdiction, a state law providing for exclusive state court jurisdiction over a particular state claim cannot deprive the federal courts of pendent jurisdiction over that claim. *Thompkins v. Stuttgart School District,* 787 F.2d 439 (8th Cir. 1986).

* The district court's automatic dismissal of pendent state law claims in five different cases was reversible error because the exercise of pendent jurisdiction requires case-by-case discretion. *Perez v. Ortiz,* 849 F.2d 793 (2d Cir. 1988).

The doctrine of *Parratt v. Taylor,* 451 U.S. 527 (1981), does not require that a federal court decline pendent jurisdiction over a state law claim "simply because it rests on a state cause of action that provides the adequate post-deprivation remedy necessitating dismissal of the federal due process claim so long as the court has jurisdiction upon other grounds." *Wright v. Newsome,* 795 F.2d 964, 968 (11th Cir. 1986).

A district court declined to exercise pendent jurisdiction over state law negligence and gross negligence claims because they were "inconsistent and incompatible with civil rights claims and may confuse a jury." *Scott v. Rieht,* 690 F. Supp. 368, 372 (E.D. Pa. 1988).

A cross-claim for indemnification by the defendant police officer against the defendant City of New York was within the court's pendent jurisdiction. *Turk v. McCarthy,* 661 F. Supp. 1526 (E.D.N.Y. 1987). *See also Holman v. Walls,* 648 F. Supp. 947 (D. Del. 1986) (ancillary jurisdiction); § **14.17**.

Page 15, add to end of section:

The Eleventh Circuit ruled that there may be pendent party jurisdiction over a state law claim against a mayor. *Fundiller v. Cooper City,* 777 F.2d 1436, 1443 n.5 (11th Cir. 1985). Pendent party jurisdiction was also exercised in *Santella v. Grishaber,* 672 F. Supp. 321 (N.D. Ill. 1987) and *Montgomery v. Chicago,* 670 F. Supp. 230 (N.D. Ill. 1987).

A number of decisions, however, found that there is no pendent party jurisdiction in
* § 1983 actions. *Robinson v. Via,* 821 F.2d 913, 926 (2d Cir. 1987); *Mow v. Cheeseborough,* 696 F. Supp. 1360 (D. Haw. 1988) (no jurisdiction over defendants who are not § 1983 "persons"); *Washco v. Darby Borough Police Department,* 688 F. Supp. 1026 (E.D. Pa. 1988) (pendent plaintiff); *Donahey v. Wellman,* 687 F. Supp. 194 (W.D. Pa. 1988) (private defendants); *Hynson v. City of Chester,* 684 F. Supp. 1294 (E.D. Pa. 1988) (same); *Barton v. Gulf States Entertainment,* 655 F. Supp. 782 (M.D. La. 1987); *Rojas v. Alexander's Dep't Store,* 654 F. Supp. 856, 859 (E.D.N.Y. 1986); *Steele v. Stephan,* 633 F. Supp. 950 (D. Kan. 1986); *Sullivan v. Marshall,* 628 F. Supp. 1080 (D. Mass. 1985) (rejecting jurisdiction over the claim of a pendent plaintiff); *Nunnelley v. Douglas County,* 622 F. Supp. 124 (D. Nev. 1985); *Miletich v. Raley's,* 593 F. Supp. 124 (D. Nev. 1984). While the Seventh Circuit recognized that pendent party jurisdiction may apply in § 1983 actions, it stated that jurisdiction should not be

exercised with respect to a state law claim against an official who has been relieved of the obligation to stand trial on the § 1983 claim by successful assertion of qualified immunity. *Justice v. Town of Blackwell,* 820 F.2d 238 (7th Cir. 1987). In *Doe v. Bobbitt,* 682 F. Supp. 388 (N.D. Ill. 1988), the court determined that there may be pendent party jurisdiction over a defendent that is suable under § 1983, such as a municipality, but not over a defendant not suable under § 1983, such as a nonstate actor private
* party. In *Valliere v. Kaplan,* 694 F. Supp. 517 (N.D. Ill. 1988), the court found that it had pendent party jurisdiction against a municipality, but in its discretion declined that jurisdiction.

§ 1.6 State Court Jurisdiction

Page 15, add to first paragraph of section:

The Supreme Court reiterated that federal and state courts have concurrent jurisdiction over § 1983 claims. *Felder v. Casey,* 108 S. Ct. 2302 (1988); *Arkansas Writers' Project v. Ragland,* 107 S. Ct. 1722, 1730 (1987). A state court's lack of familiarity with § 1983 is not a basis for declining jurisdiction. *Seibring v. Parcell's, Inc.,* 159 Ill. App. 3d 376, 512 N.E.2d 394 (1987).

Citing this text, a federal district court observed that § 1983 claims are "routinely" litigated in the state courts. *Glover v. City of Portland,* 675 F. Supp. 398, 406 (M.D. Tenn. 1987).

Page 15, note 83, update Chamberlain v. Brown cite:

Chamberlain, overruled by Poling v. Goins, 713 S.W.2d 305 (Tenn. 1986) (holding that § 1983 actions may be brought and tried in Tennessee state courts).

Page 15, add to footnote 83:

The New York Court of Claims does not have jurisdiction over § 1983 claims. *Gittens v. New York,* 132 Misc. 2d 399, 504 N.Y.S.2d 969 (Ct. Cl. 1986).

§ 1.8 —Pertinent Factors

Page 19, add at end of section:

On the interplay of removal and pendent jurisdiction, *see Carnegie-Mellon University v. Cohill,* 108 S. Ct. 614 (1988), discussed in **§ 1.5** of this supplement.

Recent decisions confirm that state court § 1983 claims may be removed to federal
* court. *Dorsey v. City of Detroit,* 858 F.2d 338 (6th Cir. 1988); *Harris v. Birmingham Board of Education,* 817 F.2d 1525 (11th Cir. 1987); *Aben v. Dailwig,* 665 F. Supp. 523 (E.D. Mich. 1987); *Spencer v. South Florida Water Management District,* 657 F. Supp. 66 (S.D. Fla. 1986).

* When a § 1983 claim and a state law claim are removed to federal court, may the removal stand if the court declines pendent jurisdiction over the state claim? In

Harrison v. Texas Department of Corrections, 694 F. Supp. 226 (E.D. Tex. 1988), the court ruled that the action may be removed only if the federal claim is "separate and independent" of the state claim. When the two claims are not separate and independent, as in *Harrison,* the district court may remand the entire case to the state court.

CHAPTER 2

PERSONS PROTECTED

§ 2.2 Individuals

Page 22, add after carryover paragraph:

In a Second Circuit case, the plaintiffs were current and former members of the Ku
* Klux Klan bringing suit to vindicate their federal rights under § 1983. The Court observed the irony, since the original version of § 1983 was "passed in an effort to protect freedmen and loyal whites from deprivation of their constitutional 'rights, privileges, or immunities' at the hands of the Ku Klux Klan and cognate groups." *Wilkinson v. Forst,* 832 F.2d 1330, 1337 (2d Cir. 1987), *cert. denied,* 108 S. Ct. 1593 (1988).

Page 22, add to footnote 4:

Since a fetus is not a "person" protected by the Fourteenth Amendment, a § 1983 claim may not be based upon conduct which occurred while plaintiff was in utero. Ruiz Romero v. Gonzalez Caraballo, 681 F. Supp. 123 (D.P.R. 1988).

Page 22, add to second full paragraph:

Since a deceased is not a "person" who may bring a § 1983 action, a § 1983 claim may not be based upon violations of federal rights which occurred after a claimant's death. *Hudak v. D'Elia,* 120 A.D.2d 667, 502 N.Y.S.2d 261 (2d Dep't 1986).

§ 2.3 Entities

Page 26, add at end of section:

A corporation is a "person" protected by the due process clause. *San Bernardino Physicians' Services Medical Group v. San. Bernardino,* 825 F.2d 1404, 1407 (9th Cir. 1987).

The Eleventh Circuit adheres to the view that a municipal corporation is not a "person" which may bring suit under § 1983. *United States v. Alabama,* 791 F.2d 1450 (11th Cir. 1986), *cert. denied sub nom. Board of Trustees v. State Board,* 107 S. Ct. 1287 (1987); *Randolph County v. Alabama Power Co.,* 784 F.2d 1067 (11th Cir.), *modified,* 798 F.2d 425 (11th Cir. 1986), *cert. denied,* 107 S. Ct. 878 (1987). The Sixth Circuit, however, holds that the ruling in *Monell v. Department of Social Services,* 436 U.S. 658 (1978) – that municipal entities are proper § 1983 defendants – logically means that they are proper § 1983 plaintiffs as well. *South Macomb Disposal Authority v. Township,* 790 F.2d 500 (6th Cir. 1986). The court determined that whether municipalities may assert a constitutional claim depends upon the nature of the claim. They cannot assert violations of the privileges and immunities, equal protection, or due process clauses of the Fourteenth Amendment. In dicta, the court referred to cases allowing municipal bodies to bring suit under the supremacy clause.

* A municipality does not have standing to claim that state legislation violates its rights under the impairment of contracts clause. *Town of Charlestown v. United States,* 696 F. Supp. 800 (D.R.I. 1988).

A state agency cannot bring suit against the State to redress an uncompensated taking of property. *Board of Levee Commissioners v. Huls,* 852 F.2d 140 (5th Cir. 1988).

Two district court decisions held that while a conjugal partnership, an independent entity under Puerto Rico law, may be a proper § 1983 plaintiff, it did not have standing to assert a violation of its constitutional rights, because the right asserted belonged to a spouse and not to the partnership. *Rosario Nevarez v. Torres Gaztambide,* 633 F. Supp. 287 (D.P.R. 1986), *rev'd on other grounds,* 820 F.2d 525 (1st Cir. 1987); *Rodriguez Hernandez v. Almodovar,* 631 F. Supp. 960 (D.P.R. 1986). * *See also Soto Gomez v. Lopez-Feliciano,* 698 F. Supp. 28 (D.P. R. 1988) (conjugal partnership has standing to sue under § 1983 only if *it* has suffered direct injury as a result of deprivation of *its* constitutional rights); *Anaya Serbia v. Lavsell,* 646 F. Supp. 1236 (D.P.R. 1986).

Native American tribes are "other persons" which may bring suit under § 1983. *Lac Courte Oreilles Band v. Wisconsin,* 663 F. Supp. 682 (W.D. Wis.), *appeal dismissed,* 829 F.2d 601 (7th Cir. 1987).

§ 2.4 General Principles

Page 27, add after note 31 reference:

When standing is challenged on the basis of the pleadings, the Supreme Court accepts as true the material allegations of the complaint and construes them in plaintiff's favor. A party who contests the constitutionality of a legislative enactment must show a "realistic danger" of direct injury from its enforcement. While the record in this case leaves much to be desired in this regard, the Court applied the standard leniently because the case arose in a state court. In future cases, the parties should supplement the record to enable the Supreme Court to resolve the standing question with as much precision as possible. *Pernell v. San Jose,* 108 S. Ct. 849 (1988) (non-§ 1983 action).

The Supreme Court held that a school board member, who was sued in an official capacity, had no standing to appeal a district court judgment in his individual capacity, when the board determined not to appeal. *Bender v. Williamsport Area School District,* 475 U.S. 934, 106 S. Ct. 1326 (1986). The school board member did not have a sufficient personal stake in his individual capacity, because the suit against him in his official capacity was tantamount to suit against the entity under the teachings of *Brandon v. Holt,* 469 U.S. 464 (1985) and *Kentucky v. Graham,* 473 U.S. 159 (1985). See § **6.1**. "Generally speaking, members of collegial bodies do not have standing to perfect an appeal the body itself has declined to take." *Bender,* 106 S. Ct. at 1333.

Relying on *Bender,* the Supreme Court dismissed the appeal in *Karcher v. May,* 108 S. Ct. 388, 393 (1987). "The fact that Karcher and Orechio participated in this litigation in their official capacities as presiding officers on behalf of the legislature does not mean that they became parties in all of their personal and professional capacities." Justice White, concurring, noted that "we again leave for another day the issue whether individual legislators have standing to intervene and defend legislation for which they voted." *Id.* at 396 (White, J., concurring).

Page 27, add after third paragraph:

The Supreme Court found that a private physician did not have standing to defend the constitutionality of the Illinois abortion law which, inter alia, imposes criminal liability for the performance of an abortion under certain circumstances. *Diamond v. Charles,* 476 U.S. 54, 106 S. Ct. 1697 (1986). There was no standing "[b]ecause a private party whose own conduct is neither implicated nor threatened by a criminal statute has no judicially cognizable interest in the statute's defense . . . ." 106 S. Ct. at 1700.

The physician in *Diamond* was also denied third-party standing to assert his daughter's interest, because he had "not shown that his daughter is currently a minor or that she is otherwise incapable of asserting her own rights." *Id.* at 1706. "Nor can Diamond assert any constitutional rights of the unborn fetus. Only the State may invoke regulatory measures to protect that interest and only the State may invoke the power of the courts when those regulatory measures are subject to challenge." *Id.* at 1706.

"[W]hen a licensing statute vests unbridled discretion in a government official over whether to permit or deny expressive activity, one who is subject to the law may challenge it facially without the necessity of first applying for, and being denied, a license." *City of Lakewood v. Plain Dealer Publishing Co.,* 108 S. Ct. 2138, 2143 (1988).

§ 2.5 Injunctive and Declaratory Relief

Page 30, add at end of page:

The Supreme Court found that the plaintiff booksellers had standing to lodge a pre-enforcement facial challenge to an antipornography statute where the state did not suggest that the law would not be enforced and there was no reason to assume otherwise. Plaintiffs "alleged an actual and well-founded fear that the law will be enforced against them. Further, the alleged danger of the statute is, in large measure, one of self-censorship; a harm that can be realized even without an actual prosecution." *Virginia v. American Booksellers Association,* 108 S. Ct. 636, 642 (1988).

Applying the doctrine of *City of Los Angeles v. Lyons,* 461 U.S. 95 (1983), several courts denied plaintiffs standing to seek injunctive relief. *Brown v. Fauver,* 819 F.2d 395
* (3d Cir. 1987); *Travelers Social Club v. Pittsburgh,* 685 F. Supp. 929 (W.D. Pa. 1988); *Jones v. Bowman,* 664 F. Supp. 433 (N.D. Ind. 1987); *Alvarez v. Chicago,* 649 F. Supp. 43 (N.D. Ill. 1986); *Weisner v. Koch,* 632 F. Supp. 1369 (S.D.N.Y. 1986); *Minne v. Indiana,* 627 F. Supp. 1189 (N.D. Ind. 1986). Other decisions found *Lyons* distinguish-
* able and granted plaintiffs standing to seek injunctive relief. *Ward v. Portland,* 857 F.2d 1373 (9th Cir. 1988); *Goff v. Nix,* 803 F.2d 358, 361 n.6 (8th Cir. 1986), *cert. denied,* 108 S. Ct. 115 (1987); *Daryl H. v. Coler,* 801 F.2d 893, 896 n.3 (7th Cir. 1986); *Quinones v. Coler,* 651 F. Supp. 1028 (N.D. Ill. 1987). While the complaint in *Smith v. City of*

Fontana, 818 F.2d 1411 (9th Cir.), *cert. denied,* 108 S. Ct. 1311 (1987), did not establish a credible threat of future injury, plaintiffs were given leave to amend on remand because the complaint had been filed prior to the decision in *Lyons.*

Plaintiff demonstrated a sufficient threat of future enforcement of the contested ordinance, since he testified that he was willing to engage in the prohibited conduct in the future and had previously been arrested four times pursuant to the ordinance. *City of Houston v. Hill,* 107 S. Ct. 2502, 2508 n.7 (1987). In *Doe v. Duling,* 782 F.2d 1202 (4th Cir. 1986), the court found that plaintiffs had no standing to attack a criminal statute prohibiting fornication and cohabitation by unmarried persons because they were not subject to a realistic threat of prosecution.

While several courts found *Lyons* fully applicable to class actions, *Tucker v. Phyfer,* 819 F.2d 1030 (11th Cir. 1987); *Howard v. City of Greenwood,* 783 F.2d 1311, 1313 n.2 (5th Cir. 1986); *Schaefer v. Wilcock,* 676 F. Supp. 1092 (D. Utah 1987); *Strandell v. Jackson County,* 634 F. Supp. 824 (S.D. Ill. 1986), one court found that a named plaintiff with standing to seek damages may represent a class of persons seeking prospective relief. *Robinson v. Chicago,* 638 F. Supp. 186 (N.D. Ill. 1986).

§ 2.6 Rights of Third Parties; Organizations; Class Actions

Page 33, add at end of section:

When First Amendment rights are alleged, a party may assert the rights of others. *Virginia v. American Booksellers Ass'n,* 108 S. Ct. 636, 642 (1988) (booksellers permitted to allege infringement of First Amendment rights of bookbuyers).

A physician contesting a state abortion law was denied standing to assert the rights of his daughter and an unborn fetus. It was not shown that his daughter was incapable of asserting her own rights, and only the state may seek to protect the fetus. *Diamond v. Charles,* 106 S. Ct. 1697 (1986).

The Supreme Court applied the three-part test for association standing established by *Hunt v. Washington Apple Advertising Commission,* 432 U.S. 333 (1977). *New York State Club Association v. City of New York,* 108 S. Ct. 2225 (1988). The Court determined that a nonprofit association had standing to sue on behalf of its member associations, because those member associations had standing to sue on behalf of their individual members. The Court also reiterated that the state courts have power to fashion their own standing and justiciability rules free of the Article III "case" and "controversy" limitations. *Id.* at 2231 n.2.

CHAPTER 3

PROTECTED RIGHTS

§ 3.1 Protected Rights – Introduction

Page 36, add at end of section:

The Fifth Circuit ruled that consent decrees do not establish rights enforceable under § 1983. *Green v. McKaskle,* 788 F.2d 1115 (5th Cir. 1986). "[A] remedial court order, standing alone, does not serve as a basis for § 1983 liability." *Id.* at 1124. *Green* reasons that remedial decrees correct constitutional violations, do not create or enlarge constitutional rights, and are enforceable by contempt rather than through § 1983.

* An allegation of a conspiracy is not sufficient to state a claim under § 1983. The plaintiff must allege a conspiracy to violate a federally protected right. *Easter House v. Felder,* 852 F.2d 901, 920 (7th Cir.), *reh'g granted,* 861 F.2d 494 (7th Cir. 1988).

§ 3.2 Constitutional Rights: Protected and Unprotected Rights

Page 37, add after carryover paragraph:

Elections

In an action brought by unsuccessful candidates for political office, the Fourth Circuit ruled that § 1983 damage actions normally do not lie for "garden variety election irregularities," even if of constitutional dimension. *Hutchinson v. Miller,* 797 F.2d 1279, 1283 (4th Cir. 1986), *cert. denied,* 107 S. Ct. 1295 (1987). To rule otherwise "could intrude on the role of states and Congress to conduct elections and adjudge results." 797 F.2d at 1285. In a similar vein, the Seventh Circuit determined that candidates for political office who seek relief under § 1983 for election irregularities must show willful misconduct and not mere negligence. *Bodine v. Elkhart County*
* *Election Board,* 788 F.2d 1270 (7th Cir. 1986). The Ninth Circuit also endorsed a "restrained approach to election challenges," holding that an individual who participates in an extensive election campaign with full knowledge of the alleged infirmity, and who makes no attempt to seek equitable relief to correct it, may not recover damages under § 1983. *Soules v. Kauaians for Nukolii Campaign Committee,* 849 F.2d 1176 (9th Cir. 1988). Under these circumstances the damages were "self-inflicted." *Id.* at 1182.

The Eleventh Circuit also takes the position that "garden variety" election disputes do not give rise to § 1983 claims. *Thompson v. Woodall,* 819 F.2d 1052, 1053 (11th Cir. 1987); *Curry v. Baker,* 802 F.2d 1302 (11th Cir.), *cert. dismissed,* 479 U.S. 1023 (1986).

PROTECTED RIGHTS

Property Interests

While contracts can create constitutionally protected property rights, they do not always do so; the farther away one gets from employment contracts, the "prime protected category," the less likely it becomes that a contract will create a constitutionally created property interest. *San Bernardino Physicians' Services Medical Group v. San Bernardino,* 825 F.2d 1404 (9th Cir. 1987) (contract between physicians' group and county to supply medical service to the county did not create a protected property right).

The Second and Sixth Circuits cited *San Bernardino* with approval. *S&D Maintenance Co. v. Goldin,* 844 F.2d 962 (2d Cir. 1988); *Ramsey v. Board of Education,* 844 F.2d 1268 (6th Cir. 1988). The Second Circuit, concerned that every action by a state alleged to be in breach of contract would give rise to a § 1983 action if the concept of entitlement is given a broad interpretation, opined that ordinary commercial contracts are "qualitatively different" from public employment and essential public benefits. "And even if all public contract rights warranted the procedural protection of due process, there would be a substantial argument that in most circumstances post-deprivation state court remedies would provide all the process that is due." *S&D Maintenance Co.,* 844 F.2d at 966.

Quoting *San Bernardino* with approval, the Sixth Circuit, while finding that employment benefits, such as accumulated sick leave, may constitute a deprivation of property, held "that an interference with a property interest in a pure benefit of employment, as opposed to an interest in the tenure nature of the employment itself, is an interest that can be and should be redressed by a state breach of contract action and not be a federal action under section 1983." *Ramsey,* 844 F.2d at 1274-75.

The authors believe that the Supreme Court procedural due process cases provide no basis for distinguishing between employment contracts and other contracts with respect to the existence of a protected property interest. *See Medical Laundry Service* * *v. Board of Trustees,* 840 F.2d 840 (11th Cir.), *cert. denied,* 109 S. Ct. 77 (1988) (contract to provide laundry service to state university created property interest). Of course, the strength of the private interest is a relevant factor in the *Matthew v.* * *Eldridge,* 424 U.S. 319 (1976), test used to determine the process which is due. When the plaintiff asserted due process claims arising out of a breach of contract, the district court concluded that (1) the procedural due process claim is defeated by an adequate state remedy for breach of contract, and (2) a state actor's breach of contract does not violate substantive due process. *Pinehurst Enterprises v. Town of Southern Pines,* 690 F. Supp. 444 (M.D.N.C. 1988).

There is dicta in *S&D Maintenance Co.* that "rare cases might be imagined where denial of a contract right, if deemed to be Fourteenth Amendment property, would violate substantive due process." 844 F.2d at 966, citing *Schaper v. City of Huntsville,* 813 F.2d 709, 716-18 n.8 (5th Cir. 1987) (collecting cases).

* Judge Posner, after tracing the meaning of property back to Blackstone and Locke, concluded that "[t]he continued appropriateness of using federal courts to resolve run-of-the-mine contract disputes between public employees and their employers may deserve fresh consideration by the Supreme Court, but at our level the issue is foreclosed." *Patterson v. Portch,* 853 F.2d 1399, 1405 (7th Cir. 1988).

§ 3.2 CONSTITUTIONAL RIGHTS

The Sixth Circuit, in an en banc opinion, interpreted *Cleveland Board of Education v. Loudermill,* 470 U.S. 532 (1985), as giving the discharged public employee only the right to reply before the official responsible for the discharge. Under this reading of *Loudermill,* the employee does not have the right to a pre-termination hearing before a neutral decisionmaker. *Duchesne v. Williams,* 849 F.2d 1004 (6th Cir. 1988) (en banc). The authors are persuaded by the dissenting opinion's argument that *Loudermill* contemplates a meaningful hearing conducted by one who is reasonably impartial. *Id.* at 1010 (Judge Ryan, dissenting).

Criminal Procedure

Subjecting an individual to an "unduly suggestive lineup" does not constitute a violation of constitutional rights actionable under § 1983, unless it results in denial of a fair trial. *Hensley v. Corey,* 818 F.2d 646 (7th Cir.), *cert. denied,* 108 S. Ct. 456 (1987). * By contrast, the Fifth Circuit ruled that a police officer who procures a false identification by unlawful means and deliberately conceals exculpatory evidence violates "clearly established" contitutional rights. *Geter v. Fortenberry,* 849 F.2d 1550 (5th Cir. 1988). A § 1983 claim may not be based upon failure to give *Miranda* * warnings, because they are not constitutionally guaranteed. *Johnson v. Carroll,* 694 F. Supp. 500, 504 (N.D. Ill. 1988); *Hensley v. Carey,* 633 F. Supp. 1251 (N.D. Ill. 1986). Similarly, because entrapment does not constitute a constitutional violation, it does not give rise to a § 1983 claim. *Mullinax v. McElhenney,* 672 F. Supp. 1449 (N.D. Ga. * 1987). The alleged denial of a fair trial cannot give rise to a § 1983 claim "where the [Federal Court] plaintiff was acquitted of the crime charged." *Schiavone Construction Co. v. Merola,* 678 F. Supp. 64, 66 (S.D.N.Y.), *aff'd,* 848 F.2d 43 (2d Cir.), *cert. denied,* 109 S. Ct. 144 (1988).

Privileges and Immunities

A § 1983 claim may be based upon a violation of rights protected by Article IV, § 2 of the privileges and immunities clause. *International Organization of Masters, Mates and Pilots v. Andrews,* 831 F.2d 843 (9th Cir. 1987), *cert. denied,* 108 S. Ct. 1228 (1988).

Land Use

Local zoning decisions that are alleged to violate a land owner's constitutional rights * give rise to claims for relief under § 1983. *Bateson v. Geisse,* 857 F.2d 1300 (9th Cir. 1988); *Bello v. Walker,* 840 F.2d 1124 (3d Cir.) *cert. denied,* 109 S. Ct. 176 (1988); *Sullivan v. Town of Salem,* 805 F.2d 81 (2d Cir. 1986). *But see Lemke v. Cass County,* 846 F.2d 469 (8th Cir. 1987) (whether denial of zoning permit may give rise to substantive due process claim is an "open question" in Eighth Circuit).

Chilling Effect

In *Gibson v. United States,* 781 F.2d 1334 (9th Cir. 1986), *cert. denied,* 107 S. Ct. 928 (1987), plaintiffs alleged that members of the Los Angeles Police Department engaged in frequent low-altitude helicopter flights over their residences in order to inhibit their political advocacy. While *Laird v. Tatum,* 408 U.S. 1, *reh'g denied,* 409 U.S. 901 (1972), forbids suit on the basis of a speculative "chill" due to generalized and legitimate law-enforcement activities, the Ninth Circuit found that plaintiffs stated a proper § 1983 claim by alleging "discrete acts of police surveillance and intimidation directed solely at silencing them." *Gibson,* 781 F.2d at 1338.

Affirmative versus Negative Rights

* The United States Supreme Court determined, by a six-to-three vote, that the due process clause does not impose an affirmative obligation upon public authorities to protect a child from parental abuse, even when they know that the child faces special danger and undertake some steps to protect him. *De Shaney v. Winnebago County Department of Social Services,* 57 U.S.L.W. 4218 (U.S. 1989) (No. 87-154). In an opinion by the Chief Justice, the Court read the due process clause as generally not imposing an affirmative obligation on the state to provide assistance or services. "If the Due Process Clause does not require the State to provide its citizens with particular protective services, it follows that the State cannot be held liable under the Clause for injuries that could have been averted had it chosen to provide them. As a general matter, then, we conclude that a State's failure to protect an individual against private violence simply does not constitute a violation of the Due Process Clause." *Id.* at 4220.

Rejecting a general "special relationship" doctrine, the Court in *De Shaney* read its prior decisions as recognizing a constitutional obligation to provide services only to those in state custody, such as prisoners and involuntarily committed mental patients. "Taken together, they stand only for the proposition that when the State takes a person into its custody and holds him there against his will, the Constitution imposes upon it a corresponding duty to assume some responsibility for his safety and general well-being." *Id.* The fact that the state at one point took Joshua De Shaney into custody does not change the result, "for when it returned him to his father's custody, it placed him in no worse position than that in which he would have been had it not acted at all; the State does not become the permanent guarantor of an individual's safety by having once offered him shelter." *Id.* at 4221. The Court in dicta opined that a state's placement of a child in foster care "might" be "sufficiently analogous to incarceration or institutionalization to give rise to an affirmative duty to protect," but expressed no view on the validity of this analogy. *Id.* at 4221, n.9.

While the permanent brain damage suffered by Joshua De Shaney is "undeniably tragic," the child welfare authorities faced a difficult predicament because, if they had moved too soon to take custody of the child, "they would likely have been met with charges of improperly intruding into the parent-child relationship . . . ." *Id.* at 4211. Any remedy in this case should depend upon state tort law rather than the due process clause. The Court declined to consider, because not raised below, whether the state child protection statutes created a property interest protected by substantive due process. *Id.* at 4219 n.2. It did indicate that a "State may not, of course, selectively deny its protective services to certain disfavored minorities without violating the Equal Protection Clause." *Id.* at 4220 n.3.

Justice Brennan's dissenting opinion criticizes the Court for overemphasizing the action-inaction dichotomy, and for failing to give sufficient consideration to the actions in fact taken by the local officials on Joshua's behalf, because such actions can amount to a limitation on the individual's freedom to protect himself or herself or obtain help from others. The majority fails "to see that inaction can be every bit as abusive of power as action, that oppression can result when a State undertakes a vital duty and then ignores it. Today's opinion construes the Due Process Clause to permit a State to displace private sources of protection and then, at the critical moment, to shrug its shoulders and turn away from the harm that it has promised to try to prevent." *Id.* at 4224.

Justice Blackman, dissenting, lamenting the plight of "[p]oor Joshua," also criticizes the Court's overly formalistic distinction between action and reaction.

The Eleventh Circuit, following the decision in *Doe v. Department of Social Services,* 649 F.2d 134 (2d Cir. 1981), *cert. denied,* 464 U.S. 864 (1983), ruled that state and county officials who place a child in foster care have a constitutional (due process) obligation to insure the continuing safety of the environment in which the child is placed, and will be liable if they are grossly negligent or deliberately indifferent to the welfare of the child. *Taylor v. Ledbetter,* 818 F.2d 791 (11th Cir. 1987) (en banc). In these circumstances there is a special relationship between the state and the child. "The State's action in assuming the responsibility of finding and keeping the child in a safe environment placed an obligation on the State to insure the continuing safety of the environment." *Id.* at 795.

In *Lopez v. Houston Independent School District,* 817 F.2d 351 (5th Cir. 1987), the court ruled that because the defendant school bus driver was entrusted with the care of students attending school pursuant to the state compulsory education law, his failure to protect a student from a beating by other students, or to render emergency aid, would violate the due process clause "if the jury finds it rose to the level of callous indifference and was a cause of the injury." *Id.* at 356.

* The Third Circuit reasoned that because students in public school pursuant to a compulsory education law are in the "functional custody" of school authorities during school hours, school officials have a due process duty "to take some affirmative action to investigate and protect students from a teacher's sexual abuse of which they were made aware, and to take steps to eliminate rather than condone an atmosphere in which teachers could sexually harass students with impunity." *Stoneking v. Bradford Area School District,* 856 F.2d 594, 603-04 (3d Cir. 1988).

In *Wells v. Walker,* 852 F.2d 368 (8th Cir. 1988), the plaintiffs, relatives and representatives of the deceased, alleged that prison officials accelerated the release date of a prisoner, transported him to the closest "pick up" point, a store operated by Ms. Sanderlin and, after dropping him off there, the prisoner murdered her. The plaintiffs' allegations that the defendants failed to conduct an adequate investigation, and that such an investigation would have shown that the prisoner had "violent propensities," could state a proper due process claim to protection, because the officials had placed Ms. Sanderlin in a "position of danger." The Eighth Circuit concluded, however, that the complaint did not state a proper due process claim because it alleged only negligence. See **§ 3.5**.

The Ninth Circuit found that the plaintiff wife alleged a "special relationship" because the police had repeated notice of her hustand's threats against her and the state court had issued a temporary restraining order forbidding the husband from having any contact with her. These circumstances are sufficient to state a claim that the police owed the plaintiff a duty to take reasonable steps to protect her from her husband. "The relationship between defendants' failure to arrest or investigate, and [plaintiff's] emotional disturbances presents a causation question separate from the special relationship and duty of protection issues." *Balistreri v. Pacifica Police Department,* 855 F.2d 1421, 1426-1427 (9th Cir. 1988). The authors note that the reasoning in *Balistreri* and reliance upon the "special relationship" doctrine appear to be inconsistent with the Supreme Court's decision in *De Shaney.*

* When confronted with the issue, most courts, even before the Supreme Court's decision in *De Shaney,* found no special relationship and no constitutional obligation on the state to provide protection or other services. The Eleventh Circuit's position is fairly typical: "a constitutional duty can arise only when a state or municipality, by exercising a significant degree of control over an individual, places that person in a worse situation than he would have been had the government not acted at all." *Wideman v. Shallowford Community Hospital,* 826 F.2d 1030, 1035 (11th Cir. 1987) (county policy of using its emergency vehicles to transport patients only to county hospitals which guarantee payment of county's medical bills is not unconstitutional). See also *Archie v. City of Racine,* 847 F.2d 1211 (7th Cir. 1988) (en banc) (no constitutional right to rescue services); *Carlson v. Conklin,* 813 F.2d 769 (6th Cir. 1987) (state has no constitutional obligation to provide protection); *Ketchum v. Alameda County,* 811 F.2d 1243 (9th Cir. 1987) (no constitutional right to protection from attack by third parties, absent a special relationship); *Washington v. District of Columbia,* 802 F.2d 1478 (D.C. Cir. 1986) (prison guards have no constitutional right to a safe workplace); *Escamilla v. City of Santa Ana,* 796 F.2d 266 (9th Cir. 1986) (no constitutional right to police protection); *Walker v. Rowe,* 791 F.2d 507 (7th Cir.) (prison guards have no constitutional right to safe working conditions), *cert. denied,* 107 S. Ct. 597 (1986); *Bradberry v. Pinellas County,* 789 F.2d 1513 (11th Cir. 1986) (county has no constitutional obligation to provide a sufficient number of adequately trained lifeguards); *Estate of Gilmore v. Buckley,* 787 F.2d 714 (1st Cir.) (state has no constitutional obligation to provide police protection). *cert. denied,* 107 S. Ct. 270 (1986); *McClary v. O'Hare,* 786 F.2d 83 (2d Cir. 1986) (failure of officials to follow health and safety laws does not violate Constitution).

The special relationship cases frequently have been discussed in conjunction with the problem of proximate cause. See discussion in **§ 4.3**.

A police officer, whether supervisory or otherwise, may be liable for failing to intervene when a constitutional violation, such as an unprovoked beating by another officer, takes place in his or her presence. *Byrd v. Clark,* 783 F.2d 1002 (11th Cir. 1986). *Accord, O'Neil v. Krzeminski,* 839 F.2d 9 (2d Cir. 1988); *Fundiller v. Cooper City,* 777 F.2d 1436, 1441-42 (11th Cir. 1985); *Borek v. Town of McLeansboro,* 629 F. Supp. 657 (S.D. Ill. 1986). The Seventh Circuit agrees with this principle, but notes that under the Supreme Court's decisions in *Daniels* and *Davidson,* discussed in **§ 3.5**, the defendant onlooking officer may not be held liable for negligently "failing to perceive that the other officers were inflicting illegal summary punishment rather than using lawful force to subdue a violent inmate." *Rascon v. Hardiman,* 803 F.2d 269, 276 (7th Cir. 1986). The Second Circuit holds that the onlooking officer may be liable only if there is an episode "of sufficient duration to support a conclusion that an officer who stood by without trying to assist the victim became a tacit collaborator." *O'Neil v. Krzeminski,* 839 F.2d 9, 11-12 (2d Cir. 1988).

§ 3.2 CONSTITUTIONAL RIGHTS

Unequal Services

A claimed inequality in the provision of municipal services on the basis of such factors as race or sex may give rise to an equal protection clause violation that is
* cognizant under § 1983. *Watson v. Kansas City,* 857 F.2d 690 (10th Cir. 1988) (claimed police department policy of not providing assistance to victims of spousal abuse in the same manner as other assault victims states a proper equal protection claim); *Balistreri v. Pacifica Police Department,* 855 F.2d 1421 (9th Cir. 1988) (gender discrimination claim); *Hawk v. Perillo,* 642 F. Supp. 380 (N.D. Ill. 1985) (race); *Bartalone v. County of Berrien,* 643 F. Supp. 574 (W.D. Mich. 1986) (gender). See also *Sherrell v. Longview,* 683 F. Supp. 1108 (E.D. Tex. 1987) (police department policy giving favored treatment to police officers accused of domestic violence). The court in *Bartalone* quoted *Thurman v. City of Torrington,* 595 F. Supp. 1521, 1527 (D. Conn. 1984), for the proposition that "[i]f officials have notice of the possibility of attacks on women in domestic relationships or other persons, they are under an affirmative duty to take reasonable measures to protect the personal safety of such persons in the community. Failure to perform this duty would constitute a denial of equal protection of the laws."

* Right to Die

In what is believed to be the first § 1983 "right to die" case, a district court ruled that the constitutionally protected right of privacy encompasses the right to refuse life-sustaining treatment. *Gray v. Romeo,* 697 F. Supp. 580 (D.R.I. 1988).

Page 38, add after carryover paragraph:

The Handicapped Children's Protection Act of 1986 (HCPA) overruled *Smith v. Robinson,* 468 U.S. 992 (1984), by amending 28 U.S.C. § 1415 of the EHA so as to provide, inter alia, that the EHA shall not limit a person's right to bring suit under any other federal statute or provision of the federal Constitution. Pub. L. No. 99-372, § 3 (1986). The EHA thus no longer restricts any remedies under § 1983. The Eighth Circuit found that under the 1986 amendment plaintiff "was entitled to bring a section 1983 action based on alleged violations of EHA or the due process and equal protection clauses of the fourteenth amendment." *Digre v. Roseville Schools,* 841 F.2d 245, 250 (8th Cir. 1988).

The new HCPA requires that "before the filing of a civil action under such laws seeking relief that is also available under [the EHA], the procedure under [the EHA] shall be exhausted to the same extent as would be required had the action been brought under this part." *Id.* See § **8.3**.

The circuit courts have determined that the 1986 amendment making § 1983 available should be applied retroactively. *Mrs. W. v. Tirozzi,* 832 F.2d 748 (2d Cir. 1987); *Board of Education v. Diamond,* 808 F.2d 987 (3d Cir. 1986); *Jackson v. Franklin County,* 806 F.2d 623 (5th Cir. 1986).

With respect to the effect of the EHA amendment on claims for attorney's fees under § 1988, see § **15.16**.

Page 38, add to end of page:

The clear trend is to allow a federal constitutional claim to be asserted under § 1983 even if the same facts upon which it is based give rise to a claim under Title VII. *Keller v. Prince George's County,* 827 F.2d 952 (4th Cir. 1987); *Ratliff v. Milwaukee,* 795 F.2d 612 (7th Cir. 1986); *Harvey v. Little Rock,* 787 F.2d 1223 (8th Cir. 1986). The Fifth Circuit, however, takes the position that § 1983 employment discrimination constitutional claims must be based "on grounds different from those available under Title VII." *Parker v. Department of Public Welfare,* 811 F.2d 925, 927 n.3 (5th Cir. 1987).

On the issue of whether a constitutional claim based upon age discrimination in employment may be based upon § 1983, *compare Price v. County of Erie,* 654 F. Supp. 1206 (W.D.N.Y. 1987) (Age Discrimination in Employment Act does not preclude § 1983 equal protection clause claim) *with Ring v. Crisp County Hospital Authority,* 652 F. Supp. 477 (M.D. Ga. 1987) (ADEA preempts equal protection age discrimination claims though not due process or First Amendment claims).

Page 39, add after note 27 reference:

* Several courts followed the weight of authority in concluding that supremacy clause preemption claims do not give rise to § 1983 claims. *Golden State Transit Corp. v. Los Angeles,* 857 F.2d 631 (9th Cir. 1988); *Air Transport Association v. Public Utilities Commission,* 833 F.2d 200 (9th Cir. 1987); *Segundo v. City of Rancho Mirage,* 813 F.2d 1387, 1394 (9th Cir. 1987); *White Mountain Apache Tribe v. Williams,* 810 F.2d 844 (9th Cir.), *cert. denied,* 107 S. Ct. 940 (1987); *New York Airlines v. Dukes County,* 623 F. Supp. 1435 (D. Mass. 1985); *Pesticide Public Policy v. Village of Wauconda,* 622 F. Supp. 423 (N.D. Ill. 1985), *aff'd,* 826 F.2d 1068 (7th Cir. 1987); *Central Machinery Co. v. State,* 152 Ariz. 134, 730 P.2d 843 (1986); *Ramah Navajo School Board v. Bureau of Revenue,* 104 N.M. 302, 720 P.2d 1243 (Ct. App.), *cert. denied,* 479 U.S. 940 (1986). In the last cited case, the court, after concluding that "the Supremacy Clause alone does not create federal substantive rights but merely is a policy of federalism[,]" 720 P.2d at 1252, went on to find that the federal statute at issue, the Indian Self-Determination and Education Assistance Act, created a right enforceable under § 1983.

Page 40, add after note 30 reference:

Alleged violations of the commerce clause do not give rise to claims for relief under § 1983. *Pesticide Public Policy v. Village of Wauconda,* 622 F. Supp. 423 (N.D. Ill. 1985), *aff'd,* 826 F.2d 1068 (7th Cir. 1987); *Private Truck Council v. Secretary of State,* 503 A.2d 214 (Me.), *cert. denied,* 106 S. Ct. 1997 (1986).

* § 3.2A —Retaliation Claims (New)

A large number of § 1983 claims consist of alleged retaliation by public officials for engaging in constitutionally protected activity. These claims should be evaluated under the framework established in *Mount Healthy School District v. Doyle,* 429 U.S. 274 (1977).

In *Rakovich v. Wade,* 850 F.2d 1180, 1189 (7th Cir.) (en banc), *cert. denied,* 109 S. Ct. 497 (1988), the Court stated that "an investigation conducted in retaliation for comments protected by the first amendment could be actionable under section 1983."

The retaliation need not consist of the deprivation of a constitutional right. Rather, it may consist of the deprivation of any non-trivial commodity because the individual engaged in constitutionally protected activity. *See Georgia Association of Educators v. Gwinnett County School District,* 856 F.2d 142 (11th Cir. 1988) (denial of union dues checkoff privileges allegedly in retaliation for first amendment activity); *Howland v. Kilquist,* 833 F.2d 639, 644 (7th Cir. 1987) (" '[A]n act in retaliation for the exercise of a constitutional right is actionable under [§] 1983 even if the act, when taken for different reasons, would have been proper." '), quoting from *Buise v. Hudkins,* 584 F.2d 223, 229 (7th Cir. 1978), *cert. denied,* 440 U.S. 916 (1979); *Franco v. Kelly,* 854 F.2d 584, 590 (2d Cir. 1988) (same). *Franco* is discussed in **§ 3.6.** In the employment context, the Second and Third Circuits took the position that the retaliation may be less than a discharge. *Lieberman v. Reisman,* 857 F.2d 896 (2d Cir. 1988) (denial of compensatory and vacation time); *Bennis v. Gable,* 823 F.2d 723, 731 (3d Cir. 1987) (demotion: ". . . the constitutional violation is not in the harshness of the sanction applied, but in the imposition of any disciplinary action for the exercise of permissible free speech").

Evidence which shows a reasonable probability of improper motive should go to the jury, but a "mere possibility . . . is insufficient to get to the jury." *Hughes v. Halifax County School Board,* 855 F.2d 183, 186 (4th Cir. 1988), *cert. denied,* 109 S. Ct. 867 (1989).

§ 3.3 Excessive Force Cases—"Shock the Conscience" Standard

Page 44, add at end of section:

A number of circuit court decisions applied the *shock the conscience* theory of substantive due process to claims of excessive force by law enforcement officers (cases listed by circuit):

Fernandez v. Leonard, 784 F.2d 1209 (1st Cir. 1986); *Robison v. Via,* 821 F.2d 913 (2d Cir. 1987); *Graham v. City of Charlotte,* 827 F.2d 945 (4th Cir. 1987); *Justice v. Dennis,* 834 F.2d 380 (4th Cir. 1987) (en banc); *Hinojosa v. City of Terrell,* 834 F.2d 1223 (5th Cir. 1988); *Stevens v. Corbell,* 832 F.2d 884 (5th Cir. 1987), *cert. denied,* 108 S. Ct. 2018 (1988); *Lynch v. Cannatella,* 810 F.2d 1363 (5th Cir. 1987); *Dale v. Janklow,* 828 F.2d 481 (8th Cir. 1987), *cert. denied,* 108 S. Ct. 1486 (1988); *Griffin v. Hilke,* 804 F.2d 1052 (8th Cir. 1986), *cert. denied,* 107 S. Ct. 3185 (1987); *New v. Minneapolis,* 792 F.2d 724 (8th Cir. 1986); *Burton v. Livingston,* 791 F.2d 97 (8th Cir. 1986); *Patzner v. Burkett,* 779 F.2d 1363 (8th Cir. 1985); *Rinker v. Napa County,* 831 F.2d 829 (9th Cir. 1987); *Gaut v. Sunn,* 810 F.2d 923 (9th Cir. 1987); *McRorie v. Shimoda,* 795 F.2d 780 (9th Cir. 1986); *Rutherford v. City of Berkeley,* 780 F.2d 1444 (9th Cir. 1986); *Trujillo v. Goodman,* 825 F.2d 1453 (10th Cir. 1987); *Popham v. City of Kennesaw,* 820 F.2d 1570 (11th Cir. 1987); *Leslie v. Ingram,* 786 F.2d 1533 (11th Cir. 1986); *Owens v. Atlanta,* 780 F.2d 1564 (11th Cir. 1986); *Fundiller v. Cooper City,* 777 F.2d 1436 (11th Cir. 1985).

In a non-§ 1983 context, Justice Rehnquist recognized that "[s]o-called 'substantive due process' prevents the government from engaging in conduct that 'shocks the conscience'. . . ." *United States v. Salerno,* 107 S. Ct. 2095, 2101 (1987).

The Fourth Circuit, sitting en banc, upheld the district court's refusal to give an instruction stating that the standard of liability in an excessive force arrest case is force which is greater than "reasonably necessary." The district court properly instructed the jury that force is " 'unconstitutionally excessive if the officer used means so brutal, demeaning and harmful as literally to shock the conscience of a court' and that the jury must determine whether the force 'was so disproportionate to the need presented and was so inspired by malice or sadism rather than a merely careless or unwise excess of zeal that it amounts to a brutal or inhumane abuse of official power literally shocking to the conscience.' " *Justice v. Dennis,* 834 F.2d 380, 382 (4th Cir. 1987) (en banc) (quoting from unreported district court opinion). The dissenting opinion chided the majority for not analyzing the issue in Fourth Amendment terms.

Several decisions held that the Fourth Amendment and not the due process clause
* governs claims of excessive force in making arrests. *Heath v. Henning,* 854 F.2d 6 (2d Cir. 1988); *Davis v. Little,* 851 F.2d 605 (2d Cir. 1988); *Martin v. Malhoyt,* 830 F.2d 237, 260-61 (D.C. Cir. 1987); *Lester v. Chicago,* 830 F.2d 706 (7th Cir. 1987), overruling *Gumz v. Morrissette,* 772 F.2d 1395 (7th Cir. 1985), *cert. denied,* 106 S. Ct. 1644 (1986).
* *See also Martin v. Gentile,* 849 F.2d 863 (4th Cir. 1988) (substantive due process provides "residual protection" in this context). See § **3.4**. According to the Tenth Circuit, however, "the use of *excessive* force against an arrestee or pretrial detainee, like Meade, is actionable under section 1983 as a deprivation of life or liberty without due process of law. . . ." *Meade v. Grubbs,* 841 F.2d 1512, 1527 (10th Cir. 1988) (emphasis in original). See also *Sample v. Atlanta,* 846 F.2d 1328 (11th Cir. 1988); *Smith v. City of Fontana,* 818 F.2d 1411, 1417 (9th Cir.), *cert. denied,* 108 S. Ct. 311 (1987); *Griffin v. Hilke,* 804 F.2d 1052, 1056 (8th Cir. 1986), *cert. denied,* 107 S. Ct. 3185 (1987).

* The Third Circuit ruled that the plaintiff has the burden of proving the use of excessive force by a preponderance of the evidence. *Edwards v. Philadelphia,* 860 F.2d 568 (3d Cir. 1988). *Accord, Wing v. Britton,* 748 F.2d 494 (8th Cir. 1984). Although expressing doubt about the propriety of defense counsel's opening statement, a "Golden Rule" argument asking the jury to place itself in the police officer's shoes, the *Edwards* court found that any error was cured by a curative final instruction. This instruction directed the jurors to perform their duties without bias, prejudice, or sympathy, to consider only the evidence, and that counsel's statements are not evidence.

The Fifth Circuit, calling for en banc review to resolve a conflict in its own decisional law, ruled by a two-to-one vote that under the controlling law in the circuit a showing of "severe injury" is a necessary element of a shock-the-conscience claim. Judge Thornbury dissented. *Johnson v. Moral,* 843 F.2d 846 (5th Cir. 1988).

The Fifth Circuit stated that the "constitutional line" is "drawn at conduct that was not only disproportionate under the circumstances, but also was inspired by malice, so as to amount to an abuse of official power that shocks the conscience." *Stevens v. Corbell,* 832 F.2d 884, 889 (5th Cir. 1987), *cert. denied,* 108 S. Ct. 2018 (1988). Plaintiff need not show, however, "that the state officer actually knew that his actions were in *violation of the law.*" *Id.* at 890 (emphasis in original).

The shock-the-conscience test normally presents a jury issue. *Trujillo v. Goodman,* 825 F.2d 1453 (10th Cir. 1987) (no error in submitting excessive force claim to jury). In *Robison v. Via,* 821 F.2d 913, 927 (2d Cir. 1987), the court stated that "the jury should be advised as to any difference between the excessiveness requirements of the § 1983 claim and those of the state-law battery claim." One of the issues which the jury should consider is whether defendant acted in good faith or maliciously or sadistically. *Justice v. Dennis,* 834 F.2d 380 (4th Cir. 1987) (en banc); *Graham v. City of Charlotte,* 827 F.2d 945 (4th Cir. 1987), *cert. granted,* 109 S. Ct. 54 (1988). In a case involving an officer's use of a chokehold, the Ninth Circuit found that it was not improper to instruct the jury that it might consider the officer's state of mind. *Maddox v. Los Angeles,* 792 F.2d 1408 (9th Cir. 1986). *See also Trujillo v. Goodman,* 825 F.2d 1453 (10th Cir. 1987).

The Eighth Circuit found that the district court properly granted a directed verdict for defendants in *Dale v. Janklow,* 828 F.2d 481, 486 (8th Cir. 1987), *cert. denied,* 108 S. Ct. 1486 (1988) ("Although few cases have considered the propriety of a decision of reasonable force as a matter of law, there is support for this position"). The court stated that "the test for officers facing a life threatening situation must be whether the officers were objectively acting in good faith under the circumstances." *Id.* at 487.

In *Burton v. Livingston,* 791 F.2d 97 (8th Cir. 1986), the court ruled that a complaint alleging that a prison guard's terrorizing and threatening to kill the plaintiff prisoner, accompanied by racial epithets, without provocation, for the apparent purpose of retaliating against the prisoner for having filed a federal court action, stated claims for relief under the First Amendment and due process and equal protection clauses. "The complaint describes . . . a wanton act of cruelty which, if it occurred, was brutal despite the fact that it resulted in no measurable physical injury to the prisoner." 791 F.2d at 100.

In *Checki v. Webb,* 785 F.2d 534 (5th Cir. 1986), the plaintiff alleged that he was forced to travel at speeds of over 100 miles per hour in order to flee a "terrorizing" police officer. The court found that there was a factual issue as to whether the officer's conduct constituted negligence, which would not be a constitutional violation (see § **3.5**) or an intentional wrong, rising to a substantive due process violation, even absent physical injury. Just as a police officer who terrorizes a civilian by brandishing a cocked gun in his face may be liable under § 1983, even if no physical injury results, "where a police officer uses a police vehicle to terrorize a civilian and he has done so with malicious abuse of official power shocking the conscience, a court may conclude that the officers have crossed the 'constitutional line.'" 785 F.2d at 538. *But see Johnson v. Moral,* 843 F.2d 846 (5th Cir. 1988) (severe injury is necessary element of shock-the-conscience claim); *Gaut v. Sunn,* 810 F.2d 923 (9th Cir. 1987) (threat of bodily harm does not give rise to § 1983 claim).

The use of a roadblock by the police which caused a collision could violate substantive due process. *Brower v. Inyo County,* 817 F.2d 540 (9th Cir. 1987), *cert. granted,* 108 S. Ct. 2869 (1988).

The Eighth Circuit applied the shock-the-conscience test in a child abuse context in *Fitzgerald v. Williamson,* 787 F.2d 403, 408 (8th Cir. 1986), but found its conscience not shocked by the fact that "caseworkers responsible for an allegedly abused child arranged for the child to be examined by a psychologist and, after receiving confirmation of child abuse, reduced the parents' visitation rights and permitted the child to remain with her foster parent when the foster parent moved out of the parents' geographical area." In *Vinson v. Campbell County Fiscal Court,* 820 F.2d 194, 198 (6th Cir. 1987), the court found that a juvenile probation officer's procurement of a technically invalid summons to answer charges of child neglect or abuse is not "an egregious abuse of governmental power sufficient to state a substantive due process violation." *Id.* at 201.

In *Wood v. Ostrander,* 851 F.2d 1212 (9th Cir. 1988), the plaintiff alleged that the defendant police officer arrested the driver of the car in which she was a passenger and left her stranded alone in a high crime area at 2:30 a.m. She subsequently accepted a ride with a man who raped her. The court found a triable issue of fact as to whether the officer's conduct placed the plaintiff in a position of danger. It would not be an exaggeration for a jury to conclude that the officer's conduct "shocks the conscience."

The excessive use of force in the corporal punishment of public school students violates the due process clause. *Wise v. Pea Ridge School District,* 855 F.2d 560, 564 (8th Cir. 1988); *Metzger v. Osbeck,* 841 F.2d 518 (3d Cir. 1988); *Garcia v. Miera,* 817 F.2d 650 (10th Cir. 1987) ("at some point of excessiveness or brutality, a public school child's substantive due process rights are violated by beatings administered by government-paid school officials"), *cert. denied,* 108 S. Ct. 1220 (1988).

A police officer sued for excessive force may counterclaim for assault and battery. *Bates v. McKeon,* 650 F. Supp. 476 (D. Conn. 1986). *Accord, Law v. Cullen,* 613 F. Supp. 259 (S.D.N.Y. 1985); *Smith v. City of New York,* 611 F. Supp. 1080, 1087 (S.D.N.Y. 1985).

§ 3.4 –Fourth Amendment Theory

Page 46, add after note 74 reference:

Several circuit court decisions applied a Fourth Amendment analysis to claims of excessive force (decisions listed by circuit):

Martin v. Malhoyt, 830 F.2d 237 (D.C. Cir. 1987); *Fernandez v. Leonard,* 784 F.2d 1209 (1st Cir. 1986); *Heath v. Henning,* 854 F.2d 6 (2d Cir. 1988); *Davis v. Little,* 851 F.2d 605 (2d Cir. 1988); *Dodd v. City of Norwich,* 827 F.2d 1, 7-8 (2d Cir. 1987) (on reargument), *cert. denied,* 108 S. Ct. 701 (1988); *Martin v. Gentile,* 849 F.2d 863 (4th Cir. 1988); *Robinette v. Barnes,* 854 F.2d 909 (6th Cir. 1988); *Jones v. Sherrill,* 827 F.2d 1102 (6th Cir. 1987); *Cameron v. City of Pontiac,* 813 F.2d 782 (6th Cir. 1987); *Leber v. Smith,* 773 F.2d 101 (6th Cir. 1985), *cert. denied,* 475 U.S. 1084 (1986); *Ford v. Childers,* 855 F.2d 1271 (7th Cir. 1988) (en banc); *Sherrod v. Berry,* 856 F.2d 802 (7th Cir. 1988) (en banc); *Lester v. Chicago,* 830 F.2d 706 (7th Cir. 1987); *Griffin v. Hilke,* 804 F.2d 1052 (8th Cir. 1986), *cert. denied,* 107 S. Ct. 3185 (1987); *New v. Minneapolis,* 792 F.2d 724 (8th Cir. 1986); *Smith v. City of Fontana,* 818 F.2d 1411 (9th Cir.), *cert. denied,* 108 S. Ct. 311 (1987); *Brower v. Inyo County,* 817 F.2d 540 (9th Cir. 1987), *cert. granted,* 108

S. Ct. 2869 (1988); *Ryder v. Topeka,* 814 F.2d 1412 (10th Cir. 1987); *Brown v. City of Clewiston,* 848 F.2d 1534 (11th Cir. 1988).

Several circuit court decisions take the position that claims of excessive force in making arrests should be based solely on the Fourth Amendment. *Heath v. Henning,* 854 F.2d 6 (2d Cir. 1988); *Davis v. Little,* 851 F.2d 605 (2d Cir. 1988); *Martin v. Malhoyt,* 830 F.2d 237, 261-62 (D.C. Cir. 1987); *Lester v. Chicago,* 830 F.2d 706 (7th Cir. 1987). *See also Martin v. Gentile,* 849 F.2d 863 (4th Cir. 1988) (due process provides "residual protection" in this context). In an important opinion, the court in *Lester* concluded that, under the Fourth Amendment, subjective inquiry into the officer's motive is incompatible with a Fourth Amendment objective reasonableness analysis. "Under the Fourth Amendment, a police officer's use of force in arresting a suspect violates the Constitution if, judging from the totality of the circumstances at the time of the arrest, the officer used greater force than was reasonably necessary to make the arrest." *Id.* at 713. Because this standard does not implicate the officer's state of mind or the seriousness of plaintiff's injury, it differs from a substantive due process approach. *See also Heath v. Henning,* 834 F.2d at 9 (the consideration of such subjective factors is inconsistent with the fourth amendment balancing test articulated in *Garner*); *Martin v. Gentile,* 849 F.2d at 869.

In *Sherrod v. Berry,* 856 F.2d 802 (7th Cir. 1988), the court concluded that the jury should not consider any information or facts not known to the officer. "When a jury measures the objective reasonableness of an officer's action, it must stand in *his* shoes and judge the reasonableness of his actions based upon the information he possessed and the judgment he exercised in responding to that situation." *Id.* at 804-05 (emphasis in original). It was thus reversible error for the trial court to allow the plaintiff to introduce evidence that the deceased in fact was not armed, because the officer did not have this information.

In *Ford v. Childers,* 855 F.2d 1271 (7th Cir. 1988), the court, relying upon *Sherrod,* ruled that (1) the officer's "reasonable belief that danger exists may be formed by reliance on appearances[,]" (2) there is no constitutional requirement that a warning shot be fired before the officer employs deadly force, and (3) consideration should be given to the fact that the officer may have to make critical split-second judgments. *Id.* at 1275-76. In this case the use of deadly force was reasonable: Officer "Childers, after warning Ford on two separate occasions, fired at Ford because he reasonably believed that the suspect had committed a felony involving the use of deadly force, was armed with a deadly weapon, and was likely to pose a danger of serious harm to others if not immediately apprehended." *Id.* at 1275.

In *Martin v. Gentile,* 849 F.2d at 863, the Fourth Circuit stressed that the "wholly objective" *Garner* test is less stringent than the shock the conscience standard. As applied to the circumstances of this case, a sergeant who rammed a loaded shotgun through the plaintiff's windshield, sending glass flying in all directions, did not act unreasonably. Circuit Judge Murnaghan, concurring in part and dissenting in part, laments that although perhaps his "conscience is insufficiently toughened," it nevertheless "is disturbed." *Id.* at 872.

Not all courts agree with the position that excessive force arrest claims should be analyzed solely under the Fourth Amendment, and that the Fourth Amendment inquiry differs from a substantive due process analysis. In *Griffin v. Hilke,* 804 F.2d 1052 (8th Cir. 1986), *cert. denied,* 107 S. Ct. 3185 (1987), the court stated that

> [a]llegations of brutality by law enforcement personnel apprehending a suspect or effectuating an arrest are typically analyzed in terms of fourth amendment and liberty interests. If sufficiently egregious, a deliberate use of excessive force in this context can implicate the substantive fourth amendment guarantee against unreasonable seizures, the substantive due process right to be free from abusive governmental conduct "offensive to human dignity," or both.

804 F.2d at 1056. *Accord, Himple v. Moore,* 673 F. Supp. 758 (E.D. Va. 1987). In *Smith v. City of Fontana,* 818 F.2d 1411 (9th Cir. 1987), the Ninth Circuit took the position that the Fourth Amendment and due process inquiries overlap, and that whether a seizure was excessive under the Fourth Amendment depends upon an evaluation of the requirements for the officer's safety, the motivation for the arrest and the extent of the injury inflicted. See also *Meade v. Grubbs,* 841 F.2d 1512, 1527 (10th Cir. 1988) (use of excessive force against arrestees and pretrial detainees gives rise to due process claims).

The authors believe that there is no basis for concluding that the Fourth Amendment claim somehow "preempts" the due process claim. Moreover, both claims should be based upon a standard of objective reasonableness. This would promote objectivity and uniformity and eliminate the anomaly pursuant to which arrestees receive greater constitutional protection against excessive force than do detainees and convicted prisoners when different constitutional standards are applied. *See* Comment, *Excessive Force Claims: Removing the Double Standard,* 53 Chi. L. Rev. 1369 (1984); Schwartz, *Public Interest Litigation,* N.Y.L.J., Feb. 16, 1988, at 1, col. 1.

The Ninth Circuit found that the use of a roadblock to stop a fleeing driver is not a seizure "in the constitutional sense." *Brower v. Inyo County,* 817 F.2d 540, 546 (9th Cir. 1987), *cert. granted,* 108 S. Ct. 2869 (1988); Judge Pregeson, dissenting, relied on the Fifth Circuit decision in *Jamieson v. Shaw,* 772 F.2d 1205 (5th Cir. 1985), to support his position that a police roadblock operates to "seize" its victims.

An officer's high-speed pursuit of a furloughed prisoner, resulting in the death of another driver (plaintiff's decedent), did not constitute a Fourth Amendment seizure of the driver, since the officers did not intend to apprehend him. *Jones v. Sherrill,* 827 F.2d 1102 (6th Cir. 1987). See also *Galas v. McKee,* 801 F.2d 200 (6th Cir. 1986).

In *Robinette v. Barnes,* 854 F.2d 909 (6th Cir. 1988), the court articulated two factors to determine whether the officer used deadly force: (1) the intent of the officer, and (2) the probability that the use of the particular device created a substantial risk of causing death or serious bodily harm. Following this approach, the court found that the use of a properly trained police dog to apprehend a felony suspect did not constitute deadly force, even though the dog in fact killed the suspect. In addition, even if the use of the dog constituted deadly force, it was not unreasonable under the circumstances. The decision might have been different if the officer had intended to inflict death or serious bodily harm, or if the dog had been improperly trained.

In an Eleventh Circuit case, there was a conflict between the state law and the chief of police's manual regarding the use of deadly force. The evidence showed that the manual represented the city policy. The manual set forth a more restrictive policy and the police chief instructed his officers to follow it. *Brown v. City of Clewiston,* 848 F.2d 1534 (11th Cir. 1988).

It is unsettled whether the Fourth Amendment reaches negligent conduct. The Second Circuit ruled that it does not. *Dodd v. City of Norwich,* 827 F.2d 1, 7-8 (2d Cir. 1987), *cert. denied,* 108 S. Ct. 701 (1988). The Tenth Circuit disagrees, concluding that "no specific mental state is required to violate the Fourth Amendment." *Specht v. Jensen,* 832 F.2d 1516, 1523 (10th Cir. 1987). *Accord, Borunda v. Richmond,* 860 F.2d 937 (9th Cir. 1988) (*Daniels v. Williams,* 474 U.S. 327 (1986) no-negligence rule has "little relevance" to claim of arrest without probable cause); *Austin v. East Grand Rapids,* 685 F. Supp. 1396 (W.D. Mich. 1988); *McKenna v. Clayton County,* 657 F. Supp. 221 (N.D. Ga. 1987); *Patterson v. Fuller,* 654 F. Supp. 418 (N.D. Ga. 1987); *Uberoi v. University of Colorado,* 713 P.2d 894 (Colo. 1986).

There is a split in the circuits over whether *Garner* should be applied retroactively. The Second Circuit, finding that *Garner* simply applied a "traditional Fourth Amendment balancing test," gave it retroactive effect. *Davis v. Little,* 851 F.2d 605, 609 (2d Cir. 1988). By contrast, the Sixth and Tenth Circuits view *Garner* as "novel" and "unexpected," and thus denied retroactive effect. *Mitchell v. City of Sapulpa,* 857 F.2d 713 (10th Cir. 1988); *Carter v. City of Chattanooga,* 850 F.2d 1119 (6th Cir. 1988), *cert. denied,* 109 S. Ct. 795 (1989).

Applying *Garner,* the state appellate court in *Guider v. Smith,* 157 Mich. App. 92, 403 N.W.2d 505 (1987), ruled that (1) "[t]he fact that the plaintiff had a duty to refrain from resisting arrest is not relevant to the determination of whether the force used was reasonable" (*id.* at 509), and (2) a police department policy allowing the use of deadly force against nonassaultive and unarmed citizens suspected of committing nonviolent crimes against property violates the Fourth Amendment.

§ 3.4A —Eighth Amendment Theory (New)

Under the Eighth Amendment, a prisoner who complains of the use of force by prison officials must show more than the lack of due care; he or she must show obdurate or wanton behavior. *Whitley v. Albers,* 106 S. Ct. 1078 (1986). Whether the measure that was taken "inflicted unnecessary and wanton pain" turns on application of the *Johnson v. Glick,* 481 F.2d 1028 (2d Cir.), *cert. denied,* 414 U.S. 2033 (1973), factors discussed in § 3.3.

Under *Whitley,* prison officials who take security measures are entitled to broad deference. While this deference "does not insulate from review actions taken in bad faith and for no legitimate purpose, . . . it requires that neither judge nor jury freely substitute their judgment for that of officials who have made a considered choice." 106 S. Ct. at 1085. Courts should hesitate "to critique in hindsight decisions necessarily made in haste, under pressure, and frequently without the luxury of a second chance." *Id.* at 1085.

The Court in *Whitley* determined that the Eighth Amendment is the primary source of substantive protection "to convicted prisoners who challenge the use of force" as excessive and unjustified. In these circumstances, substantive due process affords "no greater protection than does the Cruel and Unusual Punishment Clause." *Id.* at 1088.

Applying these principles, the Court in *Whitley* held that a prison inmate who was shot by prison officials in the course of attempting to quell a prison riot did not suffer a violation of constitutional rights.

A number of circuit court decisions dealt with the *Whitley* standard. The D.C. Circuit Court of Appeals ruled that prison authorities have an Eighth Amendment obligation to protect prisoners from unreasonable threats of violence by fellow inmates and that, under *Whitley,* deliberate indifference is the proper constitutional standard. The record supported findings that defendants' deliberate indifference to the inmates' security was the proximate cause of plaintiff's injury. The emergencies present in *Whitley* which justified the decision made in haste were not present here. *Martin v. District of Columbia,* 824 F.2d 1049 (D.C. Cir. 1987).

The Second Circuit interpreted *Whitley* to mean that "the extent of injury is but one of the factors to be considered." *Corselli v. Coughlin,* 842 F.2d 23, 26 (2d Cir. 1988).

* In *Stubbs v. Dudley,* 849 F.2d 83 (2d Cir. 1988), the Second Circuit ruled that the evidence supported a finding that the corrections officer violated the prisoner's Eighth Amendment right by "deliberate indifference" in failing to protect him from injury by other prisoners. The Eighth Amendment standard does not require a showing of malice, and the "obdurate and wantonness" standard is limited to the use of force to quell prison riots.

The Fourth Circuit applied the *Whitley* standard to a claim by a prisoner growing out of an attack by a fellow inmate in *Ruefly v. Landon,* 825 F.2d 792 (4th Cir. 1987). "The relevant question is whether Ruefly has alleged that the defendants wantonly and obdurately failed to take precautions for his safety in deliberate indifference to a specific risk of harm posed by [inmate] Scottie Lowe." *Id.* at 793.

The Fifth Circuit ruled that the *Whitley* standard does not extend to all prison disciplinary cases but only to those where prison security is involved, *Foulds v. Coiley,* 833 F.2d 52 (5th Cir. 1987), and does not apply to prison condition cases. *Gillespie v. Crawford,* 833 F.2d 47, 50 (5th Cir. 1987) (Supreme Court has not made intent an element of prison condition cases).

* The Sixth Circuit applied the *Whitley* "deliberate indifference" standard to the rape of an inmate by another inmate. *Roland v. Johnson,* 856 F.2d 764 (6th Cir. 1988); *see also McGhee v. Foltz,* 852 F.2d 876 (6th Cir. 1988).

The Seventh Circuit concluded that *Whitley* does not require "severe injury." *Williams v. Boles,* 841 F.2d 181 (7th Cir. 1987). In *Walsh v. Mellas,* 837 F.2d 789 (7th Cir.), *cert. denied,* 108 S. Ct. 2832 (1988), the court found that defendant prison officials violated the Eighth Amendment by their deliberate indifference in failing to institute procedures and safeguards to determine whether an inmate to be housed with a gang member is targeted by a prison gang.

Applying *Whitley,* the Ninth Circuit ruled that a prisoner's claim that a prison guard used "unjustified and excessive force against him" stated a proper Eighth Amendment claim. *McRorie v. Shimoda,* 795 F.2d 780, 784 (9th Cir. 1986).

In a case in which a prisoner was murdered, presumably by another inmate, the Tenth Circuit concluded "that wanton or obdurate disregard of or deliberate indifference to the prisoner's right to life . . . is a substantive deprivation whether it falls under the due process clause or the Eighth Amendment." *Harris v. Maynard,* 843 F.2d 414, 416 (10th Cir. 1988).

The Eleventh Circuit applied *Whitley* to the assault of an inmate by a prison guard. *Brown v. Smith,* 813 F.2d 1187 (11th Cir. 1987)

§ 3.4B Pretrial Detainees (New)

A "deliberate indifference" standard governs the due process rights of pretrial detainees. *Molten v. Cleveland,* 839 F.2d 240 (6th Cir. 1987); *Colburn v. Upper Darby Township,* 838 F.2d 663 (3d Cir. 1988); *Anderson v. Gutschenritter,* 836 F.2d 346 (7th Cir. 1988).

§ 3.5 Supreme Court Due Process Negligence Cases

Page 49, add at end of section:

In *Cannon v. Taylor,* 782 F.2d 947 (11th Cir. 1986), the court held "that a person injured in an auto accident caused by negligent, or even grossly negligent, operation of a motor vehicle by a policeman acting in the line of duty has no § 1983 cause of action for violation of a federal right." 782 F.2d at 950. See also *Jones v. Sherrill,* 827 F.2d 1102 (6th Cir. 1987).

In *Rinker v. Napa County,* 820 F.2d 295 (9th Cir. 1987), the court found that a police officer's shooting of plaintiff during a drug raid did not violate the due process clause. The decision shows that it is not always easy to distinguish negligent from intentional conduct: "Although [defendant] Fitt 'intended,' in a literal sense, to shoot Rinker, this is not the type of intent of which the courts speak. The shooting here resulted from a spontaneous reaction, albeit a negligent reaction." *Id.* at 298.

A difficult issue under *Daniels-Davidson* is whether, in procedural due process cases, the pertinent conduct is that which results in the deprivation of a protected interest or that which resulted in the procedural deficiencies. In *Franklin v. Aycock,* 795 F.2d 1253 (6th Cir. 1986), the court concluded that a negligent failure to afford sufficient process gave rise to a due process claim because an intentional act caused the deprivation of liberty. Under *Daniels-Davidson,* the relevant conduct is that which caused the deprivation, not the conduct resulting in procedural deficiencies. "The conduct which allegedly injured Franklin's liberty interest, and which is therefore the focus of our *Daniels* inquiry, is the Disciplinary Board's decision to place him in disciplinary segregation, rather than the Board's alleged failure to afford adequate procedures by not rendering a post-hearing written statement." 795 F.2d at 1262. On the other hand, the Seventh Circuit ruled that the negligent failure to give notice of a hearing does not give rise to a due process claim. *Brunken v. Lance,* 807 F.2d 1325, 1331 (7th Cir. 1986).

Under *Daniels-Davidson,* if the contested conduct was intentional, it is "not necessary for the district court to make any other state of mind finding." *Sourbeer v. Robinson,* 791 F.2d 1094, 1105 (3d Cir. 1986), *cert. denied sub nom. Patton v. Sourbeer,* 107 S. Ct. 3276 (1987). "We know of no authority for the proposition that an intentional deprivation of life, liberty or property does not give rise to a due process violation because the failure to provide due process was without fault." *Id.*

Daniels-Davidson does not diminish the rule that sufficiently egregious brutal behavior may violate substantive due process. *New v. Minneapolis,* 792 F.2d 724 (8th Cir. 1986).

Most circuit courts take the position that recklessness or deliberate indifference may
* give rise to a due process claim. *Committee of United States Citizens Living in*

Nicaragua v. Reagan, 859 F.2d 929, 949 (D.C. Cir. 1988) (" . . . some reckless acts may constitute due process violations while others may not"); *Balistreri v. Pacifica Police Department,* 855 F.2d 1421 (9th Cir. 1988); *Archie v. City of Racine,* 847 F.2d 1211 (7th Cir. 1988) (en banc) (recklessness); *Harris v. Maynard,* 843 F.2d 414, 416 (10th Cir. 1988) (wanton or obdurate disregard or deliberate indifference); *Morales v. Department of Corrections,* 842 F.2d 27 (2d Cir. 1988) (deliberate indifference); *Taylor v. Ledbetter,* 818 F.2d 791 (11th Cir. 1987) (en banc) (deliberate indifference); *Lopez v. Houston Independent School District,* 817 F.2d 351 (5th Cir. 1987) (callous indifference); *Jacquez v. Procunier,* 801 F.2d 789 (5th Cir. 1986) (same). *But see Washington v. District of Columbia,* 802 F.2d 1487, 1481 (D.C. Cir. 1986) (recklessness not enough).

The Third, Sixth, and Ninth Circuits take the position that even gross negligence may
* serve as the basis of a due process violation. *Hammond v. County of Madera,* 859 F.2d 797 (9th Cir. 1988); *Fargo v. San Juan Bautista,* 857 F.2d 638 (9th Cir. 1988); *Wood v. Ostrander,* 851 F.2d 1212 (9th Cir. 1988); *Estate of Conners v. O'Connor,* 846 F.2d 1205 (9th Cir. 1988); *Metzger v. Osbeck,* 841 F.2d 518, 520 n.1 (3d Cir. 1988); *Colburn v. Upper Darby Township,* 838 F.2d 663, 668 & n.3 (3d Cir. 1988); *Jones v. Sherrill,* 827 F.2d 1102, 1106 (6th Cir. 1987); *Vinson v. Campbell County Fiscal Court,* 820 F.2d 194, 199-200 (6th Cir. 1987); *Nishiyama v. Dickson County,* 814 F.2d 277 (6th Cir. 1987) (en banc). The Seventh and Eighth Circuits have come to the opposite conclusion. *Archie v. City of Racine,* 847 F.2d 1211, 1220 (7th Cir. 1988) (" 'Recklessness' is a proxy for intent; 'gross negligence' is not"); *Tallman v. Reagan,* 846 F.2d 494 (8th Cir. 1988); *Myers v. Morris,* 810 F.2d 1437, 1468 (8th Cir.), *cert. denied,* 108 S. Ct. 97 (1987). The Seventh Circuit believes that the line between negligence and gross negligence cannot be "policed" and thus is not worth drawing in constitutional law. *Archie v. City of Racine,* 847 F.2d at 1219.

The Sixth Circuit found that the alleged gross negligence or reckless indifference of a sheriff and his deputy, in entrusting a fully-equipped patrol car to an inmate who killed plaintiff's decedent after pulling her over to the side of the road, stated a proper § 1983 due process claim. While *gross negligence* is not easy to define, a person may be liable under § 1983 "if he intentionally does something unreasonable with disregard to a known risk or a risk so obvious that he must be assumed to have been aware of it and of a magnitude that it is highly probable that harm will follow." *Nishiyama v. Dickson County,* 814 F.2d at 282. See also *Stanulonis v. Marzec,* 649 F. Supp. 1536, 1543 (D. Conn. 1986) (distinction between negligence, gross negligence, and recklessness is the difference between " 'a fool, a damned fool, and a God-damned fool' ").

In *Jones v. Sherrill,* 827 F.2d 1102, 1106 (6th Cir. 1987), the court stated that gross negligence requires an allegation of "outrageous conduct or arbitrary use of government power."

The Seventh Circuit, citing *Daniels* preceded by "[s]ee generally," held that election irregularities implicate § 1983 only when there is willful misconduct. *Bodine v. Elkhart County Election Board,* 788 F.2d 1270 (7th Cir. 1986). See also *Lunde v. Oldi,* 808 F.2d 219 (2d Cir. 1986).

* Contrary to the training he received, an officer held his gun in his hand while he handcuffed the suspect. As he started to handcuff him the gun went off, shooting the suspect in the shoulder. The Ninth Circuit found that a jury question was presented as to the officer's gross negligence, and that the violation of police procedures is relevant in assessing this question. *Fargo v. San Juan Bautista,* 857 F.2d 638 (9th Cir. 1988).

In *Harris v. Maynard,* 843 F.2d 414, 416 (10th Cir. 1988), the Court determined that under the Eighth Amendment and due process clause "prison officials may not exercise their responsibility with wanton or obdurate indifference to the preservation of the life of the inmate."

* The *Daniels-Davidson* no-negligence rule does not impose a scienter or other culpability requirement superseding the *Youngberg v. Romeo,* 457 U.S. 307 (1982), professional judgment standard, which is utilized to determine the constitutional rights of involuntarily committed mental patients. *Estate of Conners v. O'Connor,* 846 F.2d 1205 (9th Cir. 1988).

The Second Circuit ruled that the Fourth Amendment does not reach negligent conduct. *Dodd v. City of Norwich,* 827 F.2d 1, 7-8 (2d Cir. 1987) (on reargument), *cert. denied,* 108 S. Ct. 701 (1988). Citing "*Cf. Daniels*[,]" a district court held that there is no Fourth Amendment violation "when a police officer is alleged to have negligently included material false statements in an affidavit accompanying a warrant application." *Willocks v. Dodenhoff,* 110 F.R.D. 652, 657 (D. Conn.), *aff'd,* 805 F.2d 392 (2d Cir. 1986). Several courts, however, found that negligence may give rise to a Fourth
* Amendment claim. *Borunda v. Richmond,* 860 F.2d 937 (9th Cir. 1988) (*Daniels* no negligence rule has "little relevance to claim of arrest without probable cause");
* *Specht v. Jensen,* 832 F.2d 1516 (10th Cir. 1987); *Austin v. East Grand Rapids,* 685 F. Supp. 1396 (W.D. Mich. 1988) (right to reasonably prompt probable cause hearing may be violated by negligence); *McKenna v. Clayton County,* 657 F. Supp. 221 (N.D. Ga. 1987); *Patterson v. Fuller,* 654 F. Supp. 418 (N.D. Ga. 1987). The Colorado Supreme Court held that the *Daniels* no-negligence rule applies to due process claims but not to First, Fourth, Fifth, and Tenth Amendment claims. *Uberoi v. University of Colorado,* 713 P.2d 894 (Colo. 1986).

The *Daniels* rule was applied retroactively in *Stanulonis v. Marzec,* 649 F. Supp. 1536 (D. Conn. 1986).

§ 3.6 Other Constitutional Torts–Malicious Prosecution

Page 51, add at end of section:

In a case that was expected to answer the question of whether malicious prosecution constitutes a constitutional tort, the United States Supreme Court dismissed the writ of certiorari as improvidently granted. *Cerbone v. Conway,* 107 S. Ct. 390 (1986).

The circuit courts have expressed different views on this issue. In a *Bivens* action, the D.C. Circuit Court of Appeals recognized that a constitutional tort of retaliatory prosecution may be based upon a practice of pursuing criminal charges against individuals because they refused to waive their civil suits against the arresting officers. The decision in *Town of Newton v. Rumery,* 107 S. Ct. 1187 (1987), discussed in **§ 14.5**, did not sanction such an abuse of prosecutorial power. *Haynesworth v. Miller,* 820 F.2d 1245 (D.C. Cir. 1987).

* The Second Circuit reiterated that malicious prosecution can form the basis of § 1983 liability. The fact that the prosecutor and grand jury advance the prosecution

does not necessarily insulate a complaining witness from liability. Although a grand jury indictment is prima facie evidence of probable cause in the malicious prosecution action, it may be rebutted by proof that the defendant misrepresented, withheld, or falsified evidence. *White v. Frank,* 855 F.2d 956 (2d Cir. 1988). *White* analyzes the issue of witness immunity. See **§ 7.9**.

Like the Second Circuit, the Third Circuit takes the position that "the elements of liability for the constitutional tort of malicious prosecution under § 1983 coincide with those of the common law tort." Note how the court handles the qualified immunity issue:

> Because the law pertaining to the controlling Pennsylvania statute of limitations was unclear and the investigators sought the advice of counsel before filing charges, they could reasonably believe that their actions were lawful. On this record, no reasonable jury could find that the unlawfulness of the investigators' actions were [was] so apparent that their claim of qualified immunity must be denied.

Lee v. Mihalich, 847 F.2d 66, 70, 73 (3d Cir. 1988).

The Fifth Circuit holds that abuse of civil process, without more, does not rise to a constitutional violation. *Whatley v. Philo,* 817 F.2d 19 (5th Cir. 1987). In *Cougan v. City of Wixon,* 820 F.2d 170, 175 (5th Cir. 1987), the court adhered to its position that misuse of a legal proceeding is unconstitutional when it is sufficiently "egregious." The Fifth Circuit analyzed the issue in more detail in *Hand v. Gary,* 838 F.2d 1420 (5th Cir. 1988). The court set forth four principles: (1) bad faith prosecution violates constitutional rights; (2) when plaintiff makes a prima facie case of malicious prosecution, the burden shifts to defendant to show that his or her actions did not result from improper motivation; (3) those who join prosecutors in malicious prosecutions may be liable for damages; and (4) "simply obtaining an indictment is not enough to insulate state actors from an action for malicious prosecution under § 1983." *Id.* at 1426. The defendant in *Hand* demonstrated that the prosecution was not malicious by showing that prior to bringing charges probable course was reascertained, departmental procedures were followed, and no relevant information was withheld from the grand jury. In *Thomas v. Kippermann,* 846 F.2d 1009 (5th Cir. 1988), the court found that allegations that the defendant police officer maliciously supplied information knowing that it was false, and that this information formed the basis for the plaintiff's arrest, detention, and prosecution, stated claims for false arrest, false imprisonment, and malicious prosecution under § 1983.

In *McMaster v. Cabinet for Human Resources,* 824 F.2d 518 (6th Cir. 1987), the court, citing this text, stated that, to support a constitutional claim, plaintiffs must show that they were subject to incarceration and that the prosecution shocks the conscience.

The Seventh Circuit held that a county's "mere unsuccessful attempt to secure an injunction under an allegedly unconstitutional ordinance does not make out a deprivation of constitutional rights." *Andree v. Ashland County,* 818 F.2d 1306, 1312 (7th Cir. 1987). In dicta, however, the court indicated that the result might be different if the action was tantamount to a malicious prosecution or abuse of process, or if the ordinance sought to be enforced "is palpably unconsitutional." *Id.* at 1313. In *Easter House v. Felder,* 852 F.2d 901, 910 (7th Cir. 1988), the court, responding to the plaintiffs' claim of malicious administrative investigation, concluded that malicious prosecution standing alone does not violate a constitutional right. In a subsequent case, Judge Posner, terming the issue "open" in the Seventh Circuit, found it unnecessary to examine the "difficult question whether malicious prosecution can ever count as a deprivation of liberty without due process of law when defendant is not imprisoned . . . ." *Jones v. Chicago,* 856 F.2d 985, 992 (7th Cir. 1988).

The Ninth Circuit took the position that malicious prosecution is not actionable under § 1983 if a state judicial remedy is available to redress it. "However, 'an exception exists to the general rule when a malicious prosecution is conducted with the intent to deprive a person of equal protection of the law or is otherwise intended to subject a person to a denial of constitutional rights.' " *Usher v. Los Angeles,* 828 F.2d 556, 562 (9th Cir. 1987), quoting *Bretz v. Kelman,* 773 F.2d 1026, 1031 (9th Cir. 1985) (en banc). *See also Karim-Panahi v. Los Angeles Police Department,* 839 F.2d 621, 624 (9th Cir. 1988); *McCarthy v. Mayo,* 827 F.2d 1310 (9th Cir. 1987); *Johnson v. Barker,* 799 F.2d 1396 (9th Cir. 1986).

* The Eleventh Circuit follows the Fifth Circuit rule that there is a federal constitutional right to be free of malicious prosecution. *Strength v. Hubert,* 854 F.2d 421 (11th Cir. 1988). *Strength* also analyzes the question of witness immunity. See § **7.9**.

The Second Circuit ruled that no constitutional violation results from a prison official's lodging of false disciplinary charges against a prisoner so long as fair procedures are provided. "Plaintiff suffered as a result of the finding of guilty by the prison disciplinary committee hearing, and not merely because of the filing of unfounded charges . . . ." *Freeman v. Rideout,* 808 F.2d 949, 953 (2d Cir. 1986), *reh'g denied,* 826 F.2d 194 (2d Cir. 1987), *cert. denied,* 108 S. Ct. 1273 (1988). *Accord, Hanrahan v. Lane,* 747 F.2d 1137 (7th Cir. 1984). *See contra, United States v. Wallace,* 673 F. Supp. 205 (S.D. Tex. 1987); *Morrison v. LeFever,* 592 F. Supp. 1052 (S.D.N.Y.
* 1984). The Second Circuit narrowed its holding in *Freeman* in *Franco v. Kelly,* 854 F.2d 584 (2d Cir. 1988). The *Franco* court ruled that an inmate's allegations that prison officials intentionally filed false disciplinary charges against him because he cooperated in a state investigation of inmate abuse stated a proper § 1983 claim of retaliation for exercising the constitutional right to petition the government for redress of grievances.

§ 3.7 —False Arrest and False Imprisonment

Page 52, add at end of section:

Plaintiff's allegation of being detained for 40 hours following a warrantless arrest, without a probable cause hearing before a magistrate, stated a proper § 1983 claim. *King v. Massarweh,* 782 F.2d 825 (9th Cir. 1986). Plaintiff's arrest and subsequent jailing for 23 days as a material witness, when the case for which his testimony was sought had already been closed, violated his due process rights. *Mairena v. Foti,* 816 F.2d 1061 (5th Cir. 1987), *cert. denied,* 108 S. Ct. 697 (1988).

* Relatively short delays in releasing an individual who is entitled to be released are not unconstitutional. In *Lewis v. O'Grady,* 853 F.2d 1366 (7th Cir. 1988), the court

ruled that the plaintiff's detention in custody for approximately 11 hours after a state court had determined that he was not the person named in the arrest warrant did not by itself violate his constitutional rights. A reasonable time is allowed for carrying out administrative tasks incident to release, such as transportation, identity verification, and processing. It is for the jury to determine whether the time it took to discharge the plaintiff was reasonable. In *Clark v. Link,* 855 F.2d 156 (4th Cir. 1988), the court determined that when an arrest is made under a valid warrant, a three-hour delay in the plaintiff's release does not violate due process.

Arrests and searches which do not violate the Fourth Amendment do not violate the due process clause. *Patton v. Przybylski,* 822 F.2d 697, 699 (7th Cir. 1987). The Seventh Circuit found that a police officer's execution of an arrest warrant against the wrong person was not unconstitutional where the officer did not act unreasonably. The plaintiff's name, race, and birthdate were the same as the person named in the warrant. *Id.* See also *Howard v. Regional Transit Authority,* 667 F. Supp. 540 (N.D. Ohio 1987). In *Brown v. Patterson,* 823 F.2d 167 (7th Cir.), *cert. denied,* 108 S. Ct. 162 (1987), the court ruled that the arresting officer acted constitutionally in executing an arrest warrant which was regular on its face, even though the address and birthdate on the warrant did not match the information on the arrestee's driver's license, where the officer reasonably believed the arrestee was using an alias and false address and birthdate.

> Although a prolonged confinement of an arrested person without a hearing to determine whether he is the person named in the warrant would be a deprivation of liberty without due process of law and thus violate the Fourteenth Amendment, there is no suggestion that 24 hours was unreasonable in the circumstances.

823 F.2d at 169.

The fact that the federal court plaintiff pleaded guilty in a state criminal proceeding was not conclusive proof that there was probable cause for his arrest. *Hinshaw v. Doffer,* 785 F.2d 1260, 1267 (5th Cir. 1986). See also *Davis v. City of Charleston,* 827 F.2d 317, 321 (8th Cir. 1987) (rejecting argument that plaintiff's conviction collaterally
* estopped him from contesting constitutionality of his arrest). The Fifth Circuit, citing an array of circuit court decisions, observed that "[t]he effect of a conviction on the issue of probable cause in a civil setting is less than etched in stone in this circuit." *Brumfield v. Jones,* 849 F.2d 152, 155 (5th Cir. 1988). In *Cameron v. Fogarty,* 806 F.2d 380 (2d Cir. 1986), *cert. denied,* 107 S. Ct. 1894 (1987), the court, applying New York state law, ruled that plaintiff's conviction defeated his § 1983 unlawful arrest claim. The authors believe that there was no basis for applying a state law defense to a federal constitutional § 1983 claim in this context, and that the proper approach is to apply the state law of preclusion to the conviction. *See Adamson v. Volkmer,* 680 F. Supp. 1191 (N.D. Ill. 1987).

* Putting together a smorgasbord of res judicata, qualified immunity, and state law immunity a la *Cameron v. Fogarty,* the Sixth Circuit concluded that a state court finding of guilt following a plea of nolo contendere defeated the federal court plaintiff's (criminal defendants) § 1983 claim for false arrest. Rule 410 of the Federal Rules of Evidence does not preclude the defendant officers' use of the plea for collateral

estoppel purposes. "Rule 410 was intended to protect a criminal defendant's use of the nolo contendere plea to defend himself from future civil *liability*. We decline to interpret the rule so as to allow the former [criminal] defendants to use the plea offensively, in order to obtain damages, after having admitted facts which would indicate no civil liability on the part of the arresting police." *Walker v. Schaeffer,* 854 F.2d 138, 143 (6th Cir. 1988) (emphasis in original).

The Ninth Circuit reaffirmed its prior decision in the *Smiddy v. Varney* case (655 F.2d 261) that police officers normally are not liable for damages for an unlawful arrest that is followed by a criminal prosecution, because there is "a rebuttable presumption that a prosecutor exercises independent judgment regarding the existence of probable cause [to arrest] in filing a complaint." *Smiddy v. Varney,* 803 F.2d 1469, 1471 (9th Cir. 1986), *modified,* 811 F.2d 504 (9th Cir. 1987).

> The presumption can be overcome, for example, by evidence that the officers knowingly submitted false information or pressured the prosecutor to act contrary to her independent judgment. *Smiddy,* [665 F.2d] at 266-267. Unless overcome, however, the presumption insulates the arresting officer from liability for pain suffered after the prosecutor initiated formal prosecution.

803 F.2d at 1471.

The court in *Smiddy* held that the Supreme Court's decision in *Malley v. Briggs,* 106 S. Ct. 1092 (1986), which deals with police officer qualified immunity (see **§ 7.16**), neither addressed nor altered these rules. See also *Hand v. Gary,* 838 F.2d 1420 (5th Cir. 1988). *See contra, Mitchel v. City of Hartford,* 674 F. Supp. 60 (D. Conn. 1986).

* The Ninth Circuit, applying its original decision in *Smiddy,* found that plaintiffs rebutted the presumption by demonstrating that the defendant police officers "procured the filing of the criminal complaint by making misrepresentations to the prosecuting attorney." *Borunda v. Richmond,* 860 F.2d 937, 943 (9th Cir. 1988). The court in *Borunda* also ruled that the *Daniels* no-negligence rule has "little relevance" to a claim of arrest without probable cause.

The Seventh Circuit took the position that when the plaintiff claimed false arrest and imprisonment resulting from a police officer's deliberate supplying of misleading information to prosecutorial authorities, the officers "cannot escape liability by pointing to the decisions of prosecutors or grand jurors or magistrates to confine or prosecute him. They cannot hide behind the officials whom they have defrauded." *Jones v. Chicago,* 856 F.2d 985, 994 (7th Cir. 1988).

§ 3.8 Procedural Due Process Claims: *Parratt v. Taylor*

Page 56, add before first full paragraph:

* The *Parratt-Hudson* doctrine applies to deprivations of liberty as well as property. *Birkenholz v. Sluyter,* 857 F.2d 1214 (8th Cir. 1988); *Watts v. Burkhart,* 854 F.2d 839 (6th Cir. 1988); *Wood v. Ostrander,* 851 F.2d 1212 (9th Cir. 1988).

Disagreeing with the reasoning of *Bretz v. Kelmon,* 773 F.2d 1026 (9th Cir. 1985) (en banc), the Fifth Circuit held that the *Parratt-Hudson* doctrine is not limited to minor deprivation of liberty or property. *Holloway v. Walker,* 790 F.2d 1170 (5th Cir.) (en banc), *cert. denied,* 107 S. Ct. 571 (1986). *Accord, Byrd v. Stewart,* 803 F.2d 1168 (11th Cir. 1986). The Ninth Circuit rejected the argument that the *Parratt* doctrine is limited to prisoner cases. *Lake Nacimiento Ranch Co. v. San Luis Obispo County,* 830 F.2d 977, 983 (9th Cir.), *amended,* 841 F.2d 872 (9th Cir. 1987). *See Goolsby v. City of Montgomery,* 805 F.2d 1008 (11th Cir. 1987), applying *Parratt* in an employment termination context.

The courts have been experiencing considerable difficulty determining when a deprivation of a protected due process interest is random and unauthorized so as to invoke the *Parratt-Hudson* doctrine. Decisions of the Second, Third, Seventh, Eighth, Ninth, and Eleventh Circuits take the position that even if the deprivation is in violation of state law, it is not random and unauthorized if carried out pursuant to a practice or policy established by senior officials with authority to grant predeprivation hearings. *Burch v. Apalachee Community Health Services,* 840 F.2d 797 (11th Cir. 1988) (en banc) (*Parratt* does not apply to unauthorized nonrandom conduct); *R.R. Village Association v. Denver Sewer Corp.,* 826 F.2d 1197, 1204 (2d Cir. 1987) ("the action of a high-ranking official body, such as the Town Board, which has final authority over the decision-making process cannot be considered random and unauthorized"); *Dwyer v. Regan,* 777 F.2d 825, 832 (2d Cir. 1985) ("where the depriving actions were taken by a high-ranking official having final authority over the decision-making process, . . . they were not random or unauthorized"), *modified,* 793 F.2d 457 (2d Cir. 1986); *Berlanti v. Bodman,* 780 F.2d 296 (3d Cir. 1985); *Brown v. Trench,* 787 F.2d 167, 171-72 (3d Cir. * 1986); *Matthiesen v. North Chicago School District,* 857 F.2d 404, 407 n.3 (7th Cir. 1988); *Westborough Mall v. City of Cape Girardeau,* 794 F.2d 330, 337 (8th Cir. 1986); *Brower v. Inyo County,* 817 F.2d 540, 544-45 (9th Cir. 1987), *cert. granted,* 108 S. Ct. * 2869 (1988). In *Watts v. Burkhart,* 854 F.2d 839 (6th Cir. 1988), *Parratt-Hudson* was found inapplicable because the deprivation was pursuant to the established state procedure. The court rejected the argument that, because the state procedures on their face comported with due process, any conduct which violated due process was necessarily random and unauthorized. According to *Watts,* the key to *Parratt-Hudson* is whether the state is in a position to provide predeprivation process. That the state was in such a position was demonstrated by the fact that it actually provided predeprivation notice and a hearing. In *Merritt v. Mackey,* 827 F.2d 1368 (9th Cir. 1987), the court stated that "[p]ostdeprivation remedies satisfy due process only when the conduct at issue was both unauthorized *and* random" (emphasis in original). In an en banc decision, dealing with involuntary commitment, the Eleventh Circuit read *Parratt* as not applying to unauthorized but nonrandom conduct. The focus should be on the practicality with which state officials with authority could provide a prior hearing. *Burch v. Apalachee Community Mental Health Services,* 840 F.2d 797 (11th Cir. 1988) (en banc). Judge Tjoflat's dissenting opinion takes the position that the controlling inquiry is whether the state was in a position to forecast the deprivation and provide a prior hearing. It is not in such a position when its officials act in contravention of state policy.

In contrast, the Fifth Circuit held "[t]hat ability of the individual state employee to provide predeprivation process does not determine whether a due process violation has taken place" and that "[w]hen state procedures provide due process and are violated by a random or unauthorized act of a state employee, even a high-ranking state employee, *Parratt-Hudson* established that no federal constitutional due process * violation has occurred." *Holloway v. Walker,* 790 F.2d 1170, 1173 (5th Cir. 1986). The Fourth Circuit followed *Holloway* in *Fields v. Durham,* 856 F.2d 655 (4th Cir. 1988).

The court in *Holloway v. Walker,* further disagreeing with the Ninth Circuit's position in *Bretz v. Kelmon, supra,* found that *Parratt-Hudson* applies to an illegal conspiracy that abuses the state process itself. *Accord, Schaper v. City of Huntsville,* 813 F.2d 709, * 715 (5th Cir. 1987) (state cannot be expected to anticipate conspiracies). Disagreeing with *Holloway,* the Seventh Circuit concluded that the *Parratt-Hudson* doctrine did not encompass a conspiracy by high-level officials to use the authority of a state licensing agency to transfer property from one private citizen to another. "The absence of statutory or regulatory authorization for the defendants' misuse of the regulatory process does not . . . establish that the conduct at issue was random and unauthorized." *Easter House v. Felder,* 852 F.2d 901, 915 (7th Cir.), *reh'g granted,* 861 F.2d 494 (7th Cir. 1988). *Labov v. Lalley,* 809 F.2d 220, 223 (3d Cir. 1987) (an intentional conspiracy under color of state law "is not the kind of isolated, and thus unpreventable conduct with which the Supreme Court purports to deal in the *Parratt* . . . line of cases").

In *Lake Nacimiento Ranch Co. v. San Luis Obispo County,* 830 F.2d 977 (9th Cir.), *opinion amended,* 841 F.2d 872 (9th Cir. 1987), a zoning controversy, the court determined that a claim based upon a decisionmaker's alleged conflict of interest is an attack on the decisionmaking process and is thus within the *Parratt* doctrine.

In *Yates v. Jamison,* 782 F.2d 1182 (4th Cir. 1986), the plaintiffs complained about the city's demolition of their house without prior notice. The majority concluded that since plaintiffs "alleged that their house was destroyed without notice because defendants were 'willfully and recklessly negligent' in failing to comply with the notice and hearing procedures mandated by state law," they were claiming "that their house was destroyed without notice only because the defendants violated established state procedure." 782 F.2d at 1185. This brought the case within *Parratt-Hudson.* Circuit Judge Ervin, dissenting, saw it differently. In his view, plaintiffs alleged that the demolition without notice represented a city custom or policy; if this was so, *Parratt-Hudson* does not apply even if the custom or policy may have violated state law. For a criticism of the majority opinion in *Yates, see Esquivel v. Village of McCullom Lake,* 633 F. Supp. 1199 (N.D. Ill. 1986).

The Second Circuit applied *Parratt* to a claim that an administrative law judge's failure to strike the testimony of a witness violated procedural due process, finding that a judicial review proceeding provided all the process that was due. *Marino v. Ameruso,* 837 F.2d 45 (2d Cir. 1988).

The Second Circuit, in dicta, acknowledged the relationship between the *Parratt-Hudson* doctrine and the *Monell* policy requirement by stating that if plaintiff has no claim for municipal liability because the contested conduct was unauthorized, the action might be dismissed if the state provided an adequate postdeprivation remedy. *Sullivan v. Town of Salem,* 805 F.2d 81, 86 (2d Cir. 1986). The Seventh Circuit took the same position, stating that if the contested conduct was in accord with "official policy" it could not be random and unauthorized. "Therefore, a complaint asserting municipal liability under *Monell* by definition states a claim to which *Parratt* is inapposite." *Wilson v. Civil Town of Clayton,* 839 F.2d 375, 380 (7th Cir. 1988). The court also stated that "[b]ecause *Parratt* applies only to actions that are random *and* unauthorized, it does not apply to the claims against the Trustees in their official capacities." *Id.* at 382. *But see Vinson v. Campbell County Fiscal Court,* 820 F.2d 194, 199 (6th Cir. 1987) (distinguishing the *Monell* and *Parratt* issues).

Page 57, add after carryover paragraph:

Another issue that gives the courts difficulty is whether the state remedy is adequate. The following have been found to be adequate postdeprivation remedies: workers' compensation, *McClary v. O'Hare,* 786 F.2d 83 (2d Cir. 1986); *Hayes v. Vessey,* 777 F.2d 1149 (6th Cir. 1985); *Coollick v. Town of Windham,* 7 Conn. 142, 508 A.2d 46 (Ct. App. 1986); a wrongful death action, *McGowan v. Riley,* 628 F. Supp. 1087 (N.D. Miss. 1985); *Miga v. City of Holyoke,* 398 Mass. 343, 497 N.E.2d 1 (1986); *Enright v. School Directors Board,* 118 Wis. 2d 236, 346 N.W.2d 771 (1984); an administrative appeal or judicial review proceeding, *Campo v. Employees' Retirement System,* 843 F.2d 96 (2d Cir.), *cert. denied,* 109 S. Ct. 220 (1988); *Marino v. Ameruso,* 837 F.2d 45 (2d Cir. 1988); *Alfaro Motors v. Ward,* 814 F.2d 883, 888 (2d Cir. 1987) (dicta); *Myrick v. Dallas,* 810 F.2d 1382, 1388 (5th Cir. 1987); *Lee v. Hutson,* 810 F.2d 1030 (11th Cir. 1987); *Sullivan v. Town of Salem,* 805 F.2d 86 (2d Cir. 1986) (dictum); a replevin action, *Storey v. United States,* 629 F. Supp. 1174, 1179 (N.D. Miss. 1986); a state tort claims act * remedy, *Hossman v. Spradlin,* 812 F.2d 1019 (7th Cir. 1987); a *Bivens*-type remedy (*Bivens v. Six Unknown Named Agents,* 403 U.S. 388 (1971)) under the state constitution, *Huron Valley Hospital v. City of Pontiac,* 686 F. Supp. 608 (E.D. Mich. 1988); *Hikel v. King,* 659 F. Supp. 337 (E.D.N.Y. 1987); *Sheets v. Department of Corrections,* 656 F. Supp. 733 (S.D. Ind. 1986); a collective bargaining grievance procedure, *Costello v. Town of Fairfield,* 811 F.2d 782 (2d Cir. 1987); and a state court habeas corpus and false imprisonment damages remedy, *Martin v. Dallas County,* 822 F.2d 553 (5th Cir. 1987).

To be adequate, the state remedy need not afford all the relief that is available under § 1983. *Economic Development Corp. v. Stierheim,* 782 F.2d 952, 955 (11th Cir. 1986) (unavailability of punitive damages does not render state remedy inadequate); *Davey v. Tomlinson,* 627 F. Supp. 1458, 1464 (E.D. Mich. 1986) (fact that state remedy does not authorize attorney's fees does not render it inadequate).

"An investigation of 'adequacy' must, of course, consider the extent to which a state has waived its sovereign immunity and whether individual defendants are somehow insulated from liability." *Burch v. Apalachee Community Mental Health Services,* 804 F.2d 1549, 1556 n.11 (11th Cir. 1986), *rev'd on other grounds,* 840 F.2d 797 (11th Cir. 1988) (en banc). Most courts hold that the mere fact that state immunity law may deprive a plaintiff of a remedy does not itself render the state remedy inadequate. *Taylor v. Ledbetter,* 791 F.2d 881, 884 (11th Cir. 1986); *National Communication Systems v. Public Service Commission,* 789 F.2d 370 (6th Cir.) (availability of good faith immunity did not render state remedy inadequate), *cert. denied,* 107 S. Ct. 182 (1986); *Taylor v. Watters,* 636 F. Supp. 181, 188 (E.D. Mich. 1986). See also *Williams v. St. Louis County,* 812 F.2d 1079, 1082 (8th Cir. 1987) (noting "debate" over whether state * law immunity renders state remedies inadequate). A district court determined that the *Parratt-Hudson* doctrine does not bar a § 1983 procedural due process claim when the state remedy would be defeated by absolute immunity. *Soto v. Lord,* 693 F. Supp. 8, 15-16 (S.D.N.Y. 1988). In *Hight v. Burden,* 180 Ga. 716, 350 S.E.2d 471, 473 (1986), however, the court found the state remedy inadequate because "claims against the State of Georgia fall far short of amounting to the significant waiver of sovereign immunity which is provided by the tort claim procedure of the State of Nebraska which is approved in *Parratt.*"

A state remedy is not inadequate solely because it is barred by the state statute of limitations. *Harris v. Missouri Conservation Commission,* 790 F.2d 678, 681 (8th Cir. 1986) ("The state provided a remedy, but plaintiffs failed to pursue it").

"[W]here an indigent plaintiff presents a non-frivolous state-law claim, the denial of *in forma pauperis* status or similar relief for no apparent reasons renders an otherwise adequate postdeprivation remedy inadequate under *Parratt.*" *Williams v. St. Louis County,* 812 F.2d 1079, 1083 (8th Cir. 1987).

The Sixth Circuit adheres to its requirement that a § 1983 plaintiff who asserts a procedural due process claim has the burden of pleading and proving that state damages remedies are inadequate. *Sproul v. City of Wooster,* 840 F.2d 1267 (6th Cir. 1988).

§ 3.9 Substantive Constitutional Rights: Reconciling *Parratt* and *Monroe*

Page 59, add at end of section:

The circuits are in accord that the *Parratt-Hudson* doctrine does not apply to claimed violations of substantive constitutional rights. A listing of the leading recent circuit court decisions follows:

1st Cir.	*Simmons v. Dickhaut,* 804 F.2d 182 (1st Cir. 1986)
2d Cir.	*Robison v. Via,* 821 F.2d 913, 925 (2d Cir. 1987);
	Morello v. James, 810 F.2d 344 (2d Cir. 1987);
	McClary v. O'Hare, 786 F.2d 83 (2d Cir. 1986)
5th Cir.	*Martin v. Dallas County,* 822 F.2d 553 (5th Cir. 1987);
	Jackson v. Procunier, 789 F.2d 307 (5th Cir. 1986)
6th Cir.	*Vinson v. Campbell County Fiscal Court,* 820 F.2d 194 (6th Cir. 1987);
	Dugan v. Brooks, 818 F.2d 513 (6th Cir. 1987);
	Hayes v. Vessey, 777 F.2d 1149 (6th Cir. 1985)
7th Cir.	*Bailey v. Andrews,* 811 F.2d 366 (7th Cir. 1987)
8th Cir.	*McIntosh v. Arkansas Republican Party,* 816 F.2d 409 (8th Cir. 1987);
	Martin v. Salem, 801 F.2d 324 (8th Cir. 1986);

		Littlefield v. City of Afton, 785 F.2d 596 (8th Cir. 1986)
*	9th Cir.	*Wood v. Ostrander,* 851 F.2d 1212 (9th Cir. 1988);
		Smith v. City of Fontana, 818 F.2d 1411 (9th Cir.), *cert. denied,* 108 S. Ct. 311 (1987);
		Shah v. County of Los Angeles, 797 F.2d 743 (9th Cir. 1986);
		McRorie v. Shimoda, 795 F.2d 780 (9th Cir. 1986);
		Sanders v. Kennedy, 794 F.2d 478 (9th Cir. 1986);
		New v. Minneapolis, 792 F.2d 724 (8th Cir. 1986);
		King v. Masarweh, 782 F.2d 825 (9th Cir. 1986);
		Mann v. Tuscon, 782 F.2d 790 (9th Cir. 1986);
		Rutherford v. City of Berkeley, 780 F.2d 1444 (9th Cir. 1986)
	11th Cir.	*Lee v. Hutson,* 810 F.2d 1030 (11th Cir. 1987);
		Depew v. City of St. Mary's, 787 F.2d 1496 (11th Cir. 1986);
		Leslie v. Ingram, 786 F.2d 1533 (11th Cir. 1986);
		Love v. Sheffield, 777 F.2d 1453 (11th Cir. 1985);
		Fundiller v. Cooper City, 777 F.2d 1436 (11th Cir. 1985)

Two district court opinions found the *Parratt-Hudson* doctrine inapplicable to claimed deprivations of life in violation of substantive due process. *Strandell v. Jackson County,* 634 F. Supp. 824 (S.D. Ill. 1986); *Doty v. Carey,* 626 F. Supp. 359 (N.D. Ill. 1986).

§ 3.10 *Parratt* and Just Compensation Claims

Page 60, add at end of section:

The Supreme Court ruled that the just compensation clause requires that compensation be provided for temporary regulatory takings, and that invalidation of the ordinance without payment of just compensation for use of the property during the taking period is a constitutionally insufficient state remedy. *First English Evangelical Lutheran Church v. Los Angeles County,* 107 S. Ct. 2378 (1987). The Court dealt with a regulation-taking controversy in a § 1983 action in *Keystone Bituminous Coal Co. v. DeBenedictis,* 107 S. Ct. 1232 (1987). *Keystone* involved a statutory scheme virtually identical to that at issue in the landmark case of *Pennsylvania Coal Co. v. Mahon,* 260 U.S. 393 (1922) and, although not directly overruling *Mahon,* reached a directly opposite result. In *Nollan v. California Coastal Commission,* 107 S. Ct. 3141 (1987), the Court ruled that when the government imposes conditions upon the use of land, those conditions must have a close relationship to the asserted state interests.

A takings claim asserted by landlords against a rent control ordinance provision allowing a hearing officer to consider, inter alia, "hardship to a tenant," was premature because the hearing officer had not yet applied the clause. Because the takings analysis is essentially ad hoc, the challenge should await an actual factual setting. *Pennell v. San Jose,* 108 S. Ct. 849 (1988).

The First Circuit found that the *Williamson* prematurity doctrine applies to both takings and due process claims. "If reviewed strictly as a due process claim, the money damages claim was likewise premature, because the amount of damages could not be estimated where the developer had failed to apply for variances from the challenged regulations." *Culebras Enterprises v. Rivera Rios,* 813 F.2d 506, 511-12 (1st Cir. 1987). The court also ruled that the fact that the Commonwealth election-of-remedy law provided that obtaining a remedy against either the Commonwealth or against the individual official barred a remedy against the other did not render the state remedy inadequate.

While mysteriously not citing *Williamson,* the Eighth Circuit ruled that, assuming that plaintiffs are correct that their state remedy is barred by the statute of limitations, their federal court just compensation and due process claims are without merit. *Harris v. Missouri Conservation Commission,* 790 F.2d 678, 681 (8th Cir. 1986) ("The state provided a remedy but plaintiffs failed to pursue it").

The Ninth Circuit has been especially active in applying *Williamson.* In *Kinzli v. Santa Cruz,* 818 F.2d 1449 (9th Cir.), *amended,* 830 F.2d 968 (9th Cir. 1987), *cert. denied,* 108 S. Ct. 775 (1988), the court determined that to assert a regulatory takings claim, plaintiff must show "(1) that the regulation has gone so far that it has 'taken' plaintiff's property, and (2) that any compensation tendered is not 'just' " (*id.* at 1453). The first component requires a final determination from an authoritative decision-maker, and this requires at least an application by the landowner for a favorable administrative determination. In this case plaintiffs neither submitted a development plan for approval nor applied for a variance. While it is unclear when a state remedy should be found "futile," "[t]he Supreme Court has indicated that *at least one* application must be submitted before the futility exception applies." *Id.* at 1454 (emphasis in original). With respect to the second component, plaintiff must seek compensation from the state if adequate procedures are available. Plaintiffs failed to do so. The court rejected plaintiff's contention that California does not have an adequate procedure for obtaining compensation for inverse condemnation.

In another case, the Ninth Circuit ruled that plaintiff's failure to pursue the state inverse condemnation remedy rendered the federal court just compensation claim premature; it also found that there is no constitutional right to pretaking notice and an opportunity to be heard, or to pretaking compensation. *Cassettari v. Nevada County,* 824 F.2d 735 (9th Cir. 1987).

In *Herrington v. County of Sonoma,* 857 F.2d 567 (9th Cir. 1988), *amending* 834 F.2d 1488 (9th Cir. 1987), the court (1) read Ninth Circuit decisions as applying the same takings ripeness standards, which require developers to obtain the planning commission's "final definitive position" as to how it will apply the regulations to the land in issue, to equal protection and substantive due process claims and, in this case, to the plaintiff's procedural due process claim; (2) found that, even though the plaintiff had not submitted a development plan that was "formally complete," the requirement of a rejected development plan was satisfied because to require its completion or application for a variance would be futile, and (3) concluded that the trial court should not have submitted the ripeness issue to the jury because it is an issue of law for the trial court subject to de novo appellate review.

In *Bateson v. Geisse,* 857 F.2d 1300 (9th Cir. 1988), the court clarified that there is no requirement that just compensation be sought from state authorities before bringing a substantive due process claim.

In *Shelter Creed Development Corp. v. City of Oxnard,* 838 F.2d 375 (9th Cir.), *cert. denied,* 109 S. Ct. 134 (1988), the court reiterated that the ripeness requirement applies to both takings and substantive due process claims. Plaintiffs' claim that the contested zoning ordinance was unconstitutional as applied was not ripe for adjudication because plaintiff never applied for a variance or special use permit.

Just compensation must be sought from the state even when the state inverse condemnation remedy is uncertain and undeveloped. The remedy must be pursued until the state courts declare it to be unavailable. The court also applied *Williamson* retroactively, because it affects the "jurisdiction" to hear taking claims. *Austin v. Honolulu,* 840 F.2d 678 (9th Cir.), *cert. denied,* 109 S. Ct. 136 (1988). With respect to an as-applied takings claim, the court found that the county's denial of plaintiff's informal development proposal was "not a final and authoritative decision exposing the nature and extent of permissible development." *Lake Nacimiento Ranch Co. v. San Luis Obispo County,* 841 F.2d 872, 876 (9th Cir. 1987).

A regulatory takings claim is not ripe until a variance and compensation are sought. The claim in *Lai* was not ripe because, although there was no state procedure for compensation claims, plaintiff did not seek a variance. The *Lai* court quoted from *McDonald, Somer & Frates v. Yolo County,* 477 U.S. 340, 106 S. Ct. 2561, 2566 (1986): "The court cannot determine whether a regulation has gone 'too far' unless it knows how far the regulation goes." *Lai v. Honolulu,* 841 F.2d 301 (9th Cir.), *cert. denied,* 109 S. Ct. _____ (1988).

Analyzing the adequacy of state remedies, the Eleventh Circuit found (1) that Florida did not provide an adequate remedy for monetary relief, (2) entirely discretionary state remedies, such as filing a claims bill in the state legislature for restitution, are not adequate state remedies, and (3) the availability of a state court § 1983 claim is not the type of *state* remedy contemplated by *Williamson. Corn v. City of Lauderdale Lakes,* 816 F.2d 1514 (11th Cir. 1987), *cert. denied,* 109 S. Ct. 79 (1988).

Williamson applied to procedural and substantive due process and just compensation claims, but not to an equal protection racial discrimination claim, because this claim did not attack the propriety of land use regulations. *East-BibbTwiggs Neighborhood*

Association v. Macon Bibb Planning & Zoning Commission, 662 F. Supp. 1465 (M.D.
* Ga. 1987). A district court interpreted the *Williamson* ripeness requirement as applying only to takings claims; it was inapplicable to a plaintiff's claim that a building inspector's decision that a proposed use required a special permit violated the rights of privacy and equal protection. *P.L.S. Partners v. City of Cranston,* 696 F. Supp. 788 (D.R.I. 1988).

The *Williamson* doctrine applies to federal court claims for equitable as well as monetary relief. *Golemis v. Kirby,* 632 F. Supp. 159 (D.R.I. 1985).

A just compensation claim was found premature when the federal court plaintiff obtained injunctive relief in state court, but had not attempted to obtain damages or compensation in the state court proceeding. *Schafer v. Waupaca,* 637 F. Supp. 176 (E.D. Wis. 1986).

* A perceptive analysis of the preclusion issues created by the *Williamson* ripeness requirement is contained in *Peduto v. North Wildwood,* 696 F. Supp. 1004 (D.N.J. 1988). The court discussed, but did not resolve, whether an exception to claim preclusion should be carved out for state inverse condemnation proceedings brought pursuant to *Williamson,* but held that issue preclusion does apply. "[A]n exception would not be appropriate where a party actually litigated the federal issues in state court." *Id.* at 1012. Note the cited cases: *Paulucci v. Duluth,* 826 F.2d 780 (8th Cir. 1987) (res judicata and collateral estoppel applied to ruling in eminent domain proceeding that property was taken for a public use); *Moore v. Costa Mesa,* 678 F. Supp. 1448 (C.D. Cal. 1987); *Mitchell v. Mills County,* 673 F. Supp. 332, 336 (S.D. Iowa 1987) (citing *Paulucci* with approval), *aff'd,* 847 F.2d 486 (8th Cir. 1988). *But see Norco Construction v. Kings County,* 801 F.2d 1143, 1146-47 (9th Cir. 1986) (applying state preclusion law; decision in state mandamus proceeding does not bar § 1983 damages claim).

The Eleventh Circuit found that a state court ruling on a consitutional claim in an inverse condemnation proceeding precluded relitigation of that claim in a federal court § 1983 action. *Fountain v. Metropolitan Atlanta Rapid Transit,* 849 F.2d 1412 (11th Cir. 1988).

Williamson was applied in a state court § 1983 action. *Allingham v. Seattle,* 109 Wash. 2d 947, 749 P.2d 160 (1988).

§ 3.11 Federal Statutory Rights

Page 62, add after second full paragraph:

In *Wright v. Roanoke Redevelopment and Housing Authority,* 107 S. Ct. 766 (1987), the Supreme Court determined, by a five-to-four vote, that tenants in federally assisted public housing may enforce Brooke Amendment limitations on the maximum amount that may be charged for rent and utilities in a § 1983 action. Justice White wrote the majority opinion which was joined by Justices Brennan, Marshall, Blackmun, and Stevens. Justice O'Connor wrote a dissenting opinion in which Chief Justice Renquist and Justices Powell and Scalia joined.

The *Wright* plaintiffs, tenants residing in a low-income federally assisted public housing project, alleged that the defendant housing authority "overbilled them for their utilities and thereby violated the rent ceiling imposed by the Brooke Amendment to the Housing Act of 1937, and . . . implementing [HUD] regulations." 107 S. Ct. at 768-69. They sought recovery of the improper charges.

The Brooke Amendment generally limits the tenant's "rent" to no more than 30 percent of the family's monthly "adjusted income." HUD regulations have consistently considered "rent" to include a "reasonable amount" for the use of utilities, and have defined this "reasonable amount" as that which is "equal to or less than the amount determined by the [Public Housing Authority] to be a reasonable part of the rent paid by low-income tenants." *Id.* at 769.

The majority found that the Brooke Amendment and its implementing regulations create rights and do not just declare policy. The Brooke Amendment itself "could not be clearer," since the 30 percent limitation focuses "on the individual family and its income." *Id.* at 774. Thus, "[t]he intent to benefit tenants is undeniable." *Id.*

The HUD regulations were also found to grant the tenants enforceable rights. The Court reasoned that HUD's regulations constitute an interpretation of the statute entitled to "deference," especially since Congress "in the course of amending [the Brooke Amendment] has not disagreed with it." *Id.* While the housing authority argued that the "reasonable allowance for utilities" standard "is too vague and amorphous" to create rights enforceable under § 1983, the Court found that "they specifically set out guidelines that the PHA's were to follow in establishing utility allowance[s]." *Id.* at 775. The Congressional regulatory scheme is thus "sufficiently specific and definite to qualify as enforceable rights under . . . § 1983." *Id.*

The dissenters found that Congress did not intend to create an enforceable right to reasonable charges for utilities. Assuming without deciding that federal regulations may create rights that are enforceable under § 1983, the dissenters believed that the utility regulations were not capable of judicial enforcement because the wide discretion given to local housing authorities provides "no basis for calculating an individual's utility allowance or for providing a remedy if there is a violation." *Id.* at 778 (O'Connor, J., dissenting).

Two significiant principles emerge from the *Wright* Court's analysis of the enforceable rights issue. First, the majority appears to hold that valid federal regulations may create rights enforceable under § 1983, at least when (1) the federal statute pursuant to which the regulations were promulgated itself creates enforceable rights; (2) the regulation is within the scope of the statute; and (3) the regulation itself was intended to create enforceable rights.

Once it is determined that the federal provision at issue does create enforceable rights, there is a presumption that those rights may be enforced under § 1983, and the burden shifts to the defendant to demonstrate "by express provision or other specific evidence from the statute itself that Congress intended to foreclose . . . private enforcement [i.e., under § 1983]." *Id.* at 771. To make clear that this is not an easy burden to satisfy, the Court in *Wright* quoted *Smith v. Robinson,* 468 U.S. 992, 1012 (1984), for the proposition that " '[w]e do not lightly conclude that Congress intended to preclude reliance on § 1983 as a remedy' for the deprivation of a federally secured right." 107 S. Ct. at 771.

While the federal statutes and regulations in *Wright* set forth some specific remedies, including a mandated local housing authority tenant grievance procedure and HUD enforcement mechanisms, they did not indicate an intent to preclude enforcement under § 1983. "Not only are the Brooke Amendment and its legislative history devoid of any express indication that exclusive enforcement authority was vested in HUD, but there have also been both congressional and agency actions indicating that enforcement authority is not centralized and that private actions were anticipated." *Id.*

Administrative grievance procedures are available to tenants in federally assisted public housing projects, but the regulations establishing these procedures state that a decision in a grievance proceeding shall not affect any of the tenant's available judicial remedies. The *Wright* Court concluded that the agency interpretation of the statute which it administers was entitled to deference.

Moreover, the Court indicated that administrative remedies will not normally preclude resort to § 1983. While in *Middlesex County Sewage Authority v. National Sea Clammers Association,* 453 U.S. 1 (1981), and *Smith v. Robinson,* 468 U.S. 992 (1984), the statutes "themselves provided for private judicial remedies, thereby evidencing congressional intent to supplant the § 1983 remedy [t]here is nothing of that kind found in the Brooke Amendment or elsewhere in the Housing Act." 107 S. Ct. at 773. More generally, relying upon the no-exhaustion of administrative remedies rule of *Patsy v. Board of Regents,* 457 U.S. 496 (1982), the Court stated that "the existence of a state administrative remedy does not ordinarily foreclose resort to § 1983." 107 S. Ct. at 773. In addition, the only specific remedies that will defeat the § 1983 claim are federal court remedies. Thus, the fact that the tenants could sue on their leases in state court "is hardly a reason to bar an action under § 1983, which was adopted to provide a federal remedy for the enforcement of federal rights." *Id.* at 774. Finally, HUD's statutory authority "to audit, enforce annual contributions contracts [with local authorities], and cut off federal funds" are "generalized powers" which "are insufficient to indicate a congressional intent to foreclose § 1983 remedies." *Id.* at 773.

The Tenth Circuit, citing *Wright,* stated that "[i]n at least some instances, violations of rights provided under federal regulations provide a basis for § 1983 suits." *DeVargas v. Mason & Hanger-Silas Mason Co.,* 844 F.2d 714, 724 n.19 (10th Cir. 1988).

The Eleventh Circuit followed the decision in *Wright* in *Hill v. Ogburn,* 812 F.2d 679 (11th Cir. 1987).

Page 63, add to end of section:

The following federal statutes were found by the lower courts to grant rights enforceable under § 1983:

* **Cable Communication Policy Act** (47 U.S.C. § 605 (a, b)): *Van Meter v. Township of Maplewood,* 696 F. Supp. 1024 (D.N.J. 1988).

Development Disability Act (re services and habilitation plan, 42 U.S.C. §§ 6022, 6023): *Gieseking v. Schafer,* 672 F. Supp. 1249 (W.D. Mo. 1987). *See contra, Garrity v. Gallen,* 522 F. Supp. 171 (D.N.H. 1981).

Extradition Statute (18 U.S.C. § 3182): *Draper v. Coombs,* 792 F.2d 915 (9th Cir. 1986).

Family Education Rights and Privacy Act (20 U.S.C. § 1232g): *Fay v. South Colonie Central School District,* 802 F.2d 21, 33 (2d Cir. 1986) ("Although FERPA authorizes extensive enforcement procedures created by regulation, see 34 C.F.R. §§ 99.60-.67 (1985), these regulations do not demonstrate a congressional intent to preclude suits under section 1983 to remedy violations of FERPA").

* **Federal-Aid Highway Act** (23 U.S.C. § 101 *et seq.*): *Clallam County v. Department of Transportation,* 849 F.2d 424 (9th Cir. 1988), *cert. denied,* 109 S. Ct. 790 (1989).

Food Stamp Act (expedited food stamps; 7 U.S.C. § 2011 *et seq.*): *Gonzalez v. Pingree,* 821 F.2d 1526 (11th Cir. 1987); *Victorian v. Miller,* 813 F.2d 718 (5th Cir. 1987) (en banc).

* **Foster Care Title of Social Security Act** (42 U.S.C. §§ 671, 675): *J.L. v. Massinga,* 838 F.2d 118 (4th Cir. 1988), *cert. denied,* 109 S. Ct. 816 (1989).

Indian Self-Determination and Educational Assistance Act (25 U.S.C. §§ 450-450a): *Ramah Navajo School Board v. Bureau of Revenue,* 104 N.M. 302, 720 P.2d 1243 (Ct. App.), *cert. denied,* 107 S. Ct. 423 (1986).

Medicaid Chapter of Federal Social Security Act: *Coos Bay Care Center v. Oregon Department of Human Resources,* 803 F.2d 1060 (9th Cir. 1986) (claims by health care provider and Medicaid patient), *vacated,* 108 S. Ct. 52 (1987); *Nebraska Health Care Association v. Dunning,* 778 F.2d 1291 (8th Cir. 1985), *cert. denied,* 107 S. Ct.
* 947 (1987); *Connecticut Legal Sources v. Heintz,* 689 F. Supp. 82 (D. Conn. 1988) (bidder for legal services contract with state Medicaid agency). *See also Silver v. Baggiano,* 804 F.2d 1211 (11th Cir. 1986) (court discussed but did not decide whether health care providers may sue under § 1983 to enforce Medicaid provisions of Social
* Security Act). *Contra Vantage Healthcare Corp. v. Virginia Board of Medical Assistance Services,* 684 F. Supp. 1329 (E.D. Va. 1988) (health care providers do not have enforceable rights under Medicaid chapter of Social Security Act).

Public Health Service Act (42 U.S.C. §§ 300, 300a *et seq.*): *Planned Parenthood v. Montana,* 648 F. Supp. 47 (D. Mont. 1986).

* **Rehabilitation Act § 504** (29 U.S.C. § 794): *Cordero-Martinez v. Aponte-Roque,* 685 F. Supp. 314 (D.P.R. 1988); *Conlon v. Long Beach,* 676 F. Supp. 1289 (E.D.N.Y. 1987).

* **Section 8 of United States Housing Act** (42 U.S.C. § 1437f): *Drake v. Pierce,* 691 F. Supp. 264 (W.D. Wash. 1988); *Holly v. Housing Authority,* 684 F. Supp. 1363 (E.D. La. 1988).

Uniform Relocation Assistance and Real Property Acquisitions Policies Act (42 U.S.C. § 4625): *Pietroniro v. Borough of Oceanport,* 764 F.2d 976 (3d Cir.), *cert. denied,* 474 U.S. 1020 (1985).

The following statutes were found not to grant rights that are enforceable under § 1983:

Adoption Assistance Act (42 U.S.C. §§ 620-628): *Scrivner v. Andrews,* 816 F.2d 261 (6th Cir. 1987) (no enforceable right to "meaningful visitation"); *Lesher v. Lavrich,* 784 F.2d 193 (6th Cir. 1986) (claim for retrospective relief).

Age Discrimination in Employment Act (29 U.S.C. § 623 *et seq.*): *Price v. County of Erie,* 654 F. Supp. 1206 (W.D.N.Y. 1987); *Ring v. Crisp County Hospital Authority,* 652 F. Supp. 477 (M.D. Ga. 1987); *Morgan v. Humboldt County School District,* 623 F. Supp. 440 (D. Nev. 1985).

Airport and Airway Development Act (49 U.S.C. § 2210): *Rocky Mountain Airways v. Pitkin County,* 674 F. Supp. 312 (D. Colo. 1987); *Hillman Flying Service v. City of Roanoke,* 652 F. Supp. 1142 (W.D. Va. 1987). *See contra, New York Airlines v. Dukes County,* 623 F. Supp. 1435 (D. Mass. 1985).

Aviation Act: *Western Air Lines, Inc. v. Port Authority,* 817 F.2d 222 (2d Cir. 1987) (49 U.S.C. §§ 1305(a) and 1349(a)); *Montauk-Caribbean Airways v. Hope,* 784 F.2d 91, 98 (2d Cir.) ("The comprehensive enforcement scheme provided in the federal Aviation Act manifests congressional intent to foreclose an action under § 1983"), *cert. denied,* 107 S. Ct. 248 (1986).

Civil Rights Act of 1964 (Title VII) (42 U.S.C. § 2000e *et seq.*): *Foster v. Wyrick,* 823 F.2d 218 (8th Cir. 1987).

* **Comprehensive Employment and Training Act** (29 U.S.C. § 801 *et seq.*): *Davis v. Mobile Consortium of CETA,* 857 F.2d 737 (11th Cir. 1988).

Consumer Credit Protection Act (exemption from wage garnishment, 15 U.S.C. § 1673): *Follette v. Vitanza,* 658 F. Supp. 492 (N.D.N.Y.), *modified,* 658 F. Supp. 514 (N.D.N.Y. 1987), *vacated in part,* 671 F. Supp. 1362 (N.D.N.Y. 1988).

Copyright Act: *Dodd v. Fort Smith Special School District,* 666 F. Supp. 1278 (W.D. Ark. 1987).

Hill-Burton Act (42 U.S.C. § 291 *et seq.*): *Lile v. University of Iowa Hospitals & Clinics,* 674 F. Supp. 288 (S.D. Iowa 1987).

Indian Trader Act (25 U.S.C. §§ 261-264): *Central Machinery Co. v. State,* 152 Ariz. 134, 730 P.2d 843 (1986) (en banc).

Legal Services Corporation Act (42 U.S.C. § 2996 *et seq.*): *Fultz v. Neighborhood Legal Services,* 654 F. Supp. 881 (W.D. Pa. 1987) (no right to meaningful representation).

Low Income Home Energy Assistance Energy Act (42 U.S.C. § 8261 *et seq.*): *Hunt v. Robeson County Department of Social Services,* 816 F.2d 150 (4th Cir. 1987).

* **National Labor Relations Act** (29 U.S.C. § 151 *et seq.*): *Golden State Transit Corp. v. Los Angeles,* 857 F.2d 631 (9th Cir. 1988).

Rehabilitation Services Provision of Social Security Act (42 U.S.C. § 422): *Smith v. Kirk, 821 F.2d 980 (4th Cir. 1987).*

Rehabilitation Act (29 U.S.C. § 791 *et seq.*): *Fallet v. United States Postal Service,* 644 F. Supp. 625 (N.D. Tex. 1986).

Tax Withholding Statutes (26 U.S.C. §§ 3402-3403): *DiGiovanni v. City of Rochester,* 680 F. Supp. 80 (W.D.N.Y. 1988).

United States Housing Act (provision setting forth policy of providing federally assisted "decent, safe and sanitary dwellings for families of lower income," 42 U.S.C. § 1437): *Edwards v. District of Columbia,* 821 F.2d 651 (D.C. Cir. 1987). *But see Concerned Tenants Association v. Pierce,* 685 F. Supp. 316 (D. Conn. 1988) (relying upon congressional amendment intended to overrule *Edwards).*

While rights under a federal treaty may be asserted under § 1983, in this case there was no dispute that rights existed under the treaty at issue; the only dispute involved an interpretation of the treaty. Under these circumstances "the Tribes' treaty interpretation claims do not give rise to a claim cognizable under § 1983." *United States v.*

Washington, 813 F.2d 1020, 1023 (9th Cir. 1987), *cert. denied,* 108 S. Ct. 1593 (1988). *See also Lac Courte Oreilles Band v. Wisconsin,* 663 F. Supp. 682 (W.D. Wis.) (federal treaties may be "laws" securing rights cognizable under § 1983), *appeal dismissed,* 829 F.2d 601 (7th Cir. 1987).

§ 3.12 —Section 1983 and Implied Rights of Action

Page 64, add after note 2 reference:

The Supreme Court reiterated the four-part *Cort v. Ash* test in *Merrell Dow Pharmaceuticals v. Thompson,* 106 S. Ct. 3229, 3234 (1986). The Court described the test as "guides" used to determine congressional intent in *Thompson v. Thompson,* 108 S. Ct. 513 (1988). The focus on congressional intent, however, does not mean that members of Congress actually had in mind the creation of a private cause of action. *Id.* at 516.

The questions of whether a federal statute is enforceable under § 1983, or creates an implied private right of action, involve separate inquiries. *Victorian v. Miller,* 813 F.2d 718 (5th Cir. 1987); *Coos Bay Care Center v. Oregon Department of Human Resources,* 803 F.2d 1060, 1062 n.1 (9th Cir. 1986), *vacated,* 108 S. Ct. 52 (1987); *Fay v. South Colonie Central School District,* 802 F.2d 21 (2d Cir. 1986) (claim found under § 1983 even though no private cause of action). *See also Haskins v. Stanton,* 794 F.2d 1273 (7th Cir. 1986) (since there is a private right of action under the Food Stamp Act, there is no need to discuss whether a claim lies under § 1983). In *Victorian v. Miller,* 813 F.2d at 721, the court reasoned that plaintiffs bear a lesser burden under § 1983 than under the implied right of action doctrine because "Congress is presumed to legislate against the background of section 1983 and thus to contemplate private enforcement of the relevant statute against state actors absent discernible congressional intent to the contrary."

CHAPTER 4

CULPABLE CONDUCT

§ 4.3 Proximate Cause

Page 72, add at end of section:

* The Supreme Court read *Martinez v. California,* 444 U.S. 277 (1980), as based upon a causation analysis; it should not be read to imply a general "special relationship" doctrine. *De Shaney v. Winnebago County Department of Social Services,* 57 U.S.L.W. 4218, ____, n.4 (U.S. Feb. 22, 1989) (No. 87-154) (see § 3.2).

Applying the *Martinez v. California,* 444 U.S. 277 (1980), proximate cause requirement, several circuit court decisions found that the defendant's conduct was not the proximate cause of the claimed deprivation of plaintiff's rights.

In *Estate of Gilmore v. Buckley,* 787 F.2d 714 (1st Cir.), *cert. denied,* 107 S. Ct. 270 (1986), the plaintiff, administrator of the estate of the deceased, brought suit under § 1983 against various prison officials and other county employees. The administrator complained that the officials had granted a prisoner a two-day furlough and that while on leave the prisoner killed the deceased. The court ruled that, even if the officials had knowledge that the prisoner posed a special danger to the deceased, "the state did nothing to render Gilmore any more or less capable of defending herself from a violent attacker than any other member of the general public." 787 F.2d at 721. There was no special relationship between the defendants and the deceased. For there to be such a relationship, the state must be more directly implicated than it was in the victim's death. *Id.* at 722.

The Third Circuit, applying *Martinez* to a murder by an escaped inmate, dismissed claims against prison and county officials because they had no knowledge of any special danger to the deceased; the brief interval between the escape and the murder was not sufficient to distinguish this case from *Martinez. Commonwealth Bank & Trust Co. v. Russell,* 825 F.2d 12 (3d Cir. 1987).

Martinez was applied where a plaintiff was injured in a halfway house. "We do not consider the *Martinez* holding to extend only to cases alleging due process violations." *Carlson v. Conklin,* 813 F.2d 769, 772 (6th Cir. 1987). In another Sixth Circuit case, the court found that where police officers killed plaintiff's decedent accidently during a high-speed chase while attempting to apprehend a furloughed prisoner, it could not be said that granting the furlough was the proximate cause of the violation of decedent's constitutional rights. *Jones v. Sherrill,* 827 F.2d 1102 (6th Cir. 1987).

In *Janan v. Trammell,* 785 F.2d 557 (6th Cir. 1986), the court found that the defendant parole board's release of a prisoner was not the proximate cause of the parolee's murder of an individual. The fact that the murder occurred less than two months after the prisoner's release, rather than the five months in *Martinez,* was not a basis for distinction. "Rather, the proper analysis is whether a special relationship exists between the criminal and the victim or between the victim and the state or whether there is some showing that the victim, as distinguished from the public at large, faces a special danger by the parolee's release." *Id.* at 560.

In *Hayes v. Vessey,* 777 F.2d 1149 (6th Cir. 1985), the Sixth Circuit, applying *Martinez,* found that the defendant correctional officers' conduct was not the proximate cause of the rape of the plaintiff prisoner in a prison school.

The *Martinez* standard was satisfied where defendants sheriff and deputy sheriff allegedly entrusted a fully equipped patrol car to a convicted felon who used the car to pull a woman off to the side of the road and then killed her. "[T]he officers gave Hartman the car *and* the freedom to commit the crime." *Nishiyama v. Dickson County,* 814 F.2d 277, 281 (6th Cir. 1987)(en banc).

The state was not responsible for the assault and rape of the plaintiff by an escaped prisoner where the incident occurred two months after the escape and the state was not on notice that plaintiff was subject to any special risk. *Ketchum v. Alameda County,* 811 F.2d 1243 (9th Cir. 1987).

It is fairly common for a court to avoid the proximate cause determination by finding that the defendant's action or inaction did not violate plaintiff's constitutionally protected rights, or to combine a no-proximate-cause finding with a no-constitutional-violation ruling. A circuit-by-circuit summary of recent leading cases follows.

D.C. Circuit. *Washington v. District of Columbia,* 802 F.2d 1478 (D.C. Cir. 1986). Prison guards have no constitutional right to safe conditions because, absent a custodial relationship, one has no constitutional right to be protected by the state. "Prison guards, unlike the prisoners in their custody, are not held in state custody." *Id.* at 1482.

First Circuit. *Estate of Gilmore v. Buckley,* 787 F.2d 714 (1st Cir.), *cert. denied,* 107 S. Ct. 270 (1986), discussed above, is based upon both a lack of proximate cause and the lack of a deprivation of constitutional rights. Absent a custodial or other special relationship, the state has no constitutional obligation to provide protection from the acts of third parties.

Second Circuit. *McClary v. O'Hare,* 786 F.2d 83 (2d Cir. 1986). The administrator of the decedent's estate brought a § 1983 claim, arguing that the decedent died when a wire cable on a mobile crane truck operated by a fellow employee broke, causing the boom to fall and strike decedent on the head. The court held that substantive due process does not require a public employer to provide safe working conditions.

Third Circuit. *Estate of Bailey v. County of York,* 768 F.2d 503 (3d Cir. 1985). State has a constitutional duty to protect a child from danger where it is aware of a special
* danger. The special relationship doctrine is not limited to custodial relationships. The authors believe that the decision in *Estate of Bailey* appears to have been undercut by the Supreme Court's recent decision in the *De Shaney* case.

Stoneking v. Bradford Area School District, 856 F.2d 594 (3d Cir. 1988) (school officials have affirmative obligation to take reasonable steps to protect students from sexual abuse by teachers; see § 3.2).

Fourth Circuit. *Fox v. Custis,* 712 F.2d 84 (4th Cir. 1983). State has no constitutional obligation to protect an individual from wrongful acts of parolees.

Fifth Circuit. Because a school bus driver was entrusted with students' safety, his failure to protect a student from a beating by other students or to render emergency aid would violate the due process clause if "it rose to the level of callous indifference and was a cause of injury." *Lopez v. Houston Independent School District,* 817 F.2d 351 (5th Cir. 1987).

Sixth Circuit. *Carlson v. Conklin,* 813 F.2d 769 (6th Cir. 1987), discussed above, where the court agreed with the Seventh Circuit's position that there is no constitutional right to protection by the state from being murdered by third parties.

Seventh Circuit. The state has no constitutional obligation to provide rescue services. It is better to "jettison" special relationship language and understand that it is only a "shorthand" to describe "cases in which the state either deliberately inflicted injury or greatly increased risk while constricting access to self-help . . . ." *Archie v. City of Racine,* 847 F.2d 1211, 1223 (7th Cir. 1988)(en banc).

The court determined in *Walker v. Rowe,* 791 F.2d 507 (7th Cir.), *cert. denied,* 107 S. Ct. 597 (1986), that the defendant supervisory prison officials did not violate the constitutional rights of the plaintiff guards, three of whom were killed and others injured by prison inmates. The principle that the state must protect those it has placed in its custody did not apply because, while

> [t]he state must protect those it throws into snake pits, [it] need not guarantee that volunteer snake charmers will not be bitten. It may not throw Daniel into the lion's den, but if Daniel chooses to be a lion tamer in the state's circus, the state need not separate Daniel from his charges with an impenetrable shield.

791 F.2d at 511.

Eighth Circuit. The Eighth Circuit rejects the position of the Third and Fourth Circuits that there is a general special relationship doctrine. "Without the control [i.e., found in the prison environment] there is no constitutionally mandated duty to protect one private citizen from another. We do not believe that the concept of special relationship was intended to extend beyond prison or prison-like environments." *Harpole v. Arkansas Department of Human Services,* 820 F.2d 923, 927 (8th Cir. 1980.)
* *See also Wells v. Walker,* 852 F.2d 368 (8th Cir. 1988) (see § **3.2**).

Ninth Circuit. *Ketchum v. Alameda County,* 811 F.2d 1243 (9th Cir. 1987), followed the principle that a state is not constitutionally obligated to protect an individual against criminal attacks. "The prevailing rule in the circuits is that citizens have no constitutional right to be protected by the state from attack by private third parties, absent some special relationship between the state and the victim or the criminal and the victim from the general public." *Id.* at 1247.

The court had taken the same position in *Escamilla v. City of Santa Ana,* 796 F.2d 266 (9th Cir. 1986). Plaintiffs, the children of the innocent victim of a barroom shooting, claimed that the defendant undercover officers, who were present at the scene, should have taken direct action to prevent the shooting. Their claim was held to be without merit because, absent a special relationship, the state has no constitutional obligation to protect citizens from a dangerous situation which state officials neither created nor exacerbated.

* The Ninth Circuit found that the plaintiff's allegations that a state court had issued a temporary restraining order in her favor against her husband, and that the police had repeated notice of the husband's threats against her, were sufficient to present a triable issue whether there was a "special relationship." *Balistreri v. Pacifica Police Department,* 855 F.2d 1421 (9th Cir. 1988). The authors believe that the decision in *Balistreri* has been undercut by the Supreme Court's decision in the *De Shaney* case.

Eleventh Circuit. In *Wideman v. Shallowford Community Hospital,* 826 F.2d 1030 (11th Cir. 1987), the court found no constitutional infirmity in a county policy of using its emergency medical vehicles to transport patients only to hospitals which guaranteed payment of the county's medical bills. "[A] constitutional duty can arise only when a state or municipality, by exercising a significant degree of custody or control over an individual, places that person in a worse situation than he would have been had the government not acted at all." *Id.* at 1035. In *Bradberry v. Pinellas County,* 789 F.2d 1513 (11th Cir. 1986), the court determined that the county was not liable for allegedly failing to provide a sufficient number of adequately trained lifeguards on a beach where the decedent drowned. Since the states have no constitutional obligation to expend their resources to guard against accidents, "it would be anomalous to hold them liable when they attempt to do so and fail in their effort." *Id.* at 1517. The state does not deprive one of life "when it grossly negligently trains one of its agents who then fails in an attempt to rescue that person from an existing peril not created by the governmental agency." *Id.*

Sitting en banc, the Eleventh Circuit found that state and county officials who placed a child in foster care have a due process obligation to insure the continuing safety of the child's environment, and will be liable if they are grossly negligent or deliberately indifferent to the welfare of the child. There is a special relationship between the state and the child. *Taylor v. Ledbetter,* 818 F.2d 791 (11th Cir. 1987)(en banc), following *Doe v. Department of Social Services,* 649 F.2d 134 (2d Cir. 1981), *cert. denied,* 464 U.S. 864 (1983).

§ 4.4 Rule against Respondeat Superior Liability

Page 73, add after note 35 reference:

The rule against vicarious liability applies to private corporations. *DeVargas v. Mason & Hanger-Silas Mason Co.,* 844 F.2d 714, 723 (10th Cir. 1988)(dicta); *Auster Oil & Gas v. Stream,* 835 F.2d 597, 601 (5th Cir. 1988)(without discussion of the public-private distinction, court applied no respondeat superior rule to private defendant); *Scutieri v. Estate of Revitz,* 683 F. Supp. 795 (S.D. Fla. 1988); *Fraser v. Schultze,* 663 F. Supp. 512 (N.D. Ill. 1987); *Holdeman v. Consolidated Rail Corp.,* 649 F. Supp. 1188 (N.D. Ind. 1986), *aff'd,* 840 F.2d 20 (7th Cir. 1988). Under *Pembaur v. City of Cincinnati,* 106 S. Ct. 1292 (1986), private corporations "may be liable for the actions of policy-making employees." *Jones v. Preuit & Mauldin,* 808 F.2d 1435, 1449 n.3 (11th Cir.), *modified,* 822 F.2d 998 (11th Cir. 1987).

Page 73, add after note 37 reference:

When plaintiff has a constitutional claim under § 1983, that is the exclusive remedy, and a *Bivens*-type claim may not be asserted directly under the Constitution. *Thomas v. Shipka,* 818 F.2d 496 (6th Cir.), *modified,* 829 F.2d 570 (6th Cir. 1987).

Where an entity fails to request a "*Monell* instruction, it is deemed to have consented to respondeat superior liability." *Frett v. Virgin Islands,* 839 F.2d 968, 979 (3d Cir. 1988).

§ 4.6 Municipal Policy

Page 76, add at end of section:

The jury instructions should define what is meant by *official policy,* because it is not a phrase readily understood without instructions. *Westborough Mall v. City of Cape Girardeau,* 794 F.2d 330 (8th Cir. 1986), *cert. denied,* 107 S. Ct. 1373 (1987).

There is a difference of opinion as to meaning of *Los Angeles v. Heller,* 106 S. Ct. 1571 (1986). In *Heller,* the Supreme Court ruled that a jury determination that an officer acted constitutionally required dismissal against the city, in circumstances in which the city was sued only because it was "thought legally responsible for the officers' actions" (*id.* at 1573) by adopting "a policy of condoning excessive force in making arrests." *Id.* at 1574 (Stevens, J., dissenting). Some circuit courts take the position that, while municipal liability may be imposed even though the defendant official is not liable because of a good faith immunity, it may not be imposed "if the officers acted constitutionally." *Palmerin v. City of Riverside,* 794 F.2d 1409, 1415 (9th Cir. 1986). *Accord, Dodd v. City of Norwich,* 827 F.2d 1 (2d Cir. 1987) (on reargument), * *cert. denied,* 108 S. Ct. 701 (1988). *See also Watson v. Kansas City,* 857 F.2d 690, 697 (10th Cir. 1988) ("While it would be improper to allow a suit to proceed against the city if it was deteremined that the officers' action did not amount to a constitutional violation, [*Heller*], there is nothing anomalous about allowing such a suit to proceed when immunity shields the individual defendants."); *Ford v. Childers,* 855 F.2d 1271, 1277 (7th Cir. 1988) (en banc) (although not citing *Heller,* the court ruled that a determination that the police officer's use of force was reeasonable means that the Chief of Police and City "cannot, as a matter of law, be held liable to Ford as their liability was dependent upon the unreasonableness of Officer Childers' actions."); *Frost v. Hawkins County Board of Education,* 851 F.2d 822, 827 (6th Cir.) ("a jury's findings that a police officer inflicted no constitutional injury on a plaintiff is conclusive not only as to the officer's liability, but also as to the liability of the city and its police commission"), *cert. denied,* 109 S. Ct. 529 (1988); *Swink v. City of Pagedale,* 810 F.2d 791 (8th Cir.)(where city was sued only because it was thought to be responsible for police officers' actions, a jury verdict in favor of officers required dismissal against city), *cert. denied,* 107 S. Ct. 3274 (1987).

This is the correct conclusion where the municipality's liability is closely related to and derivative of the *named* officer's liability. However, this is not always the case. For example, a municipal body may be liable where, "[a]lthough the acts or omissions of no one employee may violate an individual's constitutional rights, the combined acts or omissions of several employees acting under a governmental policy or custom may violate an individual's constitutional rights." *Anderson v. Atlanta,* 778 F.2d 678, 686 (11th Cir. 1985), quoting *Garcia v. Salt Lake County,* 768 F.2d 303, 310 (10th Cir. 1985).

The authors believe that the Supreme Court in *Heller* did not intend to impose an absolute rule that a municipality must be exonerated every time the officer defendant is found not to have violated the Constitution, but intended only that the municipality should be exonerated under the particular facts of that case. *See Praprotnik v. St. Louis,* 798 F.2d 1168, 1172 n.3 (8th Cir. 1986), *rev'd on other grounds,* 108 S. Ct. 915 (1988); *Dodd v. City of Norwich,* 827 F.2d 1, 9 (2d Cir. 1987)(Pratt, J., dissenting). A narrow reading of *Heller* is supported by the fact that it was a per curiam summary determination. Also, it should be emphasized that under *Monell* individual officer liability is not a prerequisite to municipal liability, the only requirements being a showing of a municipal policy or custom which is the proximate cause of the violation of plaintiff's federally protected rights. Viewed in this light, it is apparent that the *Heller* problem is obviated if plaintiff does not name an official individually as a defendant.

It is essential that the municipal action or inaction be the proximate cause of the constitutional violations. In *Busch v. Viterna,* 795 F.2d 1203 (5th Cir. 1986), the court found that the defendant Texas Commission on Jail Standards was not responsible for unconstitutional jail conditions because, assuming that the breach of a state-created duty may be the proximate cause of a constitutional wrong, the commission had no state-imposed legal duty to correct unconstitutional jail conditions. The state duty imposed on the commission to regulate, monitor, inspect, and advise was "not accompanied by an obligation to extirpate constitutionally substandard conditions or activities that may be encountered." *Id.* at 1208.

Finding surprisingly little law on the issue, and not unsympathetic to the county's dilemma, one court held that a municipality may be liable when it adopts a policy subsequently declared unconstitutional, even though the policy was mandated by state law. *Davis v. City of Camden,* 657 F. Supp. 396 (D.N.J. 1987). What happens if a municipality adopts a policy or custom in violation of state law? Dubious dicta in *Thompson v. County of Rock,* 648 F. Supp. 861, 871 (W.D. Wis. 1986) states: "If a municipal custom were present in this case it would be one of noncompliance with state criminal procedure mandates. Such a 'custom' clearly would not establish any wrongdoing on the part of the municipalities."

Conflicting regulations are not the type of policy upon which municipal liability may be based; this is not a single course of action selected from alternatives but rather a conflict indicating a lack of policy. *Byers v. City of Reno,* 633 F. Supp. 94 (D. Nev. 1987).

§ 4.7 Who Makes Municipal Policy

Page 77, add after third paragraph:

In *Pembaur v. City of Cincinnati,* 106 S. Ct. 1292 (1986), a badly splintered Court ruled that one act by one municipal policymaker may be a municipal policy that provides the basis for the imposition of municipal liability. The Court specifically concluded that "[i]n ordering the Deputy Sheriffs to enter petitioner [Pembaur's medical] clinic the County Prosecutor was acting as the final decision-maker for the county, and the county may therefore be held liable under § 1983." *Id.* at 1301.

In Part II-A of his opinion the Court, Justice Brennan reiterated the statement in *Oklahoma City v. Tuttle,* 105 S. Ct. 2427, 2436 (1985), that "once a municipal policy is established, it requires only one application . . . to satisfy fully *Monell's* requirement that a municipal corporation be held liable only for constitutional violations resulting from the municipality's official policy." *Pembaur,* 106 S. Ct. at 1297, n.6. Rules formally promulgated by local legislative bodies obviously represent municipal policy. Like other legislative enactments, these rules "establish fixed plans of action to be followed under similar circumstances consistently and over time." *Id.* at 1299. This, however, is not the only way that municipal policy may be established, since local legislative bodies do not have the exclusive power to establish policy and policy is not always adopted for recurrent situations. Rather,

> a government frequently chooses a course of action tailored to a particular situation and not intended to control decisions in later situations. If the decision to adopt that particular course of action is properly made by that government's authorized decisionmakers, it surely represents an act of official government "policy." . . . More importantly, where action is directed by those who establish government policy, the municipality is equally responsible whether that action is to be taken only once or to be taken repeatedly.

Id.

The critical issue in *Pembaur* was who, besides legislative officials, are municipal policymakers. The Court looked to state law to decide this question. An official who has policymaking authority may delegate that authority to another official, *id.,* and "municipalities often spread policymaking authority among various officers and official bodies." *Id.*

An official may have policymaking authority with respect to one function, though only discretion with respect to another. Justice Brennan provided the following example:

> The County Sheriff may have discretion to hire and fire employees without also being the county official responsible for establishing county employment policy. If this were the case, the Sheriff's decisions respecting employment would not give rise to municipal liability, although similar decisions with respect to which the Sheriff *is* the official policymaker, *would* give rise to municipal liability. Instead, if county employment policy was set by the Board of County Commissioners, only that body's decisions would provide a basis for county liability . . . even if the Board left the Sheriff discretion to hire and fire employees and the Sheriff exercised that discretion in an unconstitutional manner; the decision to act unlawfully would not be a decision of the Board. However, if the Board delegated its power to establish final employment policy to the Sheriff, the Sheriff's decisions *would* represent county policy and could give rise to municipal liability.

Id. at 1300 n.12 (emphasis in original).

Justice White's concurring opinion adds another dimension to the problem. In his view, the mere fact that a municipal official has final authority to make certain decisions does not mean that those decisions represent municipal policy. Since decisionmaking authority must be exercised in accordance with the requirements of state and local law, "[w]here the controlling law places limits on [an official's] authority, [she] cannot be said to have the authority to make contrary policy." *Id.* at 1302. Justice Stevens's concurring opinion reiterates the position in his dissenting opinion in *Tuttle* that respondeat superior liability should apply to § 1983 actions against municipal entities.

Justice Powell, joined by Chief Justice Burger and Justice Rehnquist, dissenting, criticized the Court for its "circular" reasoning "that policy is what policymakers make, and policymakers are those who have authority to make policy," *id.* at 1308. They also criticized the majority for finding a policy based upon "nothing more than a brief response [by the Prosecutor] to a single question over the telephone [by the Sheriff]." *Id.* at 1307. In their view, whether a policy exists should depend upon an evaluation of two factors. First, a court should consider the nature of the decision reached or action taken. Most policies "embody a rule of general applicability" that serve to distinguish them from "mere *ad hoc* decisions." *Id.* at 1309. Second, a court should consider the process by which the decision was reached or action taken. Formal deliberate decisions are more likely to reflect policy than are actions such as the prosecutor's telephone response in *Pembaur.*

The Supreme Court returned to the issue in *City of St. Louis v. Praprotnik,* 108 S. Ct. 915 (1988). Again, the Court was badly splintered. Justice O'Connor's plurality opinion, in which the Chief Justice and Justices White and Scalia joined, takes the position that the identification of policymakers is a question of state law. The pertinent inquiry is whether the state law gives the official authority to make *final* policy. It is critical to distinguish authority to make final policy from authority to exercise discretion. An official's exercise of discretion within the bounds of policy established by another official or body does not constitute the formulation of policy but rather the implementation of previously established policy. "When an official's discretionary decisions are constrained by policies not of that official's making, those policies, rather than the subordinate's departures from them, are the act of the municipality." *Id.* at 926.

The plurality's emphasis upon *final* authority to set policy means that, when a subordinate's decision is subject to review by superior policymaking officers, the subordinate's determination does not constitute policy because the superiors "have retained the authority to measure the official's conduct for conformance with *their* policies." *Id.* (emphasis in original). If the policymakers approve a subordinate's decision and the basis for it, this ratification is a final determination chargeable to the city. The fact that the policymakers fail to review, however, does not automatically mean that the subordinate's decision represents the formulation of policy.

The fact that the review procedure is "circumscribed" and gives "substantial deference" to the original decisionmaker does not mean that he or she exercised policymaking authority. Rather, limited review is consistent with a presumption that decisionmaking officials are acting in accordance with the established policies. *Id.* at 927.

Justice Brennan's concurring opinion, in which Justices Marshall and Blackmun joined, takes the position that the issue should not be resolved solely by references to state law. State law sources will not always identify those with policymaking authority in a particular area and, even when they do, "real and apparent authority may diverge . . . ." *Id.* at 934. While state law is an appropriate starting point, the pertinent issue is one of fact for the jury which "must determine where such policymaking authority actually resides, and not simply 'where the applicable law purports to put it.' " *Id.*

While Justice Brennan agreed with the basic distinction between the authority to set final policy and the authority to exercise discretion in carrying out policy, he strongly disagreed with the plurality's analysis of final policymaking authority. Reviewing authorities may choose not to exercise their review authority or may exercise it in a highly circumscribed or deferential fashion. Under either of these circumstances, the practical reality is that the subordinate's decision is the "final municipal pronouncement on the subject" and these considerations should be considered by the jury. *Id.*

Both the O'Connor and Brennan groups agreed that when a city's actual practices differ from its expressly stated policies, the practices represent the actual policy. *Id.* at 927-28, 935 n.7. Thus, for example, a declared city policy against employment discrimination would not insulate the city from liability for the consequences of persistent discriminatory practices. *Id.* at 935 n.7.

The specific issue in *Praprotnik* was whether the director of a community development agency, who allegedly transferred employee Praprotnik to another agency in retaliation for filing an appeal with the Civil Service Commission, had authority to set policy. Both the plurality and concurring Justices agreed that he had no authority to set employment policy, which was lodged in the mayor, aldermen, and Civil Service Commission, but only discretion to effectuate policy, and that the policymakers had not adopted a policy of retaliation. The fact that the commission, which had review authority over the director's decisions, operated under a narrow scope of review did not call for a different result.

Justice Stevens, dissenting, continues to believe that Congress intended to impose respondeat superior liability under § 1983. *Id.* at 937 n.1. This, of course, would obviate the seemingly losing battle of attempting to define municipal policy. If respondeat superior is not applied, Justice Stevens believes that the pertinent inquiry is not what constitutes policy, but when should the city be liable for acts of its agents? In his view, it should be liable for the acts of its high officials, because they control their subordinates, and their acts and decisions are in substance "statements" about how similar decisions should be carried out in the future. The decisions of high-ranking officials are thus likely to have "City-wide ramifications, both through their similar response to a like class of situations, and through the response of subordinates who follow their lead." *Id.* at 948 (Stevens, J., dissenting).

Of the members of the Court who have expressed their views on the issue, Justice Stevens takes the most expansive view of municipal liability. It is thus fair to conclude that he is more closely aligned with the views of the Brennan group than with those of the O'Connor plurality. Viewed in this light, there emerges in *Praprotnik* a four-to-four split among the Justices. Justice Kennedy, who did not participate in the decision, appears to hold the pivotal vote.

A large number of circuit court decisions finds that the acts or determinations of
* high-ranking officers constitute municipal policy. *Video International Production v. Warner-Amex Cable Co.*, 858 F.2d 1075, 1087 (5th Cir. 1988) (board of adjustment and building inspector had final authority to interpret and enforce zoning code); *Bateson v.*

Geisse, 857 F.2d 1300 (9th Cir. 1988) (city council's decision to withhold building permit represents official policy); *Parker v. Williams,* 862 F.2d 1471 (11th Cir. 1988) (sheriff had final authority to hire employees for county jail); *Anderson v. Gutschenritter,* 836 F.2d 346 (7th Cir. 1988)(county sheriff is policymaker regarding operation of county jail); *Lucas v. O'Loughlin,* 831 F.2d 232 (11th Cir. 1987)(sheriff was a county policymaker with respect to appointment and control of deputies; while state law requires sheriff's election, he or she is a county official), *cert. denied,* 108 S. Ct. 1595 (1988); *Bennis v. Gable,* 823 F.2d 723, 733 n.11 (3d Cir. 1987)(mayor was policymaker for promotions and demotions); *Webb v. City of Chester,* 813 F.2d 824 (7th Cir. 1987)(Board of Fire and Police Commissioners' firing of policy officer); *Messick v. Leavins,* 811 F.2d 1439 (11th Cir. 1987)(superintendent of public works' decision to burn a barge); *Weber v. Dell,* 804 F.2d 796 (2d Cir. 1986)(by ordering strip searches of arrestees, sheriff established county policy); *Williams v. Butler,* 802 F.2d 296 (8th Cir. 1986)(when municipal judge had final authority to fire court clerk, the firing constituted municipal policy), *vacated,* 108 S. Ct. 1102 (1988); *Mazanec v. North Judson-San Pierre School Corp.,* 798 F.2d 230 (7th Cir. 1986)(school officials' pursuit of prosecution of parents for taking their children out of school was act of an authorized policymaker); *Small v. Inhabitants of Belfast,* 796 F.2d 544 (1st Cir. 1986)(if city manager had final authority to revoke plaintiff's appointment as a special police officer, liability could attach to city); *Shaw v. Department of Alcoholic Beverage Control,* 788 F.2d 600, 611 (9th Cir. 1986)(chief of police was policymaker regarding police matters); *Malak v. Associated Physicians,* 784 F.2d 277 (7th Cir. 1986)(chief executive officer of public hospital is its policymaker); *Hollins v. Powell,* 773 F.2d 191 (8th Cir. 1985)(mayor's exercise of authority represents official policy), *cert. denied,* 106 S. Ct. 1635 (1986); *Saye v. St. Vrain Valley School District,* 650 F. Supp. 716 (D. Colo. 1986)(where school officials' recommendations to school district were, for all intents and purposes, the district decision, they represented district's policy); *Jackson v. Chicago,* 645 F. Supp. 926 (N.D. Ill. 1986)(police superintendent's decision not to implement a policy of preventing suicides in lockup cells was municipal policy).

* For recent cases rejecting claims that the official was a policymaker, *see Samarzia v. Clark County,* 859 F.2d 88, 91 (9th Cir. 1988) (department director's "decision was merely ratified by a supervisor[;] it was not constrained or subjected to review by an authorized policymaker as required by *Praprotnik*"); *Hughes v. Halifax County School Board,* 855 F.2d 183 (4th Cir. 1988) (school maintenance supervisor is not a policymaker with respect to authority to terminate employees), *cert. denied,* 109 S. Ct. 867 (1989); *Morrash v. Strobel,* 842 F.2d 64 (4th Cir. 1987)(director of public safety not a policymaker regarding transfer of employee where other officials had authority to countermand his personnel decisions); *Lake Nacimiento Ranch Co. v. San Luis Obispo County,* 841 F.2d 872, 879 (9th Cir. 1987)("Under California law, [County Supervisor] Markins did not have final authority to establish the County's official policy regarding participation in decisionmaking by an official with a conflict of interest"); *Bigford v. Taylor,* 834 F.2d 1213, 1222 (5th Cir.) (local justice of the peace was not a county policymaker but was carrying out state policy: "His 'deliberate or mistaken departure * from the controlling law' cannot be said to represent county policy"), *cert. denied,* 109 S. Ct. 135 (1988). When an employee is found to be acting on behalf of the state, his or her determinations do not represent municipal policy. *Baez v. Hennessy,* 853 F.2d 73 (2d Cir. 1988) (in prosecuting criminal cases, district attorneys in New York act as

state officials and do not establish county policy), *cert. denied,* 109 S. Ct. 805 (1989); *Soberbeck v. Burnett County,* 821 F.2d 446 (7th Cir. 1987)(under state law, county
* sheriff found to be acting on behalf of state, not county); *Woods v. Michigan City,* 694 F. Supp. 1344 (N.D. Ind. 1988) (judges of Indiana courts are state officers who do not make county policy); *Bendiburg v. Dempsey,* 692 F. Supp. 1354 (N.D. Ga. 1988) (judge of Georgia Juvenile Court is a state officer and not a county policymaker); *Owens v. Fulton County,* 690 F. Supp. 1024 (N.D. Ga. 1988) (Georgia prosecutor makes state, not county, policy); *Stokes v. Chicago,* 660 F. Supp. 1459 (N.D. Ill. 1987)(assistant attorney general, in carrying out prosecutorial functions, acted on behalf of state, not
* county). *Cf. Crane v. Texas,* 766 F.2d 193 (5th Cir.), *cert. denied,* 474 U.S. 1020 (1985) (under Texas law, district attorney is a county official). It should be recalled that *Pembaur* found that under Ohio law, the prosecutor acted as a county official. *Pembaur v. Cincinnati,* 106 S. Ct. 1292 (1986).

In *Brown v. City of Clewiston,* 848 F.2d 1534 (11th Cir. 1988), the court was faced with a conflict between the state law and the chief of police's manual regarding the use of deadly force. The evidence showed that the manual represented city policy. The manual set forth a more restrictive policy and the chief instructed his officers to follow it.

The Fifth Circuit continues to adhere to the standards of *Webster v. Houston,* 735 F.2d 838, 841 (5th Cir. 1984)(en banc), quoted on page 79 of the main volume. *Lopez v. Houston Independent School District,* 817 F.2d 351 (5th Cir. 1987).

§ 4.8 Custom or Usage

Page 80, add at end of section:

In *Bohen v. East Chicago,* 799 F.2d 1180, 1189 (7th Cir. 1986), the court found that

> sexual harassment was the general, ongoing, and accepted practice at the East Chicago Fire Department, and higher-ranking, supervisory, and management officials responsible for working conditions at the department knew of, tolerated, and participated in the harassment. This satisfies § 1983's requirement that the actions complained of be the policy or custom of the state entity.

See also *Harris v. City of Pagedale,* 821 F.2d 499 (8th Cir.)(city's failure to take remedial action after receiving notice of sexual misconduct of its police officers was a custom of deliberate indifference which was the proximate cause of a police officer's sexual assault on plaintiff), *cert. denied,* 108 S. Ct. 504 (1987); *Garza v. Omaha,* 814 F.2d 553, 556 (8th Cir. 1987)(evidence was sufficient for jury to conclude that the discrimination "was so permanent and well settled as to constitute a custom with the force of law").

The existence of a written municipal policy against discrimination cannot insulate the municipality from liability where the actual discriminatory practices constitute an official policy. "Indeed the actual practices of officials often constitute the official policy of a municipality, while an ordinance, regulation or manual may be routinely ignored." *Young v. Sedgwick,* 660 F. Supp. 918, 925 (D. Kan. 1987). This is consistent with position taken in dicta in *St. Louis v. Praprotnik,* 108 S. Ct. 915, 927-28 (1988); *id.* at 935 n.7 (Brennan, J., concurring).

* In *Watson v. Kansas City,* 857 F.2d 690 (10th Cir. 1988), the court found that the plaintiff's evidence, if believed, is sufficient to support a finding that the police department is following a policy of not providing assistance to victims of spousal abuse in the same manner as to other assault victims. The evidence consisted of (1) statistics showing a significantly lower arrest rate for domestic assault cases than other assault cases; (2) proof that police officers are trained to defuse domestic violence situations and to use arrest as a last resort; and (3) proof that in the plaintiff's particular case, the police denied her protection over a lengthy period. As to the first item, the court rejected the defendants' argument that the statistics are irrelevant without a finding of probable cause. Whether probable cause exists is not susceptible of statistical quantification. In addition, it is possible or even probable that the officers' assessment of probable cause is colored by the fact that the disturbance is a domestic as opposed to non-domestic dispute and thus subject to the same allegedly discriminatory policy.

There was sufficient evidence of persistent understaffing of prison medical personnel to justify the imposition of city liability for deliberate indifference to the medical needs of the plaintiff pretrial detainees. *Anderson v. Atlanta,* 778 F.2d 678 (11th Cir. 1985).

The evidence in *Brandon v. Allen,* 645 F. Supp. 1261, 1269 (W.D. Tenn. 1986), showed that "[t]he police officers who knew of the mistreatment of civilians uniformly suppressed the information, and their supervisors, although well aware that criminal conduct was being concealed in this manner, made no apparent effort to impose sanctions on any of the officers involved in the cover-up." The court determined that this "code of silence . . . is precisely the type of custom with which the framers of section 1983 were concerned." *Id.*

A municipal policy may consist of a practice or "standard operating procedure" even if it is contrary to a court order or decision. *Wright v. Newsome,* 795 F.2d 964 (11th Cir. 1986); *Anela v. City of Wildwood,* 790 F.2d 1063, 1069 (3d Cir.)("We hold that the practice of the police officers of the City of Wildwood in routinely following a bail schedule established by the City municipal judge in violation of a rule of the New Jersey Supreme Court . . . is attributable to the City"), *cert. denied,* 107 S. Ct. 434
* (1986). *Cf. Brown v. City of Clewiston,* 848 F.2d 1534 (11th Cir. 1988) (chief of police's manual represented city policy regarding use of deadly force even though manual was inconsistent with state law).

Plaintiffs' evidence of police misconduct fell short of demonstrating a persistent or pervasive practice in *Carter v. District of Columbia,* 795 F.2d 116, 124 (D.C. Cir. 1986)("the assorted actual instances of misconduct . . . do not line up to compose a common widespread pattern of misbehavior adequate to establish § 1983 municipal liability").

A showing of approximately twelve racial employment incidents in two-and-a-half years in the fire department was insufficient to constitute a pattern "that would warrant imputation of constructive knowledge" to the department's higher ranking officers, especially since the evidence showed that when higher officers learned of such incidents, "they promptly acted to discourage them, reprimanding those responsible and noting the incidents in the offenders' files." *Hamilton v. Rodgers,* 791 F.2d 439, 443 (5th Cir. 1986).

§ 4.9 Training and Supervision

Page 83, add at end of section:

* The United States Supreme Court, in an opinion by Justice White, unanimously determined that a municipality's inadequate training may give rise to § 1983 liability when it is deliberately indifferent to the rights of the city's inhabitants and actually causes the plaintiff's injury. *City of Canton v. Harris,* 109 S. Ct. ____, 57 U.S.L.W. 4270 (U.S. Feb. 28, 1989) (No. 86-1088). While all the courts of appeals had agreed that inadequate training may serve as the basis of municipal liability, they differed as to the degree of culpability required. In adopting the deliberate indifference standard, the court specifically rejected gross negligence as a basis of liability in this situation. At the same time, in finding that inadequate training may give rise to municipal liability, the Court rejected the city's argument that only unconstitutional municipal policies are actionable under § 1983. A policy may be constitutional on its face but applied in a manner that causes a violation of federally protected rights. In stressing that the inadequate training must be closely related to the violation of plaintiff's federal rights, the Court in substance adopted the approach in Justice O'Connor's dissenting opinion in *City of Springfield v. Kibbe,* 107 S. Ct. 1114 (1987), discussed below.

The Court provided two examples of deliberately inadequate training: (1) instances in which the need for more or different training is obvious and the inadequacy is likely to result in the violation of constitutional rights, such as the failure to train police officers as to the constitutional limitations upon the use of deadly force established in *Tennessee v. Garner,* 471 U.S. 1 (1985); and (2) a failure to provide obviously needed additional training in the face of repeated constitutional violations by subordinate employees.

The District of Columbia Circuit Court of Appeals took the position that deliberate indifference exhibited by a pattern of inadequate training, supervision, and discipline of police officers gives rise to municipal liability "provided there is a causal connection between such inadequacies and the risk of harm to others." In this case the evidence showed a "clear pattern" of inadequately trained officers in terms of arrest procedure and physical aptitude, as well as inadequate discipline; following "serious injuries to an innocent man" there were "no consequent sanctions or even reprimands." *Parker v. District of Columbia,* 850 F.2d 708, 712-13 (D.C. Cir. 1988).

In a lengthy opinion, the Fourth Circuit concluded that either deficient training and supervision or a failure to correct a widespread pattern of unconstitutional conduct by police officers, or both, may be the basis of municipal liability where the deficiencies rise to the level of deliberate indifference or reckless disregard.

> The most critical substantive difference between the two theories is that municipal fault may be ascribed for the first specific violation that results from proven policy, . . . while fault for a violation resulting from condoned custom can only be ascribed when a pattern of comparable practices has become actually or constructively known to responsible policymakers.

Spell v. McDaniel, 824 F.2d 1380, 1391 (4th Cir. 1987), *cert. denied,* 108 S. Ct. 752 (1988). While there is no requirement that the policy itself be unconstitutional, it must be the proximate cause of the violation of constitutional rights. "[A]s in the case of deficient training policy, failure to correct the known practices must be such as to make the specific violation 'almost bound to happen, sooner or later,' rather than merely 'likely to happen in the long run,' " 824 F.2d at 1391.

The Third Circuit stated that "[i]f the procedure that a municipality chooses violates or is contrary to state law, but meets federal standards, we may not set it aside." *Talbert v. Kelly,* 799 F.2d 62, 68 (3d Cir. 1986). This is not consistent with the notion that a municipal policy valid on its face may be applied in an unconstitutional manner.

In a case in which the district court gave a jury instruction almost identical to the instruction struck down in *Tuttle* (discussed at pages 81-83 of the main volume), the Tenth Circuit stated that it is "reluctant to read *Tuttle* as foreclosing harmless error analysis because of the Supreme Court's routine application of such analysis even in criminal cases involving important constitutional rights." *Lusby v. T.G.&Y. Stores,* 796 F.2d 1307, 1311 (10th Cir.), *cert. denied,* 107 S. Ct. 275 (1986). The court, however, did not resolve the issue because the city failed to object to the instruction at trial.

Under the decisions in *Daniels* and *Davidson,* discussed in § 3.5, a policy of merely negligent training or supervision may not serve as the basis of municipal liability. *McKenna v. Memphis,* 785 F.2d 560 (6th Cir. 1986); *Cannon v. Taylor,* 782 F.2d 947, 951 (11th Cir. 1986). Similarly, negligent hiring cannot provide a basis of municipal liability. *Stokes v. Bullins,* 844 F.2d 269 (5th Cir. 1988). Plaintiff Stokes alleged that the town was responsible for police brutality because it was grossly negligent in hiring the police officer. However, the court found that the fact that the town did not order a National Crime Information Center check on the officer's full arrest history and did not more completely investigate his background did not constitute gross negligence. The officer had lived in the town for two or three years before being hired, the mayor and alderman lived in close proximity to him and had not observed any suspicious behavior, and he was interviewed several times and revealed some of his arrests. "[T]o hold the town . . . liable here would march municipal liability too far down a path toward liability based on simple negligence." *Id.* at 274-75.

In a case involving "at least ten officers and three separate shooting incidents, in which three different officers fired their weapons," the First Circuit distinguished *Tuttle* and ruled that "a jury reasonably could have found that it was the [police] department's gross negligence in training that caused the premature use of deadly force against Thurston." *Kibbe v. Springfield,* 777 F.2d 801 (1st Cir. 1985), *cert. granted,* 106 S. Ct. 1374 (1986). *See also Wierstak v. Heffernan,* 789 F.2d 968 (1st Cir. 1986)(genuine issues of material fact regarding defendants' alleged gross negligence or willful indifference, with regard to alleged failure to train, supervise, and monitor prison conditions). The United States Supreme Court in *Kibbe* subsequently dismissed the writ of certiorari as improvidently granted. *City of Springfield v. Kibbe,* 107 S. Ct. 1114 (1987). The Court had granted certiorari to determine: (1) whether a municipality can be liable under § 1983 based on the inadequate training of its employees; (2) "whether the 'single incident rule' of *Oklahoma City v. Tuttle,* 471 U.S. 808 (1985), is limited in application to one act by one officer"; (3) "whether a policy of inadequate training may be inferred from the conduct of several officers during a single incident absent evidence of prior misconduct in the department or a conscious decision by policymakers," and (4) the "fairly included" related question of "whether more than *negligence* in training is required in order to establish such liability." 107 S. Ct. 1115 (emphasis in original), and 1115 fn. The writ was dismissed largely because the city failed to object to the pertinent jury instruction at trial. Fed. R. Civ. P. 51.

Four dissenting Justices believed that the Court should have reached the inadequate training issue. In an opinion by Justice O'Connor, joined by the Chief Justice and

Justices White and Powell, the dissenters opined that 'inadequacy of police training may serve as the basis for § 1983 liability only where the failure to train amounts to a reckless disregard for or deliberate indifference to the rights of persons within the city's domain." 107 S. Ct. at 1121.

The dissenters stated that the key to the training issue is the proximate cause requirement:

> At the time of the officers' alleged misconduct, any number of other factors were also in operation that were equally likely to contribute or play a predominant part in bringing about the constitutional injury; the disposition of the individual officers, the extent of their experience with similar incidents, the actions of the other officers involved, and so forth.

Id. at 1120.

§ 4.10 Discipline, Remedial Action, and Indemnification

Page 84, add at end of section:

Municipal liability may be based upon a grossly negligent or reckless failure to correct a pattern of widespread unconstitutional conduct if such failure was the proximate cause of the violation of plaintiff's federally protected rights. *Spell v. McDaniel,* 824 F.2d 1380 (4th Cir. 1987), *cert. denied,* 108 S. Ct. 752 (1988)(discussed in § **4.9**); *Harris v. City of Pagedale,* 821 F.2d 499 (8th Cir.), *cert. denied,* 108 S. Ct. 504 (1987)(see § **4.8**).

In an action for damages arising from numerous alleged abuses during a prison shakedown, the Ninth Circuit stated that "[p]olicy or custom may be inferred if after the shakedown, the prison officials took no steps to reprimand or discharge the guards, or if they otherwise failed to admit the guards' conduct was in error." *McRorie v. Shimoda,* 795 F.2d 780, 784 (9th Cir. 1986).

The Eleventh Circuit, in a case involving several incidents of excessive force, found that "the city had knowledge of improper police conduct, but failed to take proper remedial action"; "[t]he continued failure of the city to prevent known constitutional violations by the police force is precisely the type of informal policy or custom that is actionable under section 1983." *Depew v. City of St. Mary's,* 787 F.2d 1496, 1499 (11th Cir. 1986).

Similarly, in *Fiacco v. City of Rensselaer,* 783 F.2d 319 (2d Cir. 1986), *cert. denied,* 107 S. Ct. 1384 (1987), the Second Circuit found that a municipal policy may be based upon a city's deliberate indifference to the use of excessive force by police officers. The city failed to implement procedures set forth in the city charter for lodging charges against police officers and failed to make reasonable investigations into complaints against policemen. The city's response to complaints of excessive force was so superficial that it reflected a policy of indifference to the use of excessive force.

In *Coon v. Ledbetter,* 780 F.2d 1158 (5th Cir. 1986), the court found that the sheriff's defense of his deputies, based upon their version of the contested incident, did not constitute a municipal policy. Since the deputies' "version did not show that the deputies' actions were manifestly indefensible," the sheriff did not defend lawless conduct. "[I]t is unreasonable to infer from his defense of his men a county policy approving reckless police behavior." *Id.* at 1162. The court in *Coon* gave a narrow reading to *Grandstaff v. City of Borger,* 767 F.2d 161 (5th Cir. 1985), *cert. denied,* 107 S. Ct. 1369 (1987), stating that it was based on "highly peculiar," "extraordinary facts" and "does *not* stand for the broad proposition that if a policymaker defends his subordinates and if those subordinates are later found to have broken the law, then the illegal behavior can be assumed to have resulted from an official policy." *Coon,* 780 F.2d at 1158 (emphasis in original).

The city was not responsible for failing to take corrective action in *Jones v. Chicago,* 787 F.2d 200 (7th Cir. 1986). In that case, two patients complained that a city health clinic physician sexually assaulted them during gynecological examinations. The court rejected plaintiffs' argument that the city should be held responsible for the alleged wrongs because it failed to monitor and supervise its physicians, did not require a chaperone, and did not adequately investigate the first instance of misconduct. There was no showing that the city was deliberately indifferent to the patients' rights, as there was no record of prior complaints of sexual misconduct or improprieties by city physicians. "[T]he quantum of evidence needed is considerably greater where, as here, the particular custom that [plaintiffs'] claim resulted in their injuries involves a course of municipal inaction that is a good deal removed from the constitutional deprivation alleged." "Where the custom itself does not establish wrongdoing, there must be evidence of a course of events or circumstances that permit [sic] an inference of deliberate indifference or tacit authorization of the offensive acts." *Id.* at 204-05.

§ 4.11 Supervisory Liability

Page 87, add at end of section:

The District of Columbia Circuit Court of Appeals found that supervisory liability requires a showing that the supervisor "was responsible for supervising the wrongdoer; that a duty to instruct the subordinate to prevent constitutional harm arose from the surrounding circumstances; and that, as a result of the official's failure to instruct, the plaintiff was harmed in the manner threatened." *Haynesworth v. Miller,* 820 F.2d 1245, 1262 (D.C. Cir. 1987). More than negligence must be shown to satisfy the *Rizzo v. Goode,* "affirmative link" requirement. *Haynesworth* contains a discussion of the distinction between supervisory and training liability and policymaking liability. *See also Clay v. Conlee,* 815 F.2d 1164 (8th Cir. 1987).

The Second Circuit summarized the law of supervisory official liability, stating that a supervisor may be liable by directly participating in an infraction, by failing to remedy a wrong after learning of it, by creating "a policy or custom under which unconstitutional practices occurred, or allowed such a policy or custom to continue," or by being "grossly negligent in managing subordinates who caused the unlawful condition or event . . . ." *Williams v. Smith,* 781 F.2d 319, 323-24 (2d Cir. 1986). In that case, the court concluded that prison officer Morgan's involvement did not fall within any of these categories. His mere filing of an inmate misbehavior report did not implicate him in constitutional violations which occurred in a subsequent prison disciplinary hearing. However, the allegation that prison superintendent Smith affirmed plaintiff's disciplinary violation was a sufficient allegation that Smith was personally involved in the contested deprivation of plaintiff's right to call witnesses at the disciplinary hearing.

A superior officer's liability may be based upon "personal direction" or "actual knowledge and acquiescence." Allegations concerning these matters, however, "must be made with appropriate particularity." *Rode v. Dellarciprete,* 845 F.2d 1195, 1207 (3d Cir. 1988).

* The Sixth Circuit determined that a showing that supervisory officials were aware of the sexual harassment of an employee but failed to take appropriate action is an insufficient basis for imposing supervisory liability. *Poe v. Haydon,* 853 F.2d 418 (6th Cir. 1988), *cert. denied,* 109 S. Ct. 788 (1989).

The Seventh Circuit found that gross negligence does not provide a basis for supervisory liability. A § 1983 claimant who seeks to impose supervisory liability carries a heavy burden of showing that the supervisors know about the unconstitutional conduct and "facilitate it, approve it, condone it, or turn a blind eye for fear of what they might see. They must in other words act either knowingly or with deliberate, reckless indifference." *Jones v. Chicago,* 856 F.2d 985, 992-93 (7th Cir. 1988). In another case the Seventh Circuit concluded that if the police officer did not use excessive force, the chief of police could not be liable because the chief's liability was dependent upon the constitutionality of the officer's conduct. *Ford v. Childers,* 855 F.2d 1271, 1276-77 (7th Cir. 1988) (en banc).

In an Eighth Circuit case, the plaintiff's evidence made out a "colorable claim" of supervisory liability for inadequate medical care to prisoners. "Most prominent among Boswell's allegations is that inadequately trained jailers were directed to use their own judgment about the seriousness of prisoners' medical needs, rather than being directed to consult trained medical personnel." *Boswell v. Sherburne County,* 849 F.2d 1117, 1121 (8th Cir. 1988).

The Eighth Circuit stated that "regardless of the [law enforcement] officers' initial training on the use of excessive force, Sheriff Bohen could nonetheless be liable for breach of duty if, once his officers were certified, he showed deliberate indifference in his supervision and control of their actions." *Anderson v. Roberts,* 823 F.2d 235 (8th Cir. 1987).

The Tenth Circuit stated that "[u]nless a supervisor has established or utilized an unconstitutional policy or custom, a plaintiff must show that the supervisory defendant breached a duty imposed by state or local law which caused the constitutional violation." The complaint in the subject case sufficiently alleged a claim against the sheriff individually "for improperly hiring, training, supervising and disciplining his deputies." *Meade v. Grubbs,* 841 F.2d 1512, 1528 (10th Cir. 1988).

The Eleventh Circuit ruled that a complaint alleged a proper claim against city safety director Pozar in *Fundiller v. Cooper City,* 777 F.2d 1436 (11th Cir. 1985). The complaint "alleges that Pozar is responsible for disciplining police officers and setting police department policy, and that Cooper City police officers have engaged in a pattern of excessive force." *Id.* at 1443.

The courts continue to follow the rule described on page 87 of the main volume that "[i]f a police officer, whether supervisory or not, fails or refuses to intervene when a constitutional violation such as an unprovoked beating takes place in his presence, the officer is directly liable under Section 1983." *Byrd v. Clark,* 783 F.2d 1002, 1007 (11th Cir. 1986). *Accord, Rascon v. Hardiman,* 803 F.2d 269, 276 (7th Cir. 1986); *Fundiller v. Cooper City,* 777 F.2d 1436, 1441-42 (11th Cir. 1985). For the doctrine to apply, there must be an episode of sufficient duration to enable the officer to intervene. *O'Neil v. Krzeminski,* 839 F.2d 9 (2d Cir. 1988). In *Rascon,* the court stated that under the *Daniel-Davidson* rule, the police officer may not be held liable for *negligently* "failing to perceive that the other officers were inflicting illegal summary punishment rather than using lawful force to subdue a violent inmate." *Rascon v. Hardiman,* 803 F.2d at 276.

A police officer's duty to intervene to protect an individual applies only when a fellow police officer employs excessive force. Therefore, police officers and other town officers who witnessed an assault by the town supervisor had no constitutional duty to intervene. *Borek v. Town of McLeansboro,* 629 F. Supp. 657 (S.D. Ill. 1986).

Because sexual harassment by transit authority staff attorneys was not action under color of law, their supervisor could not be held responsible for allegedly recklessly disregarding the staff attorneys' behavior. The non-color-of-law conduct did not violate plaintiff's constitutionally protected rights, and thus did not provide a basis of superior officer liability. The supervisors could be held liable, however, if it is shown that they themselves "*intended* plaintiff to be the victim of discrimination through the medium of the staff attorneys." *Murphy v. Chicago Transit Authority,* 638 F. Supp. 464, 469 (N.D. Ill. 1986)(emphasis in original). The color-of-law issue in *Murphy* is discussed in § 5.4.

§ 4.12 Pleading Municipal Policy and Custom

Page 88, add at end of section:

There continues to be a difference of opinion over the degree of specificity necessary to plead a municipal policy or custom. Most courts reject conclusory allegations of municipal policy or custom, insisting upon specific factual allegations. *Patton v. Przybylski,* 822 F.2d 697 (7th Cir. 1987)(specific allegations required to establish superior officer liability); *Monitor v. Chicago,* 653 F. Supp. 1294 (N.D. Ill. 1987)(complaint dismissed with leave to amend); *Alvarado v. Chicago,* 648 F. Supp. 994 (N.D. Ill. 1986); *Hornung v. Village of Park Forrest,* 634 F. Supp. 540 (N.D. Ill. 1986); *Bartalone v. County of Berrien,* 643 F. Supp. 574 (W.D. Mich. 1986); *Zwarton v. Chicago,* 625 F. Supp. 1211 (N.D. Ill. 1985); *Loza v. Lynch,* 625 F. Supp. 850 (D. Conn. 1986); *Camarano v. City of New York,* 624 F. Supp. 1144 (S.D.N.Y. 1986).

The opposite result was reached in *Shah v. County of Los Angeles,* 797 F.2d 743, 747 (9th Cir. 1986), where the court found it sufficient that the complaint contain a "bare allegation that the individual officers' conduct conformed to official policy, custom, or practice." *See also Karim-Panahi v. Los Angeles Police Department,* 839 F.2d 621, 624 (9th Cir. 1988)(following *Shah*); *Haile v. Village of Sag Harbor,* 639 F. Supp. 718, 722 (E.D.N.Y. 1986)(no enhanced pleading requirement under § 1983). In *Shaw v. Department of Alcoholic Beverage Control,* 788 F.2d 600, 610 (9th Cir. 1986), the court stated that "[t]he plaintiffs need not specifically allege a custom or policy; it is enough if the custom or policy can be inferred from the allegation of the complaint."

Dicta in the Second Circuit's decision in *Oliveri v. Thompson,* 803 F.2d 1265 (2d Cir. 1986), *cert. denied,* 107 S. Ct. 1373 (1987), supports the position that it is inappropriate to require detailed allegations of municipal policy or custom:

> We recognize . . . that when commencing a suit of this type neither the plaintiff nor his attorney is likely to know much about the relevant internal operations of the police department, nor about the disciplinary history and record of the particular police officers involved. In view of the strong policies favoring suits protecting the constitutional rights of citizens, we think it would be inappropriate to require plaintiffs and their attorneys before commencing suit to obtain the detailed information needed to prove a pattern of supervisory misconduct in the form of inadequate training, improper policies, and toleration of unconstitutional actions by individual police officers.

803 F.2d at 1279.

* The Second Circuit found that the district court abused its discretion in dismissing "the suits against the police officers in their official capacities without giving the plaintiffs an opportunity to amend their complaints to conform to the requirements of an official capacity suit." *Perez v. Ortiz,* 849 F.2d 793, 798 (2d Cir. 1988).

§ 4.13 Municipal and Individual Liability: Ethical Considerations

Page 90, add at end of section:

While observing that government attorneys and insurance counsel have routinely represented officials sued in their individual capacities, and acknowledging the "great potential for conflict in this field," the Sixth Circuit found that the city attorney's representation of police officers sued for damages in their individual capacities did not create a conflict of interest. *Gordon v. Norman,* 788 F.2d 1194, 1199 (6th Cir. 1986). The officers failed to show prejudice from the representation, since the city was not a party to the action and the city attorney raised the good faith immunity issue and vigorously defended the suit.

Distinguishing the Second Circuit's decision in *Dunton v. Suffolk County,* 729 F.2d 903 (2d Cir.), *amended on other grounds,* 748 F.2d 69 (2d Cir. 1984), the Seventh Circuit found no conflict from the village attorney's representation of the village and its officials where (1) the attorney conceded that the actions of the officials were in their official capacities, and (2) "the claims against the Village and the individual defendants were completely different." *Coleman v. Smith,* 814 F.2d 1142, 1148 (7th Cir. 1987).

The New Jersey Supreme Court recognized the potential conflicts when a municipal attorney represents both the entity and the officer, but refused to adopt an absolute ban against joint representation. *In re Petition for Review of Opinion 552,* 102 N.J. 194, 507 A.2d 233 (1986). The conflict issue should be resolved on a case-by-case basis. For example, joint representation would be proper if the entity agrees that the official was acting within the scope of his or her duties, waives any claim of reimbursement of legal expenses, and agrees to indemnify the official for any individual judgment.

There was little danger of a conflict of interest from joint representation by the attorney general of the state officials in their official and individual capacities because the official capacity claim was barred by the Eleventh Amendment, leaving only the individual capacity claim, for which defense counsel would have no reason to undercut the qualified immunity defense. Defendants must give their "informed consent" to continued representation by the attorney general's office. *Galvin v. Lloyd,* 663 F. Supp. 1572 (D. Conn. 1987).

CHAPTER 5

SECTION 1983 DEFENDANTS: COLOR OF LAW AND STATE ACTION

§ 5.2 Section 1983 Persons

Page 94, add at end of section:

The weight of authority remains that a state or state agency is not a "person" which may be sued under § 1983. *Harris v. Missouri Court of Appeals,* 787 F.2d 427, 429 (8th Cir.) (state court is not a "person" within the meaning of § 1983), *cert. denied,* 107 S. Ct. 179 (1986); *Vest v. Schafer,* 757 P.2d 588 (Alaska 1988); *Smith v. Department of Public Health,* 428 Mich. 540, 410 N.W.2d 749 (1987), *cert. granted sub nom. Will v. Department of State Police,* 108 S. Ct. 1466 (1988); *Beck v. Kansas Adult Authority,* 241 Kan. 13, 735 P.2d 222 (1987); *Aase v. State,* 400 N.W.2d 269 (S.D. 1987); *Wickwire v. State,* 725 P.2d 695, 704 n.9 (Alaska 1986); *Hontz v. State,* 105 Wash. 2d 302, 714 P.2d 1176 (1986). *Contra, Uberoi v. University of Colorado,* 713 P.2d 894 (Colo. 1986).

The First Circuit held that a state is a "person" under § 1983 when it has waived its Eleventh Amendment protection because, when such a waiver occurs, there is no reason to distinguish between state and local entities. *Della Grotta v. Rhode Island,* 781 F.2d 343 (1st Cir. 1986). The court in *Della Grotta* observed that it is usually not necessary to resolve the "person" issue because relief against a state or state agency normally will be barred by the Eleventh Amendment.

The Commonwealth of Northern Mariana Islands, a United States Territory, is a "person" subject to § 1983 liability. The Covenant establishing this commonwealth, which was entered into by the United States and the Mariana Political Status Commission and subsequently enacted into law by Congress, waives its Eleventh Amendment immunity. *Fleming v. Department of Public Safety,* 837 F.2d 401 (9th Cir.), *cert. denied,* 109 S. Ct. 222 (1988). *Accord, Sablan v. Department of Finance,* 856 F.2d 1317 (9th Cir. 1988). The Ninth Circuit also ruled that because Guam is a *federal* instrumentality, it is not a "person" subject to § 1983 liability. Thus a § 1983 claim may not be asserted against Guam, its police department, or its police officers in their official capacities. But the court holds that a § 1983 claim may be asserted against the officers in an individual capacity. *Ngiraingas v. Sanchez,* 858 F.2d 1368 (9th Cir. 1988). The authors believe that it is inconsistent to characterize Guam as a federal instrumentality and yet hold that its officers individually may be sued under § 1983. If Guam is a federal instrumentality, it follows that its officers act under color of federal, rather than state, law.

§ 5.4 State and Local Officials—Misuse of State Power

Page 96, add at end of section:

The Supreme Court reaffirmed the general rule that state employees who carry out their official responsibilities act under color of state law and are state actors even when they act in violation of state law. *West v. Atkins,* 108 S. Ct. 2250, 2255-56 (1988). The decision in *Polk County v. Dodson,* 454 U.S. 312 (1981), is the only case that reached a contrary result. See § **5.5**.

The purely private act of a state official is not state action. Thus, a state official's invocation of the state law right to initiate a petition to recall an election, a right granted to all citizens of Mississippi, was not state action. *Smith v. Winter,* 782 F.2d 508, 512 (5th Cir. 1986).

* A New York state police officer did not act under color of New York law when all of the contested conduct took place in Connecticut, because the officer had neither actual nor apparent official authority to act in that state. State action could be found, however, based upon the officer's alleged conspiracy with a Connecticut police officer. *Firman v. Abreu,* 691 F. Supp. 811 (S.D.N.Y. 1988).

Off-duty police officers who were involved in a personal altercation did not exercise state power and thus did not engage in state action. Although the officers carried police identification and weapons and state law deemed them on duty at all times, the officers did not identify themselves as police officers, did not display their badges or other police identification, and did not arrest the plaintiff. *Manning v. Jones,* 696 F. Supp. 1231 (S.D. Ind. 1988).

In *Murphy v. Chicago Transit Authority,* 638 F. Supp. 464, 468 (N.D. Ill. 1986), the court concluded that staff attorneys of the defendant transit authority, who engaged in sexual harassment, did not act under color of state law because "the abusive conduct was not in any way related to the duties and powers incidental to the job of CTA staff attorney. That the conduct occurred on the CTA work premises is not enough to render it 'related to' the state authority conferred on the defendants."

The Eighth Circuit stated that if court-appointed guardians, therapists, and attorneys acted beyond the scope of their official duties in reporting the results of their inquiries to law enforcement personnel, they did not act under color of state law. *Myers v. Morris,* 810 F.2d 1437, 1467 (8th Cir.), *cert. denied,* 108 S. Ct. 97 (1987).

§ 5.5 —*Polk County v. Dodson*

Page 97, add at end of section:

* In holding that the NCAA was not engaged in state action under the joint participation theory (see § **5.13**), the Supreme Court analogized from *Polk County v. Dodson,* 454 U.S. 312 (1981):

> Just as a state-compensated public defender acts in a private capacity when she represents a private client in a conflict with the State . . . the NCAA is properly viewed as a private actor at odds with the State when it represents the interests of its entire membership in an investigation of one public university.

NCAA v. Tarkanian, 109 S. Ct. 454, 464 (1988).

Several lower federal court decisions applied the Supreme Court's decision in *Polk County v. Dodson,* 454 U.S. 312 (1981). In *Eling v. Jones,* 797 F.2d 797 (8th Cir. 1986), *cert. denied,* 107 S. Ct. 1371 (1987), the Eighth Circuit determined that the public defender's denial of his clients' requests for copies of transcripts was not under color of state law. It was not an administrative function, but involved an exercise of independent professional judgment.

The Fifth Circuit ruled that retained counsel had not acted under color of state law. *Russell v. Millsap,* 781 F.2d 381 (5th Cir. 1985), *cert. denied,* 107 S. Ct. 103 (1986). The Tenth Circuit found that a guardian ad litem lien does not act under color of state law because the guardian owes no duty to the state, but owes undivided loyalty to the minor, and must exercise independent, professional judgment on the minor's behalf. *Meeker v. Kercher,* 782 F.2d 153 (10th Cir. 1986). *Accord, Doe v. Bobitt,* 665 F. Supp. 691 (N.D. Ill 1987). By contrast, the Fourth Circuit found that a guardian who participated in admitting his ward to a state hospital did act under color of state law. *Thomas S. v. Morrow,* 781 F.2d 367 (4th Cir.), *cert. denied,* 107 S. Ct. 235 (1986). The guardian's reliance on *Polk County* was misplaced because there was language in *Polk County* indicating that one who carries out a "custodial function" acts under color of law and a "guardian has custody of his ward." *Thomas S.,* 781 F.2d at 377. In addition, the court relied upon the joint participation state action doctrine, finding that the guardian joined with state officials in bringing about various placements.

The Supreme Court unanimously determined that a physician's provision of medical services to prison inmates pursuant to a contract with the state constituted "state action" and action "under color of state law." *West v. Atkins,* 108 S. Ct. 2250 (1988). The court found that *Polk County v. Dodson* was distinguishable since the defender in that case acted as an adversary of the state. This was not so with respect to a prison doctor whose provision of medical services enabled the state to carry out its constitutional and state law obligations to its inmates. While the doctor, like the defender, exercised professional judgment, this does not mean that there is no state action.

The result is the same whether the physician is an employee or acts pursuant to contract. It is significant that the physician provides services at the state prison and under the considerable influence of prison policy; nor did the fact that the doctor worked part-time for the state change the result.

The decision in *West* prevents the state from avoiding its Eighth Amendment obligation to provide medical care to prisoners pursuant to the "deliberate indifference to serious medical needs" standard established by *Estelle v. Gamble,* 429 U.S. 97 (1976). A ruling that the prison doctor is not a state actor would enable the state to avoid its *Estelle* obligation by contracting out the provision of prison medical services to private physicians.

The *West* decision is not couched in terms of any of the traditional state action doctrines. The critical indicia of state action in *West* are (1) the provision of services, pursuant to state contract, which the state is constitutionally obligated to provide, (2) in a state facility, (3) to individuals with no other access to those services, and (4) under the heavy influence of state authority.

The authors believe that *West* strongly supports the conclusion that the operations of a private prison constitute state action.

§ 5.6 Federal Officials; State Officials Acting Pursuant to Federal Authority; Tribal Authority

Page 98, add at end of section:

National Guard officials engage in state action in carrying out their administrative functions. *Johnson v. Orr,* 780 F.2d 386 (3d Cir.), *cert. denied,* 107 S. Ct. 107 (1986). In a case in which a member of the National Guard alleged a violation of federal rights, the Fifth Circuit found that the State Adjunct General, a National Guard official, had engaged in state action. *Holdiness v. Stroud,* 808 F.2d 417 (5th Cir. 1987). See also *Stinson v. Hornsby,* 821 F.2d 1537 (11th Cir. 1987), reaffirming the analysis of *Mindes v. Seaman,* 453 F.2d 197 (5th Cir. 1971), *cert. denied,* 109 S. Ct. 402 (1988). See also **§ 7.17A.**

State officials who enforce federal Medicaid policy act under color of state law. *Rose v. Heintz,* 806 F.2d 389 (2d Cir. 1986); *Mitson v. Coler,* 670 F. Supp. 1568 (S.D. Fla. 1987). However, a state official's denial of federal disaster unemployment benefits pursuant to federal law was not under color of state law. *Rosas v. Brock,* 826 F.2d 1004 (11th Cir. 1987). "Where the challenged action by state employees is nothing more than application of federal rules, the federal involvement in those actions is so pervasive that the actions are taken under color of federal and not state law." *Id.* at 1007.

Indian Tribes are not state actors and do not act under color of state law. *Chapoose v. Hodel,* 831 F.2d 931 (10th Cir. 1987). "Redress for an alleged deprivation of civil rights accomplished under color of tribal law must be sought in the appropriate tribal court under the Indian Civil Rights Act, 25 U.S.C. §§ 1301-1303 . . . . Relief is not available under either a 42 U.S.C. § 1983 state action analogy theory or *Bivens* doctrine theory." *Evans v. Little Bird,* 656 F. Supp. 872, 874 (D. Mont. 1987).

Interpreting 28 U.S.C. § 1343, the Ninth Circuit concluded that Mexican government officials and employees do not act under color of state law. *Gerritsen v. Madrid Hurtado,* 819 F.2d 1511 (9th Cir. 1987).

The filing of a federal tax lien by a federal official was not state action because "the state is merely a passive agent of the federal government in maintaining records of such liens." *Church of Human Potential v. Vorsky,* 636 F. Supp. 93, 97 (D.N.J. 1986). The Secretary of Health and Human Services acted under color of federal rather than state law in administering the federal Medicaid program, and thus was not subject to suit under § 1983. *Estate of Smith v. Heckler,* 622 F. Supp. 403 (D. Colo. 1985). In *Savage v. Toan,* 636 F. Supp. 156, 158 (W.D. Mo. 1986), the court, applying the joint participation test, found that "the federal defendant . . . acted 'under color of state law' by pressuring the State defendants to violate plaintiff's medicaid rights." *See also Schrader v. Idaho Department of Health and Welfare,* 631 F. Supp. 1426, 1429 (D. Idaho 1986) ("[T]he federal defendants' threats of defunding meet the requirements to find state action and a violation of Section 1983").

§ 5.8 The State Action Requirement

Page 100, add to note 57:

The same tests are used for state and federal government action. San Francisco Arts & Athletics, Inc. v. United States Olympic Comm., 107 S. Ct. 2971 (1987).

Page 100, add at end of section:

* In the typical state action case, a private party is engaged in conduct claimed to be injurious and the issue is "whether the State was sufficiently involved to treat the decisive conduct as state action.... Thus in the usual case we ask whether the State provided a mantle of authority that enhanced the power of the harm-causing individual actor." *NCAA v. Tarkanian,* 109 S. Ct. 454, 462 (1988). In *Tarkanian,* however, the harm was inflicted by the University of Nevada, Las Vegas (UNLV), a state university which was unquestionably engaged in state action. The issue in *Tarkanian* was whether the role of the NCAA, a private association of public and private colleges and universities, constituted state action when it brought about the contested suspension of coach Tarkanian by UNLV. "This case uniquely mirrors the traditional state action case" and this "mirror image" required the Court "to step through an analytical looking glass to resolve it." *Id.* at 462. The Court ruled that the NCAA, in adopting and enforcing its rules, did not exercise state power. The Court rejected state action arguments under the public function, close nexus, and joint participation theories. (See §§ **5.11-5.13**.)

The Court in *Tarkanian* observed the similarity between the antitrust state action exemption and the Fourteenth Amendment state action doctrine.

> Although by no means identical, analysis of the existence of state action justifying immunity from antitrust liability is somewhat similar to the state action injury conducted pursuant to § 1983 and the Fourteenth Amendment. In both contexts, for example, courts examine whether the rule in question is a rule of the State.... The degree to which the activities of the State entity and the arguable private entity are intertwined also is pertinent.

109 S. Ct. at 463 n.14. In *Ezpeleta v. Sisters of Mercy Health Corp.,* 800 F.2d 119 (7th Cir. 1986), the court ruled that because the plaintiff's antitrust claim against a private hospital was barred by the state action antitrust immunity, the hospital's conduct did not necessarily constitute state action within the meaning of the Fourteenth Amendment.

The Fifth Circuit held that the *Noerr-Pennington* doctrine, which generally exempts from antitrust liability bona fide attempts by private parties to obtain relief from government, is applicable to § 1983 liability as well. "[W]e hold that any behavior by a private party that is protected from antitrust liability by the *Noerr-Pennington* doctrine is also outside the scope of section 1983 liability." The co-conspirator exception to *Noerr-Pennington* is also an exception which would justify the imposition of § 1983 liability. *Video International Production v. Warner-Amex Cable Communications,* 858 F.2d 1075, 1084 (5th Cir. 1988).

§ 5.9 Tests to Determine State Action – In General

Page 103, add at end of section:

* The Supreme Court ruled that the NCCA's successful efforts to induce a state university to suspend its basketball coach did not constitute state action. The NCAA's adoption of its rules did not constitute the exercise of state power. Rather, its rulemaking power came from the collective memebership of numerous private and public colleges and university. Nor had the state university delegated the NCAA the power to sanction a university employee. There was no basis for applying the public function, close nexus, or joint participation theories. The NCAA and the state university acted more like adversaries than partners. Four Justices, however, would have found state action under the joint participation theory. See **§ 5.13**. *NCAA v. Tarkanian,* 109 S. Ct. 454 (1988).

The Supreme Court ruled that the United States Olympic Committee's refusal to allow a nonprofit organization to use the word "Olympic" was not government action within the meaning of the due process clause of the Fifth Amendment, even though Congress granted the committee its corporate charter and the exclusive use of the word "Olympic." *San Francisco Arts and Athletics, Inc. v. United States Olympics Committee,* 107 S. Ct. 2971 (1987). The Court reiterated the rules that the conferral of government benefits, extensive government regulation, the carrying out of an important function, and government acquiescence are insufficient bases for finding government action. The Fifth and Fourteenth Amendment state action standards are
* identical. *Id.* at 2987 n.21. Four Justices dissented from the Court's no-state action ruling.

The Third Circuit found that because "the factual existence of state action was not a question of jurisdiction[,]" the district court should not have treated a finding (made on a preliminary injunction motion) that there was no state action, as conclusive for the purpose of subject matter jurisdiction. *Kulick v. Pocono Downs Racing Association,* 816 F.2d 895 (3d Cir. 1987).

§ 5.10 – The Symbiotic Relationship Test

Page 105, add at end of section:

* The Supreme Court rejected the plaintiff's reliance upon *Burton v. Wilmington Parking Authority,* 365 U.S. 715 (1961), in *NCAA v. Tarkanian,* 109 S. Ct. 454, 464 n.16 (1988).

> In the case before us the state and private parties' relevant interests do not coincide, as they did in *Burton*; rather, they have clashed throughout the investigation, the attempt to discipline Tarkanian, and this litigation. UNLV and the NCAA were antagonists, not joint participants, and the NCAA may not be deemed a state actor on this ground.

Id.

The Eleventh Circuit, in the course of holding that a union's exclusion of a broadcast network from the union's convention was not state action even though the union leased its facilities from the city, rejected the *Burton* symbiotic relationship doctrine. *Burton* does not extend to all lessees of public property. *National Broadcasting Co. v. Communication Workers of America,* 860 F.2d 1022 (11th Cir. 1988).

In *Adams v. Vandemark,* 855 F.2d 312 (6th Cir. 1988), *cert. denied,* 109 S. Ct. 868 (1989), the court, distinguishing *Burton,* found that the defendant anti-poverty organization was not engaged in state action even though it received significant governmental funding (90-99 percent of its budget), leased space from the city for 30 years at $1 per year, was subject to governmental regulation, and state law required that one-third of its directors be public officials. Judge Merritt, dissenting, chided the court for not considering "the effect of all individual 'links' together on the 'symbiosis.' " *Id.* at 319.

> This entity was created by government, is sustained by government, is required to further government purposes, and cannot exist without government. It is strange indeed to characterize such an animal as 'private,' a real confusion of categories, like The *Man Who Mistook His Wife For a Hat* (Dr. Oliver Sacks, Summit Books, 1986) or the Greek goddess who mistook the Unicorn for a Centaur.

Id. at 322.

The Fourth Circuit relied in part upon the symbiotic relationship theory in finding that a bail bondsman who entered a home to apprehend a fugitive from justice was engaged in state action. *Jackson v. Pantazes,* 810 F.2d 426 (4th Cir. 1987).

The Fifth Circuit found that *Burton* was the "controlling precedent" in the case of a hospital which was a "public corporation created by statute to serve a public purpose[,]" the facilities of which "were publicly owned and were constructed with public funds." *Jatoi v. Hurst-Euless-Bedford Hospital Authority,* 807 F.2d 1214, 1221 (5th Cir.), *modified,* 819 F.2d 545 (5th Cir. 1987), *cert. denied,* 108 S. Ct. 709 (1988). *See also Artist v. Virginia International Terminals,* 679 F. Supp. 587 (E.D. Va.) (state-owned port authority terminal operated by private entity is state actor), *aff'd,* 857 F.2d 977 (4th Cir. 1988).

§ 5.11 –The Public Function Test

Page 107, add at end of section:

The Supreme Court held that the coordination of amateur sports by the United States Olympic Committee has not been a "traditional governmental function." *San Francisco Arts and Athletics, Inc. v. United States Olympic Committee,* 107 S. Ct. 2971, 2985 (1987). The fact that the committee carries out a "representational function can hardly be called traditionally governmental." *Id.* at 2985 n.27. Justice Brennan's dissenting opinion criticized the exclusivity aspect of the public function doctrine because it can "freeze into law a static conception of Government." *Id.* at 2988 n.1.

* The Supreme Court rejected the argument that the NCAA carried out a traditional public function. *NCAA v. Tarkanian,* 109 S. Ct. 454, 465 n.18 (1988). Although the

plaintiff had the good sense, in light of *San Francisco Arts and Athletics,* not to argue that fostering amateur college athletics is a public function, he did argue that the NCAA assumed the state function of disciplining public employees. The Court rejected the argument because NCAA rules prohibited it from taking direct action against a university employee, and because discipline of a university employee was but one means available to the NCAA to bring about university compliance with its rules.

Despite the Supreme Court's requirement that a public function be the *exclusive* prerogative of the state, a number of lower federal courts continue to find state action under the public function doctrine. *Williams v. St. Louis,* 783 F.2d 114 (8th Cir. 1986) (city's delegation to redevelopment corporation of powers to set housing standards for residential properties and of eminent domain are delegations of traditional * governmental powers under color of state law); *Pitt v. Pine Valley Golf Club,* 695 F. Supp. 778 (D.N.J. 1988) (where private golf club owned all land in borough, its enforcement of rule restricting home ownership in borough to golf club members is analogous to enforcement of public zoning power); *Fialkowski v. Greenwich Home for Children,* 683 F. Supp. 103 (E.D. Pa. 1987) (care to mentally retarded is a public function); *Schaefer v. Wilcock,* 676 F. Supp. 1092 (D. Utah 1987) (social worker retained to perform psychological assessment of state employee is state actor); *Plain v. Flicker,* 645 F. Supp. 898 (D.N.J. 1986) (private physicians' certification of civil commitment is state action under public function doctrine); *Libin v. Town of Greenwich,* 625 F. Supp. 393 (D. Conn. 1985) (volunteer fire department is a state actor under public function and symbiotic relationship tests). In *Davenport v. Saint Mary Hospital,* 633 F. Supp. 1228 (E.D. Pa. 1986), the court found that a question of fact existed as to whether the state delegated to the defendant private hospital its responsibilities for the care and custody of involuntarily committed individuals. Dictum in *Plain v. Flicker,* 645 F. Supp. at 907, states that "if a state contracted with a private corporation to run its prisons, it would no doubt subject the private prison employees to § 1983 suits under the public function doctrine." *See West v. Atkins,* 108 S. Ct. 2250 (1988), discussed in § **5.5**.

A number of recent lower court cases rejected arguments that state action existed * under the public function doctrine. *National Broadcasting Co. v. Communications Workers of America,* 860 F.2d 1022, 1026 (11th Cir. 1988) ("Selecting media stations to cover a speech has never been an exclusive function of the government . . . "); *Robison v. Canterbury Village,* 848 F.2d 424 (3d Cir. 1988) (company town's evictions do not constitute state action); *McCormack v. National Collegiate Athletic Association,* 845 F.2d 1338 (5th Cir. 1988) (coordination and oversight of intercollegiate athletics); *Medical Institute v. National Association of Trade and Technical Schools,* 817 F.2d 1310, 1315 (8th Cir. 1987) (accreditation of educational institutions not exclusive governmental function); *Graham v. National Collegiate Athletic Association,* 804 F.2d 953 (6th Cir. 1986) (regulation of intercollegiate athletics is not a public function); *Carlin Communication v. Southern Bell Telephone and Telegraph Co.,* 802 F.2d 1352 (11th Cir. 1986) (utility company's refusal to allow transmittal of sexually explicit tape-recorded messages is not a traditional state function); *Harris v. Arkansas Book Co.,* 794 F.2d 358 (8th Cir. 1986) (book depository which stores textbooks for publishing companies pending distribution to schools does not perform a function that has been traditionally the exclusive prerogative of the state); *Malachowski v. City of Keene,* 787 F.2d 704 (1st Cir.) (nonprofit organization that makes foster homes available for state

agencies and provides recommendations regarding child placement to juvenile court does not perform a function that has been traditionally the exclusive prerogative of the
* state), *cert. denied,* 107 S. Ct. 107 (1986); *Mineo v. Transportation Management of Tennessee,* 694 F. Supp. 417 (M.D. Tenn. 1988) (mass transportation is not an exclusively governmental function); *Transport Careers v. National Home Study Council,* 646 F. Supp. 1474, 1479 (N.D. Ind. 1986) (accreditation of educational entities has been a private function); *Vargas v. Salvation Army,* 649 F. Supp. 763 (N.D. Ill. 1986) (care for sick and elderly not exclusive governmental function); *Nygren v. Predovich,* 637 F. Supp. 1083 (D. Colo. 1986) (private forensic research laboratory engaged in scientific testing of physical evidence does not perform an essential public function); *Giannattasio v. Stamford Youth Hockey Association,* 621 F. Supp. 825 (D. Conn. 1985) (a youth hockey organization does not carry out a public function); *Gardner v. Governor Apartments Associates,* 396 Mass. 661, 488 N.E.2d 3 (1986) (rehabilitation of decadent housing not an exclusive government function).

In *Malachowski v. City of Keene,* the First Circuit found that "child care and placement is not traditionally the exclusive prerogative of the state." 787 F.2d at 711. By contrast, a federal district court, without mentioning the public function doctrine, found that a child care agency's acceptance and care of foster children constituted state action under the "sufficiency close nexus" test because the state and city remained ultimately responsible for the child's welfare, and the agency's decisions were directly circumscribed by state and city regulations. *Wilder v. Bernstein,* 645 F. Supp. 1292 (S.D.N.Y. 1986).

In a finding that a telephone company's institution of a policy of excluding all adult entertainment messages from its services was not a public function, the court reasoned that censorship without a prior judicial determination is something the states may *not* do and only private parties may do. *Carlin Communication v. Mountain States Telephone and Telegraph Co.,* 827 F.2d 1291, 1297 (9th Cir. 1987), *cert. denied,* 108 S. Ct. 1586 (1988).

* In *Robison v. Canterbury Village,* 848 F.2d 424 (3d Cir. 1988), the Third Circuit stated that although the defendant is a company town, not all of its activities are state action. Rather, "only the actions or decisions connected with exercise of governmental functions are those that may be regarded as state action, such as a company town's refusal to permit persons to leaflet on the town's sidewalks or a park owner's refusal to admit blacks." 848 F.2d at 429. Similarly, the town's provision of municipal services would constitute state action. By contrast, the contested evictions were carried out by the president of the defendant village in his "private landlord role" and thus do not constitute state action. *Id.* On remand, the district court should consider whether the president's "alleged conduct as *de facto* employer of municipal employees should be treated as state action." *Id.*

§ 5.12 —The Nexus Test

Page 109, add at end of section:

There was an insufficient nexus between the federal government and the United States Olympic Committee's refusal to allow a nonprofit organization to use the word

"Olympic" because "[t]here is no evidence that the Federal Government coerced or encouraged the USOC in the exercise of its right." *San Francisco Arts and Athletics, Inc. v. United States Olympic Committee,* 107 S. Ct. 2971, 2986 (1987).

* In holding that the NCAA's conduct in persuading a state university (UNLV) to suspend its coach did not constitute state action, the Supreme Court in *NCAA v. Tarkanian,* 109 S. Ct. 454 (1988), found that although the state university had some impact upon NCAA policy determinations, so did the numerous other private and public member colleges and universities. In this context the source of the rules was not the state university but the collective membership. "The situation would, of course, be different if the membership consisted entirely of institutions located within the same state, many of them public institutions created by the same sovereign." *Id* at 462 n.13. Nor did the NCAA's investigation, enforcement proceedings, and recommended sanctions represent the exercise of state power. The state university "delegated no power to the NCAA to take specific action against any university employee. The commitment by UNLV to adhere to NCAA enforcement procedures was enforceable only by sanctions that the NCAA might impose on UNLV itself." *Id.* at 464. Finally, even if it is assumed that UNLV had no choice but to comply with the NCAA's demands, it doesn't follow that the NCAA was engaged in state action. *Id.* at 465.

In *Albert v. Carovano,* 851 F.2d 561 (2d Cir. 1988) (en banc), the court held that the fact that state law requires colleges to adopt student disciplinary rules and file them with the state does not justify a finding that a private college's suspension of students constituted state action when state officials were not responsible for any particular sanction. "[E]ven if the state had specifically required . . . Hamilton [College] to adopt the precise rules set forth in its [code], the ultimate power to select a particular sanction in individual cases would rest with the private party." *Id.* at 571.

Under the unique facts of the case, the Fifth Circuit in *Howard Gault Co. v. Texas Rural Legal Aid,* 848 F.2d 544 (5th Cir. 1988), found that private parties who filed suit in state court were engaged in state action. The parties were represented by attorneys who were also employed by the county as district attorneys and these attorneys utilized the resources of the state's attorney general's office and the sheriff's office. The state "significantly encouraged" the state court litigation and there was joint participation between the public and private sectors.

In *National Broadcasting Co. v. Communication Workers of America,* 860 F.2d 1022 (11th Cir. 1988), a union's exclusion of a broadcast network from the union's convention, which was held in facilities leased from the city, was not state action because the city neither compelled nor significantly encouraged the exclusion.

Defendant telephone company's termination of plaintiff's adult entertainment message service was state action because it resulted from the exercise of coercive state power in the form of a threat to prosecute. However, defendant's adoption of a new policy excluding all adult entertainment messages from its services was not state action because it was not the product of state coercion and was not a public function. *Carlin Communication v. Mountain States Telephone and Telegraph Co.,* 827 F.2d 1291 (9th Cir. 1987), *cert. denied,* 108 S. Ct. 1586 (1988).

The enforcement by civic center employees of the center's "no camera" rule provided the necessary state action, regardless of whether the employees were paid by the center or by a private company. *D'Amario v. Providence Civic Center Authority,* 783

F.2d 1 (1st Cir. 1986). The determinative factor in finding an employment relationship was that the employees remained within the control and direction of the civic center, and the enforcement of the no-camera rule by the employees supplied the "state involvement nexus that is a jurisdictional requisite under 42 U.S.C. § 1983." *Id.* at 3.

In *Sims v. Jefferson Downs Racing Association,* 778 F.2d 1068 (5th Cir. 1985), the defendant race track's eviction of a trainer was state action because the track solicited and utilized state power to carry out the eviction.

The nexus test was not satisfied in *Jarrell v. Chemical Dependency Unit,* 791 F.2d 373 (5th Cir. 1986). While the state may have placed its authority behind the plaintiff's compulsory commitment, there was no nexus between the state's authority and the alleged deprivation of plaintiff's rights during the course of his treatment.

§ 5.13 –The Joint Participation Test

Page 112, add at end of section:

* The Supreme Court rejected the argument that the NCAA and a state university were joint participants because they acted much more like adversaries than like partners. *NCAA v. Tarkanian,* 109 S. Ct. 454 (1988). The university used its best efforts to retain its winning coach, a goal diametrically opposite to that of the NCAA, which sought to bring about the suspension of the coach as a sanction to further its goal of rule enforcement. "[T]he NCAA is properly reviewed as a private actor at odds with the State when it represents the interests of its entire membership in an investigation of one public university." *Id.* at 464.

Justice White's four-Justice dissenting opinion finds state action under the joint participation test because

1. "Tarkanian was suspended for violations of NCAA rules, which UNLV embraced in its agreement with the NCAA"
2. "[T]he NCAA and UNLV also agreed that the NCAA would conduct hearings concerning violations of its rules" and
3. "[T]he NCAA and UNLV agreed that the findings of fact made by the NCAA at the hearings it conducted would be binding on UNLV."

Id. at 466-67. The fact that the university had the opportunity to become an opponent of its partner does not undermine the agreement itself. The key is that ultimately UNLV suspended Tarkanian pursuant to its agreement to abide by NCAA rules and findings. *Id.* at 468.

The Seventh Circuit found state action on the basis of a conspiracy to transfer a license from one private party to another. *Easter House v. Felder,* 852 F.2d 901 *reh'g granted,* 861 F.2d 494 (7th Cir. 1988).

The utilization of public attorneys and resources on behalf of private litigants satisfied the joint participation test. *Howard Gault Co. v. Texas Rural Legal Aid,* 848 F.2d 544 (5th Cir. 1988).

The mere fact that a private party requests relief from a municipality does not constitute state action; the private party and the city were not engaged in a conspiracy. *Video International Production v. Warner-Amex Cable Communications,* 858 F.2d 1075 (5th Cir. 1988).

A supermarket security guard's detention of a customer was not state action when there was no prearranged plan with the police. *Gramenos v. Jewel Cos.,* 797 F.2d 432 (7th Cir. 1986), *cert. denied,* 107 S. Ct. 1952 (1987). The fact that a merchant detains a customer pursuant to a state shoplifting statute does not by itself provide a basis for finding state action, *Hurt v. G.C. Murphy,* 624 F. Supp. 512 (S.D. W. Va. 1986), but a store detective's arrest was found to be state action where the detective was designated a "special patrolman" by the New York City Police Commissioner and given the power to arrest. *Rojas v. Alexander's Department Store,* 654 F. Supp. 856 (E.D.N.Y. 1986). *See also Merola v. National Railroad Passenger Corp.,* 683 F. Supp. 935 (S.D.N.Y. 1988).

The fact that an individual makes a "citizen's arrest," transfers the arrestee to the police station, and reports suspected criminal activity to the police is not a sufficient basis for finding state action, where there is no evidence of a prearranged plan or concerted action. *Lee v. Town of Estes Park,* 820 F.2d 1112 (10th Cir. 1987). *See also Carey v. Continental Airlines,* 823 F.2d 1402 (10th Cir. 1987); *Benavidez v. Gunnell,* 722 F.2d 615 (10th Cir. 1983).

The fact that a private landlord called the police, who subsequently searched the premises and made an arrest, did not make the landlord a participant in the arrest, where the landlord exercised no control over the officers' decision to search and arrest. *King v. Massarweh,* 782 F.2d 825 (9th Cir. 1986).

The Fourth Circuit, relying upon the symbiotic relationship and joint participation theories, found that a bail bondsman who entered a home to apprehend a fugitive from justice was engaged in state action. *Jackson v. Pantazes,* 810 F.2d 426 (4th Cir. 1987).

In a case with a theatrical and bizarre fact pattern, the court found that defendant Anderson was not a mere complainant of criminal wrongdoing, but was a joint participant with the deputy chief of police in having plaintiff arrested and detained. The circumstantial evidence showed that Anderson "possessed and exerted influence over the Worcester police, and conspired with them to have Wagenmann arrested and kept under wraps in order to safeguard his son's wedding from unwanted intrusion." *Wagenmann v. Adams,* 829 F.2d 196, 211 (1st Cir. 1987).

A guardian who worked with a state hospital and local officials to have his ward admitted to the hospital was engaged in state action under the *Lugar v. Edmondson Oil Co.,* 457 U.S. 922 (1982), joint participation test. *Thomas S. v. Morrow,* 781 F.2d 367 (4th Cir.), *cert. denied,* 107 S. Ct. 235 (1986).

The Seventh Circuit applied *Lugar* in *Del's Big Saver Foods v. Carpenter Cook,* 795 F.2d 1344 (7th Cir. 1986). The court found that the creditor's repossession of the debtor's property was state action because "[t]he state court order gave [the creditor] Carpenter Cook the powers of the sheriff, and if [debtor] Del's had resisted the attachment the sheriff would have popped in and taken over from Carpenter Cook; the order directed the sheriff to assist." *Id.* at 1346.

There was a question of fact as to whether an attorney's advice to a bank as to the legality of prejudgment attachment and the institution of attachment proceedings was joint participation. *Watertown Equipment Co. v. Norwest Bank,* 830 F.2d 1487 (8th Cir. 1987), *cert. denied,* 108 S. Ct. 1723 (1988).

In *Pennzoil Co. v. Texaco,* 107 S. Ct. 1519 (1987), Justices Brennan, Blackmun, and Stevens, in separate concurring opinions, found that a judgment creditor's invocation of postjudgment collection procedures constitutes state action. The Court, however, did not reach the issue, deciding the case instead on the basis of *Younger* abstention. See § **12.6**.

The contractual relationship between a city employer and the union of city employees, based upon the collective bargaining agreement, rendered the union a state actor under the joint participation test. *McGlumphy v. Fraternal Order of Police,* 633 F. Supp. 1074, 1079 n.10 (N.D. Ohio 1986).

More than mere encouragement and endorsement of legislation that turns out to be unconstitutional is necessary to find state action on a conspiracy theory. *Culebras Enterprises v. Rivera Rios,* 813 F.2d 506, 519 (1st Cir. 1987). A federal district court concluded: "An agreement with the state to do what a private person already has the legal authority to do simply does not, by itself, transform the private action into state action." *Hudson v. S.D. Warren Co.,* 665 F. Supp. 937, 939 (D. Me. 1987).

Proof of a conspiracy requires a showing of agreement or meeting of the minds between the private persons and government agents. All must, at least, share common objectives or purpose. *United Steelworkers v. Phelps Dodge,* 833 F.2d 804 (9th Cir. 1987).

§ 5.14 Application of State Action Doctrines

Page 113, add to end of Creditors' Rights subsection:

* *Hassett v. Lemay Bank & Trust Co.,* 851 F.2d 1127 (8th Cir. 1988) (private party's misuse of replevin statute is not state action); *Carlin Communication v. Mountain States Telephone and Telegraph Co.,* 827 F.2d 1291 (9th Cir. 1987) (termination of adult entertainment message service was state action because it was the result of a threat to prosecute; telephone company's adoption of new policy to exclude all adult entertainment messages from its services was not state action because the policy was not the product of state coercion), *cert. denied,* 108 S. Ct. 1586 (1988); *Carlin Communication v. Southern Bell Telephone and Telegraph Co.,* 802 F.2d 1352 (11th Cir. 1986) (termination of utility service is not state action); *Del's Big Saver Foods v. Carpenter Cook,* 795 F.2d 1344 (7th Cir. 1986) (creditor's repossession of debtor's property was state action where state court order gave creditor powers of sheriff and directed sheriff to assist).

While the Court did not resolve the issue, Justices Brennan, Blackmun, and Stevens, in their concurring opinions, took the position that a judgment creditor's invocation of postjudgment collection procedures constitutes state action. *Pennzoil Co. v. Texaco,* 107 S. Ct. 1519 (1987).

Page 114, add after second line:

* **Educational and Athletic Institutions.** *NCAA v. Tarkanian,* 109 S. Ct. 454 (1988) (state university officials who perform their official functions are engaged in state action; NCAA found not engaged in state action); *San Francisco Arts and Athletics, Inc. v. United States Olympic Committee,* 107 S. Ct. 2971 (1987) (Olympic Committee's enforcement of "Olympic" trademark not governmental action within meaning of Fifth Amendment); *McCormack v. National Collegiate Athletic Association,* 845 F.2d 1338 (5th Cir. 1988) (athletic association's coordination and oversight of intercollegiate athletics not state action); *Sinn v. The Daily Nebraskan,* 829 F.2d 662 (8th Cir. 1987) (state university college newspaper's refusal to accept certain advertisements not state action because there were insufficient indicia of state control over the paper's editorial
* process); *Albert v. Carovano,* 851 F.2d 561 (2d Cir. 1988) (en banc) (state did not coerce or significantly encourage private college's suspension of plaintiff students
* merely by requiring colleges to adopt disciplinary rules); *Gay and Lesbian Students Association v. Gohn,* 850 F.2d 361 (8th Cir. 1988) (state university student senate's denial of funding to gay and lesbian association was state action because university had final say over funding decisions); *Griffin High School v. Illinois High School Association,* 822 F.2d 671 (7th Cir. 1987) (association, made up of 85 percent public and 15 percent private secondary schools, for the purpose of regulating interscholastic athletics, is engaged in state action because of its "overwhelming public character"); *Medical Institute v. National Association of Trade and Technical Schools,* 817 F.2d 1310 (8th Cir. 1987) (accrediting agency's denial of reaccreditation not state action); *Karamanos v. Baker,* 816 F.2d 258 (6th Cir. 1987) (athletic association's regulation of intercollegiate athletics is not state action); *Graham v. National Collegiate Athletic Association,* 804 F.2d 953 (6th Cir. 1986) (athletic association's regulation of intercollegiate athletics is not state action); *Transport Careers v. National Home Study Council,* 646 F. Supp. 1474 (N.D. Ind. 1986) (accrediting commission's decision to terminate accreditation of home study school not state action); *Jones v. Grunewarld,* 644 F. Supp. 256 (S.D.N.Y. 1986) (private college that runs a prison educational program; no state action); *Nygren v. Predovich,* 637 F. Supp. 1083 (D. Colo. 1986) (forensic research laboratory's scientific testing of physical evidence is not state action); *Giannattasio v. Stamford Youth Hockey Association,* 621 F. Supp. 825 (D. Conn. 1985) (youth hockey organization; no state action).

Page 115, add after second line, at end of Health Care subsection:

* *West v. Atkins,* 108 S. Ct. 2250 (1988) (physician's provision of care to prison inmates pursuant to contract with state is state action); *Tunca v. Lutheran General Hospital,* 844 F.2d 411 (7th Cir. 1988) (private hospital's denial of staff privileges is not state action); *Tarabishi v. McAlester Regional Hospital,* 827 F.2d 648 (10th Cir. 1987) (defendant hospital is a state actor because it is "public trust" governed by trustees who are public officials); *Pariser v. Christian Health Care Systems,* 816 F.2d 1248 (8th Cir. 1987) (private hospital's suspension of medical staff privileges; no state action); *Savin v. Samaritan Health Center,* 813 F.2d 755 (6th Cir. 1987) (private hospital's revocation of staff privileges; no state action); *Jatoi v. Hurst-Euless-Bedford Hospital Authority,* 807 F.2d 1214 (5th Cir.), *modified,* 819 F.2d 545 (5th Cir. 1987), *cert. denied,*

108 S. Ct. 709 (1988) (hospital, which is public corporation with publicly owned facilities constructed with public funds, is state actor); *Ezpeleta v. Sisters of Mercy Health Corp.,* 800 F.2d 119 (7th Cir. 1986) (private hospital's termination of staff privileges; no state action); *Jarrell v. Chemical Dependency Unit,* 791 F.2d 373 (5th Cir. 1986) (defendant's provision of treatment not state action); *Fialkowski v. Greenwich Home for Children,* 683 F. Supp. 103 (E.D. Pa. 1987) (organization which provides care to the mentally retarded is engaged in state action); *Plain v. Flicker,* 645 F. Supp. 898 (D.N.J. 1986) (physician's certification of civil commitment is state action); *Davenport v. Saint Mary Hospital,* 633 F. Supp. 1228 (E.D. Pa. 1986) (question of fact exists as to whether state delegated to defendant hospital the responsibilities for care and custody of involuntarily committed individuals).

Page 116, add after second line, at end of Judicial Participants subsection:

The Supreme Court found that a state court's "pervasive and substantial" involvement with a provision of Oklahoma's probate laws, which required certain claims to be presented to the executor or executrix within two months of publication of notice advising creditors of the commencement of probate proceedings, constituted state action. While a self-executing statute of limitations does not constitute state action (*Texaco v. Short,* 454 U.S. 516 (1982)), in this case the "nonclaim" statute becomes operative only after commencement of probate proceedings. The probate court appoints the executor or executrix and directs the publication of notice, and copies of the notice must be filed with the court. "[W]hen private parties make use of state procedures with the direct, significant assistance of state officials, state action may be found." *Tulsa Professional Collection Services v. Pope,* 108 S. Ct. 1340, 1345 (1988).

The mere fact that a private party is a participant in a judicial proceeding does not make that party a state actor. *Tunstall v. Office of Judicial Support,* 820 F.2d 631 (3d Cir. 1987); *McDougald v. Jenson,* 786 F.2d 1465 (11th Cir.), *cert. denied,* 107 S. Ct. 207 (1986); *Fleming v. Moore,* 780 F.2d 438 (4th Cir. 1985), *cert. denied,* 475 U.S. 1123 (1986); *Ross v. Hatfield,* 640 F. Supp. 708 (D. Conn. 1986) (claim that defendants threatened to seek judicial enforcement of restrictive covenant; no state action); *Mabe*
* *v. Galveston Park Board,* 635 F. Supp. 105 (S.D. Tex. 1986). *Tunstall* also holds that a private party who purchases property at a sale conducted by a municipality to collect delinquent taxes is not engaged in state action. In *Mabe,* the court ruled that (1) the city's request for an injunction was not state action because it did not involve the exercise of governmental power but was analogous to a private party bringing suit, and (2) the state court's issuance of an injunction did not make the city a state actor.

* Under the unique facts of this case, the Fifth Circuit found that private parties who filed suit in state court were state actors because they were represented by attorneys who were employed by the county as district attorneys and those attorneys utilized the resources of the state's attorney general's office and the county sheriff's office. *Howard Gault Co. v. Texas Rural Legal Aid,* 848 F.2d 544 (5th Cir. 1988). The court relied upon the joint action and significant encouragement theories.

Public officials brought a state court proceeding to remove a county official from office. Even though state law prohibited the officials from bringing the suit in their official capacities, their institution of the suit constituted state action because they used public funds and the suit "was merely the culmination of a whole series of earlier actions taken by the defendants in their official capacities as commissioners with the intent of removing [the county official] from office." *Jones v. Duncan,* 840 F.2d 359, 363 (6th Cir. 1988).

* The Fifth Circuit held that a private litigant's exercise, in federal district court, of a peremptory challenge on allegedly racial grounds constitutes governmental action within the meaning of the due process clause of the Fifth Amendment. *Edmonson v. Leesville Concrete Co.,* 860 F.2d 1308 (5th Cir. 1988). The government summons the venire, the right to peremptory challenges is granted by federal statute, and the judge excuses the juror. The government is thus "intimately involved" in the peremptory challenge. Judge Gee, dissenting, opined that the judge "performs the merely ministerial function of excusing veniremen cut by counsel from further attendance in the case." *Id.* at 1316.

Court-appointed guardians, a therapist, and an attorney who reported the results of their inquiries to law enforcement officials would not be engaged in state action if they acted beyond the scope of their official duties. *Myers v. Morris,* 810 F.2d 1437, 1467 (8th Cir.), *cert. denied,* 108 S. Ct. 97 (1988).

Most cases which raise the question of whether private individuals become state actors when involved with law enforcement activities are analyzed under the joint participation doctrine. See § **5.13**. It is settled that the mere fact that a private party files a criminal complaint does not constitute state action. *Daniel v. Ferguson,* 839 F.2d 1124, 1130 (5th Cir. 1988); *Emswiler v. McCoy,* 622 F. Supp. 786 (S.D. W. Va. 1985). One who merely assists an organized crime task force in obtaining evidence is not a state actor. *Della Pietra v. New York State Organized Crime Task Force,* 630 F. Supp. 986 (W.D.N.Y. 1986). See also *Manax v. McNamara,* 842 F.2d 808 (5th Cir. 1988) (provision of information to state board of medical examiners in an attempt to convince board to revoke a doctor's medical license is not state action).

Taking the position that the question of whether government informers are governmental actors should be decided on a case-by-case basis, the Sixth Circuit found that an informer was not a governmental actor because any unconstitutional acts were committed on his own behalf, he was already a member of the organization which he infiltrated when approached by the FBI, and the FBI did not place him there. *Ghandi v. Police Department,* 823 F.2d 959 (6th Cir. 1987), *cert. denied,* 108 S. Ct. 774 (1988). The court indicated that government action is more likely to be found when a full-time informant is paid a salary to infiltrate an organization, as opposed to receiving periodic payments for discrete projects. *Id.* at 964.

The courts have different views on whether the action of a court constitutes government action. In *Grandbouche v. Clancy,* 825 F.2d 1463, 1466 (10th Cir. 1987), the court concluded that "the magistrate's order compelling discovery and the trial court's enforcement of that order provide the requisite governmental action that invokes First Amendment scrutiny."

The Eleventh Circuit found that a state's mere provision of a judicial forum is a "neutral act" which does not constitute state action.

> Thus, state court involvement in a private civil action cannot rise to the level of state action until the state has placed its weight behind a position adverse to the federal plaintiff's federal right in the form of an "immediately enforceable" state court judgment . . . , and, except in extraordinary circumstances, in order to be immediately enforceable a state court judgment must have been approved by the highest court of the state.

Paisey v. Vitale, 807 F.2d 889, 894 (11th Cir. 1986).

According to the Ninth Circuit, "state enforcement of private rights generally will not itself meet the state action requirement." *International Olympic Committee v. San Francisco Arts and Athletics, Inc.,* 781 F.2d 733, 737 (9th Cir.), *aff'd on other grounds,* 107 S. Ct. 2971 (1987).

A bar association's termination of the plaintiff's employment was not state action where the state court, which had a close relationship with the association, was not involved in the termination. *Niehaus v. Kansas Bar Association,* 793 F.2d 1159 (10th Cir. 1986).

A court-appointed receiver acts under color of state law. *Scutieri v. Estate of Revitz,* 683 F. Supp. 795 (S.D. Fla. 1988).

A legal services organization's denial of services did not constitute state action. *Fultz v. Neighborhood Legal Services,* 654 F. Supp. 881 (W.D. Pa. 1987).

Other judicial participants are discussed in **§ 5.5**.

Page 116, add to end of Subsidized Housing subsection:

Gallman v. Pierce, 639 F. Supp. 472 (N.D. Cal. 1986) (§ 8 landlord's termination of tenancy was state action); *Gardner v. Governor Apartments Associates,* 396 Mass. 661, 488 N.E.2d 3 (1986) (rehabilitator of decadent housing; no state action);

Page 116, add at end of section:

Child Care. *Malachowski v. City of Keene,* 787 F.2d 704 (1st Cir.) (nonprofit organization that made foster homes available and provided child placement recommendations to court; no state action), *cert. denied,* 107 S. Ct. 107 (1986); *Swayne v. L.D.S. Social Services,* 670 F. Supp. 1537 (D. Utah 1987) (adoption agency's termination of illegitimate father's parental rights is state action where it is mandated by state statute; insuring that child will be placed in care of appropriate substitute parents is within public function doctrine); *Wilder v. Bernstein,* 645 F. Supp. 1292 (S.D.N.Y. 1986) (child care agency's acceptance and care of children placed with it by city agency is state action).

* **Community Organizations.** *Adams v. Vandemark,* 855 F.2d 312 (6th Cir. 1988) (nonprofit antipoverty organization; no state action), *cert. denied,* 109 S. Ct. 868 (1989); *Nail v. Community Action Agency,* 805 F.2d 1500 (11th Cir. 1986) (nonprofit
* community agency's discharge of teacher's aide; no state action); *Cassiano v. Amigos Del Valle,* 776 F.2d 1300 (5th Cir. 1985) (nonprofit organization which provides services to elderly; no state action); *Vargas v. Salvation Army,* 649 F. Supp. 763 (N.D. Ill. 1986) (discharge of employee not state action).

Race Tracks. *Sims v. Jefferson Downs Racing Association,* 778 F.2d 1068 (5th Cir. 1985) (race track's expulsion of trainer was state action). *Sims* collects the leading race track state action decisions. *Roberts v. Louisiana Downs,* 742 F.2d 221 (5th Cir. 1984); *Bier v. Fleming,* 717 F.2d 308 (6th Cir. 1983), *cert. denied,* 465 U.S. 1026 (1984); *Fitzgerald v. Mountain Laurel Racing,* 607 F.2d 589 (3d Cir. 1979), *cert. denied,* 446 U.S. 956 (1980).

CHAPTER 6

GOVERNMENTAL LIABILITY AND IMMUNITY

§ 6.1 Section 1983 Liability: Introduction

Page 119, add after carryover paragraph:

The Supreme Court reiterated the rule that "the real party in interest in an official capacity suit is the entity represented and not the individual officeholder." *Karcher v. May,* 108 S. Ct. 388, 393 (1987). The Seventh Circuit concluded that where the plaintiff sued the mayor officially and the city, in reality there was only one defendant, because suing the mayor in an official capacity was equivalent to suing the city. "Nothing was added by suing the mayor in his official capacity." *Jungels v. Pierce,* 825 F.2d 1127, 1129 * (7th Cir. 1987). In *Kennedy v. Hardiman,* 684 F. Supp. 540 (N.D. Ill. 1988), however, the court, although acknowledging that a claim against a municipal official in an official capacity is equivalent to a claim against the entity, ruled that the plaintiff may choose to name more than one official capacity defendant. "By naming an individual in his official capacity, rather than merely naming the municipality itself, a plaintiff focuses the attention of the parties, the court, and perhaps later the jury, on the particular official whom he seeks to hold responsible for implementing an allegedly unlawful municipal policy." *Id.* at 542.

Courts frequently experience difficulties in determining whether an official has been sued in an individual or official capacity. In *Hadi v. Horn,* 830 F.2d 779 (7th Cir. 1987), the court found that the defendant was sued in an individual capacity because (1) the named defendants left office during the litigation of the action and the parties did not point out the need for substitution; (2) plaintiff sought money damages against state officials which, under the Eleventh Amendment, normally are not available in official-capacity suits against state officials; and (3) defendants never raised the Eleventh Amendment defense, but did raise the qualified immunity defense. In *Gregory v. Chehi,* 843 F.2d 111 (3d Cir. 1988), the court construed the complaint as naming the defendant municipal officials in their individual (in addition to official) capacities because the plaintiffs sought punitive damages against them, and this relief was recoverable against them only in their individual capacities.

* The Second Circuit relied upon the facts that the plaintiff sought punitive and compensatory damages, and the defendants moved for summary judgment on qualified immunity but not Eleventh Amendment grounds, as supporting the conclusion that the parties treated the action as a personal capacity suit. *Shabazz v. Coughlin,* 852 F.2d 697 (2d Cir. 1988).

Correcting any misimpression that may have been construed from its decision in *Jones v. Smith,* 784 F.2d 149 (2d Cir. 1986), the Second Circuit clarified that the fact that the complaint alleges that a state official was carrying out a state policy does not mean that the action can be characterized only as an official capacity suit. *Farid v.*

Smith, 850 F.2d 917 (2d Cir. 1988). As the authors pointed out in the last edition of the Supplement, "a claim for damages against an official in an individual capacity may grow out of the implementation of official policy." *Farid* correctly holds that such a personal capacity claim would not be defeated by the Eleventh Amendment.

The Seventh Circuit found that a suit should be treated as an individual capacity suit where the record showed that the litigants and at least one of the three judges successively assigned to the case treated it as an individual capacity suit. The defendants raised the good faith immunity defense, "a defense that only an individual is entitled to raise." *Shockley v. Jones,* 823 F.2d 1068, 1071 (7th Cir. 1987). *See also Fitzgerald v. McDaniel,* 833 F.2d 1516 (11th Cir. 1987); *Lundgren v. McDaniel,* 814 F.2d 600 (11th Cir. 1987). In another Seventh Circuit case, the court stated: "We recognize that complaints often fail to specify clearly whether a suit is an official-capacity suit, a personal-capacity suit, or both, and . . . that the actual result of proceedings is often the best evidence of the nature of the liability sought to be imposed." *Brunken v. Lance,* 807 F.2d 1325, 1329 (7th Cir. 1986). Just naming a defendant in an official capacity or just naming defendant and his or her office (e.g., Smith, Warden) raises a presumption that the official has been sued only in an official capacity, but the presumption may be rebutted when, as here, the case was tried as a suit against defendants as individuals. *Duckworth v. Franzen,* 780 F.2d 645 (7th Cir. 1985), *cert. denied,* 107 S. Ct. 71 (1986).

The Supreme Court of Ohio (1) ruled that the distinction between individual- and official-capacity suits is relevant only where damages are sought, and (2) determined that the Ohio state courts have jurisdiction to hear § 1983 claims for injunctive relief where it is alleged that state officials acted unconstitutionally. *Schwarz v. Board of Trustees,* 31 Ohio St. 3d 267, 510 N.E.2d 808 (1987).

When police officers were sued in their individual capacities, it was prejudicial error for plaintiff's counsel to state in closing argument that the government would be liable for the officers' unconstitutional acts. *Griffin v. Hilke,* 804 F.2d 1052 (8th Cir. 1986), *cert. denied,* 107 S. Ct. 3184 (1987). The court drew an analogy from the rule that excludes evidence of insurance coverage on the question of liability.

The principles of *Feres v. United States,* 340 U.S. 135 (1950) and *Chappell v. Wallace,* 462 U.S. 296 (1983), which generally immunize the United States and superior military officers from liability growing out of military matters, apply in § 1983 actions against officials of a state National Guard. *Holdiness v. Stroud,* 808 F.2d 417 (5th Cir. 1987); *Sebra v. Neville,* 801 F.2d 1135 (9th Cir. 1986); *Jorden v. National Guard Bureau,* 799 F.2d 99 (3d Cir. 1986). In *Jorden,* the court adopted a per se rule prohibiting damage claims against military superiors, but ruled that claims for equitable relief, including reinstatement, are reviewable. In *Stinson v. Hornsby,* 821 F.2d 1537 (11th Cir. 1987), *cert. denied,* 109 S. Ct. 402 (1988), the court adhered to *Mindes v. Seaman,* 453 F.2d 197 (5th Cir. 1971), which sets forth a series of factors to be considered in determining whether a particular constitutional claim may be asserted by members of the armed forces against their superiors. The authors believe that the concurring and dissenting judges are correct that *Mindes,* is now outdated in light of the Supreme Court's decision in *Chappell.*

* The Seventh Circuit found that claims against the State National Guard and its officials in an official capacity were barred by the Eleventh Amendment. *Meadows v. Indiana,* 854 F.2d 1068 (7th Cir. 1988).

An interstate compact creating a metropolitan area transit authority was entered into by Maryland, Virginia, and the District of Columbia, and was consented to by Congress, which provided that the authority "shall not be liable for any torts occurring in the performance of a governmental function." This congressional immunity applied to § 1983 claims. Whether defendants had been engaged in a "governmental function" was determined by federal standards, and, under these standards, it was concluded that adoption of a policy of testing employees for drugs or alcohol following job accidents or unusual operating incidents was a governmental function. *Sanders v. Washington Metropolitan Area Transit Authority,* 819 F.2d 1151 (D.C. Cir. 1987).

A congressional statute limiting the liability of the Virgin Islands does not reflect an intent to limit its § 1983 liability. *Frett v. Virgin Islands,* 839 F.2d 968 (3d Cir. 1988).

Most state courts take the position that state law sovereign immunity applies to § 1983 actions. *Hill v. Department of Corrections,* 513 So. 2d 129 (Fla. 1987), *cert. denied,* 108 S. Ct. 1024 (1988); *Greene v. Friend of Court,* 406 N.W.2d 433 (Iowa 1987); *Ramah Navajo School Board v. Bureau of Revenue,* 104 N.M. 302, 720 P.2d 1243 (Ct. App.), *cert. denied,* 107 S. Ct. 423 (1986). *See contra, Cooperman v. University Surgical Associates,* 32 Ohio St. 3d 191, 513 N.E.2d 288 (1987). When faced with the issue, federal courts typically hold that state immunity law cannot bar a § 1983 claim. * *McClary v. O'Hare,* 786 F.2d 83, 85 (2d Cir. 1986); *Stock v. Forbes Health System,* 697 F. Supp. 1399 (W.D. Pa. 1988); *DiGiovanni v. City of Rochester,* 680 F. Supp. 80 (W.D.N.Y. 1988); *Martinez v. El Paso County,* 673 F. Supp. 1030 (D. Colo. 1987); *Pillette v. Detroit Police Department,* 661 F. Supp. 1145 (E.D. Mich. 1987).

Dicta in *Felder v. Casey,* 108 S. Ct. 2302, 2307-10 (1988) takes the position that state * immunity rules may not defeat a § 1983 claim. Relying heavily upon *Felder,* the Oregon Supreme Court ruled that provisions in the state Tort Claims Act limiting the recovery for compensatory damages against state bodies and employees and prohibiting the recovery of punitive damages from these defendants may not be applied to § 1983 claims. *Rogers v. Saylor,* 306 Or. 267, 760 P.2d 232 (1988).

§ 6.2 Municipal Liability

* *Page 120, add to footnote 20:*

In re Scott County Master Docket, 672 F. Supp. 1152, 1187-90 (D. Minn. 1987) (dicta); Brotzler v. County of Scott, 427 N.W.2d 685 (Minn. Ct. App. 1988).

Page 122, add at end of section:

The fact that state law requires a municipality to indemnify its police officers does not make the municipality the real party in interest. *Haile v. Village of Sag Harbor,* 639 F. Supp. 718 (E.D.N.Y. 1986). Under *City of Newport v. Fact Concerts,* 453 U.S. 247 (1981), punitive damages may not be obtained against a municipal official in an official capacity. *Brown v. Allenstown,* 648 F. Supp. 831 (D.N.H. 1986).

§ 6.3 State Liability and the Eleventh Amendment: Introduction

Page 124, add before last sentence:

A claim for damages against a state official in an official capacity is equivalent to a claim against the state, and is thus barred by the Eleventh Amendment. *McClary v. O'Hare,* 786 F.2d 83 (2d Cir. 1986). In *Meadows v. Indiana,* 854 F.2d 1068 (7th Cir. 1988), the court found that claims against State National Guard officials in their official capacities are barred by the Eleventh Amendment. A claim against a state court is tantamount to a claim against the state, within the meaning of the Eleventh Amendment. *Harris v. Missouri Court of Appeals,* 787 F.2d 427 (8th Cir.), *cert. denied,* 107 S. Ct. 179 (1986).

The Eleventh Amendment applies to third-party claims for contribution or indemnity that fall within ancillary jurisdiction. *Holman v. Walls,* 648 F. Supp. 947, 954 (D. Del. 1986).

The Sixth Circuit found the Eleventh Amendment applicable in *Kelley v. Metropolitan County Board of Education,* 836 F.2d 986 (6th Cir. 1987), *cert. denied,* 108 S. Ct. 2844 (1988). The county board of education had been found guilty of school segregation in federal court and filed a third-party complaint against the state requesting that it be ordered to pay the full cost of implementing the district court's desegregation remedies. Because the state was not found to have been involved in ongoing constitutional violations, the relief sought against the state could not be said to be ancillary to any prospective relief. Rather, the claim was one for the recovery of money from the state for past constitutional violations, and thus barred by the Eleventh Amendment.

There is a conflict over whether the denial of Eleventh Amendment immunity is immediately appealable. The Second Circuit takes the position that an order denying a motion to dismiss on Eleventh Amendment grounds is immediately appealable because the essence of the absolute immunity provided by the amendment is the "right not to be hauled into court – a right that cannot be vindicated after trial." *Minotti v. Lensink,* 798 F.2d 607, 608 (2d Cir. 1986), *cert. denied,* 107 S. Ct. 2484 (1987). *Accord Eng v. Coughlin,* 858 F.2d 889 (2d Cir. 1988). The Second Circuit applied *Minotti* in *Smith v. Reagan,* 841 F.2d 28 (2d Cir. 1988), holding that the district court's failure to decide the state's motion to dismiss on Eleventh Amendment was immediately appealable. The court in *Smith* indicated that the result might be different "[i]f there were a showing of some need for discovery or other pre-trial proceedings related to the eleventh amendment immunity issue." *Id.* at 31. The First Circuit expressly declined to follow *Minotti,* reasoning that the concerns voiced in *Mitchell v. Forsyth,* 472 U.S. 511 (1985), "as to the pernicious consequences of lawsuits against public officials – inhibiting officials' discretion, distracting them from their duties, deterring people from entering service – are largely irrelevant" when suit is against the state. *Libby v. Marshall,* 833 F.2d 402, 405 (1st Cir. 1987). The Eleventh Amendment is not "an entitlement not to stand trial." *Id.*

In *Welch v. State Department of Highways and Public Transportation,* 107 S. Ct. 2941 (1987), the Court, over a four-Justice dissenting opinion, reaffirmed that the Eleventh

Amendment embodies a broad principle of sovereign immunity and is applicable to federally based claims. Justice Brennan's dissenting opinion advocates that the Eleventh Amendment was intended to apply only to diversity cases.

* In *Eng v. Coughlin,* 858 F.2d 889, 897 (2d Cir. 1988), the court told us what we already know all too well: "Eleventh Amendment jurisprudence has not been a model of logical symmetry, but marked rather by baffling complexity." A federal district court, however, showed compassion for elderly doctrines: "Doctrines like people are sometimes excused from the requirements of logical consistency when they are eighty years old." *Native Village of Venetie v. Alaska,* 687 F. Supp. 1380, 1384 (D. Alaska 1988).

§ 6.5 Prospective Relief: The Doctrine of *Ex Parte Young*

Page 128, add at end of section:

The doctrine of *Ex parte Young* applies to violations of federal law even if the contested conduct also violates state law. *Benjamin v. Malcolm,* 803 F.2d 46 (2d Cir. 1986), *cert. denied,* 107 S. Ct. 1358 (1987).

In a case brought by a resident of a state institution for the mentally retarded, the court held that, under *Milliken v. Bradley,* 433 U.S. 267 (1977), discussed in § **6.8**, the Eleventh Amendment does not bar an order requiring a state institution to pay for a program of services prospectively, when the program is necessary to undo the harmful effects of past constitutional violations. *Clark v. Cohen,* 794 F.2d 79 (3d Cir.), *cert.*
* *denied,* 107 S. Ct. 459 (1986). The Eleventh Circuit found that a claim for prospective relief to compel state officials to provide indigent criminal defense services meeting constitutional standards is within the *Young* doctrine, even though the relief would require the expenditure of state funds. *Walker v. Dugger,* 860 F.2d 1010 (11th Cir. 1988). The court also commented upon the proper defendants for *Young* claims: "Personal action by defendants individually is not a necessary condition of injunctive relief against state officers in their official capacity. All that is required is that the official be responsible for the challenged action." *Id.* at 1015.

The *Young* doctrine is not limited to cases in which plaintiff seeks to enjoin an unconstitutional state statute, but also applies "where the underlying authorization upon which the named official acts is asserted to be illegal under federal law, the 'violation of federal law by [the] state official is ongoing,' and the relief sought will end the violation." *Ezzell v. Board of Regents,* 838 F.2d 1569, 1571 (11th Cir. 1988), quoting from *Papasan v. Allain,* 106 S. Ct. 2932, 2940 (1986).

A third-party claim by a county against the state to reimburse the county for the costs of implementing a school desegregation decree was not within the *Young* doctrine. *Kelley v. Metropolitan County Board of Education,* 836 F.2d 986 (6th Cir. 1987), *cert. denied,* 108 S. Ct. 2848 (1988). See § **6.3**.

Several circuit court decisions dealt with the application of the Eleventh Amendment to claims by state employees. *Barnes v. Bosley,* 828 F.2d 1253 (8th Cir. 1987) (Eleventh Amendment does not bar prospective award of reinstatement and payment of salary from date of court's judgment; fact that district court stayed judgment pending appeal does not change result); *Patteson v. Johnson,* 787 F.2d 1245 (8th Cir.) (award of salary and other benefits from date of district court judgment until plaintiff is either reinstated or is awarded damages in lieu of reinstatement is prospective relief not barred by Eleventh Amendment), *cert. denied,* 107 S. Ct. 109 (1986); *Elliott v. Hinds,* 786 F.2d 298 (7th Cir. 1986) (reinstatement and expungement of personnel records are forms of prospective relief within the doctrine of *Ex parte Young*); *Dwyer v. Regan,* 777 F.2d 825 (2d Cir. 1985) (Eleventh Amendment bars a claim for back pay but not for reinstatement), *modified,* 793 F.2d 457 (2d Cir. 1986).

An injunction requiring state officials to process an employment discrimination complaint is prospective relief within the doctrine of *Ex parte Young. Bennett v. Tucker,* 827 F.2d 63 (7th Cir. 1987).

In a case challenging termination from a state university doctoral program, the circuit court ruled that reinstatement was within the *Young* doctrine. *Kashani v. Purdue University,* 813 F.2d 843 (7th Cir. 1987).

A request for expungement of a child abuse record is not barred by the Eleventh Amendment, but is a permissible form of prospective relief. *Donald M. v. Matava,* 668 F. Supp. 714 (D. Mass. 1987).

Recent circuit court decisions take the position that claims within *Young* are against the official in an official capacity. *Akins v. Board of Governors,* 840 F.2d 1371, 1377 (7th Cir. 1988); *Libby v. Marshall,* 833 F.2d 402, 406 (1st Cir. 1987).

The *Young* doctrine authorizes relief only against state officials. Thus, prospective relief against a state agency is barred even if state officials are party defendants. *Brunken v. Lance,* 807 F.2d 1325, 1328 (7th Cir. 1986).

A declaratory judgment against the state violates the Eleventh Amendment, in the absence of ongoing violations of federal law. *Watkins v. Blinzinger,* 789 F.2d 474 (7th Cir. 1986), *cert. denied,* 107 S. Ct. 1976 (1987); *Jones v. Smith,* 784 F.2d 149 (2d Cir. 1986). If injunctive relief is not barred by the Eleventh Amendment, a declaratory judgement is also not barred. *Doyle v. Dukakis,* 634 F. Supp. 1441 (D. Mass. 1986).

§ 6.6 Limiting the Fiction of *Ex Parte Young: Pennhurst II*

Page 129, add at end of section:

An extensive discussion of the impact of *Pennhurst II* upon federal court plaintiffs and the federal judiciary is contained in *Cuesnongle v. Ramos,* 835 F.2d 1486 (1st Cir. 1987). The court raised but declined to decide whether *Pullman* abstention may be invoked where the state law is clear and dispositive, but the federal court is powerless to enforce it because of *Pennhurst II.* The authors believe that it would not be appropriate to apply *Pullman* in these circumstances, because it is settled that this abstention doctrine applies only when there is an unclear issue of state law. See **§§ 12.2-12.3**.

Judge Easterbrook, dissenting, referred to the "unhappy result" brought about by *Pennhurst II* because it "may force a federal court to reach the constitutional issue though plausible state-law grounds are available for decision." *Citizens for John W. Moore v. Board of Election Commissioners,* 781 F.2d 581, 585 (7th Cir. 1986) (Easterbrook, J., dissenting).

Pennhurst II was applied to claims under a state constitution, *Dennis v. Figueroa,* 642 F. Supp. 959 (D.P.R. 1986); to a claim within pendent party jurisdiction, *Benjamin v. Malcolm,* 626 F. Supp. 1264 (S.D.N.Y.), *aff'd,* 803 F.2d 46 (2d Cir. 1986), *cert. denied,* 107 S. Ct. 1358 (1987); to a claim for indemnification or contribution within ancillary jurisdiction, *Holman v. Walls,* 648 F. Supp. 947 (D. Del. 1986); and to a claim for damages under pendent claim jurisdiction, *Picozzi v. Sandalow,* 623 F. Supp. 1571, 1575 n.3 (E.D. Mich. 1986), *aff'd,* 827 F.2d 770 (6th Cir. 1987), *cert. denied,* 108 S. Ct. 777 (1988). The last cited case stated that a federal court ruling that state officials complied with state law does not violate *Pennhurst II* because it involves no intrusion on state sovereignty. *Id.* at 1582 n.11. The authors believe that this is erroneous because, under *Pennhurst II,* the Eleventh Amendment would prevent the court from deciding the claim.

A consent decree based upon state law is within *Pennhurst II, Lelsz v. Kavanagh,* 807 F.2d 1243 (5th Cir.), *cert. denied,* 108 S. Ct. 44 (1987), while a consent decree based upon federal law is not. *Ibarra v. Texas Employment Commission,* 823 F.2d 873 (5th Cir. 1987); *Duran v. Carruthers,* 678 F. Supp. 839 (D.N.M. 1988). In *Lelsz,* the court ruled that a pre-*Pennhurst II* settlement, which was followed by a post-*Pennhurst II* coercive order, could not be construed as consent to the coercive relief based upon a pendent state law claim. Prior to *Pennhurst II,* there could not have been a knowing and intelligent Eleventh Amendment waiver, because it was assumed that the Eleventh Amendment did not apply to those pendent claims.

Incorporation of state law standards into federal law takes the case outside of *Pennhurst II. Everett v. Schramm,* 772 F.2d 1114 (3d Cir. 1985). *Cf. Silver v. Baggiano,* 804 F.2d 1211 (11th Cir. 1986) (*Pennhurst II* applied because the state law allegedly violated was not incorporated into federal law). The court in *Silver* rejected the ultra vires exception to *Pennhurst II,* because the official did not act without any authority whatever.

* *Pennhurst II* is not a bar when the plaintiff claims that a state practice violates federal statutory law. The facts that the state practice may also violate state law and that the federal court may have to determine the meaning of state law does not change the result. *Mont v. Heintz,* 849 F.2d 704 (2d Cir. 1988).

"[T]hat a constitutional right is predicated on state law does not bring a claim within *Pennhurst II.*" *Libby v. Marshall,* 653 F. Supp. 359, 363 (D. Mass. 1986), *appeal dismissed,* 833 F.2d 402 (1st Cir. 1987). Where plaintiffs have state and federal claims, the court may bifurcate them and hear only the federal claims in federal court. "Numerous post-*Pennhurst* courts have found the alternative of bifurcation acceptable, or even preferable, to abstention in Eleventh Amendment cases." *Society for Good Will to Retarded Children v. Cuomo,* 652 F. Supp. 515, 526 (E.D.N.Y. 1987).

A district court concluded that, while *Pennhurst II* applies to violations of state law even if the state law is alleged to be unconstitutional, the Eleventh Amendment does not prohibit the introduction of evidence of state law violations when it is probative of the intent of state officials to violate federal constitutional obligations. *Board of School Directors v. Wisconsin,* 649 F. Supp. 82 (E.D. Wis. 1985).

Pennhurst II covers state law claims against state officials in an official capacity. *Lach v. Robb,* 679 F. Supp. 508, 514 (W.D. Pa. 1988).

§ 6.9 *Quern v. Jordan* Notice Relief

Page 134, add to end of section:

The Eleventh Amendment barred a claim for notice relief when there were no ongoing violations of federal law. *Dial v. Coler,* 791 F.2d 78 (7th Cir. 1986). *Quern* notice relief was not barred by the Eleventh Amendment when it was ancillary to a retroactive award of food stamp benefits. *Cotton v. Mansour,* 634 F. Supp. 1094 (E.D. Mich. 1986).

The Eleventh Amendment does not bar *Quern* notice relief even though the state may have to bear some expense in notifying the plaintiff class. *Ward v. Hunt,* 667 F. Supp. 782 (N.D. Ala. 1987); *Wilson v. Lyng,* 662 F. Supp. 1391, 1396 (E.D.N.C. 1987); *Anderson v. Lyng,* 652 F. Supp. 1237 (M.D. Ala. 1987).

§ 6.11 Personal, Municipal, and Hybrid Entity Liability

Page 136, add to end of section:

"[E]very court that has considered the issue has rejected, rightly in our view, the argument that an indemnity statute brings the Eleventh Amendment into play." *Duckworth v. Franzen,* 780 F.2d 645, 650 (7th Cir. 1985), *cert. denied,* 107 S. Ct. 71 (1986). *Accord, Blaylock v. Schwinden,* 862 F.2d 1352 (9th Cir. 1988); *Farid v. Smith,* 850 F.2d 917 (2d Cir. 1988); *Griess v. Colorado,* 841 F.2d 1042 (10th Cir. 1988).

"The decision whether a state institution or entity is an arm of the state for Eleventh Amendment purposes should not be made without a full examination of all the factors." *Ainsworth Aristocrat International Pty. v. Tourism Co. of Puerto Rico,* 818 F.2d 1034, 1038 (1st Cir. 1987).

The following entities were found to be protected by the Eleventh Amendment: The Port Authority of New York and New Jersey, created by interstate compact, *Port Authority Police Benevolent Association v. Port Authority of New York and New Jersey,* 819 F.2d 413 (3d Cir.), *cert. denied,* 108 S. Ct. 344 (1987); *see also Clarke v. Washington Metropolitan Area Transit Authority,* 654 F. Supp. 712 (D.D.C. 1985) (transit authority created by interstate compact); *Sanders v. Washington Metro Area Transit Authority,* 652 F. Supp. 765 (D.D.C. 1986) (same), *aff'd,* 819 F.2d 1151 (D.C. Cir. 1987); the Board of Regents of the University of Michigan, *Estate of Ritter v. University of Michigan,* 851 F.2d 846, 850 (6th Cir. 1988) ("the most important factor if not the absolutely determinative factor . . . is whether the judgment for retroactive monetary relief would be paid out of the state treasury"); a state system of higher education, *Skehan v. State System of Higher Education,* 815 F.2d 244 (3d Cir. 1987); Charity Hospital of Louisiana and the state Department of Health and Human Resources,

Darlak v. Bobear, 814 F.2d 1055 (5th Cir. 1987); Purdue University, *Kashani v. Purdue University,* 813 F.2d 843, 845 (7th Cir.), *cert. denied,* 108 S. Ct. 141 (1987) ("the most important factor is the extent of the entity's financial autonomy from the state"); * Indiana University, *Shannon v. Bepko,* 684 F. Supp. 1465 (S.D. Ind. 1988); an adult probation department, *Clark v. Tarvant County,* 798 F.2d 736 (5th Cir. 1986); a state unemployment appeals commission, *Fincher v. Department of Labor,* 798 F.2d 1371 (11th Cir. 1986), *cert. denied,* 107 S. Ct. 1262 (1987); a state bar association, *Lewis v. State Bar Association,* 792 F.2d 493 (5th Cir. 1986).

The following were found not protected by the Eleventh Amendment: a park and planning commission, *Ram Ditta v. Maryland National Capital Park and Planning Commission,* 822 F.2d 456 (4th Cir. 1987); Rutgers University, *Kovats v. Rutgers, the State University,* 822 F.2d 1303 (3d Cir. 1987); a board of levee commissioners, *McDonald v. Board of Mississippi Levee Commissioners,* 832 F.2d 901 (5th Cir. 1987); a school district, *Fay v. South Colonie Central School District,* 802 F.2d 21 (2d Cir. 1986).

Retroactive food stamps were not barred by the Eleventh Amendment when they were payable by a local department of social services. *Biggs v. Block,* 629 F. Supp. 1574 (E.D.N.Y. 1986). Courts have granted retroactive food stamps over Eleventh Amendment objections, on the grounds that the benefits were payable out of federal funds. *Griffin v. Coler,* 667 F. Supp. 1233 (C.D. Ill. 1986); *Cotton v. Mansour,* 634 F. Supp. 1094 (E.D. Mich. 1986). See also *Wilson v. Lyng,* 662 F. Supp. 1391, 1396 (E.D.N.C. 1987).

In a non-§ 1983 case, the Seventh Circuit ruled that a local entity is not entitled to Eleventh Amendment protection merely because the state provided it with federal rules and the entity acted pursuant to state rules in order to carry out a federal program. *Gary A. v. New Trier High School District,* 796 F.2d 940 (7th Cir. 1986). An entity not otherwise protected by the Eleventh Amendment does not acquire "immunity by virtue of its role in a state administered federal aid program." *Id.* at 946.

The Eleventh Amendment is not applicable to a private party state actor because the judgment would not be payable out of the state treasury. *Artist v. Virginia International Terminals,* 679 F. Supp. 587 (E.D. Va. 1988), *aff'd,* 857 F.2d 977 (4th Cir. 1988).

§ 6.12 Eleventh Amendment Waivers

Page 139, add at end of section:

While a state statute on its face did not waive the state's Eleventh Amendment protection, a state supreme court decision construing the statute did effectuate an Eleventh Amendment waiver, and this decision was binding upon the federal courts. *Della Grotta v. Rhode Island,* 781 F.2d 343 (1st Cir. 1986). *Grotta* also held that, having waived its Eleventh Amendment immunity, the state was a "person" subject to suit under § 1983. See § **5.2**.

A state attorney's argument in support of a stay of an order of reinstatement of a wrongfully discharged state employee operated to waive the state's Eleventh Amendment immunity from liability for back pay. *Barnes v. Bosley,* 625 F. Supp. 81 (E.D. Mo. 1985), *appeal dismissed,* 790 F.2d 718 (8th Cir. 1986).

In *Garcia v. Board of Education,* 777 F.2d 1403 (10th Cir. 1985), *cert. denied,* 107 S. Ct. 66 (1986), the court found that the attorney for the school board had no authority to waive the board's Eleventh Amendment immunity. While the court sympathized with the fact that plaintiff and the trial court had been "sandbagged" by defendant's abandonment of the Eleventh Amendment at trial, such an abandonment does not prevent defendant from raising the Eleventh Amendment on appeal. See *Sosna v. Iowa,* 419 U.S. 393, 396 n.2 (1975); *Neuwirth v. State Board of Dentistry,* 845 F.2d 553 (5th Cir. 1988) (Eleventh Amendment raised for first time on appeal may be considered by court).

A state statute did not waive the state's Eleventh Amendment immunity even though it waived state tort law liability (but excluded constitutional torts from the waiver), created a state self-insurance fund to the extent the state might be held liable under § 1983, and required state indemnification of judgments against its officials in their individual capacities if they did not act in bad faith. *Gamble v. Florida Department of Health and Rehabilitative Services,* 779 F.2d 1509 (11th Cir. 1986).

Removal of a suit by the state as defendant from state court to federal court does not operate as an Eleventh Amendment waiver. *Estate of Ritter v. University of Michigan,* 851 F.2d 846 (6th Cir. 1988); *Silver v. Baggiano,* 804 F.2d 1211 (11th Cir. 1986); *Keenan v. Washington Metropolitan Area Transit Authority,* 643 F. Supp. 324 (D.D.C. 1986). *See contra, Maine Association of Interdependent Neighborhoods v. Petit,* 659 F. Supp. 1309 (D. Me. 1987). *Petit* takes the position that the issue depends upon whether the official who removes has authority to waive the Eleventh Amendment. *Accord Stephans v. Nevada,* 685 F. Supp. 217, 219 (D. Nev. 1988) ("[R]emoval by State officials of a case to federal court does not amount to waiver of Eleventh Amendment immunity unless those state officials are authorized to waive such immunity").

A settlement entered into pre-*Pennhurst II* did not waive the Eleventh Amendment. *Lelsz v. Kavanagh,* 807 F.2d 1243 (5th Cir.), *cert. denied,* 108 S. Ct. 44 (1987). See § **6.6**.

Congress waived the Eleventh Amendment immunity of the Commonwealth of The Northern Mariana Islands. *Fleming v. Department of Public Safety,* 837 F.2d 401 (9th Cir.), *cert. denied,* 109 S. Ct. 222 (1988). *Accord Sablan v. Department of Finance,* 856 F.2d 1317 (9th Cir. 1988).

There is a conflict in the circuits as to whether Congress's enactment of the Education of the Handicapped Act reflects an intent to abrogate the Eleventh Amendment. *Compare, e.g., Muth v. Central Bucks School District,* 839 F.2d 113 (3d Cir. 1988) (finding waiver) *with Kerr Center Parents Association v. Charles,* 842 F.2d 1052 (9th Cir. 1988) (finding no waiver).

CHAPTER 7

INDIVIDUAL LIABILITY: COMMON-LAW IMMUNITIES

§ 7.1 Common-Law Immunities in General

Page 142, add at end of section:

The Supreme Court reaffirmed that the same common law immunities apply to § 1983 and *Bivens* suits. *Malley v. Briggs,* 106 S. Ct. 1092, 1096 n.2 (1986).

§ 7.2 Absolute and Qualified Immunity: The Functional Approach

Page 144, add at end of section:

The Supreme Court reaffirmed (1) the functional approach to § 1983 immunities, (2) that absolute immunity is to be applied in only limited circumstances, and (3) the burden is on the defendant official to demonstrate entitlement to absolute immunity. *Forrester v. White,* 108 S. Ct. 538 (1988). *Forrester* specifically deals with the scope of judicial immunity. See § 7.3.

§ 7.3 Judicial Immunity

Page 148, add at end of section:

A judge's alleged alteration of a transcript and record are judicial acts protected by absolute judicial immunity. *Eades v. Sterlinske,* 810 F.2d 723 (7th Cir.), *cert. denied,* 108 S. Ct. 143 (1987).

Absolute judicial immunity was accorded a judge who held contempt proceedings, found a party in contempt, and ruled on a recusal motion, since these are judicial acts and the judge did not act in the clear absence of all jurisdiction. *Liles v. Reagan,* 804 F.2d 493 (8th Cir. 1986).

A judge's initiation of a prosecution is a judicial act protected by absolute judicial immunity when it arises "out of judicial proceedings brought before him by independent parties." *Harris v. Deveaux,* 780 F.2d 911, 915 (11th Cir. 1986).

The Ninth Circuit, reversing its prior decisional law, now holds "that a conspiracy between judge and prosecutor to predetermine the outcome of a judicial proceeding, while clearly improper, does not pierce the immunity extended to judges and prosecutors. As long as the judge's ultimate acts are judicial actions taken within the court's subject matter jurisdiction, immunity applies." *Ashelman v. Pope,* 793 F.2d 1072, 1078 (9th Cir. 1986) (en banc). *See also Scott v. Schmidt,* 773 F.2d 160, 164 n.6 (7th Cir. 1985) (dicta).

* A judge who acts in the clear absence of his or her "territorial jurisdiction" is not protected by judicial immunity. *Maestri v. Jutkofsky,* 860 F.2d 50 (2d Cir. 1988).

In a non-§ 1983 case, federal judges were protected by absolute judicial immunity for the "extrajudicial" statements they made to lawyers for a defendant in a federal action that concerned the lawsuits before them. *Patterson v. Aiken,* 628 F. Supp. 1068 (N.D. Ga. 1985), *aff'd,* 784 F.2d 403 (11th Cir. 1986). The fact that the judges' statements about a party were derogatory did not change the result, since "such statements are quite common in settlement negotiations." *Id.* at 1074.

The Supreme Court ruled that, under the functional approach, a judge's employment decisions (e.g., hiring, demotion, and firing), are not judicial acts and thus not protected by absolute judicial immunity. There is no need to extend judicial immunity to a judge's administrative activities. "[A] judge who hires or fires a probation officer cannot meaningfully be distinguished from a district attorney who hires or fires assistant district attorneys, or indeed from any other executive branch official who is responsible for making such employment decisions." *Forrester v. White,* 108 S. Ct. 538, 545 (1988). While the Court leaves open the question of whether a judge is protected by qualified immunity, the authors believe it is apparent that qualified immunity does apply in these circumstances.

* The Seventh Circuit found *Forrester* fully applicable to a judge's firing of a public defender. *Kurowski v. Krajewski,* 848 F.2d 767 (7th Cir.), *cert. denied,* 109 S. Ct. 309 (1988). The fact that the firing occurred pre-*Forrester* was of no moment. Rejecting the defendant judge's attempt to limit *Forrester* to the firing of probation officers, the court suggested that litigants "take adverse decisions more gracefully." *Id.* at 773.

On remand from the Supreme Court for reconsideration in light of *Forrester,* the Sixth Circuit adhered to its prior decision that bar admission decisions made by members of the state judiciary and by its Committee on Character and Fitness are judicial acts protected by judicial immunity. *Sparks v. Character and Fitness Committee,* 859 F.2d 428 (6th Cir. 1988). *See also Childs v. Reynoldson,* 777 F.2d 1305 (8th Cir. 1985). *Sparks* relied in part upon *Bradley v. Fisher,* 80 U.S. (13 Wall.) 335, 20 L. Ed. 646 (1871) (judicial immunity covers disbarment decision). *Accord Forrester v. White,* 108 S. Ct. at 544 (dictum).

The Supreme Court remanded the following cases for reconsideration in light of *Forrester: Crooks v. Maynard,* 820 F.2d 329 (9th Cir. 1987) (judge who held court clerks in contempt for violating his administrative order was protected by judicial immunity), *vacated,* 108 S. Ct. 744 (1988); *Ohse v. Hughes,* 816 F.2d 1144 (7th Cir. 1987) (judge's investigation of probation officer protected by judicial immunity), *vacated,* 108 S. Ct. 1070 (1988). * The Ninth Circuit subsequently remanded *Crooks* to the district court to determine whether the act was a judicial act and whether it was in the clear absence of all jurisdiction. *Crooks v. Maynard,* 851 F.2d 1562 (9th Cir. 1988).

§ 7.4 –Prospective Relief

Page 149, add at end of section:

* The *Pulliam* rule, denying judicial immunity to claims for prospective relief, was applied to a request by a discharged employee for reinstatement. *McDonald v. Krajewski,* 649 F. Supp. 370 (N.D. Ill. 1986).

Several cases illustrate that federal court complaints seeking relief against judges often fail for reasons other than immunity. These claims have been defeated by mootness, *Eitel v. Holland,* 787 F.2d 995, 997 (5th Cir. 1986), *see also Carras v. Williams,* 807 F.2d 1286 (6th Cir. 1986); the *Rooker-Feldman* doctrine, *Hollins v. Wessel,* 819 F.2d 1073 (11th Cir. 1987); a finding that the judge was not engaged in * state action, *Paisey v. Vitale,* 807 F.2d 889 (11th Cir. 1986); lack of standing, *Sterling v. Calvin,* 694 F. Supp. 1382 (E.D. Mo. 1988); failure to establish "substantial and immediate irreparable injury" and *Younger v. Harris* abstention, *Williams v. North,* 685 F. Supp. 502, 507-08 (D. Md. 1988); and a holding that the judge was not a proper party defendant, *Alcan Aluminum Corp. v. Lyntel Products,* 656 F. Supp. 1138, 1143 (N.D. Ill. 1987). In *Smith v. Wood,* 649 F. Supp. 901 (E.D. Pa. 1986), *Pulliam* was distinguished as a case involving a constitutional challenge to a state judge's *practice.* Where, as in *Smith,* the state court litigant is simply disappointed with the state court ruling, there is no case or controversy between the litigant and the judge.

The Ninth Circuit, by a two-to-one vote, ruled that the decision in *Pulliam* does not apply to *Bivens* actions. *Mullis v. United States Bankruptcy Court,* 828 F.2d 1385 (9th Cir. 1987), *cert. denied,* 108 S. Ct. 2031 (1988).

§ 7.5 —Enforcers of Court Orders, Clerks, Court Reporters

Page 150, add at end of section:

Court-appointed guardians, therapists, and attorneys are entitled to absolute quasi-judicial immunity for providing reports and recommendations to the state court and for questioning children in a child abuse proceeding. "[N]onjudicial persons who fulfill quasi-judicial functions intimately related to the judicial process have absolute immunity for damage claims arising from their performance of the delegated functions." *Myers v. Morris,* 810 F.2d 1437, 1466-67 (8th Cir.), *cert. denied,* 108 S. Ct. 97 (1987). The Eighth Circuit also determined that a psychiatrist appointed by the court to perform a competency examination performs a function essential to the judicial process and is thus entitled to absolute judicial immunity. The fact that plaintiff pleaded a conspiracy does not defeat the immunity. *Moses v. Parwatikar,* 813 F.2d 891 (8th Cir.), *cert. denied,* 108 S. Ct. 97 (1987).

The Ninth Circuit accorded family court counselors quasi-judicial immunity for carrying out their statutory duties relating to child visitation at the direction of the court. *Meyers v. Contra Costa County Department of Social Services,* 812 F.2d 1154 (9th Cir.), *cert. denied,* 108 S. Ct. 98 (1987).

Sheriffs and police officers who enforce a judgment pursuant to a facially valid court order are entitled to quasi-judicial immunity. *Henry v. Farmer City State Bank,* 808 F.2d 1228 (7th Cir. 1986). Similarly, a clerk who issues an arrest warrant at the direction of the court is protected by absolute judicial immunity. *Rogers v. Bruntrager,* 841 F.2d 853 (8th Cir. 1988).

A child protective service worker who obtained custody of a child, and removed her from her home pursuant to court order, was entitled to quasi-judicial immunity. *Coverdell v. Department of Social Services,* 834 F.2d 758 (9th Cir. 1987).

A court reporter and court clerk who allegedly prepared and filed a false certificate summarizing an instruction conference allegedly never held, and who altered the docket to reflect that falsity, were protected by absolute quasi-judicial immunity. They exercised discretion with respect to duties integrally related to the judicial process. *Eades v. Sterlinske,* 810 F.2d 723 (7th Cir.), *cert. denied,* 108 S. Ct. 143 (1987). *See also Mullis v. United States Bankruptcy Court,* 828 F.2d 1385, 1390 (9th Cir. 1987), *cert. denied,* 108 S. Ct. 2031 (1988) (*Bivens* action: "Court clerks have absolute quasi-judicial immunity from damages for civil violations when they perform tasks that are an integral part of the judicial process").

A judge's law clerk performs judicial discretionary functions and is protected by absolute judicial immunity. *Oliva v. Heller,* 839 F.2d 37, 40 (2d Cir. 1988) (*Bivens* action: " 'Law clerks are simply extensions of the judges at whose pleasure they serve' "). In a federal tort claims case, the Ninth Circuit held that the Clerk of the United States Supreme Court was entitled to absolute immunity because his challenged activities were "an integral part of the judicial process." *Sharma v. Stevas,* 790 F.2d 1486 (9th Cir. 1986). A court clerk who issued a prejudgment writ of attachment was protected by absolute judicial immunity. *McCrory v. Johnson,* 296 Ark. 231, 755 S.W.2d 566 (1988). On the other hand, a court clerk who carries out ministerial, nonjudicial duties is entitled only to qualified good faith immunity. *Barnes v. Smith,* 654 F. Supp. 1244 (E.D. Mo. 1987).

The failure of county officials to provide sign language interpreters to enable deaf individuals to serve as jurors was not protected by judicial or legislative immunity. Defendants were entitled to claim qualified immunity, which they waived. *Greater Los Angeles Council on Deafness v. Zolin,* 812 F.2d 1103 (9th Cir. 1987).

§ 7.6 –Parole and Probation Officers

Page 152, add at end of section:

The immunity to which parole officers are entitled depends upon the function performed. *Stewart v. Lattanzi,* 832 F. 2d 12 (2d Cir. 1987).

Probation officers are entitled to absolute judicial immunity for preparation of pretrial release and presentence reports. *Turner v. Barry,* 856 F.2d 1539 (D.C. Cir. 1988) (presentence reports); *Freeze v. Griffith,* 849 F.2d 172 (5th Cir. 1988) (presentence report); *Dorman v. Higgins,* 821 F.2d 133 (2d Cir. 1987) (presentence report); *Tripati v. United States Immigration and Naturalization Service,* 784 F.2d 345 (10th Cir. 1986) (pretrial release and presentence reports), *cert. denied,* 108 S. Ct. 755 (1988); *Demoran v. Witt,* 781 F.2d 155 (9th Cir. 1986) (presentence report). *See also Chitty v. Walton,* 680 F. Supp. 683 (D. Vt. 1987) (caseworker supervisor and parole officer who prepared reports for parole board given absolute immunity); *Weseman v. Meeker County,* 659 F. Supp. 1571 (D. Minn. 1987) (juvenile probation officer's investigation and report regarding child placement protected by absolute judicial immunity). *But see LaFrance v. Rampone,* 678 F. Supp. 72 (D. Vt. 1988) (declining to follow *Chitty*). In *Dorman v. Higgins,* the court also ruled that (1) an allegation of conspiracy does not defeat the absolute immunity, and (2) under *Pulliam* (see § 7.4), the absolute immunity is limited to claims for damages and does not bar the granting of injunctive relief.

The First Circuit found that, although parole board members who perform adjudicatory functions enjoy absolute liability, an arresting parole board officer is entitled only to qualified immunity. *Johnson v. Rhode Island Parole Board Members,* 815 F.2d 5 (1st Cir. 1987).

A Third Circuit decision determined that (1) a parole official who serves as a hearing examiner is entitled to absolute immunity; (2) a probation officer who charges the criminal defendant with wrongdoing and presents evidence to that effect performs an essentially executive function for which qualified immunity applies; and (3) probation officers have qualified immunity for their general responsibilities. *Harper v. Jeffries,* 808 F.2d 281 (3d Cir. 1986). The Fifth Circuit, however, ruled that absolute immunity applies not only to officers who conduct parole revocation hearings but also to those who present evidence at the hearing, a prosecutorial function. *Farrish v. State Parole* * *Board,* 836 F.2d 969 (5th Cir. 1988). *See also Miller v. Garrett,* 695 F. Supp. 740 (S.D.N.Y. 1988) (filing of notice of parole violation and presentation of case at parole revocation proceeding protected by absolute immunity). *Farrish* also determined that the failure of the commissioner of corrections to establish adequate rules and policies for preliminary parole revocation hearings and to advise parole officers of the commissioner's subpoena power was administrative activity within qualified immunity.

A parole board member's grant or denial of parole is protected by absolute * immunity. *Fuller v. State Board of Pardons & Paroles,* 851 F.2d 1307, 1310 (11th Cir. 1988); *Knoll v. Webster,* 838 F.2d 450 (10th Cir. 1988); *Serio v. Members of State Board of Pardons,* 821 F.2d 1112 (5th Cir. 1987).

Parole board members are entitled to absolute immunity for the quasi-judicial function of granting parole, and "[w]hether claimant is an inmate appealing denial of parole or a victim of parolee's criminal actions is irrelevant." *Nelson v. Balazic,* 802 F.2d 1077, 1079 (8th Cir. 1986). *Nelson* also held that a parole officer's decision to not take a parolee into custody immediately is analogous to the function carried out by police officers in determining whether to make an arrest, and is thus accorded qualified immunity. *See also Doe v. United Social and Mental Health Services,* 670 F. Supp. 1121 (D. Conn. 1987) (parole board members have absolute immunity for granting parole, though qualified immunity for their alleged failure to supervise the parolee).

In *Wright v. McClain,* 626 F. Supp. 1073 (W.D. Tenn. 1986), the court ruled that a parole officer was entitled to absolute immunity for evidentiary rulings made at a preliminary parole revocation hearing.

§ 7.7 –Hearing Officers, Arbitrators, Mediators, Others Who Carry Out Judicial Functions

Page 153, add before last paragraph:

Following the Supreme Court's decision in *Cleavinger v. Saxner,* 106 S. Ct. 496 (1985), the Sixth Circuit determined that prosecutors who sit on a concealed weapons licensing board are not entitled to absolute judicial immunity. *Joseph v. Patterson,* 795 F.2d 549 (6th Cir. 1986). While the board performs some adjudicatory functions, "it does not adjudicate in the formal 'classic' sense" because the board members are not impartial and are vested with wide discretion based on "local needs." *Id.* at 558. Thus, the board members were entitled to qualified immunity.

* Two decisions distinguished *Cleavinger* and accorded prison hearing officers absolute judicial immunity. *Shelly v. Johnson,* 849 F.2d 228 (6th Cir. 1988) (full time independent professional hearing officer); *Shaddy v. Gunter,* 690 F. Supp. 860 (D. Neb. 1988).

Plaintiff complained that members of a public utilities commission engaged in the following conduct during his hearing on his interstate trucking application: "interference with the evidence producing process, ex parte contacts, performing audits and inspections, issuing cease and desist letters and complaints . . ., making press statements, and advising shippers that if they engage the services of [plaintiff Schlegel], they may face legal action." *Schlegel v. Bebout,* 841 F.2d 937, 944 (9th Cir. 1988). The court ruled that the commission officers were acting in a regulatory, not adversarial capacity, and were thus accorded qualified immunity.

The consideration of applications for admission to the bar by members and employees of a character and fitness committee, pursuant to duties imposed by the state supreme court, is protected by absolute quasi-judicial immunity. *Sparks v.*
* *Kentucky Character and Fitness Committee,* 859 F.2d 428 (6th Cir. 1988).

Judicial immunity extends to members of a state tax appeals commission. *Pryzina v. Ley,* 813 F.2d 821 (7th Cir. 1987).

§ 7.8 Prosecutorial Immunity

Page 157, add at end of section:

The formulation of general prosecutorial policies is protected by absolute prosecutorial immunity. *Haynesworth v. Miller,* 820 F.2d 1245 (D.C. Cir. 1987) (*Bivens* claim).

Where it is claimed that a prosecutor acted beyond his or her jurisdiction, absolute immunity applies unless it is shown that he or she acted in the clear absence of all jurisdiction. *Barr v. Abrams,* 810 F.2d 358 (2d Cir. 1987). *See also McCarthy v. Mayo,* 827 F.2d 1310 (9th Cir. 1987) (prosecutorial immunity not lost because prosecutors lacked state law authority).

* Absolute prosecutorial immunity protected a prosecutor who, misreading a juror's voting sheet, which showed a decision not to indict, prepared an indictment in the belief that the vote had been in favor of indictment. *Baez v. Hennessy,* 853 F.2d 73 (2d Cir. 1988), *cert. denied,* 109 S. Ct. 805 (1989).

A prosecutor who participates in a coroner's inquest as an advocate for the state, in order to decide whether to initiate criminal proceedings, is within the scope of the absolute prosecutorial immunity. The inquest "was a quasi-judicial proceeding analogous to a grand-jury inquisition" and "investigation to secure the information necessary to the prosecutor's decision to initiate criminal proceedings is within the quasi-judicial aspect of the prosecutor's job and therefore is absolutely immune from civil suit for damages." *Williams v. Hartje,* 827 F.2d 1203, 1209-10 (8th Cir. 1987). The Eighth Circuit, following *Williams,* ruled that a prosecutor's participation in electronic surveillance to determine whether criminal charges should be lodged against a particular individual and to protect a "key witness" and insure her attendance at trial, was within absolute prosecutorial immunity. *Lewellen v. Raff,* 843 F.2d 1103 (8th Cir. 1988).

§ 7.8 PROSECUTORIAL IMMUNITY

The prosecutor enjoys absolute immunity for the factual investigation necessary to prepare a case, including interviewing witnesses before presenting them to the grand jury. "Offering a witness immunity in exchange for his testimony is a necessary adjunct to that factual development." On the other hand, only qualified immunity attaches to a prosecutor's "direct participation with the police in conducting a search" and "entrapping someone into committing a prosecutable offense." Both of these activities "undeniably constitute[ ] investigative behavior." *Mullinax v. McElhenney,* 817 F.2d 711, 715 (11th Cir. 1987).

A federal prosecutor " 'who submits information to the United States Parole Commission is cloaked with absolute immunity.' " *Allen v. Thompson,* 815 F.2d 1433, 1434 (11th Cir. 1987).

In *Martinez v. Winner,* 778 F.2d 553 (10th Cir. 1985), the court modified its prior opinion (771 F.2d 424) which contained an error of fact. Since the prosecutor's affidavit, which was the basis for plaintiff's claim of an alleged cover-up, was in fact filed in a criminal prosecution and not, as the court previously believed, in an attorney disciplinary proceeding, the prosecutor was entitled to absolute prosecutorial immunity. The Tenth Circuit subsequently found the action to be moot. *Martinez v. Winner,* 800 F.2d 230 (10th Cir. 1986).

There is no exception to the rule of absolute prosecutorial immunity for the bad faith withholding of exculpatory evidence. *Campbell v. Maine,* 787 F.2d 776 (1st Cir. 1986).

The court analyzed several issues concerning prosecutorial immunity in *Joseph v. Patterson,* 795 F.2d 549 (6th Cir. 1986), *cert. denied,* 107 S. Ct. 1910 (1987). The court (1) found that absolute prosecutorial immunity applied to the prosecutor's filing of criminal complaints, issuance of arrest warrants, and decisions to pursue charges and appeal the dismissal of charges; (2) applied qualified immunity to a prosecutor's participation in a search with the police and to investigators' "self-initiated" investigation (i.e., not at the direction of the prosecutor); (3) remanded for further development of the record the question of degree of immunity to which the prosecutor is entitled for interrogation of a witness while in police custody, because the allegations could support a finding that the prosecutor acted in an investigatory capacity; (4) determined that a factual inquiry was necessary to determine whether the prosecutor's directing the police to secure further evidence was part of the prosecutorial or investigatory function; and (5) ruled that whether the prosecutor is entitled to absolute immunity for opposing requests to expunge records depends on whether the prosecutor had discretion, since if he had no discretion, it was not an advocacy function.

A prosecutor who is involved in a conspiracy with a judge to predetermine the outcome of a case is entitled to absolute immunity. *Ashelman v. Pope,* 793 F.2d 1072 (9th Cir. 1986) (en banc). See § **7.3**.

Disagreeing with the Tenth Circuit's decision in *Benavidez v. Gunnell,* 722 F.2d 615 (10th Cir. 1983), the Seventh Circuit ruled that a prosecutor who provides advice to the police functions in a quasi-judicial capacity, and is thus entitled to absolute prosecutorial immunity. *Henderson v. Lopez,* 790 F.2d 44 (7th Cir. 1986). The Tenth Circuit subsequently declined the invitation to follow *Henderson* and overrule *Benavidez,* and adhered to its position "that a prosecutor is entitled to only qualified immunity for giving such advice [i.e., regarding the seizure and disposition of property] to police officers." *Wolfenbarger v. Williams,* 826 F.2d 930, 937 (10th Cir. 1987). The Eighth Circuit takes the position that a prosecutor's advice to law enforcement officials concerning the existence of probable cause to arrest and the legality of arrests is protected by absolute prosecutorial immunity. *Myers v. Morris,* 810 F.2d 1437 (8th Cir.), *cert. denied,* 108 S. Ct. 97 (1987).

* Observing that the "dividing line" between prosecutorial and executive and administrative functions is "amorphous," the Eleventh Circuit made these rulings: (1) absolute immunity protects a prosecutor's rendering of legal advice to police officers concerning the existence of probable cause to made an arrest; (2) absolute immunity does not apply to a prosecutor's announcement to the media of the discontinuation of a prosecution; (3) absolute immunity covers action taken to secure information necessary to determine whether to initiate and pursue a prosecution, such as interviewing the victim of the crime; and (4) with respect to the allegation that the prosecutors distributed explicit photographs of a rape victim's injuries to "other law enforcement officers," the record was not sufficiently developed to determine whether the activity was prosecutorial, because the record did not reveal the identity of the persons to whom the photographs were allegedly distributed or the purposes for the distribution. *Marx v. Gumbinner,* 855 F.2d 783 (11th Cir. 1988).

Prosecutors are protected by only qualified immunity for engaging in investigatory activities prior to the filing of criminal charges. *Higgs v. District Court,* 713 P.2d 840 (Colo. 1985). The activities in *Higgs* involved a photographic identification procedure, procurement of nontestimonial identification evidence, and requests for arrest and search warrants.

A prosecutor who revealed the identity of a witness to the subject of a prosecution and who refused to provide protection for that witness was not entitled to absolute prosecutorial immunity. This case "falls within the ambit of law enforcement supervision and the gathering of evidence"; these investigatory activities receive qualified immunity. *Barbera v. Smith,* 836 F.2d 96, 101 (2d Cir. 1987).

A prosecutor is protected by absolute immunity when her investigation focuses upon a particular person. *Chicipee Lions Club v. District Attorney,* 396 Mass. 244, 485 N.E.2d 673 (1985).

* In *Joseph v. Patterson,* 795 F.2d 549, 560 (6th Cir. 1986) the Sixth Circuit analyzed the immunity for investigators in the district attorney's office: an investigator

> who takes ministerial actions intimately related to the judicial process pursuant to the express direction and control of a prosecutor, who is directing the activity in the fulfillment of a quasi-judicial responsibility . . . has absolute immunity . . . . However, when the nonjudicial official undertakes action on his own initiative or when he carries out administrative or investigatory functions of the prosecutor, he can only claim . . . qualified immunity.

Accord Bittner v. Smith, 697 F. Supp. 144, 153 (S.D.N.Y. 1988). The Eleventh Circuit ruled that an investigator who performs investigative work at the direction of an assistant district attorney is not protected by absolute prosecutorial immunity. *Rich v. Dollar,* 841 F.2d 1558 (11th Cir. 1988).

The alleged failure of a state attorney general and health commissioner to initiate civil or criminal proceedings against other state officials was within absolute prosecutorial immunity. *Meade v. Grubbs,* 841 F.2d 1512 (10th Cir. 1988).

An assistant state attorney general was entitled to absolute immunity for his role in defending the state in a civil action because "he should not be inhibited in the faithful performance of his duties by the threat of harassing lawsuits against him." *Barrett v. United States,* 798 F.2d 565, 572 (2d Cir. 1986). *See also Murphy v. Morris,* 849 F.2d 1101 (8th Cir. 1988) (absolute immunity applied to state attorney general's defense of state officials in civil rights litigation); *Pryzina v. Ley,* 813 F.2d 821 (7th Cir. 1987) (state attorney general and his assistant are absolutely immune for defending state court judicial review proceeding). Although expressing approval with the Second Circuit's decision in *Barrett v. United States,* that a government attorney's defense of civil actions is protected by absolute immunity, the Seventh Circuit ruled that government defense counsel receive only qualified immunity "for pretrial investigations that occur outside the rules of discovery." *Auriemma v. Montgomery,* 860 F.2d 273, 278 (7th Cir. 1988).

An agency attorney who prosecuted an employment discrimination case was entitled to absolute prosecutorial immunity, even though her dual representation of the agency and the individual complainant created a possible conflict of interest. *Rudow v. City of New York,* 822 F.2d 324 (2d Cir. 1987). Agency attorneys performing prosecutorial functions are afforded absolute immunity so long as their conduct is "colorably prosecutorial" and not "in the clear absence of jurisdiction." *Id.* at 328.

Members of a state board of medical examiners, who are empowered to take disciplinary action against physicians by initiating charges, holding hearings, and rendering decisions, carry out prosecutorial and adjudicatory functions and are thus protected by absolute immunity. *Horwitz v. State Board of Medical Examiners,* 822 F.2d 1508 (10th Cir. 1987), *cert. denied,* 108 S. Ct. 453 (1988). *See also Ivancie v. State Board of Dental Examiners,* 678 F. Supp. 1496 (D. Colo. 1988) (*Horowitz* not undermined by Supreme Court decision in *Forrester v. White,* 108 S. Ct. 538 (1988)). On the other hand, the Eighth Circuit found that neither judicial nor prosecutorial immunity applied to an administrative determination requiring the inspection of a campground, and the summary suspension of a license to operate a campground for refusal to allow the inspection. *Freeman v. Blair,* 793 F.2d 166 (8th Cir. 1986), *vacated,* 107 S. Ct. 3254 (1987). "These decisions are analogous to to the kind of administrative or investigative functions to which courts ordinarily do not extend absolute immunity to prosecutors . . . ." *Id.* at 171.

In *Schlegel v. Bebout,* 841 F.2d 937 (9th Cir. 1988), the court determined that the following activities of the public utilities commissioner and his assistants were not within the prosecutorial immunity: "interference with the evidence producing process, ex parte contacts, performing audits and inspections, making press statements, and advising shippers that if they engage the services of Schlegel they may face legal action." *Id.* at 944. The court also found that the hearings for trucking route authorizations were not adversarial but regulatory, and that qualified immunity thus applied.

A juvenile officer who files a delinquency petition with the court performs a prosecutorial function protected by absolute immunity. *Malachowski v. City of Keene,* 787 F.2d 704 (1st Cir.), *cert. denied,* 107 S. Ct. 107 (1986).

A number of decisions dealt with the immunities applicable in child abuse and neglect proceedings. The Second Circuit determined that an assistant state attorney and state trooper who took a child into custody on a complaint of child abuse performed an investigatory function, and were entitled not to absolute prosecutorial immunity but to qualified immunity. Defendants had "not sustained their burden of showing that the seizure, without a court order, of children in order to pursue an investigation of child abuse should be accorded absolute immunity." *Robison v. Via,* 821 F.2d 913, 919 (2d Cir. 1987). *See also Czikalla v. Malloy,* 649 F. Supp. 1212 (D. Colo. 1986).

The Fifth Circuit followed *Robison* in *Hodorowski v. Ray,* 844 F.2d 1210 (5th Cir. 1988), finding that child protective workers who seize children from their home without a court order function in a manner "more akin to the function of police than prosecutors." *Id.* at 1214. The court expressly disagreed with three district court decisions which reached a contrary result.

The Fifth Circuit determined that child protection workers who investigate reports of child abuse and neglect and file complaints with the district attorney are governed by qualified immunity. They do not receive absolute prosecutorial immunity because, under the state law, the district attorney initiates abuse proceedings. *Austin v. Borel,* 830 F.2d 1356 (5th Cir. 1987).

The Eighth Circuit found that court-appointed guardians, therapists, and assigned counsel are protected by absolute quasi-judicial immunity for providing reports and recommendations to the court and for questioning children in child abuse proceedings. These individuals "were appointed to fulfill quasi-judicial responsibilities under court direction." *Myers v. Morris,* 810 F.2d 1437, 1467 (8th Cir.), *cert. denied,* 108 S. Ct. 97 (1987). The court also ruled that the county attorney was protected by absolute prosecutorial immunity for (1) providing advice to law enforcement officials regarding the existence of probable cause and the prospective legality of arrests; (2) questioning children to determine "whom to charge and to prepare for the presentation of her cases[,]" 810 F.2d at 1451; and (3) for initiating neglect proceedings.

The Ninth Circuit concluded that "social workers are entitled to absolute immunity in performing quasi-prosecutorial functions connected with the initiation and pursuit of child dependency proceedings[,]" but only qualified immunity for ordering a parent away from his home until after the juvenile court hearing, because this "can be characterized neither as advocacy or quasi-judicial." *Meyers v. Costa County Department of Social Services,* 812 F.2d 1154, 1152 (9th Cir.), *cert. denied,* 108 S. Ct. 98 (1987). The court also ruled that family court counselors are protected by quasi-judicial immunity in carrying out their statutory duties at the direction of a court.

The Ninth Circuit followed its decision in *Meyers* in *Coverdell v. Department of Social and Health Services,* 834 F.2d 758 (9th Cir. 1987). The court in *Coverdell* ruled that social workers were absolutely immune for their quasi-prosecutorial functions connected with initiating and pursuing child dependency proceedings, and that a child protection worker who obtained custody of a child and removed her from her home pursuant to court order came within quasi-judicial immunity.

A county attorney who brings and litigates paternity actions on behalf of indigent mothers is covered by absolute prosecutorial immunity. *Duersherl v. Foley,* 681 F. Supp. 1364 (D. Minn. 1987), *aff'd,* 845 F.2d 1027 (8th Cir. 1988).

* The Ninth Circuit rejected the argument of hospital administrators that their initiation and pursuit of employee disciplinary proceedings are quasi-prosecutorial in nature. These are executive functions within qualified immunity. *Schwartzman v. Valenzuela,* 846 F.2d 1209 (9th Cir. 1988).

The Fifth Circuit ruled that private prosecutors received qualified immunity because "[t]he public policy concerns which justify absolute immunity for prosecutors are not present when the party seeking immunity is acting in a private prosecutorial role." *Howard Gault Co. v. Texas Rural Legal Aid,* 848 F.2d 544, 556 (5th Cir. 1988).

§ 7.9 Attorneys, Witnesses, and Jurors

Page 160, add after carryover paragraph:

* Witnesses who testify before a grand jury are entitled to absolute immunity. *Strength v. Hubert,* 854 F.2d 421 (11th Cir. 1988); *Alioto v. City of Shively,* 835 F.2d 1173 (6th Cir. 1987); *Kompare v. Stein,* 801 F.2d 883 (7th Cir. 1986); *Strength v. Hubert,* 660 F. Supp. 878 (M.D. Ala. 1987), *adhered to,* 670 F. Supp. 322 (M.D. Ala. 1987); *Behre v. Thomas,* 665 F. Supp. 89, 95 (D.N.H. 1987), *aff'd,* 843 F.2d 1385 (1st Cir. 1988). * The witness in *Strength* was an investigator in the office of the attorney general. Although he received absolute immunity for his grand jury testimony, his investigatory activity prior to his testimony was cloaked in qualified immunity.

In *Daloia v. Rose,* 849 F.2d 74 (2d Cir.), *cert. denied,* 109 S. Ct. 242 (1988), the Second Circuit applied the absolute witness immunity to an adversarial pretrial suppression hearing. In *White v. Frank,* 855 F.2d 956 (2d Cir. 1988), the court, applying common law immunity rules, concluded that a witness who merely testifies before the grand jury is protected by absolute immunity, but a complaining witness who testifies before the grand jury is not entitled to absolute immunity. The court also ruled that the role of the prosecutor and grand jury in advancing the prosecution does not insulate the witness from liability for malicious prosecution. The authors question the validity of the court's treatment of the complaining witness. It would seem that, under the Supreme Court's functional approach, the lodging of a complaint would be an executive task within qualified immunity and the giving of the testimony protected by the absolute witness immunity.

The Third Circuit concluded that a witness who testified at a preliminary hearing and suppression hearings is protected by *Briscoe* absolute immunity. *Williams v.* * *Hepting,* 844 F.2d 138 (3d Cir.), *cert. denied,* 109 S. Ct. 135 (1988).

The Ninth Circuit applied the *Briscoe* absolute immunity to a witness who testified at an adversarial pretrial proceeding in a criminal action. The court read language in *Briscoe* (460 U.S. at 329 n.5) "as reserving the question of immunity for witnesses at probable-cause hearings in particular, rather than all pre-trial proceedings in general." *Holt v. Castaneda,* 832 F.2d 123, 126 (9th Cir. 1987), *cert. denied,* 108 S. Ct. 1275 (1988).

A district court determined that *Briscoe* absolute witness immunity applies to adversarial hearings such as the pretrial probable cause hearing to suppress evidence, but not to nonadversarial hearings like grand jury proceedings, which are ex parte and lack the procedural safeguards of an adversarial hearing. *White v. Frank,* 680 F. Supp. 629 (S.D.N.Y. 1988).

Under *Briscoe,* guardians, therapists, and an attorney who testified in family court child abuse proceedings are protected by absolute immunity. *Myers v. Morris,* 810 F.2d 1437, 1466 (8th Cir.), *cert. denied,* 108 S. Ct. 97 (1987). "We think the immunity extends beyond oral testimony to providing their reports and recommendations to the family court." *Id.*

Witnesses who testify at administrative hearings are entitled to absolute immunity. *Lepley v. Dresser,* 681 F. Supp. 418 (W.D. Mich. 1988) (attorney and judicial misconduct proceedings); *Kukla v. Village of Antioch,* 647 F. Supp. 799, 815 (N.D. Ill. 1986) (employee disciplinary proceeding).

* In *Freeze v. Griffith,* 849 F.2d 172 (5th Cir. 1988), the court applied absolute immunity to a juror who allegedly perjured himself during the voir dire phase of a criminal trial in order to be selected as a juror, and who used undue influence over the jury in order to secure a conviction. The juror was accorded absolute immunity either as a petit juror or as a witness.

§ 7.10 Legislative Immunity

Page 163, add after carryover paragraph:

* Legislative immunity did not protect city council members who had acted in violation of a consent judgment–which had been agreed to by the city and approved by the city council–from contempt sanctions. Although the court "would seriously doubt" that legislative immunity insulates legislative officials from "orders requiring them to comply with remedial decrees redressing constitutional violations," it was not necessary to "definitively decide whether as a general matter a district court may order city council members to vote in favor of a particular ordinance, even to implement remedies for constitutional violations." This case presented the narrower question of whether contempt sanctions may be imposed when the city agreed to a consent judgment committing itself to enact implementing legislation, the city council voted in favor of the decree, but the council members voted against the promised legislation. The fact that a particular councilman voted against the decree neither exempted him from the responsibility to act in accordance with the decree nor insulated him from contempt sanctions. *United States v. City of Yonkers,* 856 F.2d 444, 456, 457 (2d Cir. 1988).

Legislative immunity was not applicable to a borough council's abolition of a police force by vote rather than by enactment of an ordinance, where state law provided that the legislative powers of boroughs shall be carried out by ordinance and all other powers exercised by vote. *Donivan v. Dallastown Borough,* 835 F.2d 486 (3d Cir. 1987), *cert. denied,* 108 S. Ct. 1596 (1988).

Recognizing that local legislative officials who carry out their legislative functions are entitled to absolute immunity, the Fifth Circuit ruled that

> [i]f absolute immunity is urged by the School Board members in the district court, that court must determine whether, under the statutory scheme in Louisiana, school board members' decisions whether to appropriate funds to pay a particular tort judgment involve the degree of discretion and public-policy making traditionally associated with legislative functions or merely an administrative application of existing policies.

Minton v. St. Bernard Parish School Board, 803 F.2d 129, 135 (5th Cir. 1986). *See also Callaway v. Hafeman,* 628 F. Supp. 1478 (W.D. Wis. 1986).

A public employer's promulgation of rules governing the conduct of clerical employees is an administrative rather than legislative act. Because defendants acted in the capacity of employer governing agency internal affairs, they were accorded qualified immunity rather than absolute legislative immunity. *Gutierrez v. Municipal Court,* 838 F.2d 1031 (9th Cir. 1988).

§ 7.10 LEGISLATIVE IMMUNITY

The mayor and town commissioners' decision to contract out police services was protected by absolute legislative immunity. *Healy v. Town of Pembroke Park,* 831 F.2d 989 (11th Cir. 1987). The Ninth Circuit found that the failure of county officials to provide sign language interpreters to enable deaf individuals to serve as jurors was not protected by legislative immunity because the decision did not involve rulemaking but rather the execution of legislative mandates. Hence, qualified immunity controlled. *Greater Los Angeles Council on Deafness v. Zolin,* 812 F.2d 1103 (9th Cir. 1987).

Officials who adopt or amend zoning laws carry out legislative functions protected by legislative immunity. Officials who rule on variance applications receive quasi-judicial immunity because they must hold hearings, construe the ordinances, and apply them to particular pieces of land. *Jodeco v. Hahn,* 674 F. Supp. 488 (D.N.J. 1987). Legislative immunity protected members of a board of supervisors who denied a zoning permit where the state law considered it to be a legislative function. *Pendleton Construction Corp. v. Rockbridge County,* 652 F. Supp. 312 (W.D. Va. 1987), *aff'd,* 837 F.2d 178 (4th Cir. 1988).

Legislative officials who vote for resolutions eliminating job titles are protected by legislative immunity. *Ditch v. Board of County Commissions,* 650 F. Supp. 1245 (D. Kan.), *amended,* 669 F. Supp. 1553 (D. Kan. 1986). The court in *Ditch* contrasted the conduct to the hiring or firing of a particular employee, which is an administrative act.

* The city council's denial of a building permit was not a legislative act. "This decision neither applied to the general community, nor involved the promulgation of legislative policy as a defined and binding rule of conduct . . . . Rather, it was directed specifically and solely at a single individual . . . ." *Bateson v. Geisse,* 857 F.2d 1300, 1304 (9th Cir. 1988). *See also Epstein v. Township of Whitehall,* 693 F. Supp. 309 (E.D. Pa. 1988) (legislative immunity not applicable to denial of development plan); *De Botton v. Marple Township,* 689 F. Supp. 477 (E.D. Pa. 1988) (refusal to grant curative amendment to denial of zoning variance is an administrative, not legislative act); *Creekside Associates v. City of Wood Dale,* 684 F. Supp. 201 (N.D. Ill. 1988) (city council's rejection of development plan is an administrative act).

Legislative immunity did not extend to (1) a city alderman's communication of complaints to members of a liquor commission in order to delay the issuance of plaintiff's liquor license, (2) an agreement between the alderman and plaintiff regarding the issuance of the license, or (3) the alderman's instructions to police to harass customers at plaintiff's liquor establishments. *Mirshak v. Joyce,* 652 F. Supp. 359
* (N.D. Ill. 1987). *See also Polenz v. Parrott,* 694 F. Supp. 599 (E.D. Wis. 1988) (alderman's denial of liquor license is administrative act).

A number of decisions dealt with the issue of whether legislative immunity covers the employment decisions of legislative officials. In *Browning v. Clerk, United States House of Representatives,* 789 F.2d 923, 929 (D.C. Cir.), *cert. denied,* 107 S. Ct. 601 (1986), a non-§ 1983 case involving the speech and debate clause, the court ruled that the House's discharge of its official reporter was protected by the absolute immunity of the speech and debate clause, because "the employee's duties were *directly related to the due functioning of the legislative process*" (emphasis in original). A number of federal district courts have applied absolute legislative immunity to legislative employment decisions regarding employees involved in the legislative process itself. *Birdsong v. Dirck,* 633 F. Supp. 54 (E.D. Mo. 1984) (fiscal analyst); *Bostick v. Rappleyea,* 629 F. Supp. 1328 (N.D.N.Y. 1985) (budget analyst); *Lasa v. Colberg,* 622 F.

Supp. 557 (D.P.R. 1985) (advisor and formulator of plans). *See also Rateree v. Rockett,* 630 F. Supp. 763 (N.D. Ill. 1986) (termination of public employees for budgetary reasons is a legislative act). The issue should be reevaluated in light of the Supreme Court's recent decision in *Forrester v. White,* 108 S. Ct. 538 (1988), discussed in § **7.3**. The authors believe that, under the rationale of *Forrester,* individual employment decisions made by legislative officials are executive acts which fall within qualified immunity even if the employee's duties relate closely to the legislative process. *See Kukla v. Village of Antioch,* 647 F. Supp. 799, 814 (N.D. Ill. 1986) ("A legislator making an employment decision functions not as a legislator but essentially as any other employer would"); *Kuchka v. Kile,* 634 F. Supp. 502 (M.D. Pa. 1985) (discharge of one employee is an administrative rather than legislative act because it does not involve the promulgation of general or prospective legislation).

* In a post-*Forrester* decision, the Seventh Circuit ruled that the employment decisions of legislators generally are administrative acts, but this is not so when, as here, a position is eliminated altogether as a result of a budgetary decision. Budget decisions are core legislative activities because they involve the ordering of policy priorities in the face of limited financial resources. *Rateree v. Rockett,* 852 F.2d 946 (7th Cir. 1988).

§ 7.11 Executive and Administrative Officials: Qualified Good Faith Immunity in General

Page 165, add at end of section:

In a *Bivens* action, the Supreme Court ruled that qualified good faith immunity applies to law enforcement officials who engage in warrantless searches. *Anderson v. Creighton,* 107 S. Ct. 3034 (1987). See § **7.16**. The Court was "unwilling to complicate qualified immunity analysis by making the scope of extent of immunity turn on the precise character of the particular rights alleged to have been violated." *Id.* at 3040. Also, the fact that the government might reimburse the official does not call for a different immunity. *Id.* at 3040 n.3.

Qualified good faith immunity applies to a claim for nominal damages against an official in an individual capacity. *Hartley v. Fine,* 780 F.2d 1383, 1388 (8th Cir. 1985).

A medical examiner who performs an autopsy that leads to a criminal prosecution performs a function analogous to that of a police officer who investigates a suspected homicide, and is thus protected by qualified immunity. *Kompare v. Stein,* 801 F.2d 883 (7th Cir. 1986).

* The Fifth Circuit reaffirmed the rule of *Folsom Investment Co. v. Moore,* 681 F.2d 1032 (5th Cir. 1982), that a private party who invokes a presumptively valid state statute is protected by good faith immunity. *Howard Gault Co. v. Texas Rural Legal Aid,* 848 F.2d 544 (5th Cir. 1988).

According to the Sixth Circuit, the *Harlow* objective good faith *immunity* is not applicable to *private* party defendants, because they did not enjoy this immunity at common law, and the policy reasons for applying this immunity to public officials are not applicable to private parties. The defendant, however, may have a "good faith *defense.*" For example, where, as here, the § 1983 claim is based upon malicious prosecution or wrongful attachment, it is a valid defense that a private party in good faith relied upon the advice of counsel in invoking presumptively valid state statutes. *Duncan v. Peck,* 844 F.2d 1261 (6th Cir. 1988). *See also Howerton v. Gabica,* 708 F.2d 380, 385 n.10 (9th Cir. 1983) (private parties not protected by good faith immunity).

The Tenth Circuit ruled "that when private party defendants act in accordance with the duties imposed by a contract with a governmental body, perform a governmental function, and are sued solely on the basis of those acts performed pursuant to contract, qualified immunity is proper." *DeVargas v. Mason & Hanger-Silas Mason Co.,* 844 F.2d 714, 722 (10th Cir. 1988).

The Eleventh Circuit recognized a qualified good faith immunity for private party
* defendant state actors in *Jones v. Preuit & Mauldin,* 851 F.2d 1321 (11th Cir. 1988) (en banc). The court found that *Harlow* governed a claim against a private party who had utilized a state attachment procedure. "When a citizen undertakes in good faith to utilize a proceeding at law provided by his state legislature, he should do so with confidence that he need not fear liability resulting from the legislature's constitutional error of which he was unaware." *Id.* at 1325. Judge Vance, dissenting, observed that "[u]nlike public officials, private defendants do not exercise official discretion, nor do they formulate policy" and opined that "none of the policy considerations which support the qualified immunity doctrine is present in this case . . . ." *Id.* at 1343.

The Supreme Court of Montana recognized a good faith defense for a private party defendant. *Stensvad v. Towe,* 759 P.2d 138 (Mont. 1988).

* Qualified immunity is not a bar to injunctive relief. *Prisco v. Department of Justice,* 851 F.2d 93 (3d Cir. 1988); *Akins v. Board of Governors,* 840 F.2d 1371, 1378 (7th Cir. 1988).

§ 7.12 —The *Harlow v. Fitzgerald* Standard

Page 168, add at end of section:

The "clearly established law" aspect of the good faith test requires an analysis of the particular federal right at issue. *Anderson v. Creighton,* 107 S. Ct. 3034 (1987).

> The contours of the right must be sufficiently clear that a reasonable official would understand that what he is doing violates that right. That is not to say that an official action is protected by qualified immunity unless the very action in question has previously been held unlawful, . . . but it is to say in the light of preexisting law the unlawfulness must be apparent.

Id. at 3039.

A "conclusory and unsupported allegation of conspiratorial purpose fails to defeat an assertion of qualified immunity by a defendant otherwise entitled to that defense." *Myers v. Morris,* 810 F.2d 1437, 1453 (8th Cir.), *cert. denied,* 108 S. Ct. 97 (1987).

The First Circuit ruled that the defendant official's legal experience as judge and law school dean are irrelevant to the good faith immunity issue, because the *Harlow* test focuses on the objective reasonableness of the official's conduct; the immunity "is not affected by the defendant's particular state of knowledge about the law." *Raffucci Alvarado v. Sonia Zayas,* 816 F.2d 818, 820 (1st Cir. 1987).

The Eighth Circuit cited this text for the proposition that the fact defendants sought the advice of counsel may be an "extraordinary circumstance" protecting an official from liability even if he or she violated clearly established law. This is a pertinent factor, but was not controlling, because defendants did not confront a "perilous" or "unique" situation and the case did not present any special public concerns. *Watertown Equipment Co. v. Norwest Bank,* 830 F.2d 1487 (8th Cir. 1987), *cert. denied,* 108 S. Ct. 1723 (1988). The Third Circuit considered advice of counsel a pertinent factor in the qualified immunity equation in *Lee v. Mihalich,* 847 F.2d 66, 72 (3d Cir. 1988) (malicious persecution claim; because the statute of limitations was unclear and the investigators sought advice of counsel before filing criminal charges, they acted with a reasonable belief that their actions were lawful). *See also Harper v. Washington,* 110 Wash. 2d 873, 759 P.2d 358, 366 (1988) ("While reliance on advice of counsel is not an absolute defense, it is a factor to be considered on the issue of good faith.").

The district court committed error in determining that the inquiry under the *Harlow* good faith test is the same as in a contempt proceeding; while the good faith inquiry in a contempt proceeding focuses on whether a party acted willfully or intentionally, the *Harlow* test centers on objective good faith. *I.A. Durbin, Inc. v. Jefferson National Bank,* 793 F.2d 1541 (11th Cir. 1986).

The courts are experiencing difficulties applying the *Harlow* objective standard to constitutional claims for which intent is a relevant element. *See Feliciano-Angulo v. Rivera-Cruz,* 858 F.2d 40, 46 (1st Cir. 1988) ("*Harlow* will not bar inquiry into a defendant's state of mind when the applicable law makes the defendant's state of mind (as distinct from defendant's *knowledge* of the law) an essential element of plaintiff's constitutional claim.") (emphasis in original); *Coen v. Runner,* 854 F.2d 374 (10th Cir. 1988); *Poe v. Haydon,* 853 F.2d 418 (6th Cir. 1988), *cert. denied,* 109 S. Ct. 788 (1989); *Pueblo Neighborhood Health Centers v. Losavio,* 847 F.2d 642 (10th Cir. 1988); *Musso v. Hourigan,* 836 F.2d 736, 743 (2d Cir. 1988) ("*Harlow* does not require us . . . to ignore the fact that intent is an element of the relevant cause of action"); *Wade v. Hegner,* 804 F.2d 67, 70 (7th Cir. 1986) ("Intent is relevant to the threshold question of whether the defendant violated plaintiff's constitutional rights but is ignored for a question of whether that right was clearly established at the time of the incident").

The application of *Harlow* to constitutional claims requiring intent was discussed in detail in *Martin v. Metropolitan Police Department,* 812 F.2d 1425 (D.C. Cir.), *reh'g denied,* 824 F.2d 1240 (D.C. Cir. 1987). The problem, stated the court, is that "[t]he 'clearly established law' and 'objective reasonableness' facets of current qualified immunity doctrine tug in opposite directions where, as here, the 'clearly established law' itself contains a subjective component." Adhering to its decision in *Hobson v. Wilson,* 737 F.2d 1 (D.C. Cir. 1984), *cert. denied,* 470 U.S. 1084 (1985), the court held that when intent is an essential element of plaintiff's constitutional claim, the court must consider that intent in evaluating the qualified immunity defense. Plaintiff "must be afforded an opportunity to overcome an asserted immunity with an offer of proof of the defendant's alleged unconstitutional purpose." *Martin,* 812 F.2d at 1433. The court then discussed procedural aspects of the immunity issue in this context:

> once defendant has moved for pretrial judgment based on a showing of the objective reasonableness of his actions, then plaintiff, to avert dismissal short of trial, must come forward with something more than inferential or circumstantial support for his allegation of unconstitutional motive. That is, some direct

> evidence that the officials' actions were improperly motivated must be produced if the case is to proceed to trial.

Id. at 1435. Discovery should be allowed on the intent issue and, after the limited authorized discovery, if plaintiff "has not presented an amended complaint containing nonconclusory allegations of [unconstitutional] intent, . . . his constitutional tort claims must be dismissed." *Id.* at 1438.

The Ninth Circuit followed *Martin's* analysis of the interplay between *Harlow* immunity and constitutional intent and plaintiff's pleading burden. *Gutierrez v. Municipal Court,* 838 F.2d 1031, 1052 (9th Cir. 1988) ("in order to survive a motion to dismiss, plaintiffs must state in their complaint nonconclusory allegations setting forth evidence of unlawful intent"). The court left open the question of whether to follow the *Martin* court's limited pretrial discovery rule.

* Several other courts followed the approach taken by *Martin* and *Gutierrez. Poe v. Haydon,* 853 F.2d 418 (6th Cir. 1988), *cert. denied,* 109 S. Ct. 788 (1989); *Coen v. Runner,* 854 F.2d 374 (10th Cir. 1988); *Pueblo Neighborhood Health Centers v. Losavio,* 847 F.2d 642 (10th Cir. 1988). *See also Rakovich v. Wade,* 850 F.2d 1179 (7th Cir.) (en banc) (applying *Harlow* standard in a *Mt. Healthy [School District v. Doyle]* mixed motive context, *cert. denied,* 109 S. Ct. 497 (1988).

Feliciano-Angulo v. Rivera-Cruz, 858 F.2d 40 (1st Cir. 1988), involved a claim by a public employee that he had been dismissed for engaging in First Amendment activity. The court concluded that there was a factual issue as to why the plaintiff was dismissed, and the qualified immunity issue could not be decided until this factual issue was resolved.

The Seventh Circuit observed that a § 1983 conspiracy claim presents a "tension" between the *Harlow* objective standard "and the centrality of motivation to conspiracy claims . . . ." This tension would be troubling except for two important limits on conspiracy claims: (1) the plaintiff must plead specific facts tending to show that a conspiracy existed, and (2) the plaintiff must allege a conspiracy to violate a clearly established constitutional right. If these requirements are complied with, the allegation of conspiracy should be considered in determining whether the defendants violated a clearly established federal right. The court concluded that a reasonable official could not have concluded that the law of due process in 1974 "permitted licensing decisions to be made by officials engaged in a conspiracy to transfer property from one licensee to another." *Easter House v. Felder,* 852 F.2d 901, 919 (7th Cir.), *reh'g granted,* 861 F.2d 494 (7th Cir. 1988).

While language in *Harlow v. Fitzgerald,* 457 U.S. 800, 818 (1982) refers to "officials performing discretionary functions," the *Harlow* standard has been applied to officials carrying out ministerial duties. *McIntosh v. Weinberger,* 810 F.2d 1411, 1432 (8th Cir. 1987), *vacated,* 108 S. Ct. 2870 (1988); *Gagne v. City of Galveston,* 805 F.2d 558 (5th Cir. 1986), *cert. denied,* 107 S. Ct. 3266 (1987). *See contra, Breault v. Chairman,* 401 Mass. 26, 513 N.E.2d 1277 (1987) (*Harlow* limited to discretionary acts), *cert. denied,* 108 S. Ct. 1078 (1988).

The Supreme Court determined that the *Barr v. Mateo,* 360 U.S. 564 (1959), absolute immunity from state tort liability enjoyed by federal officials who act within the "outer perimeter" of their line of duty only extends to discretionary acts. "When an official's conduct is not the product of independent judgment, the threat of liability cannot detrimentally inhibit that conduct." *Westfall v. Erwin,* 108 S. Ct. 580, 584 (1988). Although Congress effectively overturned the result in *Westfall,* Pub. L. No. 100-694, the authors believe that the rationale of *Westfall* may prove to be pertinent with respect to the immunity rule for state and local officials performing ministerial acts.

The fact that an official "was acting pursuant to [superior's] orders does not provide a basis for a broader immunity." *Patzner v. Burkett,* 779 F.2d 1363, 1371 (8th Cir. 1985).

§ 7.13 —Clearly Established Law

Page 169, add at end of section:

An official protected by qualified immunity can be held to violate clearly established law even though the "very action in question" was not previously held unlawful. *Anderson v. Creighton,* 107 S. Ct. 3034, 3039 (1987). The right allegedly violated must be clearly established in a relatively "particularized" sense. *Id.* For liability to attach, the unlawfulness must have been "apparent" in light of "preexisting law." *Id.*

The Seventh Circuit, recognizing that the right must be sufficiently particularized to put potential defendants on notice that their conduct probably is unlawful, concluded "that the test for immunity should be whether the law was clear in relation to the specific facts confronting the public official when he acted." *Colaizzi v. Walker,* 812 F.2d 304, 308 (7th Cir. 1987). *Accord Rakovich v. Wade,* 850 F.2d 1180, 1211 (7th Cir.) (en banc), *cert. denied,* 109 S. Ct. 497 (1988).

In evaluating whether the law was clearly established, the courts have had difficulties determining (1) the degree of factual correspondence required between the relevant precedents and the case at hand, and (2) the appropriate body of case law. Most courts adopt a flexible approach, requiring some but not precise factual correspondence with pertinent precedent. *Boswell v. Sherburne County,* 849 F.2d 1117 (8th Cir. 1988); *Eastwood v. Department of Corrections,* 846 F.2d 627 (10th Cir. 1988); *Abel v. Miller,* 824 F.2d 1522, 1533 (7th Cir. 1987); *Garcia v. Miera,* 817 F.2d 650 (10th Cir. 1987), *cert. denied,* 108 S. Ct. 1220 (1988); *Lappe v. Loeffelholz,* 815 F.2d 1173 (8th Cir. 1987); *Sourbeer v. Robinson,* 791 F.2d 1094 (3d Cir. 1986), *cert. denied sub nom. Patton v. Sourbeer,* 107 S. Ct. 3276 (1987). The Third Circuit in *Sourbeer* concluded that "[a] reasonable official should not fail to respect a person's constitutional rights because the rationale behind the cases establishing those rights may be faulty." 791 F.2d at 1104. In *Lappe,* the Eighth Circuit pointed out that "[a] defendant who knows the appropriate legal standard . . . does not necessarily know how to apply that standard when faced with a unique situation." 815 F.2d at 1180 n.7.

After acknowledging that a precedent need not be on "all-fours" with the instant case, the Fifth Circuit observed that "[a] commanding precedent is also referred to as a 'Goose' case in Louisiana, 'Spotted Horse' or 'Spotted Dog' cases in Alabama, 'Cow cases' in Kansas, and 'White Horse' or 'White Pony' cases in Texas." *Jefferson v. Ysleta Independent School District,* 817 F.2d 303, 305 n.1 (5th Cir. 1987) (citations omitted).

The First Circuit stated that for the law to be clearly established there need not be precedent covering the

> precise situation at hand. It is enough that there existed case law sufficient to clearly establish that, if a court *were* presented with such a situation, the court would find that plaintiff's rights were violated . . .. [T]he fact that no court had put these pieces together in the precise manner we do today does not absolve defendants of liability. No police officer reasonably aware of the law could have failed to appreciate that confining Bancroft Hall until he agreed to forfeit the right to sue violated his civil rights.

Hall v. Ochs, 817 F.2d 920, 925 (1st Cir. 1987) (emphasis in original).

Whether a right was clearly established should not be decided solely by reference to decisions of the United States Supreme Court. *Benson v. Allphin,* 786 F.2d 268 (7th Cir.), *cert. denied,* 107 S. Ct. 172 (1986). When the constitutional principle requires a balancing of interests, there must be a close factual correspondence between the facts of the existing case law and the instant case. The court observed that "qualified immunity typically casts a wide net to protect government officials from damage liability whenever balancing is required." 786 F.2d at 276. *See also Rakovich v. Wade,* 850 F.2d 1180, 1213 (7th Cir.) (en banc), *cert. denied,* 109 S. Ct. 497 (1988); *Noyola v. Texas Department of Human Resources,* 846 F.2d 1021 (5th Cir. 1988); *Warner v. Graham,* 845 F.2d 179 (8th Cir. 1988). On the other hand, the mere fact that the constitutional law requires a balancing of interests does not mean that the law was not clearly established. *Roth v. Veteran's Administration,* 856 F.2d 1401, 1408 (9th Cir. 1988) ("[A]t the time the defendants acted, case law had clearly established that Roth's criticisms regarding wastefulness, ethical and statutory violations, and risk to the patients and public were protected speech relating to matters of public concern.").

The Sixth Circuit stated that, to be clearly established, the issue must be decided either by the highest state court in the state where the case arose, by a United States Court of Appeals, or by the United States Supreme Court. In dicta, the court opined that it is not reasonable to charge a police officer with knowledge of a decision four days after it was issued. *Robinson v. Bibb,* 840 F.2d 349 (6th Cir. 1988).

In *Hensley v. Wilson,* 850 F.2d 269, 275 (6th Cir. 1988), the court stated that "[a] single recent case from a neighboring circuit holding a particular way . . . hardly suffices to make the law 'clearly established' in this circuit." Defendant prison officials are entitled to act "somewhat at variance" with circuit court precedent interpreting a Supreme Court decision because they might reasonably believe the Sixth Circuit would interpret the Supreme Court decision differently.

The Sixth Circuit elaborated upon the "clearly established" standard in *Ohio Civil Service Employees Association v. Seiter,* 858 F.2d 1171, 1177-78 (6th Cir. 1988):

> [I]n the ordinary instance, to find a clearly established constitutional right, a district court must find binding precedent by the Supreme Court, its court of appeals or itself. In an extraordinary case, it may be possible for the decisions of other courts to clearly establish a principle of law. For the decisions of other courts to provide such 'clearly established law' these decisions must both point unmistakably to the unconstitutionality of the conduct complained of and be so clearly foreshadowed by the applicable direct authority as to leave no doubt in the mind of a reasonable officer that his conduct, if challenged on constitutional grounds, would be found wanting. Here a mere handful of decisions of other circuit and district courts, which are admittedly novel, cannot form the basis for a clearly established constitutional right in this circuit.

In *Rakovich v. Wade,* 850 F.2d at 1209, the Seventh Circuit ruled that a court should consider not only binding precedent, but whatever decisional law is available to ascertain whether the law was clearly established.

In another Sixth Circuit decision, the court found that it was not until the Supreme Court's 1982 decision in *Youngberg v. Romeo,* 457 U.S. 307 (1982), that a mental patient could "assert the existence of a clearly established constitutional right to be protected from self-injury." *Davis v. Holly,* 835 F.2d 1175, 1181 (6th Cir. 1987). "A single idiosyncratic opinion from the court of appeals for another circuit was hardly sufficient to put defendants on notice of where this circuit might come out on the issue in question." *Id.* at 1182. Judge Jones, dissenting, found that the law requiring protection of the personal security of patients in mental institutions was clearly established in 1979. *See also Knight v. Mills,* 836 F.2d 659 (1st Cir. 1987) (civilly committed psychiatric patients did not have an established constitutional right to treatment in 1981); *Savidge v. Fincannon,* 836 F.2d 898, 908 (5th Cir. 1988) ("[A]s a general matter the duty to provide institutionalized retardees with constitutionally adequate care was firmly established in this circuit by 1980".) Surely, Judge Gee is right when he says that "the meaning of 'clearly established' is not yet clearly established." *Id.* at 910 (Judge Gee, concurring in part and dissenting in part).

In the absence of binding Supreme Court or Ninth Circuit precedent, the Ninth Circuit considers decisions of other courts and the likelihood that the Supreme Court or the Ninth Circuit would adopt the analysis of the other courts. *Kirkpatrick v. Los Angeles,* 803 F.2d 485 (9th Cir. 1986); *Ward v. San Diego County,* 791 F.2d 1329 (9th Cir. 1986), *cert. denied,* 107 S. Ct. 3263 (1987). In *Ward,* the court observed that law enforcement officials are responsible for keeping abreast of constitutional developments, though not to the same extent as law professors and academicians. *Id.* at 1332. The court concluded that "[i]f no reasonable ground existed for [sheriff] Duff's blanket strip search policy as applied to Ward, . . . the law . . . was sufficiently clear to subject Duffy to liability for civil damages." *Id.* at 1333.

In another Ninth Circuit case, defendants were not protected by qualified immunity, even though a decision on point did not come down from a state appellate court until three years after the federal case was filed. Defendants "cannot use the absence of case law directly on point to shield them from liability. The unlawfulness of their conduct should have been apparent to them in light of preexisting case law." *Ostlund v. Bobb,* 825 F.2d 1371, 1374 (9th Cir. 1987), *cert. denied,* 108 S. Ct. 2016 (1988).

In *Garcia v. Miera,* 817 F.2d 650, 658 (10th Cir. 1987), *cert. denied,* 108 S. Ct. 1220 (1988), the Tenth Circuit reasoned that, while a conflict in the circuits is relevant to the *Harlow* inquiry, it is not controlling because "[t]o give preclusive effect to a conflict among the circuits would effectively bind this circuit by the decisions of others." 817 F.2d at 658. The court found that, at least by May 13, 1983, "the law was clearly established that excessive corporal punishment could deny substantive due process."*Id.* at 657.

"[A] district court decision does not 'clearly establish' the law even of its own circuit, much less that of other circuits." *Hawkins v. Steingut,* 829 F.2d 317, 321 (2d Cir. 1987). *Accord, Muhammad v. Wainwright,* 839 F.2d 1422, 1425 (11th Cir. 1987).

Public officials are not charged with knowledge of decisions that were unreported on the date of the contested conduct. *Williams v. Smith,* 781 F.2d 319 (2d Cir. 1986).

In *Salahuddin v. Coughlin,* 781 F.2d 24 (2d Cir. 1986), the defendant officials were charged with their attorneys' knowledge of a state court oral order, but were protected by qualified immunity because the order was unclear in light of a conflicting written judgment. In these circumstances, failure to follow the oral order could not be said to constitute the violation of clearly established law.

A consent decree cannot be applied retroactively to allow automatic damages for its violation, because to do so would deprive an official of the "right" to assert the good faith immunity defense. *Green v. McKaskle,* 788 F.2d 1115 (5th Cir. 1986). While remedial decrees may provide notice to officials of clearly established rights, they do not create rights and "at some point it becomes unreasonable to expect a prison official to learn the details of thousands of pages of stipulations and compliance plans. We conclude therefore that a remedial court order, standing alone, does not serve as the basis for § 1983 liability." *Id.* at 1124.

* § 7.13A —Specific Applications of Clearly Established Law (New)

The First Circuit found that by December 1976 the use of excessive force by governmental officials was a well-established violation of due process and the Fourth Amendment. *Fernandez v. Leonard,* 784 F.2d 1209 (1st Cir. 1986). *See also Stevens v. Corbell,* 832 F.2d 884, 890 (5th Cir. 1987) ("the defense of qualified immunity is unavailable to a police officer who the plaintiff has alleged . . . used excessive force"), *cert. denied,* 108 S. Ct. 2018 (1988). The Eleventh Circuit held "that shooting a suspected felon who was apparently neither fleeing nor threatening the officers or others was—even in July, 1983—an unreasonable seizure and clearly violated fourth amendment law." *Lundgren v. McDaniel,* 814 F.2d 600, 603 (11th Cir. 1987) (footnote omitted). The law does not clearly establish a duty on police officers to use disabling force before using deadly force. *Clark v. Evans,* 840 F.2d 876 (11th Cir. 1988).

* The Fifth Circuit concluded "that a police officer cannot avail himself of a qualified immunity defense if he procures false identification by unlawful means or deliberately conceals exculpatory evidence, for such activity violates clearly established constitutional principles." *Geter v. Fortenberry,* 849 F.2d 1550 (5th Cir. 1988).

A blanket policy of strip searching all misdemeanor arrestees was clearly established to be unconstitutional as early as 1983. *Weber v. Dell,* 804 F.2d 796 (2d Cir. 1986), *cert. denied,* 107 S. Ct. 3263 (1987). *See also Walsh v. Franco,* 849 F.2d 66 (2d Cir. 1988).

The Ninth Circuit held "that it was clearly established by 1984 that body cavity searches of inmates must be conducted in a reasonable manner . . . ." *Vaughan v. Ricketts,* 859 F.2d 736, 741 (9th Cir. 1988).

The Eighth Circuit was "confident that a pretrial detainee's right to emergency medical care was both clearly established and clearly contoured before March 1984 . . . ." *Boswell v. Sherburne County,* 849 F.2d 1117, 1121 (8th Cir. 1988).

The Sixth Circuit ruled that it was not until 1982 that a mental patient had a clearly established constitutional right to be protected from self-injury. *Davis v. Holly,* 835 F.2d 1175 (6th Cir. 1987). The First Circuit found that civilly committed patients did not have an established constitutional right to treatment in 1981. *Knight v. Mills,* 836 F.2d 659 (1st Cir. 1987). By contrast, the Fifth Circuit found that "as a general matter the duty to provide institutionalized retardees with constitutionally adequate care was firmly established in this circuit by 1980." *Savidge v. Fincannon,* 836 F.2d 898, 908 (5th Cir. 1988).

The Seventh Circuit concluded that a reasonable official in 1974 could not have believed that due process "permitted licensing decisions to be made by officials engaged in a conspiracy to transfer property from one licensee to another." *Easter House v. Felder,* 852 F.2d 901, 919 (7th Cir.), *reh'g granted,* 861 F.2d 494 (7th Cir. 1988).

The Third Circuit found that by 1979, school officials had a clear constitutional duty to take reasonable steps to protect students from sexual abuse by teachers. *Stoneking v. Bradford Area School District,* 856 F.2d 594 (3d Cir. 1988). The Ninth Circuit found that it was clearly established in 1984 that a due process violation results when a police officer is deliberately indifferent after placing an individual in danger. *Wood v. Ostrander,* 851 F.2d 1212 (9th Cir. 1988).

The Fifth Circuit opined that because of the "case-by-case" balancing that must take place in first amendment public employment cases, "[t]here will rarely be a basis for *a priori* judgment that the termination or discipline of a public employee violated 'clearly established' constitutional rights." *Noyola v. Texas Department of Human Resources,* 846 F.2d 1021, 1025 (5th Cir. 1988). The Ninth Circuit, however, stressed that there are cases in which the result of the balancing will be obvious. Declining "to adopt a rule that would effectively eviscerate whistleblower protection for public employees," the court concluded that it was clearly established that the plaintiff's "criticisms regarding wastefulness, ethical and statutory violations, and risk to the patients and public were protected speech relating to matters of public concern." *Roth v. Veteran's Administration,* 856 F.2d 1401, 1408 (9th Cir. 1988).

The Eighth Circuit reasoned that when there is a good faith dispute as to the adequacy of the available state remedies under the *Parratt-Hudson* doctrine, it could not be said that the defendant's failure to grant the plaintiff a hearing violated clearly established law. *Birkenholz v. Sluyter,* 857 F.2d 1214 (8th Cir. 1988).

A federal district court concluded that prison officials' dissemination to nonmedical personnel of information that the plaintiff prisoner had tested positive for the AIDS virus violated the clearly established right of privacy as interpreted in *Whalen v. Roe,* 429 U.S. 589 (1977). *Woods v. White,* 689 F. Supp. 874 (W.D. Wis. 1988).

The Fifth Circuit analyzed the clearly established standard in the context of federal statutory claims in *Del A. v. Edwards,* 855 F.2d 1148 (5th Cir.), *reh'g granted,* 862 F.2d 1107 (5th Cir. 1988). In this context the only pertinent inquiry is whether a reasonable official would know how the statute required the official to act. Whether it is clearly established that the federal statute gives rise to a § 1983 claim for relief is irrelevant to the immunity issue. *Id.* at 1152. *See also J.L. v. Massinga,* 838 F.2d 118, 122 (4th Cir. 1988), *cert. denied,* 109 S. Ct. 816 (1989).

§ 7.14 —The Subjective Prong after *Harlow*

Page 170, add at end of section:

Language in Supreme Court opinions continues to create uncertainty over whether the subjective prong was totally eliminated by *Harlow.* In *Malley v. Briggs,* 106 S. Ct. 1092, 1096 (1986), the Court stated: "Under the *Harlow* standard, . . . an allegation of malice is not sufficient to defeat immunity if the defendant acted in an objectively reasonable manner." On the other hand, *Anderson v. Creighton,* 107 S. Ct. 3034, 3038,

3040 (1987), states that good faith "generally turns on the 'objective legal reasonableness' of the action," and that *Harlow* sought to "minimize" inquiry into subjective intent.

In the opinion of the Seventh Circuit, the *Harlow* test is entirely objective, and inquiry into the official's state of mind is not appropriate. *Benson v. Allphin,* 786 F.2d 268 (7th Cir.), *cert. denied,* 107 S. Ct. 172 (1986).

§ 7.15 –Violations of State Law: *Davis v. Scherer*

Page 172, add at end of section:

An official who violates state regulations may be found liable for damages under § 1982 only if he or she also violated clearly established federal constitutional or federal statutory rights. *Deane v. Dunbar,* 777 F.2d 871 (2d Cir. 1985).

§ 7.16 Arrests and Searches

Page 173, add at end of section:

The United States Supreme Court, in a *Bivens* action, ruled that the *Harlow* objective good faith test applies to warrantless searches by law enforcement officers. *Anderson v. Creighton,* 107 S. Ct. 3034 (1987). "The relevant question . . . is the objective (albeit fact-specific) question whether a reasonable officer could have believed Anderson's warrantless search to be lawful, in light of clearly established law and the information the searching officers possessed. Anderson's subjective beliefs about the search are irrelevant." *Id.* at 3040. An officer might reasonably but mistakenly believe that probable cause or exigent circumstances are present. *Id.* at 3039. The dissenting Justices accuse the majority of applying a "double standard of reasonableness." *Id.* at 3043 (Stevens, J., dissenting). While *Anderson* deals specifically with a warrantless search, its rationale covers warrantless arrests as well.

* A number of recent circuit court cases applied *Anderson v. Creighton* to warrantless arrests and searches. *Osabutey v. Welch,* 857 F.2d 220 (4th Cir. 1988) (searches: "the exigencies of the situation, coupled with the personal corroboration of a tip from a known and reliable informant, provide sufficient basis for a finding that the officers are acting within the protection of the qualified immunity discussed in *Anderson*"); *Jones v. Chicago,* 856 F.2d 985 (7th Cir. 1988) (no immunity when a reasonable officer could not have made a decision to arrest based upon the available information); *McIntosh v. Arkansas Republican Party,* 856 F.2d 1185 (8th Cir. 1988) (arrest); *Jones v. Denver,* 854 F.2d 1206 (10th Cir. 1988) (arrest); *Herren v. Bowyer,* 850 F.2d 1543 (11th Cir. 1988) (arrest; factual dispute precluded summary judgment on immunity grounds); *Turner v. Dammon,* 848 F.2d 440, 446 (4th Cir. 1988) (factual dispute existed as to whether police officers carried out a disproportionately large number of administrative searches of a topless bar: "The basic standards governing administrative searches condemn the baseless isolation of a single establishment for grossly disproportionate intrusions."); *Sevigny v. Dicksey,* 846 F.2d 953, 956-57 (4th Cir. 1988) ("a warrantless arrest made either because of an unreasonable misapprehension of the arrestee's

conduct or of the scope of the crime thought to have been committed, or certainly of both in combination, could not be one made on the basis of a reasonably held belief that the arrest was justified.").

In *Richardson v. Bonds,* 860 F.2d 1427, 1433 (7th Cir. 1988), the court concluded that "at the time of the arrest, it was not clearly established that an off-duty police officer could not be arrested for failure to identify himself as required by a police department regulation."

The Eleventh Circuit applied the *Anderson* test to a *Tennessee v. Garner* (471 U.S. 1 (1985)) claim regarding the use of deadly force against a prisoner who attempted to escape. *Clark v. Evans,* 840 F.2d 876 (11th Cir. 1988). Under *Anderson,* the immunity issue

> is whether a reasonable officer with the information available to [prison guard] Coleman could have believed less violent means were not reasonably available. In other words, could a reasonable officer under these circumstances have believed it was lawful to shoot rather than permit [prisoner] Sharp to proceed in reliance upon the ability of [guard] Prescott to subdue Sharp without using deadly force?

Id. at 881.

A federal district court interpreted *Anderson* to mean that "to win summary judgment on the ground of qualified immunity, defendants must establish *either* that the law establishing the right allegedly violated was not clearly established, *or* that, in light of the facts and circumstances known to those officers and the clearly established law, a 'reasonable' police officer could have believed that the challenged action was lawful." *Vitalone v. Curran,* 665 F. Supp. 964, 974 (D. Me. 1987) (emphasis in original).

In a pre-*Anderson* case, a district court cogently observed that, in the context of warrantless arrests and searches, the *Harlow* standard operates "better in theory than in practice . . . because it often will be impossible to assess the objective reasonableness of the defendant's conduct without a resolution of the factual disputes surrounding the incident from which the action arises." *McGaughey v. Chicago,* 664 F.
* Supp. 1131, 1138 (N.D. Ill. 1987), *vacated in part,* 690 F. Supp. 707 (N.D. Ill. 1988). *See also Martin v. City of Eastlake,* 686 F. Supp. 620, 629 (N.D. Ohio 1988) (it is rare for a qualified immunity defense not to raise an issue of fact).

The Fourth Circuit observed that there is often a "legitimate question" as to whether a search or seizure violates the Fourth Amendment. "The precise action or combination of actions . . . which will infringe a particular suspect's fourth amendments rights is often difficult for even the constitutional scholar to discern because the legal doctrine has developed and continues to develop incrementally." *Tarantino v. Baker,* 825 F.2d 772, 775 (4th Cir. 1987).

A number of lower federal court decisions applied the Supreme Court's decision in *Malley v. Briggs,* 106 S. Ct. 1092 (1986), discussed in the main volume, that police officers who furnish information to magistrates are not automatically immune from liability for an unlawful arrest or search because the magistrate issued an arrest or search warrant. Their immunity is gauged by an objective good faith standard. In *Schulte v. Dodge City,* 630 F. Supp. 327, 331 (D. Kan. 1986), the court ruled that, under *Malley,* civil liability may not be imposed "for a search warrant which, through the simple negligence of the officers preparing the affidavit, contains incorrect information." Rather, to impose liability, *Malley* requires a showing of gross neglect or reckless disregard for the truth.

Malley was distinguished in *Willocks v. Dodenhoff,* 110 F.R.D. 652 (D. Conn.), *aff'd,* 805 F.2d 392 (2d Cir. 1986). While in *Malley* the plaintiff claimed that the magistrate erred in finding that an arrest warrant contained information adequate to support probable cause, in the instant case the plaintiffs conceded that the allegations in the affidavit in support of the warrant application were sufficient to establish probable cause. "[A]s the plaintiffs in this case have conceded that the search warrant shows probable cause on its face, there is no question that the defendants retain their shield of immunity against any section 1983 claims based upon the adequacy of the information contained on the face of the warrant application." *Id.* at 655.

The Seventh Circuit, observing in dicta that *Malley* did not deal "specifically with the question of potential liability for *withholding* information from a magistrate or judicial officer[,]" opined that "[o]nly where a reasonable officer can conclude that a withheld fact is irrelevant to probable cause should an officer who withholds a known (or recklessly disregarded) fact be protected with qualified immunity." *Olson v. Tyler,* 825 F.2d 1116, 1120-21 (7th Cir. 1987) (emphasis in original). *See also Shertz v. Waupaca County,* 683 F. Supp. 1551, 1570 (E.D. Wis. 1988).

In *Odgen v. District of Columbia,* 676 F. Supp. 324 (D.D.C. 1987), the court dealt with an affidavit in support of the search warrant which on its face established probable cause; however, plaintiff argued that facts omitted from the warrant could have negated probable cause. "Such sub-facial attack is relevant, because if an officer seeking a warrant deliberately or recklessly withholds material facts, the officer may be liable for a civil rights violation." *Id.* at 326. The court found the *Malley* test applicable: whether a reasonably well-trained officer would have known that his or her affidavit failed to establish probable cause and that he or she should not have applied for the warrant.

The Eleventh Circuit determined that the *Malley* standard applies only when it is shown, or there is at least a genuine issue of fact, that the officer's request for a warrant allegedly caused an unconstitutional arrest. Absent such a showing, a claim against an officer is governed by the *Harlow* test. *Rich v. Dollar,* 841 F.2d 1558 (11th Cir. 1988). The court believes that the *Malley–Harlow* distinction is important because, while *Malley* did not alter the basic *Harlow* standard, it did establish a hybrid form of the *Harlow* objective reasonableness test that is applicable only to claims of qualified immunity advanced by officers whose warrant requests caused unconstitutional arrests.

Malley did not decide the liability of the officer who executes the warrant. The Second Circuit held that those who act pursuant to facially valid court-issued arrest warrants are protected by the *Harlow* good faith immunity. Unlike the officers in *Malley,* "[h]ere the investigators did not apply for the warrant but simply executed it in a concededly proper manner." *Barr v. Abrams,* 810 F.2d 358, 362 (2d Cir. 1987).

In *Morris v. County of Tehama,* 795 F.2d 791, 795 (9th Cir. 1986), the court ruled that, since a police officer who executes an arrest warrant is entitled to assume it was validly obtained (*Whiteley v. Warden,* 401 U.S. 560 (1971)), "for purposes of section 1983 immunity, an officer is entitled to assume the validity of a *search* warrant secured by fellow officers" (emphasis in original). *See also Heine v. Connelly,* 644 F. Supp. 1508, 1514 n.6 (D. Del. 1986) (*Malley* inapplicable to officers who execute warrants).

Morris was decided post-*Malley* but did not refer to it. In a more recent case, the plaintiffs complained, inter alia, that the search warrant "was mistakenly executed at their residence and carried out in an unreasonable and excessive manner[.]" *Bergquist v. Cochise County,* 806 F.2d 1364, 1367 (9th Cir. 1986). The court ruled that under *Malley* an officer's reliance on a warrant issued by a magistrate is not per se reasonable, and that "an officer's conduct in executing a search warrant is always subject to judical review as to its reasonableness. Officers may face § 1983 liability for executing a warrant in an unreasonable manner." *Id.* at 1368-69 (citations omitted). *Morris* and *Bergquist* are not in conflict. Read together, a police officer may rely upon the facial validity of a warrant but must act reasonably in executing it.

The Eighth Circuit found summary judgment inappropriate because, while plaintiff had a clearly established Fourth Amendment right to be free of unreasonable searches, a question of fact existed as to the reasonableness of the prison strip search of the plaintiff visitor. *Smothers v. Gibson,* 778 F.2d 470 (8th Cir. 1985).

The defendant officers were protected by good faith immunity when they had a warrant to search and the law was uncertain "as to what exactly may be seized when innocent material is intermixed with relevant material." *Crooker v. Mulligan,* 788 F.2d 809, 812 (1st Cir. 1986).

When a warrantless search is sought to be justified by exigent circumstances, the immunity issue is whether a reasonably well-trained officer could have found exigent circumstances based upon the information available to him or her. *Elwood v. Rice,* 423 N.W.2d 671 (Minn. 1988). The court in *Elwood* concluded: "Given the volatility of domestic disputes, we are reluctant to second-guess the officers' judgment on these facts; at the very least officers of reasonable competence could have disagreed about the proper response." *Id.* at 676.

§ 7.17 Professionals

Page 174, add to end of section:

The *Youngberg v. Romeo,* 457 U.S. 307 (1982), professional judgment standard governs the question of whether health professionals violated constitutionally protected rights. *Estate of Connors v. O'Connor,* 846 F.2d 1205 (9th Cir. 1988); *Dautremont v. Broadlawns Hospital,* 827 F.2d 291 (8th Cir. 1987); *Wells v. Franzen,* 777 F.2d 1258 (7th Cir. 1985). In *Wells,* the court stated:

> Freedom of bodily movement is a substantive right derived from the due process clause, and it is breached when a prisoner is bodily restrained except pursuant to an appropriate exercise of judgment by a health professional ....
>
> Long-term restraint decisions should be made by psychiatric personnel. Shorter-term decisions are appropriately made by nurses and non-psychiatric physicians .... If nonprofessional prison employees arbitrarily and without good reason (such as safety) preempt the exercise of judgment by professionals, they risk violation of due process rights of prisoners.

Id. at 1261-63 (citations omitted).

In *Gibson v. Merced County Department of Human Resources,* 799 F.2d 582 (9th Cir. 1986), the court applied the *Youngberg* professional judgment standard to a county agency's removal of a child from foster parents, and found the removal reasonable and constitutional.

The *Youngberg* budgetary restraint defense is an absolute defense to claims for damages but not for injunctive relief. *Thomas S. v. Morrow,* 781 F.2d 367, 375 (4th Cir.), *cert. denied,* 107 S. Ct. 235 (1986).

§ 7.17A National Guard Officials (New)

Under the prevailing view, the rationale of *Feres v. United States,* 340 U.S. 135 (1950) and *Chappell v. Wallace,* 462 U.S. 296 (1983), which generally immunize the United States and superior military officers from liability growing out of military matters, applies to § 1983 claims against state National Guard officials. *Holdiness v. Stroud,* 808 F.2d 417 (5th Cir. 1987); *Sebra v. Neville,* 801 F.2d 1135 (9th Cir. 1986); *Jorden v. National Guard Bureau,* 799 F.2d 99 (3d Cir. 1986), *cert. denied,* 108 S. Ct. 66 (1987); *Crawford v. Texas Army National Guard,* 794 F.2d 1034 (5th Cir. 1986). *But see Stinson v. Hornsby,* 821 F.2d 1537 (11th Cir. 1987) (adhering to the *Mindes v. Seaman,* 453 F.2d 197 (5th Cir. 1971), formula), *cert. denied,* 109 S. Ct. 402 (1988). While the Third Circuit in *Jorden* absolutely barred claims for damages against military personnel, it did allow for review of equitable claims.

§ 7.18 Burdens, Summary Judgment, and Appeals

Page 175, add at end of Burdens of Pleading and Proof subsection:

Seventh and Ninth Circuit decisions state that defendants have the burden of proof on the good faith immunity issue. *Williams v. Lane,* 851 F.2d 867, 882 (7th Cir. 1988); *Benigni v. City of Hemet,* 853 F.2d 1519, 1525 (9th Cir. 1988); *Guerra v. Sutton,* 783 F.2d 1371, 1374 (9th Cir. 1986). Most courts take the position that if the defendant properly raises the issue of qualified immunity, plaintiff has the burden of showing that the law was clearly established. *Alvarado v. Picur,* 859 F.2d 448 (7th Cir. 1988); *Coen v. Runner,* 854 F.2d 374 (10th Cir. 1988); *Poe v. Haydon,* 853 F.2d 418 (6th Cir. 1988), *cert. denied,* 109 S. Ct. 788 (1989); *Klein v. Ryan,* 847 F.2d 368, 371 (7th Cir. 1988); *Connor v. Reinhard,* 847 F.2d 384 (7th Cir. 1988); *Dominque v. Telb,* 831 F.2d 673 (6th Cir. 1987); *Hynson v. City of Chester,* 827 F.2d 932 (3d Cir. 1987), *cert. denied,* 108 S. Ct. 702 (1988); *Abel v. Miller,* 824 F.2d 1522, 1534 (7th Cir. 1987); *Whatley v. Philo,* 817 F.2d 19 (5th Cir. 1987); *Lutz v. Weld County School District,* 784 F.2d 340 (10th Cir. 1986). In *Lutz,* the court determined that plaintiff's failure to meet this burden "does not raise a jury question, but rather calls for entry of judgment in favor of the defendants." 784 F.2d at 1343. Defendants are entitled to a jury instruction on the qualified immunity defense only as to whether there were "exceptional circumstances" justifying the immunity. *Id.*

The Seventh Circuit views qualified immunity as an issue of law for the court, not the jury. *Alvarado v. Picur,* 859 F.2d 448, 451 (7th Cir. 1988); *Rakovich v. Wade,* 850 F.2d 1180, 1201-02 (7th Cir.) (en banc), *cert. denied,* 109 S. Ct. 407 (1988). The Ninth Circuit stated that "[w]hether a reasonable official would know that she is violating . . . clearly established law is a question for the jury." *Brady v. Gebbie,* 859 F.2d 1543, 1556 (9th

Cir. 1988), citing *Schlegel v. Bebout,* 841 F.2d 937, 945 (9th Cir. 1988). This appears to be contrary to the Supreme Court's intent that, by defining the immunity in objective terms, qualified immunity would be an issue of law to be determined pretrial and prediscovery whenever possible. *See Anderson v. Creighton,* 107 S. Ct. 3034 (1987); *Mitchell v. Forsyth,* 472 U.S. 511 (1985); *Harlow v. Fitzgerald,* 457 U.S. 800 (1982).

The Eighth Circuit ruled that pleading absolute immunity as a defense also raised qualified immunity, because "assertions of absolute immunity clearly encompassed the lesser degree of qualified immunity as well." *Hartley v. Fine,* 780 F.2d 1383, 1387 (8th Cir. 1985). On the other hand, the Second Circuit found that defendant waived qualified immunity by raising only absolute immunity in the motion for summary judgment and requesting a charge to the jury on the qualified immunity issue, because qualified immunity is an issue for the court, not the jury. *Stein v. Board of Education,* 792 F.2d 13, 18 (2d Cir.), *cert. denied,* 107 S. Ct. 572 (1986).

* The Seventh Circuit found that the defendants properly raised qualified immunity in a pretrial brief and motion for a directed verdict. *Rakovich v. Wade,* 850 F.2d at 1204.

Defendant's failure to file timely objections to a magistrate's report, which recommended denial of a motion to dismiss raising the qualified immunity defense, operated as a waiver of the defense. *Ivey v. Wilson,* 832 F.2d 950 (6th Cir. 1987).

While defendants waived the qualified immunity defense by failing to plead it as an affirmative defense and only raising it on a motion to dismiss, plaintiff waived this procedural objection by failing to object to the use of the dismissal motion to raise the immunity defense. As a result, the defendant was allowed to present the immunity defense. *Thurston v. United States,* 810 F.2d 438 (4th Cir. 1987).

Some courts impose a heightened pleading requirement upon the plaintiff in § 1983 * actions raising the immunity issue. *Marx v. Gumbinner,* 855 F.2d 783, 792 (11th Cir. 1988) (prosecutorial immunity); *Poe v. Haydon,* 853 F.2d 418 (6th Cir. 1988), *cert. denied,* 109 S. Ct. 788 (1989); *Geter v. Fortenberry,* 849 F.2d 1550 (5th Cir. 1988); *Pueblo Neighborhood Health Centers v. Losavio,* 847 F.2d 642 (10th Cir. 1988); * *Eastwood v. Department of Corrections,* 846 F.2d 627 (10th Cir. 1988); *Dominque v. Telb,* 831 F.2d 673, 676 (6th Cir. 1987); *Brown v. Texas A&M University,* 804 F.2d 327 (5th Cir. 1986); *Martin v. Malhoyt,* 830 F.2d 237, 253 (D.C. Cir. 1987).

With respect to the pleading burden when the constitutional right asserted requires a showing of intent, see the discussion in **§ 7.12.**

Page 176, add at end of Summary Judgment and Discovery subsection:

* The Seventh Circuit observed that although the benefit of qualified immunity as an "immunity from suit is effectively lost once the parties go to trial, we allow plaintiffs to use qualified immunity at any stage of the litigation." *Alvarado v. Picur,* 859 F.2d 448, 451 n.3 (7th Cir. 1988).

A federal district court pointed out that qualified immunity may arise at four stages of the proceedings: (1) on motions to dismiss, (2) for summary judgment, (3) for a directed verdict, or (4) for judgment notwithstanding the verdict. In this court's experience, "the theory and the reality of making an early decision on whether a defendant is entitled to qualified immunity are entirely different." Because it is rare for a qualified immunity defense not to raise a factual issue, "the well-intentioned goal of the early termination of frivolous cases against law enforcement officials is generally ineffective because of the realities of the practice of law." *Martin v. City of Eastlake,* 686 F. Supp. 620, 629 (N.D. Ohio 1988).

A district court should first determine if the actions defendant allegedly took were those a reasonable officer could have believed lawful. If they were, defendant is entitled to dismissal prior to discovery. If they were not, and defendant claims to have engaged in conduct different from that alleged in the complaint – conduct a reasonable officer could have believed lawful – then discovery on the immunity issue may be necessary before defendant's summary judgment motion based on qualified immunity can be resolved. *Anderson v. Creighton,* 107 S. Ct. 3034, 3042 n.6 (1987). Where the constitutional claim requires a showing of intent, discovery may be necessary on the intent issue in order to resolve the immunity issue. *Martin v. District of Columbia Metropolitan Police Department,* 812 F.2d 1425 (D.C. Cir.), *reh'g denied,* 824 F.2d 1240 (D.C. Cir. 1987).

* The Fifth Circuit authorized limited discovery pertaining to the resolution of a factual issue necessary to determine the qualified immunity issue. *Geter v. Fortenberry,* 849 F.2d 1550 (5th Cir. 1988). *See also Unwin v. Campbell,* 863 F.2d 124, 132 n.5 (1st Cir. 1988).

A district court may defer a ruling on a motion for summary judgment on qualified immunity grounds and call for additional discovery when discovery is needed to oppose the motion. Discovery, however, should be allowed only if there is a showing that the information sought would undercut the defendant's claim of objectively reasonable conduct. In this case, the plaintiff failed to demonstrate "any connection between the information he would seek in discovery and the validity of the officers' qualified immunity." *Jones v. Denver,* 854 F.2d 1206, 1211 (10th Cir. 1988).

Discovery may be appropriate when the plaintiff alleges a constitutional claim implicating the official's motive. *Martin v. Metropolitan Police Department,* 812 F.2d 1425 (D.C. Cir.), *reh'g denied,* 824 F.2d 1240 (D.C. Cir. 1987) (see discussion in **§ 7.12**). In *Poe v. Haydon,* 853 F.2d 418, 432 (6th Cir. 1988), *cert. denied,* 109 S. Ct. 788 (1989), the court stated that when discovery has taken place on the motive issue, and the defendant has moved for summary judgment, the plaintiff must produce direct evidence of improper motive in order to have any hope of defeating the motion. *Poe* also ruled that when the "defendant takes an interlocutory appeal, all discovery must cease." *Id.* at 425.

Once it has been determined that defendant is protected by qualified immunity, there is no need to determine the constitutional claim. *Hernandez v. Estelle,* 788 F.2d 1154, 1157 (5th Cir. 1986). *See also Benson v. Allphin,* 786 F.2d 268, 279 n.26 (7th Cir.), *cert. denied,* 107 S. Ct. 172 (1986). *Cf. Kovats v. Rutgers, The State University,* 822 F.2d 1303 (3d Cir. 1987) (where factual issues of merits and qualified immunity issue were intertwined, district court did not err in denying defendant's motion for summary judgment based upon qualified immunity).

Page 176, add at end of Appeals subsection:

* Recent circuit court immunity decisions concerning appeals from denial of immunity place considerable emphasis upon language in *Mitchell v. Forsyth,* 472 U.S. 511, 525-26 (1985), that an "essential attribute" of qualified immunity is "an entitlement not to stand trial under certain circumstances" and thus is "an immunity from suit rather than a mere defense to liability." The Supreme Court subsequently described the *immunity* as "the right to be free of the burdens of a trial." *Van Cauwenberghe v. Biard,* 108 S. Ct. 1945, 1951 (1988).

The denial of absolute immunity was not immediately appealable where defendant reserved for a later pretrial proceeding his claim to qualified immunity. "We hold that where a defendant claims both qualified and absolute immunity, we will not entertain an interlocutory appeal on one of the claims while the other is reserved for later pre-trial proceedings." *Kaiter v. Town of Boxford,* 836 F.2d 704, 708 (1st Cir. 1988). Under this view, a defendant who claims immunity is limited to one interlocutory appeal. Thus, where a defendant raises absolute immunity and intends to raise qualified immunity, both issues should be resolved by the district court before an interlocutory appeal is taken. *See also Unwin v. Campbell,* 863 F.2d 124, 132 n.5 (1st Cir. 1988). The Eighth Circuit disagreed with *Kaiter* in *Murphy v. Morris,* 849 F.2d 1101 (8th Cir. 1988), holding that denial of absolute immunity is immediately appealable even though the official intends to raise qualified immunity. "If public officials are required to wait to appeal an adverse decision regarding absolute immunity until the court has also ruled on the qualified immunity defense, freedom from as many of the costs, risks, and disruptions of the trial process as possible, would be lost." *Id.* at 1104.

In *Group Health v. Blue Cross Association,* 793 F.2d 491 (2d Cir. 1986), *cert. denied* 107 S. Ct. 1566 (1987), the court refused to allow an immediate appeal from the denial of absolute immunity, because the immunity issue could not be resolved without addressing the merits, and because the immunity issue sought to be appealed was "closely intertwined" with an immunity issue that was not presently before the circuit court. Under these circumstances, the absolute immunity question was not completely separate from the merits, did not present solely a question of law, and judicial economy suggested that all of the immunity issues proceed together in the district court, so that ultimately they could be resolved together on appeal.

The district court's denial of qualified immunity was not immediately appealable where it did not present a purely legal issue separate from the merits, but presented a disputed factual issue. *Velasquez v. Senko,* 813 F.2d 1509 (9th Cir. 1987). The Eleventh Circuit ruled that there is no immediate appeal from the denial of immunity when there is a factual issue which impacts upon the reasonableness of the official's conduct and thus upon the immunity. *Goddard v. Urrea,* 847 F.2d 765 (11th Cir. 1988). Judge Johnson, dissenting, believes that qualified immunity appeals raise issues of law because they assume the validity of the plaintiff's version of the facts.

The denial of qualified immunity is not immediately appealable when its resolution depends upon questions of fact and law. *Mahoney v. Hankin,* 844 F.2d 64 (2d Cir. 1988). Where the immunity issue is "inextricably bound" to the merits, a circuit court will normally dismiss the appeal. But where, as here, the district court has already adjudicated the merits of the liability issue (though not the issue of relief), the circuit court "can entertain the appeal of the denial of qualified immunity and exercise pendent jurisdiction to review the liability determinations." *Bolden v. Alston,* 810 F.2d 353, 356 (2d Cir.), *cert. denied,* 108 S. Ct. 229 (1987).

The Fifth Circuit ruled that an order denying a motion to dismiss was subject to immediate appeal because it effectively denied defendant's claim of qualified immunity. *Jacquez v. Procunier,* 801 F.2d 789 (5th Cir. 1986). The Fifth Circuit allowed an immediate appeal from a district court's refusal to consider a motion for summary judgment based on qualified immunity. *Helton v. Clements,* 787 F.2d 1026 (5th Cir. 1986) (per curiam). The court in *Helton* remanded the immunity issue to the district court for its determination. The Eighth Circuit followed *Helton* in *Craft v. Wipf,* 810

F.2d 170 (8th Cir. 1987), as did the Second Circuit in *Musso v. Hourigan,* 836 F.2d 736 (2d Cir. 1988). The Second Circuit, observing that to deny the interlocutory appeal would deprive defendant of her potential entitlement not to stand trial, remanded the case with instructions that the district court consider the qualified immunity issue. * *Accord Eng v. Coughlin,* 858 F.2d 889, 895 (2d Cir. 1988); *Francis v. Coughlin,* 849 F.2d 778 (2d Cir. 1988).

The Sixth Circuit held that, in order to preserve an immediate appeal, it is necessary that the official file a timely notice of appeal from the interlocutory order. *Kennedy v. City of Cleveland,* 797 F.2d 297 (6th Cir. 1986), *cert. denied,* 107 S. Ct. 1334 (1987). * *Accord Webster v. Sowders,* 846 F.2d 1032 (6th Cir. 1988). On the other hand, defendant's failure to take an immediate appeal from the district court's denial of her motion for summary judgment based on immunity grounds is not a waiver of the defense and does not bar defendant from raising the defense on appeal after trial. * *Matherne v. Wilson,* 851 F.2d 752 (5th Cir. 1988); *Kurowski v. Krajewski,* 848 F.2d 767 (7th Cir.), *cert. denied,* 109 S. Ct. 309 (1988); *McIntosh v. Weinberger,* 810 F.2d 1411, 1431 n.7 (8th Cir. 1987), *vacated,* 108 S. Ct. 2870 (1988).

The qualified immunity issue is a purely legal question which the appellate court reviews de novo. *Garionis v. Newton,* 827 F.2d 306 (8th Cir. 1987); *Tomer v. Gates,* 811 F.2d 1240 (9th Cir. 1987). While the qualified immunity issue is immediately appealable only when it turns on an issue of law, these appeals normally do raise questions of law because the propriety of a denial of summary judgment is a question of law. For example, in *White v. Pierce County,* 797 F.2d 812 (9th Cir. 1986), the court found that, while the questions of probable cause for a search and the reasonableness of the force used in making an arrest are ordinarily questions of fact for the jury, when these issues are raised as part of an official's claim of qualified immunity, they are questions of law for the district and circuit courts. As questions of law, the district court's determination receives de novo review in the circuit court.

In *Wright v. South Arkansas Regional Health Center,* 800 F.2d 199 (8th Cir. 1986), the plaintiff claimed that he had been retaliated against for having exercised his First Amendment rights. While there was no doubt that the right to be free of such official retaliation had been clearly established for some time, the question in the case was whether the defendant in fact retaliated against the plaintiff. The court viewed the district court's denial of defendant's motion for summary judgment as raising a question of law, i.e., "whether, when all the facts are viewed in the light most favorable to plaintiff, there is any genuine issue, triable to a jury, of improper motivation." *Id.* at 203. *See also DeVargas v. Mason & Hanger-Silas Mason Co.,* 844 F.2d 714, 719 (10th Cir. 1988) (*Wright* illustrates "proper solution").

The Eighth Circuit denied an immediate appeal to private defendant state actors who sought to appeal from the denial of a summary judgment motion based in part on qualified immunity. *Chicago and North Transportation Co. v. Ulery,* 787 F.2d 1239 (8th Cir. 1986). The rationale behind allowing interlocutory appeals, namely, protecting public officials from the burden of discovery and trial if they did not act in violation of clearly established federal rights, is not applicable when the defendants are private party state actors. The court indicated that the result might have been different if some of the defendants had been public officials entitled to an immediate appeal, in which case "it might make sense to allow the interlocutory appeal to proceed as to all appellants, public and private." *Id.* at 1241 n.1. On this last point, *see Myers v. Morris,*

810 F.2d 1437, 1441 (8th Cir.), *cert. denied,* 108 S. Ct. 97 (1987) (private party allowed immediate appeal where public officials took immediate appeal). In *DeVargas v. Mason & Hanger-Silas Mason Co.,* 844 F.2d 714 (10th Cir. 1988), the court ruled that private parties who carry out their obligations under a governmental contract may bring interlocutory appeals from the denial of qualified immunity. "Forcing such private contractor parties to defend meritless damages actions at trial creates the same distractions from public duties as it does for public employees." *Id.* at 717.

Numerous recent decisions hold that an immediate appeal lies from the denial of qualified immunity even though, in addition to a claim for damages against the official individually, plaintiff asserts a claim for injunctive relief against the official in an
* official capacity. *Marx v. Gumbinner,* 855 F.2d 783 (11th Cir. 1988); *Jones v. Denver,* 854 F.2d 1206 (10th Cir. 1988); *Giacalone v. Abrams,* 850 F.2d 79 (2d Cir. 1988); *Young v. Lynch,* 846 F.2d 960 (4th Cir. 1988), *overruling England v. Rockefeller,* 739 F.2d 140 (4th Cir. 1984) and *Bever v. Gilbertson,* 724 F.2d 1083 (4th Cir. 1984); *DeVargas v. Mason & Hanger-Silas Mason Co.,* 844 F.2d 714 (10th Cir. 1988); *Drake v. Scott,* 812 F.2d 395 (8th Cir.), *cert. denied,* 108 S. Ct. 455 (1987); *Scott v. Lacy,* 811 F.2d 1153 (7th Cir. 1987); *Kennedy v. City of Cleveland,* 797 F.2d 297 (6th Cir. 1986). *cert. denied,* 107 S. Ct. 1334 (1987); *De Abadia v. Izquierdo Mora,* 792 F.2d 1187 (1st Cir. 1986); *Tubbesing v. Arnold,* 742 F.2d 401 (8th Cir. 1984). *See also Musso v. Hourigan,* 836 F.2d 736, 742 n.1 (2d Cir. 1988) (interlocutory appeal lies with respect to immunity issue on one constitutional claim, even though defendant may have to undergo trial on another constitutional claim); *Justice v. Town of Blackwell,* 820 F.2d 238 (7th Cir. 1987) (denial of qualified immunity immediately appealable even though third-party defendant has to defend state law claim); *Brown v. Texas A&M University,* 804 F.2d 327 (5th Cir. 1986) (denial of qualified immunity is immediately appealable even though defendant faces another claim (under the ADEA) in which he is a nominal defendant facing no
* monetary or other personal liability). *Contra Prisco v. Department of Justice,* 851 F.2d 93 (3d Cir. 1988).

These decisions stress the significant differences between a claim for damages against an official individually and a claim for injunctive relief against the official in an official capacity, including the facts that the emotional and physical responsibilities are not likely to be as great with respect to claims for injunctive relief. *See, e.g., Scott v. Lacy,* 811 F.2d 1153 (7th Cir. 1987) ("As a practical matter, a public official who is a defendant in a suit seeking an injunction is not on trial at all"). By contrast, the claim for damages is likely to divert the official from his or her official responsibilities and may require that he or she retain independent counsel. The cases cited above thus recognize an immediate appeal from the denial of a claim of qualified immunity from damages liability, even though a prayer for injunctive relief is pending.

* Overruling its decisions in *Bonitz v. Fair,* 804 F.2d 184 (1st Cir. 1986), the First Circuit determined that upon an interlocutory appeal from the denial of a summary judgment motion made on qualified immunity grounds, the circuit court may "consider all the materials that were properly before the lower court, including depositions, in connection with such motion." *Unwin v. Campbell,* 863 F.2d 124, 128 (1st Cir. 1988).

The Seventh Circuit concluded "that when considering a qualified immunity issue on a motion for summary judgment, a district court should consider all of the undisputed evidence in the record, read in the light most favorable to the non-movant." *Green v.*
* *Carlson,* 826 F.2d 647, 650 (7th Cir. 1987). *Accord Rakovich v. Wade,* 850 F.2d 1180,

1204-05 (7th Cir.) (en banc), *cert. denied,* 109 S. Ct. 497 (1988); *Turner v. Dammon,* 848 F.2d 440 (4th Cir. 1988); *DeVargas v. Mason & Hanger-Silas Mason Co.,* 844 F.2d 714 (10th Cir. 1988); *Trapnell v. Ralston,* 819 F.2d 182, 184 n.1 (8th Cir. 1987); *Myers v. Morris,* 810 F.2d 1437, 1459 (8th Cir.), *cert. denied,* 108 S. Ct. 97 (1987).

Following the decision in *Bonitz v. Fair,* several circuit court decisions held that, on an interlocutory appeal from denial of qualified immunity, there is no pendent * appellate jurisdiction to consider other issues. *Brown v. United States,* 851 F.2d 615 (3d Cir. 1988) (*Bivens* claim); *Francis v. Coughlin,* 849 F.2d 778, 780-81 (2d Cir. 1988); *Emery v. Holmes,* 824 F.2d 143 (1st Cir. 1987); *Vazquez Rios v. Hernandez Colon,* 819 F.2d 319, 320 n.3 (1st Cir. 1987). *See also Hynson v. City of Chester,* 827 F.2d 932 (3d Cir. 1987) (issue on appeal is "limited to the purely legal question of whether the facts alleged support a violation of clearly established law"), *cert. denied,* 108 S. Ct. 702 (1988).

Some courts, however, acknowledge, either explicitly or implicitly, the existence of pendent appellate jurisdiction to determine closely related issues. *Feaster v. Miksch,* 846 F.2d 21 (6th Cir. 1988) (on appeal from denial of qualified immunity, court may determine *Younger* abstention issue); *Craft v. Wipf,* 836 F.2d 412, 418 (8th Cir. 1987) ("an appellate court has jurisdiction to consider whether substantial evidence exists to support an equal protection claim at the same time it considers a denial of qualified immunity for the alleged violation"); *Anderson v. Roberts,* 823 F.2d 235 (8th Cir. 1987) (court may determine if there are genuine issues of material fact relating to merits of constitutional claims); *Carlson v. Conklin,* 813 F.2d 769 (6th Cir. 1987) (court may decide if plaintiff has been deprived of a constitutional right); *Drake v. Scott,* 812 F.2d 395 (8th Cir. 1987) (court may consider closely related issues of law); *Bolden v. Alston,* 810 F.2d 353 (2d Cir.) (pendent jurisdiction over liability determinations), *cert. denied,* 108 S. Ct. 229 (1987).

Federal "district courts should state for the record, and for the benefit of the circuit court on appeal their reasons for denying immunity." *Schaper v. City of Huntsville,* 813 F.2d 709, 713 (5th Cir. 1987).

The denial of a motion to amend the answer to include the qualified immunity defense is not immediately appealable. *Justice v. Town of Blackwell,* 820 F.2d 238 (7th Cir. 1987).

* A grant of immunity is not immediately appealable. *Feliciano-Angulo v. Rivera-Cruz,* 858 F.2d 40, 42 n.1 (1st Cir. 1988)("Such an appeal must await resolution of the case by a complete final judgment."); *Theis v. Smith,* 827 F.2d 260 (7th Cir. 1987); *Coe v. Ziegler,* 817 F.2d 29 (6th Cir. 1987).

An immediate appeal does not lie from the denial of a protective order based upon qualified immunity. *Graham v. Gray,* 827 F.2d 679 (10th Cir. 1987). In *Lion Boulos v. Wilson,* 834 F.2d 504 (5th Cir. 1987), the court ruled that defendant could not appeal a district court's order compelling limited discovery where the discovery material was needed to resolve the qualified immunity issue.

* The Ninth Circuit criticized state governmental defendants for apparently deeming "it mandatory to bring these [interlocutory] appeals from any adverse ruling, no matter how clearly correct the trial court's decision." *Schwartzman v. Valenzuela,* 846 F.2d 1209, 1210 (9th Cir. 1988).

Whether state officials have the right to an immediate appeal from the denial of qualified immunity claimed solely under state law depends upon whether the state's qualified immunity doctrine, like the federal doctrine, "provides a true immunity from suit and not a simple defense to liability." *Sorey v. Kellett,* 849 F.2d 960, 962 (5th Cir. 1988). *Accord Marrical v. Detroit News,* 805 F.2d 169 (6th Cir. 1986).

A number of state courts have adopted the federal rule allowing interlocutory appeal from a denial of immunity. *Breault v. Chairman,* 401 Mass. 26, 513 N.E.2d 1277 (1987), *cert. denied,* 108 S. Ct. 1078 (1988); *Robinson v. Beaumont, 291 Ark. 477, 725 S.W.2d 839 (1987); Anderson v. City of Hopkins,* 393 N.W.2d 363 (Minn. 1986). *Contra,* * *Pizzato's v. City of Berwyn,* 168 Ill. App. 3d 796, 523 N.E.2d 51 (1988); *Noyola v. Flores,* 740 S.W.2d 493 (Tex. Ct. App. 1987).

CHAPTER 8

EXHAUSTION OF STATE REMEDIES

§ 8.1 Exhaustion Defenses: Introduction

Page 178, add at end of section:

Section 1983 claimants cannot complain about a violation of procedural due process when they "have made no attempt to avail themselves of existing state procedures." *Boston Environmental Sanitation Inspections Association v. Boston,* 794 F.2d 12, 13 (1st Cir. 1986); *Kauth v. Hartford Insurance,* 852 F.2d 951, 955 (7th Cir. 1988) ("Kauth simply cannot refuse to pursue the available state remedies and then come into federal court complaining that he was not afforded due process."); *Narumanchi v. Board of Trustees,* 850 F.2d 70, 72 (2d Cir. 1988) (plaintiff's failure to submit to the grievance procedures precludes consideration of the fairness of thos procedures in practice); *Myrick v. Dallas,* 810 F.2d 1382 (5th Cir. 1987); *Suarez v. Illinois Valley Community College,* 688 F. Supp. 376 (N.D. Ill. 1988); *Lavelle v. Quinones,* 679 F. Supp. 253 (E.D.N.Y. 1988); *Gonzales Martinez v. Autoridad de Energia Electrica,* 644 F. Supp. 364 (D.P.R. 1986), *vacated,* 831 F.2d 280 (1st Cir. 1987). The Eleventh Circuit viewed the failure to request a hearing available under established procedures as a waiver of a procedural due process claim. *Grandison v. Smith,* 779 F.2d 637, 641 (11th Cir. 1986). *See also Tavarez v. O'Malley,* 826 F.2d 671, 676 (7th Cir. 1987) (dicta). *Cf. Jones v. Preuit & Mauldin,* 808 F.2d 1435, 1443 (11th Cir.) (failure to request hearing not a waiver where pretaking procedures not available), *modified,* 822 F.2d 998 (11th Cir.), *vacated,* 833 F.2d 1436 (11th Cir. 1987). On the other hand, the existence of available grievance procedures is irrelevant when the § 1983 claimant asserts a violation of First Amendment rights. *Narumanchi v. Board of Trustees,* 850 F.2d at 73, citing *Parrett v. City of Connersville,* 737 F.2d 690, 697 (7th Cir. 1984), *cert. dismissed,* 469 U.S. 1145 (1985).

§ 8.2 Exhaustion of State Judicial Remedies

Page 180, add at end of section:

The fact that the claimant pursues judicial remedies in state and federal court does not preclude a § 1983 federal court claim. *Brandman v. North Shore Guidance Center,* 636 F. Supp. 877 (E.D.N.Y. 1986). The authors observe that this course of action may create res judicata and *Colorado River* abstention problems.

While "exhaustion of state remedies is not required in section 1983 actions, under *Parratt,* the availability of state procedures is important in ascertaining whether due process is available." *Lee v. Hutson,* 810 F.2d 1030, 1033 (11th Cir. 1987). *See also Birkenholz v. Sluyter,* 857 F.2d 1214 (8th Cir. 1988); *Campo v. Employees Retirement*

System, 843 F.2d 96 (2d Cir.), *cert. denied,* 109 S. Ct. 220 (1988); *Marino v. Ameruso,* 837 F.2d 45, 47 (2d Cir. 1988).

The rule of *Williamson County Regional Planning Commissioner v. Hamilton Bank,* 473 U.S. 172 (1985), see **§ 3.10**, is not inconsistent with § 1983's no-exhaustion rule. *Cassettari v. Nevada County,* 824 F.2d 735, 739 (9th Cir. 1987).

§ 8.3 Exhaustion of State Administrative Remedies

Page 182, add at end of section:

An amendment to the Education of the Handicapped Act (EHA), which provides that the EHA does not restrict or limit any remedies under § 1983 (see **§ 3.2**), states that "before the filing of a civil action under [§ 1983] seeking relief that is also available under [the EHA], the procedures under [the EHA] shall be exhausted to the same extent as would be required had the action been brought under [the EHA]." Public L. No. 99-372, § 3, 20 U.S.C. § 1415(f). The Senate Report makes clear that "[e]xhaustion of E.H.A. administrative remedies would thus be excused where they would not be required to be exhausted under the E.H.A., such as when resort to those proceedings would be futile." S. Rep. No. 112, 99th Cong., 2d Sess. 15 (1986).

Asserting claims under the EHA and § 1983, plaintiffs in one case alleged that the state agency adopted a policy that was contrary to law and "that they are unlikely to receive adequate relief because a due process hearing officer lacks the authority to effectuate class action and system-wide relief." *Mrs. W. v. Tirozzi,* 832 F.2d 748, 757 (2d Cir. 1987). The Second Circuit found that plaintiffs "pleaded an entitlement to an exemption from exhaustion of administrative remedies sufficient to overcome a motion for judgment on the pleadings." *Id.* at 757. Also, because plaintiffs' claims involved purely legal questions, there was no basis for invoking the doctrine of primary jurisdiction. *See also J.G. v. Board of Education,* 830 F.2d 444 (2d Cir. 1987) (EHA exhaustion excused where claimed systemic wrongs could not be corrected administratively). Exhaustion was found futile in another case when plaintiffs had been denied a hearing and the school district determined that it would not provide the funds necessary for plaintiff's education. *Kerr Center Parents Association v. Charles,* 842 F.2d 1052 (9th Cir. 1988).

The *Patsy* no-exhaustion of administrative remedies rule in § 1983 action applies to claims based upon the Federal Medicaid Act. *Alacare, Inc.-North v. Baggiano,* 785 F.2d 963 (11th Cir.), *cert. denied,* 107 S. Ct. 111 (1986). While there are express and perhaps implied congressional exceptions to the *Patsy* rule, there must be firm evidence, lacking in *Alacare,* of a congressional intent to justify an exception to the rule against exhaustion.

The district court's certification that Wisconsin's inmate grievance remedies are in compliance with the attorney general's regulations promulgated under the Civil Rights of Institutionalized Persons Act (CRIPA), 42 U.S.C. § 1997e, was premature. The district court did not determine if the inmates participated in the formulation, implementation, and operation of the grievance system or were afforded the opportunity to ask questions about the procedures. *Lewis v. Meyer,* 815 F.2d 43 (7th Cir. 1987).

During CRIPA's 90-day exhaustion period, the inmate must not only commence the grievance procedure but also appeal to the highest administrative body available. *Maulick v. Central Classification Board,* 659 F. Supp. 24 (E.D. Va. 1986). The district court has power to dismiss if the inmate fails to pursue his or her administrative remedies, but should not dismiss without considering whether the inmate "had reasonably and in good faith pursued his administrative remedies." *Rocky v. Vittorie,* 813 F.2d 734, 736 (5th Cir. 1987). In *Robinson v. Young,* 674 F. Supp. 1356 (W.D. Wis. 1987), the court determined that defendants waived any possible exhaustion defense by dismissing the inmate's administrative complaint pending the outcome of the litigation.

Some courts require exhaustion of administrative remedies in § 1983 actions brought by members of the National Guard because of the importance of judicial deference to the military. *Stinson v. Hornsby,* 821 F.2d 1537 (11th Cir. 1987), *cert. denied,* 109 S. Ct. 402 (1988); *Crawford v. Texas Army National Guard,* 794 F.2d 1034 (5th Cir. 1986); *Furman v. Edwards,* 657 F. Supp. 1243 (D. Vt. 1987). Many of these claims are dismissed under the *Feres-Chappell* doctrine. See § **7.17A.**

* When a discharged CETA employee's claim is based upon the Constitution or upon a federal statute other than CETA, such as § 1983, the plaintiff need not exhaust administrative remedies. *Black v. Broward Employment and Training Administration,* 846 F.2d 1311 (11th Cir. 1988).

In the course of holding that state notice of claim requirements do not apply to state court § 1983 claims, see § **11.9**, the Supreme Court determined that the no-exhaustion of administrative remedies rule stablished by *Patsy v. Board of Regents,* 457 U.S. 496 (1982), applies to both federal and state court § 1983 actions. Congress did not contemplate "that those who sought to vindicate their federal rights in state courts could be required to seek redress in the first instance from the very state officials whose hostility to those rights precipitated their injuries." *Felder v. Casey,* 108 S. Ct. 2302, 2311 (1988).

§ 8.3A —Ripeness (New)

Although it is well established that exhaustion of state remedies is not a prerequisite for commencing suit under § 1983 (see §§ **8.2-8.3**), a constitutional claim must progress to the point where it is "ripe." This requirement has been specifically applied by the Supreme Court in *Williamson County Regional Planning Commission v. Hamilton Bank,* 473 U.S. 172 (1985), in the context of just compensation taking claims (see § **3.10**). The Third Circuit, analogizing from the principles developed in *Williamson,* found that a challenge to an attorney advertising rule was not ripe. *Felmeister v. Office of Attorney Ethics,* 856 F.2d 529 (3d Cir. 1988). The court in *Felmeister* relied upon the approach in the leading case of *Abbott Laboratories v. Gardner,* 387 U.S. 136 (1967), which requires consideration of two competing concerns: the fitness of the issue for judicial review and the hardship to the parties if review is delayed. The *Felmeister* court concluded that "until it is shown that plaintiffs wish to engage in an activity that would be prohibited under the revised attorney advertising rule, their challenge lacks the level of factual specificity necessary to make the matter ripe for adjudication." *Id.* at 537.

The authors point out that ripeness overlaps in concept with the standing requirements to obtain injunctive relief (see § **2.5**).

§ 8.6 Section 1983 and Federal Habeas Corpus: Determining the Appropriate Remedy

Page 191, add at end of section:

In a case inadvertently omitted from the text, the Seventh Circuit ruled that a corporation that has been convicted and fined may not challenge the constitutionality of the conviction in a federal court § 1983 action; federal habeas corpus is the exclusive remedy to challenge a conviction and the fact that habeas corpus is not available because the corporation is not in "custody" does not render § 1983 available. *Waste Management of Wisconsin v. Fokakis,* 614 F.2d 138 (7th Cir.), *cert. denied,* 449 U.S. 1060 (1980), *reh'g denied,* 450 U.S. 960 (1981).

When a § 1983 damages claim is based upon the alleged unconstitutionality of the conviction, the district court should stay, rather than dismiss, the action pending state court review of the conviction. *Williams v. Hepting,* 844 F.2d 138 (3d Cir. 1988) (applying *Deakins v. Monaghan;* see § **12.7**).

A claim that a habitual offender statute is unconstitutional cannot be lodged under § 1983. "This is an attack on the duration of confinement and must therefore be treated as a petition for habeas corpus . . . ." *Feeney v. Auger,* 808 F.2d 1279 (8th Cir. 1986). Habeas corpus was the appropriate remedy where plaintiff sought release from parole, alleging that parole officials filed fabricated charges against him. However, plaintiff's claim for damages should not be dismissed, but should be stayed pending exhaustion of state remedies. *Harper v. Jeffries,* 808 F.2d 281 (3d Cir. 1986).

A claim seeking the restoration of good time credits is within federal habeas corpus, not § 1983, and exhaustion of state remedies is required, even though not raised by the state in the district or circuit courts. Applying the decision in *Granberry v. Greer,* 107 S. Ct. 1671 (1987), the court concluded: "Because the exhaustion doctrine implicates values that may transcend the concerns of the parties to an action, it is not inappropriate for the court, on its own motion, to invoke the doctrine; and we do so here." *Brown v. Fauver,* 819 F.2d 395, 398 (3d Cir. 1987).

In an unusual twist, a prisoner seeking reinstatement in a work release program invoked federal habeas corpus, while the defendant warden claimed that § 1983 was the proper remedy. Habeas corpus was found proper because participation in New Hampshire's work release program was closely connected to the prisoner's impending release. *Brennan v. Cunningham,* 813 F.2d 1 (1st Cir. 1987).

Claims for declaratory relief and damages for the alleged unlawful deprivation of good time credits are not within § 1983 even though restoration of the credits is not sought. *Hanson v. Heckel,* 719 F.2d 93 (7th Cir. 1986). "[T]o entertain Hanson's challenge would be tantamount to a decision on his entitlement to speedier release . . . ." *Id.* at 96. Similarly, the Seventh Circuit determined that a claim for damages for the allegedly unconstitutional denial of parole must await the exhaustion of state remedies. *Crump v. Lane,* 807 F.2d 1394 (7th Cir. 1986).

The Eighth Circuit took the position that a § 1983 claims for damages and declaratory relief for the withholding of good time credits should be stayed pending the exhaustion of state remedies. *Offet v. Solem,* 823 F.2d 1256 (8th Cir. 1987).

The Fifth Circuit continues to hold that while a general procedural due process attack may be lodged under § 1983, *Johnson v. Pfeiffer,* 821 F.2d 1120 (5th Cir. 1987) (general challenge to criteria used in parole release determinations), a challenge to a single defective parole release hearing requires the exhaustion of state remedies. *Serio v. Members of State Board of Pardons,* 821 F.2d 1112 (5th Cir. 1987).

Habeas corpus is the exclusive remedy to contest the right to be released from confinement resulting from a civil contempt adjudication. *Leonard v. Hammond,* 804 F.2d 838 (4th Cir. 1986).

Habeas corpus is not a proper remedy and § 1983 is available when a prisoner seeks release from administrative segregation to the general prison population. *Toussaint v. McCarthy,* 801 F.2d 1080, 1102-03 (9th Cir. 1986), *cert. denied,* 107 S. Ct. 2462 (1987).

Disagreeing with the First Circuit's decision in *Dickerson v. Walsh,* 750 F.2d 150 (1st Cir. 1984), which is discussed in the main text, the Sixth Circuit ruled that federal habeas corpus is not an appropriate remedy to challenge the constitutionality of state post-conviction proceedings, because this does not constitute a challenge to the fact or duration of confinement. *Kirby v. Dutton,* 794 F.2d 245 (6th Cir. 1986). The court did not discuss the availability of § 1983.

A claim that the seriousness of the offense is too broad a reason to justify the denial of parole may be raised in a § 1983 action or in a federal habeas corpus proceeding. *Huggins v. Isenbarger,* 798 F.2d 203 (7th Cir. 1986).

The Second Circuit determined that a claim for damages based upon an alleged Sixth Amendment violation by a sheriff and deputy sheriff's failure to produce a witness, but which does not seek immediate or speedier release and does not contest the constitutionality of the conviction, may be asserted under § 1983. However, because a state court appeal of the conviction was pending, the federal action was stayed pending termination of the state court criminal proceeding. *Mack v. Varelas,* * 835 F.2d 995 (2d Cir. 1987). The Seventh Circuit faced a similar issue in *Smith v. Springer,* 859 F.2d 31 (7th Cir. 1988). Following his release from confinement, the plaintiff commenced a § 1983 action for damages against three police officers for allegedly fabricating evidence against him to secure his conviction. Under the "unique" facts of the case the court read the complaint as a proper § 1983 action, challenging only the conduct of the officers, but not the state court procedures culminating in the conviction nor the conviction itself. "Although the correctness of Smith's conviction may be seriously undermined if he succeeds in his claim, he does not seek this result directly." *Id.* at 33.

The Second Circuit determined that a patient in a psychiatric center can challenge the validity of his or her confinement, as opposed to the conditions of confinement, only in a federal habeas corpus proceeding following exhaustion of state remedies. *Buthy v. Commissioner of Office of Mental Health,* 818 F.2d 1046, 1051 (2d Cir. 1987).

When some asserted claims attack the conviction or sentence, and are thus within federal habeas corpus, while others are proper § 1983 claims (e.g., for illegal arrest and excessive force), the district court may, but need not, proceed with the § 1983 claims while holding the habeas claims in abeyance pending exhaustion. *Hernandez v. Spencer,* 780 F.2d 504 (5th Cir. 1986). The district court may, as it did here, choose to hold all of the claims in abeyance until completion of exhaustion as a matter of "good judicial administration," and because there "is no obligtion on the part of the busy trial judge to pick through such a mass of ambiguous matter, sorting out one type of claim from the other." *Id.* at 506.

CHAPTER 9

RES JUDICATA AND COLLATERAL ESTOPPEL

§ 9.3 State Criminal Proceedings

Page 193, add at end of section:

Where probable cause was found against the criminal defendant in an adversarial preliminary hearing, he was collaterally estopped from raising the probable cause issue in a § 1983 claim for malicious prosecution. The accused had a full and fair opportunity to litigate the issue in the state proceeding and in fact did so. *Coogan v. City of Wixom,* 820 F.2d 170 (6th Cir. 1987) (see § **9.8**).

A ruling in a probable cause hearing that there was probable cause to proceed on disorderly conduct charges did not collaterally estop a § 1983 plaintiff from contesting the constitutionality of his arrest. The § 1983 arrest issue – whether the arrest was in bad faith because the officer could not have reasonably believed plaintiff was engaged in disorderly conduct – was not the same issue determined in the probable cause hearing and, in any case, the § 1983 claimant did have a full and fair opportunity to litigate the probable cause issue in the probable cause hearing. *Bailey v. Andrews,* 811 F.2d 366 (7th Cir. 1987).

* A ruling in a state court suppression hearing that a search was reasonable, which was followed by a judgment of acquittal, was not binding in a federal court § 1983 action because of the interlocutory nature of the state court ruling. *Pachaly v. City of Lynchburg,* 696 F. Supp. 180 (W.D. Va. 1988).

The Eighth Circuit rejected defendant's argument that a conviction bars a § 1983 claim for unlawful arrest, because the issue of guilt or innocence of the charge is not identical to the claim of unlawful arrest based upon an absence of probable cause. *Davis v. City of Charleston,* 827 F.2d 317 (8th Cir. 1987). *See also Hornung v. Village of Park Forest,* 634 F. Supp. 540 (N.D. Ill. 1986); *Adamson v. Volkmer,* 680 F. Supp. 1191 (N.D. Ill. 1987) (state law of preclusion determines if a conviction conclusively establishes probable cause for an arrest; under Illinois law, the conviction is not
* conclusive but does establish a prima facie case that probable cause did exist). A court conviction for resisting arrest and rejection of the defense of self-defense did not bar a § 1983 claim for excessive force in making the arrest because "the state court made no findings as to the amount of force used in making the arrest . . . ." *O'Leary v. Luongo,* 692 F. Supp. 893, 903 (N.D. Ill. 1988).

The Second Circuit, applying New York State law, ruled that plaintiff's conviction defeated his § 1983 unlawful arrest claim. *Cameron v. Fogarty,* 806 F.2d 380 (2d Cir. 1986), *cert. denied,* 107 S. Ct. 1894 (1987). The court did not employ a § 1738 analysis but simply imported the state law defense into the § 1983 claim. The authors believe that this is an erroneous state law intrusion of the federal § 1983 remedy.

A state court criminal defendant who obtains a favorable ruling in the state proceeding may seek to invoke offensive collateral estoppel against a federal court § 1983 defendant. See § **9.12**. In two cases, however, circuit courts found reasons for rejecting offensive collateral estoppel under the particular circumstances. In *Williams v. Kobel,* 789 F.2d 463 (7th Cir. 1986), a determination in a state court preliminary hearing, that there was no probable cause to have the suspect bound over for trial, did not preclude the federal court defendant police officers from contesting the plaintiff's claim that there was no probable cause for his arrest. Probable cause to arrest was not an issue at the preliminary hearing and the defendant officers were not parties to the state court proceeding, and thus did not have a full and fair opportunity to litigate the probable cause issue in state court. In *Kunzelman v. Thompson,* 799 F.2d 1172 (7th Cir. 1986), the court denied offensive collateral estoppel to the state court's dismissal of criminal charges because the federal court defendant officials were not parties or privies to the state criminal action and were not "sufficiently involved in the conduct of the state court litigation to actuate principles of collateral estoppel." *Id.* at 1178. *See also Gutierrez v. Coughlin,* 841 F.2d 484 (2d Cir. 1988) (decision in judicial review proceeding brought by inmate did not collaterally estop § 1983 defendant officials who could not have been personally liable in the judicial review proceeding); *Urban v. Henley,* 654 F. Supp. 870 (D. Kan. 1987) (decision in state court habeas corpus proceeding in favor of prisoner did not collaterally estop § 1983 defendants who were not parties to the habeas proceeding).

Two other cases dealt with the preclusive effect of guilty pleas. *Rodriguez v. Schweiger,* 796 F.2d 930 (7th Cir. 1986) (guilty plea collaterally estopped federal court plaintiff from claiming that police officers fired first shot; plaintiff may not collaterally attack his own guilty plea), *cert. denied,* 107 S. Ct. 1899 (1987); *Wall v. Heath,* 622 F. Supp. 105 (S.D. Miss. 1985) (guilty plea did not bar § 1983 action based upon warrantless searches).

§ 9.4 State Judicial Review Proceedings

Page 199, add at end of section:

A judgment in a state court judicial review proceeding bars a federal court § 1983 action when the state proceeding provided a full and fair opportunity to litigate federal claims. *Gargiul v. Tompkins,* 790 F.2d 265 (2d Cir. 1986); *Sharpley v. Davis,* 786 F.2d 1109 (11th Cir. 1986); *Bartel Dental Books v. Schultz,* 786 F.2d 486 (2d Cir.), *cert. denied,* 106 S. Ct. 3298 (1986); *Genova v. Southampton,* 776 F.2d 1560 (2d Cir. 1985); *Albenga v. Ward,* 635 F. Supp. 660 (S.D.N.Y. 1986). A judgment in a state judicial review proceeding will not preclude a federal court § 1983 claim when the federal plaintiff did not have a full and fair opportunity to litigate the federal claim in the judicial review proceeding. *Hill v. Coca Cola Bottling Co.,* 786 F.2d 550 (2d Cir. 1986).

In *Davidson v. Capuano,* 792 F.2d 275 (2d Cir. 1986), the court ruled that a judgment in a New York judicial review proceeding did not bar a federal court § 1983 action for damages, because it was unlikely that the damages claim could have been asserted in the judicial review proceeding. *Accord, Davis v. Halpern,* 813 F.2d 37 (2d Cir. 1987); *Giano v. Flood,* 803 F.2d 769 (2d Cir. 1986); *Fay v. South Colonie Central School District,* 802 F.2d 21 (2d Cir. 1986). *Davidson* was distinguished in *Kirkland v. City of*

Peekskill, 828 F.2d 104 (2d Cir. 1987). In that case, the court found that a determination in a judicial review proceeding barred plaintiff's § 1983 employment discrimination claim, because the state court proceeding was brought to review the determination of an agency which had power to award back pay and compensatory damages. See also § **9.9**.

* The Second Circuit, applying New York preclusion law, ruled that because the state law regards dismissal of a judicial review proceeding on limitations grounds as being sufficiently close on the merits to bar a second action, the state court dismissal barred the plaintiff's federal court § 1981 and Title VII claims. *Bray v. New York Life Insurance,* 851 F.2d 60 (2d Cir. 1988).

The Seventh Circuit, applying Illinois preclusion law, found that a determination in a state court mandamus proceeding barred a § 1983 claim for damages. *Wozniak v. DuPage County,* 845 F.2d 677 (7th Cir. 1988).

§ 9.5 Plenary Civil Actions: Claim Preclusion

Page 200, add at end of section:

In *Gargiul v. Tompkins,* 790 F.2d 265 (2d Cir. 1986), the court applied the claim preclusion principle of *Migra v. Warren City School District,* 465 U.S. 75 (1984), in a "complex setting." The court, inter alia, applied *Migra* retroactively, and ruled that a state court dismissal on limitations grounds does not deny a litigant a full and fair opportunity to be heard. *See also Kirkland v. City of Peekskill,* 828 F.2d 104 (2d Cir. 1987) (dismissal on limitations grounds is on the merits); *De Vargas v. Montoya,* 796 F.2d 1245 (10th Cir. 1986) (state court dismissal on limitations grounds precludes federal court § 1983 action when the state law regards the ruling as being on the merits). *Gargiul* also observed that "New York law generally holds that a suit against an individual in his official capacity will bar a later suit, arising out of the same
* transaction, against him in his individual capacity." 790 F.2d at 272. *See also Bray v. New York Life Insurance,* 851 F.2d 60 (2d Cir. 1988); *Lawrence v. McGuire,* 651 F. Supp. 312 (S.D.N.Y. 1987).

Under *Migra,* the preclusive effect of a ruling in a state court habeas corpus proceeding is determined by the state law of preclusion. *Coe v. Ziegler,* 657 F. Supp. 182 (S.D. Ohio 1987).

Where claimant obtained equitable relief in state court, the state court judgment barred his § 1983 federal court claim for damages. Under § 1738, state law controlled the preclusive effect of the state court judgment. *Pasterczyk v. Fair,* 819 F.2d 12 (1st Cir. 1987). *See also Wozniak v. DuPage County,* 845 F.2d 677 (7th Cir. 1988) (determination in state mandamus proceeding barred § 1983 claim for damages).

In *Gregory v. Chehi,* 843 F.2d 111 (3d Cir. 1988), a discharged police officer unsuccessfully contested his termination in a state court proceeding in which he raised only state law claims against the town and specified officials in their official capacity. His federal court § 1983 action was against these and other defendants, the officials being sued in their individual and official capacities. In the state action the issue was whether plaintiff's hearing was politically biased; in the federal action the issue was whether his discharge was politically motivated. Applying § 1738, the Third Circuit made the following rulings: (1) the fact that the relief available in state court was limited to reinstatement and back pay did not deprive the state court ruling of preclusive effect; (2) the state court judgment precluded litigation of the federal claim against the defendant town and officials in their official capacities, the judgment in favor of the town being binding as to official capacity claims even as to officials not named in the state action; and (3) issue preclusion did not apply to the claims against the officials in their individual capacities because the issues in the state and federal actions were different.

Some circuit court decisions, instead of following the § 1738 approach, simply hold that the attainment of at least some relief in state court operates as an election of remedies that bars the § 1983 claim. *Campbell v. City of Allen Park,* 829 F.2d 576 (6th Cir. 1987); *Punton v. City of Seattle,* 805 F.2d 1378 (9th Cir. 1986), *cert. denied,* 107 S. Ct. 1954 (1987). *See also Robinson v. Boyer,* 825 F.2d 64 (5th Cir. 1987) (claimant was fully compensated by state court judgment, thereby rendering it unnecessary to resolve his constitutional claims). The authors believe that there is no federal authorization for disposing of § 1983 claims in this fashion, and that the correct approach is for the federal court to utilize § 1738.

The *Migra* rule applies to state court civil defendants. *Pliska v. City of Stevens Point,* 823 F.2d 1168 (7th Cir. 1987); *Golkin v. Abrams,* 803 F.2d 55 (2d Cir. 1986).

* A state court federal constitutional law ruling in an inverse condemnation proceeding was binding in a federal court § 1983 action. *Fountain v. Metropolitan Atlanta Rapid Transit Authority,* 849 F.2d 1412 (11th Cir. 1988). The Eighth Circuit gave preclosure effect to a ruling in an eminent domain proceeding that property had been taken for a public use. *Paulucci v. City of Duluth,* 826 F.2d 780 (8th Cir. 1987).

A federal district court, in a cogent opinion, gave careful consideration to the preclusion issues that arise out of *Williamson* ripeness requirements (see **§ 3.10**). *Peduto v. North Wildword,* 696 F. Supp. 1004 (D.N.J. 1988). The court discussed, but did not resolve, whether an exception to claim preclusion should exist for state court inverse condemnation proceedings brought pursuant to *Williamson.* The court did hold that issue preclusion applies because "an exception would not be appropriate where a party actually litigated the federal issues in state court." *Id.* at 1012. For other preclusion cases in the land use context, *see Moore v. Costa Mesa,* 678 F. Supp. 1448 (C.D. Cal. 1987); *Mitchell v. Mills County,* 673 F. Supp. 332, 336 (S.D. Iowa 1987), *aff'd,* 847 F.2d 486 (8th Cir. 1988).

The Seventh Circuit analyzed "the mysteries of Illinois res judicata doctrine . . . ." *La Salle National Bank v. County of DuPage,* 856 F.2d 925, 933 (7th Cir. 1988). *See also Hagee v. City of Evanston,* 729 F.2d 510 (7th Cir. 1984).

For decisions applying the California primary rights doctrine, *see, e.g., Clark v. Yosemite Community College District,* 785 F.2d 781 (9th Cir. 1986); *Takahashi v. Board of Trustees,* 783 F.2d 848 (9th Cir.), *cert. denied,* 106 S. Ct. 2916 (1986).

§ 9.6 Preclusive Effect of State Court Judgments: Summary

Page 201, add at end of section:

A federal court should first determine whether plaintiff's claim is barred under state preclusion law and, if it is, then determine whether the plaintiff had a full and fair opportunity to litigate his or her federal claims in the state proceedings. *Gahr v. Trammel,* 796 F.2d 1063, 1066 (8th Cir. 1986).

§ 9.7 *Migra and Pennhurst II:* A Powerful Tandem

Pages 203, add at end of section:

Since an *England v. Board of Medical Examiners,* 375 U.S. 411 (1964), reservation may be utilized only following the invocation of *Pullman* abstention, one may not reserve a federal constitutional claim in a state court proceeding instituted in the first instance. *Tarpley v. Salerno,* 803 F.2d 57, 59-60 (2d Cir. 1986); *Fuller Co. v. Ramon I. Gil, Inc.,* 782 F.2d 306, 312 (1st Cir. 1986). An exception exists where the state case is filed first in anticipation of *Pullman* abstention, which is in fact invoked by the federal court. In these circumstances, the reservation may be made in state court. *Wicker v. Board of Education,* 826 F.2d 442 (6th Cir. 1987). See § **12.5**.

§ 9.8 Full and Fair Opportunity to Be Heard

Page 206, add to end of section:

For cases holding that there was a full and fair opportunity to litigate in the state court proceeding, *see Brookins v. General Motors,* 843 F.2d 879 (6th Cir. 1987) ("no progress" dismissal in state court); *Gargiul v. Tompkins,* 790 F.2d 265 (2d Cir. 1986) (fact state court ruling was on limitations grounds does not mean there was no full and fair opportunity to be heard); *Bartel Dental Books v. Schultz,* 786 F.2d 486 (2d Cir.) (failure to hold hearing does not mean there was no full and fair opportunity to be heard), *cert. denied,* 106 S. Ct. 3298 (1986). For cases finding no full and fair opportunity to litigate in state court, *see Thourner v. Meyer,* 803 F.2d 1093 (10th Cir. 1986) (one-day notice and four-day total life of state court action); *Scroggins v. Kansas,* 802 F.2d 1289, 1293 (10th Cir. 1986) (judicial review "both narrow and conclusory"); *Williams v. Kobel,* 789 F.2d 463 (7th Cir. 1986) (arresting officers not parties to state court proceeding); *Hill v. Coca Cola Bottling Co.,* 786 F.2d 550 (2d Cir. 1986) (racial discrimination claim not considered in agency proceedings that preceded judicial review).

In *Garza v. Henderson,* 779 F.2d 390 (7th Cir. 1985), a judgment in favor of a criminal defendant in a federal habeas corpus proceeding did not preclude the § 1983 defendant prison officials from contesting the issue of liability for the alleged violation of constitutional rights, because the officials were not parties to the habeas corpus proceeding. "These defendants did not have the opportunity to engage in any discovery or assert any defense that could shield them from liability." *Id.* at 394. *See also Gutierrez v. Coughlin,* 841 F.2d 484 (2d Cir. 1988); *Kunzelman v. Thompson,* 799 F.2d 1172 (7th Cir. 1986); *Williams v. Kobel,* 789 F.2d 463 (7th Cir. 1986); *Urban v. Henley,* 654 F. Supp. 870 (D. Kan. 1987).

A judgment against the city in a federal court Title VII action did not preclude a subsequent federal court action under, inter alia, § 1983 against individual police officers. While plaintiff could have joined all of her claims in the first action, she was not required to do so. Res judicata did not bar the second action because the officials individually were not parties to the first suit and were not in privity with the city. Thus, "litigation involving officials in their official capacity does not preclude relitigation in their personal capacity." *Headley v. Bacon,* 828 F.2d 1272, 1279 (8th Cir. 1987). *See also Gregory v. Chehi,* 843 F.2d 111 (3d Cir. 1988); *Gutierrez v. Coughlin,* 841 F.2d 484 (2d Cir. 1988). *But see Thurston v. United States,* 810 F.2d 438 (4th Cir. 1987).

The full and fair opportunity issue may arise when federal issues are determined in a state court criminal proceeding. In *Coogan v. City Wixom,* 820 F.2d 170 (6th Cir. 1987), the court determined that a ruling in an adversarial preliminary hearing against the accused collaterally estopped him from litigating the issue in a federal court § 1983 action, where he had an opportunity to contest the ruling and in fact did so.

> [W]e do not hold that every determination in a preliminary hearing should be given preclusive effect in a subsequent 1983 action. Some preliminary hearings are little more than formalities. Also, even when an opportunity for full adversary proceedings is afforded, strategic concerns may counsel against engaging in such an exercise at the early stages of a criminal proceeding. However, where the state affords an opportunity for an accused to contest probable cause at a preliminary hearing and the accused does so, a finding of probable cause by the examining magistrate or state judge should foreclose relitigation of that finding in a subsequent 1983 action.

Id. at 175.

There was no full and fair opportunity to litigate the federal issue in a probable cause hearing where it was ex parte, the arresting officer was not required to appear, and the criminal defendant was not allowed to present any evidence or cross-examine the state's witness. Moreover, the issue determined at the hearing, that there was probable cause to proceed with the criminal prosecution, was not the same as the § 1983 issue, i.e., probable cause to arrest. *Bailey v. Andrews,* 811 F.2d 366 (7th Cir. 1987).

§ 9.9 Preclusive Effect of Arbitration Decisions

Page 208, add at end of section:

The Seventh Circuit distinguished the Supreme Court's decision in *McDonald v. City of West Branch,* 466 U.S. 284 (1984) in *Papapetropoulous v. Milwaukee Transport Services,* 795 F.2d 591 (7th Cir. 1986). While the plaintiff in *McDonald* had a claim against the defendant employer based upon a constitutional violation independent of the arbitration process itself, no such claim was presented in the *Papapetropoulous* case, and plaintiff's claimed procedural due process deficiencies in the arbitration process were without merit. Here, plaintiff "seeks nothing but a review of the arbitrator's decision under the guise of a section 1983 action." *Id.* at 597.

§ 9.10 Preclusive Effect of Administrative Determinations

Page 211, add at end of section:

There has been a good deal of litigation involving *University of Tennessee v. Elliott,* 106 S. Ct. 3220 (1986).

For cases giving preclusive effect to administrative determinations, *see Eilrich v. Remas,* 839 F.2d 630 (9th Cir.), *cert. denied,* 109 S. Ct. 60 (1988); *Kirkland v. City of Peekskill,* 828 F.2d 104 (2d Cir. 1987); *DeCintio v. Westchester County Medical Center,* 821 F.2d 111 (2d Cir.), *cert. denied,* 108 S. Ct. 455 (1987); *Buckhalter v. Pepsi-Cola General Bottlers,* 820 F.2d 892 (7th Cir. 1987) (§ 1981 claim); *Abramson v. Council Bluffs Community School District,* 808 F.2d 1307 (8th Cir. 1987); *Yancy v. McDevitt,* 802 F.2d 1025 (8th Cir. 1986); *Derertich v. Office of Administrative Hearings,* 798 F.2d 1147 (8th Cir. 1986); *Valley Wood Preserving v. Paul,* 785 F.2d 751 (9th Cir. 1986).

For cases denying preclusive effect, *see Healy v. Town of Pembroke Park,* 831 F.2d 989 (11th Cir. 1987) (agency did not have the power to award relief sought); *Gjellum v. City of Birmingham,* 829 F.2d 1056 (11th Cir. 1987) (*Elliott* limited to issue preclusion and does not extend to issues which could have been litigated before agency); *Scroggins v. Kansas,* 802 F.2d 1289 (10th Cir. 1986) (no full and fair opportunity); *Fay v. South Colonie Central School District,* 802 F.2d 21 (2d Cir. 1986) (agency determination not * on the merits, and unclear whether agency procedures quasi-judicial); *Yates v. Philip Morris,* 690 F. Supp. 180 (S.D.N.Y. 1988) (§ 1981); *Alder v. Columbia Historical Society,* 690 F. Supp. 9 (D.D.C. 1988).

Most courts take the position that *Elliott* was intended to apply to an agency's factfinding, not legal, conclusions. *Perry v. Brakke,* 826 F.2d 740, 746 (8th Cir. 1987) ("Elliot directs that an agency's fact-finding is to be given preclusive effect in a subsequent 1983 action"); *Cook v. Board of Education,* 671 F. Supp. 1110 (S.D. W. Va. 1987); *Wool v. Maryland National Capital Park and Planning Commission,* 664 F. Supp. 225 (D. Md. 1987). In *Eilrich v. Remas,* 839 F.2d 630 (9th Cir.), *cert. denied,* 109 S. Ct. 60 (1988), however, the court read *Elliott* as not distinguishing between issues of fact and law. *Id.* at 634. The court also rejected the argument that *Elliott* is limited to *state* agency determinations, and applied administrative res judicata to a determination of a local agency.

Both parties to the agency proceedings may be bound by the agency's factual findings. *Barnes v. McDowell,* 647 F. Supp. 1307 (E.D. Ky. 1986), *aff'd in part, rev'd & remanded in part,* 848 F.2d 725 (6th Cir. 1988), *cert. denied,* 109 S. Ct. ____ (1989).

Because judicial review proceedings were pending, the court did not give preclusive effect to the agency determination. Instead it stayed the § 1983 action until completion of the judicial review proceeding. *Crot v. Byrne,* 646 F. Supp. 1245 (N.D. Ill. 1986).

§ 9.12 Miscellaneous Preclusion Issues

Page 212, add at end of Successive Federal Actions subsection:

* *Conner v. Reinhard,* 847 F.2d 384 (7th Cir.) (judgment in action against city did not preclude subsequent action against city officials in the individual capacities; under

federal law, official sued individually and city are not in privity), *cert. denied,* 109 S. Ct. 147 (1988); *Headley v. Bacon,* 828 F.2d 1272 (8th Cir. 1987) (judgment against city on Title VII claim did not preclude § 1983 claim against individual officers; see **§ 9.8**); *Smith v. Chicago,* 820 F.2d 916 (7th Cir. 1987) (denial of petition for relief under consent decree on grounds of laches and statute of limitations was on the merits and precluded civil rights action for damages based upon same grievance); *Holloway v. Lockhart,* 813 F.2d 874 (8th Cir. 1987) (findings in defendant's favor in action brought by an inmate did not bar subsequent action brought by different inmate who was neither a party nor in privity with a party to the first action); *Thurston v. United States,* 810 F.2d 438 (4th Cir. 1987) (*Bivens* action: judgment in favor of government collaterally estopped plaintiff from litigating claim against officials in their individual capacities).

* In *Conner v. Reinhard,* 847 F.2d at 384, the court drew a distinction between issue preclusion and claim preclusion. As a matter of claim preclusion, a judgment in favor of a city will not preclude an action against city officials in their individual capacities. However, issue preclusion applies to the second action because it "does not require the same mutuality of parties that is necessary for claim preclusion." *Id.* at 396.

Page 212, add at end of Federal Judgment Asserted in State Courts subsection:

See Puckett v. City of Emmelt, 113 Idaho 639, 747 P.2d 48 (1987) (federal court determination of federal issues did not preclude litigation of state claim in state court where federal court would not have exercised pendent jurisdiction over state claim); *Massengil v. Scott,* 738 S.W.2d 629 (Tenn. 1987) (federal court determination of § 1983 claim did not preclude litigation of state law claim where federal court declined pendent jurisdiction); *Peery v. Department of Agriculture,* 402 N.W.2d 695 (S.D. 1987) (a federal district court's § 1983 determination cannot be contested in state court); *Lawler v. Eugene Wuesthoff Memorial Hospital Association,* 497 So. 2d 1261 (Fla. Dist. Ct. App. 1986) (federal court judgment in civil rights action precluded state court § 1983 claim).

Page 212, add at end of section:

Offensive Collateral Estoppel. While this doctrine is potentially applicable in federal court § 1983 actions, most courts find reasons for not applying it because of the circumstances of the particular case. *Gutierrez v. Coughlin,* 841 F.2d 484 (2d Cir. 1988) (judgment in favor of inmate in judicial review proceeding did not collaterally estop officials in federal court § 1983 action because they could not have been personally liable and could not raise immunity and other personal defenses in that proceeding); *Kunzelman v. Thompson,* 799 F.2d 1172 (7th Cir. 1986) (federal court defendants neither parties nor sufficiently involved with state court proceedings); *Williams v. Kobel,* 789 F.2d 463 (7th Cir. 1986) (constitutional issue not addressed in state court proceeding and federal court defendants not parties to that proceeding); *Polk v. Montgomery County,* 782 F.2d 1196 (4th Cir. 1986) (first action was not sufficiently final; it could not be determined whether the issues in the two actions were identical, and instant plaintiff could have but did not join in final suit); *Garza v. Henderson,* 779 F.2d 390 (7th Cir. 1985) (defendants not parties to first proceeding); *Urban v. Henley,* 654 F. Supp. 870 (D. Kan. 1987) (decision in prisoner's favor in state court habeas corpus proceeding did not collaterally estop § 1983 defendants who were not parties to the habeas corpus proceeding).

Offensive collateral estoppel was applied in *Benjamin v. Coughlin,* 643 F. Supp. 351 (S.D.N.Y. 1986) (issues identical and defendant officials had a full and fair opportunity to litigate in the state court action).

CHAPTER 10

LAW APPLIED IN § 1983 ACTIONS

§ 10.2 Operation of the Interstices Statute

Page 217, add at end of section:

The Supreme Court took the position that the interstices provision in 42 U.S.C. § 1988 applies only to federal court § 1983 claims; when the application of state law to state court § 1983 claims is at issue, the question is essentially one of preemption. *Felder v. Casey,* 108 S. Ct. 2302 (1988) (see **§ 10.9**).

§ 10.4 –Accrual of Claim

Page 219, add at end of section:

Reversing its prior decisions, the Tenth Circuit now holds "that federal law controls questions relating to accrual of federal causes of action." *Newcomb v. Ingle,* 827 F.2d 675, 678 (10th Cir. 1987). *Accord, Mullinax v. McElhenney,* 817 F.2d 711, 716 (11th Cir. 1987). *But see Glover v. Johnson,* 831 F.2d 99 (5th Cir. 1987) (citing state law as governing accrual issue).

In a *Bivens* action, the court ruled that claims brought under the Fourth and Fifth Amendments for unreasonable searches and seizures and the deprivation of property without due process of law accrue when the property is seized. The fact that defendants retained the property does not extend the accrual date on a damages claim, because the retention is merely a consequence of the seizure. *Shannon v. Recording Industry Association,* 661 F. Supp. 205 (S.D. Ohio 1987).

A claim for malicious prosecution does not accrue until the allegedly malicious action is terminated in favor of the federal court plaintiff. *McCune v. Grand Rapids,* 842 F.2d 903 (6th Cir. 1988); *Rohena Encarnacion v. Department of Treasury,* 665 F. Supp. 102 (D.P.R. 1987).

A claim for wrongful arrest accrues at the time of the arrest rather than upon reversal of a conviction. *McCune v. Grand Rapids, supra; Davis v. Harvey,* 789 F.2d 1332 (9th Cir. 1986). In *McCune,* the court determined that the wrongful incarceration following the false arrest "constitutes an ill effect from the original false arrest" and is thus "not independently actionable." 842 F.2d at 907. Recognizing that federal law determines the accrual date, the Ninth Circuit ruled that a cause of action in inverse condemnation accrues when the governmental authorities have made a final determination as to the status of the property. *Norco Construction v. King County,* 801 F.2d 1143 (9th Cir. 1986). *See also McMillan v. Goleta Water District,* 792 F.2d 1453 (9th Cir. 1986) (claim for just compensation accrues when state makes final decision on claim), *cert. denied,* 107 S. Ct. 1348 (1987).

Plaintiff, a probationary teacher, claimed he was retaliated against for bringing Title IX grievances. The retaliation, he alleged, consisted of negative teacher evaluations, and denial of tenure. The statute of limitations accrued when the negative evaluations occurred and when tenure was denied. "[T]he two 'not effective' evaluations and the denial of tenure are more properly considered two separate retaliatory acts than cause and effect." *Lendo v. Garret County Board of Education,* 820 F.2d 1365, 1367 (4th Cir. 1987).

Since a cause of action for conspiracy accrues "in accordance with the last overt act doctrine," "the cause of action runs separately from each overt act that is alleged to cause damage to the plaintiff." *Gibson v. United States,* 781 F.2d 1334, 1340 (9th Cir. 1986), *cert. denied,* 107 S. Ct. 928 (1987). *Accord, Scherer v. Balkema,* 840 F.2d 437 (7th Cir.), *cert. denied,* 108 S. Ct. 2035 (1988); *Helton v. Clements,* 832 F.2d 332, 335 (5th Cir. 1987) ("the actionable civil injury to a plaintiff results from the overt acts of the defendants, not from the mere continuation of a conspiracy . . . . Therefore, any cause of action against the defendants accrued as soon as plaintiff knew or should have known of the overt acts involved in the alleged conspiracy"); *Jones v. Coughlin,* 665 F. Supp. 1040 (S.D.N.Y. 1987). In *Scherer v. Balkema,* 840 F.2d 437 (7th Cir. 1988), the Seventh Circuit determined that, since the cause of action runs separately from each overt act alleged to cause injury, it follows that while the injury must be within the limitations period the agreement need not be within it. The fact that the agreement is not within the limitations period does not prevent the court from determining whether an agreement existed.

False arrest, malicious prosecution, and the wrongful suppression of exculpatory evidence are discrete wrongs rather than continuing violations. The accrual date must thus be determined for each of these wrongs. As indicated above, the false arrest claim accrues on the date of arrest and the malicious prosecution claim upon favorable termination of the criminal proceeding. There was no injury from the suppression of exculpatory evidence because the criminal proceeding terminated in plaintiff's favor. *McCune v. Grand Rapids,* 842 F.2d 903 (6th Cir. 1988). For cases dealing with continuing violations, *see DeLeon Otero v. Rubero,* 820 F.2d 18 (1st Cir. 1987); *Selzer v. Board of Education,* 113 F.R.D. 165 (S.D.N.Y. 1986); *Jackson v. Galan,* 631 F. Supp. 409 (E.D. La. 1986); *Storey v. United States,* 629 F. Supp. 1174 (N.D. Miss. 1986).

Since Rule 3 of the Federal Rules of Civil Procedure determines when a § 1983 action is commenced for limitations purposes, there is no deficiency in the federal law and thus no need to turn to state law. *Martin v. Demma,* 831 F.2d 69 (5th Cir. 1987); *Del Raine v. Carlson,* 826 F.2d 698, 706-07 (7th Cir. 1987). The Supreme Court's decision in *West v. Conrail,* 107 S. Ct. 1538 (1987), substantiates that conclusion. *Del Raine v. Carlson,* 826 F.2d at 706 (decision in *Checki v. Webb,* 785 F.2d 534, 537 (5th Cir. 1986), which relied upon state law to determine commencement, is a "dubious exception" in light of *West*); *Martin v. Demma,* 831 F.2d 698 (7th Cir. 1987). In *West,* brought under the Railway Labor Act, the Supreme Court broadly stated that

> when the underlying cause of action is based on federal law and the absence of an express federal statute of limitations makes it necessary to borrow a limitations period from another statute, the action is not barred if it has been "commenced" in compliance with Rule 3 [of the Federal Rules of Civil Procedure] within the borrowing period.

107 S. Ct. at 1541. "[W]hen it is necessary for us to borrow a statute of limitations for a federal cause of action, we borrow no more than necessary." *Id.* at 1542.

* A federal district court set forth two basic federal accrual rules: (1) under the "discovery rule," the claim accrues when the "plaintiff becomes aware, of both the fact of injury and its causal connection to the defendant, although the plaintiff need not know that the defendant's conduct is tortious or unlawful," and (2) the "active concealment of a defendant tolls the running of the statute until a plaintiff discovers the cause of action or discovers facts that reasonably put her on notice of it." *Sowers v. Bradford Area School District,* 694 F. Supp. 125, 136, 136 n.12 (W.D. Pa. 1988).

§ 10.6 –The Aftermath of *Wilson v. Garcia*

Page 224, add at end of section:

A large number of decisions deal with the application of the Supreme Court's decision in *Wilson v. Garcia,* 471 U.S. 261 (1985), which requires selection of the state personal injury limitations period. The following is a state-by-state summary of the litigation to date.

State	Limitations Period in Years	Leading Decisions
Alabama	6	*Preuit & Mauldin v. Jones,* 763 F.2d 1250 (11th Cir. 1985), *cert. denied,* 106 S. Ct. 893 (1986)
Alaska	2	*Jenkins v. Daniels,* 751 P.2d 19 (Alaska 1988)
Arizona	2	*DeLuna v. Farris,* 841 F.2d 312 (9th Cir. 1988); *Marks v. Parla,* 785 F.2d 1419 (9th Cir. 1986); *Rivera v. Green,* 775 F.2d 1381 (9th Cir. 1985), *cert. denied,* 475 U.S. 1128 (1986)
Arkansas	3	*Williams v. Hartje,* 827 F.2d 1203 (8th Cir. 1987)
California	1	*Usher v. Los Angeles,* 828 F.2d 556 (9th Cir. 1987); *McMillan v. Goleta Water District,* 792 F.2d 1453 (9th Cir. 1986), *cert. denied,* 107 S. Ct. 1348 (1987); *Gibson v. United States,* 781 F.2d 1334 (9th Cir. 1986), *cert. denied,* 107 S. Ct. 928 (1987)

State	Limitations Period in Years	Leading Decisions
Colorado	2	*Arko v. United States Air Force Reserve Officer Training Program,* 661 F. Supp. 31 (D. Colo. 1987)
Connecticut	2	*See LaCroix v. Board of Education,* 844 F.2d 88 (2d Cir. 1988) (not resolving whether period is three-year intentional tort period or two-year other personal injury period)
Delaware	2	*Carter v. Three Unknown Police Officers*, 112 F.R.D. 48 (D. Del. 1986); *Vanaman v. Palmer,* 506 A.2d 190 (Del. 1986)
* District of Columbia	3	*Banks v. Chesapeake and Potomac Telephone Co.,* 802 F.2d 1416 (D.C. Cir. 1986) (§ 1981); *Alder v. Columbia Historical Society,* 690 F. Supp. 9 (D.D.C. 1988); *Greenfield v. District of Columbia,* 623 F. Supp. 47 (D.D.C. 1985)
* Florida	4	*Baker v. Gulf & Western Industries,* 850 F.2d 1480 (11th Cir. 1988) (§ 1981)
* Georgia	2	*Giles v. Garwood,* 853 F.2d 876 (11th Cir. 1988); *Mullinax v. McElhenney,* 817 F.2d 711, 716 n.2 (11th Cir. 1987); *Williams v. Atlanta,* 794 F.2d 624 (11th Cir. 1986)
Guam	2	*Ngiraingas v. Sanchez,* 858 F.2d 1368 (9th Cir. 1988) (though applying pre-*Wilson* three-year period)
Idaho	2	*Henderson v. Idaho,* 110 Idaho 318, 715 P.2d 978, *cert. denied,* 106 S. Ct. 3282 (1986)
Illinois	2	*Anton v. Lehpamer,* 787 F.2d 1141 (7th Cir. 1986)
Indiana	2	*Dugan v. Ball State University,* 815 F.2d 1132 (7th Cir. 1987); *Loy v. Clamme,* 804 F.2d 405 (7th Cir. 1986)

State	Limitations Period in Years	Leading Decisions
Iowa	2	*Dautremont v. Broadlawns Hospital,* 827 F.2d 291 (8th Cir. 1987); *Ridgway v. Wapello County,* 795 F.2d 646 (8th Cir. 1986); *Wycoff v. Menke,* 773 F.2d 983 (8th Cir. 1985)
Kansas	2	*Derstein v. Van Buren,* 828 F.2d 653 (10th Cir. 1987); *Newcomb v. Ingle,* 827 F.2d 675 (10th Cir. 1987)
Kentucky	1	*Bass v. NKC,* 644 F. Supp. 24 (W.D. Ky. 1985); *Frisby v. Board of Education,* 707 S.W.2d 359 (Ky. Ct. App. 1986). *See also McSurely v. Hutchinson,* 823 F.2d 1002 (6th Cir. 1987) (*Bivens* action applying *Wilson v. Garcia*), *cert. denied,* 108 S. Ct. 1107 (1988)
* Louisiana	1	*Freeze v. Giffith,* 849 F.2d 172 (5th Cir. 1988); *Auster Oil & Gas v. Stream,* 835 F.2d 597 (5th Cir.), *cert. denied,* 108 S. Ct. 2007 (1988); *St. Amant v. Benoit,* 806 F.2d 1294, 1296 n.1 (5th Cir. 1987); *Washington v. Breaux,* 782 F.2d 553 (5th Cir. 1986)
Maine	6	*Small v. Inhabitants of Belfast,* 796 F.2d 544 (1st Cir. 1986)
Maryland	3	*Jones v. Frederick County Board of Education,* 689 F. Supp. 535 (D. Md. 1988)
Massachusetts	3	*Roberts v. Murphy,* 684 F. Supp. 759 (D. Mass. 1988)
Michigan	3	*McCune v. Grand Rapids,* 842 F.2d 903 (6th Cir. 1988); *Carroll v. Wilkerson,* 782 F.2d 44 (6th Cir.) *cert. denied,* 107 S. Ct. 330 (1986)
Minnesota	6	*Jane Does 1-100 v. Omodt,* 813 F.2d 910 (8th Cir. 1987)
Mississippi	1	*Shelby v. McAdory,* 781 F.2d 1053 (5th Cir. 1986); *Gates v. Spinks,* 771 F.2d 916 (5th Cir. 1985), *cert. denied,* 106 S. Ct. 1378 (1986)

	State	Limitations Period in Years	Leading Decisions
	Missouri	5	*Chandler v. Presiding Judge,* 838 F.2d 977 (8th Cir. 1988)
*	Nebraska	4	*Bridgeman v. Nebraska State Penn,* 849 F.2d 1076 (8th Cir. 1988)
	New Jersey	2	*Craig v. Ewing Township,* 678 F. Supp. 1106 (D.N.J. 1988); *Plain* v. *Flicker,* 645 F. Supp. 898 (D.N.J. 1986)
	New Mexico	2	*Walker v. Maruffi,* 106 N.M. 763, 737 P.2d 544 (Ct. App. 1987)
*	New York	3	*Owens v. Okure,* 109 S. Ct. 573 (1989); *423 South Salina Street, Inc. v. Syracuse*, 68 N.Y.2d 474, 503 N.E.2d 63, 510 N.Y.S.2d 507, *appeal dismissed,* 107 S. Ct. 1880 (1987)
*	North Dakota	2	*Kessel v. Schaff,* 697 F. Supp. 1102 (D.N.D. 1987)
	Ohio	1	*Vodila v. Clelland,* 836 F.2d 231 (6th Cir. 1987); *Thomas v. Shipka,* 818 F.2d 496 (6th Cir.), *on reh'g,* 829 F.2d 570 (6th Cir. 1987); *Jones v. Shankland,* 800 F.2d 77, (6th Cir. 1986); *cert. denied*, 107 S. Ct. 2177 (1987); *Mulligan v. Hazard,* 777 F.2d 340 (6th Cir. 1985) *cert. denied,* 106 S. Ct. 2902 (1986)
	Oklahoma	2	*Meade v. Grubbs,* 841 F.2d 1512 (10th Cir. 1988)
*	Oregon	2	*Davis v. Harvey,* 789 F.2d 1332 (9th Cir. 1986); *Sanok v. Grimes,* 306 Or. 259, 760 P.2d 228 (1988)
	Pennsylvania	2	*Bartholomew v. Fischl,* 782 F.2d 1148 (3d Cir. 1986); *Fitzgerald v. Larson,* 769 F.2d 160 (3d Cir. 1985); *Smith v. Pittsburgh,* 764 F.2d 188 (3d Cir.), *cert. denied,* 106 S. Ct. 349 (1985); *Knoll v. Springfield Township School District*, 763 F.2d 584 (3d Cir. 1985)
	Puerto Rico	1	*De Leon Otero v. Rubero,* 820 F.2d 18 (1st Cir. 1987)

	State	Limitations Period in Years	Leading Decisions
	South Dakota	3	*Hughes v. Sheriff,* 814 F.2d 532, 533 n.1 (8th Cir.), *appeal dismissed & cert. denied,* 108 S. Ct. 46 (1987); *Nichols v. Rysavy,* 809 F.2d 1317, 1334 n.19 (8th Cir.), *cert. denied,* 108 S. Ct. 147 (1987)
	Tennessee	1	*Bendt v. Tennessee,* 796 F.2d 879 (6th Cir. 1986)
	Texas	2	*Helton v. Clements,* 832 F.2d 332 (5th Cir. 1987); *Glover v. Johnson,* 831 F.2d 99 (5th Cir. 1987); *see also Price v. Digital Equipment Corp.,* 846 F.2d 1026 (5th Cir. 1988)
	Utah	4	*Maddocks v. Salt Lake City Corp.,* 740 P.2d 1337 (Utah 1987)
*	Washington	3	*Continental Life Insurance Co. v. Pierce County,* 690 F. Supp. 930 (W.D. Wash. 1987)
*	West Virginia	2	*Sattler v. Johnson,* 857 F.2d 224 (4th Cir. 1988); *Rodgers v. Corporation of Harpers Ferry,* 371 S.E.2d 358 (W.Va. 1988)
*	Wisconsin	3	*Ratzel v. Marinette County,* 694 F. Supp. 606 (E.D. Wis. 1988) (three years); *Hanson v. Madison Service Corp.,* 125 Wis. 2d 138, 370 N.W.2d 586 (Ct. App. 1985) (three years).

* Following the decision in *Wilson v. Garcia,* the lower federal courts experienced difficulties in resolving the limitations issue for states which have multiple personal injury limitations periods. The Supreme Court recently ended the confusion. In *Owens v. Okure,* 109 S. Ct. 573 (1989), the Court unanimously ruled that "where state law provides multiple statutes of limitations for personal injury actions, courts considering § 1983 claims should borrow the general or residual statute for personal injury actions." 109 S. Ct. at 582. The limitations period for intentional torts is "manifestly inappropriate." The decision in *Owens* should add certainty because "[i]n marked contrast to the multiplicity of state intentional tort statutes of limitations, every state has one general or residual statute of limitations governing personal injury actions." *Id.* at 580.

The authors point out that prior precedents establishing limitation periods in states with more than one personal injury period should be reevaluated in light of the decision in *Owens*. *See, e.g., Mulligan v. Hazard,* 777 F.2d 340 (6th Cir. 1985), *cert. denied,* 106 S. Ct. 2902 (1986) (Ohio: selection of intentional tort period over period for bodily injury); *Gates v. Spinks,* 771 F.2d 916 (5th Cir. 1985), *cert. denied,* 106 S. Ct. 1378 (1986) (Mississippi: selection of intentional tort period over residual period); *Jones v. Preuit & Mauldin,* 763 F.2d 1250 (11th Cir. 1985), *cert. denied,* 106 S. Ct. 893 (1986) (Alabama: selection of intentional tort period over residual period).

Dicta in *Felder v. Casey,* 108 S. Ct. 2302, 2307 (1988), says that state limitations periods which provide "only a truncated period of time within which to file suit" conflict with the policies of § 1983, citing *Burnett v. Grattan,* 468 U.S. 42 (1984). Justice White's concurring opinion observes that "[i]t has since been assumed that *Wilson v. Garcia* governs the timeliness of section 1983 suits brought in state as well as federal court." *Felder v. Casey,* 108 S. Ct. at 2315 (White, J. concurring) (collecting numerous state court cases).

§ 10.7 –Retroactivity of *Wilson v. Garcia*

Page 225, add at end of section:

For circuit court cases applying *Wilson v. Garcia,* 471 U.S. 261 (1985), retroactively * so as to defeat the § 1983 claim, *see Baker v. Gulf & Western Industries,* 850 F.2d 1480 (11th Cir. 1988); *Bridgeman v. Nebraska State Penn,* 849 F.2d 1076 (8th Cir. 1988); *Vodila v. Clelland,* 836 F.2d 231 (6th Cir. 1987); *Thomas v. Shipka,* 829 F.2d 570 (6th Cir. 1987); *Dautremont v. Broadlawns Hospital,* 827 F.2d 291 (8th Cir. 1987) (*Wilson* applied retroactively to one claim though not another); *Mullinax v. McElhenney,* 817 F.2d 711, 716 n.2 (11th Cir. 1987); *Jones v. Shankland,* 800 F.2d 77 (6th Cir. 1986); *Williams v. Atlanta,* 794 F.2d 624 (11th Cir. 1986); *Bartholomew v. Fischl,* 782 F.2d 1148 (3d Cir. 1986); *Mulligan v. Hazard,* 777 F.2d 340 (6th Cir. 1985), *cert. denied,* 106 S. Ct. 2902 (1986).

As noted on page 225, note 91 of the text, at times *Wilson* is applied retroactively to allow for the assertion of a § 1983 claim that would otherwise be time-barred. *See Rowlett v. Anheuser-Busch,* 832 F.2d 194 (1st Cir. 1987); *Small v. Inhabitants of Belfast,* 796 F.2d 544, 549 n.6 (1st Cir. 1986); *Farmer v. Cook,* 782 F.2d 780 (8th Cir. 1986). *Wilson* was denied retroactive effect in *Derstein v. Van Buren,* 828 F.2d 653 (10th Cir. 1987); *Eades v. Thompson,* 823 F.2d 1055 (7th Cir. 1987); *Young v. Biggers,* 820 F.2d 727 (5th Cir. 1987); *Jane Does 1-100 v. Omodt,* 813 F.2d 910 (8th Cir. 1987); *Brown v. Foley,* 810 F.2d 55 (3d Cir. 1987); *Pratt v. Thornburgh,* 807 F.2d 355 (3d Cir. 1986), *cert. denied,* 108 S. Ct. 125 (1987); *Ridgway v. Wapello County,* 795 F.2d 646 (8th Cir. 1986); *Gibson v. United States,* 781 F.2d 1334 (9th Cir. 1986), *cert. denied,* 107 S. Ct. 928 (1987).

Because the pre-*Wilson* period was five years but the *Wilson* period is two years, the Seventh Circuit required that the case be commenced "within the shorter period of either five years from the date his action accrued or two years after *Wilson*." *Anton v. Lehpamer,* 787 F.2d 1141, 1146 (7th Cir. 1986). *See also Karim-Panahi v. Los Angeles*

Police Department, 839 F.2d 621 (9th Cir. 1988); *Hanner v. Mississippi,* 833 F.2d 55 (5th Cir. 1987); *Usher v. Los Angeles,* 828 F.2d 556 (9th Cir. 1987); *Dugan v. Ball State University,* 815 F.2d 1132 (7th Cir. 1987); *Loy v. Clamme,* 804 F.2d 405 (7th Cir. 1986).

Applying the *Chevron Oil Co. v. Huson,* 404 U.S. 97 (1971), factors in a 42 U.S.C. § 1981 case, the United States Supreme Court upheld a determination that *Wilson* not be applied retroactively. *Saint Francis College v. Al-Khazraji,* 107 S. Ct. 2022 (1987). A decision specifying a new limitations period should be applied only prospectively where "it overruled clearly established circuit precedent on which a complaining party was entitled to rely," "retroactive application would be inconsistent with the purpose of the substantive statute," and where retroactive "application would be manifestly inequitable." *Id.* at 2025-26. *Cf. Goodman v. Lukens Steel Co.,* 107 S. Ct. 2617 (1987) (§ 1981; limitations period applied retroactively where there was no clear precedent upon which plaintiffs could have relied).

§ 10.8 —Tolling Limitations Periods

Page 227, add before Class Actions subsection:

A state tolling rule which tolls the limitations period for those who are imprisoned but not for "federal civil rights cases" may not be applied to § 1983 claims, because it discriminates against § 1983 claimants. The fact that a state need not provide for tolling during imprisonment "does not mean that a state may provide tolling for state claims but refuse to do so for analogous federal claims and have this discrimination incorporated as federal law." *Hughes v. Sheriff,* 814 F.2d 532, 535 (8th Cir.), *appeal dismissed & cert. denied,* 108 S. Ct. 46 (1987). The court applied the state tolling rule free of the discriminatory provision.

The Sixth Circuit ruled that a state statute which in effect tolled prisoners' claims during their incarceration and allowed suit to be brought within one year after release is in conflict with the policies of § 1983, because imprisonment does not disable prisoners from bringing § 1983 actions and "application of a lengthy tolling period is clearly counterproductive to sound federal policy in attempting to deal with § 1983 claims as promptly as practicable." *Higley v. Michigan Department of Corrections,* 835 F.2d 623, 626-27 (6th Cir. 1987). *See also Mangels v. City of Orange,* 678 F. Supp. 1452 (C.D. Cal. 1988); *Perotti v. Carty,* 647 F. Supp. 39 (S.D. Ohio 1986), *aff'd,* 848 F.2d 193 (6th Cir. 1988). *But see Lagon v. Barry,* 658 F. Supp. 55 (D.D.C. 1987) (state rule providing for tolling during imprisonment is not inconsistent with § 1983 because prisoners are burdened by lack of counsel of their choice and inability to assist fully in
* gathering evidence). The Sixth Circuit subsequently adhered to *Higley* in a case in which the Supreme Court granted certiorari. *Hardin v. Straub,* 836 F.2d 549 (6th Cir. 1987) (full opinion on LEXIS), *cert. granted,* 109 S. Ct. 217 (1988).

Since exhaustion of administrative remedies is not a prerequisite for filing suit under § 1983, the limitations period is not tolled during plaintiff's voluntary pursuit of his or her administrative remedies. *Black v. Broward Employment and Training Administra-*
* *tion,* 846 F.2d 1311 (11th Cir. 1988).

Page 228, add at end of Class Actions subsection:

The federal court adopted a state tolling rule, which embraced the federal tolling principle of *American Pipe and Construction Co.,* discussed on page 227 of the text. Applying this state rule, the court found that the limitations period on a federal court § 1983 claim was tolled for unnamed class members during the pendency of a state court class action, even though the state and federal actions were litigated on the basis of separate legal theories, where the asserted factual bases of the state and federal claims were the same. *Cullen v. Margiotta,* 811 F.2d 698 (2d Cir.), *cert. denied,* 107 S. Ct. 3226 (1987).

Since there is no federal rule governing tolling for voluntarily dismissed federal suits, the court adopted the applicable state tolling provision. *Flores v. Chicago,* 682 F. Supp. 950 (N.D. Ill. 1988).

§ 10.9 –Notice of Claim Provisions

Page 229, add at end of section:

In *Felder v. Casey,* 108 S. Ct. 2302 (1988), the Supreme Court, by a seven-to-two vote, determined that state notice of claim requirements may not be applied to state court § 1983 claims. Viewing the question as essentially one of preemption, the court found that state notice of claim rules conflict with the remedial and deterrent purposes of § 1983 claims by burdening the assertion of these claims and discriminating against them.

In reaching this conclusion, the court expressed full agreement with the "near unanimous consensus" of lower federal court decisions, most notably *Brown v. United States,* 742 F.2d 1498 (D.C. Cir. 1984) (en banc), *cert. denied,* 471 U.S. 1073 (1985), holding that state notice of claim provisions do not apply to federal court § 1983 claims. While these decisions are not dispositive with respect to state court § 1983 claims, their reasoning is instructive with respect to these claims.

Felder found that a state notice of claim requirement imposes preconditions upon § 1983 claimants not authorized by § 1983. This burden is not the neutral result of an otherwise uniformly applicable state law, but applies only to claims brought against governmental defendants, the precise claims created by Congress. Notice of claim requirements thus stand in stark contrast to state service of process and substitution of party rules.

The notice of claim provision also imposes an exhaustion of state remedies requirement which is inconsistent with the no-exhaustion rule of *Patsy v. Board of Regents,* 457 U.S. 496 (1982). Congress did not contemplate "that those who sought to vindicate their federal rights in state courts could be required to seek redress in the first instance from the very state officials whose hostility to those rights precipitated their injuries." Felder, 108 S. Ct. at 2311. The states "may not adulterate or dilute the predominant feature of the federal right by imposing mandatory settlement periods. *Id.* at 2312.

The court also applied a type of reverse *Erie* principle, pursuant to which state courts may not refuse to hear otherwise properly presented federal claims by imposing substantive conditions upon the assertion of those claims. "State courts simply are not free to vindicate the substantive interests underlying a state rule of decision at the expense of the federal right." *Id.* at 2314.

In sum, since Congress intended that § 1983 would enable those deprived of their civil rights to obtain full compensation from the responsible governmental officials,

> [a] state law that conditions that right of recovery upon compliance with a rule designed to minimize governmental liability, and that directs injured persons to seek redress in the first instance from the very targets of the federal legislation, is inconsistent in both purpose and effect with the remedial objectives of the federal civil rights law.

Id. at 2314.

Felder recognizes that federal courts entertaining state law claims are obligated to
* apply the state's notice-of-claim rules. 108 S. Ct. at 2313. *See also Courtemanche v. Enlarged City School District,* 686 F. Supp. 1025, 1032 (S.D.N.Y. 1988); *Piesco v. City of New York,* 650 F. Supp. 896 (S.D.N.Y. 1987).

* In *Piesco v. City of New York,* 693 F. Supp. 86, 87 n.1 (S.D.N.Y. 1988), the court rejected the argument that only a state court can grant leave to file a late notice of claim; the federal court may hear the application when this is the forum in which the state law claim is asserted.

CHAPTER 11

SURVIVORSHIP, WRONGFUL DEATH, AND SUCCESSOR OFFICIALS

§ 11.2 Survivorship of Claim

Page 236, add at end of section:

In an important decision, the Seventh Circuit followed *Bell v. City of Milwaukee,* 746 F.2d 1205 (7th Cir. 1984), and *Bass v. Wallenstein,* 769 F.2d 1173 (7th Cir. 1985), in allowing the decedent's estate to recover not only for the economic loss suffered by decedent but also for the intrinsic value of decedent's life itself. The court also upheld the district court's ruling allowing an economist to testify to the "hedonic value" of * human life. *Sherrod v. Berry,* 827 F.2d 195 (7th Cir. 1987). The panel opinion, however, was subsequently vacated, the case was set for rehearing en banc (835 F.2d 1222 (1988)), and upon rehearing, the en banc court reversed the judgment of the district court on evidentiary grounds. *Sherrod v. Berry,* 856 F.2d 802 (7th Cir. 1988) (en banc) (see discussion in § 3.4).

The Eighth Circuit held that the fact that Arkansas law abated plaintiff's § 1983 cause of action upon his death did not render the state law inconsistent with § 1983's policies of deterrence and compensation. *Parkerson v. Carrouth,* 782 F.2d 1449 (8th Cir. 1986). Since plaintiff was "suing merely as executrix of her husband's estate . . . for this Court to override Arkansas law by mandating survival of this action would not further the section 1983 goal of compensating those injured by civil rights violations." *Id.* at 1455. The authors believe that the court's approach is inconsistent with the mandate of *Robertson v. Wegmann,* 436 U.S. 584 (1978), that the federal court determine whether the state law generally is hospitable to the survival of § 1983 claims. Under the Eighth Circuit's approach, abatement of plaintiff's claim would never be inconsistent with § 1983, except perhaps when the defendant's allegedly illegal behavior caused plaintiff's death.

§ 11.3 Wrongful Death Claims

Page 240, add at end of section:

The First Circuit determined that stepparents and siblings were not deprived of their federally protected constitutional rights by the loss of companionship of their adult son and brother who was allegedly beaten to death by prison guards:

> We decline, on this record, to make the leap ourselves from the realm of governmental action directly aimed at the relationship between a parent and a young child to an incidental deprivation of the relationship between appellants and their adult relative . . . . Although distinguished courts have taken such a step, their cases have involved at least one legal parent, who arguably has the strongest claim for a constitutional remedy in these circumstances. We have before us a stepfather and siblings.

Ortiz v. Burgos, 807 F.2d 6, 9 (1st Cir. 1986).

The Seventh Circuit reaffirmed its rulings in *Bell v. City of Milwaukee,* 746 F.2d 1205 (7th Cir. 1984), and *Bass v. Wallenstein,* 769 F.2d 1173 (7th Cir. 1985), that a police officer's causing the death of a child may violate the due process clause's protection of the parent-child relationship. The court distinguished the Tenth Circuit's decision in *Trujillo v. Board of County Commissioners,* 768 F.2d 1186 (10th Cir. 1985), discussed on page 240 of the text, which requires a specific intent to sever the protected relationship, as based upon a First Amendment right of parental association. By contrast, the due process clause does not require specific intent. *Sherrod v. Berry,* 827 F.2d 195 (7th Cir. 1987). The court in *Sherrod* originally upheld an award of damages, for the death of plaintiff's 19-year-old son, on the survival claim, of $850,000 for the value of the life of the deceased and $300,000 for the pecuniary loss to the estate; $1,700 funeral expenses; and, on the wrongful death claim, $450,000 for the loss of parental rights. However, after vacating the panel opinion and setting the case for en banc review (835 F.2d 1222 (1988)), the en banc court reversed the judgment of the district court on evidentiary grounds. *Sherrod v. Berry,* 856 F.2d 802 (7th Cir. 1988) (en banc) (see discussion in § **3.4**).

In another Seventh Circuit case, the court determined that the plaintiff parents had no standing to seek damages under § 1983 for the injuries sustained by their deceased child. Their complaint "did not plead any individual injuries but only sought recovery for injuries sustained by the decedent." In other words, this was a potential survival claim that belonged to decedent's estate. *Estate of Johnson v. Village of Libertyville,* 819 F.2d 174, 177-78 (7th Cir. 1987).

The Eighth Circuit ruled that the plaintiff grandmother did not suffer a deprivation of constitutional rights as a result of the alleged wrongful behavior of the Department of Human Services in causing the death of her grandchildren.

> We do not believe that the drafters of the Fourteenth Amendment intended to protect from government interference every conceivable family relationship, no matter how far removed. Further, it is illogical to believe that federal law requires that money be paid to a grandmother whose grandchild is injured by the state. Protecting familial relationships does not necessarily encompass relatives who suffer as a result of wrongful state conduct, especially when the loss is an individual result of that conduct.

Harpole v. Arkansas Department of Human Services, 820 F.2d 923, 928 (8th Cir. 1987).

The Ninth Circuit found that the plaintiffs (minor and adult children) did not have standing to maintain a Fourth Amendment cause of action for the alleged use of excessive force that led to the death of plaintiffs' father. "The children were not directly subjected to the excessive use of state force and therefore cannot maintain personal causes of action under section 1983 in reliance on this Fourth Amendment theory." *Smith v. City of Fontana,* 818 F.2d 1411, 1417 (9th Cir. 1987). However, both the minor and adult plaintiff children could assert a substantive due process claim based upon the violation of their own right to the continuation of their relationship with their father. This relationship is "a cognizable liberty interest" and "the state has no legitimate interest in interfering with this liberty interest through the use of *excessive* force by police officers." *Id.* at 1420 (emphasis in original). The court declined to follow the Tenth Circuit's specific intent requirement imposed by *Trujillo v. Board of County Commissioners,* 786 F.2d 1186 (10th Cir. 1985).

A federal district court ruled that illegitimate children could sue under § 1983 for the loss from the death of their father. The federal court's exercise of jurisdiction to determine whether the deceased was the father of the children did not constitute an impermissible finding of paternity but was incidental to the court's power to decide the § 1983 claim. *Greene v. City of New York,* 675 F. Supp. 110, 115 (S.D.N.Y. 1987). In dicta, the court opined that to bar children recovery because they were born out of wedlock would conflict with the compensatory and deterrence policies underlying § 1983. The court also held that damages for the wrongful death claim are measured by state law, which in this case was found to be consistent with § 1983. *Id. See also Sharpe v. City of Lewisburg,* 677 F. Supp. 1362 (M.D. Tenn. 1988) (relying upon state law for conclusion that damages for wrongful death may include loss of society and companionship).

* A federal district court in Pennsylvania read *Estate of Bailey v. County of York,* 768 F.2d 503 (3d Cir. 1985), as allowing parents to sue for the wrongful death of an adult married child when there was a close relationship between them. The court also ruled that state law may not limit the damages recoverable for a constitutional violation. *Agresta v. Sambor,* 687 F. Supp. 162 (E.D. Pa. 1988).

Whether the assertion of a § 1983 wrongful death claim extinguishes a pendent state wrongful death claim depends upon the interpretation of the state wrongful death statute. In this case the federal district court interpreted the state law as not extinguishing the state wrongful death claim. *Miltier v. Beorn,* 696 F. Supp. 1086 (E.D. Va. 1988).

Dicta in *Felder v. Casey,* 108 S. Ct. 2302 (1988), says that state statutory limits on monetary recovery are preempted by § 1983 because "partial immunities inconsistent with section 1983 must yield to the federal right." *Id.* at 2309. If accepted, this would substantiate the conclusion that state limits on wrongful death recovery may not be applied to § 1983 claims.

§ 11.4 Successor Officials

Page 242, add at end of section:

Referring to Fed. R. Civ. P. 25(d)(1) and Fed. R. App. P. 43(c)(i), the Supreme Court observed that these "rules effectuating automatic substitution of public officers were specifically designed to prevent suits involving public officers from becoming moot due to personnel changes." *Karcher v. May,* 108 S. Ct. 388, 395 (1987). In this case, however, while the case did not become unreviewable because the officials left office, the "controversy ended when the losing party – the New Jersey Legislature – declined to pursue its appeal." *Id.*

A newly developed successor town may be liable for prospective injunctive relief when there are findings that the successor will continue the predecessor's practices. *Lodestar Company v. County of Mono,* 639 F. Supp. 1439 (E.D. Cal. 1986).

CHAPTER 12

THE ABSTENTION DOCTRINES

§ 12.1 Introduction

Page 244, add at end of section:

At times, courts appear to combine abstention doctrines, and do not spell out which branch they are relying upon. In *Fields v. Rockdale County,* 785 F.2d 1558 (11th Cir.), *cert. denied,* 107 S. Ct. 571 (1987), the court relied upon aspects of *Pullman, Burford,* * and *Colorado River* abstention. *See also Franza v. Abrams,* 695 F. Supp. 747, 749 (S.D. N.Y. 1988) ("elements of *Younger, Colorado River, Burford* and *Pullman* abstention doctrines present in this case"). In *Pennzoil Co. v. Texaco,* 107 S. Ct. 1519, 1526 n.9 (1987), the Court stated that "[t]he various types of abstention are not rigid pigeonholes into which federal courts must try to fit cases. Rather, they reflect a complex of considerations designed to soften the tensions inherent in a system that contemplates parallel judicial processes."

§ 12.2 *Pullman* Abstention – General Principles

Page 246, add at end of section:

Consistent with the discussion on page 246 of the text, three decisions held that *Pullman* abstention does not apply to supremacy clause preemption claims. *United Services Automobile Association v. Muir,* 792 F.2d 356 (3d Cir. 1986), *cert. denied,* 107 S. Ct. 875 (1987); *Federal Home Loan Bank Board v. Empie,* 778 F.2d 1447 (10th Cir. 1985); *Housatonic Cable Vision v. Department of Public Utility Control,* 622 F. Supp. 798 (D. Conn. 1985).

§ 12.3 – Unclear Issues of State Law

Page 248, add at end of section:

Pullman abstention is inapplicable when "the unconstitutionality of the particular state action under challenge is clear . . . ." *Thornburgh v. American College of Obstetricians,* 106 S. Ct. 2169, 2176 (1986). This is true even where the state courts have never interpreted the state statute. "[W]here municipal courts have regularly applied an unambiguous statute, there is certainly no need for a federal court to abstain until state appellate courts have an opportunity to construe it." *City of Houston v. Hill,* 107 S. Ct. 2502, 2514 (1987).

Without mentioning *Pullman* abstention, the Supreme Court in a First Amendment controversy certified two state law questions to the Virginia Supreme Court. Since the attorney general does not bind the state courts or law enforcement authorities, the Court was unable to accept her interpretation of the law as authoritative. Under the "unusual circumstances" of this case, where the state will decline to defend the statute if read one way and where plaintiffs' constitutional challenge is drastically altered if it is read another way, "it is essential that we have the benefit of the law's authoritative construction from the" state court. *Virginia v. American Booksellers Association,* 108 S. Ct. 636, 644 (1988).

"Generally, an administrative interpretation of a facially ambiguous state statute will not remove the ambiguity for *Pullman* purposes." *United Services Automobile Association v. Muir,* 792 F.2d 356, 362 (3d Cir. 1986), *cert. denied,* 107 S. Ct. 875 (1987).

Pullman abstention is not appropriate where the potential lack of clarity is in a parallel state constitutional provision, even if that provision is given an independent interpretation by the highest state court. *Guiney v. Roache,* 833 F.2d 1079 (1st Cir. 1987).

The First Circuit raised but did not decide whether *Pullman* abstention may be invoked when the state law questions are clear and dispositive but the federal court is powerless to enforce the state law under the Eleventh Amendment as interpreted in *Pennhurst II. Cuesnongle v. Ramos,* 835 F.2d 1486 (1st Cir. 1987). The authors believe that *Pullman* is not appropriate in these circumstances, because the doctrine depends upon an unclear issue of state law.

§ 12.4 –Balancing Benefits from Abstaining against Harm from Delay

Page 249, add at end of section:

The Supreme Court reiterated its reluctance to invoke *Pullman* abstention in cases involving facial challenges under the First Amendment. In addition, while defendant's failure to raise *Pullman* until after three years of litigation on the merits, and not until after it lost on the merits in the court of appeals, did not prevent the Supreme Court from considering the abstention issue, it did "undercut the force of the City's argument." *City of Houston v. Hill,* 107 S. Ct. 2502, 2512 n.16 (1987). While the existence of a state certification procedure is an "important factor" in determining whether to abstain, "it is not in itself sufficient to render abstention appropriate." *Id.* at 2514. For a rare First Amendment case in which *Pullman* was invoked, *see Almodovar v. Reiner,* 832 F.2d 1138 (9th Cir. 1987).

The Second Circuit observed the burdens created by *Pullman* abstention and the fact that they can be mitigated by a state certification procedure:

> Although intellectually attractive, *Pullman* abstention places heavy burdens on plaintiffs, who traditionally must commence or continue separate proceedings in state court. At best, a suit becomes more costly and its disposition is delayed. At worst, abstention transforms our dual court system into a jurisdictional labyrinth from which even the hardiest litigant is unlikely to emerge. . . .
>
> These difficulties, however, can be ameliorated by use of certification of state law questions to a state's highest court where this procedure is available.

Griffin Hospital v. Commissions on Hospitals and Health Care, 782 F.2d 24, 25-26 (2d Cir. 1986) (citation omitted).

The First Circuit rejected *Pullman* because the case was already seven years old and the highest state court had previously refused to resolve the state law issues. *Cuesnongle v. Ramos,* 835 F.2d 1486 (1st Cir. 1987).

§ 12.5 –Procedural Aspects

Page 250, add at end of section:

The *England* reservation procedure requires that all federal claims either be tendered to the state court or reserved in the state court. Thus, when plaintiffs submitted to the state court a preemption claim but failed to submit due process and equal protection claims, these later claims were deemed abandoned. *White Mountain Apache Tribe v. Williams,* 798 F.2d 1205, 1216-17 (9th Cir. 1984), *opinion amended,* 810 F.2d 844 (9th Cir.), *cert. denied,* 107 S. Ct. 940 (1987).

Two circuit courts ruled that the *England* reservation applies only following the invocation of *Pullman* abstention, and may not be employed simply because a litigant institutes a state court proceeding prior to bringing suit in federal court. *Tarpley v. Salerno,* 803 F.2d 57 (2d Cir. 1986); *Fuller Co. v. Ramon I. Gil, Inc.,* 782 F.2d 306 (1st Cir. 1986). The *England* procedure does apply, however, where a litigant, anticipating *Pullman* abstention, commences suit in state court prior to bringing the federal court action, and the federal court in fact invokes *Pullman* abstention. In these circumstances, the state court plaintiff may reserve the right to litigate the federal constitutional claim in the federal action. "That a party may anticipate a federal abstention order by filing suit in state court . . . offends neither the principles underlying abstention nor the procedures laid out in *England.*" *Wicker v. Board of*
* *Education,* 826 F.2d 442, 445 (6th Cir. 1987). *See also Barnes v. McDowell,* 848 F.2d 725, 732 (6th Cir. 1988) ("we do not view the absence of an *England* reservation as a factor which distinguishes the applicability of *Wicker* to this case."), *cert. denied,* 109 S. Ct. 789 (1989).

§ 12.6 *Younger v. Harris* Abstention – Introduction

Page 252, add at end of section:

The Seventh Circuit limits the doctrine of *Mitchum v. Foster,* 407 U.S. 225 (1972), discussed in the main volume, to constitutional violations. As a result, when a § 1983 claimant seeks relief against a pending state court proceeding based on an alleged violation of a federal statute, the relief is barred by the anti-injunction statute and is not within its "expressly authorized" exception. *Hickey v. Duffy,* 827 F.2d 234 (7th Cir. 1987). The authors agree with Judge Flaum's position in his concurring opinion that this is an "innovative and troubling proposition." *Id.* at 244.

Some federal courts take the position that preemption claims are exempt from *Younger,* because there is no legitimate state interest in these cases. *See, e.g., Middle South Energy v. Public Service Commission,* 772 F.2d 404 (8th Cir. 1985), *cert. denied,* 106 S. Ct. 884 (1986); *Champion International Corp. v. Brown,* 731 F.2d 1406 (9th Cir. 1984). The Third Circuit, while recognizing these authorities, appears to regard preemption as a pertinent factor in the *Younger* equation, stating that it would "be an overstatement to suggest that *Younger* abstention is never appropriate when the question presented is one of preemption." *Kentucky West Virginia Gas Co. v. Public Utility Commission,* 791 F.2d 1111, 1117 (3d Cir. 1986). The Fourth Circuit takes the position that there is no valid reason for excluding preemption claims from the reach of *Younger. Potomac Electric Power Co. v. Sachs,* 802 F.2d 1527 (4th Cir. 1986), *vacated,* 108 S. Ct. 743 (1988).

In *Kentucky West Virginia Gas Co., supra, Younger* was inapplicable because the federal court plaintiffs, who raised a preemption claim, were also state court plaintiffs and did not seek to enjoin a state judicial proceeding.

The *Younger* doctrine does not apply to claims for federal court relief against a pending *federal* court criminal proceeding. The district court judge, however, may defer action in the civil case pending resolution of the criminal proceedings. *Juluke v. Hodel,* 811 F.2d 1553 (D.C. Cir. 1987).

§ 12.7 – State Criminal Proceedings

Page 256, add at end of section:

* The *Younger* doctrine is applicable when the federal plaintiff does not seek to enjoin the state criminal proceeding, but seeks to interfere with it by allowing it to "proceed only under conditions imposed by the federal judiciary." *Davis v. Lansing,* 851 F.2d 72, 77 (2d Cir. 1988).

The Fifth Circuit, following the decision in *United Books v. Conte,* 739 F.2d 30 (1st Cir. 1984), found the *Younger* abstention doctrine applicable to a claim for prospective relief against future prosecutions, because a grant of such relief would affect the outcome of presently pending state proceedings. The court also found abstention appropriate under the *O'Shea v. Littleton,* 414 U.S. 488 (1974), branch of *Younger* because the relief sought would require "monitoring" of state court procedures. *Ballard v. Wilson,* 856 F.2d 1568 (5th Cir. 1988).

In *Potomac Electric Power Co. v. Sachs,* 802 F.2d 1527 (4th Cir. 1986), the court applied *Younger* abstention to a grand jury proceeding because the federal claim could be presented as a defense to the pending criminal proceeding. "The grand jury, although separate, is an integral part of state criminal enforcement proceedings . . . ." *Id.* at 1532.

The Third Circuit reached a contrary result in *Monaghan v. Deakins,* 798 F.2d 632 (3d Cir. 1986). After finding that a request in federal court for the return of seized documents that were to be used in the grand jury proceeding was not exempted from the *Younger* doctrine, the court ruled that *Younger* did not defeat the prayer for federal court relief, because the grand jury had no authority to adjudicate anything and

Younger does not justify dismissal based "upon the mere availability of a state judicial proceeding." *Id.* at 638.

After granting certiorari, the Supreme Court found that plaintiffs' claims for equitable relief were mooted by subsequent events in the state criminal proceeding, including the return of an indictment by the grand jury, the failure of the prosecutor to submit the seized documents to the grand jury, a state court ruling ordering the return of the documents, and a pending state court motion for the return of other documents. In light of these developments, the plaintiffs represented that they no longer desired to pursue their claims for equitable relief. *Deakins v. Monaghan,* 108 S. Ct. 523 (1988). This left for resolution the question of whether plaintiffs' federal court claims for monetary relief were barred by the *Younger* doctrine. The Third Circuit found it "settled" in that circuit "that a district court, when abstaining from adjudicating a claim for injunctive relief, should stay and not dismiss accompanying claims for damages and attorney fees when such relief is not available from the ongoing state proceedings." 798 F.2d at 635. The fact that a § 1983 action could be filed in state court does not change the result. The Supreme Court in *Deakins* agreed with this conclusion. Finding no reason to "decide the extent to which the *Younger* doctrine applies to a federal court action seeking only monetary relief," the Supreme Court concluded that "the District Court has no discretion to dismiss rather than to stay claims for monetary relief that cannot be redressed in the state proceeding." 108 S. Ct. at 529. In this context, the involvement of the federal courts cannot be "blamed" for the piecemeal litigation. "Because the state criminal proceeding can provide only equitable relief, any action for damages would necessarily be separate." *Id.* at 530. Justice White, concurring, chided the majority for not adequately explaining "why the federal courts must or may stay, rather than proceed to adjudicate federal constitutional claims for damages." *Id.* at 532 (White, J., concurring). In his view, because "[a] judgment in the federal damages action may decide several questions at issue in the state criminal proceeding," and presumably these rulings would be entitled to preclusive effect in the criminal proceeding, he would resolve that under *Younger* "the lower courts *may not* adjudicate respondents' damages claims until the completion of the pending state criminal proceedings." *Id.* at 533 (emphasis in original).

The Second Circuit held "that *Younger* does not invariably require dismissal of § 1983 damage actions." *Suggs v. Brannon,* 804 F.2d 274, 279 (2d Cir. 1986). The court recognized, however, that a federal court in its discretion may stay its proceedings pending a state court decision, in order to avoid duplicate litigation and obtain the benefit of the views of the state court.

The Fifth Circuit indicates that claims for damages are not within the *Younger* doctrine. *Thomas v. State Board of Medical Examiners,* 807 F.2d 453, 457 (5th Cir. 1987).

The Sixth Circuit ruled "that a federal court should not abstain from a case seeking monetary relief when the suit arises from a state judicial proceeding to which the state is not a party, absent extraordinary circumstances." *Carras v. Williams,* 807 F.2d 1286, 1291-92 (6th Cir. 1986). The court believes that claims for monetary relief are "much less intrusive" than claims for injunctive or declaratory relief. *Id.* at 1291. In a subsequent case, the Sixth Circuit ruled "that when disposition of a federal action for damages necessarily requires the resolution of issues that will determine the outcome of pending state criminal proceedings, *Younger* requires that the federal action not proceed." *Feaster v. Miksch,* 846 F.2d 21, 24 (6th Cir. 1988). The court reached this result even though plaintiff asserted a Fourth Amendment violation which, under *Stone v. Powell,* 428 U.S. 465 (1976), could not be raised in a federal habeas corpus proceeding.

The Ninth Circuit follows those courts that abstain when a damages action will have "a substantially disruptive effect" upon ongoing state criminal proceedings. *Mann v. Jett,* 781 F.2d 1448, 1449 (9th Cir. 1986).

The proper time to determine the applicability of *Younger* is the date on which the federal complaint is filed; if a state prosecution is pending on that date, *Younger* requires federal noninterference absent extraordinary circumstances. *Zalman v. Armstrong,* 802 F.2d 199 (6th Cir. 1986). Applying this rule, the court ruled that the fact that the state dismissed an indictment, in accordance with the judgment of the federal district court, did not preclude the state from challenging in the circuit court of appeals the district court's interference with the pending state proceeding. The Sixth Circuit
* found that the district court should have abstained. *See also Beltran v. California,* 857 F.2d 542 (9th Cir. 1988) (*Younger* doctrine applicable if state proceedings pending when federal action commenced, though completed when federal court determines the merits).

State court proceedings were pending, within the meaning of *Younger,* even though they were not commenced until after the filing of the federal action. When the state action was commenced, proceedings of substance had not taken place in federal court. Since the state court complaint was filed two days before the hearing in federal court on plaintiff's motion for a preliminary injunction, the federal action had not gone beyond the "embryonic state." The state court action, however, did not implicate sufficiently weighty state interests to justify the invocation of *Younger.* The state court action, a state-instituted declaratory judgment action regarding the constitutionality of the state obscenity law, was not a state enforcement action, but merely sought a declaratory judgment on the same issue involved in the federal court action. *Polykoff v. Collins,* 816 F.2d 1326 (9th Cir. 1987).

The *Younger* doctrine applied to federal court claims for relief asserted by Sequoia Books and two of its employees, Patroff and Collins, even though Collins was not a party to the pending state court proceeding. Sequoia Books and Patroff were parties to the state proceedings, and they and Collins shared the same interest in the state litigation regarding an obscenity issue. *Collins v. Kendall County,* 807 F.2d 95 (7th Cir. 1986), *cert. denied,* 107 S. Ct. 3228 (1987).

* In *Blackwelder v. Satnauer,* 689 F. Supp. 106 (N.D.N.Y. 1988), three families challenged the state's alleged interference with the home education of children. One of these families was involved in a pending state proceeding, but this did not justify *Younger* abstention as to the other two. Even though the three families were represented by the same attorney and asserted similar legal claims, their claims were not so interrelated as to justify involving *Younger* against the two families who were not parties to pending state proceedings. With respect to the family involved in pending state proceedings, the court rejected its argument that *Younger* should not apply because the federal action was filed before the state proceedings. The filing of an amended complaint and intervention by the state did not constitute federal court proceedings of substance on the merits.

§ 12.8 –State Civil Proceedings

Page 258, add at end of section:

In *Pennzoil Co. v. Texaco,* 107 S. Ct. 1519 (1987), the Court, relying upon *Juidice v. Vail,* 430 U.S. 327 (1977), found *Younger* applicable to federal court relief that would interfere with the enforcement of a state court judgment. The Court relied upon the important state interest in the enforcement of judgments. The Court denied the position in Justice Stevens's concurring opinion that the *Younger* doctrine was now applicable to all private civil litigation.

For other decisions applying *Younger* to state proceedings implicating important state interests, *see Beltran v. California,* 857 F.2d 542 (9th Cir. 1988) (state interest in collective bargaining); *Allen v. Board of Dentistry,* 835 F.2d 100 (5th Cir. 1988) (dentistry license revocation proceeding); *Kitchens v. Bowen,* 825 F.2d 1337 (9th Cir. 1987) (state-instituted proceeding to establish paternity and collect support on behalf of AFDC children), *cert. denied,* 108 S. Ct. 1109 (1988); *Jacobson v. Northbrook Municipal Corp.,* 824 F.2d 567 (7th Cir. 1987) (quasi-criminal enforcement proceeding growing out of unpaid traffic fines); *World Famous Drinking Emporium v. City of Tempe,* 820 F.2d 1079, 1083 (9th Cir. 1987) (action instituted by city board to compel compliance with anti-public nuisance ordinance: "Such an action, in aid of and closely related to Tempe's zoning prosecution, clearly involves an important state interest"); *Brunken v. Lance,* 807 F.2d 1325, 1330 (7th Cir. 1986) (proceeding to determine custody of child allegedly sexually abused by father: "In a practical sense the State is a party to the proceedings in a fashion analogous to its role in a standard criminal proceeding"); *Malachowski v. City of Keene,* 787 F.2d 704 (1st Cir.) (juvenile delinquency), *cert. denied,* 107 S. Ct. 107 (1986); *P. Edward A. v. Williams,* 696 F. Supp. 1432 (D. Utah 1988) (state proceeding involving family matters); *Franza v. Abrams,* 695 F. Supp. 747 (S.D.N.Y. 1988) (drug paraphernalia forfeiture action); *Pincham v. Judicial Inquiry Board,* 681 F. Supp. 1309 (N.D. Ill. 1988) (judicial discipline proceeding); *Blake v. Lang,* 669 F. Supp. 584, 589 (S.D.N.Y. 1987) (state proceeding to revoke license to practice medicine); *Metropolitan Hospital v. Thornburgh,* 667 F. Supp. 208 (E.D. Pa. 1987) (state proceeding involving distribution of health care services); *Crazy Eddie v. Cotter,* 666 F. Supp. 503 (S.D.N.Y. 1987) (state-instituted action to enforce energy regulation); *Ganoe v. Lummis,* 662 F. Supp. 718 (S.D.N.Y. 1987) (probate proceeding); *Blount v. Redmond,* 649 F. Supp. 319 (D. Me. 1986) (truancy proceeding); *Cronson v. Clark,* 645 F. Supp. 793 (C.D. Ill. 1986) (state mandamus proceeding to compel auditor to conduct audit), *aff'd,* 810 F.2d 662 (7th Cir.), *cert. denied,* 108 S. Ct. 199 (1987).

For cases holding *Younger* inapplicable to purely private state civil litigation, *see First Alabama Bank v. Parsons Steel,* 825 F.2d 1475 (11th Cir. 1987), *cert. denied,* 108 S. Ct. 1015 (1988); *Martori Brothers Distributors v. Massengale,* 781 F.2d 1349 (9th Cir.), *amended,* 791 F.2d 799 (9th Cir.), *cert. denied,* 107 S. Ct. 435 (1986).

Younger was held inapplicable to a state-instituted declaratory judgment action seeking a ruling that the state obscenity law was constitutional. This was not the type of state enforcement proceeding justifying *Younger.* Rather, the state action sought a declaratory judgment on the same federal issue involved in the federal action.

"*Younger* abstention principles do not require federal courts to forego the exercise of jurisdiction to decide a federal constitutional question under the Declaratory Judgment Act whenever a state prefers to litigate the question of declaratory relief in state court." *Polykoff v. Collins,* 816 F.2d 1326, 1333 (9th Cir. 1987).

Several decisions dealt with application of the decision in *Ohio Civil Rights Commission v. Dayton Christian Schools,* 106 S. Ct. 1718 (1986), cited in the text at page 258, note 20. In a non-§ 1983 suit, the Second Circuit interpreted *Dayton Christian Schools* as requiring three inquiries: "(1) whether there is an ongoing state proceeding; (2) whether an important state interest is involved; and (3) whether the federal plaintiff has an adequate opportunity for judicial review of his constitutional claims during or after the proceeding." *Christ The King Regional High School v. Culvert,* 815 F.2d 219, 224 (2d Cir.), *cert. denied,* 108 S. Ct. 102 (1987). *See also University Club v. City of New York,* 842 F.2d 37 (2d Cir. 1988).

The First Circuit distinguished the *Dayton* rule from the no-exhaustion rule established by *Patsy v. Board of Regents,* 457 U.S. 496 (1982). The crucial distinction is that in the *Dayton* situation the federal court plaintiff seeks to enjoin a pending administrative proceeding which is claimed to be unconstitutional, while in the *Patsy* situation the administrative proceeding is an option available to the federal court plaintiff on his or her own initiative to redress a wrong inflicted by the state. "In the former case, abstention is appropriate, in the latter, the *Patsy* rule prevails." *Kercado Melendez v. Aponte-Roque,* 829 F.2d 255, 261 (1st Cir.), *cert. denied,* 108 S. Ct. 2037 (1987). *See also University Club v. City of New York,* 842 F.2d 37, 42 (2d Cir. 1988) (proceedings relevant to *Patsy* exhaustion issue were remedial; proceedings relevant to *Dayton* are coercive).

The Third Circuit found *Dayton-Younger* inapplicable to a pending administrative proceeding because, inter alia, the federal court plaintiffs, a class of alcoholics in need of rehabilitation services, were not parties to the pending administrative proceedings, they could not "request in the state proceeding all relief available in federal court[,]" and they were threatened with irreparable injury from the lack of treatment. *Sullivan v. Pittsburgh,* 811 F.2d 171 (3d Cir.), *cert. denied,* 108 S. Ct. 148 (1987).

The Fifth Circuit applied *Dayton-Younger* to a utility rate-setting administrative proceeding. *New Orleans Public Service v. New Orleans,* 798 F.2d 858 (5th Cir. 1986),
* *cert. denied,* 107 S. Ct. 1910 (1987), *subsequent history,* 850 F.2d 1069 (5th Cir. 1988), *cert. granted,* 109 S. Ct. 780 (1989).

The Sixth Circuit found that *Dayton-Younger* applies to administrative disciplinary proceedings against dentists because they implicate important state interests, but found the doctrine inapplicable to the case at hand because the state law provided for judicial review only if the board determines to revoke the dentist's license.

> We find that an opportunity for judicial review which is contingent upon the type of disciplinary action taken is insufficient to trigger *Younger* abstention. Rather, for a federal court to abstain from reaching the merits of the case under *Younger,* it must be assured that there exists a definite opportunity to raise his constitutional claims on direct state judicial review of the state administrative proceedings. Since that is clearly not the case here, abstention is inappropriate and we may reach the merits of this case.

Parker v. Board of Dentistry, 818 F.2d 504, 509 (6th Cir. 1987).

The Sixth Circuit applied *Dayton* to a proceeding to suspend and revoke the license of a physician in *Watts v. Burkhart,* 854 F.2d 839 (6th Cir. 1988). *Dayton-Younger* was applied to an administrative driver's license and motor vehicle registration suspension proceeding, because it implicated important state interests and was in aid of and closely related to the enforcement of the state criminal law. *Ronwin v. Dunham,* 818 F.2d 675 (8th Cir. 1987).

Dayton was denied retroactive effect because it marks a "clear break" with past law. *Perry v. Brakke,* 826 F.2d 740 (8th Cir. 1987).

§ 12.9 –Exceptions

Page 262, add at end of section:

The loss of child custody, which might prove to be temporary, did not suffice to take the case outside of *Younger. Malachowski v. City of Keene,* 787 F.2d 704 (1st Cir.), *cert. denied,* 107 S. Ct. 107 (1986).

The "flagrantly and patently" unconstitutional exception has never been found applicable by the United States Supreme Court "since it first announced the exception in *Younger.*" *Zalman v. Armstrong,* 802 F.2d 199, 205 (6th Cir. 1986). The authors observe that while the exception was "announced" in *Younger,* the *Younger* Court had in fact quoted from *Watson v. Buck,* 313 U.S. 387, 402 (1941). See discussion on page 260 of the main volume.

The Seventh Circuit rejected the bad faith exception in *Collins v. Kendall County,* 807 F.2d 95 (7th Cir. 1986), *cert. denied,* 107 S. Ct. 3228 (1987). "[P]laintiffs have failed to set forth facts supporting an inference of bad faith prosecution or harassment. Instituting approximately thirty criminal prosecutions over a two-year period does not constitute bad faith or harassment in and of itself." *Id.* at 99. Plaintiffs failed to allege that state officials were prosecuting them with no expectation of securing convictions and only to discourage their exercise of First Amendment rights. *Id.* at 101.

The bad faith exception was invoked where it was shown that the criminal prosecution was instituted to retaliate for or to discourage the exercise of constitutional rights. This is a sufficient showing of bad faith, regardless of whether the prosecutor has a reasonable expectation of securing a valid conviction. *Lewellen v. Raff,* 843 F.2d 1103 (8th Cir. 1988). A compilation of bad faith prosecution cases is set forth in *Wichert v. Walter,* 606 F. Supp. 1516, 1521 (D.N.J. 1985).

The Fifth Circuit takes the position that double jeopardy claims are an exception to the *Younger* doctrine. "Thus federal courts are empowered to enjoin state criminal proceedings that would constitute double jeopardy." *Showery v. Samaniego,* 814 F.2d 200, 201-02 n.5 (5th Cir. 1987); *Davis v. Herring,* 800 F.2d 513, 516 (5th Cir. 1986);
* *Foster v. Murphy,* 686 F. Supp. 471 (S.D.N.Y. 1988), citing *Drayton v. Hayes,* 589 F.2d 117, 120-21 (2d Cir. 1979).

Younger does not apply when there is no adequate opportunity to litigate the constitutional claim in the pending state proceeding. *Lynk v. La Porte Superior Court,* 789 F.2d 554 (7th Cir. 1986). In *Lynk,* the Seventh Circuit found *Younger* inapplicable to a prisoner's due process claim, which was based upon the state's refusal to adjudicate his divorce proceeding. While *Younger* did not require dismissal of the federal action, because there was no showing that plaintiff could raise his federal claim in state court, comity required that the federal court plaintiff give the state court system a full opportunity to adjudicate his divorce claim before seeking federal relief against the state court. Plaintiff in the federal action for the first time had counsel and this may help him get a state court determination after he dismissed his present divorce proceeding and filed a new one making clear his grounds for divorce and his constitutional objection to denying him a divorce.

* The fact that the highest court in the state had previously rejected the federal constitutional claim does not mean that there is no adequate opportunity to raise the constitutional claim in the pending state proceeding. "If this Court were to rule that adverse state court precedent requires federal court intervention, we would open the door for federal courts to overrule state court decisions without the avenue of a state appeal." *Ballard v. Wilson,* 856 F. 2d 1568, 1571 (5th Cir. 1988).

The Ninth Circuit holds that "[p]robation is not a pending action for *Younger* purposes" because it does offer an opportunity to raise federal constitutional questions. *Almodovar v. Reiner,* 832 F.2d 1138, 1141 (9th Cir. 1987).

The burden is on the federal court plaintiff to demonstrate an inability to litigate the federal claim in state court. Federal courts should not "assume that state judges will interpret ambiguities in state procedural law to bar presentation of federal claims." *Pennzoil Co. v. Texaco,* 107 S. Ct. 1519, 1528 (1987).

§ 12.10 – Procedural Aspects

Page 263, add at end of section:

"Federal courts are not compelled to abstain on *Younger* grounds when the state voluntarily submits to adjudication in a federal forum." *Umphlet v. Connick,* 815 F.2d 1061, 1063 (5th Cir. 1987).

The First Circuit refused to consider *Younger* where it was raised in the district court, but not in the court of appeals. *Shannon v. Telco Communications,* 824 F.2d 150 (1st Cir. 1987), citing *Brown v. Hotel and Restaurant Employees Local 54,* 468 U.S. 491, 500 n.9 (1984) ("Since the State's Attorney General has . . . agreed to our adjudication of the controversy, considerations of comity are not implicated, and we need not address the merits of the *Younger* abstention claim").

§ 12.11 *Colorado River* Abstention

Page 265, add at end of section:

"[T]he general rule is that a suit is duplicative of another suit if the parties, issues and available relief do not significantly differ between the two actions." *I.A. Durbin, Inc. v. Jefferson National Bank,* 793 F.2d 1541 (11th Cir. 1986). *See also Crawley v. Hamilton County Commissioners,* 744 F.2d 28 (6th Cir. 1984) (claims not parallel where claims and parties different). In *Lumen Construction v. Brant Construction Co.,* 780 F.2d 691, 695 (7th Cir. 1986), the court stated that it looks "not for formal symmetry between the two actions, but for a substantial likelihood that the state litigation will dispose of all claims presented in the federal case." *See also Interstate Material Corporation v. Chicago,* 847 F.2d 1285 (7th Cir. 1988) (facts that parties are not identical and only federal action sought class action relief do not destroy parallel nature of the cases); *Weiser v. Koch,* 632 F. Supp. 1369, 1370 (S.D.N.Y. 1986).

The Eleventh Circuit rejects *Colorado River* abstention in § 1983 cases. *Alacare, Inc.-North v. Baggiano,* 785 F.2d 963, 969 (11th Cir.), *cert. denied,* 107 S. Ct. 111 (1986). Despite its general hesitancy to apply the doctrine in § 1983 cases, the Fifth Circuit applied it in *Allen v. Board of Dentistry,* 835 F.2d 100 (5th Cir. 1988), and in *Eitel v. Holland,* 798 F.2d 815 (5th Cir. 1986), as did the Seventh Circuit in *Oliver v. Fort Wayne Education Association,* 820 F.2d 913 (7th Cir. 1987) and in *Lumen Construction v. Brant Construction,* 780 F.2d 691 (7th Cir. 1986). The court in *Lumen* also held that when *Colorado River* is invoked, the federal suit should be stayed, not dismissed, in order to protect against the running of the statute of limitations should the state suit not dispose of all of the claims on the merits.

The Second Circuit found that the federal district court did not abuse its discretion in dismissing the § 1983 action under *Colorado River. American Disposal Services v. O'Brien,* 839 F.2d 84 (2d Cir. 1988). In a case brought by homeless families with children, the Second Circuit found that the district court did not abuse its discretion in abstaining under *Colorado River* and *Burford. Cannady v. Valentin,* 768 F.2d 501 (2d Cir. 1985). Citing this text, a federal district court applied *Colorado River* in a § 1983 action in *Glover v. City of Portland,* 675 F. Supp. 398 (M.D. Tenn. 1987).

Colorado River was denied under the particular circumstances in *Bath Memorial Hospital v. Maine Health Care Finance Commission,* 853 F.2d 1007 (1st Cir. 1988); *Zemsky v. New York City,* 821 F.2d 148 (2d Cir.), *cert. denied,* 108 S. Ct. 456 (1987), and in *Polykoff v. Collins,* 816 F.2d 1326 (9th Cir. 1987). A federal district court rejected *Colorado River* because of the importance of a federal forum to hear § 1983 claims and the danger that the preclusive effect of a state court judgment could preclude plaintiff from litigating the § 1983 claim in federal court. *Tucker v. Callahan,* 663 F. Supp. 375 (M.D. Tenn. 1987).

Colorado River abstention does apply in declaratory judgment actions. *Lumbermen's Mutual Casualty Co. v. Connecticut Bank and Trust Co.,* 806 F.2d 411 (2d Cir. 1986); *Fuller Co. v. Ramon I. Gil, Inc.,* 782 F.2d 306 (1st Cir. 1986).

Although curiously not mentioning *Colorado River,* the Ninth Circuit stayed a federal court § 1983 action pending the outcome of a parallel state court action. *Ollie v. Riggin,* 848 F.2d 1016 (9th Cir. 1988).

A determination declining *Colorado River* abstention is not immediately appealable to the circuit court of appeals. *Gulfstream Aerospace Corp. v. Mayacamas Corp.,* 108 S. Ct. 1133 (1988).

§ 12.12 *Burford* Abstention

Page 267, add at end of section:

Finding no precedent applying *Burford* to First Amendment claims, and doubting whether it would ever be appropriate to invokc *Burford* when substantial First

Amendment claims are asserted, the Third Circuit rejected *Burford* in an action attacking attorney advertising rules on free speech grounds. The case "does not present the sort of complex, technical, regulatory scheme to which the *Burford* abstention doctrine usually is applied." *Felmeister v. Office of Attorney Ethics,* 856 F.2d 529, 534 (3d Cir. 1988).

Without explicitly discussing *Burford* abstention, but "mindful that federal courts should not become zoning boards of appeal," the Second Circuit held that the district courts may resolve zoning disputes in § 1983 cases raising federal constitutional or statutory claims. *Sullivan v. Town of Salem,* 805 F.2d 81, 82 (2d Cir. 1986).

Burford abstention was applied to a § 1983 claim, especially because plaintiff advanced a "tenuous" constitutional claim. *Coin Call v. Southern Bell Telephone and Telegraph Co.,* 636 F. Supp. 608 (N.D. Ga. 1986).

The Third Circuit follows the weight of authority (see cases cited on page 266, note 91 of the main volume) in holding *Burford* abstention inapplicable to preemption claims. *Kentucky West Virginia Gas Co. v. Public Utility Commission,* 791 F.2d 1111 (3d Cir. 1986). The Fifth Circuit, however, withdrew its prior opinion on this point (782 F.2d 1236) and now holds that *Burford* abstention may be applied to preemption claims. *New Orleans Public Service v. New Orleans,* 798 F.2d 858 (5th Cir. 1986), *cert.* * *denied,* 107 S. Ct. 1910 (1987), *subsequent history,* 850 F.2d 1069 (5th Cir. 1988), *cert. granted,* 109 S. Ct. 780 (1989).

The Fourth Circuit invoked *Burford* abstention in a land use case because the local zoning provisions were a "complex state regulatory scheme" and there were "several levels of state review of zoning decisions." *Merredith v. Talbot County,* 828 F.2d 228, 232 (4th Cir. 1987). *See also Northern Virginia Law School v. City of Alexandria,* 680 F. Supp. 222 (E.D. Va. 1988).

The mere fact that an action contests land use policy, however, does not mean that *Burford* should be invoked. The Third Circuit rejected *Burford* because plaintiff asserted a federal claim and the local regulatory scheme was not especially complex. "In this case an express, narrow, and quite specific federal provision threatens, at most, only a minimal disruption of a broad state policy." *Izzo v. Borough of Riveredge,* 843 * F.2d 765, 769 (3d Cir. 1988). *See also Epstein v. Township of Whitehall,* 693 F. Supp. 309 (E.D. Pa. 1988). The authors observe that (1) the assertion of a federal claim (2) against a land use policy are factors which cut in opposite directions in assessing the applicability of *Burford.*

A district court applied *Burford* to a § 1983 action dealing with the rights of mental patients, because of the state's demonstrated "interest in comprehensive and unitary decision making." *Hartshorn v. Heydinger,* 647 F. Supp. 73, 77 (S.D. W. Va. 1986). *See also Jordi v. Sauk Prairie School Board,* 651 F. Supp. 1566 (W.D. Wis. 1987) (applying * *Burford* to § 1983 claim). In a case brought by homeless families with children, the Second Circuit found that the district court did not abuse its discretion in abstaining under *Burford* and *Colorado River. Cannady v. Valentin,* 768 F.2d 501 (2d Cir. 1985).

Burford abstention was rejected because, while worker's compensation "involves a relatively complex state system[,]" the state has not set up "special tribunals" to resolve these claims. *Michigan Injured Workers v. Blanchard,* 647 F. Supp. 571, 575 (W.D. Mich. 1986).

Burford is not applicable to a challenge to the constitutionality of a state statute on its face, because such claims do not threaten the uniform application of a regulatory * scheme. *Bath Memorial Hospital v. Maine Health Care Finance Commission,* 853 F.2d 1007 (1st Cir. 1988); *Long Island Lighting Co. v. Cuomo,* 666 F. Supp. 370, 399 (N.D.N.Y. 1987).

§ 12.13 Tax Injunction Act

Page 269, add at end of section:

The Tax Injunction Act applies not only to federal court § 1983 actions attacking the validity of state tax laws, but also to attacks upon the administration of state tax laws. *Brooks v. Nance,* 801 F.2d 1237 (10th Cir. 1986).

The inability to pay taxes imposed by the state and consequential unavailability of a state refund remedy does not render the state remedy inadequate. *Adams v. Indiana,* 795 F.2d 27 (7th Cir. 1986). Nor does the absence of a class action procedure render the state remedy inadequate. *Waldron v. Collins,* 788 F.2d 736 (11th Cir.), *cert. denied,* 107 S. Ct. 274 (1986). The necessity for filing 67 class actions in 67 counties did not render the state remedy inadequate in view of "the several hundred thousand members of the class and several hundred million dollars in question." *Winicki v. Mallard,* 783 F.2d 1567, 1571 (11th Cir.), *cert. denied,* 107 S. Ct. 70 (1986). *Winicki* also held that a federal court claim for relief will be defeated by the principles of federalism that underlie the Tax Injunction Act, even when a state tax statute had been declared unconstitutional and is no longer operational, and only retroactive relief is sought in federal court.

Plaintiffs claimed that Illinois state court tax procedures may be challenged in federal court because they are deficient, in that they fail to allow discovery and lack of "set standard" of proof. The court held that these were procedural challenges which could not be characterized as frivolous or unreasonable. *Hamer v. Lake County,* 819 F.2d 1362 (7th Cir. 1987).

In *Coleman v. McLaren,* 631 F. Supp. 749 (N.D. Ill. 1985), the court found the state remedy adequate even though (1) it does not provide for class, injunctive, or systematic relief; (2) it does not guarantee identical results; (3) each remedy is not speedy; (4) it requires exhaustion of administrative remedies; (5) costs are not recoverable; (6) the state remedy is costly; and (7) there is uncertainty as to the availability of discovery.

Plaintiffs challenged the "systematic underassessment" of certain property for tax purposes. Without deciding whether relief which would *enhance* the collection of taxes is within the Tax Injunction Act, the court found the claim for relief barred by the principles of comity underlying the Act. "[T]he scope of federal court deference based on principles of comity is substantially broader that that required under the Tax Injunction Act." *In re Gillis,* 836 F.2d 1001, 1006 (6th Cir. 1988).

The Sixth Circuit determined that a state statutory requirement that parolees make monthly payments into parole supervision and victim compensation funds was within the Tax Injunction Act, because this is a revenue-raising measure. *Wright v. McClain,*

835 F.2d 143 (6th Cir. 1987). On the other hand, a district court ruled that state bar membership dues are not a tax within the meaning of the Act because they are not a part of the "state's revenue raising operations." *Levine v. Supreme Court of Wisconsin,* 679 F. Supp. 1478, 1489 (W.D. Wis. 1988).

* The Tax Injunction Act applied to an attack upon the state tax refund policy. *Goodman v. Burris,* 695 F. Supp. 973 (N.D. Ill. 1988).

Whether the Tax Injunction Act applies to state court § 1983 cases "is not entirely clear." *Arkansas Writers' Project v. Ragland,* 107 S. Ct. 1722, 1730 n.7 (1987), citing Note, *Section 1983 in State Court: A Remedy for Unconstitutional State Taxation,* 95 Yale L.J. 414, 420-21 (1985). Several recent state court decisions dealt with this issue. The Mississippi Supreme Court reads *Fair Assessment in Real Estate Association v. McNary,* 454 U.S. 100 (1981), as holding that state courts have authority to hear § 1983 actions attacking the constitutionality of state tax statutes. *Marx v. Truck Rental and Leasing Association,* 520 So. 2d 1333 (Miss. 1987). The Supreme Court of Kansas took the same position. *Allison v. Johnson County Board of County Commissioners,* 241 Kan. 266, 737 P.2d 6 (1987). The Supreme Court of North Dakota determined that, although the Tax Injunction Act does not apply in state court, it does provide the proper standard for § 1983 tax suits:

> Thus, although we conclude that the Tax Injunction Act does not *per se* apply to state court actions, we nevertheless conclude that imposition of similar limitations under *state* law upon § 1983 actions brought in state court challenging the levy is appropriate. We therefore hold that a taxpayer may not bring a § 1983 action in state court seeking to enjoin, suspend, or restrain the assessment, levy, or collection of any tax under state law where an adequate state remedy is available.

Linderkamp v. Bismarck School District, 397 N.W.2d 76, 80 (N.D. 1986) (emphasis in original), following *Zizka v. Water Pollution Control Authority,* 195 Conn. 682, 490 A.2d 509 (1985). The Georgia Court of Appeals, following *Backus v. Chilivis,* 236 Ga. 500, 224 S.E.2d 370 (1976), concluded that § 1983 is not available to contest an allegedly nonuniform and nonequal property tax appraisal procedure. *Vann v. Board of Tax Assessors,* 186 Ga. App. 208, 367 S.E.2d 43 (1988).

§ 12.14 Johnson Act

Page 270, add at end of section:

The Johnson Act was inapplicable when the plaintiff did not challenge utility rates but contested a tariff allowing termination of telephone service because of the content of recorded messages. *Carlin Communication v. Southern Bell Telephone and Telegraph Co.,* 802 F.2d 1352 (11th Cir. 1986).

The Johnson Act is not applicable to preemption claims because, when these claims are asserted, federal court jurisdiction is not based solely on a claim that the utility rate order is repugnant to the federal Constitution; preemption claims require federal statutory interpretation. *Hawaii Telephone Co. v. Public Utilities Commission,* 827 F.2d 1264 (9th Cir. 1987), *cert. denied,* 108 S. Ct. 2870 (1988); *New Orleans Public Service v.*

New Orleans, 782 F.2d 1236 (5th Cir.), *modified on other grounds,* 798 F.2d 858 (5th * Cir. 1986), *cert. denied,* 107 S. Ct. 1910 (1987), *subsequent history,* 850 F.2d 1069 (5th Cir. 1988), *cert. granted,* 109 S. Ct. 780 (1989).

The Johnson Act is not limited to injunctive relief, but also covers claims for monetary and declaratory relief. *Miller v. NYS Public Service Commission,* 807 F.2d 28 (2d Cir. 1986).

Plaintiff cannot avoid the Johnson Act by failing to pursue a speedy and efficient state court remedy. *People's National Utility Co. v. Houston,* 837 F.2d 1366 (5th Cir. 1988).

§ 12.15 Domestic Relations Doctrine (New)

The federal courts traditionally decline to exercise jurisdiction over domestic relations controversies "when the core issue involves the status of parent and child or husband and wife." *Coats v. Woods,* 819 F.2d 236, 237 (9th Cir.), *appeal dismissed & cert. denied,* 108 S. Ct. 46 (1987). The domestic relations doctrine was invoked in this § 1983 case which, "while raising constitutional issues, is at its core a child custody dispute." *Id. See also Daniels v. Stovall,* 660 F. Supp. 301 (S.D. Tex. 1987) (issues involving divorce and child custody).

CHAPTER 13

MOOTNESS OF CLAIM AND ACTION

§ 13.2 Federal Court Mootness Principles

Page 273, add after second full paragraph:

When a case becomes moot on appeal, the Supreme Court normally vacates the judgment of the court below. *United States v. Munsingwear,* 340 U.S. 36 (1950). In *Karcher v. May,* 108 S. Ct. 388 (1987), however, the Court ruled that the fact that former public officials, who are parties to the action, do not have standing to appeal to defend the constitutionality of the contested statute, does not render the case moot. The case became neither moot nor unreviewable, because successor officials were automatically substituted as parties (see § **11.4**), and they could have chosen to appeal. "The rules effectuating automatic substitution of public officers were specifically designed to prevent suits involving public officers from becoming moot due to personnel changes." 108 S. Ct. at 395.

§ 13.3 Claims for Monetary Relief

Page 276, add at end of section:

The release of the plaintiffs on parole did not moot their challenge to parole release procedures, because they asserted claims for damages and the defendants parole officers' immunity from monetary liability had not been resolved by the Supreme Court. *Board of Pardons v. Allen,* 107 S. Ct. 2415, 2417 n.1 (1987).

While the village's stipulation not to terminate water service at plaintiffs' property rendered plaintiffs' request for declaratory relief moot, it did not moot the action, because plaintiffs asserted a "colorable" claim for damages. *Stokes v. Village of Wurtsboro,* 818 F.2d 4 (2d Cir. 1987).

A prisoner's claims for injunctive and declaratory relief were mooted when he was moved to another prison unit, but he retained standing to assert a claim for damages. *Martin v. Sargent,* 780 F.2d 1334 (8th Cir. 1985).

Consistent with the "better view" asserted on page 275 of the main volume, a claim for nominal damages is found sufficient to create a case or controversy. *Green v. McKaskle,* 788 F.2d 1116, 1124 (5th Cir. 1986).

A party who is offered all of the relief demanded may not refuse the offer and go to trial, because that party is not aggrieved. A party may not choose "to forfeit that relief to obtain a chance on a precedent that would help only strangers." *Alliance to End Repression v. Chicago,* 820 F.2d 873, 876 (7th Cir. 1987).

* The Fifth Circuit stated that attorneys' "[f]ees are allowed even through the injunction is dismissed as moot." *Nash v. Chandler,* 859 F.2d 1210, 1211 (5th Cir. 1988).

§ 13.4 Voluntary Cessation of Allegedly Illegal Conduct

Page 278, add at end of section:

In a § 1983 suit, the Supreme Court reiterated the doctrine of *United States v. W.T. Grant Co.,* stressing that defendant must show that it is " '*absolutely clear* that the allegedly wrongful behavior could not reasonably be expected to recur.' " *G. Waltney of Smithfield v. Chesapeake Bay Foundation,* 108 S. Ct. 376, 386 (1987) quoting from *United States v. Concentrated Phosphate Export Association,* 393 U.S. 199, 203 (1968) (emphasis in original). *See Steele v. Van Buren Public School District,* 845 F.2d 1492 (8th Cir. 1988) (disavowal of intent to resume prayers in class not sufficient to moot case).

Statutory or regulatory amendments may render a case moot. *United States Department of Treasury v. Galioto,* 106 S. Ct. 2683 (1986) (amendment to federal * statute); *Ransom v. Marrazzo,* 848 F.2d 398, 409 (3d Cir. 1988); *Dial v. Coler,* 791 F.2d 78 (7th Cir. 1986) (federal program changed and new regulations promulgated). *Cf. Green v. McCall,* 636 F. Supp. 101 (D. Conn. 1986) (rule changes did not moot case where agency continued to violate court order), *aff'd,* 822 F.2d 284 (2d Cir. 1987).

§ 13.5 Capable of Repetition, Yet Evading Review

Page 281, add at end of section:

The Court applied the "capable of repetition, yet evading review" doctrine in an Education of the Handicapped Act (EHA) setting in *Honig v. Doe,* 108 S. Ct. 592 (1988). This doctrine may save a case from mootness if there is either a "demonstrated probability" or a "reasonable expectation" that the same controversy will recur. *Id.* at 601 n.6. The issue is whether the controversy is "*capable* of repetition and not . . . whether the claimant had demonstrated that a recurrence of the dispute was more probable than not." *Id.* at 602 n.6 (emphasis in original).

The Chief Justice, concurring in *Honig,* advocates an "exception" to the mootness doctrine "for those cases where the events which render the case moot have supervened since our grant of certiorari or noting of probable jurisdiction in the case." *Id.* at 608 (Rehnquist, C.J., concurring).

The Supreme Court also applied the "capable of repetition, yet evading review" doctrine in *Burlington Northern Railroad v. Brotherhood of Maintenance of Way Employees,* 107 S. Ct. 1841 (1987) (labor dispute) and *Brock v. Roadway Express,* 107 S. Ct. 1740 (1987) (procedural due process).

The doctrine was applied to a claimed denial of assigned counsel to indigents found in civil contempt and incarcerated for failure to make child support payments. *Leonard v. Hammond,* 804 F.2d 838 (4th Cir. 1986).

§ 13.6 Mootness and Class Actions

Page 285, add at end of section:

The settlement of the named plaintiff's claim for damages and the probable mooting of his individual claims for injunctive and declaratory relief did "not necessarily moot the potential class action." *Ball v. Wagers,* 795 F.2d 579, 581 (6th Cir. 1986). The action was remanded to determine if the plaintiff "is yet" a proper class representative. *Id.* at 582.

The Eleventh Circuit ruled that because the named plaintiff's claims for equitable relief became moot by the time he moved for class certification, he could not represent a class of individuals seeking equitable relief, even though he asserted a live claim for damages. *Tucker v. Phyfer,* 819 F.2d 1030 (11th Cir. 1987). The authors believe that this is erroneous. The circuit court ignored (1) the possibility that in some instances class certification may relate back to the filing of the complaint, and (2) Supreme Court decisions deemphasizing the significance of the timing of the class action order for mootness purposes. See discussion in the main volume at page 282.

CHAPTER 14

DAMAGES AND OTHER RELIEF

§ 14.1 Remedies in § 1983 Actions – Introduction

Page 289, add at end of section:

In a non-§ 1983 action raising a Fourth Amendment claim against federal defendants, the Fourth Circuit broadly concluded that "[t]he denial of a constitutional right, if denial is established, constitutes irreparable harm for purposes of equitable jurisdiction." *Ross v. Meese,* 818 F.2d 1132, 1135 (4th Cir. 1987). On the other hand, the First Circuit ruled that "[t]he alleged denial of procedural due process, without more, does not automatically trigger such a finding" of irreparable injury. *Public Service Co. v. Town of West Newbury,* 835 F.2d 380, 382 (1st Cir. 1987). The court read cases holding that a deprivation of constitutional rights is sufficient to constitute irreparable injury as "almost entirely restricted to . . . free speech, association, privacy or other rights as to which temporary deprivation is viewed of such quantitative importance as to be irremediable by any subsequent relief." *Id.*

The same general equitable remedial principles developed by the Supreme Court in the school desegregation cases are applicable in Eighth Amendment prison condition
* cases. *Inmates v. Barry,* 844 F.2d 828 (D.C. Cir. 1988). In *Williams v. Lane,* 851 F.2d 867, 885 (7th Cir. 1988), the court stated that under § 1983 "prisoners may receive remedies comparable to all civil litigants[,]" including damages and injunctive relief to present continuing violations of constitutional rights.

When a state statute is found to be unconstitutional, a federal court can enjoin its enforcement in favor of all similarly situated persons, even though the action was not brought as a class action. "When a state statute has been ruled unconstitutional, state actors have an obligation to desist from enforcing that statute." *Soto-Lopez v. Civil Service Commission,* 840 F.2d 162, 168 (2d Cir. 1988), citing *Cooper v. Aaron,* 358 U.S. 1 (1958). In these circumstances class certification is largely a formality.

"[T]he availability of injunctive relief fails to affect an attendant claim for damages." *Parrish v. Johnson,* 800 F.2d 600, 606 (6th Cir. 1986).

* In employment discrimination cases under Title VII and § 1983, back pay and reinstatement are "presumptively favored" equitable remedies. Back pay "should include the salary, including any raises which plaintiff would have received but for the discrimination, as well as sick leave, vacation pay, pension benefits and other fringe benefits she would have received but for discrimination." *Gutzwiller v. Fenik,* 860 F.2d 1317, 1333 (6th Cir. 1988).

Reinstatement may be an appropriate remedy for a public employee who was discharged in violation of her constitutional rights, even if the remedy violates state law and may have "disturbing consequences." *Banks v. Burkich,* 788 F.2d 1161 (6th Cir. 1986).

* The Ninth Circuit ruled that the proper remedies for a public employee discharged in violation of procedural due process are to order the process that is due and "any attendant damages which directly resulted from the failure to give the proper procedure." There may be a right to reinstatement when a violation of a substantive constitutional right "coexists with the right to procedural due process[,]" but it is not an available remedy for a violation of procedural due process alone. *Brady v. Gebbie,* 859 F.2d 1543, 1552 (9th Cir. 1988). *See also Perry v. Brakke,* 826 F.2d 740, 747 (8th Cir. 1987) ("Reinstatement may not be an appropriate remedy for an employee who was terminated for cause but denied procedural due process").

In wrongful discharge cases, the plaintiff is entitled to reinstatement absent "unusual circumstances." Such circumstances existed, however, where the wrongfully discharged sheriff's term had expired during the litigation. *Lucas v. O'Loughlin,* 831 F.2d 232 (11th Cir. 1987), *cert. denied,* 108 S. Ct. 1595 (1988).

* Cases analyzing the remedies in due process stigma cases are discussed in **§ 14.5.**

Front pay is an equitable remedy that may be awarded in lieu of reinstatement, in an appropriate case, to an employee discharged in violation of his constitutional rights.
* *Haskins v. City of Boaz,* 822 F.2d 1014 (11th Cir. 1987). In *Johnson v. Chapel Hill Independent School District,* 853 F.2d 375, 382-383 (5th Cir. 1988), the court stated that "reinstatement rather than front pay is the preferred remedy for a victim of employment discrimination[,]" "front pay may be awarded as a supplement to reinstatement or to encourage the employee to promptly return the discrimination victim to his rightful job" and has been "characterized as an extension of defendant's back pay liability until the employer makes an offer of reinstatement."

Expungement of a record may be a proper § 1983 remedy. *Hall v. Six Unknown Named Agents,* 647 F. Supp. 136 (N.D.N.Y. 1986) (prison misconduct report), *rev'd in*
* *part, aff'd in part,* 825 F.2d 642 (2d Cir. 1987). A court's inherent authority to expunge, however, is narrow. The court should balance the harm caused the plaintiff by the continued existence of the record against the government's interest in maintaining the record. *Feagin v. Broglin,* 693 F. Supp. 741 (N.D. Ind. 1988).

§ 14.2 Trial by Jury

Page 292, add at end of section:

The Tenth Circuit, finding that the lower courts have been "far from consistent" in their treatment of back pay as a legal or equitable remedy, concluded that generally the issue has depended upon "whether the plaintiff has requested back pay as an adjunct to the equitable remedy of reinstatement, in which case it has been characterized as equitable, . . . or as an element of plaintiff's damages for the breach of his employment contract." In this case, although the plaintiff requested reinstatement, the focus of his complaint is on the recovery of damages for an allegedly discriminatory discharge. Under these circumstances back pay is a legal remedy to which the right to trial by jury attaches. *Skinner v. Total Petroleum,* 859 F.2d 1439, 1443-44 (10th Cir. 1988).

A jury verdict on a § 1983 claim for legal relief in defendant's favor was binding on a parallel Title VII claim. *Ward v. Texas Employment Commission,* 823 F.2d 907 (5th
* Cir. 1987). *See also Gutzwiller v. Fenik,* 860 F.2d 1317, 1333 (6th Cir. 1988); *Skinner v. Total Petroleum,* 859 F.2d at 1439; *Roebuck v. Drexel University,* 852 F.2d 715 (3d Cir. 1988); *Wade v. Orange County Sheriff's Office,* 844 F.2d 951 (2d Cir. 1988). In *Roebuck v. Drexel University,* 852 F.2d at 737-38, the Third Circuit determined that because the jury's findings on a § 1981 claim are binding on the trial judge's resolution of a concurrently tried Title VII claim, "a district court should not render judgment on a Title VII claim prior to the return of the jury verdict on a related § 1981 claim."

In *Hussein v. Oshkosh Motor Truck Co.,* 816 F.2d 348 (7th Cir. 1987), the court analyzed the interplay between the right to trial by jury and collateral estoppel. The district court dismissed plaintiff's § 1981 claims for legal relief. (Plaintiff had a right to trial by jury on these claims and demanded this right.) The district court then held a bench trial on plaintiff's Title VII claim and made findings of fact and entered judgment in favor of defendant. The circuit court found the dismissal of the § 1981 claim improper, which presented the issue of whether the findings on the Title VII claim collaterally estopped plaintiff from trying the § 1981 claim before a jury. In rejecting collateral estoppel, the circuit court concluded that plaintiff should not be deprived of the opportunity to have his § 1981 claims tried to a jury simply because the trial judge erroneously dismissed these claims. If they had not been dismissed, the jury findings on the § 1981 claim would have been binding on the Title VII claim. *See also Volk v. Coler,* 845 F.2d 1422 (7th Cir. 1988).

The Fourth Circuit reached the opposite conclusion in *Ritter v. Mount St. Mary's College,* 814 F.2d 986 (4th Cir.), *cert. denied,* 108 S. Ct. 260 (1987). The court determined that the district court's findings on a Title VII claim in defendant's favor collaterally estopped plaintiff's remanded claims under the Equal Pay Act and Age Discrimination in Employment Act, which had been erroneously dismissed by the trial court. While this conclusion did deprive plaintiff of his jury trial right on the remanded claims, interests of finality and judicial economy were considered of overriding
* concern in this setting. The authors believe that *Ritter* is contrary to the weight of authority and impermissibly deprives the plaintiff of the right to trial by jury on the legal claims. The Fourth Circuit, although not overruling *Ritter,* "cut back" its holding in *Swentek v. USAFR,* 830 F.2d 532 (4th Cir. 1987). *See Roebuck v. Drexel University,* 852 F.2d at 737 n.39 (discussing *Ritter* and *Swentek*).

For an analysis of the application of the Seventh Amendment right to trial by jury to congressionally created causes of action, *see Tull v. United States,* 107 S. Ct. 1831 (1987).

§ 14.3 Damages in General

Page 294, add at end of section:

Damages received in settlement of a free speech claim are considered for personal injuries and thus are excludable from gross income under the Internal Revenue Code. *Bent v. Commissioner,* 835 F.2d 67 (3d Cir. 1987).

§ 14.5 Damages for Procedural Due Process Violations

Page 298, add at end of section:

In a case involving a public employee who claimed that he was discharged for stigmatizing reasons without a hearing, the Eighth Circuit ruled that if the district court on remand finds that the reasons for termination were publicized and true, plaintiff "will not be entitled to actual damages or reinstatement, but only nominal damages and attorneys fees." *Hogue v. Clinton,* 791 F.2d 1318, 1325 (8th Cir.), *cert. denied,* 107 S. Ct. 648 (1986). Judge Lay, concurring in part and dissenting in part, opined that the damages principles established by *Carey v. Piphus,* 435 U.S. 247 (1987), were meant to apply to deprivations of liberty interests, and not to public employees deprived of protected property interests in violation of procedural due process. He reasoned that "[w]ithout the deterrent of a back pay award, no incentive remains for the employer to do anything more than provide only a post-termination hearing." 107 S. Ct. at 1328. The authors point out, however, that *Carey* found that the potential availability of punitive damages and attorney's fees provides not inconsequential "assurance that agents of the State will not deliberately ignore due process rights." *Carey v. Piphus,* 435 U.S. at 257 n.11.

* The District of Columbia Circuit Court of Appeals concluded that a delayed grant of a name-clearing hearing does not necessarily remedy the procedural due process injury because, by its very nature, such a hearing "loses value the longer it is delayed" and the delay itself may constitute compensable due process injury. *Lyons v. Barrett,* 851 F.2d 406 (D.C. Cir. 1988). The court also discussed the contours of the name-clearing hearing, finding that the district court has discretion to tailor the form of the hearing to the particular circumstances. *Id.* at 411.

Damages for procedural due process violations in public employee–stigma liberty interest cases "may not include back pay or reinstatement since the liberty interest protects only reputation, as opposed to a property interest in continued employment." *Willbanks v. Smith County,* 661 F. Supp. 212, 220 (E.D. Tex. 1987). Substantial damages, however, may be awarded for deprivation of the liberty interest. In this case, the jury found that the plaintiff deputy sheriff's employment was terminated for alleged thefts of property and that this charge had been publicized. The district court upheld a jury award of $23,000 compensatory damages and $2,000 punitive damages.

The Fifth Circuit found that the district court committed error in instructing the jury that "mental anguish" and "pain and suffering" are separate items of damages, since the concepts overlap and *Carey* lumps them together as "distress." *Fowler v. Carrollton Public Library,* 799 F.2d 976 (5th Cir. 1986). In addition, injury to reputation and distress are not separate but are "linked" as compensable psychic injury. *Id.* at 983.

§ 14.6 Damages for Violations of Substantive Constitutional Rights—In General

Page 301, add after note 3 reference:

The Fifth Circuit found that the district court's instruction that actual damages could be awarded for the intrinsic value of the deprivation of constitutional rights violated the Supreme Court's teachings in *Memphis Community School District v. Stachura,* 106 S. Ct. 2537 (1986). *Auster Oil & Gas v. Stream,* 835 F.2d 597 (5th Cir.), *cert. denied,* 108 S. Ct. 2007 (1988). In another case in which the jury instruction violated *Stachura,* the circuit found that the error was harmless because plaintiff received "minimal damages" even though the record substantiated that he suffered considerable emotional and physical harm. *Vosburg v. Solem,* 845 F.2d 763 (8th Cir. 1988).

The Sixth Circuit read the Supreme Court's decision in *Memphis Community School District v. Stachura* as authorizing awards of presumed damages for First Amendment violations and for some Eighth Amendment violations, presumably meaning in an appropriate case. *Parrish v. Johnson,* 800 F.2d 600 (6th Cir. 1986). *See also Walje v. City of Winchester,* 827 F.2d 10 (6th Cir. 1987). See §§ **14.8** and **14.10.**

The Sixth Circuit applied the decision in *Stachura* retroactively. Even though the jury instruction given pre-*Stachura* was not objected to at trial, it may be contested for the first time on appeal. The jury was erroneously instructed to consider as a partial measure of compensatory damages the intrinsic value and importance of the First Amendment. The objection may be made for the first time on appeal when, as here, it was clearly incorrect under a Supreme Court decision rendered during the pendency of the appeal. *Ratliff v. Board of Education,* 820 F.2d 792 (6th Cir. 1987).

Dicta in an Eighth Circuit decision reads the Supreme Court's decision in *Stachura* as disapproving the Eighth Circuit's decision in *Herrera v. Valentine,* 653 F.2d 1220 (8th Cir. 1981), discussed on page 300 of the main volume. *Harris v. City of Pagedale,* 821 F.2d 499, 505 n.8 (8th Cir.), *cert. denied,* 108 S. Ct. 504 (1987).

§ 14.8 —First Amendment Rights

Page 303, add at end of section:

The Third Circuit read the Supreme Court's decision in *Memphis Community School District v. Stachura,* 106 S. Ct. 2537 (1986), as holding that presumed damages may be awarded when plaintiff is unable to prove emotional distress. In this case plaintiff's claim did not "fall within the narrow category of cases in which damages may be presumed." *Spence v. Board of Education,* 806 F.2d 1198, 1200 (3d Cir. 1986). Judge Higginbotham, concurring in the result, read *Carey* and *Memphis* as meaning that "it is the *injury,* not a precise measure of damages, that must be clearly established in the record before a plaintiff may recover any damages." *Id.* at 1203 (emphasis in original).

Under *Stachura,* presumed damages are not available "for plaintiffs like Lewis, whose damages are readily measurable." *Lewis v. Harrison School District,* 805 F.2d 310, 317 (8th Cir. 1986), *cert. denied,* 107 S. Ct. 2481 (1987). The Sixth Circuit read

Stachura as authorizing presumed damages for First Amendment violations, presumably meaning in an appropriate case. *Parrish v. Johnson,* 800 F.2d 600 (6th Cir. 1986).

In an ambiguous opinion, the Sixth Circuit read *Stachura* as meaning that the "focus of damage awards for constitutional torts should be compensatory and that it is proper to look to common law tort principles in granting presumed damages in cases where specific damages are difficult to establish." *Walje v. City of Winchester,* 827 F.2d 10, 13 (6th Cir. 1987). The relevance of this point to the case at hand is unclear, as the court went on to determine that the *evidence* supported the district court's award of "general damages" of $5,000 for the suspension of plaintiff from his public employment in violation of his First Amendment rights.

The Sixth Circuit also applied *Stachura* retroactively and allowed a jury instruction to be challenged for the first time on appeal. The instruction was clearly incorrect under *Stachura,* which was decided during the pendency of the instant appeal. *Ratliff v. Board of Education,* 820 F.2d 792 (6th Cir. 1987).

In *City of Watseka v. Illinois Public Action Council,* 796 F.2d 1547 (7th Cir. 1986), *aff'd,* 107 S. Ct. 919 (1987), the court found that damages were properly awarded for the specific compensable harm suffered rather than the abstract value of the First Amendment right at issue.

In *Sykes v. McDowell,* 786 F.2d 1098 (11th Cir. 1986), the court found that the district court's award of $60,000 to the plaintiff public employee, who had been fired in violation of his First Amendment rights, was not excessive. The plaintiff suffered embarrassment among his peer employees, and in a small community the humiliation of a public firing is evident.

A police officer, who was fired in violation of his First Amendment rights, was awarded front pay in lieu of reinstatement, back pay, lost benefits, and damages for the pain and suffering from the wrongful loss of his career. *Wulf v. City of Wichita,* 644 F. Supp. 1211 (D. Kan. 1986).

§ 14.9 – Racial Discrimination

Page 304, add at end of section:

Under 42 U.S.C. § 1981, general compensatory damages for racial discrimination in employment may include compensation for emotional pain and suffering. Such damages will not be presumed, but must be based upon evidence. *Gunby v. Pennsylvania Electric Co.,* 840 F.2d 1108 (3d Cir. 1988).

§ 14.9A – Sex Discrimination (New)

The Seventh Circuit upheld an award of $30,000 compensatory damages to a police officer whose termination was the product of gender discrimination. Of the $30,000, $20,250 represented compensation for embarrassment and humiliation and $9,750 was for lost wages. The opinion contains a valuable compilation of awards "for embarrassment, humiliation, emotional distress, and the like" in § 1981 and § 1983 employment discrimination termination cases. *Webb v. City of Chester,* 813 F.2d 824, 836-37 (7th Cir. 1987).

§ 14.10 –Excessive Force, Unreasonable Searches and Seizures, and Unlawful Arrests

Page 306, add at end of section:

The compensation principles of *Carey v. Piphus,* 435 U.S. 247 (1978), apply to Fourth Amendment claims. *Aubin v. Fudala,* 782 F.2d 280 (1st Cir. 1983). The principle of *Memphis Community School District v. Stachura,* 106 S. Ct. 2537 (1986), that damages may not be based upon the "abstract value" or importance of a constitutional right, was applied to Fourth Amendment violations in *Carter v. District of Columbia,* 795 F.2d 116, 133-35 (D.C. Cir. 1986).

For other examples of damages awards, *see Hagge v. Bauer,* 827 F.2d 101 (7th Cir. 1987) (police brutality: $75,000 compensation damages, $6,457 special damages and $25,000 punitive damages); *Hall v. Ochs,* 817 F.2d 920 (1st Cir. 1987) ($160,000 to arrestee for false arrest, false imprisonment, and excessive force, $5,000 to arrestee's daughter for being struck by a police officer, $210,000 punitive damages, and $60,000 prejudgment interest); *Hinshaw v. Doffer,* 785 F.2d 1260 (5th Cir. 1986) ($60,000 for false arrest, $25,000 for excessive force, and $2,000 punitive damages); *Aubin v, Fudala,* 782 F.2d 280 (1st Cir. 1983) ($30,000 for injuries from shooting); *Dennis v. Warren,* 779 F.2d 245 (5th Cir. 1985) ($6,000 compensatory and $10,000 punitive damages for unlawful arrest and detention); *Brown v. Triche,* 660 F. Supp. 281 (N.D. Ill. 1987) ($9,000 compensatory damages and $15,000 punitive damages to pretrial detainees beaten by deputy sheriff).

* In its original panel opinion in a case involving a police officer's killing of a 19-year-old male, the Seventh Circuit reaffirmed that loss of life is compensable to the decedent's estate, found that the district court did not commit error in allowing an economist to testify to the hedonic value of life, and upheld an award of damages of over $1.6 million. *Sherrod v. Berry,* 827 F.2d 195 (7th Cir. 1987). However, after vacating the panel opinion and granting en banc review, 835 F.2d 1222, the en banc court reversed the judgment of the district court on evidentiary grounds. *Sherrod v. Berry,* 856 F.2d 802 (7th Cir. 1988) (en banc) (see discussion in **§ 3.4**).

Two district courts turned to state law to determine the measure of damages for § 1983 wrongful death claims. *Sharpe v. Lewisburg,* 677 F. Supp. 1362 (M.D. Tenn. 1988); *Greene v. City of New York,* 675 F. Supp. 110 (S.D.N.Y. 1987). See **§ 11.3**.

§ 14.11 –Unconstitutional Prison Conditions

Page 306, add at end of section:

Because the Eighth Amendment prohibition against cruel and unusual punishment encompasses such a variety of wrongs, the Sixth Circuit adopted an ad hoc approach to determine whether presumed damages may be awarded for an Eighth Amendment violation. *Parrish v. Johnson,* 800 F.2d 600 (6th Cir. 1986). The court ruled specifically that presumed damages may be awarded for an Eighth Amendment violation for conduct that constitutes a common-law assault.

A prisoner's compensatory damages may include "only pain and suffering and not medical costs or lost earnings." *Thompkins v. Belt,* 828 F.2d 298, 301 (5th Cir. 1987).

A compilation of damages awards for improper prison confinement is set forth in *Ustrak v. Fairman,* 781 F.2d 573, 579 (7th Cir.), *cert. denied,* 107 S. Ct. 95 (1986). *See also Adams v. Wolff,* 624 F. Supp. 1036, 1040 (D. Nev. 1985).

In a prison sexual assault case, the Eighth Circuit observed that in sexual assault cases damage awards can easily reach the six-figure level. *Vosburg v. Solem,* 845 F.2d 763 (8th Cir. 1988).

For recent monetary awards in prisoner cases, *see Sourbeer v. Robinson,* 791 F.2d 1094 (3d Cir. 1986) ($1,970 for administrative confinement during period plaintiff should have been in general prison population; computed on basis of $10 per day), *cert. denied sub nom. Patton v. Sourbeer,* 107 S. Ct. 3276 (1987); *Soto v. Lord,* 693 F. Supp. 8, 21-22 (S.D.N.Y. 1988) ($50 for each day of punitive segregation confinement and $1.25 per day for lost prison wages); *Smith v. Montgomery County,* 643 F. Supp. 435 (D. Md. 1986) (class members whose Fourth Amendment rights were violated by strip searches entitled to awards of "nominal damages" of $200 to deter future violations and to vindicate the interests of the class); *Adams v. Wolff,* 624 F. Supp. 1036 (D. Nev. 1985) (expungement of violation from prison record; $16 per week for denial of right to outdoor exercise; loss of prison wages; $40 per week for unlawful punitive segregation).

§ 14.12 Mitigation of Damages

Page 308, add at end of section:

Assuming that § 1983 requires the mitigation of damages, only "reasonable attempts" to mitigate are required, which occurred here. *City of Watseka v. Illinois Public Action Council,* 796 F.2d 1547 (7th Cir. 1986), *aff'd,* 107 S. Ct. 919 (1987).

The Eleventh Circuit found that a federal rule of mitigation applies to § 1983 damages claims. In this case the mitigation rule justified reducing a back pay award by the amount of the plaintiff's earnings between his employment termination and the trial. "By requiring an award of back pay to be offset by interim earnings, courts compensate the plaintiff for the actual loss he suffered as a result of the defendant's unconstitutional action." *Murphy v. City of Flagler Beach,* 846 F.2d 1306, 1309 (11th Cir. 1988).

Disagreeing with decisions of the Seventh and Eighth Circuits allowing an offset for unemployment compensation, the Fifth Circuit holds that "whether to allow testimony of offset is within the discretion of the district court . . . ." *Matherne v. Wilson,* 851 F.2d 752, 762 (5th Cir. 1988).

§ 14.13 Punitive Damages

Page 313, add at end of section:

Applying the decision in *Smith v. Wade,* 461 U.S. 30 (1983), to a § 1981 intentional racial discrimination claim, the First Circuit upheld an instruction allowing the jury to award punitive damages if it finds that the racial discrimination was the result of malice or callous and reckless indifference. There is no requirement that the instruction use language like "extraordinary" or "outrageous." *Rowlett v. Anheuser-Busch,* 832 F.2d 194, 205-06 (1st Cir. 1987).

While it is necessary to establish a reckless or callous disregard of plaintiff's rights in order to trigger an inquiry into punitive damages, the fact that such a showing is made does not automatically entitle plaintiff to receive punitive damages. Rather, punitive damages are within the discretion of the trier of fact, which must weigh the nature of the conduct, the wisdom of pecuniary punishment, and the advisability of a deterrent. *Fairley v. Jones,* 824 F.2d 440 (5th Cir. 1987).

"A plaintiff may recover nominal as well as punitive damages even if a violation of his civil rights causes no actual injury." *Green v. McKaskle,* 788 F.2d 1115, 1124 (5th Cir. 1986). In *Hollins v. Powell,* 773 F.2d 191 (8th Cir. 1985), *cert. denied,* 106 S. Ct. 1635 (1986), the court ruled that the amount of punitive damages should bear a reasonable relationship to the injury inflicted and that it is appropriate to consider
* defendant's net worth. In a subsequent decision the Eighth Circuit determined that although the amount of punitive damages must bear a reasonable relationship to the amount of compensatory damages awarded, this rule does not apply to an award of nominal damages. "To apply a proportionality rule to a nominal damages award would invalidate most punitive damages awards . . . ." *Edwards v. Jewish Hospital,* 855 F.2d 1345, 1352 (8th Cir. 1988).

The Third Circuit ruled that evidence of a defendant's financial status is not a prerequisite to the imposition of punitive damages. In this case the defendants "had every opportunity to present evidence of their financial worth and chose not to do so." *Bennis v. Gable,* 823 F.2d 723, 734 n.14 (3d Cir. 1987).

Punitive damages are appropriate in cases of racially discriminatory employment practices. *Brown v. Freedman Baking Co.,* 810 F.2d 6 (1st Cir. 1987). In *Hall v. Ochs,* 817 F.2d 920, 927 (1st Cir. 1987), the court upheld a jury award for $200,000 punitive damages for the "shocking and brutal racial discrimination. As a conscience of the community, the jury responded accordingly."

A punitive damages award of $50,100 was upheld in the case of deliberate indifference to serious medical needs. "The callous indifference required for punitive damages is essentially the same as the deliberate indifference required for a finding of liability on the § 1983 claim; the propriety of a guilty verdict on the latter thus supports the punitive damage award as well." *Cooper v. Dyke,* 814 F.2d 941, 948 (4th Cir. 1987).

In light of plaintiff's "protected property interest in his tenured position as a teacher, Kirksey's callous refusal to comply with the letter and spirit of the settlement agreement reached justifies an award of punitive damages." *Washington v. Kirksey,* 811 F.2d 561, 565 (11th Cir.), *cert. denied,* 108 S. Ct. 96 (1987).

The district court's punitive damages award of $185,000 was not excessive. The district court judge had observed that he "had heard many excessive force cases in eight years of jury trials, but none so shocked the conscience of this court as did this one." *O'Neil v. Krzeminski,* 839 F.2d 9, 13 (2d Cir. 1988).

Punitive damages of $31,500 were awarded where the plaintiff local resident was forcibly removed from city commission chambers and arrested with "callous indifference" to his First Amendment rights. The opinion contains a compilation of punitive damage awards in First Amendment cases. *Jones v. Key West,* 679 F. Supp. 1547 (S.D. Fla. 1988).

Plaintiff was a state university professor whose employment was terminated because she spoke out against preferential treatment given to university athletes. The jury awarded her punitive damages of $2.3 million. "As far as the court is aware, this might be the largest amount of punitive damages of record in a § 1983 case involving public employees or officers (particularly university administrators)." *Kemp v. Ervin,* 651 F. Supp. 495, 507 (N.D. Ga 1986). The court found the amount "shockingly excessive" and reduced it to a maximum of $400,000 ($200,000 against each of the two defendants).

Where the trial judge probably should have charged the jury on punitive damages but the jury found for defendants on every issue, finding no actual damages, the issue of punitive damages was moot. *King v. Jones,* 824 F.2d 324, 327 (4th Cir. 1987).

Punitive damages were not proper against a mayor where "he acted at all times under the advice of the duly selected city attorney." *Angell v. Leslie,* 832 F.2d 817, 821 (4th Cir. 1987).

State law may not abrogate or limit the right to recover punitive damages under § 1983. *Gordon v. Norman,* 788 F.2d 1194, 1199 (6th Cir. 1986). The fact that the state law required the municipality to indemnify its employees neither made the municipality the real party in interest nor immunized the official from liability for punitive damages. *Haile v. Village of Sag Harbor,* 639 F. Supp. 718, 723 (E.D.N.Y. 1986).

Where there are multiple defendants, punitive damages may not be the subject of joint and several liability. *Shields v. Martin,* 109 Idaho 32, 706 P.2d 21 (1985).

§ 14.14 Multiple Defendants and Contribution

Page 315, add at end of section:

The Fifth Circuit, without analysis, relied upon state law to determine that defendants should be jointly and severally liable for damages resulting from a violation of First Amendment rights. *Sims v. Jefferson Downs Racing Association,* 778 F.2d 1068, 1081-82 (5th Cir. 1985). In a subsequent decision, the same court, in reversing a judgment against one of two jointly and severally liable tortfeasors, found that since federal law did not address the effect of the reversal on the tortfeasors who remained liable, it was necessary under 42 U.S.C. § 1988 to resolve the issue under state law. *Hinshaw v. Doffer,* 785 F.2d 1260 (5th Cir. 1986). Under the applicable state law, the adjudged tortfeasors remained fully liable for the judgment, and this rule was found consistent with § 1983's goals of fully "compensating plaintiffs who suffer a violation of constitutional rights and preventing abuses by those acting under color of state law." *Id.* at 1269.

* Relying upon the analysis in the text, a federal district court held that whether a settlement with one of two joint tortfeasors may be pleaded as an affirmative defense by the remaining defendant should be determined under 42 U.S.C. § 1988 by reference to state law. A state common law rule denying contribution among joint tortfeasors, but providing that the plaintiff is entitled to only one satisfaction of his damages, thus requiring a set-off to the extent of the settlement, is consistent with § 1983's compensatory purpose. "Allowing double recovery would conflict with § 1983's basic purpose–to provide compensation, not a windfall." *Hoffman v. McNamara,* 688 F. Supp. 830, 834 (D. Conn. 1988).

The trial court instructed the jury that " 'when the defendants act together, the law permits the injured party to treat all concerned in the injury jointly; and all are liable to the plaintiff in a total sum as damages.' " This instruction was recognized as "a correct statement of joint liability under § 1983." *Hall v. Ochs,* 817 F.2d 920, 926 (1st Cir. 1987).

Apportionment of damages is appropriate if there is a factual basis for some rough estimate limiting a defendant's liability to that part of the harm he caused. The Third Circuit upheld the district court's charge: "The trial court stated that compensatory damages could be awarded only once, and when the harm inflicted by separate torts does not lend itself to definite or satisfactory proof, apportionment may properly be left to the jury's estimate." *Bennis v. Gable,* 823 F.2d 723, 734 n.14 (3d Cir. 1987).

Rejecting the argument of the defendant district attorney that the jury's apportionment of damages was "unconscionable," the Fifth Circuit set forth the rule that apportionment is a factual matter, subject to review under the deferential reasonableness standard. *Mairena v. Foti,* 816 F.2d 1061, 1065 (5th Cir. 1987), *cert. denied,* 108 S. Ct. 697 (1988).

When the defendants acted concurrently and produced indivisible harm to plaintiffs, joint and several liability was proper with respect to compensatory but not punitive damages. *Shields v. Martin,* 109 Idaho 32, 706 P.2d 21 (1985).

While § 1983 provides no cause of action for indemnification, the defendant may implead a third-party defendant on the basis of a state law claim for indemnification. *Holman v. Walls,* 648 F. Supp. 947 (D. Del. 1986); *Banks v. City of Emeryville,* 109 F.R.D. 535 (N.D. Cal. 1985). Note, however, that when the third-party claim seeks indemnification against the state treasury, it will be barred by the Eleventh Amendment. *Holman v. Walls,* 648 F. Supp. at 954 ("A state's Eleventh Amendment immunity extends as well to third-party claims for contribution or indemnity that fall within a federal court's ancillary jurisdiction").

A settling joint tortfeasor does not have a right to contribution under § 1983. *Medina County Agricultural Society v. Swagler,* 34 Ohio App. 3d 336, 518 N.E.2d 589 (1987).

§ 14.15 Settlement, Waiver, and Release

Page 316, add at end of section:

A waiver of a § 1983 claim was valid when it was negotiated as part of a settlement of a civil action by sophisticated and experienced businessmen represented by counsel. *Trans Sterling v. Bible,* 804 F.2d 525 (9th Cir. 1986).

In *Town of Newton v. Rumery,* 107 S. Ct. 1187 (1987), the Supreme Court ruled that an agreement in which a criminal defendant releases his right to file a § 1983 action in return for a prosecutor's dismissal of pending criminal charges is not automatically invalid. Although the Court agreed "that in some cases these agreements may infringe important interests of the criminal defendant and of society as a whole, we do not believe that the mere possibility of harm to these interests calls for a *per se* rule." *Id.* at 1192. Rather, the validity of these agreements should be determined on a case-by-case basis. The issue provoked three separate opinions. Justice Powell wrote the opinion of the Court, in which the Chief Justice and Justices Whites, O'Connor, and Scalia joined, except with respect to Part III-B, in which only three other Justices joined, because Justices O'Connor disassociated herself from that part of the Court's opinion. Justice O'Connor wrote a separate opinion, concurring in part. Justice Stevens wrote a dissenting opinion, which was joined in by Justices Brennan, Marshall, and Blackmun.

Despite these various opinions, there are several important areas of agreement. First, all the Justices seem to agree that the validity of release-dismissal agreements presents a question of federal law.

Second, all the Justices rejected a rule of per se invalidity, although the dissenters did so with much reluctance. Third, all the Justices agreed that, to be valid, the agreement must be voluntary and not the product of overreaching by the prosecutor. Justice O'Connor's concurring opinion details some of the important factors on the question of voluntariness:

> The knowledge and experience of the criminal defendant and the circumstances of the execution of the release, including, importantly, whether the defendant was counselled, are clearly relevant. The nature of the criminal charges that are pending is also important, for the greater the charge, the greater the coercive effect. The existence of a legitimate criminal justice objective for obtaining the release will support its validity, and, importantly, the possibility of abuse is clearly mitigated if the release-dismissal agreement is executed under judicial supervision.

Id. at 1197 (O'Connor, J., concurring).

All of the Justices also agreed that the validity of the agreements should be determined on a case-by-case basis, and seem to be in agreement that, in evaluating the validity of an agreement, the pertinent considerations, in addition to voluntariness, are whether the agreement was the product of the prosecutor's overreaching or other misconduct and whether the agreement adversely affects the public interest.

There is disagreement, however, over whether release-dismissal agreements should be presumed valid or invalid. In Part III-B of Justice Powell's opinion, which represents the position of four Justices, emphasis is placed upon the broad realm of prosecutorial discretion and the deference courts normally give to the exercise of that discretion. "Against this background of discretion, the mere opportunity to act improperly does not compel an assumption that all or even a significant number of release-dismissal agreements stem from the prosecutors abandoning 'the independence of judgment required by [their] public trust[.]' " *Id.* at 1194, quoting from *Imbler v. Pachtman,* 424 U.S. 409, 423 (1976).

On the other hand, because "release-dismissal agreements potentially threaten the integrity of the criminal process and preclude vindication of federal civil rights[,]" Justice O'Connor would place the burden on the defendant to "establish that a particular release executed in exchange for the dismissal of a criminal charge was voluntarily made, not the product of prosecutorial overreaching, and in the public interest." 107 S. Ct. at 1197. Moreover, the dissenting Justices found "that the federal policies reflected in the enactment and enforcement of § 1983 mandate a *strong presumption* against the enforceability of such agreements . . . ." *Id.* at 1205. (emphasis added.) When Justice O'Connor's concurrence is added to the four dissenting Justices, there are five Justices who would invoke a presumption against the enforcement of release-dismissal agreements.

When a plaintiff alleged that the release of his § 1983 claim in return for the dropping of criminal charges was not voluntary, he was entitled to a hearing on the question of the voluntariness of the release. *Sexton v. Ryan,* 804 F.2d 26 (2d Cir. 1986). A state court judge took the position that "defendant, as the party relying upon the release, has the burden of establishing that the agreement is neither involuntary nor the product of an abuse of the criminal process." *Cowles v. Brownell,* 127 A.D.2d 325, 329, 515 N.Y.S.2d 131, 133 (3d Dep't 1987) (Judge Kane, concurring).

A release-dismissal agreement was not voluntary where plaintiff was arrested and held in jail solely to coerce him to sign the agreement, where he refused to sign it three times and ultimately signed it to obtain his release. "Reduced to its essence the choice was this: forget your liberty and face criminal charges or forfeit your right to bring suit. . . . No waiver executed under such circumstances can be called voluntary." *Hall v. Ochs,* 817 F.2d 920, 923-24 (1st Cir. 1987).

The decision in *Rumery* does not sanction the abuse of prosecutorial power in the form of a prosecution motivated by a desire to prevent the criminal defendant from seeking judicial redress for alleged police misconduct. *Haynesworth v. Miller,* 820 F.2d 1245 (D.C. Cir. 1987) (*Bivens* claim).

"The failure to object to a rule promulgated by a 'state' agency during the notice and comment period does not constitute a waiver of one's right to bring a section 1933 action in federal court challenging the legality of a regulation." *Samuels v. District of Columbia,* 669 F. Supp. 1133, 1141 (D.D.C. 1987).

A release-dismissal agreement was valid under *Rumery* where it was voluntarily entered into by the criminal defendant, the prosecutor neither manipulated nor coerced the federal plaintiff into giving up her civil claims in return for dismissal of the criminal charge, the prosecutor sought the release for a number of legitimate objectives, negotiations occurred only after the state court found probable cause, and the agreement was executed under judicial supervision. *Hammond v. Bales,* 843 F.2d 1320 (10th Cir. 1988).

A settlement agreement pursuant to which an inmate agreed to drop his § 1983 suit in exchange for treatment of his eye condition was enforceable. *Merritt v. Faulkner,* 823 F.2d 1150 (7th Cir. 1987).

The Sixth Circuit, sitting en banc, upheld the validity of a state statute providing that the filing of suit in state court against the state operates to waive claims against the state officials based upon the same conduct, as applied to federal court § 1983 claims against the appeals. The state was not required to waive its state law immunity in

state court, and could choose to offer such a waiver only to those who agree not to sue its officials based on the same transactions. Judge Keith, dissenting, objects that the majority "characterizes the effect of its holding in terms of a single contractual metaphor, as if Constitutional rights are bushels of wheat and the Constitution itself the *Restatement (Second) of Contracts.*" *Leaman v. Ohio Department of Mental Retardation and Developmental Disabilities,* 825 F.2d 946, 958 (6th Cir. 1987) (en
* banc), *cert. denied,* 108 S. Ct. 2844 (1988). *See also White v. Gerbitz,* 860 F.2d 661 (6th Cir. 1988) (extending *Leaman* to administrative remedy before Tennessee Claims Commission).

The First Circuit ruled that the bringing of a § 1983 claim does not automatically operate as a waiver of plaintiff's attorney-client privilege as to matters involved in the civil rights suit. Rather, a court should balance the importance of the privilege against the defending party's need for the information in making its defense. *Greater Newburyport Clamshell Alliance v. Public Service Co.,* 838 F.2d 13 (1st Cir. 1988).

The controversy in *Greater Newburyport* came about when a government informant infiltrated meetings between criminal defendants (who were also the federal court § 1983 claimants) and their attorneys and overheard communications and trial strategy. The § 1983 complaint alleged that this violated the plaintiff's Sixth Amendment right to the effective assistance of counsel. The federal court defendants sought discovery of material related to the criminal case and plaintiffs claimed they were privileged. Defendants countered by claiming that plaintiffs waived the privilege by bringing the § 1983 claim. The court stated that parties should not be presented with the "Hobson's choice" of either dropping the § 1983 claim or revealing all confidential communications related to a criminal defense. "The scope of required disclosure should not be so broad as to effectively eliminate any incentive to vindicate the constitutional right through a section 1983 suit." *Id.* at 22.

* The Second Circuit articulated principles governing the modification of consent decrees in constitutional reform litigation. Although some flexibility is warranted, the guiding principle is that modification is favored only when necessary to carry out the purposes of the original decree. Total compliance with a consent decree is not an absolute precondition to modification, but tolerance of noncompliance is more appropriate in cases involving broad-ranging decrees

> affecting the entire prison system of state. Where, as here, a consent decree seems to achieve precise objectives at a single location, modification of essential provisions ought to be disfavored until those seeking change demonstrate that they are in substantial compliance with the decree and that the proposed future change will have no adverse effect on future compliance.

Badgley v. Santacroce, 853 F.2d 50, 53-54 (2d Cir. 1988).

§ 14.16 Other Issues: Consortium and Prejudgment Interest

Page 317, add at end of section:

There is no constitutional right to consortium. *Gresham v. Dell,* 630 F. Supp. 1135 (N.D. Ga. 1986).

The Seventh Circuit generally regards prejudgment interest to be a component of full compensation. *Williamson v. Handy Button Machine Co.,* 817 F.2d 1290 (7th Cir. 1987) (§ 1981 and Title III).

The First Circuit stated that prejudgment interest is a matter for determination by the jury. *Aubin v. Fudala,* 782 F.2d 287 (1st Cir. 1983). Disagreeing with this view, a federal district court applied the common law tort rule disallowing prejudgment interest on unliquidated damages, because compensatory and punitive damages already effectuate § 1983's purpose of compensation and deterrence. *Strandell v. Jackson County,* 634 F. Supp. 824 (S.D. Ill. 1986). While not resolving the issue, the Seventh Circuit opined that common law policies disallowing prejudgment interest would be inconsistent with the policy of the federal civil rights laws. *Hunter v. Allis-Chalmers Corp.,* 797 F.2d 1417, 1425-26 (7th Cir. 1986).

* In a Title VII case, the Supreme Court characterized prejudgment interest as "an element of complete compensation." *Loeffler v. Frank,* 108 S. Ct. 1965, 1971 (1988), quoting from *West Virginia v. United States,* 479 U.S. 305, 310 (1987).

§ 14.17 Collateral Source Rule (New)

The collateral source rule, pursuant to which payments made to injured parties by third parties do not reduce the damages plaintiff may recover, applies to § 1983 claims. *Perry v. Larson,* 794 F.2d 279, 285-86 (7th Cir. 1986).

§ 14.18 Enforcement of Judgment (New)

Two circuit courts ruled that when a judgment is obtained against an official in an individual capacity and there is a state law basis, such as an indemnification statute, for enforcing that judgment against a nonparty municipality, the federal courts have jurisdiction over enforcement proceedings against the municipality. *Argento v. Village of Melrose Park,* 838 F.2d 1483 (7th Cir. 1988); *Skevofilax v. Quigley,* 810 F.2d 378 (3d Cir.) (en banc), *cert. denied,* 107 S. Ct. 1956 (1987). *See contra, Berry v. McLemore,* 795 F.2d 452 (5th Cir. 1986). The Seventh Circuit in *Argento* found that it had ancillary and "supplementary" jurisdiction, while the Third Circuit in *Skevofilax* bottomed its ruling upon ancillary jurisdiction. The court in *Argento* also applied its jurisdictional holding to an enforcement of judgment claim against an insurance company.

* The Tenth Circuit ruled that the propriety of filing a notice of lis pendens in a § 1983 action is governed by state law. *Hamilton v. Smith,* 808 F.2d 36, 37 (10th Cir. 1986).

PART II

ATTORNEY'S FEES LITIGATION AND AWARDS UNDER 42 U.S.C. § 1988

Introduction
The Development of the Lodestar Adjustment Method for Calculating Reasonable Attorney's Fees

Pages 320 and 321, update Delaware Valley citations in notes 9 and 12:

478 U.S. 546, 563, 564 (1986).

Page 321, update Delaware Valley and Rivera citations in note 13:

Delaware Valley, 478 U.S. 546 (1986); Rivera, 477 U.S. 561 (1986).

The Relevance to § 1988 of Fee Decisions Arising Under Other Fee-Shifting Statutes

Page 323, update Delaware Valley citation in note 17:

478 U.S. 546, 559-60 (1986).

Pages 324-25, add at end of note 21:

State courts occasionally have balked at giving full effect to the principle, established by the legislative history of § 1988 and binding Supreme Court precedent, that the plaintiff who succeeds on a state law claim joined with a related, but unadjudicated, federal constitutional claim that is not frivolous is a prevailing party for § 1988 fee purposes. See discussion at **§ 15.17** of supplement. Analyzed in **§ 16.8** of the supplement is the substantial issue of whether, and to what extent, state law principles of sovereign immunity may insulate state defendants from § 1988 fee liability to prevailing plaintiffs in state court § 1983 actions, in the absence of the applicability of the Eleventh Amendment.

CHAPTER 15

QUALIFYING THE SUCCESSFUL CIVIL RIGHTS PLAINTIFF FOR § 1988 FEES – THE PREVAILING PARTY REQUIREMENT

§ 15.1 Introduction

Page 329, change sentence in third line of note 5 to read:

See Introduction to Part II of this book.

Pages 329-30, delete the continuation sentence that begins on bottom of page 329, together with note 6, and substitute the following:

In *North Carolina Dep't of Transp. v. Crest Street Community Council, Inc.*, 479 U.S. 6 (1986), the Supreme Court ruled that an "action or proceeding" in which § 1988 fees can be awarded is limited to a court suit involving the merits of the underlying civil rights claim, and does not include an independent court suit instituted for the sole purpose of recovering attorney's fees for the plaintiff's success in prior administrative proceedings. The Court indicated that this principle is operative not only when the plaintiff has successfully pursued *optional* administrative proceedings on claims arising, for example, under Title VI of the Civil Rights Act of 1964 (42 U.S.C. §§ 2000d *et seq.*), as in the *Crest Street* case, or under § 1983, but as well when the plaintiff succeeds in *mandatory* administrative proceedings pursuant to Title VII (42 U.S.C. §§ 2000e *et seq.*) which *must* be exhausted prior to the initiation of a court action. 479 U.S. at 13-14. As Justice Brennan observed in his dissenting opinion in *Crest Street,* the net effect of the narrow reading given by the majority to "action or proceeding" under § 1988 is to create an incentive for plaintiffs' lawyers to institute protective court suits on their substantive civil rights claims concurrently with the exhaustion of administrative remedies, in order to ensure the availability of a judicial forum for recovery of statutory attorney's fees should the plaintiff achieve complete success at the administrative stage. Alternatively, the plaintiff asserting civil rights claims, such as those enforceable through § 1983 or Title VI, for which administrative exhaustion is not mandatory, may forego altogether resort to available administrative proceedings and proceed directly to court. 479 U.S. at 21-25.

Page 330, add the following new paragraph after the continuation paragraph ending with note 7 reference:

The courts are generally in agreement that the prevailing plaintiff's failure to specifically cite § 1983 (or other applicable fee-generating provision) in his complaint or during the course of the merits litigation is not fatal to his claim for § 1988 attorney's fees, provided that the pleading sufficiently asserts that the plaintiff was deprived of a federally protected right by a person acting under color of law. This result is consistent with the liberal rules of notice pleading that prevail under the Federal Rules of Civil Procedure and under the civil procedural rules of most states. *See Americans United for Separation of Church and State v. School District,* 835 F.2d 627 (6th Cir. 1987) (prevailing plaintiff was entitled to § 1988 fees notwithstanding absence of specific reference to § 1983 in the complaint; complaint contained allegations sufficient to state a § 1983 cause of action, and complaint's recitation of 28 U.S.C. § 1343(a)(3) as a jurisdictional basis indicated that suit was more than merely a declaratory judgment action); Solomon v. City of Gainesville, 796 F.2d 1464 (11th Cir. 1986) (although prevailing plaintiff had waived his § 1983 damages claim on appeal and had pled only 28 U.S.C. §§ 2201-02 as a basis for declaratory and injunctive relief on his successful constitutional claim, he nonetheless was entitled to § 1988 fees since § 1983 is available as the basis for enforcement of the constitutional claim); *Maldonado v. Nebraska Dep't of Public Welfare,* 223 Neb. 485, 391 N.W.2d 105, 107-09 (1986); *Ramah Navajo School Bd. v. Bureau of Revenue,* 104 N.M. 302, 720 P.2d 1243, 1246-47 (Ct. App.), *cert. denied,* 479 U.S. 940 (1986); *cf. Client's Council v. Pierce,* 778 F.2d 518, 520-21 (8th Cir. 1985) (although their amended complaint deleted reference to 42 U.S.C. §§ 1981 and 1982, the prevailing plaintiffs nonetheless were entitled to a § 1988 fee award against the federal defendants on the basis of those provisions, since the underlying equal protection claim remained in the pleading and was successful). *But see Ball v. School Dist. of Grand Rapids,* 641 F. Supp. 1 (W.D. Mich. 1986) (denying § 1988 fees to the plaintiff who failed to plead § 1983 in support of his successful constitutional claim). Similarly, § 1988 need not specifically have been pled in the complaint in order for the prevailing plaintiff to recover fees under that provision, provided that this basis for an award is fairly embraced within a general request in the complaint for attorney's fees or costs. *See Ramah Navajo School Bd. v. Bureau of Revenue,* 720 P.2d at 1247; *Kay v. David Douglas School Dist.,* 79 Or. App. 384, 719 P.2d 875, 881-82 (1986) (declining to apply the more specific pleading requirement imposed by state civil procedure rule), *cert. denied,* 108 S. Ct. 740 (1988); *City of Arlington v. Byrd,* 713 S.W.2d 224, 228-29 (Tex. Ct. App. 1986). On the other hand, a plaintiff who has succeeded on a nonfee claim in the litigation may not recover § 1988 fees on the basis of a substantial § 1983 claim that is found to have been abandoned during the litigation or inserted belatedly into the case solely for the purpose of qualifying the plaintiff for statutory fees. See § **15.15**.

§ 15.2 Types of Prevailing Parties

Page 330, add to note 8:

However, while recognizing that intervenor-plaintiffs are eligible for § 1988 fee awards, a court may carefully scrutinize the intervenor's role in the litigation in relation to the results achieved, to insure that the intervenor who recovers fees has contributed significantly to a favorable outcome gained primarily by the original plaintiff. *See* ECOS, Inc. v. Brinegar, 671 F. Supp. 381, 386-88 (M.D.N.C. 1987); American Booksellers Ass'n, Inc. v. Hudnut, 650 F. Supp. 324, 331-33 (S.D. Ind. 1986).

Page 330, add to note 13:

Jones v. Wilkinson, 800 F.2d 989, 991-92 (10th Cir. 1986) (prevailing corporation), *judgment aff'd,* ____ U.S. ____, 94 L.Ed.2d 753 (1987).

Page 330, add at end of section:

Prevailing party status for § 1988 purposes is limited to actual parties to the litigation. Thus the Fifth Circuit in *Morales v. Turman,* 820 F.2d 728 (5th Cir. 1987), denied § 1988 fees to organizations which participated as amici curiae, but not as parties, in a class action suit successfully challenging conditions at institutions for delinquent juveniles. Because amici were not parties, and indeed lacked standing to intervene in the suit, they could not qualify as prevailing parties under § 1988, even though they concededly provided services beneficial to the plaintiff class. *Id.* at 732-33.

§ 15.3 –The Pro Se Litigant as Prevailing Party

Page 331, add to cases cited in note 16:

Coleman v. Turner, 838 F.2d 1004, 1005 (8th Cir. 1988); Gonzales v. Kangas, 814 F.2d 1411 (9th Cir. 1987).

Page 331, add to cases cited in note 18:

Merrell v. Block, 797 F.2d 740, 742 (9th Cir. 1986) (dictum); Shakman v. Democratic Org. of Cook County, 634 F. Supp. 895, 901 (N.D. Ill. 1986) (noting that lawyer *pro se* litigant, "unlike a layperson, actually performs legal services and actually suffers pecuniary loss due to the time lost from his practice" and that the "difficulty in measuring the value of a lay litigant's services is not present when a party attorney seeks compensation").

Page 332, add to note 20 following the Duncan case:

In Shakman v. Democratic Org. of Cook County, 634 F. Supp. 895, 901-02 (N.D. Ill. 1986), the court concluded that a lawyer appearing *pro se* was not ethically obligated to withdraw as counsel when it became apparent that his trial testimony was necessary since, given the lawyer's "extensive knowledge of and involvement in this case, his refusal to testify would have resulted in a 'substantial hardship' " to the plaintiffs. However, the court denied the lawyer fee compensation for time spent "preparing his own affidavits and testimony," and, "[g]iven the sensitive nature of Shakman's dual role as litigant and advocate," for time spent counseling other persons about possible legal violations in the case.

* *Page 332, delete last sentence in section, together with notes 21 and 22, and substitute:*

However, several courts have rejected purported distinctions between nonlawyer and lawyer pro se litigants, and have concluded that both groups are ineligible for § 1988 fees. *Levine v. Heffernan,* 691 F. Supp. 173 (W.D. Wisc. 1988); *Lawrence v. Staats,* 586 F. Supp. 1375, 1378-80 (D.D.C. 1984).

§ 15.4 Requirement of Success on the Merits

Page 332, add after sentence in mid-paragraph ending with "discovery sanctions.":

* *See also Tribble v. Gardner,* 860 F.2d 321, 328 (9th Cir. 1988) (plaintiff did not prevail by obtaining appellate affirmance of district court's denial of summary judgment to defendants on qualified immunity grounds, since at trial defendants might still establish their qualified immunity from § 1983 liability); *Palmer v. City of Chicago,* 806 F.2d 1316, 1321 (7th Cir. 1986) (plaintiffs were not prevailing parties where the only relief they obtained, an appellate court order directing defendant to retain certain files for plaintiffs' inspection, was "in the nature of a discovery order" that did not lead to the winning of any merits relief); *Shah v. County of Los Angeles,* 797 F.2d 743, 747 (9th Cir. 1986) (plaintiff did not prevail on appeal in securing a reversal of the dismissal of his suit and a remand for further proceedings); *Proctor v. Consolidated Freightways Corp.,* 795 F.2d 1472, 1478-79 (9th Cir. 1986) (plaintiff did not prevail on appeal where she obtained only a reversal of the district court's grant of summary judgment in favor of defendant and a remand for a trial); *Ekanem v. Health & Hosp. Corp.,* 778 F.2d 1254, 1258 (7th Cir. 1985) (plaintiffs' success in obtaining appellate reversal of district court's definition of the relevant labor pool in evaluating claim of employment race discrimination represented success on an evidentiary matter only and did not qualify plaintiffs as prevailing parties).

Page 333, add following the continuation sentence ending with note 30 reference:

The plaintiff's interlocutory success in obtaining a preliminary injunction or in prompting the defendant to take voluntary remedial action also does not qualify the plaintiff as a prevailing party where his suit ultimately is judicially determined, on appeal or at final judgment, to be unmeritorious. See §§ **15.13, 15.20.** *See Palmer v. City of Chicago,* 806 F.2d 1316, 1320-24 (7th Cir. 1986) (plaintiffs were not prevailing parties on basis of preliminary injunction and defendant's remedial action, where court of appeals subsequently reversed the injunction on the grounds of plaintiffs' lack of standing to sue and abstention principles, and issued only a discovery-type order that yielded no success to plaintiffs when they later effectively abandoned their suit); *Ward v. County of San Diego,* 791 F.2d 1329, 1333-34 (9th Cir. 1986) (plaintiff did not prevail when preliminary injunction was reversed on appeal for plaintiff's lack of standing to seek injunctive relief); *Tucker v. Summers,* 784 F.2d 654, 656-57 (5th Cir. 1986) (plaintiff did not prevail on basis of injunctions obtained in appellate and district courts that subsequently were found to have been inappropriately entered in view of supervening Supreme Court decision establishing the federal court's lack of subject-matter jurisdiction over the dispute); *Ekanem v. Health & Hosp. Corp.,* 778 F.2d 1254, 1258 (7th Cir. 1985) (plaintiffs did not become prevailing parties by obtaining preliminary injunction, when injunction was reversed on appeal and district court subsequently dismissed the suit). Finally, in *Jensen v. City of San Jose,* 806 F.2d 899 (9th Cir. 1986), the Ninth Circuit, sitting *en banc,* ruled that the plaintiff who has lost on the merits of his civil rights case cannot recover § 1988 fees as a prevailing party on the basis of his appellate success in obtaining the reversal of the district court's award of fees to the defendant that rested on the erroneous finding that plaintiff's losing civil rights claims were frivolous. The success that qualifies the plaintiff as a prevailing party under § 1988, the court concluded, must be success on some aspect of the merits of his underlying civil rights claims. In accord is *Ekanem v. Health & Hosp. Corp.,* 778 F.2d 1254, 1258 (7th Cir. 1985).

Page 333, add following the sentence ending with note 33 reference:

In a number of other cases the plaintiff has been found to be a prevailing party by winning relief on a discrete and significant merits issue even though he does not or may not succeed on other merits claims. In *Grano v. Barry,* 783 F.2d 1104, 1108-10 (D.C. Cir. 1986), the District of Columbia Court of Appeals found that the plaintiffs prevailed for § 1988 purposes when they obtained an injunction prohibiting the demolition of an historic tavern until a scheduled voter referendum concerning the fate of the tavern could be held. This conclusion was not altered by the ruling of the court of appeals, following the referendum, that the issue of the validity of a *post*-election injunction must be resolved by the local courts, which then in turn held that the voter initiative was unconstitutional and could not prevent the demolition of the tavern. The court of appeals concluded that the plaintiffs had prevailed under § 1988 because they had obtained final success on the merits of their civil rights claim, ultimately mooted by the holding of the election, that the tavern should not be demolished until the referendum was conducted, even though they ultimately lost on the separate and independent issue of the validity of the referendum itself. This is to be distinguished from a case like *Palmer v. City of Chicago,* 806 F.2d 1316 (7th Cir. 1986), in which the plaintiff was denied prevailing party status on the basis of a preliminary injunction that subsequently was undone by an appellate ruling that the underlying suit should have been dismissed.

Page 333, add at end of page:

In *Hewitt v. Helms,* 107 S.Ct. 2672 (1987), the Supreme Court held that a civil rights plaintiff becomes a prevailing party under § 1988 only when he obtains *relief,* or establishes *entitlement to relief,* on the merits of a legal claim. Thus, the Court concluded in *Hewitt* that a plaintiff does not become a prevailing party under § 1988 merely by obtaining a favorable appellate ruling on the merits of his legal claim that does not establish his entitlement to some relief on the merits, but rather leaves open the possibility that the plaintiff ultimately may obtain no merits relief in the case. Accordingly, neither procedural victories that do not involve the merits of plaintiff's legal claims, as in *Hanrahan v. Hampton,* 446 U.S. 754 (1980), nor favorable legal rulings that do not grant merits relief, as in *Hewitt,* can qualify the plaintiff as a prevailing party under § 1988.

In *Hewitt,* the plaintiff state prisoner in a non-class action suit claimed due process violations in the lack of a prompt and adequate hearing on misconduct charges that led to his administrative segregation and in his conviction for misconduct on the basis of uncorroborated hearsay testimony. He sought declaratory and injunctive relief, damages, and expungement of his prison disciplinary record. The plaintiff ultimately lost on his due process hearing claim in the Supreme Court. However, the court of appeals found that his misconduct conviction based only on uncorroborated hearsay evidence violated due process and instructed the district court to enter summary judgment for plaintiff on that claim unless defendants could establish an immunity defense. On remand to the district court, plaintiff pursued only his damages claim, without seeking entry of a declaratory judgment that his constitutional rights had been violated or an injunction requiring expungement of his misconduct conviction. The district court granted summary judgment for defendants on the basis of their immunity defense. On plaintiff's appeal, defendants argued that plaintiff had waived his claims for declaratory and injunctive relief in failing to pursue them in the district court and that, in any event, they had been rendered moot by plaintiff's release from prison on parole. During the pendency of the appeal, the state defendant revised its prison regulations to include procedures restricting the use of confidential-source information in prison disciplinary proceedings. The district court's decision was affirmed without opinion. *Id.* at 2674-75.

The Supreme Court ruled in *Hewitt* that the plaintiff did not prevail for § 1988 purposes by winning the favorable legal ruling from the court of appeals on his uncorroborated hearsay due process claim, where that ruling did not itself grant, or establish entitlement to, any judicial relief for the plaintiff on the merits of the claim, and the plaintiff ultimately obtained none in the district court. (Neither, the Court ruled, could the plaintiff achieve prevailing party status on the basis of the state defendant's promulgation of ameliorative regulations, as discussed in **§ 15.12** of the supplement.) The favorable judicial statement by the court of appeals that the plaintiff's due process rights had been violated did not establish plaintiff's entitlement to any relief on the merits of the due process claim, since it "explicitly left it to the District Court 'to determine the appropriateness and availability of the requested relief.' " *Id.* at 2676. The Court rejected the contention that the favorable court of appeals ruling was "a form of" or "the equivalent of" a declaratory judgment that would establish the plaintiff as a prevailing party, since by itself it granted plaintiff no relief or entitlement to relief on the due process claim. *Id.* The favorable appellate ruling gave plaintiff only the "moral satisfaction of knowing that a federal court concluded that his rights had been violated." *Id.* The plaintiff ultimately failed to obtain *any* judicial relief that would have gained him prevailing party status, since in the district court he was denied damages relief on immunity grounds, and his counsel "never took the steps necessary to have a declaratory judgment or expungement order properly entered." *Id.*

Hewitt requires careful evaluation of favorable appellate legal rulings, in order to distinguish between those that establish the plaintiff's "entitlement to some relief on the merits of his claims" (*Hanrahan v. Hampton,* 446 U.S. 754, 757 (1980)), and thereby confer prevailing party status on the plaintiff under § 1988, and those that do not by themselves grant any merits relief, or entitlement to relief, to the plaintiff and therefore do not make the plaintiff a prevailing party. Thus a favorable appellate ruling that unequivocally "established the liability of the opposing party, although final remedial orders had not been entered" (*Hanrahan,* 446 U.S. at 757) suffices to establish the plaintiff as a prevailing party on appeal. *See Wharton v. Knefel,* 562 F.2d 550, 556, 558 (8th Cir. 1977) (favorably cited in *Hanrahan,* 446 U.S. at 758 n.4), where plaintiff prevailed when the court of appeals reversed the district court's judgment for defendant in a housing race discrimination suit and ruled that "[r]acial discrimination has been established both as a matter of fact and law," while remanding issues of remedial relief for further developments in the district court. In *Ganey v. Garrison,* 813 F.2d 650 (4th Cir. 1987), the court found that although the plaintiff prisoner did not win money damages or any equitable relief sought in his complaint, he nonetheless became a prevailing party under § 1988 by obtaining a jury verdict and judgment that the defendant prison warden had violated plaintiff's constitutional rights. On the other hand, the plaintiff does not become a prevailing party merely by winning an appellate ruling, as in *Hewitt,* that recognizes a legal right or finds that plaintiff's legal rights were violated, no matter how important the legal rights so vindicated, if the plaintiff is not thereby granted at least a declaratory judgment that plaintiff's rights were violated or a ruling that plaintiff is entitled unconditionally to a declaratory judgment in his favor. *See also Healy v. Town of Pembroke Park,* 831 F.2d 989, 994 (11th Cir. 1987) (ruling that plaintiff-appellant who obtained a remand to the district court for consideration of his § 1983 claim for damages – the only merits relief sought in his federal suit – was not yet entitled to § 1988 fees, because "[a]t this stage, the plaintiff has not obtained any relief on the merits of his § 1983 claim"); *McQuillen v. Wisconsin Education Association Council,* 830 F.2d 659, 666 (7th Cir. 1987) (declining to render advisory opinion on legality of defendant's affirmative action plan, when a favorable ruling would not entitle plaintiff to any relief on the merits in his unsuccessful Title VII hiring discrimination suit and would not establish his eligibility for statutory attorney's fees; "[s]imply having a favorable statement of law in an order that denies all relief does not entitle a plaintiff to attorney's fees as a prevailing party").

Of debatable validity after *Hewitt* is the Ninth Circuit's decision in *Mantolete v. Bolger,* 791 F.2d 784 (9th Cir. 1986), finding the plaintiff a prevailing party under the Rehabilitation Act, 29 U.S.C. § 794a(b), on the basis of appellate rulings establishing several significant legal precedents, whether or not she ultimately succeeded on her claim that she was improperly denied a job due to her handicap. The significant legal rulings on which the Ninth Circuit relied in finding the plaintiff a prevailing party significantly strengthened the protections of the Rehabilitation Act with respect to substantive standards and burden of proof, but they did not grant relief or establish entitlement to relief to the plaintiff on her claim that the defendant illegally refused her a job because of her epileptic condition. *Id.* at 786-87. The court suggested, nonetheless, that the favorable appellate rulings in effect granted relief to the plaintiff because even if she "does not prevail on her claim that the Postal Service discriminated against her in this specific instance, the standards established by our opinion will aid her in any future application for employment," and "even though this case was not certified as a class action, we consider it important that Ms. Mantolete's success on appeal generally benefits all handicapped persons seeking employment." *Id.* at 787. It is arguable, however, that the plaintiff lacked standing to seek any of that relief. Accordingly, the result in *Mantolete* stretches the boundaries of the *Hewitt* decision. An interesting variant on the *Hewitt* principle was addressed in *Alliance to End Repression v. City of Chicago,* 820 F.2d 873 (7th Cir. 1987). In that case, the Seventh Circuit held that the plaintiffs were not entitled to § 1988 fees for obtaining a judicial ruling, following the entry of a consent agreement for an injunction and the payment of money damages, that the plaintiffs' constitutional rights had been violated by the police misconduct at issue in the litigation. The parties had agreed to seek adjudication of the underlying legal issue but not to appeal the result, with successful plaintiffs retaining their damages settlements and unsuccessful plaintiffs losing them. Three of the plaintiffs who entered into the agreement obtained the sought-after judicial declaration and then applied for additional attorney's fees for the effort. The Seventh Circuit concluded that these plaintiffs were not entitled to § 1988 fees for that stage of the litigation, because the legal precedent obtained by the plaintiffs did not give them any relief that they had not already gained by the injunction and money damages settlements. Thus, after the consent agreement, there remained no justiciable controversy concerning the legality of defendants' conduct, and the plaintiffs were requesting only an advisory opinion. The court likened the dispute to a "pure wager of law", by which the plaintiffs "staked" their money damages settlements on the gaining of a legal precedent which, while perhaps of value to others in subsequent suits, could not further benefit the plaintiffs. *Id.* at 875-76.

In *Rhodes v. Stewart,* 109 S. Ct. 202 (1988), the Supreme Court elaborated upon *Hewitt* by ruling that the plaintiff prisoners who had obtained a favorable declaratory judgment that their constitutional rights had been violated by prison officials were not prevailing parties entitled to § 1988 fees, since the favorable judgment was obtained *after* their claims had become moot due to the death of one plaintiff and the release of the other. The Court reasoned that since the case, a non-class action suit, was moot before judgment issued, the declaratory judgment had been improperly granted and the plaintiffs, in effect, obtained no relief whatsoever. The principle of *Rhodes,* that the plaintiff is not a prevailing party under § 1988 when he obtains relief that was improperly granted, should be confined to cases where the defect in the merits judgment "goes to the court's jurisdiction, as mootness does." *Id.* at 205 (Blackmun, J., dissenting).

Page 334, add at end of section:

Significantly, the requirement that the prevailing plaintiff achieve *merits* success against a particular defendant in order to secure § 1988 fee liability against that defendant is relaxed in connection with fee awards against an intervenor who has voluntarily entered the litigation to support the primary defendant's resistance to the relief sought by the plaintiff. See complete discussion at § **16.11**.

§ 15.6 –Prevailing on Appeal

Page 335, add to note 40 following the continuation sentence:

See Toussaint v. McCarthy, 826 F.2d 901, 904 n.3 (9th Cir. 1987) (plaintiffs who were prevailing parties under § 1988 in the court of appeals were not entitled to § 1988 fees for their unsuccessful certiorari petition to the Supreme Court; "[t]ime spent on the certiorari petition cannot reasonably be said to have been expended in the course of the instant appeal"); Clark v. City of Los Angeles, 803 F.2d 987, 989-90, 993 (9th Cir. 1986) (plaintiffs were prevailing parties in district court where their trial success on the merits prompted defendants to cease the challenged conduct, but were not prevailing parties on appeal where court of appeals reversed the district court judgment and remanded case for further proceedings).

Page 335, add to first part of note 41 the following cases in which the plaintiff-appellant did not prevail on appeal:

Palmer v. City of Chicago, 806 F.2d 1316, 1321 (7th Cir. 1986) (appellate relief "in the nature of a discovery order"); Shah v. County of Los Angeles, 797 F.2d 743, 747 (9th Cir. 1986) (appellate reversal of dismissal of suit and remand for further proceedings); Proctor v. Consolidated Freightways Corp., 795 F.2d 1472, 1478-79 (9th Cir. 1986) (appellate reversal of summary judgment for defendant and remand for trial); Ekanem v. Health & Hosp. Corp., 778 F.2d 1254, 1258 (7th Cir. 1985) (reversal on evidentiary grounds).

Page 335, add at end of note 42:

Cf. Akbar v. Fairman, 788 F.2d 1273, 1279 (7th Cir. 1986) (plaintiffs who were prevailing parties in district court and court of appeals were not prevailing parties on their unsuccessful petition for a writ of certiorari in Supreme Court and, accordingly, were not entitled to an award of costs for the Supreme Court work).

Page 335, line after note 42 reference, change "appellant reversal" to "appellate reversal."

Page 335, insert at beginning of note 43:

Also a prevailing party on appeal is the plaintiff-appellant who obtains an appellate reversal of the trial court's denial of § 1988 fees and a ruling awarding him fees. EWAP, Inc. v. City of Ontario, 177 Cal. App. 3d 1108, 223 Cal. Rptr. 422, 430 (1986).

Page 336, add to note 45:

Cf. Jordan v. Multnomah County, 815 F.2d 1258, 1264 (9th Cir. 1987) (plaintiff-appellants were entitled to § 1988 fees for partial success on their fee appeal, when they obtained a reversal of the district court's fee award and a remand for redetermination of the award, in accordance with the court of appeals' findings that the district court had substantially reduced the plaintiffs' requested hours and hourly rates without justification).On the other hand, the plaintiff-appellant who succeeds in obtaining an appellate reversal of the district court's fee award to the winning defendants, based on the appellate court's finding that the plaintiff's losing civil rights claims were nonfrivolous, is *not* the prevailing party on the appeal, since he failed to succeed on the merits of the underlying civil rights claim. Jensen v. City of San Jose, 806 F.2d 899 (9th Cir. 1986) (en banc); Ekanem v. Health & Hosp. Corp., 778 F.2d 1254, 1258 (7th Cir. 1985).

Page 336, add after sentence ending with note 45 reference:

However, *Hewitt v. Helms,* 107 S.Ct. 2672 (1987), holds that the plaintiff-appellant prevails on appeal under § 1988 only if the appellate court, in reversing the lower court, grants the plaintiff some *relief,* or *entitlement to relief,* on the merits of his claim.

Thus, the plaintiff is not the prevailing party on appeal where he wins only a favorable ruling from the appellate court that his legal rights were violated and a remand to the district court that leaves open the possibility that he ultimately may obtain no relief, whether of a liability or remedial nature, on his claims. See complete discussion of *Hewitt* at § 15.4 of the supplement. If on remand to the trial court the plaintiff gains the entry of a judgment that grants him some declaratory, injunctive, or damages relief on the merits of his claim, then he becomes the prevailing party under § 1988 in the trial court, and in the appellate court as well.

Page 336, add the following cases to note 46:

Chalmers v. City of Los Angeles, 796 F.2d 1205, 1213 (9th Cir. 1986); Patteson v. Johnson, 790 F.2d 712, 713 (8th Cir. 1986) (prevailing plaintiff-appellees).

Page 336, add at end of note 46:

On the other hand, the plaintiff-appellee whose successful result in the trial court is completely reversed by the appellate court not only is not the prevailing party on appeal, but as well loses his prevailing party status in the trial court. Diamond v. Charles, 476 U.S. 54, 70-71 (1986) (dictum); Merkel v. Scovill, Inc., 787 F.2d 174, 181 (6th Cir. 1986).

Page 336, add to cases cited in note 47:

Aubin v. Fudala, 821 F.2d 45, 47 (1st Cir. 1987); Ganey v. Garrison, 813 F.2d 650, 652 (4th Cir. 1987) (awarding § 1988 fees on appeal for plaintiff-appellee's successful defense of district court's fee award).

Page 336, insert after "See" in first line of note 48:

Grano v. Barry, 783 F.2d 1104, 1113 (D.C. Cir. 1986) (plaintiffs were entitled to § 1988 fees on appeal for work done in successfully opposing defendant's motions for expedited consideration of its appeal and for summary reversal of the district court's injunction, with the result that the referendum election sought by plaintiffs occurred and the appeal was rendered moot); Local 17, Int'l Ass'n v. Young, 775 F.2d 870 (7th Cir. 1985) (denial of defendant's petition for certiorari).

Page 336, add at end of note 49:

When the plaintiff succeeds on one issue on appeal but loses on another issue presented on the appeal or in a cross-appeal, and the two issues are sufficiently unrelated to require that the prevailing party analysis be applied independently to each of the two issues, then the plaintiff will be a prevailing party on the winning issue on appeal but not on the losing issue. *See* Clark v. City of Los Angeles, 803 F.2d 987, 993 (9th Cir. 1986) (plaintiffs were entitled to § 1988 fees for success in defending on appeal their fee award for district court work, but were not eligible for fees on their cross-appeal unsuccessfully seeking reversal of district court's denial of fees for a prior losing appeal).

In awarding § 1988 fees to the plaintiffs who succeeded to a limited extent as appellees on appeal, the Ninth Circuit in Toussaint v. McCarthy, 826 F.2d 901, 904 (9th

Cir. 1987), rejected defendant's argument that appellate fees are available only when the fee applicant is " 'better off' after the appeal than it was before the appeal." The court noted that this theory would deny fees to "a party obtaining a partial or complete affirmance on appeal," and "[o]nly those parties obtaining *additional* relief on appeal would be entitled to fees." *Id* at 904. Of course, in order to be a prevailing party under § 1988, the plaintiff-appellee must achieve appellate success on the merits of a fee-generating claim. *Cf.* Hamman v. Southwestern Gas Pipeline, Inc., 832 F.2d 55 (5th Cir. 1987) (ruling that successful plaintiff-appellees were not entitled to statutory fees on appeal when the defendant had appealed only the portion of the district court judgment involving non-fee-generating state law claims). The prevailing plaintiff-appellee is not entitled to recover statutory fees for time expended on unsuccessful issues on the appeal that are unrelated to and hence severable from winning issues. Hall v. Ochs, 817 F.2d 920, 929-30 (1st Cir. 1987); Brown v. Freedman Baking Co., Inc., 810 F.2d 6, 12 (1st Cir. 1987); *cf.* Wagenmann v. Adams, 829 F.2d 196, 227 (1st Cir. 1987) ("Unlike trial proceedings, where apportionment of time and charges is often impractical because of interconnectedness, such allocation should ordinarily prove more feasible in an appellate milieu").

Pages 336-37, delete the incomplete sentence beginning at bottom of page 336 and substitute the following:

On the other hand, if the plaintiff-appellee does not obtain a full appellate affirmance on *any* merits or fee issue, but instead gains only reduced or diminished success on each issue appealed, then he is not considered a prevailing party on appeal. Thus, when the court of appeals reduces the plaintiff's damage award, where the *amount* of damages is the only question presented on appeal, then the plaintiff-appellee is left in a worse position than before the appeal and is not a prevailing party on appeal.[50]

Page 337, add the following phrase at the end of the sentence in the middle of the continuation paragraph that concludes with "claiming the award is too high":

while not disputing the defendant's underlying liability for statutory fees.

* *Page 337, add after sentence ending with note 51:*

The Seventh Circuit takes the expansive view that the plaintiff-appellee is a prevailing party on appeal even when the court of appeals substantially reduces the § 1988 fee awarded to the plaintiff by the district court. The court's rationale is that the plaintiff "[a]s the prevailing party in the underlying civil rights action . . . is entitled to reimbursement of fees reasonably incurred in the original civil rights trial and appeal, fees incurred in proving those fees, or fees incurred in defending the district court's fee award." *Ustrak v. Fairman,* 851 F.2d 983, 990 (7th Cir. 1988). The plaintiff is entitled to reasonable attorney's fees incurred in defending against defendant's appeal of the fee award, since plaintiff "had no choice but to incur them or forfeit his victory in the district court." *Id.* at 990. *See also Jackson v. Illinois Prisoner Review Board,* 856 F.2d 890, 896 (7th Cir. 1988). On the other hand, the plaintiff-appellant who seeks to *increase* the fees awarded him in the district court, and "fails utterly in his appeal," is not a prevailing party on appeal, "even though he remains the prevailing party in the underlying litigation." *Ustrak,* at 990.

Page 337, add at end of note 51:

Contrast Clark v. City of Los Angeles, 803 F.2d 987, 993 (9th Cir. 1986), in which the plaintiffs-appellees were awarded § 1988 fees on appeal although the court of appeals reduced the amount of fees awarded to the plaintiffs, since defendants also unsuccessfully challenged on appeal their liability for attorney's fees.

Page 337, add to note 53:

See also Charles v. Daley, 846 F.2d 1057, 1070-73 (7th Cir. 1988) (concluding that plaintiffs were entitled to § 1988 fees for work done in defeating intervenors' appeal to Supreme Court on jurisdictional grounds, notwithstanding that Supreme Court did not award costs to plaintiffs pursuant to Court rule).

§ 15.7 –Prevailing on the Fee Application

Page 338, add at end of last paragraph in section:

* See § **15.6** in this supplement for a discussion of the plaintiff-appellee's entitlement to § 1988 fees on appeal, in cases in which the defendant has succeeded in obtaining an appellate reduction of the fees awarded to plaintiff by the district court. It also has been held that the plaintiff who has lost on the merits of his civil rights claims does not become a prevailing party merely by gaining an appellate reversal of the district court's award of § 1988 fees to the winning defendant. *Jensen v. City of San Jose,* 806 F.2d 899 (9th Cir. 1986) (en banc); *Ekanem v. Health & Hosp. Corp.,* 778 F.2d 1254, 1258 (7th Cir. 1985).

§ 15.8 –Prevailing at the Remedy Stage of the Litigation

Page 338, add to cases cited in first part of note 59:

First Circuit: Brewster v. Dukakis, 786 F.2d 16, 18-20 (1st Cir. 1986) (rejecting defendants' argument that, because of the existence of a defendant-funded court-appointed monitor, plaintiffs should receive § 1988 fees for postjudgment monitoring work only under a rigorous standard requiring plaintiffs to show that "their efforts produced a better result than otherwise would have occurred").

Fourth Circuit: Alexander v. Hill, 625 F. Supp. 567, 568 (W.D.N.C. 1985) (plaintiffs' monitoring which uncovered deficiencies in defendants' compliance with court orders).

Ninth Circuit: Keith v. Volpe, 833 F.2d 850, 855-58 (9th Cir. 1987) (holding that a "finding of contempt or obstruction of implementation is not a prerequisite to an award of attorney's fees for reasonable postjudgment monitoring of a consent decree," and that the existence of separate monitoring entities created by the decree did not bar the award of fees to plaintiffs for monitoring activities which were not duplicative of the services rendered by the monitoring entities).

Eleventh Circuit: Turner v. Orr, 785 F.2d 1498, 1501-04 (11th Cir. 1986) (postjudgment monitoring and enforcement work of plaintiffs' monitoring committee, as contemplated by consent judgment settling Title VII suit).

Page 338, update Delaware Valley citation in note 59:

478 U.S. 546, 559 (1986).

Page 338, add at end of paragraph:

In *Pennsylvania v. Delaware Valley Citizens' Council,* 478 U.S. 546 (1986), the Supreme Court appeared to place its imprimatur on the reasonable monitoring approach to the award of statutory attorney's fees for postjudgment enforcement activity. There the Court noted that several courts have held under § 1988 that "postjudgment monitoring of a consent decree is a compensable activity for which counsel is entitled to a reasonable fee." *Id.* at 559. An analysis of the lower court cases cited approvingly by the Supreme Court yields the principle that under the reasonable monitoring standard the plaintiff is entitled to fee compensation for postjudgment monitoring and enforcement work which was reasonably necessary to ensuring defendant's compliance with the underlying judgment and which contributed to defendant's compliance, even if it did not result in concrete judicial relief. *See Garrity v. Sununu,* 752 F.2d 727, 738-39 (1st Cir. 1984); *Bond v. Stanton,* 630 F.2d 1231, 1233 (7th Cir. 1980); *Miller v. Carson,* 628 F.2d 346, 347-48 (5th Cir. 1980); *Northcross v. Board of Education,* 611 F.2d 624, 637 (6th Cir. 1979), *cert. denied,* 447 U.S. 911 (1980). In *Delaware Valley Citizens' Council,* the Court approved the award of statutory fees under the Clean Air Act, 42 U.S.C. § 7604(d), for two postjudgment phases of litigation in which the plaintiff sought to safeguard and enforce rights and relief achieved in a consent decree through participation in state and federal administrative regulatory proceedings. The Supreme Court found that such participation was "crucial to the vindication of Delaware Valley's rights under the consent decree" and "helped to protect the relief awarded under the consent decree." 478 U.S. at 561. Even under the lenient reasonable monitoring standard, however, compensation could be withheld for postjudgment monitoring or enforcement efforts that were shown to have made no significant contribution to achieving compliance with a decree. *Cf. Stewart v. General Motors Corp.,* 756 F.2d 1285, 1294 (7th Cir. 1985).

The reasonable monitoring standard also may not be stretched to justify attorney's fee compensation for *all* time expended in the post-judgment phase of litigation, in total disregard of the level of success achieved or of the relevance of the work to enforcement of the underlying judgment. *See In re Burlington Northern, Inc.,* 832 F.2d 422, 426-27 (7th Cir. 1987) (rejecting plaintiffs' contention that they were entitled to fees for post-settlement activities that gained them an increased recovery from the settlement fund, when the additional sums recovered did not increase the defendant's overall liability but instead only reduced the settlement monies available to other plaintiffs); *Cooper v. Williamson County Board of Education,* 820 F.2d 180, 184 (6th Cir. 1987) (declining to award Title VII attorney's fees to plaintiff, on a reasonable monitoring theory, for post-judgment work done in resisting state agency dismissal charges that did not relate to enforcement of the Title VII race discrimination remedy obtained in federal court, or for counsel's activities in following media reports and advising plaintiff on day-to-day administrative matters after his job reinstatement), *cert. denied,* 108 S. Ct. 699 (1988); Foster v. Board of School Commissioners, 810 F.2d 1021, 1024-25 (11th Cir.) (rejecting plaintiffs' argument that they were automatically entitled to attorney's fees for *all* time expended at second stage of litigation, involving individual discrimination claims, following establishment of class-wide employment discrimination and issuance of general injunctive relief at first stage; reduction of award was warranted by fact that less than one-third of class members succeeded on their individual claims), *cert. denied,* 108 S. Ct. 99 (1987).

Page 339, update Delaware Valley Citizens' Council citation in note 60:

478 U.S. 546, 549 (1986).

Page 339, update Daggett citation in note 63:

vacated in part on other grounds, 811 F.2d 793, 800-01 (3d Cir. 1987) (approving § 1988 fee eligibility of plaintiffs who achieved at least partial success in remedy phase of reapportionment case).

§ 15.9 Extent of Success Required to Prevail

Page 341, add a new paragraph following the continuation paragraph at top of page:

While not addressing the issue of the degree of merits success needed to satisfy the prevailing party requirement of § 1988, the Supreme Court in *Hewitt v. Helms,* 107 S.Ct. 2672 (1987), held that the plaintiff becomes a prevailing party only when he obtains, by way of court order or defendant's remedial action, some *relief,* or *entitlement to relief,* on the merits of his claims. Thus, a plaintiff-appellant is not a prevailing party on appeal when he wins only an appellate ruling that his legal rights were violated, without gaining relief or entitlement to relief on the merits on his claims, and with the possibility that on remand he will obtain no merits relief, whether in the form of a declaratory judgment, injunction, or damages. The favorable legal ruling on appeal does not by itself make the plaintiff a prevailing party no matter how significant is the legal right or legal violation that is recognized. See complete discussion of *Hewitt* at **§ 15.4** of the supplement.

Page 341, add to cases cited in note 72:

Second Circuit: Henry v. Gross, 803 F.2d 757, 769 (2d Cir. 1986).
Third Circuit: Ashley v. Atlantic Richfield Co., 794 F.2d 128, 131, 134 (3d Cir. 1986).
Ninth Circuit: But see BSA, Inc. v. King County, 804 F.2d 1104, 1112 (9th Cir. 1986) (finding not clearly erroneous the district court's ruling that one plaintiff was not a prevailing party because of its "limited success" in obtaining an injunction against only two sections of a county ordinance which plaintiff sought to enjoin in its entirety and in unsuccessfully challenging the validity of the "major" provisions of the ordinance).

§ 15.10 —The Any Significant Issue Test of Required Success

Page 342, add at end of note 80:

The plaintiff who loses on the merits of his civil rights case does not become a prevailing party under § 1988 by obtaining an appellate reversal of the district court's award of attorney's fees to the winning defendant that was based on the erroneous finding that plaintiff's losing civil rights claims were frivolous. Jensen v. City of San Jose, 806 F.2d 899 (9th Cir. 1986) (en banc); Ekanem v. Health & Hosp. Corp., 778 F.2d 1254, 1258 (7th Cir. 1985).

Page 343, add to cases cited in note 85:

Van Sant v. United States Postal Services, 805 F.2d 141, 142 (4th Cir. 1986) (plaintiff prevailed under Equal Access to Justice Act, 28 U.S.C. § 2412, although "in a very limited sense," by succeeding on his claim that his notice of termination from employment was premature, although he was denied reinstatement, recovered damages of only $5,600 out of the $400,000-500,000 sought, and established "no new significant principles of law"); Ashley v. Atlantic Richfield Co., 794 F.2d 128, 132-36 (3d Cir. 1986) (plaintiff in employment race discrimination suit became a prevailing party on her claims for non-monetary relief by obtaining settlement agreement which gained her "some of the benefit sought" in the litigation, and, furthermore, was a prevailing party on her claims for monetary relief provided that she can demonstrate on remand that the $7,500 received by her in the settlement agreement constituted significant success on that claim and did not represent merely a nuisance settlement); Grano v. Barry, 783 F.2d 1104, 1108-10 (D.C. Cir. 1986) (plaintiffs achieved significant success entitling them to § 1988 fees where they obtained an injunction prohibiting the demolition of an historic tavern until a scheduled voter referendum concerning the fate of the tavern could be held); Bibbs v. Block, 778 F.2d 1318, 1324 (8th Cir. 1985) (en banc) (plaintiff prevailed in Title VII race discrimination suit by obtaining a declaratory judgment of intentional discrimination and an injunction prohibiting continued discrimination, although a remand was required on the issues of retroactive promotion and back pay); *But see* BSA, Inc. v. King County, 804 F.2d 1104, 1112 (9th Cir. 1986) (affirming, as not clearly erroneous, district court's finding that one plaintiff was not a prevailing party under § 1988 in view of its "limited success" in the litigation, although plaintiff had secured an injunction against two sections of a challenged ordinance that was otherwise upheld by the court; another plaintiff was found to be a prevailing party in obtaining an injunction against three of eight sections of a challenged ordinance).

Page 344, add to cases cited in note 87:

Derr v. Gulf Oil Corp., 796 F.2d 340, 344 (10th Cir. 1986) (plaintiff employee in Title VII suit who obtained ruling of unlawful sex discrimination against her and who therefore "will be entitled to at least nominal damages" is a prevailing party in the suit, whether or not she proves constructive discharge on remand and wins back pay and reinstatement); Williams v. St. Louis County, 643 F. Supp. 1150, 1152 (E.D. Mo.), *aff'd,* 785 F.2d 631 (8th Cir. 1986) (plaintiff who won one dollar in nominal damages from the one defendant against whom jury verdict was returned, and who failed on all counts against remaining eight defendants, was a prevailing party under § 1988).

Pages 344-45, update Ganey citation and delete last sentence in note 88:

Ganey v. Garrison, 813 F.2d 650, 651-52 (4th Cir. 1987) (reaffirming that plaintiff prevailed under § 1988 by obtaining jury verdict and judgment that his constitutional rights had been violated, although no damages or injunctive relief was granted).

Page 344, add after sentence with note 88 reference:

Without considering the degree of success required to establish the plaintiff as a prevailing party under § 1988, the Supreme Court in *Hewitt v. Helms,* 107 S.Ct. 2672 (1987) held that the plaintiff must win relief, or entitlement to relief, on the merits of a legal claim in order to qualify as a prevailing party under § 1988. See complete discussion of *Hewitt* at § **15.4** of the supplement.

Page 346, add to cases cited in note 1:

* Counsel v. Dow, 849 F.2d 731, 739-41 (2d Cir. 1988) (Education of the Handicapped Act, 20 U.S.C. § 1415(e); plaintiff did not succeed on any significant issue against the local defendants who, along with state defendants, signed consent decree, since the decree disclaimed any admission of liability or legal violation by defendants and imposed no obligations or expenses on the local defendants; neither did plaintiff prevail at administrative level against local defendant because of hearing officer's "limited finding of fiscal responsibility" by local defendant which brought plaintiff "no closer to the relief he sought"); Mazanec v. North Judson-San Pierre School Corp., 798 F.2d 230, 236-37 (7th Cir. 1986) (plaintiffs were not prevailing parties on basis of district court's ruling under state law that their children's home education was sufficient to constitute the equivalent of public school education, when that finding was "not something the Mazanecs 'sought' to achieve in bringing this lawsuit," and plaintiffs did not obtain the sought-after ruling on their constitutional claim concerning parents' rights to educate their children at home based on religious convictions and received no monetary or equitable relief).

Page 346, add the following case to note 2:

Thorne v. City of El Segundo, 802 F.2d 1131, 1140 n.9 (9th Cir. 1986) (plaintiff did not prevail for § 1988 fee purposes since defendants were found to be immune from § 1983 damages liability for their constitutional violations); *cf.* Zabkowicz v. West Bend Co., 789 F.2d 540, 552 (7th Cir. 1986) (plaintiff in Title VII suit did not prevail on her tort and labor claims since her stipulated dismissal of those claims was not the "result of any action by defendants that served to remedy civil rights violations").

Page 347, add following sentence with note 5 reference:

The Third Circuit in *Ashley v. Atlantic Richfield Co.,* 794 F.2d 128, 131-35 (3d Cir. 1986), has specifically held that the nuisance settlement argument may not be invoked to displace the "conventional inquiry" under the prevailing party analysis of whether the plaintiff has achieved significant success in the litigation that qualifies him for § 1988 fees. "To hold otherwise," the court concluded, "would permit the wholesale preemption of fee awards to plaintiffs who have in fact prevailed on their claims." *Id.* at 134 n.9. On the other hand, the court ruled that the nuisance settlement theory may be advanced as a potential special circumstance that might defeat the prevailing plaintiff's entitlement to § 1988 fees in a case in which "plaintiff's claim clearly appears to be legally or factually non-meritorious and, accordingly, in which it appears that the 'some benefit obtained' has been conferred by the defendant *solely* as a means of saving litigation expense." *Id.* See **§ 16.5** in this supplement.

Page 347, add to cases cited in note 6:

Maloney v. City of Marietta, 822 F.2d 1023, 1027 (11th Cir. 1987) (dictum); American Booksellers Ass'n, Inc. v. Hudnut, 650 F. Supp. 324, 331-33 (S.D. Ind. 1986) (denying § 1988 fees to intervenor-plaintiffs for their attorneys' efforts in "monitoring this litigation . . . [when] it did not contribute significantly to the ultimate success of the plaintiffs").

Page 347, add at end of section:

In *In re Burlington Northern, Inc.*, 832 F.2d 422, 425-27 (7th Cir. 1987), the Seventh Circuit concluded that plaintiffs did not become prevailing parties entitled to statutory fees from the defendant merely by obtaining increased amounts from the settlement fund created in the overall settlement of a Title VII employment race discrimination suit. The court noted that the increased amounts obtained decreased the amounts available to other plaintiffs from the settlement fund, but not at the expense of the defendant, whose total liability had been fixed by the settlement agreement.

§ 15.11 —The Central Issue Test of Required Success

Page 347, add to note 9:

Although generally continuing to declare its allegiance to the central issue test of the prevailing party requirement, *see e.g.,* Taylor v. City of Fort Lauderdale, 810 F.2d 1551, 1555-56 (11th Cir. 1987), the Eleventh Circuit on several occasions has lapsed into reliance on the "any significant issue" standard. Popham v. City of Kennesaw, 820 F.2d 1570, 1578 n.3 (11th Cir. 1987); Afro-American Patrolmen's League v. Atlanta, 817 F.2d 719, 725 (11th Cir. 1987).

Page 347, add to note 10:

In Trevino v. Holly Sugar Corp., 811 F.2d 896, 907 (5th Cir. 1987), the Fifth Circuit reiterated that the central issue test should be applied independently to each claim, or group of related claims, that is unrelated to other claims in the suit. But the court held in that case that the party opposing the fee request had waived a challenge on appeal to the district court's failure to make a claim-by-claim analysis by failing to raise the issue in the district court. *See also* Garner v. Wal-Mart Stores, Inc., 807 F.2d 1536,

1539-40 (11th Cir. 1987) (finding plaintiff entitled to Title VII attorney's fees on sex discrimination issue that she won, but not on unrelated constructive discharge issue that she lost).

Page 348, after sentence with note 16 reference, insert the following cases finding the plaintiff to be a prevailing party under the central issue test:

See also Solomon v. City of Gainesville, 796 F.2d 1464, 1466 (11th Cir. 1986) (plaintiff prevailed under § 1988 when he succeeded in "one of the primary objectives" of the litigation to have the challenged ordinance declared unconstitutional and to have it repealed, although he had waived his § 1983 damages claim). In *Taylor v. City of Fort Lauderdale,* 810 F.2d 1551, 1555-56 & n.17, 1558-59 (11th Cir. 1987), the Fifth Circuit stated that the "the central issue test is one of practicality, not legal formalism," and that "success on a minor or peripheral issue in a civil rights case will not support an award of attorney's fees." In *Taylor,* the court found that plaintiffs became prevailing parties under that test by obtaining a preliminary injunction on the central issue in the litigation concerning the constitutionality of the city's permit requirement as applied to the *outdoor* solicitation of religious groups. At the same time, the court noted that plaintiff's success in obtaining a judgment of the unconstitutionality of the city's requirement as applied to *indoor* solicitation did not, by itself, establish plaintiff's prevailing party status, because it did not involve the central issue in the case.

Page 349, after the sentence with note 20 reference, add the following cases finding the plaintiff not to be a prevailing party under the central issue test:

Texas State Teachers v. Garland Independent School District, 837 F.2d 190, 192-93 (5th Cir. 1988) (plaintiffs did not prevail under central issue test by succeeding, all the way to U.S. Supreme Court, on "significant secondary issues" concerning constitutionality of defendant school district's regulations, because they lost on the "central" issue in the case), *cert. granted,* 109 S. Ct. 51 (1988); *Simien v. City of San Antonio,* 809 F.2d 255, 258 (5th Cir. 1987) (plaintiff terminated city employee did not prevail under central issue test because she failed in her "primary goal" to remedy an allegedly unconstitutional residency requirement, and the procedural due process claim on which she succeeded was only a "subsidiary issue"); Howe v. Baker, 796 F.2d 1355, 1360-61 (11th Cir. 1986) (plaintiff state trooper did not prevail under § 1988 by obtaining a ruling that his suspension and transfer violated due process, when he was denied damages relief and reinstatement); *Healy v. Town of Pembroke Park,* 643 F. Supp. 1208, 1216-17 (S.D. Fla. 1986) (plaintiffs who obtained favorable constitutional ruling and judgment in federal court in their employment discharge suit were not entitled to § 1988 fees, where they had obtained reinstatement and back-pay relief in separate state administrative and judicial proceedings and defendants were immune from damage awards in federal court). In *Texas State Teachers, supra,* the Supreme Court will determine the propriety of the central issue test of the plaintiff's prevailing party status.

Page 349, add after sentence with note 24 reference:

Recent decisions of that court do not clarify whether the Sixth Circuit requires greater success than on "any significant issue" in order for the plaintiff to qualify as a prevailing party under § 1988. *See Chemin v. Welchans,* 844 F.2d 322, 330 (6th Cir. 1988) (plaintiffs were not prevailing parties under § 1988 when court found "with one minor exception," that the challenged statutory scheme was constitutional); *Loudermill v. Cleveland Board of Education,* 844 F.2d 304, 312-13 (6th Cir. 1988) (plaintiff prevailed for § 1988 purposes when defendant changed its pretermination rules to comply with favorable due process ruling by the U.S. Supreme Court, although plaintiff himself did not obtain reinstatement, back pay, compensatory damages, or a declaratory judgment that the challenged statutory provision was unconstitutional); *Haskins v. United States Department of Army,* 808 F.2d 1192, 1201 (6th Cir. 1987) (entry of judgment for plaintiff, based on defendant's admission that defendant had discriminated against her, did not make her a prevailing party for purposes of recovering Title VII fees, because plaintiff was denied all remedial relief on the ground that she would not have received the job promotion even in the absence of discrimination).

Page 351, add at end of carryover paragraph:

In his dissenting opinion in *Texas State Teachers v. Garland Independent School District,* 837 F.2d 190, 193-97 (5th Cir. 1988), Judge Goldberg expressed his dismay that the Fifth Circuit "has steadfastly refused" to review *en banc* the question of the propriety of the central issue test of prevailing party status and urged the Supreme Court to grant certiorari to resolve the split in the circuits concerning the proper prevailing party standard. Judge Goldberg noted that although the Supreme Court in *Hensley v. Eckerhart,* 461 U.S. 424 (1983), did not specifically disapprove the central issue test, the Court's express declaration that "a plaintiff can be deemed the prevailing party even where only 'minor' relief was obtained" effectively condemns the central issue test and makes clear that "the method for dealing with such partial success was to withhold payment for unsuccessful claims, not to withhold fees altogether." *Id.* at 193, 194-95. Judge Goldberg emphasized that application of the central issue test requires judges to be "mind readers" in attempting to divine "plaintiff's subjective goal in bringing the lawsuit" and "enhances the likelihood of protracted litigation over attorney's fees." *Id.* at 194, 196.

§ 15.12 Prevailing Without Obtaining Formal Judicial Relief: Settlements and Informal Success

Page 352, update Smith citation in note 35:

468 U.S. 992, 1007 (1984).

Page 352, add new paragraph after incomplete paragraph ending with note 37 reference:

In *Hewitt v. Helms,* 107 S.Ct. 2672 (1987), the Supreme Court repeated the principle that the "plaintiff is deemed to have prevailed despite the absence of a formal judgment in his favor" if his lawsuit "produces voluntary action by the defendant that affords the plaintiff all or some of the relief he sought through a judgment – e.g., a monetary settlement or a change in conduct that redresses the plaintiff's grievances."

At the same time the Court made it clear in *Hewitt* that the winning of at least some of the merits *relief* sought in the lawsuit, whether by judicial order or through defendant's voluntary action prompted by the suit, is essential to the establishment of the plaintiff as a prevailing party under § 1988. The *Hewitt* Court did not consider generally the circumstances in which a defendant's remedial action taken in response to the lawsuit establishes the plaintiff as a prevailing party under § 1988. Instead, the Court simply held that the plaintiff prisoner in that case did not qualify as a prevailing party under § 1988 on the basis of the state defendant's promulgation of regulations addressing due process requirements in the administrative segregation procedures to which the plaintiff had been subjected, since at the time the regulations were promulgated, the plaintiff had been released from prison on parole, and therefore "did not and could not get redress" from their promulgation. *Id.* at 4910. The Court stated that "[a]lthough he has subsequently been returned to prison, and is presumably now benefiting from the new procedures (to the extent that they influence prison administration even when not directly being applied), that fortuity can hardly render him, retroactively, a 'prevailing party' in this lawsuit, even though he was not such when the final judgment was entered." *Id.* See complete discussion of *Hewitt* at § **15.4** of the supplement.

§ 15.13 –The *Nadeau* Test

* *Page 354, add to note 48:*

Judge Posner expressed the view that the requirement of proving a causal connection between the lawsuit and the defendant's remedial action could be questioned in a case in which plaintiff was compelled to file suit in order to obtain relief, yet is denied statutory attorney's fees because the defendant, "for reasons extrinsic to the suit, decided to cure the plaintiff's grievance." Rootberg v. Central States Pension Fund, 856 F.2d 796, 799 (7th Cir. 1988). Judge Posner noted that "[i]t could be argued that an award of attorney's fees is justifiable if the plaintiff prudently incurred reasonable fees in pursuit of a meritorious claim and then had the claim fall into its lap because the defendant for reasons wholly unrelated to the suit, dropped its objections." *Id.* at 799.

Page 354, add at end of note 50:

* Although in California Ass'n of Physically Handicapped v. F.C.C., 721 F.2d 667, 671-72 (9th Cir. 1983), the Ninth Circuit expressly determined to follow the *Nadeau* rather than the *Bonnes* standard for purposes of determining the plaintiff's prevailing party status under federal fee-shifting statutes, in subsequent decisions the court occasionally has reverted back to a *Bonnes* test. *See* Clark v. City of Los Angeles, 803 F.2d 987, 989 (9th Cir. 1986); Ward v. County of San Diego, 791 F.2d 1329, 1334 (9th Cir. 1986); Harris v. McCarthy, 790 F.2d 753, 759 (9th Cir. 1986). However, most recent Ninth Circuit decisions clearly advance the two-prong *Nadeau* standard. *See* Cunningham v. County of Los Angeles, 859 F.2d 705, 713 (9th Cir. 1988); Sablan v. Dept. of Finance, 856 F.2d 1317, 1324-25 (9th Cir. 1988); Greater Los Angeles Council on Deafness v. Community Television of S. Cal., 813 F.2d 217, 219-20 (9th Cir. 1987).

§ 15.13 THE *NADEAU* TEST

Page 355, add to cases cited in note 53:

Rose v. Heintz, 806 F.2d 389, 391-92 (2d Cir. 1986) (in concluding that plaintiffs in Medicaid eligibility suit were prevailing parties under § 1988, court found both that state defendant "had retroactively corrected ineligibility in accord with the federal government's response to the lawsuit and because of the lawsuit" and that state defendant's challenged action was taken under color of state law, thereby satisfying the requirement of a § 1983 cause of action).

Page 355, add at end of continuation paragraph at top of page:

While purporting to follow the *Nadeau* standard, the Tenth Circuit in *Supre v. Ricketts,* 792 F.2d 958 (10th Cir. 1986), has added rigor to the second prong requirement of the *Nadeau* standard concerning the necessary substantiality of the plaintiff's undecided civil rights claim. Departing from the lenient *Nadeau* requirement that the plaintiff's underlying fee-generating claim be merely nonfrivolous, the Tenth Circuit in *Supre* insisted that the concessions made by the defendant as a result of plaintiff's suit be "legally required" in order to qualify the plaintiff as a prevailing party under § 1988. * *Id.* at 962-63; *id.* at 964 (concurring opinion); *id.* at 965 (dissenting opinion). *See also Goichman v. City of Aspen,* 859 F.2d 1466, 1471 (10th Cir. 1988). As discussed in § **15.14** in this supplement, the Third Circuit recently appears to be in retreat from its commitment to the *Bonnes* test and has appended the *Nadeau* requirement that the plaintiff's unadjudicated fee-generating claims, in a case favorably resolved short of a merits decision, be nonfrivolous.

Page 355, add to note 56:

Savidge v. Fincannon, 836 F.2d 898, 904-06 (5th Cir. 1988) (ruling that evidentiary hearing was required before district court properly could decide the "intensely factual" issue of whether defendant's voluntary remedial action was prompted by the lawsuit).

Page 355, add to note 57:

Savidge v. Fincannon, 836 F.2d 898, 906-07 (5th Cir. 1988) (plaintiff's motion for injunctive relief, that was mooted by defendants' voluntary compliance, was not frivolous or groundless and was not barred by the res judicata effect of a consent decree in a related class action suit); *see also* Heath v. Brown, 807 F.2d 1229, 1233 & n.7 (5th Cir. 1987).

Page 355, add at end of paragraph that concludes with note 58 reference:

One court has held that the plaintiff seeking to establish his prevailing party status for § 1988 fee purposes is entitled to compel discovery of documents in the defendant's possession that are relevant to the issue of whether defendant's corrective action was taken in response to the lawsuit, subject to the issuance of an appropriate protective order on, for example, privilege grounds. *Cleary v. Commissioner of Public Welfare,* 21 Mass. App. 140, 485 N.E.2d 955, 963-65 (1985).

Page 355, add to cases cited in note 59:

Clark v. City of Los Angeles, 803 F.2d 987, 989-90 (9th Cir. 1986); Gekas v. Attorney Registration & Disciplinary Comm'n, 793 F.2d 846, 849-50 (7th Cir. 1986); Supre v. Ricketts, 792 F.2d 958, 961-62 (10th Cir. 1986) (all stating clearly erroneous standard of review of fact findings under *Nadeau* test). In Heath v. Brown, 807 F.2d 1229 (5th Cir. 1987), the Fifth Circuit noted that the district court's resolution of the factual question of "[w]hether or not plaintiffs' lawsuit was a substantial cause of defendants' corrective actions . . . will stand on appeal unless clearly erroneous." *Id.* at 1233-34. However, in this case the district court never made that "crucial finding," and the court of appeals vacated the § 1988 fee award and remanded for a "factual determination of * causality." *Id.* at 1234. The Fifth Circuit subsequently upheld the district court's renewed finding that the plaintiff's lawsuit was a significant catalyst in the defendant's abandonment of the challenged policy, noting that when the fact findings underlying the causation determination are "based on credibility evaluations the deference paid to decisions by the trier-of-fact is enhanced." Heath v. Brown, 858 F.2d 1092, 1094 (5th Cir. 1988).

Page 356, update Smith citation and add the following cases to note 60:

Smith, 468 U.S. 992, 1016 n.18 (1984). Supre v. Ricketts, 792 F.2d 958, 961-62 (10th Cir. 1986); *cf.* Gekas v. Attorney Registration & Disciplinary Comm'n, 793 F.2d 846, 850 (7th Cir. 1986) (stating standard of review as one for abuse of discretion for legal issues under *Nadeau* standard).

Page 356, add at end of continuation paragraph at top of page:

The Tenth Circuit has observed in *Supre v. Ricketts,* 792 F.2d 958 (1986), that in many cases the relevant inquiry on the prevailing party issue, including application of the *Nadeau* test, involves a mixed question of law and fact. This occurs "when the facts are admitted or established and the law is disputed; the sole issue is whether the law applied to the facts satisfies the statutory standard." *Id.* at 961. The court concluded that where the mixed question "involves primarily a factual inquiry, the clearly erroneous standard is appropriate," and where it "primarily involves the consideration of legal principles, then a *de novo* review by the appellate court is appropriate." *Id. See also* Gekas v. Attorney Registration & Disciplinary Comm'n, 793 F.2d 846, 850 (7th Cir. 1986).

Page 356, add to cases cited in note 62:

First Circuit: Exeter-West Greenwich Regional School v. Pontarelli, 788 F.2d 47, 52-53 (1st Cir. 1986) (plaintiffs were prevailing parties under *Nadeau* catalyst test where their § 1983 suit in federal court resulted in that court's certification of a controlling state law issue to the Rhode Island Supreme Court and the resolution of that issue in plaintiff's favor, leading to the subsequent dismissal of the § 1983 suit as moot). *Second Circuit:* Rose v. Heintz, 806 F.2d 389, 391-92 (2d Cir. 1986) (plaintiffs were prevailing parties in Medicaid eligibility suit, where the defendant welfare department halted the challenged practice and retroactively restored Medicaid eligibility "in accord with the federal government's response to the lawsuit and because of the lawsuit", and where the state defendant had acted under color of state law in illegally terminating plaintiffs' Medicaid eligibility).

Fifth Circuit: Leroy v. City of Houston, 831 F.2d 576, 580-81 (5th Cir. 1987) (finding that the "substantial factor" or "significant catalyst" test does not require plaintiff to prove that litigation was the "only causative factor" in the defendant's remedial action but only that litigation was a "significant contributing factor," among others, to defendant's action);

Seventh Circuit: Gekas v. Attorney Registration & Disciplinary Comm'n, 793 F.2d 846, 850-51 (7th Cir. 1986) (plaintiff prevailed in suit challenging constitutionality of disciplinary rule prohibiting attorney direct-mail advertising, when district court did not clearly err in concluding that the Illinois Supreme Court advanced the effective date of the rule's favorable amendment in response to the lawsuit, and plaintiff's suit was not frivolous); Lovell v. City of Kankakee, 783 F.2d 95, 96-97 (7th Cir. 1986) (plaintiffs prevailed in suit challenging constitutionality of local sign ordinance when defendants stipulated in court that they would not enforce the ordinance, resulting in the dismissal of the action as moot, and plaintiffs' suit was not frivolous); Rivera v. Coler, 629 F. Supp. 366 (N.D. Ill. 1986) (plaintiff prevailed in suit seeking immediate determination of her Medicaid eligibility and coverage for a liver transplant where, following the issuance of a temporary restraining order, the state defendant found plaintiff Medicaid-eligible under the stimulus of the suit, and the suit, although rendered moot by the plaintiff's death before a transplant could be located, was likely to succeed on the merits).

Eighth Circuit: Granville House, Inc. v. Department of H.E.W., 813 F.2d 881, 883 (8th Cir. 1987) (plaintiff treatment center prevailed under Equal Access to Justice Act, 28 U.S.C. § 2412, in challenge to government's denial of Medicaid funding by inducing defendant to promulgate relevant regulations and to continue funding to plaintiff pending final publication of regulations, although plaintiff did not obtain a formal court order entitling it to continued funding).

* *Ninth Circuit:* Sablan v. Department of Fin., 856 F.2d 1317, 1324-27 (9th Cir. 1988) (upholding district court's finding that plaintiffs prevailed under § 1988 when their lawsuit, based in nonfrivolous constitutional claims, caused government to abandon challenged practice, after which suit was dismissed by stipulation); Greater Los Angeles Council on Deafness v. Community Television, 813 F.2d 217, 219-21 (9th Cir. 1987) (plaintiffs prevailed under Rehabilitation Act, 29 U.S.C. § 794a(b), and Equal Access to Justice Act, 28 U.S.C. § 2412, by prompting defendant federal agency to find that the Rehabilitation Act establishes duties to hearing-impaired viewers on the part of public broadcasters, although plaintiffs ultimately lost in court on the merits of their claims); Clark v. City of Los Angeles, 803 F.2d 987, 989-90 (9th Cir. 1986) (plaintiffs were prevailing parties under § 1988 although jury verdict in plaintiffs' favor for defendant police harassment was vacated on appeal for evidentiary reasons, since in the interim defendants had ceased their harassment, thus avoiding a retrial and leading to plaintiffs' voluntary dismissal of the action with prejudice).

Page 359, add to cases cited in note 64:

Fifth Circuit: Sorola v. City of Lamesa, 808 F.2d 435, 437 (5th Cir. 1987) (finding that plaintiffs did not prevail in Voting Rights Act suit, 42 U.S.C. § 1973l(e), because district court's finding that plaintiffs' lawsuit did not cause defendant city to amend challenged election ballots was not clearly erroneous); Tucker v. Summers, 784 F.2d 654, 657-58 (5th Cir. 1986) (plaintiff was not prevailing party in suit challenging validity of state bar admissions rules, when the litigation "did not play a significant or relevant part in the later rules change" that mooted the suit).

Seventh Circuit: In re Burlington Northern, Inc., 832 F.2d 422, 425-26 (7th Cir. 1987) (upholding district court's finding that plaintiffs did not prevail under Title VII because the increased recoveries obtained for plaintiffs from the fixed settlement fund were gained at expense of other plaintiffs' recoveries and not at expense of defendant); Perlman v. City of Chicago, 801 F.2d 262, 268 (7th Cir. 1986) (plaintiff did not prevail under § 1988 in his suit seeking return of jewelry allegedly illegally seized by police, when district court did not clearly err in concluding that the return of the jewelry after suit was filed "could not be attributed with certainty to the filing of the lawsuit," especially since plaintiff never requested its return before filing suit); Ekanem v. Health & Hosp. Corp., 778 F.2d 1254, 1258 (7th Cir. 1985) (plaintiffs did not prevail under § 1988 in employment discrimination suit on basis of defendant's changed employment practices, when district court did not commit clear error in concluding that those changes were "in place and established prior to the lawsuit * ever being filed"). In Rootberg v. Central States Pension Fund, 856 F.2d 796 (7th Cir. 1988), the Seventh Circuit concluded that the plaintiffs were not prevailing parties under the Employee Retirement Income Security Act, 29 U.S.C. § 1415(e), since defendants' capitulation was prompted not by this lawsuit but instead by the persuasive decision in another case.

Ninth Circuit: Braafladt v. Board of Governors, 778 F.2d 1442, 1444 (9th Cir. 1985) (plaintiff did not prevail under § 1988 in suit challenging constitutionality of Oregon Bar's residency requirements, since district court did not commit clear error in finding that Oregon Supreme Court's rescission of the offending rules was prompted not by plaintiff's lawsuit but rather through efforts of Oregon Bar Association and another lawsuit). *See also* Harris v. McCarthy, 790 F.2d 753, 759-60 (9th Cir. 1986), in which the court affirmed the district court's denial, as "unripe," of plaintiff's request for § 1988 fees that was based on the claim that the suit caused defendants' improvements in prison conditions, when plaintiffs had obtained dismissal of their federal court suit so that "they could pursue a single trial of all the issues in state court". The court of appeals agreed that "not until this litigation is finally resolved [in state court] will we know the extent to which plaintiffs' legal efforts changed the defendants' conduct," and concluded that there was no basis for plaintiffs' contention that California state courts could not award § 1988 fees to the successful plaintiffs for work done in federal court as well as in state court.

Page 360, add to cases cited in note 66:

Second Circuit: Woe by Woe v. Cuomo, 638 F. Supp. 1506, 1526-27 (E.D.N.Y. 1986) (plaintiffs in suit challenging constitutionality of conditions at state mental hospital did not prevail on basis of psychiatric centers' regaining of accreditation, when "nothing in the record suggests that defendants' actions or attitudes concerning . . . accreditation have been affected by the litigation" and when, furthermore, the court found that such accreditation is not constitutionally required).

Tenth Circuit: Supre v. Ricketts, 792 F.2d 958, 962-63 (10th Cir. 1986) (ruling that plaintiff transsexual prisoner did not prevail under § 1988 in suit seeking medical treatment for gender dysphoria, when it was unclear whether plaintiff's court-ordered hormone treatment was medically necessary and "would have continued as a result of judicial intervention," when defendants' policy changes "were being studied prior to plaintiff's lawsuit", when plaintiff's release from prison was the result of plaintiff's own "repeated attempts at self-mutilation," and, furthermore, when defendants' remedial action "was not legally required").

Page 360, add following sentence ending with note 66 reference:

In *Palmer v. City of Chicago,* 806 F. 2d 1316, 1322-24 (7th Cir. 1986), *cert. denied,* 107 S. Ct. 2180 (1987), the Seventh Circuit held that the plaintiffs, whose suit challenged the constitutionality of the defendant police department's alleged practice of concealing exculpatory material collected in criminal investigations, did not prevail under § 1988 on the basis of defendant's cessation of the challenged practice. The plaintiffs did not prevail, although their constitutional claims were not frivolous, since the district court's preliminary injunction requiring retention of the material at issue was reversed on appeal, on standing and abstention grounds, and plaintiffs subsequently abandoned pursuit of the remaining damages claims. The *Palmer* court rejected the proposition that the plaintiff who has attained some practical success in the litigation, but who also receives an adverse judicial ruling finding no merit to the suit, can achieve prevailing party status on a mere showing that his legal claims were not frivolous. Thus, the court concluded, "when a suit goes through to judgment for defendants, or is abandoned as hopeless by the plaintiffs, the plaintiffs cannot be regarded as having prevailed within the meaning of the statute even if their lawsuit was not frivolous (that is, so groundless that sanctions could be imposed for having brought it) and even if the suit brought about some or for that matter all of the changes in the defendants' conduct that the plaintiffs had sought." *Id.* at 1323. The court found that this result is not altered merely because the district court's favorable ruling was reversed on standing and abstention grounds and not on the merits of plaintiffs' constitutional claims. *Id.* 1323-24. In *Janowski v. International Brotherhood of Teamsters Local No. 710,* 812 F.2d 295, 298 n.1 (7th Cir. 1987), the Seventh Circuit reiterated that "where . . . the plaintiff loses on the merits, the plaintiff is not entitled to any award of attorney's fees, even if its suit is nonfrivolous and conferred a benefit on the plaintiff."

Page 361, update Smith citation in continuation note 66:

468 U.S. 992, 1009 n.12 (1984).

§ 15.14 —The *Bonnes* Test

Page 362, add following sentence with note 74 reference:

However, current Third Circuit decisions reflect a decided ambivalence concerning the applicable standard. Indeed, recent decisions appear to make the transition from a *Bonnes* to a *Nadeau* test, without freely admitting the change, by adding the requirement that plaintiffs undecided fee-generating claim be nonfrivolous. In *Helms v. Hewitt,* 780 F. 2d 367, 369 (3d Cir. 1986), *rev'd on other grounds,* 107 S. Ct. 2672 (1987), the court articulated the standard in *Bonnes* terms, citing the prior Third Circuit cases that similarly had invoked that test. But in *Disabled in Action v. Pierce,* 789 F.2d 1016, 1019 (3d Cir. 1986), the court appeared to reverse field when confronted with defendant's argument that the more stringent *Nadeau* test should be applied to determine prevailing party status under federal fee-shifting statutes. In response, the court accommodated the *Nadeau* standard by assimilating the nonfrivolous inquiry into the causal connection requirement of the *Bonnes* standard. Thus, the court held that a "totally frivolous lawsuit which results in the defendant doing no more than it was already commmitted to do will never satisfy" the causal connection requirement, while a "lawsuit that has sufficient merit to move the defendant to do more than it was already committed to do will satisfy" that requirement. *Id.* at 1019. Subsequently, the court backpeddled by citing the *Bonnes* test again in *Durett v. Cohen,* 790 F.2d 360, 362 (3d Cir. 1986), but in *Ashley v. Atlantic Richfield Co.,* 794 F.2d 128, 131 & n.2 (3d Cir. 1986), returned to a *Nadeau*-type standard as enunciated in *Disabled in Action*. Thus, while not unequivocally making the change, the Third Circuit appears to be abandoning the *Bonnes* test for a *Nadeau*-type standard.

Page 362, add to cases cited in note 77:

Taylor v. City of Fort Lauderdale, 810 F.2d 1551, 1560 (11th Cir. 1987) (describing inquiry under "catalyst" test as whether the "lawsuit is a substantial factor or a significant catalyst in motivating defendants to end their unconstitutional behavior" but finding its application unnecessary in this case because plaintiffs prevailed on basis of judicial relief obtained).

Page 363, update Hyatt citation (Fourth Circuit) and add to cases cited in note 80:

Third Circuit: Ashley v. Atlantic Richfield Co., 794 F.2d 128, 135-36 (3d Cir. 1986) (plaintiff prevailed on her requests for nonmonetary relief in employment discrimination suit by obtaining settlement agreement that yielded "some of the benefit sought" in the litigation and impelled the defendant employer "to do something more than it was committed to do"); Durett v. Cohen, 790 F.2d 360, 361-62 (3d Cir. 1986) (mentally retarded plaintiff prevailed since his suit prompted defendant Pennsylvania officials to persuade non-party New Jersey officials to fund plaintiff's care at residential treatment facility in New Jersey and to reimburse facility for past care, thus resolving suit in plaintiff's favor); Disabled in Action v. Pierce, 789 F.2d 1016, 1018-20 (3d Cir. 1986) (plaintiff prevailed under Rehabilitation Act, 29 U.S.C. § 794a(b), when suit concluded in settlement agreement requiring federal defendant to make substantial alterations to office building that rendered it accessible to handicapped persons, actions that were not legally "gratuitous").

Fourth Circuit: Reigh v. Schleigh, 829 F.2d 1334, 1335 (4th Cir. 1987) (although plaintiffs did not obtain any success by adjudication, they prevailed under § 1988 because their suit caused defendants to amend challenged attachment procedures), *cert. denied,* 108 S. Ct. 1247 (1988); Hyatt v. Heckler, 807 F.2d 376, 381-82 (4th Cir. 1986), *aff'g* 618 F. Supp. 227, 229-30 (W.D.N.C. 1985) (affirming fee award under Equal Access to Justice Act, 28 U.S.C. § 2412, to plaintiff disability benefit claimants whose lawsuit, although not obtaining injunctive relief, gained appellate ruling disapproving defendant's nonacquiescence policy as a basis for denying benefits and resulted in the re-evaluation of the claims of several thousand applicants "free of the Secretary's nonacquiescence policy").

Eleventh Circuit: Maloney v. City of Marietta, 822 F.2d 1023, 1025-26 (11th Cir. 1987) (plaintiff prevailed under Voting Rights Act, 42 U.S.C. § 1973l(e), because lawsuit motivated defendant to meet preclearance requirement of Act); Bradley v. Heckler, 785 F.2d 954, 955-56 (11th Cir. 1986) (plaintiff prevailed under Equal Access to Justice Act, 28 U.S.C. § 2412, when his suit and the imminent issuance of an injunction prodded the federal defendant to render a determination terminating plaintiff's disability benefits, thereby ending the indefinite suspension of benefits and enabling plaintiff to obtain review of the determination through the prescribed administrative process.

Page 364, add to cases cited in note 81:

In Hewitt v. Helms, 107 S.Ct. 2672 (1987), the Supreme Court ruled that the plaintiff prisoner could not prevail through the defendant's promulgation of ameliorative regulations since he had been released from prison by that time.

Pages 363, 364, delete Crest Street Community Council case from note 80, page 363, and add the following on page 364 after the continuation sentence ending with note 81 reference:

In *North Carolina Dep't of Transp. v. Crest Street Community Council, Inc.,* 479 U.S. 6, 16 n.* (1986), a case arising out of the Fourth Circuit, the Supreme Court ruled that a community group did not qualify as a prevailing party in a federal court suit in which it sought to intervene on the side of the prevailing plaintiffs, where the motion to intervene was never ruled on, the proposed intervenor obtained no relief in the suit, and the intervenor motion had "little catalytic effect" on the relief that was granted in the suit.

§ 15.15 Prevailing by Success on Nonfee Claims Joined with Undecided Fee-Generating Claims

Page 365, update Smith citation in note 86:

468 U.S. 992, 1007 (1984).

Page 365, add at end of note 87:

As discussed in **§ 15.16** in this supplement, Congress enacted the Handicapped Children's Protection Act of 1986, Pub. L. No. 99-372, 100 Stat. 796 (1986), to authorize the award of attorney's fees to the prevailing party on claims under the Education of the Handicapped Act, 20 U.S.C. § 1400 *et seq.*

Page 365, update Daggett citation and add after the Maine v. Thiboutot citation in note 88:

Daggett, aff'd in relevant part, 811 F.2d 793 (3d Cir. 1987). *See* Schrader v. Idaho Dep't of Health and Welfare, 631 F. Supp. 1426, 1429 (D. Idaho 1986) (recognizing availability of § 1983, and hence § 1988 fees, for successful enforcement of rights to AFDC benefits under Social Security Act); Maldonado v. Nebraska Dep't of Public Welfare, 223 Neb. 485, 391 N.W.2d 105, 109 (1986) (availability of § 1983, and hence § 1988 fees, for successful enforcement of rights to AFDC, AABD, and Medicaid benefits under Social Security Act): Torres v. Perales, 121 A.D.2d 386, 388, 503 N.Y.S.2d 96 (2 Dep't 1986) (availability of § 1983, and hence § 1988 fees, for successful enforcement of rights to AFDC benefits under Social Security Act). In Nebraska Health Care Ass'n v. Dunning, 778 F.2d 1291, 1295-96 (8th Cir. 1985), *cert. denied,* 479 U.S. 1063 (1987), the Eighth Circuit found that the rights of long-term care institutions under the Social Security Act to adequate reimbursement for services under the Medicaid program are enforceable through § 1983, thereby triggering § 1988 fee eligibiltiy, and rejected the contrary argument that *Thiboutot* limited the availability of § 1983 to the enforcement of individual rights to subsistence-level benefits under the Social Security Act.

Page 365, delete the following phrase in the last sentence on the page, together with note 90:

"... the substantive education guarantees of the Education of the Handicapped Act,[90] ..."

Page 365, update the Consolidated Freightways citation in note 92, and add:

Consolidated Freightways, *cert. denied,* 469 U.S. 834 (1984); Private Truck Council v. Secretary of State, 503 A.2d 214, 221-22 (Me. 1986), *cert. denied,* 476 U.S. 1129 (1986) (three Justices dissenting).

Page 365, add the following at the beginning of note 93:

* Scurlock v. City of Lynn Haven, 858 F.2d 1521, 1529 n.9 (11th Cir. 1988) (federal preemption claims are not cognizable under § 1983); Western Air Lines, Inc. v. Port Auth., 817 F.2d 222, 226 (2d Cir. 1987); Segundo v. City of Rancho Mirage, 813 F.2d 1387, 1394 (9th Cir. 1987); United States v. State of Wash., 813 F.2d 1020, 1023 (9th Cir. 1987), *cert. denied,* 108 S.Ct. 1593 (1988); White Mountain Apache Tribe v. Williams, 810 F.2d 844, 847-52 (9th Cir.), *cert. denied,* 479 U.S. 1060 (1987) (distinguishing between preemption claims based on federal occupation of the field or conflict with federal goals, which are *not* enforceable through § 1983, and claims based on direct conflict between state law or policy and explicit federal law provisions creating enforceable rights, which may be actionable under § 1983).

Page 365, add following last sentence on the page:

On the other hand, a closely-divided Supreme Court has ruled that tenants may enforce through § 1983 their rights to limits on rents chargeable in public housing under the Brooke Amendment, Pub. L. No. 91-152, § 213, 83 Stat. 389 (1969) and (as later amended) Pub. L. No. 97-35, § 322, 95 Stat. 400 (1978), amending the United States Housing Act of 1937, 42 U.S.C. §§ 1410 *et seq. Wright v. Roanoke Redevelopment and Housing Authority,* 479 U.S. 418 (1987). Other courts occasionally have concluded that § 1983 supplies a cause of action (with accompanying § 1988 fee eligibility) to support claims under other federal statutes that are found to confer enforceable rights and to lack their own comprehensive remedial mechanisms. *See, e.g., Gonzalez v. Pingree,* 821 F.2d 1526 (11th Cir. 1987); *Victorian v. Miller,* 813 F.2d 718 (5th Cir. 1987)(*en banc*)(both finding § 1983 available to redress violations of Food Stamp Act, 7 U.S.C. § 2011 *et seq.,* thereby triggering applicability of § 1988); * *Armstrong v. Fairmont Community Hospital Association, Inc.,* 684 F. Supp. 1486 (D. Minn. 1987) (plaintiffs' successful claim that defendant hospital violated community service obligations of Hill-Burton Act, 42 U.S.C. § 291c(e), is enforceable under § 1983, thereby entitling plaintiffs to § 1988 fees); *Ramah Navajo School Bd. v. Bureau of Revenue,* 104 N.M. 302, 720 P.2d 1243, 1251-56 (Ct. App.), *cert. denied,* 479 U.S. 940 (1986) (two Justices dissenting) (rights of Indian tribe to self-government under Indian Self-Determination and Educational Assistance Act, 25 U.S.C. §§ 450a-450n, and federal treaties, and to immunity from state's imposition of gross receipts tax on Indian school board).

Page 366, update Smith citation in note 95:

468 U.S. 992, 1006-07 (1984).

Page 366, add at end of note 96:

In Clients' Council v. Pierce, 778 F.2d 518 (8th Cir. 1985), the Eighth Circuit found that the plaintiffs, who had prevailed against the federal defendants on a constitutional claim which is not fee-generating against a *federal* defendant, were entitled to § 1988 fees because they had also asserted substantial, although undecided, claims under 42 U.S.C. §§ 1981 and 1982, for which fees are available against federal defendants pursuant to 28 U.S.C. § 2412(b) and § 1988. See **§ 16.10** for a complete discussion of § 1988 fee eligibility of federal defendants.

Page 366, update Smith citation in note 97:

468 U.S. 992, 1007 & n.10 (1984).

Page 366, update Smith citation in note 98 and add the following:

Smith, 468 U.S. at 1006, 1015. *See* Seaway Drive-In, Inc. v. Township of Clay, 791 F.2d 447, 453-55 & n.12 (6th Cir.), *cert. denied,* 479 U.S. 884 (1986) (in suit invalidating township ordinance regulating drive-in theaters, plaintiff's undecided Fourteenth Amendment "taking" claim was related, for § 1988 fee purposes, to successful claim that ordinance deprived plaintiff of vested rights under state law; Ramah Navajo School Bd. v. Bureau of Revenue, 104 N.M. 302, 720 P.2d 1243, 1256 (Ct. App.), *cert. denied,* 107 S. Ct. 423 (1986) (plaintiff who prevailed on nonfee preemption claim under Supremacy Clause was entitled to § 1988 fees on basis of undecided claim, actionable under § 1983, of violation of enforceable rights under federal law). Under the analysis in Smith v. Robinson, 468 U.S. at 1013-15, a substantial undecided procedural due process claim may not suffice to trigger eligibility for § 1988 fees where the plaintiff succeeded on nonfee claims for substantive relief involving "entirely separate legal theories" and warranting "entirely different relief."

Page 366, add to cases cited in note 99:

United States v. State of Wash., 813 F.2d 1020, 1024 (9th Cir. 1987)(finding that Fourteenth Amendment claims pendent to successful but non-fee-generating federal law claim were jurisdictionally insubstantial and hence did not support entitlement to § 1988 fees), *cert. denied,* 108 S. Ct. 1593 (1988); Seaway Drive-In, Inc. v. Township of Clay, 791 F.2d 447, 451-53 (6th Cir.), *cert. denied*, 479 U.S. 884 (1986) (ruling that district court erred in replacing the correct test, of whether the undecided constitutional claims were nonfrivolous and hence jurisdictionally substantial, with an improper inquiry concerning whether, at the time of final judgment, the constitutional claims were supported by sufficient evidence to survive a summary judgment motion).

Page 367, in note 2, update Smith citation and add White Mountain Apache Tribe case:

Smith, 468 U.S. at 1009 n.12. White Mountain Apache Tribe v. Williams, 810 F.2d 844, 852-54 (9th Cir.), *cert. denied,* 479 U.S. 1060 (1987) (plaintiffs not entitled to § 1988 fees on basis of undecided constitutional claims which were pleaded in original federal complaint but were never pressed or expounded on thereafter, were abandoned in the ancillary state court proceedings, and were merely "dusted off for use in seeking a fee award under § 1988").

§ 15.16

Delete section heading and entire section and substitute the following:

§ 15.16 –Prevailing When Constitutional Claims Are Joined with Education of the Handicapped Act Claims

In *Smith v. Robinson,* 468 U.S. 992 (1984), the Supreme Court held that the plaintiff was not eligible for a § 1988 fee award on the basis of a jurisdictionally substantial, although undecided, equal protection claim (seeking a free appropriate public education for a handicapped child) that was related factually and legally to a successfully adjudicated claim under the Education of Handicapped Act (EHA), 20 U.S.C. §§ 1400 *et seq.,* for the same relief. The Court noted that the plaintiff could not recover attorney's fees on the basis of the successful EHA claim, since the EHA (at that time) did not contain a fee-shifting provision, and since 42 U.S.C. § 1983 was not recognized as available to enforce EHA claims and thereby to trigger § 1988 fee eligibility. 468 U.S. at 1008 n.11. The Court further ruled that 42 U.S.C. § 1983 was unavailable to enforce substantial equal protection claims that are "virtually identical" to EHA claims, since, the Court concluded, Congress intended the EHA, with its comprehensive procedures and guarantees, to be the "exclusive avenue" for a handicapped child's vindication of the right to a free public education adapted to that child's special needs. *Id.* at 1009-13.

The consequence was that the plaintiff's substantial but unaddressed equal protection claim, not actionable through 42 U.S.C. § 1983 because duplicative of the successful EHA claim, was not fee-generating under the circumstances and could not support a § 1988 fee award. *Id.* At the same time, the *Smith* Court suggested, without squarely deciding, that an independent procedural due process challenge could be asserted in the EHA context pursuant to 42 U.S.C. § 1983, with attendant eligibility for § 1988 fees, to remedy fundamental procedural deficiencies in the state administrative procedures prescribed by the EHA. *Id.* at 1014 n.17 (by implication). The *Smith* Court also held that a claim under § 504 of the Rehabilitation Act, 29 U.S.C. § 794, which has its own fee-shifting provision at § 505 (29 U.S.C. § 794a(b)), may not be asserted where it essentially parallels the substantive EHA claim. *Id.* at 1016-21. *See also Irving Indep. School Dist. v. Tatro,* 468 U.S. 883 (1984).

The Handicapped Children's Protection Act. Congress promptly took up the task of amending the EHA to overcome the result in *Smith*. After laboring for almost two years to reconcile opposing views on the content of the statute, Congress on August 5, 1986, enacted the Handicapped Children's Protection Act of 1986 (HCPA), Pub. L. No. 99-372, 100 Stat. 796 (1986), amending § 615 of the EHA, 20 U.S.C. § 1415. As discussed in this section, the HCPA empowers the courts to award attorney's fees for judicial success on EHA claims, as well as for success on § 1983 constitutional claims that overlap EHA claims. However, the HCPA also requires that the plaintiff asserting § 1983 constitutional claims in court seeking relief also available under the EHA first exhaust administrative remedies where mandated under the EHA. Attorney's fees are available as well to the plaintiff who prevails on his constitutional or EHA claim in the mandated administrative proceedings. As further discussed here, several significant issues remain to be resolved concerning the scope and effect of the HCPA.

The HCPA authorizes a federal or state court, "in its discretion," to "award reasonable attorney's fees as part of the costs to the parents or guardian of a handicapped child or youth who is the prevailing party" in "any action or proceeding" to secure rights under the EHA. 20 U.S.C. § 1415(e) (4) (B). The court in *Fontenot v. Louisiana Board of Elementary and Secondary Education,* 835 F.2d 117, 120 (5th Cir. 1988), concluded that handicapped students who have reached the age of majority and bring suit in their own names also are eligible for EHA fees. The legislative history of the HCPA makes it clear that the standards for the successful plaintiff's satisfaction of the "prevailing party" requirement under that statute are to be the same as the standards for determining prevailing party status under § 1988 as interpreted by the Supreme Court. H.R. Rep. No. 296, 99th Cong., 2d Sess. 5,6 (1985); S. Rep. No. 112, 99th Cong., 2d Sess. 13 (1985), *reprinted in* 1986 U.S. Code Cong. & Ad. News 1799. The HCPA also provides for attorney's fee eligibility for the plaintiff who prevails in the administrative proceedings mandated by the EHA. 20 U.S.C. § 1415(e)(4)(B) (availability of fees in an "action or proceeding"). *See* H.R. Rep. No. 296, at 5; S. Rep. No. 112, at 14. This result is consistent with the authorization for fee awards to plaintiffs who succeed on their Title VII claims in administrative proceedings mandated by that statute. See **§ 17.9**. "[T]raditional costs incurred in the course of litigating a case" are also awardable under the HCPA. Joint Explanatory Statement of the Committee of Conference, Conference Report, H.R. Rep. No. 687, at 5 (July 16, 1986), *reprinted in* 1986 U.S. Code Cong. & Ad. News 1807. See **§ 21.8**.

Congress expressly gave retroactive effect to the HCPA provisions authorizing fee awards to plaintiffs prevailing on EHA claims in administrative or judicial proceedings, so that EHA fees are available in such actions or proceedings that were pending on or instituted on or after July 4, 1984, the day prior to the Supreme Court's decision in *Smith v. Robinson.* Section 5 of the HCPA. *See* S. Rep. No. 112, at 13, 15. Most courts have had no difficulty concluding that the retroactivity provision is applicable to preserve the prevailing plaintiff's EHA fee eligibility in cases in which the appeal of the district court's denial of fees was pending on the effective date of the HCPA (*Board of Education v. Diamond,* 808 F.2d 987, 990, 994 (3d Cir. 1986); *Fontenot v. Louisiana Board of Elementary and Secondary Education,* 805 F.2d 1222 (5th Cir. 1988)), in which the fee motion was withdrawn after *Smith* was decided and refiled after the HCPA was enacted (*Tonya K. v. Board of Education,* 847 F.2d 1243 (7th Cir. 1988)), and in which the fee motion was not made at all until after the enactment of the HCPA (*Max M. v. New Trier High School District,* 859 F.2d 1297, 1298-99 (7th Cir. 1988); *Counsel v. Dow,* 849 F.2d 7311, 734-39 (2d Cir. 1988); *Abu-Sahyun v. Palo Alto Unified School District*, 843 F.2d 1250, 1252-53 (9th Cir. 1988) (finding that defendant's expectation when it entered into settlement that it would not be liable for fees was not a "special circumstance" warranting denial of EHA fees to plaintiffs)). In such cases the courts have upheld the validity of the retroactivity provision of the HCPA against challenges based on the Eleventh Amendment, vested rights principles, and other grounds. *Max M., supra,* 859 F.2d at 1245-48; *Counsel, supra,* 849 F.2d at 731; *Fontenot v. Louisiana Board of Elementary and Secondary Education,* 835 F.2d 117, 120-21 (5th Cir. 1988). However, the Eleventh Circuit has ruled that the HCPA should not be read to confer fee eligibility on the plaintiff whose initial fee motion was finally determined, without a pending appeal, prior to the effective date of the Act. *Georgia Association of Retarded Citizens v. McDaniel,* 855 F.2d 794 (11th Cir. 1988). A contrary interpretation of the HCPA, the Eleventh Circuit concluded, would violate the vested rights doctrine. *Id.* at 810-13. Local court rules prescribing the time from final judgment within which fee motions must be made should be waived or at least construed to run anew from August 5, 1986 (the effective date of the statute) in cases to which the retroactivity provision applies but in which final judgment was entered prior to that date. See **§ 24.2.** *Cf. Max M. v. New Trier High School District,* 859 F.2d 1297, 1300 (7th Cir. 1988) (upholding district court's ruling that local rule, requiring fee motions to be filed within 90 days after final judgment, was inapplicable to case in which HCPA did not become effective until more than 90 days after final judgment); *School Board of Prince William County v. Malone,* 622 F. Supp. 999, 1001 (E.D. Va. 1987) (finding that EHA fee request filed three months after effective date of HCPA was timely, notwithstanding local court rule ordinarily requiring fee request to be filed within ten days of final judgment). See generally **§ 24.2.**

The HCPA also overrules the restrictive interpretation in *Smith* of the availability of 42 U.S.C. § 1983 and § 504 of the Rehabilitation Act to enforce claimed rights to free special education for handicapped children that parallel rights under the EHA. The HCPA achieves that result by providing that the EHA is not to be construed "to restrict or limit the rights, procedures, and remedies available under the Constitution, title V of the Rehabilitation Act of 1973, or other Federal statues protecting the rights of handicapped children and youth." 20 U.S.C. § 1415(f). Congress made it clear that this provision applies to the utilization of § 1983 to enforce constitutional claims, whether sounding in equal protection or due process, that seek relief also available under the EHA. Joint Explanatory Statement of the Committee of Conference, Conference Report, H.R.Rep. No. 687, at 7 (July 16, 1986). Although not expressly made retroactive, this provision has been applied to cases pending in the district court or on appeal on August 5, 1986, the date of the enactment of the HCPA, to uphold plaintiffs' § 1983 constitutional claims asserted in EHA suits. The courts rationalize this result on the principle that a court is required to apply the law in effect at the time it renders a decision, absent a contrary congressional intent, noting that § 1415(f) "simply codifies a congressional purpose long in place which congress believed the Supreme Court [in *Smith v. Robinson*] had misinterpreted." *Mrs. W. v. Tirozzi,* 832 F.2d 748, 755 (2d Cir. 1987); *Board of Education v. Diamond,* 808 F.2d 987, 995-96 (3d Cir. 1986); *Dodds v. Simpson,* 676 F. Supp. 1045 (D. Or. 1987); *Edward B. v. Brunelle,* 662 F. Supp. 1025, 1036-37 (D.N.H. 1986); *Rollison v. Biggs,* 656 F. Supp. 1204, 1209-10 (D. Del. 1987). *But see Silano v. Tirozzi,* 651 F. Supp. 1021, 1024-26 (D. Conn. 1987) (declining to apply § 1415(f) to pending case). See § 21.10 for an extensive analysis of the applicability of a newly-enacted fee-shifting statute to cases pending on the date of the provision's enactment.

However, Congress attached a significant condition to its restoration of the availability of § 1983 and § 504 of the Rehabilitation Act to enforce claimed rights overlapping with rights under the EHA. The HCPA expressly requires that the state and local administrative proceedings mandated by the EHA must be exhausted by the plaintiff prior to instituting a judicial action asserting § 1983 constitutional or § 504 claims seeking relief also available under the EHA. 20 U.S.C. § 1415(f). At the same time, the legislative history of the HCPA details circumstances in which administrative exhaustion under the EHA, and hence for parallel § 1983 and § 504 claims, is not required, including cases in which: "(1) it would be futile to use the due process procedures (e.g., an agency has failed to provide services specified in the child's individualized educational program (IEP) or an agency has abridged a handicapped child's procedural rights such as the failure to make a child's records available); (2) an agency has adopted a policy or pursued a practice of general applicability that is contrary to the law; (3) it is improbable that adequate relief can be obtained by pursuing administrative remedies (e.g., the hearing officer lacks the authority to grant the relief sought); and (4) an emergency situation exists (e.g., the failure to take immediate action will adversely affect a child's mental or physical health)." H.R. Rep. No. 296, at 7. *See Kerr Center Parents Association v. Charles,* 842 F.2d 1052, 1059-60 (9th Cir. 1988) (exhaustion of administrative remedies not required unless futile); *Mrs. W. v. Tirozzi,* 832 F.2d 748, 756-57 (2d Cir. 1987) (excusing exhaustion of EHA administrative remedies for § 1983 and EHA claims when plaintiffs alleged system-wide violations unable to be resolved at administrative level); *J.G. v. Board of Education,* 830 F.2d 444, 446-47 (2d Cir. 1987) (excusing exhaustion of EHA administrative remedies when plaintiffs' claimed systemic wrongs were not remediable by administrative process but predicating plaintiffs' attorney's fee award on § 1988, instead of EHA, because of assertedly "troublesome question whether the right to bring a direct cause of action, which does not follow the administrative hearing and appeal route, can be found by implication in section 1415 [of EHA]").

The plaintiff who prevails in federal or state court on his § 1983 constitutional claim that is revived by the HCPA thereby becomes eligible for § 1988 attorney's fees for work done on the successful § 1983 claim in court. Furthermore, the plaintiff who prevails on his § 1983 claim in administrative proceedings mandated by the HCPA is entitled automatically to § 1988 fees for services rendered in those proceedings, just as the plaintiff is entitled to statutory fees for work done in succeeding on EHA or Title VII claims in administrative proceedings mandated by those statues. H.R. Rep. No. 296, at 7. In contrast is the limited availability of § 1988 fees for work done by the successful § 1983 plaintiff in optional administrative proceedings preceding the federal court suit, as discussed in **§ 17.9.** In *Arons v. New Jersey State Board of Education,* 842 F.2d 58 (3d Cir. 1988), the court upheld state regulations which barred lay advocates from recovering attorney's fees under the HCPA for successful representation of a handicapped child in administrative proceedings.

Special Fee Calculation Standards for Success on EHA Claims. § 1988 fees for the plaintiff who prevails on his § 1983 claim, made available by the HCPA, in court or in mandatory administrative proceedings, are calculated under the standards described elsewhere in this book for determination of reasonable § 1988 fees. See especially **Chapter 17** (compensable hours), **Chapter 18** (reasonable hourly rates), **Chapter 19** (downward lodestar adjustments), and **Chapter 20** (upward lodestar adjustments). On the other hand, the HCPA includes provisions that in important respects describe standards different from those under § 1988 for calculating reasonable attorney's fees for the plaintiff who prevails on an EHA claim in court or in mandatory administrative proceedings. Thus, while the Act provides that market-value rates prevailing in the community are to be applied in determining reasonable fee awards for the prevailing plaintiff on his EHA claim, it also stipulates that "[n]o bonus or multiplier may be used" in calculating such a fee award. 20 U.S.C. § 1415(e) (4) (C). At the same time, the legislative history makes it clear that the prohibition on upward adjustments for EHA fee awards does not limit their availability under other fee-shifting statutes, such as § 1988, as interpreted by the Supreme Court. Joint Explanatory Statement of the Committee of Conference, Conference Report, H.R. Rep. No. 687, at 6 (July 16, 1986). See **Chapter 20.** Furthermore, there is evidence that Congress intended that factors that might have entered into the awarding of an upward adjustment, such as "novelty and difficulty of the issues, the special skills required, the unpopularity of the case, its contingency nature, and the quality of representation," as well as the "timing of payment," should be taken into account in setting market-value rates for EHA fee awards. 132 Cong. Rec. H4845 (July 24, 1986) (statement of Rep. Augustus Hawkins). *See Max M. v. Illinois State Board of Education,* 684 F. Supp. 514, 528-29 (N.D. Ill. 1988) (finding delay adjustments authorized under HCPA, as not inconsistent with statutory prohibition against award of "bonuses or multipliers").

The HCPA also provides, consistent with applicable principles under other fee-shifting statutes, that appropriate reductions in the requested EHA fee award shall be made where the prevailing plaintiff "unreasonably protracted the final resolution of the controversy," seeks compensation at a rate that "unreasonably exceeds the hourly rate prevailing in the community for similar services by attorneys of reasonably comparable skill, experience, and reputation," or claims compensation for "time spent and legal services furnished" that is "excessive considering the nature of the action or proceeding." 20 U.S.C. § 1415(e)(4)(F). See **§ 17.3** and **Chapter 18.** However, § 1415(e)(4)(G) provides that the reductions described in subparagraph F shall *not* apply where the court finds that the governmental defendant "unreasonably protracted the final resolution of the action or proceeding or there was a violation of section 615" of the Act mandating procedural safeguards for handicapped children and their parents under the EHA. *See Moore v. District of Columbia,* 674 F. Supp. 901, 907 n.4 (D.D.C. 1987) (citing § 1415(e)(4)(G) to conclude that any "excessive" time spent by plaintiffs' counsel on their successful EHA claim would be compensable if "traceable to defendants' delays" in the case). Finally, consistent with the HCPA's characterization of EHA attorney's fees as an element of "costs" (20 U.S.C. § 1415(e)(4)(B)), the Act expressly makes applicable to EHA fee determinations the rule of *Marek v. Chesny,* 473 U.S. _____, 87 L. Ed. 2d 1 (1985), that the plaintiff who rejects a defendant settlement offer, made pursuant to Federal Rule of Civil Procedure 68, that is at least as favorable as the judgment finally obtained by plaintiff in the case, may not recover statutory fees accruing after the date of the rejected offer. 20 U.S.C. § 1415(e)(4)(D). See **§ 21.4.** However, 20 U.S.C. § 1415(e)(4)(E) then provides that the limitations of the *Marek* rule are *not* applicable where the prevailing plaintiff was "substantially justified" in rejecting the Rule 68 offer. Substantial justifications for rejecting the Rule 68 offer include the pendency of relevant court cases "which could have an impact on the case in question" (Joint Explanatory Statement of the Committee of Conference, Conference Report, H.R. Rep. No. 687, at 6 (July 16, 1986)) and "the lack of adequate time to assess the strength of the claim and the reasonableness of the agency's offer." 132 Cong. Rec. H4842 (July 24, 1986) (statement of Rep. Pat Williams).

Unresolved Issues under the HCPA. Several important issues remain to be resolved concerning the prevailing party's eligibility for attorney's fees under the HCPA. One significant issue is the scope of a court's authority to award attorney's fees under the HCPA to the plaintiff who has succeeded on his EHA claim or his § 1983 claim (paralleling an available EHA claim) in mandatory administrative proceedings. The legislative history of the HCPA indicates that the court (federal or state), and not an administrative hearing officer, is authorized to award EHA or § 1988 attorney's fees to the plaintiff who has prevailed in mandatory administrative proceedings to enforce EHA claims or § 1983 claims seeking relief also available under the EHA. S. Rep. No. 112, at 14. The legislative history also states that such a plaintiff who prevails at the administrative stage may file suit in court "for the limited purpose" of obtaining attorney's fees for work done in the successful administrative proceeding. H.R. Rep. No. 296, at 5. However, the Supreme Court has ruled, in *North Carolina Department of Transportation v. Crest Street Community Council, Inc.,* 479 U.S. 6 (1986), that a court can award § 1988 attorney's fees to the plaintiff who has prevailed on a fee-generating claim in an administrative proceeding *only* in a judicial action to enforce the fee-generating claim, and *not* in an independent suit seeking only attorney's fees. The Court indicated that this principle applies with equal force in the Title VII context, notwithstanding that administrative exhaustion is mandatory and the legislative history of the Title VII fee-shifting statute evinces, as it does under the HCPA, a congressional intent to permit an independent court action limited to seeking recovery of attorney's fees for success at the administrative stage. 479 U.S. at 13-14. The arguable effect, then, of the *Crest Street* decision is to leave the plaintiff who has prevailed on an EHA or § 1983 claim in mandatory administrative proceedings, that have been exhausted before the institution of a court suit on the merits, without recourse to court for purposes of recovering the statutory attorney's fees to which he is entitled under the HCPA. The result would be to encourage the plaintiff who is exhausting mandatory administrative proceedings pursuant to the HCPA to file, during the pendency of the administrative proceeding, a protective court action seeking merits relief on his EHA or parallel § 1983 claims, in order to enable him to seek statutory attorney's fees from the court in the event that he prevails at the administrative stage. *Cf. Crest Street Community Council,* 479 U.S. at 21-25. (Brennan, J., dissenting). See discussion at **§ 17.9**.

The court in *Rollison v. Biggs,* 660 F. Supp. 875 (D. Del. 1987), *denying reargument of* 656 F. Supp. 1204, 1211 (D. Del. 1987), concurred in this arguable effect of *Crest Street.* The *Rollison* court found that the legislative history reflected an "overriding congressional intent to have the HCPA attorneys' fees provision interpreted consistent with all other civil rights fee-shifting statutes" (660 F. Supp. at 877) and hence that the *Crest Street* holding, that § 1988 fees for success in administrative agency proceedings cannot be recovered in a court suit seeking only attorney's fees, is applicable to the HCPA. However, most lower courts have concluded otherwise, finding controlling Congress' clear intent to authorize a court to award EHA fees for administrative success in a suit for fees only. These courts reject the argument that in enacting the HCPA Congress "intended only to make the fees provision coextensive with other fee-shifting statutes." *Moore v. District of Columbia,* 666 F. Supp. 263, 266 (D.D.C. 1987). Noting the extensive citation of *New York Gaslight Club* in the legislative history of the HCPA, the *Moore* court reasoned that "when Congress considered the fees provision at issue here it thought that fees *were* recoverable for administrative proceedings under other fee-shifting statutes," *id.* at 266, notwithstanding the Supreme Court's subsequent disavowal in *Crest Street* of the *Gaslight Club* dicta. Thus, the *Moore* court concluded, "while it might be true that Congress wanted the Handicapped Act to parallel these other statutes, it wanted to do so to *ensure* that attorneys' fees would be awarded for administrative proceedings, not to defeat such awards." *Id. Accord Duane M. v. Orleans Parish School Board,* 861 F.2d 115 (5th Cir. 1988); *Eggers v. Bullitt County School District,* 854 F.2d 892, 894-98 (6th Cir. 1988); *Counsel v. Dow,* 849 F.2d 731, 740-41 n.9 (2d Cir. 1988); *Rossi v. Gosling,* 696 F. Supp. 1079 (E.D. Va. 1988) (federal court suit may be brought to recover EHA fees for work done in settling dispute prior to formal administrative proceeding); *Mathern v. Campbell Country Children's Center,* 674 F. Supp. 816, 817-18 (D. Wyo. 1987); *Unified School District v. Newton,* 673 F. Supp. 418, 419-23 (D. Kan. 1987); *Kristi W. v. Graham Independent School District,* 663 F. Supp. 86, 88 (N.D. Tex. 1987); *Burpee v. Manchester School District,* 661 F. Supp. 731 (D.N.H. 1987); *Prescott v. Palos Verdes Peninsula Unified School District,* 659 F. Supp. 921 (C.D. Cal. 1987). *See also Robert D. v. Sobel,* 688 F. Supp. 861, 864 (S.D.N.Y. 1988); *Michael M. v. Board of Education,* 686 F. Supp. 995, 1000-02 (E.D.N.Y. 1988) (both applying three-year statute of limitations period to federal court suits, brought in New York, seeking EHA fees for administrative success).

Another outstanding issue is whether state defendants enjoy Eleventh Amendment immunity in federal court from liability for HCPA attorney's fees based solely on the plaintiff's success on a claim arising under the EHA. In *Hutto v. Finney,* 437 U.S. 678 (1978), and *Maher v. Gagne,* 448 U.S. 122 (1980), the Supreme Court ruled that the

Eleventh Amendment affords no immunity to state defendants from § 1988 fee liability in cases in which the prevailing plaintiff's constitutional claim was successful or remained in the case as a jurisdictionally substantial claim although the plaintiff succeeded on a statutory claim or by settlement. See discussion at §§ **6.3-6.13, 15.5,** and **16.8.** But the Court in *Maher* reserved the question whether the Eleventh Amendment bars a federal court from imposing on state defendants a § 1988 fee award predicated solely on a successful federal statutory claim made enforceable by § 1983. 448 U.S. at 130, and 134-35 (Powell, J., concurring). In this regard the First Circuit has held in *David D. v. Dartmouth School Committee,* 775 F.2d 411 (1st Cir. 1985), *cert. denied sub nom. Massachusetts Dep't of Education v. David D.,* 475 U.S. 1140 (1986), that Congress effectively overrode the State's Eleventh Amendment immunity from merits relief under the EHA by its intent to enact the EHA under the enforcement provisions of § 5 of the Fourteenth Amendment in order to promote the equal protection of the law. *Accord Muth v. Central Bucks School District,* 839 F.2d 113, 128-30 (3d Cir. 1988) (following *David D.* and noting that HCPA, 20 U.S.C. § 1415(e)(4)(G), expressly contemplates that "the State or local educational agency" is liable for fees), *cert. granted,* 109 S. Ct. 52 (1988); *Fontenot v. Louisiana Board of Elementary and Secondary Education,* 835 F.2d 117, 120 (5th Cir. 1988) (concluding that "eleventh amendment is no bar to an award of attorney fees as costs" under HCPA, citing *Hutto*). *But see Kerr Center Parents Association v. Charles,* 842 F.2d 1052, 1058-59 (9th Cir. 1988) (finding that EHA did not override state's Eleventh Amendment immunity). The analysis of the Seventh Circuit in *Tonya K. v. Board of Education,* 847 F.2d 1243, 1246 (7th Cir. 1988), is most persuasive on this point. The court concluded that whether or not the HCPA overcomes the state's Eleventh Amendment immunity from damages awards, there is no Eleventh Amendment bar to the recovery of statutory attorney's fees against the state. The court noted that attorney's fees are not damages, since they "do not compensate the plaintiffs for injuries;" rather they are "part of the 'costs' of prosecuting the suit." *Id.* at 1246. On the authority of *Hutto v. Finney,* 437 U.S. 678 (1978), "awards of fees as part of costs do not exceed the federal courts' power under the eleventh amendment." *Id.* It is also arguable that Congress has overridden any Eleventh Amendment barrier that exists to an EHA fee award against the State by enactment of section 1003 of the Rehabilitation Act Amendments of 1986, Pub.L. No. 99-506, 100 Stat. ___________ (1986), providing that the State is not immune under the Eleventh Amendment from federal suit and remedies under, *inter alia,* "the provisions of any . . . Federal statute prohibiting discrimination by recipients of Federal financial assistance."

Finally, there are doubts as to the eligibility of a successful governmental *defendant* for attorney's fees under the HCPA for its efforts in defeating a frivolous EHA claim. The Senate Report suggests that successful defendants are entitled to the recovery of attorney's fees from plaintiff parents whose EHA claims are found to be "frivolous, unreasonable, or without foundation" under the standards governing defendant fee awards under § 1988. S. Rep. No. 112, at 14, see **Chapter 23.** But the HCPA by its terms confines fee awards for successful EHA claims to the "parents or guardian of a handicapped child or youth who is the prevailing party," 20 U.S.C. § 1415(e)(4)(B), thereby making no allowance for fee awards to the typical governmental defendant who defeats an EHA claim. *See* 132 Cong. Rec. H4845 (July 24, 1986) (statement of Rep. Augustus Hawkins, observing that the HCPA "only allows the award of attorney's fees to prevailing parents, whether plaintiff or defendant in an action or proceeding"). Accordingly, the Senate Report notwithstanding, the HCPA does not appear to contemplate the award of attorney's fees to the governmental defendant who * defeats a frivolous EHA claim. Another issue that occasionally has arisen is the liability of the State Commissioner of Education for EHA fees awarded for plaintiff's success in the administrative proceeding, the outcome appearing to turn on whether the State Commissioner functioned as an adjudicator or as a participant in the administrative process. *See Robert D. v. Sobel,* 688 F. Supp. 861, 866-67 (S.D. Neb. 1988); *Michael M. v. Board of Education*, 686 F. Supp. 995, 1003-04 (E.D.N.Y. 1988); *Burr v. Ambach,* 683 F. Supp. 46, 49 (S.D.N.Y.), *appeal dismissed for lack of jurisdiction,* 863 F.2d 1071, 1074-75 (2d Cir. 1988).

§ 15.17 –Prevailing by Success on a State Law Claim Pendent to a Federal Constitutional Claim

Page 371, update Smith citation in note 21:

468 U.S. 992 (1984).

Page 371, add to cases cited in note 24:

* Scurlock v. City of Lynn Haven, 858 F.2d 1521 (11th Cir. 1988) (remanding for district court determination of whether undecided constitutional claims, which were joined with a successful pendent state law claim in the case, were insubstantial in light of a recent adverse Eleventh Circuit decision on an identical claim, so as to render plaintiff ineligible for § 1988 fees); Seaway Drive-In, Inc. v. Township of Clay, 791 F.2d 447 (6th Cir.), *cert. denied,* 479 U.S. 884 (1986) (holding that *Gagne* test is satisfied where district court had pendent jurisdiction over the successful state law claims because the undecided constitutional claims were jurisdictionally substantial): Exeter-West Greenwich Regional School v. Pontarelli, 788 F.2d 47 (1st Cir. 1986) (plaintiff prevailed in federal court action that was favorably mooted, without need to adjudicate plaintiff's substantial constitutional claims, by Rhode Island Supreme Court's resolution of controlling state law question certified to it by federal district court); Woodard v. Hardee's Restaurant, 643 F. Supp. 691, 693-95 (W.D. Mo. 1986) (§ 1988 fees assessed against defendant restaurant that was found liable under state law for false arrest of plaintiff by police officer acting as security guard, when constitutional false arrest claim against restaurant, although not submitted to jury, was substantial); Elbe v. Yankton Indep. School Dist., 640 F. Supp. 1234 (D.S.D. 1986) (plaintiff succeeded on state constitutional claim, pendent to substantial federal constitutional claim, that was favorably resolved upon its certification by federal district court to South Dakota Supreme Court); Allen v. District of Columbia, 503 A.2d 1233, 1237 (D.C. App. 1986) (plaintiff was entitled to § 1988 fees against defendant police officer for his success on common law assault claim related to substantial constitutional claim on which plaintiff arguably did not prevail); Shapiro v. Chapman, 70 Md. App. 307, 520 A.2d 1330, 1333-34 (Ct. Spec. App. 1987) (finding that trial court's erroneous entry of judgment for defendant on plaintiff's § 1983 constitutional claim was not harmless, even though that claim was redundant of plaintiff's successful state law tort claim, because the

availability of § 1988 attorney's fees hinged on reversal of the adverse ruling on constitutional claim); Crane v. Commissioner of Public Welfare, 400 Mass. 46, 507 N.E.2d 751 (Supreme Judicial Court 1987) (successful state law claim joined with undecided federal statutory claim); Cepulonis v. Registrars of Voters, 396 Mass. 808, 488 N.E.2d 1166 (1986) (successful state constitutional claim joined with undecided but substantial federal constitutional claim); Doe v. Cuddy, 21 Ohio App. 3d 270, 487 N.E.2d 914, 915-17 (1985) (prevailing plaintiff succeeded in state court on state law claim joined with substantial federal constitutional claim, following federal district court's abstention decision in the case); International Ass'n of Machinists v. Affleck, 504 A.2d 468, 470-71 (R.I. 1986). The civil rights plaintiff who succeeds on a state law claim in state court, following the federal district court's abstention decision under Railroad Comm'n v. Pullman Co., 312 U.S. 496 (1941), may have the choice of seeking § 1988 fees in the state or the federal court forum. *See* Harris v. McCarthy, 790 F.2d 753, 759-60 (9th Cir. 1986) (fee request expected in state court suit that was pursued following voluntary dismissal of federal court suit); Doe v. Cuddy, 21 Ohio App. 3d 270, 487 N.E.2d 914 (1985) (fee request in state court). In White Mountain Apache Tribe v. Williams, 810 F.2d 844, 855 n.15 (9th Cir.), *cert. denied,* 479 U.S. 1060 (1987), the court reserved the question whether a "§ 1988 attorney's fees claim is sufficiently discrete from the substantive claims upon which it rests so as to allow plaintiffs to return to federal court on their fees claim after submitting all of their substantive claims to the state courts." *See also* Punton v. City of Seattle, 805 F.2d 1378 (9th Cir. 1986) (ruling that state court judgment reinstating plaintiff as police officer and awarding him back pay barred subsequent § 1983 suit in federal court for damages for emotional distress and for § 1988 attorney's fees, even though relief sought in federal court arguably was not available in state proceeding); Trujillo v. County of Santa Clara, 775 F.2d 1359, 1369-70 (9th Cir. 1985) (denying Title VII fees to plaintiff where fees were authorized under state law in state court proceedings that were pursued prior to institution of Title VII suit in federal court, and plaintiff failed to appeal denial of fees by state trial court). Successful pursuit of § 1988 fees in either forum may require that the plaintiff submit his federal constitutional, as well as his state law, claims to the state court following the federal court's abstention decision. Failure to do so leaves the plaintiff without a fee-generating claim in state court or subject to the possible conclusion by the federal court that he abandoned his constitutional fee-generating claim. *See* White Mountain Apache Tribe, 810 F.2d at 854.

Page 371, add the phrase "in the course of the merits litigation" to end of sentence with note 25 reference.

Page 371, add to cases cited at beginning of note 25:

Federation of City Employees v. City of Birmingham, 492 So. 2d 1304 (Ala. 1986) (trial court, in deciding merits of the action, ruled that the plaintiff's federal constitutional claim was "premature" and nonjusticiable); Tiffany v. Arizona Interscholastic Ass'n, Inc., 151 Ariz. 134, 726 P.2d 231 (Ct. App. 1986) (ruling against plaintiff's constitutional claim in resolving merits of the case); Allen v. Dist. of Columbia, 503 A.2d 1233, 1237-38 & n.4 (D.C. App. 1986) (directed verdict in favor of municipal defendant on plaintiff's constitutional claim); Daigle v. City of Portsmouth, 534 A.2d 689, 705 (N.H. 1987). In Heath v. Brown, 807 F.2d 1229, 1233 (5th Cir. 1987), the Fifth Circuit ruled that plaintiffs could not achieve prevailing party status by succeeding on their pendent state law claims when the constitutional claims for relief were also addressed and found to be moot and hence were not "avoided" by a decision on state law grounds. The Fifth Circuit also held in Hamman v. Southwestern Gas Pipeline, Inc., 832 F.2d 55, 57-58 (5th Cir. 1987), that statutory attorney's fees are not available for appellees' appellate success in defeating an appeal limited to pendent state law claims, and not including the fee-generating federal law claims also decided below.

Page 371, add following the Virzi Subaru case in note 25:

Keith v. Volpe, 644 F. Supp. 1317, 1320-22 (C.D. Cal. 1986); Ackerman v. Western * Elec. Co., Inc., 643 F. Supp. 836, 857-861 (N.D. Cal. 1986), *aff'd,* 860 F.2d 1514, 1520 n.5 (9th Cir. 1988) (both involving fee eligibility under California fee-shifting statute for plaintiff's success on state-law claim). The *Ackerman* decision analyzes at length the question of whether the state or federal law of fee-shifting governs the determination of the *amount* of fees awardable in federal court under a state fee statute, finally concluding that this difficult issue need not be resolved in this case since there is "no significant difference" between applicable state and federal law principles.

Page 371, add at end of first paragraph:

On the other hand, the *Gagne* principle does not give *carte blanche* to a court to deny § 1988 fees to the plaintiff who has succeeded on a state law claim by subjecting the nonfrivolous constitutional claim, which was not adjudicated at the merits stage of the litigation, to close scrutiny for the first time on the fee application and then rejecting it on the merits. This dubious practice occasionally is indulged in by state courts in denying § 1988 fees to the plaintiff who has succeeded on a state law claim joined with a federal constitutional claim. *See City of Gary v. Redmond,* 489 N.E.2d 543 (Ind. Ct. App. 1986) (appellate court, after finding that trial court failed to specify whether plaintiff succeeded on his state law tort claim or on his constitutional due process claim, proceeded to analyze the constitutional claim and, concluding that it was wholly meritless, denied plaintiff's § 1988 fee request); *Board of Trustees v. Mississippi Publishers Corp.,* 478 So. 2d 269, 280-82 (Miss. 1985); *Misuraca v. Perales,* 120 A.D.2d 592, 501 N.Y.S.2d 907 (2d Dep't 1986) (settlement agreement based on state law claim, joined with constitutional claim which court found meritless in denying § 1988 fees); *Williams v. D'Elia,* 119 A.D.2d 678, 682, 501 N.Y.S.2d 365 (2d Dep't 1986) (denying § 1988 fees after finding that plaintiff failed to show the violation of any federal law right, in succeeding on a state law claim). Other state courts have granted § 1988 fee eligibility to the plaintiff who has succeeded on a state law claim joined with a nonfrivolous constitutional or federal statutory claim only after subjecting the hitherto undecided federal claim to a rigorous analysis tantamount to an adjudication of the merits of that claim. *See Bung's Bar & Grille, Inc. v. Township Council of Florence,* 206 N.J. Super. 432, 502 A.2d 1198, 1200-18 (1985); *Torres v. Perales,* 121 A.D.2d 386, 388, 503 N.Y.S.2d 96, (2d Dep't 1986). Federal courts more readily assume the adequacy of the undecided federal constitutional claim for § 1988 fee purposes, since that claim was the jurisdictional predicate for the federal court's favorable merits decision on the pendent state law claim.

Page 372, add to note 26:

See Mazanec v. North Judson-San Pierre School Corp., 798 F.2d 230, 236-37 (7th Cir. 1986) (plaintiffs who received a favorable finding under state law but did not achieve any of the benefit sought in the litigation, and who gained no success on their constitutional claims, did not succeed on any "significant" issue in the suit and hence were not prevailing parties entitled to § 1988 fees).

§ 15.18 Prevailing by Final Success at an Interlocutory Stage of the Litigation

Page 372, add the following cases to note 30:

See also Kopunec v. Nelson, 801 F.2d 1226, 1229 (10th Cir. 1986) (plaintiff was prevailing party under Equal Access to Justice Act, 28 U.S.C. § 2412, when his success in winning "avoidance of immediate deportation by obtaining a reversal of the INS's automatic revocation of his visa and a preliminary injunction against deportation constitutes a substantial victory of his position significantly discrete from the ultimate conclusion to warrant separate treatment"); Haitian Refugee Center v. Meese, 791 F.2d 1489, 1495-96 (11th Cir. 1986) (plaintiffs prevailed under Equal Access to Justice Act, 28 U.S.C. § 2412, when they obtained a ruling invalidating the INS's program of accelerating the processing of asylum applications made by Haitians and an injunction against further deportation proceedings pending court approval of a reprocessing plan); Nebraska Health Care Ass'n v. Dunning, 778 F.2d 1291, 1296 (8th Cir. 1985), *cert. denied,* 479 U.S. 1063 (1987) (plaintiff nursing service providers prevailed under § 1988 by obtaining a ruling, affirmed on appeal, that state Medicaid reimbursement laws violated federal Social Security Act with respect to one fiscal year, although challenge with regard to second fiscal year was not ripe for determination while administrative proceedings were pending); Zamlen v. City of Cleveland, 655 F. Supp. 1451 (N.D. Ohio 1987) (granting interim award of § 1988 fees to plantiffs in employment discrimination suit for work done in gaining partial affirmative relief that "will not be reversed or undone" even if defendant "ultimately prevails"); McKenzie v. Kennickell, 645 F. Supp. 437, 441-42 (D.D.C. 1986) (plaintiffs prevailed by obtaining "substantial interlocutory relief" over a period of seven years in Title VII suit, in form of favorable liability rulings, preliminary injunctions, and interlocutory relief orders, largely upheld on appeal); Brunet v. City of Columbus, 642 F. Supp. 1214, 1254 (S.D. Ohio 1986) (plaintiffs prevailed in Title VII sex discrimination action, prior to conclusion of suit, by obtaining favorable liability ruling and remedial orders on claim that firefighter physical exam was discriminatory); King v. Palmer, 641 F. Supp. 186, 189-90 (D.D.C. 1986) (plaintiff prevailed in Title VII employment sex discrimination suit by obtaining favorable liability ruling and remedial orders, although some issues remained to be determined). *But see* Howard v. International Molders & Allied Workers Union, 779 F.2d 1546, 1553 (11th Cir. 1986) (finding no abuse of discretion in district court's refusal to award interim attorney's fees, during pendency of appeal and prior to final judgment, in Title VII employment race discrimination case in which plaintiffs obtained favorable consent agreement with defendant employer while continuing to litigate claims against defendant union); John Does 1-100 v. Ninneman, 634 F. Supp. 341, 345 (D. Minn. 1986) (declining to award interim attorney's fees to plaintiffs who obtained liability ruling against defendants, with relief issues to be determined later, since plaintiffs' counsel were handling a number of similar cases and already had received an interim fee award in one such case, and court sought "to avoid multiple fee awards for what is possibly repeated work").

Page 372, in note 31 note the reversal of the Palmer case and add the following:

On appeal in *Palmer*, the Seventh Circuit reversed the district court's preliminary injunction, concluding that plaintiffs' claims were subject to dismissal on standing and abstention grounds, and as well reversed the § 1988 fee award. Palmer v. City of Chicago, 806 F.2d 1316 (7th Cir. 1986), *cert. denied,* 107 S. Ct. 2180 (1987). The Seventh Circuit's decision recognized an important qualification to the principle stated in the text in ruling that the plaintiff who wins a preliminary injunction or succeeds "in a practical sense" through defendant's voluntary remedial action or a settlement agreement nonetheless is not a prevailing party under § 1988 when the plaintiff's suit finally is determined to be unmeritorious. *Id.* at 1322-24. Thus, the *Palmer* court held that "when a suit goes through to judgment for defendants, or is abandoned as hopeless by the plaintiffs, the plaintiffs cannot be regarded as having prevailed within the meaning of the [fee] statute even if their lawsuit was not frivolous (that is, so groundless that sanctions could be imposed for having brought it) and even if the suit brought about some or for that matter all of the changes in the defendants' conduct that the plaintiffs had sought." *Id.* at 1323.

Page 373, add at end of last paragraph in section:

Finally, *Hewitt v. Helms,* 107 S. Ct. 2672 (1987), requires that any interlocutory order that qualifies the plaintiff as a prevailing party under § 1988 must grant *relief,* or establish *entitlement to relief,* on the merits of a legal claim, rather than merely providing a favorable statement of plaintiff's legal rights. See complete discussion of *Hewitt* at § 15.4 of the supplement.

§ 15.19 —Prevailing Party's Right to Immediate Payment of an Interim Fee Award

Pages 373 and 374, update Palmer citation in notes 37, 38, 40, and 43:

rev'd, 806 F.2d 1316 (7th Cir. 1986), *cert. denied,* 107 S. Ct. 2180 (1987).

Pages 373-74, add to cases cited in note 40:

McKenzie v. Kennickell, 645 F. Supp. 437, 452 (D.D.C. 1986) (interim fee award for seven years of work on the case, where "[i]t has now been nearly thirteen years since this case was filed, and plaintiffs' attorneys have yet to receive a penny for their highly successful efforts"); Ramos v. Lamm, 632 F. Supp. 376, 389 n.10 (D. Colo. 1986) (payment of interim fee award for a phase of successful multi-year litigation concerning prison conditions); *cf.* John Does 1-100 v. Ninneman, 634 F. Supp. 341, 345 & n.5 (D. Minn. 1986) (interim fee award denied where plaintiffs' counsel received interim fees in one of a number of similar cases handled, and court wished "to avoid multiple fee awards for what is possibly repeated work").

Page 374, add to cases cited in note 42:

McKenzie v. Kennickell, 669 F. Supp. 529 (D.D.C. 1987) (in directing payment by federal defendant of interim Title VII fee award in amount conceded to be due, court noted government's "intransigent and unreasonable attempts to delay and extend this fee litigation" and rejected government's "pauperization" principle that "would require counsel to litigate themselves into the poor house before they collect an interim fee"); King v. Palmer, 641 F. Supp. 186, 189 (D.D.C. 1986) (directing that interim fee "will be limited to the core of attorneys' fees and costs that are not seriously disputed," with determination of the disputed portion to follow); *cf.* Fadhl v. City and County of San Francisco, 804 F.2d 1097, 1099 (9th Cir. 1986) (affirming and directing payment of undisputed portion of fee award represented by lodestar amount, while retaining jurisdiction over portion of award representing upward adjustment * pending decision in relevant Supreme Court case); Black Grievance Comm. v. Philadelphia Elec. Co., 690 F. Supp. 1393, 1406 (E.D. Pa. 1988) (declining to make interim fee award where it was "not practical to attempt to determine the minimum fee to which plaintiffs are entitled").

Page 374, add to note 44:

The appellant may obtain a stay pending appeal of execution on the fee judgment by posting a bond, pursuant to Fed. R. Civ. P. 62(d).

Page 374, add at end of section:

The courts have rejected arguments of federal governmental defendants that they cannot be required to pay immediately an interim award of Title VII attorney's fees. *McKenzie v. Kennickell,* 669 F. Supp. 529, 532-35 (D.D.C. 1987); *Jurgens v. E.E.O.C.,* 660 F. Supp. 1097, 1099-1103 (N.D. Tex. 1987). These courts have concluded that statutory appropriation provisions which prohibit the payment of money judgments against the United States until an unappealed final judgment is entered must yield to the narrower, more specific Title VII fee-shifting provision, 42 U.S.C. § 2000e-5(k), which makes the United States liable for attorney's fees to the same extent as a private person. These courts also have found that Title VII provision, as interpreted in *Library of Congress v. Shaw,* 106 S. Ct. 2957, 2966 (1986), controlling in overcoming any sovereign immunity defenses to the federal government's payment of interim Title VII fee awards. Buttressing these conclusions is the recognition that the required payment of interim fee awards has the salutory effect of "prevent[ing] government attorneys from using a long delay in the payment of an award of fees as a weapon which might be used to interfere with the effective representation of Title VII plaintiffs." *Jurgens v. E.E.O.C.,* 660 F. Supp. at 1103. As the court observed in *McKenzie v. Kennickell,* 669 F. Supp. at 533, the availability of interim fee awards from the federal government has become especially important in the wake of the Supreme Court's ruling in *Shaw* foreclosing the application of current hourly rates, to account for delay, in determining

* fee awards assessed against the federal government. *See also Rosenfeld v. United States,* 859 F.2d 717, 723-27 (9th Cir. 1988) (finding that principles of sovereign immunity do not bar interim fee awards against United States under Freedom of Information Act, 5 U.S.C. § 552(a)(4)(E)).

§ 15.20 Prevailing by Nonfinal Success at an Interlocutory Stage of the Litigation

Page 375, delete the Palmer case and add the following to note 48:

Conservation Law Foundation v. Secretary of Interior, 790 F.2d 965, 968 (1st Cir. 1986) (plaintiff prevailed under Outer Continental Shelf Lands Act, 43 U.S.C. § 1349(a)(5), when, following the issuance of a preliminary injunction, defendant abandoned the challenged conduct and mooted the suit); Rivera v. Coler, 629 F. Supp. 366 (N.D. Ill. 1986) (plaintiff prevailed in suit seeking Medicaid eligibility for liver transplant when, following the issuance of a temporary restraining order, defendant determined her eligible, although plaintiff died before transplant could be located.) However, the plaintiff is not a prevailing party in a case in which a preliminary injunction is issued and the defendant grants substantial relief by voluntary action or settlement agreement, where the suit ultimately is dismissed for lack of merit. Palmer v. City of Chicago, 806 F.2d 1316, 1320-24 (7th Cir. 1986), *cert. denied,* 107 S. Ct. 2180 (1987).

Page 376, add at end of the complete paragraph:

However, such interlocutory success that preserves a favorable result for the plaintiff does *not* qualify him as a prevailing party where his suit ultimately is judicially determined, on appeal or at final judgment, to bc unmcritorious. *See Palmer v. City of Chicago,* 806 F.2d 1316, 1320-24 (7th Cir. 1986), *cert. denied,* 107 S. Ct. 2180 (1987); *Ward v. County of San Diego,* 791 F.2d 1329, 1333-34 (9th Cir. 1986); *Tucker v. Summers,* 784 F.2d 654, 656-57 (5th Cir. 1986); *Ekanem v. Health & Hosp. Corp.,* 778 F.2d 1254, 1258 (7th Cir. 1985) (see explanation of cited cases in **§ 15.4** of this supplement).

Page 377, add after sentence concluding with note 60 reference:

The application of this aspect of the prevailing party analysis is illustrated by *Taylor v. City of Fort Lauderdale,* 810 F.2d 1551 (11th Cir. 1987). The plaintiffs in *Taylor* challenged the constitutionality of the city's solicitation permit ordinance in its application to outdoor solicitation by religious oganizations. The district court first issued a preliminary injunction against the ordinance's application to both outdoor and indoor solicitation. Subsequently, the court granted partial summary judgment invalidating the ordinance only as applied to indoor solicitation, while leaving open the outdoor solicitation issue. Eventually, the city repealed the ordinance, thereby rendering the plaintiffs' suit moot. *Id.* at 1554-55.

In reviewing the district court's denial of plaintiffs' request for § 1988 attorney's fees, the Fifth Circuit agreed with the city that the grant of summary judgment against the ordinance's application to indoor solicitation did not qualify the plaintiffs as prevailing parties under § 1988, because under the Fifth Circuit's standard it did not constitute success on the central issue in the suit. *Id.* at 1558-59. See § **15.11**. The court focused on whether the preliminary injunction established plaintiffs as prevailing parties insofar as it enjoined the operation of the ordinance in its application to outdoor solicitation until the ordinance was repealed and the plaintiffs' suit rendered moot. Citing this treatise, the court noted the debate concerning whether a plaintiff becomes a prevailing party under § 1988 on the basis of a preliminary injunction that obtains a favorable result in the litigation and remains in force until the suit is rendered moot, without a *final* adjudication favorably resolving plaintiff's claims. *Id.* at 1557-58. *Cf. Kay v. David Douglas School District,* 108 S. Ct. 740 (1988) (White, J., dissenting from denial of certiorari, urging resolution of the "difficult question" of whether plaintiffs can become prevailing parties under § 1988 on the basis of a preliminary injunction that defendants comply with until the case becomes moot, when defendants "have never been finally determined to have violated the Federal Constitution or laws and have steadfastly maintained the contrary position").

The Fifth Circuit concluded in *Taylor* that the plaintiffs had established their prevailing party status by winning a preliminary injunction granting relief on the central issue in the litigation that remained in force for more than two years until the repeal of the ordinance mooted the case. 810 F.2d at 1557-58. The court correctly distinguished cases that denied prevailing party status to plaintiffs, although they had obtained preliminary injunctions, because they ultimately lost on the merits of their claims or their claims were completely eviscerated by supervening precedent. *Id.* at 1558. The Fifth Circuit's ruling that the preliminary injunction established the *Taylor* plaintiffs as prevailing parties made it unnecessary to consider whether plaintiffs independently qualified as prevailing parties on the argument that their suit prompted the city to repeal the offending ordinance, thereby favorably mooting the case. *Id.* at 1560. See § **15.14.**

Page 378, add to cases cited in note 61:

Seaway Drive-In, Inc. v. Township of Clay, 791 F.2d 447, 450 n.7 (6th Cir.), *cert. denied,* 479 U.S. 884 (1986) (following issuance of preliminary injunction, suit challenging validity of restrictive ordinances was resolved favorably to plaintiff by settlement agreement). See also cases cited in note 48 of this section.

Page 378, add to cases cited in note 62:

Cf. Rivera v. Coler, 629 F. Supp. 366 (N.D. Ill. 1986) (temporary restraining order securing interim Medicaid coverage for plaintiff's anticipated liver transplant, which continued until defendant determined plaintiff's Medicaid eligibility).

Page 378, add to cases cited in note 63:

Rivera v. Coler, 629 F. Supp. 366, 369 (N.D. Ill. 1986).

Page 378, add to note 64:

See also Webster v. Sowders, 846 F.2d 1032, 1036-38 (6th Cir. 1988) (concluding that plaintiffs did not become prevailing parties under § 1988 on basis of preliminary injunction that rested on an ambivalent and dubious district court finding of plaintiffs' probability of success on the merits).

Page 379, add to cases cited in note 65:

Cf. Harris v. McCarthy, 790 F.2d 753, 757 (9th Cir. 1986) (plaintiffs were prevailing parties on basis of issuance of preliminary injunction that gained them a substantial benefit that was "limited only by the temporary nature of their relief," although plaintiffs were denied § 1988 fees on alternative theory that the suit had caused defendants to take voluntary remedial action, since plaintiffs could seek § 1988 fees at the conclusion of the related state court suit they were pursuing after taking a voluntary dismissal of the federal action).

Page 379, add to note 66:

Palmer v. City of Chicago, 806 F.2d 1316, 1320-24 (7th Cir. 1986) (plaintiffs were not prevailing parties where appellate court reversed preliminary injunction on grounds of abstention and plaintiffs' lack of standing to sue), *cert. denied,* 107 S. Ct. 2180 (1987); Ward v. County of San Diego, 791 F.2d 1329, 1333-34 (9th Cir. 1986) (appellate reversal of preliminary injunction for plaintiff's lack of standing to seek injunctive relief); Tucker v. Summers, 784 F.2d 654, 656-57 (5th Cir. 1986) (injunctions found to have been inappropriately entered in view of supervening Supreme Court decision establishing federal court's lack of subject-matter jurisdiction over the dispute).

Page 379, add to note 67:

Ekanem v. Health & Hosp. Corp., 778 F.2d 1254, 1258 (7th Cir. 1985) (preliminary injunction reversed on appeal on the merits).

Page 379, add at end of complete paragraph:

See also Tucker v. Summers, 784 F.2d 654, 656-57 (5th Cir. 1986) (denying § 1988 fees where injunctions were found to have been inappropriately entered in view of supervening Supreme Court decision establishing federal court's lack of subject-matter jurisdiction over the dispute).

CHAPTER 16

DENYING § 1988 FEES TO THE PREVAILING PLAINTIFF–SPECIAL CIRCUMSTANCES AND DEFENDANTS' IMMUNITIES

§ 16.1 Introduction

Page 382, update Smith citation in note 1:

468 U.S. 992, 1006 (1984).

Page 382, add at end of section:

The District of Columbia Court of Appeals has held that in a case in which a "major part of the defendant's argument" focuses on the issue of whether special circumstances warrant the denial of § 1988 fees to the prevailing plaintiff, the district court "should set forth its reasoning for concluding that special circumstances [do or] do not exist." *Grano v. Barry,* 783 F.2d 1104, 1111-12 (D.C. Cir. 1986).

§ 16.3 –Financial Circumstances of the Parties and Plaintiff's Counsel

Page 383, add to cases cited in note 5:

American Booksellers Ass'n v. Commonwealth of Va., 792 F.2d 1261, 1267 (4th Cir. 1986).

Page 383, add to cases cited in note 6:

Jones v. Wilkinson, 800 F.2d 989, 991 (10th Cir. 1986), *judgment aff'd,* ____ U.S. ____, 94 L. Ed. 2d 753 (1987); American Booksellers Ass'n v. Commonwealth of Va., 792 F.2d 1261, 1266-67 (4th Cir. 1986); Duncan v. Poythress, 777 F.2d 1508, 1511 (11th Cir. 1985)(en banc); Herrington v. Sonoma County, 655 F. Supp. 1111, 1113-14 (N.D. Cal. 1987)(rejecting defendant's argument that plaintiffs should be denied § 1988 fees because they could pay their counsel's fees out of $2.5 million jury verdict).

Page 383, update Cunningham citation and add to note 7:

Cunningham, *vacated & remanded on other grounds,* 478 U.S. 1015 (1986), *reinstated,* 807 F.2d 49 (3d Cir. 1986), *cert. denied,* 107 S. Ct. 2179 (1987); Tolliver v. Amici, 800 F.2d 149, 152 (7th Cir. 1986). The Supreme Court has ruled that contingent fee principles are not relevant to the determination of reasonable fees under § 1988. City of Riverside v. Rivera, 477 U.S. 561, 586 (1986)(Powell, J., concurring). See § **21.3**.

Page 384, add to cases cited in note 8:

Duncan v. Poythress, 777 F.2d 1508, 1511 (11th Cir. 1985)(en banc).

Page 384, add to cases cited in note 9:

* Eggers v. Bullitt County School Dist., 854 F.2d 892, 898-900 (6th Cir. 1988) (prevailing plaintiffs cannot be denied attorney's fees under Education of the Handicapped Act, 20 U.S.C. § 1415(e), merely because counsel are employed by a publicly funded state agency, the Department of Public Advocacy); Mammano v. Pittston Co., 792 F.2d 1242, 1245 (4th Cir. 1986); N.A.A.C.P., Frederick County Chapter v. Thompson, 671 F. Supp. 1051, 1054 (D. Md. 1987)(no bar to § 1988 fee award that portion will go to university legal clinic).

Page 384, add to cases cited in note 10:

cf. Brewster v. Dukakis, 786 F.2d 16, 20-22 (1st Cir. 1986)(fee compensation would not be denied for work done by plaintiffs' counsel that served the interests of the plaintiff class of state mental patients, merely because counsel received funding under contract from a group of state-funded contractors).

§ 16.4 –In-House or Consultant Status of Prevailing Plaintiff's Counsel

Page 384, update Delaware Valley citation and add to note 12:

Delaware Valley, 478 U.S. 546 (1986).

On the other hand, counsel for an amicus curiae, which did not formally intervene into the suit and hence did not participate as a party to the litigation, may not receive § 1988 fees, even if counsel rendered services beneficial to the prevailing plaintiffs. Morales v. Turman, 820 F.2d 728, 732 (5th Cir. 1987).

Page 385, add to note 15:

In Jordan v. City of Greenwood, 808 F.2d 1114, 1117-18 (5th Cir.), *cert. denied,* 108 S. Ct. 89 (1987), the Fifth Circuit ruled that a lawyer could not personally be awarded § 1988 fees for work performed while employed by a federally-funded legal services office, which was primary counsel for the plaintiffs and plaintiff class in the case. The court reasoned that payment of fees to the lawyer personally would run afoul of the Legal Services Corporation Act's prohibition against the engagement by a legal services attorney in the "compensated outside practice of law." *Id.* at 1118. Instead, the § 1988 fees for those services were to be paid to the legal services organization whose staff attorneys were counsel of record in the case. *Id.* at 1119. On the other hand, the attorney was entitled personally to § 1988 fees for work done on behalf of the successful plaintiffs after he left the legal services organization and entered private practice. *Id.*

§ 16.5 —Rights Asserted and the Nature and Extent of the Plaintiff's Litigation Success

Page 386, add at end of paragraph concluding with note 20 reference:

The Third Circuit has ruled, in *Ashley v. Atlantic Richfield Co.,* 794 F.2d 128, 131-35 (3d Cir. 1986), that "the threshold determination of prevailing party status that serves to entitle a plaintiff to a reasonable award of attorney's fees may not be jettisoned by the assertion of a nuisance settlement," and that, instead, the nuisance settlement concept can only be asserted subsequently as a special circumstance that might defeat the prevailing party's right to receive § 1988 fees in narrow circumstances. *Id.* at 134. The court concluded that to consider the nuisance settlement argument – namely, that the defendant paid the plaintiff in settlement of the case only what it would minimally have cost to defend against the suit – as part of the initial prevailing party analysis "would permit the wholesale preemption of fee awards to plaintiffs who have in fact prevailed on their claims." *Id.* at 134 n.9. Considered as a special circumstance, however, the nuisance settlement argument properly may be a basis for denying fees to the prevailing party in a case in which "plaintiff's claim clearly appears to be legally or factually non-meritorious and, accordingly, in which it appears that the 'some benefit obtained' has been conferred by the defendant *solely* as a means of saving litigation expense." *Id.* But "even in these cases," the court ruled, "the focus should be on the lack of merit in the plaintiff's case, not on the defendant's motivation," and the district court should explain why awarding fees to the prevailing party "will produce an unjust result." *Id.* In the instant case, the court suggested that since defendant "was informed by the district court that 'the case was worth something, and some level of risk warranted settlement,' " the defendant's contention that it "sacrificed the minimum amount that it would have cost to defend the action in order to save itself from potentially high litigation expenses without more does not constitute a special circumstance that would render a fee award" to the prevailing plaintiff "unjust." *Id.* at 134-35 n.9.

Page 386, update Cunningham citation and add to note 21:

vacated & remanded on other grounds, 478 U.S. 1015 (1986), *reinstated,* 807 F.2d 49 (3d Cir. 1986), *cert. denied,* 107 S. Ct. 2179 (1987). In reversing the district court's denial of statutory attorney's fees to the plaintiff who succeeded in his suit to enforce compliance with the Voting Rights Act of 1965, 42 U.S.C. § 1973c, the Eleventh Circuit in Maloney v. City of Marietta, 822 F.2d 1023, 1026 (11th Cir. 1987), found that the "relevant inquiry in the prevailing party analysis is whether the plaintiff's lawsuit successfully vindicated a particular right guaranteed under a statute which authorizes the awarding of attorneys' fees, not whether the plaintiff's action somehow advanced the broader concept of minority rights." The court noted that the "actor whose litigation brings about compliance has protected important civil rights of minorities, no matter that the actor's *motives* may have been far less than altruistic." *Id.* at 1026 n.5. At the same time, the court repeated the dictum issued in Martin v. Heckler, 773 F.2d 1145, 1151 (11th Cir. 1985), that § 1988 fees might be denied to the prevailing plaintiff when the action "asserted essentially a private tort claim for money damages." 822. F.2d at 1027.

§ 16.6 –Misconduct of Plaintiff or Counsel, Refusal to Accept a Reasonable Settlement Offer, and Other Miscellaneous Factors

Page 387, add the following case after "But see" in note 26:

Joseph L. v. Office of Judicial Support, 638 F. Supp. 833, 836-37 (E.D. Pa. 1986)(relying in part on "culpability" of plaintiff, whose "wounds were self-inflicted" as special circumstance warranting denial of § 1988 fees to arguably prevailing plaintiff). The Eighth Circuit in Jenkins v. Missouri, 838 F.2d 260, 267 (8th Cir. 1988), upheld the district court's denial of § 1988 fees to the local school district defendant on its successful cross-claim against the state defendant, in a school desegregation case, based on the special circumstance that the local defendant was a "constitutional violator" in the case.

Page 388, add to cases cited in note 30:

Disabled in Action v. Pierce, 789 F.2d 1016, 1020 (3d Cir. 1986).

Page 388, add the following cases at end of paragraph concluding with note 35 reference:

See also Zipes v. Trans World Airlines, Inc., 846 F.2d 434, 441-42 (7th Cir. 1988)(rejecting as special circumstances warranting denial of Title VII fees against unsuccessful intervenor union at post-settlement phase of suit, the contentions that the fees for the *pre*-settlement phase were excessive or that the union had a duty to intervene in suit); *Afro-American Patrolmen's League v. Atlanta,* 817 F.2d 719, 725 (11th Cir. 1987)(fact that prevailing plaintiff achieved only "limited success" in Title VII suit is not a special circumstance warranting denial of statutory attorney's fees). *Mammano v. Pittston Co.,* 792 F.2d 1242, 1245-46 (4th Cir. 1986)(no special circumstances exist warranting denial of Title VII fees to prevailing plaintiffs because of plaintiffs' "limited degree of success at trial," or on basis of co-counsel's "abandonment of the lawsuit on the eve of trial" where co-counsel's withdrawal "after providing valuable services to appellees because of conflicts with local counsel in order to avoid injuring their clients' case," "would appear to be in the best interest of appellees"); *Woodard v. Hardee's Restaurant,* 643 F. Supp. 691, 692 (W.D. Mo. 1986)(refusing to deny § 1988 fees to prevailing plaintiffs "based on the speculative belief that the jury already has compensated plaintiffs for their fees herein"); *EWAP, Inc. v. City of Ontario,* 177 Cal. App. 3d 1108, 223 Cal. Rptr. 422, 427 (1986)(rejecting defendant's argument against award of § 1988 fees to prevailing plaintiff on basis that defendant's "post-answer concessions render plaintiff's success 'marginal' "). In *Culebras Enterprises Corp. v. Rivera-Rios,* 846 F.2d 94, 95-101 (1st Cir. 1988), the court ruled that § 1988 fees should not be denied to prevailing plaintiffs for pretrial work performed by two attorneys who, in conformity with Rule 3.7 of the Model Rules of Professional Conduct (as incorporated into the local district rules), had withdrawn as counsel of record as trial counsel because they were expected to testify at trial.

* *Page 388, add to cases cited in note 36:*

Bateson v. Geisse, 857 F.2d 1300, 1306 (9th Cir. 1988) (denying § 1988 appellate fees to successful plaintiff-appellee whose attorney "has not adequately briefed the issues he presents, and thereby created the need for this court to engage in extensive supplemental research").

§ 16.7 Defendant's Status as a State or Local Governmental Official or Judge Sued in an Official Capacity

Page 390, add after sentence ending with note 45 reference:

On the other hand, assessment of § 1988 fees against a governmental defendant sued in its official capacity should rest on "an explicit or implicit determination that the defendant held liable for fees is in fact the 'officer charged with responsibility for enforcing the legislative policy'." *Deary v. Guardian Loan Co., Inc.,* 623 F. Supp. 630, 633 (S.D.N.Y. 1985)(declining, "at this time," to assess § 1988 fees against state defendants as enforcement officials, "since there was never a determination that the state defendants were the officials properly charged with administering the challenged statute" pertaining to unconstitutional enforcement of judgments). *See also Durett v. Cohen,* 790 F.2d 360, 364 (3d Cir. 1986)(remanding case for district court to make express determination of basis for § 1988 fee award against defendant county officials who made the initial adverse determination in the case).

Page 390, add to cases cited in note 46:

Rose v. Heintz, 806 F.2d 389, 391-92 (2d Cir. 1986)(defendant state officials were acting under color of state law, for § 1988 fee purposes, in implementing illegal policy resulting in termination and denial of Medicaid benefits to eligible stepchildren; that state defendant "did so pursuant to a telephone conversation with an HHS official does not make . . . [state defendant's] action any less an action under color of state, as well as federal, law"); O'Brien v. Town of Westerly Housing Authority, 626 F. Supp. 1065, 1072 (D.R.I. 1986)(federally-funded public housing authority enjoyed no special status immunizing it from liability for § 1988 fees).

Page 390, add to cases cited in note 47:

Council for Periodical Distributors Ass'ns v. Evans, 827 F.2d 1483, 1486-87 (11th Cir. 1987)(upholding assessment of § 1988 fees against defendants city and its police chief, because city police officer was a member of task force that engaged in the unconstitutional prior restraint; court rejected city's "borrowed servant" argument that police officer was controlled by defendant district attorney and that city therefore should not be liable for fees, noting that a "governmental body should not be able to escape liability of assisting in unconstitutional activity simply because a different governmental body was the instigator of the illegal conduct"); Wilson v. Stocker, 819 F.2d 943, 950 (10th Cir. 1987)(rejecting defendant district attorney's contention that immunity from damages awards insulated him from liability for § 1988 fees in suit for equitable relief for unconstitutional conduct); Rose v. Heintz, 806 F.2d 389, 391-92 (2d Cir. 1986)(defendant state officials were liable for § 1988 fees for their action in enforcing an illegal policy of terminating and denying Medicaid benefits to eligible persons in accordance with the interpretation of federal law provided by federal Department of Health and Human Services; court noted that state agency was "not coerced" by federal agency in making its determination of what the law required); Savage v. Toan, 636 F. Supp. 156, 157 (W.D. Mo. 1986)(state defendants could not avoid § 1988 fee liability because their illegal change in their Medicaid eligibility regulations came under pressure from the federal defendants); Cepulonis v. Registrars of Voters, 396 Mass. 808, 488 N.E.2d 1166, 1168 (1986)(defendant voting registrars were liable for § 1988 fees notwithstanding that they were "following the requirements of State statutory law" in unconstitutionally restricting convicted felons' right to register to vote).

Page 391, update Daggett citation and add to cases cited in note 48:

Daggett, *aff'd in relevant part,* 811 F.2d 793, 795 n.2 (3d Cir. 1987); Bung's Bar & Grill, Inc. v. Township Council of Florence, 206 N.J. Super. 432, 502 A.2d 1198, 1218-19 (1985)(defendant Township Council was not immune from § 1988 fee liability in suit in which plaintiff successfully challenged validity of local improvement tax assessments and obtained injunctive relief, since when the defendant governing body "authorized the filing of the assessments in the tax office and the issuance of tax bills the action was executive" and rendered the defendant liable for § 1988 fees as an enforcement body against whom injunctive relief was issued).

Page 391, update Pulliam citations and add to note 49:

Pulliam, 466 U.S. 522, 543, 544 (1984).
See also Davis v. City of Charleston, 635 F. Supp. 197, 199 (E.D. Mo. 1986)(defendant State Circuit Judge against whom plaintiff obtained declaratory and injunctive relief for judge's failure to conduct a hearing before sentencing plaintiff to jail for nonpayment of a fine was liable for § 1988 fees); Doss v. Long, 624 F. Supp. 1078, 1080-81 (N.D. Ga. 1985)(State of Georgia was liable for § 1988 fees in plaintiffs' successful suit against defendant state court judges for operating an unconstitutional court fee system).

§ 16.8 Defendant's Official Status and the Eleventh Amendment

Page 392, add the following case to note 57:

* *See also* Tonya K. v. Board of Educ., 847 F.2d 1243, 1246 (7th Cir. 1988) (reasoning that state does not enjoy Eleventh Amendment immunity from fee liability under Education of the Handicapped Act, 20 U.S.C. § 1415(e), since statutory attorney's fees are part of "costs" incurred in obtaining permissible prospective relief); Dwyer v. Regan, 777 F.2d 825, 837 (2d Cir. 1985)(reasoning that state defendant lacks Eleventh Amendment immunity from § 1988 fee claim when it is "brought in conjunction with a claim for prospective injunctive relief based upon a constitutional cause of action" and is "ancillary to the injunctive claim"), *modified,* 793 F.2d 457 (2d Cir. 1986).

Page 393, add at end of continuation paragraph ending with note 59 reference:

In *Exeter-West Greenwich Regional School Dist. v. Pontarelli,* 788 F.2d 47, 53-54 (1st Cir. 1986), the First Circuit held that the Eleventh Amendment did not bar the award of § 1988 fees against a state defendant in an action that was dismissed as moot following the Rhode Island Supreme Court's resolution favorable to plaintiffs of a controlling state law question certified to it by the federal district court, when plaintiffs asserted a jurisdictionally substantial constitutional claim that remained in the federal court case until the disposition of the state-law issue mooted it. In so ruling, the First Circuit rejected defendant's Eleventh Amendment argument that sought to distinguish *Maher,* in which the federal court had jurisdiction over the federal statutory claim that was settled along with the constitutional claim, from the case at hand, in which the federal suit was resolved on the basis of the State Supreme Court's adjudication of a state-law issue over which the federal court had no jurisdiction against a state defendant under *Pennhurst State School & Hosp. v. Halderman,* 465 U.S. 89 (1984). *Id.* at 53-54. Discussed at **§ 15.16** of this supplement is the question of whether the Eleventh Amendment arguably confers immunity on state defendants from liability for attorney's fees under the recently enacted Handicapped Children's Protection Act, Pub. L. No. 99-372, 100 Stat. 796 (1986), for plaintiff's success based solely on federal statutory claims under the Education of the Handicapped Act, 20 U.S.C. §§ 1400 *et seq.* In *Keith v. Volpe,* 833 F.2d 850, 854-855 (9th Cir. 1987), the Ninth Circuit rejected the argument that the Eleventh Amendment bars a supplemental § 1988 fee award made against a state defendant for work performed *after* entry of a consent decree that settled litigation involving constitutional issues. However, the First Circuit has ruled in *Rogers v. Okin,* 821 F.2d 22, 27-28 (1st Cir. 1987), *cert. denied,* 108 S. Ct. 709 (1988), that the that the assessment of prejudgment interest on a § 1988 fee award against the state, in the form either of current hourly rates or an upward lodestar adjustment for delay in payment, does run afoul of the Eleventh Amendment. See further discussion at **§ 18.17.**

Page 393, add after the Crane case in note 60:

Unger v. Blum, 117 A.D.2d 607, 608, 498 N.Y.S.2d 154 (2d Dep't 1986)(state, not county, was liable for § 1988 fees since County Commissioner of Social Services who made the unlawful determination discontinuing petitioner's public assistance grant was an agent of State Commissioner of Social Services, not of the county).

Page 393, add the following case to note 62:

Doss v. Long, 624 F. Supp. 1078, 1080-81 (N.D. Ga. 1985)(State of Georgia was liable for § 1988 fees awarded against defendant state court judges whose court fee system was found unconstitutional, notwithstanding that State declined to provide representation for the defendant judges and asserted that it "had no interest in, nor benefit by, the continued course of litigation").

Page 394, add to note 65:

Barrett v. Thomas, 809 F.2d 1151, 1155-56 (5th Cir. 1987); N.A.A.C.P., Frederick County Chapter v. Thompson, 671 F. Supp. 1051, 1054-55 (D. Md. 1987)(county liable for § 1988 fees assessed against defendant official in his official capacity).

Page 394, add a new paragraph at end of section:

Although the Eleventh Amendment has no application in state court, there is a question whether, and to what extent, state law principles of sovereign immunity insulate state defendants from § 1983, and hence § 1988, liability in state court suits. The New Mexico Court of Appeals reasoned in *Ramah Navajo School Bd. v. Bureau of Revenue,* 104 N.M. 302, 720 P.2d 1243, *cert. denied,* 479 U.S. 940 (1986), that since the United States Supreme Court has held that the enactment of § 1983 did not automatically overcome the State's Eleventh Amendment immunity from certain kinds of relief in federal court, "[i]t, therefore, logically follows that Congress also did not intend, in adopting Section 1983, to abrogate the states' sovereign immunity from Section 1983 suits brought in state courts." *Id.* at 1248. Concluding that, in their application to § 1983 suits, state law sovereign immunity principles should be interpreted to parallel Eleventh Amendment immunity rules, the New Mexico court held that state defendants are immune under state law from damages relief, but not from prospective declaratory and injunctive relief under § 1983. Thus, in the case before it challenging the validity under federal law of a state tax assessment, the court ruled that the defendant state agency enjoyed sovereign immunity from relief in the form of a tax refund, but not from declaratory and injunctive relief with regard to the unlawful assessment. *Id.* at 1249-51. Correspondingly, the state defendant was not immune under state law from liability for § 1988 fees to the plaintiff who prevailed on his § 1983 claims for equitable relief. *See also Maldonado v. Nebraska Dep't of Public Welfare,* 223 Neb. 485, 391 N.W.2d 105, 109-10 (1986), in which the Nebraska Supreme Court held that the defendant state agency was not protected by sovereign immunity from assessment for § 1988 fees awarded to plaintiffs for their successful § 1983 action in state court to correct their improperly computed public assistance grants. In ruling that the state defendants had "laid down" their sovereign immunity in a case such as this, the Nebraska court relied on the state's participation in the heavily regulated federal benefit program and on a state statute which provided that the state "accepts and assents" to all applicable federal law provisions and by which the state impliedly assented to the "determination of any grievances which might arise out of its administration of the Social Security programs." *Id.* at 109-10.

The Supreme Court's recent decision in *Felder v. Casey,* 108 S. Ct. 2302 (1988), strongly fortifies the argument that a state may not apply a state law immunity doctrine to insulate itself in state court from the full scope of § 1988 fee liability as contemplated by Congress and interpreted by the Supreme Court. In *Felder,* the Court invalidated Wisconsin's restrictive notice-of-claim statute in its application to § 1983 suits in state court, on the grounds that it conflicted with the "remedial objectives" of § 1983 and would "produce different outcomes in § 1983 litigation based solely on whether the claim is asserted in state or federal court." 108 S. Ct. at 2307.

§ 16.9 Defendant's Status as a State or Local Governmental Official Sued in a Personal Capacity

Page 394, add the following to note 69:

See also Popham v. City of Kennesaw, 820 F.2d 1570, 1581-82 (11th Cir. 1987)(defendant city not liable for § 1988 fees on basis of jury verdict against defendant city police officers in their personal capacities only). Thorne v. City of El Segundo, 802 F.2d 1131, 1140 n.9 (9th Cir. 1986)(defendant City not liable for § 1988 fees on basis of finding of constitutional violations by individual defendant officials, sued in their individual capacities, who had qualified immunity from § 1983 damages); Allen v. District of Columbia, 503 A.2d 1233, 1237-38 (D.C. App. 1986)(defendant municipality not liable for § 1988 fees where plaintiff succeeded on constitutional claim against individual police officer defendant but not on constitutional claim against municipality); *cf.* Bender v. Williamsport Area School Dist., 475 U.S. 534, 543 n.6 (1986) (defendant school board member sued only in his official, and not individual, capacity lacked standing to appeal adverse judgment in § 1983 action, when defendant school board declined to appeal, and school board member as individual did not acquire standing to appeal merely because § 1988 fees were sought from him in his official capacity). Of course, the plaintiff may recover § 1988 fees against the defendant entity when it is established that the entity, as well as the defendant official, is directly liable under § 1983 for unconstitutional policy or conduct. *See* Stevens v. Gay, 792 F.2d 1000, 1003-05 (11th Cir. 1986) (state not liable for § 1988 fees on basis of constitutional violations found against individual defendant officers in their individual capacities, but state agencies may be added as defendants, and hence become liable for § 1988 fees, when it is likely that they are independently liable under § 1983 on the basis of the unconstitutional regulations relied on by individual defendants); Woodard v. Hardee's Restaurant, 643 F. Supp. 691, 693-95 (W.D. Mo. 1986)(defendant restaurant was liable for § 1988 fees, along with defendant police officer, when restaurant was independently responsible for unconstitutional false arrest of plaintiff by police officer in execution of restaurant's official policy).

Page 394, add the following cases to note 70:

Leggett v. Badger, 798 F.2d 1387 (11th Cir. 1986)(finding that Kentucky v. Graham, discussed in text, precludes joinder of state for purposes of assessment of § 1988 fees when only the individual defendant official was found liable, in his individual capacity, in the underlying § 1983 action, and finding the *Graham* principle controlling whether or not the state attorney general's office represented the individual defendant during the litigation); Stevens v. Gay, 792 F.2d 1000, 1003-05 (11th Cir. 1986)(reversing district court's assessment of § 1988 fees against state based on finding of constitutional violations by individual defendant officials who were determined to have qualified immunity from § 1983 damages liability, but also reversing district court's denial of plaintiff's motion to add as defendants state agencies whose regulations the individual defendants had relied on in their unconstitutional conduct and who likely could be liable under § 1983 and, hence, for attorney's fees under § 1988). However, state law may render the government entity directly liable to the plaintiff for both § 1983 damages and § 1988 attorney's fees that are awarded against the defendant official in his individual capacity. Argento v. Village of Melrose Park, 838 F.2d 1483, 1493-95 (7th Cir. 1988).

Page 394, add the following cases to note 71:

See Thorne v. City of El Segundo, 802 F.2d 1131, 1140 n.9 (9th Cir. 1986)(plaintiff not entitled to attorney's fees under § 1988 when individual defendant officials, sued in individual capacities, who were found to have violated plaintiff's constitutional rights enjoyed qualified immunity from § 1983 liability); Stevens v. Gay, 792 F.2d 1000, 1003 (11th Cir. 1986)(individual defendants, sued in their individual capacities, who were found to have qualified immunity from § 1983 damages liability for violation of plaintiff's constitutional rights were not liable for § 1988 fees).

§ 16.10 Defendant's Status as a Federal Governmental Official

Page 396, update Crest Street citation in note 83:

rev'd on other grounds, 479 U.S. 6 (1986).

Page 396, add the following to cases cited in note 84:

Savage v. Toan, 636 F. Supp. 156, 158 (W.D. Mo. 1986)(federal defendant was liable for § 1988 fees, through subsection (b), for pressuring state defendants to change their Medicaid eligibility regulations and for thereby engaging in "joint and concerted activity" with state defendants that violated plaintiffs' federal statutory rights); Schrader v. Idaho Dep't of Health and Welfare, 631 F. Supp. 1426, 1429 (D. Idaho 1986)(federal defendant was liable for § 1988 fees, through subsection (b), since in threatening to defund Idaho's AFDC program unless state defendant enforced an illegal state regulation, federal defendant acted jointly with state defendant in violating plaintiffs' federal statutory rights); *cf.* Olson v. Norman, 830 F.2d 811, 821 (8th Cir. 1987)(federal defendants not liable for attorney's fees under 28 U.S.C. § 2412(b) and § 1988 when evidence did not support finding that federal defendant either conspired with or placed special pressure on state defendant in the illegal termination of plaintiffs' medicaid benefits). Estate of Smith v. Heckler, 622 F. Supp. 403, 405-06 (D. Colo. 1985)(federal defendant was not liable for § 1988 fees through subsection (b), since it was acting under color of federal, not state, law in unlawfully failing to promulgate regulations implementing defendant's statutory duties). In Bergman v. United States, 844 F.2d 353 (6th Cir. 1988), the court upheld the denial of § 1988 fees, through 28 U.S.C. § 2412(b), against the United States based on the liability of defendant FBI agents, who were found liable in their individual capacities for damages under the Federal Tort Claims Act, 28 U.S.C. § 2671, and against whom undecided § 1986 damages claims were also asserted. The court rules that the potential § 1986 merits liability of the individual defendants in their personal capacities could not be attributed to the United States and hence could not be a basis for a § 1988 fee award against the United States. *Id.* at 355-56. See **§ 16.9.**

Page 397, add at end of note 85:

Disagreeing with *Trujillo* is Estate of Smith v. Heckler, 622 F. Supp. 403, 406-07 (D. Colo. 1985), where another judge in the district court of Colorado followed the "clear weight of authority" in concluding that subsection (b) does not authorize § 1988 fee awards against the federal government "in actions 'analogous' to § 1983 actions."

§ 16.11 Defendant's Status as an Intervenor

Page 398, add to cases cited in note 88:

Air Line Stewards v. Trans World Airlines, 640 F. Supp. 861, 866-67 (N.D. Ill. 1986)(intervenor union that intervened to object to elements of agreement settling Title VII employment discrimination action was liable for Title VII fees when union vigorously opposed settlement agreement, with consequence that "plaintiff classes' ultimate victory was delayed and came at a greatly increased cost"); *cf.* Diamond v. Charles, 476 U.S. 54, 70 (1986) (in finding that intervenor-defendant Diamond did not acquire standing to appeal judgment on merits of litigation merely because he was made liable for § 1988 fees, Court noted in passing that "[a]ny liability for fees is, of course, a consequence of Diamond's decision to intervene"). In Charles v. Daley, 846 F.2d 1057 (7th Cir. 1988), the Seventh Circuit, in plaintiffs' successful constitutional challenge to a state abortion statute, upheld a § 1988 fee award against intervening private physicians whose extensive legal arguments in opposition to the suit were defeated by the plaintiffs but against whom plaintiffs did not and could not obtain any finding of violation of plaintiffs' constitutional rights or any substantive merits relief. In so ruling, the court relied on the "unusual circumstances" of this case, in which the intervenors "voluntarily thrust themselves into the lawsuit and rather than attempting to minimize their participation in the litigation, tenaciously engaged the plaintiffs in a protracted and costly court battle to an extent that even the governmental defendant, the State of Illinois, was unprepared to go," and the plaintiffs thoroughly prevailed against the intervenors on the merits of all of intervenors' legal arguments. *Id.* at 1065 * & n.11. In Nash v. Chandler, 848 F.2d 567, 573-74 (5th Cir. 1988), *reh'g denied,* 859 F.2d 1210 (5th Cir. 1988), the court ruled that the State of Texas, which had appeared in this § 1983 suit as an intervenor pursuant to federal statute solely for the purpose of defending the constitutionality of a state statute, could not be held liable on the merits of the suit, and hence could not be held jointly and severally liable with the local defendants for § 1988 fees. Texas' § 1988 fee liability was limited to compensating plaintiffs for the amount of time expended by their attorneys as a result of the state's intervention. 848 F.2d at 574.

Page 399, add to cases cited in note 90:

In Reeves v. Harrell, 791 F.2d 1481, 1484-85 (11th Cir. 1986), the court held that proposed intervenors seeking to upset quota provisions in a consent decree settling an employment race discrimination suit were liable for § 1988 fees, when the district court's order granting intervention was reversed and the intervention motion was found to be frivolous as clearly time-barred. The court of appeals stated that for purposes of determining the proposed intervenors' liability for § 1988 fees, "the issue is not whether the intervenors' claims have merit, but whether their decision to pursue those claims by filing a motion to intervene was frivolous or unreasonable."

Page 399, add at end of section:

On the other hand, courts have excused intervenor-defendants from § 1988 fee liability when the intervenor was not responsible for the unconstitutional policy or practice at issue and intervened in the suit to assert in good faith a nonfrivolous, although unsuccessful, claim that the relief sought or obtained by plaintiffs was violative of the intervenor's constitutional rights. *See Reeves v. Harrell,* 791 F.2d 1481, 1484-85 (11th Cir. 1986)(intervenor white deputy sheriffs should be treated as plaintiffs, for purposes of determining their liability for § 1988 fees, when they intervened into employment race discrimination suit to claim that the consent decree's quota provision obtained by plaintiff black deputy sheriffs violated intervenors' constitutional rights, and intervenors "were not responsible for any of the alleged violations that led to the consent decree" and had not "ever violated the constitutional rights of any of the members of the plaintiff class"; however, § 1988 fees were assessed against intervenors since court of appeals found their intervention motion frivolous as clearly barred for untimeliness); *Grano v. Barry,* 783 F.2d 1104, 1112 (D.C. Cir. 1986)(affirming district court's denial of § 1988 fee award against intervenor trustees of historic property in suit successfully seeking injunction against demolition of the property pending a voter referendum on the fate of the property, where "both intervenors and plaintiffs were involved in this litigation to protect their rights under the Constitution"); *Paradise v. Prescott,* 626 F. Supp. 117 (M.D. Ala. 1985)(denying award of attorney's fees against defendant-intervenor white troopers in employment race discrimination suit, where intervenors unsuccessfully "sought to challenge a promotion scheme they honestly believed discriminated against them because of their race," so that intervenors were "functionally plaintiffs" who should not be assessed fees unless their claims were frivolous); *Kirkland v. New York State Dep't of Correctional Servs.,* 524 F. Supp. 1214 (S.D.N.Y. 1981)(white civil service employees who intervened in suit to oppose invalidation of racially discriminatory civil service examination were not liable for fees because they were not responsible for the constitutional violations and asserted in good faith their own reasonable constitutional claims); *cf. Decker v. United States Dep't of Labor,* 564 F. Supp. 1273, 1280 (E.D. Wis. 1983)(imposing § 1988 fee liability on intervenor-defendant religious organizations which unsuccessfully interposed "unmeritorious" free exercise clause defenses against

§ 1983 suit to enjoin unconstitutional use of federal CETA funds for parochial school personnel). However, the Seventh Circuit recently has rejected this "functional plaintiff" argument – that statutory attorney's fees should not be assessed against an intervening party which did not violate the legal rights established by the prevailing plaintiff and unsuccessfully made nonfrivolous arguments that the relief sought or obtained by the plaintiff violated the intervenor's own constitutional, statutory, or other legal rights. *Zipes v. Trans World Airlines, Inc.,* 846 F.2d 434 (7th Cir. 1988). In *Zipes* the court upheld a Title VII fee award to the plaintiff flight attendants against the intervenor flight attendant union, which had unsuccessfully contested a settlement agreement between the plaintiffs and the defendant airline on the grounds that it violated Title VII and the collective bargaining agreement between the airline and the union. *Id.* at 437-41. "Acceptance of a 'functional plaintiff' exception to the rule favoring fee awards to prevailing Title VII plaintiffs," the court concluded, "unnecessarily threatens to undermine what has come to be interpreted as a deliberate * statutory presumption in favor of such awards to prevailing parties." *Id.* at 439. The Supreme Court has granted certiorari in *Zipes* to consider the statutory fee liability of an intervenor-defendant whose litigation position makes it a functional plaintiff. 57 U.S.L.W. 3466 (U.S. Jan. 17, 1989).

§ 16.12 Defendant's Good Faith Generally

Page 399, add to cases cited in note 93:

Second Circuit: Rose v. Heintz, 806 F.2d 389, 391-92 (2d Cir. 1986)(state defendant was liable for § 1988 fees notwithstanding argument that its unlawful medicaid policy was implemented according to federal agency's interpretation of the law); Campaign for a Progressive Bronx v. Black, 631 F. Supp. 975, 980-82 (S.D.N.Y. 1986)(defendant Board of Election members were liable for § 1988 fees notwithstanding their good faith acts after complaint was filed).

Third Circuit: Durett v. Cohen, 790 F.2d 360, 362-63 (3d Cir. 1986)(state defendant's "'sympathetic' attitude toward the plaintiff's position in the litigation," its lack of active resistance to the suit, and its successful efforts to persuade a third party to provide relief requested did not warrant denial of § 1988 fee award against defendants).

Fourth Circuit: American Booksellers Ass'n v. Commonwealth of Va., 792 F.2d 1261, 1267 (4th Cir. 1986)(defendant's good faith does not excuse it from fee liability "even when a novel legal question is involved").

Eighth Circuit: Savage v. Toan, 636 F. Supp. 156, 157-58 (W.D. Mo. 1986)(state defendants whose amended medicaid regulations were invalidated were not excused from fee liability because the federal defendant "pressured" them to make the change).

Ninth Circuit: Schrader v. Idaho Dep't of Health and Welfare, 631 F. Supp. 1426, 1430 (D. Idaho 1986)(state defendant's claim "of being a pawn caught in the middle" between plaintiff and federal defendant in enforcing an unlawful AFDC regulation did not avoid § 1988 fee liability).

Tenth Circuit: Jones v. Wilkinson, 800 F.2d 989, 992 (10th Cir. 1986), *judgment aff'd,* _____ U.S. _____, 94 L. Ed. 2d 753 (1987) defendant's "good faith belief in the legality or constitutionality of its action" does not shield it from § 1988 fee liability).
Eleventh Circuit: Doss v. Long, 624 F. Supp. 1078, 1080-81 (N.D. Ga. 1985)(state could not avoid fee liability for unconstitutional actions of its officials by asserting that it had corrected the illegal law and that the defendant state judges had litigated the case in bad faith).
State Courts: EWAP, Inc. v. City of Ontario, 177 Cal. App. 3d 1108, 223 Cal. Rptr. 422, 427-29 (1986)(defendant's good faith belief that the challenged ordinances were constitutional and its belated concession of the ordinance's unconstitutionality did not relieve it from § 1988 fee liability).

§ 16.13 – Defendant's Exceptional Good Faith

Page 401, update Daggett citation (Third Circuit) and add to cases cited in note 96:

District of Columbia Circuit: Cf. Grano v. Barry, 783 F.2d 1104, 1111-12 (D.C. Cir. 1986)(remanding to district court to make reasoned determination whether special circumstances warranted denial of § 1988 fees against defendant District which was caught in a "squeeze play," so that "[n]o matter which course it followed" the other parties "would have claimed it was acting unconstitutionally").
Third Circuit: Daggett, 811 F.2d 793, 795 n.1 (3d Cir. 1987)(ruling discussed in text not appealed); Joseph L. v. Office of Judicial Support, 638 F. Supp. 833, 836 (E.D. Pa. 1986)(declining to assess § 1988 fees against private defendant tax sale purchaser of plaintiff's property, in successful suit challenging constitutionality of defendant county's procedures for selling real estate for tax purposes, when (1) private defendant "had no part in the alleged constitutional violation and was in fact powerless to prevent whatever violation was caused by the county" and (2) private defendant "voluntarily accommodated plaintiff, while the instant suit was pending, in every request plaintiff made in his complaint").
Eleventh Circuit: York v. Alabama State Bd. of Educ., 631 F. Supp. 78, 90-91 (M.D. Ala. 1986)(denying § 1988 fees against state defendants in action successfully challenging county defendants' adoption and use of racially discriminatory teachers' examination in the public school system, where county defendants used the examination "despite the state defendants' warnings to the contrary," the county defendants alone were culpable, and the supplemental relief obtained from the state defendants was "but necessary additional relief for the apparent wrong caused by the Mobile [County] defendants").

Page 403, add to cases cited in note 98:

Council for Periodical Distributors Ass'ns v. Evens, 827 F.2d 1483, 1486-87 (11th Cir. 1987) (city defendants cannot defeat § 1988 fee liability because they did not control the task force that engaged in the unconstitutional conduct and "may not even have fully condoned the methods used by the task force," when city defendants "did not, as they could have, either concede at the outset of the litigation that the activity was unconstitutional or agree to refuse to participate in any further intimidation of the plaintiffs"); Wilson v. Stocker, 819 F.2d 943, 951-52 (10th Cir. 1987) (defendant attorney general could not avoid § 1988 fee liability "because his office had done nothing to enforce the state statute at issue," because "neither failure to take official action to enforce a statute, nor official assurance that the law would not be enforced are special circumstances rendering an award unjust"; defendant district attorney's "assertion that fees are unjust because her participation in the litigation helped develop the law and the facts is also unpersuasive"); Rose v. Heintz, 806 F.2d 389, 391-92 (2d Cir. 1986) (state defendant's implementation of unlawful medicaid regulation in accordance with interpretation of federal law provided in a telephone conversation with a federal official did not shield state defendant from § 1988 fee liability, when state defendant was not "coerced" by federal agency to implement the improper policy and since "[a] simple telephone inquiry without a written request for confirmation hardly seems responsible state action in a situation obviously involving the eligibility for Medicaid of hundreds if not thousands of people"); Savage v. Toan, 636 F. Supp. 156, 157-58 (W.D. Mo. 1986)(state defendants could not avoid § 1988 fee liability because they assertedly "changed their Medicaid eligibility regulations only because they were pressured to do so by the federal defendant," since "[t]he fact remains that the State's change in regulations precipitated this lawsuit" and "[i]f the State fully agreed with the plaintiffs' position, it could have withstood the federal government's pressure and initiated a lawsuit challenging the Secretary on its own"); Schrader v. Idaho Dep't of Health and Welfare, 631 F. Supp. 1426, 1430 (D. Idaho 1986)(state defendant whose AFDC regulations were invalidated cannot escape § 1988 fee liability by claiming that it "was a pawn, caught between plaintiff and the federal defendant, attempting to fairly and legally administer a state eligibility plan, with its numerous rules and regulations, and simultaneously attempting to get the approval of the federal defendant to receive funding," since state defendant could have instituted a declaratory judgment action against the federal agency to obtain clarification of its obligations); Campaign for a Progressive Bronx v. Black, 631 F. Supp. 975, 980-82 (S.D.N.Y. 1986)(defendant Board of Election members were not excused from § 1988 fee liability where their good faith efforts throughout the litigation to comply with plaintiffs' demands, and their ultimate settlement of the dispute, "occurred *after,* and apparently *in response* to the complaint which was filed in this action"; court gave short shrift to defendants' contention that they should not be assessed § 1988 fees because in the future they "will be less inclined to settle and to cooperate with plaintiffs' demands, to which they may not be legally obligated to accede, than they were in the case at bar").

Page 403, add to cases cited in note 99:

See Reeves v. Harrell, 791 F.2d 1481, 1484-85 (11th Cir. 1986); Grano v. Barry, 783 F.2d 1104, 1112 (D.C. Cir. 1986); Paradise v. Prescott, 626 F. Supp. 117 (M.D. Ala. 1985) (all discussed in § **16.11** of this supplement).

Page 403, add to cases cited in note 1:

Durett v. Cohen, 790 F.2d 360, 362-63 (3d Cir. 1986) (affirming district court's reduction of § 1988 fee award against state defendant because of its " 'sympathetic' attitude toward the plaintiff's position in the litigation," its decision to "not actively contest the litigation," and its successful efforts to persuade a third party to afford the relief sought in the suit).

§ 16.14 Willingness of Private Counsel to Represent Plaintiff on a Contingent Fee Basis–The Bright Prospects Test

Page 408, update Cunningham citation in note 31:

vacated & remanded on other grounds, 478 U.S. 1015 (1986), *reinstated,* 807 F.2d 49 (3d Cir. 1986), *cert. denied,* 107 S. Ct. 2179 (1987).

Page 408, add the following case to note 33:

Jones v. Wilkinson, 800 F.2d 989, 991 n.3 (10th Cir. 1986), *judgment aff'd,* _____ U.S. _____, 94 L. Ed. 2d 753 (1987) (noting that bright prospects test has no application to suits for declaratory and injunctive relief only, and that, in any event, Tenth Circuit has rejected the test altogether).

Page 408, insert following sentence ending with note 34 reference:

While not dispositive of the issue, the Supreme Court's condemnation in *City of Riverside v. Rivera,* 477 U.S. 561, 586 (1986) (Powell, J., concurring), of the relevance of contingent fee principles to the *calculation* of § 1988 fee awards strongly suggests disapproval of the bright prospects test to deny § 1988 fees altogether to the prevailing
* plaintiff. See **§ 21.3**. In *Blanchard v. Bergeron,* 57 U.S.L.W. 4191 (U.S. Feb. 2d, 1989), the Supreme Court effectively sounded the death knell of the bright prospects test as the basis for denying § 1988 fees to the prevailing plaintiff whose § 1983 damages suit attracted competent counsel on a contingent fee basis. There, the Court stated:

> It is true that the purpose of section 1988 was to make sure that competent counsel was available to civil rights plaintiffs, and it is of course arguable that if a plaintiff is able to secure an attorney on the basis on a contingent or other fee agreement, the purpose of the statute is served if the plaintiff is bound by his contract. On that basis, however, the plaintiff should recover nothing from the defendant, which would be plainly contrary to the statute.

57 U.S.L.W. at 4192.

§ 16.15 The Grossly Exaggerated or Wholly Undocumented Fee Request

Page 490, add to note 36:

Fourth Circuit: Sun Publishing Co. V. Mecklenburg News, Inc., 823 F.2d 818 (4th Cir. 1987) (upholding complete denial of plaintiff's second supplemental petition for

attorney's fees in antitrust action as "so unreasonable and exorbitant that it shocks the conscience of this court").
Seventh Circuit: Frantz v. U.S. Powerlifting Fed'n, 836 F.2d 1063, 1065 (7th Cir. 1987)(reaffirming that a district court may deny a § 1988 fee request as a "sanction for filing an outrageously large request").

Page 410, add to note 38:

Southerland v. International Longshoremen's Local 8, 845 F.2d 796, 801 (9th Cir. 1987)(Labor-Management Reporting and Disclosure Act, 29 U.S.C. § 412; "Total denial of fees because of poor documentation is a stringent sanction, to be reserved for only the most severe of situations, and appropriately invoked only in very limited circumstances."

Page 410, add to cases cited in note 40:

Mammano v. Pittston Co., 792 F.2d 1242, 1245 (4th Cir. 1986) (assertedly " 'inflated' nature" of plaintiff's fee request is factor to be considered in determining reasonableness of Title VII fee award, but not grounds for denial altogether of fees).

CHAPTER 17

THE DETERMINATION OF COMPENSABLE HOURS

§ 17.1 The Required Elimination of Unreasonably Expended Hours: Introduction

Page 414, insert at beginning of second paragraph on page:

The Sixth Circuit in *Coulter v. Tennessee,* 805 F.2d 146, 150-51 (6th Cir. 1986), has stated that:

> Three very different kinds of issues can arise concerning excessive hours: (1) factual questions about whether the lawyer actually worked the hours claimed or is padding the account; (2) legal questions about whether the work performed is sufficiently related to the points on which the client prevailed as to be compensable; and (3) mixed questions about whether the lawyer used poor judgment in spending too many hours on some part of the case or by unnecessarily duplicating the work of co-counsel.

Page 415, add to note 11:

In Norman v. Housing Auth. of Montgomery, 836 F.2d 1292, 1301 (11th Cir. 1988), the court stated that:

> [e]xcluding excessive or otherwise unnecessary hours under the rubric of 'billing judgment' means that a lawyer may not be compensated for hours spent on activities for which he would not bill a client of means who was seriously intent on vindicating similar rights, recognizing that in the private sector the economically rational person engages in some cost benefit analysis.

"[T]he measure of reasonable hours is determined by the profession's judgment of the time that may be conscionably billed and not the least time in which it might theoretically have been done." *Id.* at 1306.

§ 17.2 Approaches to Elimination of Unreasonable Hours; Discretion of the District Court

Page 415, update Daggett citation (Third Circuit) and add to cases cited in note 13:

District of Columbia Circuit: McKenzie v. Kennickell, 645 F. Supp. 437, 442 (D.D.C. 1986) (Title VII suit; rejecting government's "invitation to undertake a line by line examination of the fee request and 'pleading by pleading examination of the copious files in this case' ").

* *First Circuit:* In United States v. Metropolitan Dist. Comm'n., 847 F.2d 12, 15-17 (1st Cir. 1988), the First Circuit upheld an unorthodox approach adopted by the district court in determining the reasonableness of time expended by plaintiffs' attorneys on a successful suit under the Clean Water Act, 33 U.S.C. § 1365(d). Instead of reducing the hours expended on the suit to eliminate excessive, duplicative, or unproductive time, the district court identified specific tasks undertaken by plaintiff's counsel and allocated to these tasks the amount of time adjudged necessary to accomplish them, thereby determining the number of compensable hours for statutory fee purposes. The court of appeals reasoned that, in the circumstances of this case, the district court appropriately focused on "what was necessary to be accomplished rather than on a welter of time sheets." *Id.* at 16. Such an approach, however, is at odds with the method endorsed by the Supreme Court in *Hensley* for determining reasonable hours compensable under § 1988.

Third Circuit: Daggett v. Kimmelman, 811 F.2d 793, 797-98 (3d Cir. 1987) (finding that district court provided adequate justification for 10% reduction in claimed hours for duplication and excessiveness, noting that "[n]o court, viewing a record of this magnitude from the distance inherent in appellate review could assess the resonability of a reduction as slight as ten percent with flawless precision").

Sixth Circuit: Coulter v. Tennessee, 805 F.2d 146, 152 (6th Cir. 1986) (holding that "[w]here duplication of effort is a serious problem, as in this case, the District Court may have to make across the board reductions by reducing certain items by a percentage figure").

Seventh Circuit: Tomazzoli v. Sheedy, 804 F.2d 93, 97-98 (7th Cir. 1986) (approving district court's approach of "cut[ting] the number of hours by a lump sum in response to appellees' claim that the time was inflated . . . as a practical means of trimming fat from a fee application").

Tenth Circuit: Mares v. Credit Bureau of Raton, 801 F.2d 1197, 1202-03 (10th Cir. 1986) (Consumer Credit Protection Act, 15 U.S.C. §§ 1601 *et seq.;* approving percentage reduction technique and stating that "[t]here is no requirement, either in this court or elsewhere, that district courts identify and justify each disallowed hour").

Page 416, add to cases cited in note 15:

City of Riverside v. Rivera, 477 U.S. 561, 573 n.6 (1986) (plurality opinion) (in affirming district court's finding regarding reasonableness of time expended on case by plaintiffs' counsel, Court noted that "the District Court was in the best position to determine whether the time expended by respondents' counsel was reasonable"); Coulter v. Tennessee, 805 F.2d 146, 152 (6th Cir. 1986) ("When the issue is a question of the lawyer's judgment in billing for a particular number of hours on a piece of work, we must depend in large measure on the fairness of the District Court in assessing the needs of the case."); Tomazzoli v. Sheedy, 804 F.2d 93, 97 (7th Cir. 1986); Mares v. Credit Bureau of Raton, 801 F.2d 1197, 1202-03 (10th Cir. 1986) (Consumer Credit Protection Act, 15 U.S.C. §§ 1601 *et seq.*); Daly v. Hill, 790 F.2d 1071, 1080 (4th Cir. 1986) (affirming reduction in claimed hours by district court, which "was in the best position to determine the amount of time reasonably necessary under the particular circumstances"); Brewster v. Dukakis, 786 F.2d 16, 22 (1st Cir. 1986) (affirming district court's reduction in claimed hours as "judgment calls . . . clearly within the discretion of the court").

Page 417, update Cunningham citation and add to cases cited in note 16:

Jacobs v. Mancuso, 825 F.2d 559, 561-62 (1st Cir. 1987) (in substantially reducing fee applicant's claimed hours, district court should identify "particular activities or practices that were inefficient, duplicative, irrelevant, or otherwise inappropriate for billing purposes"); Jordan v. Multnomah County, 815 F.2d 1258, 1263 (9th Cir. 1987) (disapproving district court's failure to make a finding on the sufficiency of the evidence supporting allowance of a "range" of compensable hours); Cunningham v. City of McKeesport, 807 F.2d 49, 52-53 (3rd Cir. 1986) (district court may not disallow claimed hours of fee applicant by "reject[ing] uncontradicted sworn affidavits because of reasons not raised by opposing counsel and on the basis of facts 'of which the trial court has no personal knowledge' "), *cert. denied,* 107 S. Ct. 2179 (1987); Gekas v. Attorney Registration & Disciplinary Comm'n, 793 F.2d 846, 852-53 (7th Cir. 1986) (vacating and remanding case for district court's redetermination of a reasonable fee, when court failed to specifically determine the number of hours reasonably expended and gave inadequate reasons for the fee reduction); *cf.* Hart v. Bourque, 798 F.2d 519, 521-23 (1st Cir. 1986) (court of appeals reversed district court's findings concerning allowable hours where the "record as a whole does not support the court's subsidiary findings," and, "[s]ince there was no trial," took the somewhat unusual step of making an appellate redetermination of the compensable hours and the maximum allowable fee).

§ 17.3 Identifying Excessive Hours

Page 417, update Hart citation and add the following cases to note 18:

Hart, *rev'd and remanded on other grounds,* 798 F.2d 519 (1st Cir. 1986); Mares v. Credit Bureau of Raton, 801 F.2d 1197, 1204, 1205 (10th Cir. 1986) (Consumer Credit Protection Act, 15 U.S.C. §§ 1601 *et seq.;* noting that plaintiffs' attorney who was "in practice for just over a year at the commencement of this case, and conceded his lack of expertise, billed every hour logged"); Diver v. Goddard Memorial Hosp., 783 F.2d 6 (1st Cir. 1986) (Fair Labor Standards Act, 29 U.S.C. § 216(b); concluding that the "present case, in which the plaintiff's counsel claims to have spent an inordinate portion of her time on a minor part of her client's lawsuit, appears to be an example of unchecked enthusiasm").

Page 418, add to note 21:

The court in Lebron v. Washington Metro. Area Transit Auth., 665 F. Supp. 923, 927-29 (D.D.C. 1987), reduced the claimed hours of plaintiff's attorneys in a First Amendment suit, with the explanation that if plaintiff's attorneys, who ordinarily practiced primarily in the area of public utility ratemaking, "are to be compensated at the market rate for First Amendment ligitators, they may be compensated only for the number of hours that a First Amendment litigator, with a comparable number of years of experience, would take to complete a particular task."

Page 418, add to cases cited in note 25:

Brewster v. Dukakis, 786 F.2d 16, 19 (1st Cir. 1986) (finding it not excessive for "attorney Schwartz to have spent about one-fourth of his time for two and one half years on this case (i.e., 1323 hours out of 5000), attorney Fleischner one-eighth (i.e., 602 hours out of 5000), and paralegal Costanzo one-eighth (i.e., 613 hours out of 5000)"); Goetz v. Ricketts, 632 F. Supp. 926, 929 (D. Colo. 1986) (court "examined the entries for the days when applicant billed in excess of 6-7 hours, and find[s] that, generally, the long days are justified"); Ramos v. Lamm, 632 F. Supp. 376, 381, 383 (D. Colo. 1986) (court stated that "special scrutiny must be given to time entries exceeding six to seven hours for a single attorney on any given day," and found that "most of the attorneys' time is comparable in amount to normal work days for lawyers in private practice in Denver", observing that "[h]owever manic such behavior may seem, I note that it is not unusual for attorneys in the private sector to put in long, continuous hours in a 'crunch' on the eve of trial or oral argument"). As the *Goetz* and *Ramos* decisions indicate, district courts in the Tenth Circuit are attentive to the court of appeals' directive in Ramos v. Lamm, discussed in note 25 in text, that courts closely "question reported time significantly in excess of the norm" in private firm practice of "six to seven billable hours per day for a five day week." 713 F.2d at 553-54. The Eleventh Circuit has noted in Norman v. Housing Auth. of Montgomery, 836 F.2d 1292, 1301 (11th Cir. 1988), that while "[g]eneralized statements that the time spent was reasonable or unreasonable of course are not particularly helpful and are not entitled to much weight," the district court will "no doubt be benefited by evidence of prevailing views among practitioners in the area" concerning whether the time claimed was excessive or unnecessary.

* Writing for the Seventh Circuit in Kurowski v. Krajewski, 848 F.2d 767 (7th Cir. 1988), Judge Easterbrook observed that "[a]wards of fees under § 1988 are supposed to give counsel the market rate for their time . . . and the kinds of billing and staffing arrangements struck when clients must pay their own lawyers are the best benchmarks of the arrangements (and bills) appropriate under § 1988." *Id.* at 776. Accordingly, Judge Easterbrook emphasized that in private practice the "standard hourly rate reflects the standard productivity of time," and "includes hours with different degrees of productivity." *Id.* This leads to the conclusion that, in measuring reasonably expended time to be compensated under § 1988, the fact that "the lawyers spent some time in blind alleys is irrelevant; this is inevitable, and the hourly rate reflects the standard productivity of time." *Id.* In a similar vein, the Eleventh Circuit has stated that "[s]worn testimony that, in fact, it took the time claimed is evidence of considerable weight on the issue of the time required in the usual case and, therefore, it must appear that the time claimed is obviously and convincingly excessive under the circumstances." Perkins v. Mobile Housing Bd., 847 F.2d 735, 738 (11th Cir. 1988). Consonant with the theme of Kurowski, above, the Perkins court suggested that "[i]n less clear cut cases where the court believes that the matter has not been handled efficiently, the court may reflect that fact by decreasing the hourly rate to the market rate charged by lawyers of less skill and experience." *Id. Cf.* Corder v. Gates, 688 F.

Supp. 1418, 1422 (C.D. Cal. 1988) ("Different litigators have different styles; that plaintiffs' counsel occasionally opts for all-nighters and summarizes depositions himself should not be held against him if his overall figure is reasonable").

Page 419, add to cases cited in note 27:

City of Riverside v. Rivera, 477 U.S. 561, 580 n.11 (1986) (plurality opinion) (noting that defendants' settlement offer in the case came late in the litigation, and observing that defendants " 'cannot litigate tenaciously and then be heard to complain about the time necessarily spent by the plaintiff in response' "); Jacobs v. Mancuso, 825 F.2d 559, 562 (1st Cir. 1987) ("[T]o the extent that defendants raised unpersuasive arguments in opposing fees, which they clearly did, they have only themselves to blame for prompting a response from plaintiffs.")

Page 419, add before sentence containing note 28 reference:

Similarly, courts often consider the number of hours expended on the case by defendant's counsel as a rough gauge of whether the hours claimed by prevailing plaintiff's attorneys are excessive. *See Chalmers v. City of Los Angeles,* 796 F.2d 1205, 1214 (9th Cir. 1986); *Thomas v. Cooper Industries, Inc.,* 640 F. Supp. 1374, 1378, 1380 (W.D.N.C. 1986); *Liverman-Melton v. British Aerospace, Inc.,* 628 F. Supp. 102, 106 (D.D.C. 1986). *But see Brantley v. Surles,* 804 F.2d 321, 326-27 (5th Cir. 1986); *Keith v. Volpe,* 644 F. Supp. 1317, 1324 (C.D. Cal. 1986) (declining to give controlling effect to number of hours expended on case by opposing counsel in determining reasonableness of hours claimed by fee applicant). See also cases cited in **§ 17.16** note 89.

In *Norman v. Housing Authority of Montgomery,* 836 F.2d 1292, 1305 n.3 (11th Cir. 1988), the court stated that "the time expended by opposing counsel is seldom relevant to a determination of hours reasonably expended on many tasks." However, the court concluded that in this case the time spent by defendants' attorneys on settlement negotiations was "some evidence" that the roughly equivalent time claimed by plaintiffs' attorneys on settlement was reasonable, because "given the cooperative nature of the settlement process, time spent by one side might be mirrored in the time spent by the other." *Id.* at 1305 & n.3. The court in *Lightfoot v. Walker,* 826 F.2d 516, 520-21 (7th Cir. 1987), held that "[w]hile it is proper to consider the number of hours found reasonable in a similar but unrelated case, merely adopting that number as reasonable in a pending case would almost certainly constitute an abuse of discretion."

Page 419, add to note 29:

In Lightfoot v. Walker, 826 F.2d 516, 522 (7th Cir. 1987), the court found that the more than 6,000 hours claimed by plaintiffs' attorneys in litigating a lengthy and complex prison conditions suit were reasonable, when the district court "carefully reviewed the attorneys' time sheets and considered their testimony regarding the division of tasks." On the other hand, the Seventh Circuit has noted that the "simplicity of the factual and legal issues involved," although "not a ground for automatically reducing a fee award," is "relevant to determining whether the hours expended by the plaintiff's attorney were reasonable." Spanish Action Comm. of Chicago v. City of Chicago, 811 F.2d 1129, 1136 (7th Cir. 1987).

Page 420, update Rivera citation in note 30:

477 U.S. 561, 585 n.2 (1986) (Powell, J., concurring).

§ 17.4 Identifying Duplicative Hours Expended by Multiple Attorneys

Page 421, add to cases cited in note 37:

Lenihan v. City of New York, 640 F. Supp. 822, 825 (S.D.N.Y. 1986) (noting the heightened efficiency achieved in complex case when the partner-in-charge brings the associate with detailed knowledge of certain issues along to court rather than attempting "to familiarize herself with all of the details of every issue in the case"; finding it reasonable for partner to revise preliminary draft of brief prepared by associate, noting that "[i]t is normal practice for attorneys to revise briefs several times before submitting them to court"); Ramos v. Lamm, 632 F. Supp. 376, 383 (D. Colo. 1986) (coordination of efforts by multiple attorneys to avoid duplication); York v. Alabama State Bd. of Educ., 631 F. Supp. 78, 84 (M.D. Ala. 1986) (noting "distinct contribution" by each of four attorneys involved in Title VII suit); Vance v. Hegstrom, 629 F. Supp. 747, 750 (D. Or. 1985) (noting that "[l]ead counsel is an attorney familiar with practice in federal court but on related type claims, while co-counsel is an expert on medicaid regulations," and concluding that "[i]t is reasonable for plaintiffs to have two lawyers with different expertise").

Page 421, add to cases cited in note 40:

Probe v. State Teachers' Retirement System, 780 F.2d 776, 785 (9th Cir. 1986) (Title VII suit) (stating that "in an important class action litigation such as this, the participation of more than one attorney does not constitute an unnecessary duplication of effort"); Ramos v. Lamm, 632 F. Supp. 376, 383 (D. Colo. 1986) (multiple attorneys in complex institutional reform litigation).

Page 421, update Daggett citation and add to cases cited in note 42:

Daggett v. Kimmelman, 617 F. Supp. 1269, 1280-81 (D.N.J. 1985) (acknowledging appropriateness of several attorneys' participation in strategy sessions, but applying 10 percent across-the-board reduction in award for duplication of effort), *aff'd in relevant part,* 811 F.2d 793, 797-98 (3d Cir. 1987); Shakman v. Democratic Organization of Cook County, 634 F. Supp. 895, 902 (N.D. Ill. 1986) (finding no duplication of effort in frequent telephone conferences between plaintiffs' attorneys where the "size and complexity of the case certainly would require conferences between plaintiffs' attorneys for coordination and strategy").

Page 421, add to cases cited in note 43:

Keith v. Volpe, 644 F. Supp. 1317, 1324 (C.D. Cal. 1986) (in order to eliminate the excessive time spent by plaintiffs' attorneys in conference with each other, which amounted to "nearly a quarter of all claimed time," court adopted the "somewhat rough-and-ready approach" of deleting "all that time reflected in nonserial entries involving conferences of three or more people"); McCullough v. Cady, 640 F. Supp. 1012, 1027 (E.D. Mich. 1986) (50 percent reduction of time claimed for attorney conferences).

Page 421, add to cases cited in note 44:

Lenihan v. City of New York, 640 F. Supp. 822, 825 (S.D.N.Y. 1986) (noting that "in a complex case such as this, it is not uncommon for an associate to accompany the partner-in-charge to court").

Page 422, add to cases cited in note 45:

Hart v. Bourque, 798 F.2d 519, 523 (1st Cir. 1986) (finding duplication of effort in "dual attendance at motion hearings," which "may have been good experience for the onlooker" but "did not advance the case"); Gregis v. Edberg, 645 F. Supp. 1153, 1161 (W.D. Pa. 1986) (denying compensation for time spent by the head of the law firm representing plaintiffs in attending, without actively participating in, a court hearing involving a member of firm); McKenzie v. Kennickell, 645 F. Supp. 437, 450 (D.D.C. 1986) (Title VII suit; "When plaintiffs choose to send two or three lawyers to sit silently in court beside the lead attorney, the defendant should not be charged for that time."); Keith v. Volpe, 644 F. Supp. 1317, 1323 (C.D. Cal. 1986) (disallowing "as unnecessarily duplicative time claimed by attorneys, paralegals, and legal clerks to attend hearings for which the court has allowed expenses for two attorneys"); Coleman v. McLaren, 635 F. Supp. 266, 269 (N.D. Ill. 1986) (defendant fee award; "Arrangements could have been made for fewer than all the defense lawyers to appear [at court status conferences], with prior discussion among them and delegation of any necessary authority to report to the Court."); Lock v. Jenkins, 634 F. Supp. 615, 621 (N.D. Ind. 1986) (disallowing time spent in meetings with co-counsel by a "recent admittee to the bar" as to whom "there is no basis for an argument that he possessed special skills or experience lacked by other counsel in this case"); Ramos v. Lamm, 632 F. Supp. 376, 384 (D. Colo. 1986) (deducting time spent by attorney in attending, but not participating in, court of appeals argument, finding that attorney's "presence at oral argument was simply not necessary even though he has devoted a significant amount of his professional career to this case and one could not reasonably expect that he would miss such a momentous event").

* *Page 422, add to note 46:*

In Kurowski v. Krajewski, 848 F.2d 767, 776 (7th Cir. 1988), the court stated that the "kinds of billing and staffing arrangements struck when clients must pay their own lawyers are the best benchmarks of the arrangements (and bills) appropriate under § 1988." Accordingly, the court approved the plaintiffs' use of two attorneys (one a professor of constitutional law), noting that the "use of two (or more) lawyers, which solvent clients commonly pay for because they believe extra help beneficial, may well reduce the total expenditures by taking advantage of division of labor," and that in this case "[t]he scholar did the research, the litigator the litigating." *Id.* at 776.

Page 422, add to cases cited in note 47:

Lenihan v. City of New York, 640 F. Supp. 822, 825 (S.D.N.Y. 1986); Dotson v. City of Indianola, 639 F. Supp. 1056, 1062 (N.D. Miss. 1986); Rogers v. Okin, 638 F. Supp. 934, 938 (D. Mass. 1986); Ramos v. Lamm, 632 F. Supp. 376, 383 (D. Colo. 1986) (all justifying multiple attorney representation of prevailing party by pointing to opposing party's deployment of a like number of lawyers). In upholding compensation for the trial work of three lawyers for the plaintiff, the court in Lenard v. Argento, 808 F.2d 1242, 1245 (7th Cir. 1987), observed that "defendants were also represented by three lawyers, and while we do not lay down a flat rule that it is always reasonable for one side to have as many lawyers as the other side, neither shall we lay down a flat rule of one plaintiff's lawyer per case."

§ 17.5 Distinguishing between Compensable and Noncompensable Activities

Page 423, add to cases cited in note 53:

Tomazzoli v. Sheedy, 804 F.2d 93, 97-98 n.5 (7th Cir. 1986) ("The volume of civil rights case law is ever-increasing and requires that a lawyer conduct research to determine whether new developments in the law affect her case in light of the issues raised. To award nothing for research time in this case, if not most civil rights cases, would be unreasonable ... especially in light of the district court's explicit requests for trial briefs and other research."); Thomas v. Cooper Industries, Inc., 640 F. Supp. 1374, 1379 (W.D.N.C. 1986) (compensation allowed for time spent in background reading of a *Fortune* magazine article about the corporate defendants, where plaintiff's attorney "had to understand the defendants in order to overcome their defenses" in Title VII suit); Goetz v. Ricketts, 632 F. Supp. 926, 931 (D. Colo. 1986) (compensation for hours spent by plaintiffs' attorneys in prison conditions suit reviewing settlement agreement in related case, which was "directly related to applicant's work on this case," and was not "purely 'background' reading"); Ramos v. Lamm, 632 F. Supp. 376, 381, 383 (D. Colo. 1986) (compensation allowed for "time spent reading cases and material specifically related to this case, which is proper and reasonable"; on the other hand, "time spent reading background materials designed to familiarize the attorney with the area of law involved in the case is normally absorbed in a private firm's general overhead and would not be billed to a client," and hence is not compensable).

Page 423, add to cases cited in note 57:

McKenzie v. Kennickell, 645 F. Supp. 437, 450 (D.D.C. 1986) (Title VII suit) ("Most important, meetings between junior and senior lawyers to discuss the progress of research and review completed assignments are reasonable and appropriate means to secure proper supervision and efficient staffing of large class actions cases such as this.").

Page 423, add to cases cited in note 59:

Baeder v. Secretary of Health and Human Services, 634 F. Supp. 1041, 1047 (D.N.J. 1986) (Equal Access to Justice Act, 28 U.S.C. § 2412; allowing time spent by plaintiff's lawyer "consulting with other attorneys" in "learning about cases in other parts of the country").

Page 424, add at end of continuation paragraph concluding with note 62 reference:

Also found to be compensable is attorney time reasonably expended in consulting with plaintiff clients about the case (*Daly v. Hill,* 790 F.2d 1071, 1079 (4th Cir. 1986); *Thomas v. Cooper Industries, Inc.*, 640 F. Supp. 1374, 1379 (W.D.N.C. 1986) (Title VII suit)), in briefing new lawyers in the case on the status of proceedings in lengthy, complex litigation in which attorney turnover is inevitable (*McKenzie v. Kennickell,* 645 F. Supp. 437, 450 & n.18 (D.D.C. 1986) (Title VII suit extending over 13 years)), in strategy conferences among plaintiff's attorneys (*City of Riverside v. Rivera,* 477 U.S. 561, 573 n.6 (1986) (plurality opinion); *McKenzie v. Kennickell,* 645 F. Supp. at 450; *Shakman v. Democratic Org. of Cook County,* 634 F. Supp. 895, 902 (N.D. Ill. 1986)), and in "moot-courting" lead counsel for plaintiffs prior to an important oral argument in an appellate court (*Trahan v. Regan,* 625 F. Supp. 1163, 1169 (D.D.C. 1985) (Equal Access to Justice Act, 28 U.S.C. § 2412)).

Page 424, update Hart citation in note 63:

Hart v. Bourque, 798 F.2d 519, 523 (1st Cir. 1986) (vacating district court's fee award but approving denial of compensation for time "devoted to continuing legal education").

Page 424, add to cases cited in note 66:

* Spell v. McDaniel, 852 F.2d 762, 768 (4th Cir. 1988) (finding it "inappropriate to charge defendants with the time necessary for replacement appellate counsel to reach the level of familiarity with the case for which trial counsel had already been compensated . . . especially where several of the legal issues had already been fully argued in the district court"); Hart v. Bourque, 798 F.2d 519, 522-23 (1st Cir. 1986) (rejecting compensation for learning time of replacement attorneys, as an "office defect, not chargeable to defendants"); Beamon v. City of Ridgeland, 666 F. Supp. 937, 942 & n.2 (S.D. Miss. 1987) (imposing 10% reduction on claimed time of both withdrawing and substituted counsel, as a "reasonable approach to dealing with the wasted time involved in the new attorney's familiarization with the case").

Page 425, update Delaware Valley citation in note 69:

aff'd in part & rev'd in part on other grounds, 478 U.S. 546 (1986).

Page 425, update Hart citation and add to cases cited in note 70:

Hart v. Bourque, 798 F.2d 519, 523 (1st Cir. 1986) (vacating district court's fee award but approving denial of compensation for time spent on "arrangements for lectures or publications about the case").

Page 425, add to cases cited in note 70:

Greater Los Angeles Council on Deafness v. Community Television, 813 F.2d 217, 221 (9th Cir. 1987) (disallowance of time spent by counsel on publicity and lobbying);

Keith v. Volpe, 643 F. Supp. 37, 43 (C.D. Cal. 1985) (elimination of time spent on "media and political activities"); Ramos v. Lamm, 632 F. Supp. 376, 381, 384 (D. Colo. 1986) (deducting time spent "attending speeches and press conferences").

Page 425, add to cases cited in note 72:

Lock v. Jenkins, 634 F. Supp. 615, 623 (N.D. Ind. 1986) (excluding hours spent by plaintiffs' lead counsel supervising and conferring with law students as part of law school clinical program, where time spent by students on the case appeared to be largely unnecessary); York v. Alabama State Bd. of Educ., 631 F. Supp. 78, 84 (M.D. Ala. 1986) (denying compensation for time spent by attorney "speaking with the author of a student law review note about teacher testing cases"). In Daggett v. Kimmelman, 811 F.2d 793, 801-02 (3d Cir. 1987), the court of appeals directed the district court on remand to determine whether some of the substantial hours claimed by plaintiffs' attorneys for the remedy phase of a congressional reapportionment case were noncompensable because they were devoted solely to maximizing the "political advantage" of the congressional plaintiffs.

§ 17.6 The Compensability of Attorney and Nonattorney Services of Varying Skill Requirements

Page 426, update Hart and Agent Orange citations and add to cases cited in note 74:

First Circuit: Jacobs v. Mancuso, 825 F.2d 559, 563 & n.6 (1st Cir. 1987) (while declining to "lay down a final rule," court rejected approaches that would either treat paralegal services as part of overhead included in counsel's fee or limit compensation for such services to actual wages, finding instead that the "use of such personnel is to be encouraged by separate compensation in order to reduce the time of more expensive counsel"). *But see* Hart v. Bourque, 608 F. Supp. 1091, 1093 (D. Mass. 1985) (denying compensation for law student time), *rev'd on other grounds,* 798 F.2d 519 (1st Cir. 1986).

Second Circuit: Lenihan v. City of New York, 640 F. Supp. 822, 825 (S.D.N.Y. 1986) (noting that law student's "much lower hourly rate more than compensates for any . . . inefficiency" in not utilizing more lawyer time in preparation of court papers). *But see In re* Agent Orange Prod. Liab. Litig., 818 F.2d 226, 238 (2d Cir. 1987) (declining to reevaluate Second Circuit rule that, at least in common fund suits, paralegal time is compensable as an expense, while recognizing that it sometimes might not be appropriate in a "large class action" to so limit compensation). Campaign for a Progressive Bronx v. Black, 631 F. Supp. 975, 983 (S.D.N.Y. 1986) (Voting Rights Act, 42 U.S.C. § 19731(e); finding that Second Circuit precedent requires that "paralegal time is to be reimbursed as an expense," but denying compensation altogether in this case for plaintiffs' failure to provide information about the wages paid to their paralegals).

* *Fourth Circuit:* Spell v. McDaniel, 852 F.2d 762, 770 (4th Cir. 1988) (finding that the "attorney's own hourly rate can properly be considered to subsume the secretarial-type services identified as having been performed by their paralegals").

Fifth Circuit: *But see* Abrams v. Baylor College of Medicine, 805 F.2d 528, 535 (5th Cir. 1986) (finding it "entirely reasonable for the court below to conclude that the cost of the services of support personnel–such as paralegals–was encompassed within the relatively high hourly billing rate awarded for the time of the plaintiffs' attorneys" in Title VII suit).

Seventh Circuit: Spanish Action Committee v. City of Chicago, 811 F.2d 1129, 1138 (7th Cir. 1987) (noting that Seventh Circuit has "expressly rejected the notion that law clerk and paralegal expenses are reflected in an attorney's fee award and has instead held that a prevailing party under § 1988 is entitled to a separate and distinct award as compensation for paralegal time reasonably expended on the case").

Eighth Circuit: Jenkins v. Missouri, 838 F.2d 260, 266 (8th Cir. 1988) (stating belief that "market considerations should govern" in setting hourly rates for paralegal and law clerk services, while concluding that "it is not necessary to adopt an ironclad rule" in this case).

Tenth Circuit: Ramos v. Lamm, 632 F. Supp. 376, 382 n.5 (D. Colo. 1986) (finding that the "law clerk and legal assistant services in this case were not part of overhead" and thus "these hours are recoverable on the same basis as those of the attorneys").

* That issue of the compensability under § 1988 of paralegal and law clerk services is before the Court in Missouri v. Jenkins, 109 S. Ct. 218 (1988), *granting cert. to* 838 F.2d 260 (8th Cir. 1988).

Page 427, add to cases cited in note 76:

McCullough v. Cady, 640 F. Supp. 1012, 1027 (E.D. Mich. 1986) (reducing time spent by senior and junior attorneys in conferences with each other, since the goal of an arrangement by which "the 'junior' lawyer does the bulk of the work at the lower rate, under the supervision of his or her senior attorney, so that the higher rates are charged only for those tasks requiring the more experienced attorney's expertise . . . is defeated if the senior attorney spends significant amounts of time consulting with junior counsel"); Lenihan v. City of New York, 640 F. Supp. 822, 825 (S.D.N.Y. 1986) (in finding reasonable the time spent by senior attorney in revising junior attorney's preliminary draft of a brief, court noted that "to the extent that [junior attorney] Sheinberg's relative inexperience increased the amount of revision required, her lower hourly rate more than compensates for such inefficiency"); Goetz v. Ricketts, 632 F. Supp. 926, 930-31 (D. Colo. 1986) (reducing attorney's claimed hours when "[m]ore of the investigative tasks, and review of correspondence, could have been accomplished by lower paid attorneys and paralegals," and other tasks "could have been performed at a lower cost to a client, such as cite checking at the state Supreme Court library, reviewing correspondence from inmates, some of the telephone work, and some of the research and drafting of interrogatories"); *cf.* Blum v. Witco Chem. Corp., 829 F.2d 367, 378-79 (3d Cir. 1987) (Age Discrimination in Employment Act, 29 U.S.C. § 626(b); urging district courts to "scrutinize . . . with care" substantial hours claimed by "senior counsel for consultation with other counsel in the firm;" "[w]e can understand the need for extensive consultation by junior counsel, but not by senior counsel"). In Daggett v. Kimmelman, 811 F.2d 793, 798-99 (3d Cir. 1987), the Third Circuit vacated the district court's 20% reduction of the lodestar award for "top-heavy" staffing of plaintiffs' case involving the exclusive use of four partners, who assertedly could have delegated many tasks to less expensive associates or paralegals. The court of appeals stated that "we are not prepared to hold on this matter of great constitutional import that it was inappropriate to use only the most experienced litigators at the early stage of this case," noting that the "insights obtained from years of experience in major litigation are often indispensable in making the most crucial, tactical judgments as to how a case should be framed and litigated." *Id.* at 798.

Page 428, add the following case to note 78:

Save Our Cumberland Mountains, Inc. v. Hodel, 622 F. Supp. 1160, 1164 (D.D.C. 1985) (Surface Mining Control and Reclamation Act, 30 U.S.C. § 1270(d); rejecting defendant's argument that it was "wasteful" to assign two senior partners of high caliber, when case was of great "importance and magnitude").

Page 428, add to note 79:

Moore v. District of Columbia, 674 F. Supp. 901, 905-06 (D.D.C. 1987) (Education of the Handicapped Act, 20 U.S.C. § 1415; rejecting defendants' criticism of plaintiffs' counsel for having partners handle their own scheduling, as "nit-picking" and an inappropriate attack on plaintiffs' counsel's "staffing patterns"); Lebron v. Washington Metro. Area Transit Auth., 665 F. Supp. 923, 929 (D.D.C. 1987) ("When a fee petition is based on a firm's normal billing rate, a court should be hesitant to challenge an allocation of tasks that is consistent with the firm's normal staffing practice.").

Page 429, add to cases cited in note 81:

Keith v. Volpe, 644 F. Supp. 1317, 1323 (C.D. Cal. 1986) (state fee statute) (disallowing hours claimed "for travel to court to file documents and similar messenger-type work which private law firms invariably absorb as an overhead and reflect within their hourly rate," and denying compensation for time spent on "routine work" of picking up copies, photocopying and distributing memos and documents, tagging exhibits, and reviewing and organizing files); Keith v. Volpe, 644 F. Supp. 1312, 1316 (C.D. Cal. 1986) (eliminating hours spent on "filing, document organization and other clerical matters that should be covered in hourly rates as normal overhead"); Catchings v. City of Crystal Springs, 626 F. Supp. 987, 989 (S.D. Miss. 1986) (Voting Rights Act, 42 U.S.C. § 1973l(e); refusing compensation for time spent on "ministerial duties such as photocopying"); Trahan v. Regan, 625 F. Supp. 1163, 1170 (D.D.C. 1985) (Equal Access to Justice Act, 28 U.S.C. § 2412; excluding attorney's time for "the clerical work of 'arrangement, photocopying, and collation' of the appendix to the appellate brief"). In Spell v. McDaniel, 824 F.2d 1380, 1401-02 (4th Cir. 1987), the Fourth Circuit upheld the district court's allowance of hours expended by plaintiff's attorneys in personal service of subpoenas on witnesses that "was accompanied by a final interview with witnesses," particularly because "many of Spell's witnesses required constant reassurance." The court also approved compensation for attorney time spent in photocopying documents, when the attorneys "screened, reviewed and arranged more than 14,000 pages of police department internal reports, 'perhaps the most important time spent on this case by plaintiff's counsel.' " *Id.* at 1402. The Fourth Circuit noted that there is no "single, correct staffing pattern exist[ing] within every law firm for every lawsuit" and that "in some circumstances, it may be more efficient and reasonable for counsel to perform such tasks." *Id.* at 1401-02.

Page 429, add to cases cited in note 82:

Jacobs v. Mancuso, 825 F.2d 559, 563 (1st Cir. 1987) (reducing the "inordinate number of attorney hours . . . claimed for reviewing and analyzing time records and preparing associated affidavits and memoranda, in view of the largely clerical skills needed for reviewing these records and the relatively uncomplicated law applicable to their analysis"). In Norman v. Housing Auth. of Montgomery, 836 F.2d 1292, 1306 (11th Cir. 1988), the Eleventh Circuit ruled that the district court must provide a "reasoned explanation for determining that some attorney time was spent on work customarily done by a paralegal or other lower-skilled person, and hence should be compensated at a reduced rate." *See also* Goetz v. Ricketts, 632 F. Supp. 926, 930 (D. Colo. 1986) (reducing award for claimed attorney time, where "[m]ore of the investigative tasks, and review of correspondence, could have been accomplished by lower paid attorneys and paralegals").

Page 430, add to cases cited in note 83:

Thomas v. Cooper Industries, Inc., 640 F. Supp. 1374, 1380 (W.D.N.C. 1986) (Title VII suit; finding that plaintiff's attorney, a solo practitioner, "cannot delegate matters to lesser-paid employees," so that "[i]t would be improper to penalize him for being a solo practitioner by discounting his time on certain matters that might, in different circumstances, be performed by 'office personnel'"); Alexander v. Hill, 625 F. Supp. 567, 569 (W.D.N.C. 1985) (rejecting defendants' contention that more paralegals, and less lawyers' time, should have been used in reviewing discovery documents and files when the "lawyers ably applied their familiarity with prior orders in this case and with regulatory requirements in this area of the law to detect both plain and subtle evasions of the terms and intent of applicable orders and rules," and as well "provided continuity" and "eliminated the need for the time-consuming training of new personnel").

Page 430, update Hart (First Circuit) and Daggett (Third Circuit) citations and add to cases in note 84:

First Circuit: Hart, *rev'd and remanded,* 798 F.2d 519, 523 (1st Cir. 1986) (but approving district court's denial of compensation for travel time).

Second Circuit: Fiacco v. City of Rensselaer, 663 F. Supp. 743, 746 (N.D.N.Y. 1987) (compensating at reduced rate time spent by plaintiff's attorney traveling from his home to federal courthouse for appellate court argument). Orshan v. Macchiarola, 629 F. Supp. 1014, 1020 n.3 (E.D.N.Y. 1986) (25 percent reduction in hours, including for travel time).

Third Circuit: Daggett, *aff'd in relevant part,* 811 F.2d 793 (3d Cir. 1987); Baeder v. Secretary of Health and Human Services, 634 F. Supp. 1041, 1048 (D.N.J. 1986) (Equal Access to Justice Act, 28 U.S.C. § 2412; allowing compensation for travel time "spent on legitimate activities – traveling to a law library and to the Court of Appeals").

Fourth Circuit: Thomas v. Cooper Industries, Inc., 640 F. Supp. 1374, 1379 (W.D.N.C. 1986) Title VII suit; allowing time "traveling to find and read possibly relevant documents", noting that "[a]s to the time counsel spent on planes, that was time when he was not working for other clients; and air travel is the fastest transportation now available"); McDowell v. Moore, 635 F. Supp. 280, 283 (W.D.N.C. 1986) (defendant fee award; reduction of travel time of out-of-town counsel, when fee applicant's affidavit did not "contain any information from which the Court may determine that it was necessary or reasonable to employ out-of-town counsel").

Fifth Circuit: Catchings v. City of Crystal Springs, 626 F. Supp. 987, 990 (S.D. Miss. 1986) (travel time allowed, but at one-half of normal hourly rate).

Seventh Circuit: Coleman v. McLaren, 635 F. Supp. 266, 269 (N.D. Ill. 1986) (defendant fee award; reduction in allowable travel time to and from depositions).

Ninth Circuit: Keith v. Volpe, 644 F. Supp. 1312, 1316 (C.D. Cal. 1986) (eliminating hours spent "traveling between meetings other than court appearances").

Tenth Circuit: Goetz v. Ricketts, 632 F. Supp. 926, 931 (D. Colo. 1986) (deducting time "associated with travel where there is no indication that any work was performed during the journey"); Ramos v. Lamm, 632 F. Supp. 376, 381, 384 (D. Colo. 1986) (disallowing travel time "unless it is demonstrated that work was performed during time spent travelling").

§ 17.8 Compensation for Postjudgment Remedial Work

Page 432, update Delaware Valley and Daggett citations and add to cases cited in note 90:

* Delaware Valley, 478 U.S. 546, 558-61 (1986); McDonald v. Armontrout, 860 F.2d 1456, 1461 (8th Cir. 1988) (upholding compensation, at full attorney rate, for work done in monitoring defendants' compliance with prison conditions consent decree, culminating in filing of contempt motion and agreement to supplement the decree); Norman v. Housing Auth. of Montgomery, 836 F.2d 1292, 1305 (11th Cir. 1988) (directing district court to grant compensation for time reasonably spent by plaintiffs' attorneys administering fund created by settlement of class action suit challenging Housing Authority rent overcharges); Keith v. Volpe, 833 F.2d 850, 857-58 (9th Cir. 1987) (existence of separate monitoring entities created by consent decree did not preclude fee award for non-duplicative monitoring services rendered by plaintiffs' attorneys; judicial finding of defendant's contempt or obstruction is not a prerequisite for an award for post-judgment monitoring activities); Brewster v. Dukakis, 786 F.2d 16, 18-19 (1st Cir. 1986); Turner v. Orr, 785 F.2d 1498, 1503-04 (11th Cir. 1986); Keith v. Volpe, 643 F. Supp. 37, 41-42 (C.D. Cal. 1985), 644 F. Supp. 1312, 1314 (C.D. Cal. 1986), and 644 F. Supp. 1317, 1325 (C.D. Cal. 1986); Alexander v. Hill, 625 F. Supp. 567, 568 (W.D.N.C. 1985) (all awarding fees for plaintiff's efforts in monitoring and enforcing defendant's compliance with judgment). *But see* Cooper v. Williamson County Bd. of Educ., 820 F.2d 180, 184 (6th Cir. 1987) (refusing fee compensation, under reasonable monitoring theory, for counsel's activities, following district court's reinstatement of plaintiff as school principal in Title VII suit, in defending plaintiff against dismissal on competency grounds in state administrative proceedings and in "follow[ing] media reports or advis[ing] him on day-to-day administrative matters

faced in his job as principal"), *cert. denied,* 108 S. Ct. 699 (1988); Daggett v. Kimmelman, 617 F. Supp. 1269, 1275-78 (D.N.J. 1985), *vacated and remanded in relevant part,* 811 F.2d 793, 800-02 (3d Cir. 1987) (vacating district court's fee award for time spent by plaintiffs' counsel in remedy phase of reapportionment case, with directions to disallow time "devoted solely to obtaining the most favorable political result" for plaintiff congressmen).

Page 433, add to cases cited in note 91:

Keith v. Volpe, 644 F. Supp. 1312, 1314 (C.D. Cal. 1986) (compensation allowed for time spent monitoring compliance with consent decree by "providing quarterly comprehensive reports to the court which summarize the progress made in implementing the decree and draw to the court's attention potential areas of difficulty").

Page 433, add to cases cited in note 95:

Argento v. Village of Melrose Park, 838 F.2d 1483, 1495, 1499 (7th Cir. 1988); Free v. Briody, 793 F.2d 807, 808-09 (7th Cir. 1986) (ERISA suit); Planned Parenthood v. State of Arizona, 789 F.2d 1348, 1352-53 (9th Cir. 1985); Gregis v. Edberg, 645 F. Supp. 1153, 1164-65 (W.D. Pa. 1986) (all granting compensation for time spent seeking to collect underlying money judgment or fee award).

§ 17.9 Compensation for Work in Ancillary Administrative or Judicial Proceedings

Page 436, add following carryover paragraph:

The Fifth Circuit, in *Leroy v. City of Houston,* 831 F.2d 576 (5th Cir. 1987), has interpreted *Webb* "to require that counsel's participation in administrative activities be tied both qualitatively and timely to the lawsuit in order to establish that such work was performed 'on the litigation,' " and hence, is compensable. *Id.* at 582. From the standpoint of timeliness, the focus is on whether the "work counsel performed in the litigation and administrative proceedings . . . is . . . easily separable, as in *Webb.*" *Id.* With regard to the "qualitative relation" between work in administrative proceedings and work performed on the litigation, the Fifth Circuit concluded that "*Webb*'s facts narrowly limit the scope of administrative work for which legal fees are recoverable." *Id.* The court noted that in *Webb* plaintiff's counsel "participated in trial-type proceedings involving precisely the issues and evidence later pertinent to plaintiff's § 1983 lawsuit," and the Supreme Court "nevertheless rejected any per se rule permitting recovery." *Id.* The Fifth Circuit further observed that a finding that work in the administrative proceeding was a catalyst in favorable resolution of the subsequent lawsuit does not by itself warrant the conclusion that administrative services are compensable under *Webb. Id.* at 583.

Page 436, update Delaware Valley citation in note 13:

478 U.S. 546, 558-61 (1986).

Page 436, delete sentence with Crest Street Community Council reference, together with note 14, and substitute the following:

In *North Carolina Dep't of Transp. v. Crest Street Community Council, Inc.*, 479 U.S. 6 (1986), the Supreme Court ruled that § 1988 attorney's fees cannot be recovered in an independent court action that seeks only the recovery of attorney's fees and does not also seek the enforcement of any of the underlying statutory provisions for which § 1988 fees are available. On that ground the Court reversed the Fourth Circuit's decision that the plaintiffs could recover § 1988 fees, in a federal court suit only for attorney's fee relief, for time expended in Title VI federal administrative proceedings, which were contemplated by Congress and expressly prescribed by federal regulations * and which gained for plaintiffs the complete merits relief sought by them.[15] *Contrast Jones v. American State Bank,* 857 F.2d 494 (8th Cir. 1988) (concluding that plaintiff seeking recovery of Title VII fees for work done in successful state administrative proceeding, mandated by Title VII, may institute federal court suit solely to recover fees). In *ECOS, Inc. v. Brinegar,* 671 F. Supp. 381, 391-93 (M.D.N.C. 1987), the court, following entry of a consent judgment on the merits, granted § 1988 fee compensation to Crest Street Community Council for services rendered in the Title VI federal administrative proceedings, concluding that "a proceeding before a federal agency, pursuant to federal regulations designed to effectuate Title VI, is . . . a 'proceeding to enforce' Title VI." Alternatively, the court found compensable under *Webb* "work performed at the administrative level [that] was obviously and ordinarily necessary to place the parties in the position to reach a settlement" in court. *Id.* at 393.

Page 437, update Delaware Valley citation in note 17:

478 U.S. 546, 559-60 (1986).

Page 437, update Delaware Valley citation in note 18:

478 U.S. at 553 n.1.

Page 437, update Crest Street Community Council citation in note 19:

769 F.2d 1025 (4th Cir. 1985), *rev'd on other grounds,* 479 U.S. 6 (1986).

Page 438, delete last two sentences in continuation paragraph and substitute the following:

As discussed above, the Supreme Court reversed the Fourth Circuit's decision in *Crest Street* on the grounds that the plaintiff may not recover § 1988 fees in an independent court suit seeking only the recovery of attorney's fees and not also seeking merits relief under one of the civil rights laws listed in § 1988.

Page 438, update Delaware Valley citation and add to cases cited in note 22:

Delaware Valley, 478 U.S. 546, 553 n.1 (1986) (upholding compensation for work done by plaintiff's counsel in submitting an *amicus curiae* brief on a related state-court appeal in which the authority of the state defendant to enter into the federal court consent decree was challenged); *cf.* Shakman v. Democratic Organization of Cook

County, 634 F. Supp. 895, 900 (N.D. Ill. 1986) (disallowing time spent by plaintiffs' attorneys on two *amicus curiae* briefs in another case when the work involved "is unrelated to the issues involved in *Shakman*" and "did not materially advance those issues").

Page 438, add after sentence ending with note 22 reference:

The Ninth Circuit has suggested in *Harris v. McCarthy,* 790 F.2d 753, 759-60 (9th Cir. 1986), that, consistent with the *Webb* decision, the California state courts could include in a § 1988 fee award for a successful civil rights suit in state court compensation for time spent in a federal court § 1983 suit between the same parties that plaintiffs voluntarily dismissed in order to pursue a single trial of all issues in state court.

Page 439, add the following case to note 23:

Exeter-West Greenwich Regional School Dist. v. Pontarelli, 788 F.2d 47, 51-52 (1st Cir. 1986) (compensation allowed for time spent by plaintiffs' counsel on integrally-related state court proceeding in Rhode Island Supreme Court, on certification to that court by the federal district court of a state law issue that was dispositive of the outcome of the federal suit).

Page 439, update Black Grievance Committee citation and add to cases cited in note 24:

Brantley v. Surles, 804 F.2d 321, 325 (5th Cir. 1986) (no § 1988 fee compensation for work done on unsuccessful state court suit asserting state law claims instituted prior to federal court suit); Black Grievance Committee v. Philadelphia Elec. Co., 802 F.2d 648, 653 (3d Cir. 1986), *aff'g in relevant part,* 615 F. Supp. 1069, 1073-74 (E.D. Pa. 1985) (denying compensation for time spent by plaintiffs' counsel in National Labor Relations Board proceeding, involving an asserted unfair labor practice by defendant, that was entirely separate from the employment discrimination class action in federal court); McCullough v. Cady, 640 F. Supp. 1012, 1025 (E.D. Mich. 1986) (disallowing time spent by plaintiff's counsel in state court proceeding that resulted in dismissal of misconduct finding against plaintiff inmate, since it was "not necessary" to the federal court § 1983 suit by inmate against prison guard); Dotson v. City of Indianola, 639 F. Supp. 1056, 1061-62 (N.D. Miss. 1986) (no compensation for time spent in related state court proceeding); Lock v. Jenkins, 634 F. Supp. 615, 622 (N.D. Ind. 1986) (denying compensation for time spent in state court proceeding); Maldonado v. Nebraska Dep't of Public Welfare, 223 Neb. 485, 391 N.W.2d 105, 110 (1986) (no § 1988 fee compensation for time expended by plaintiff's counsel in state administrative agency proceedings on her public assistance claim prior to institution of federal court suit). In Cooper v. Williamson County Bd. of Educ., 820 F.2d 180, 183-84 (6th Cir. 1987), *cert. denied,* 108 S. Ct. 699 (1988), the court denied compensation for work done in representing the Title VII plaintiff in state dismissal proceedings that did not involve employment discrimination and that occurred after the district court judgment in the Title VII suit. In so ruling, the court distinguished a case "in which the federal court abstained under the *Pullman* doctrine and required the litigants to clarify state law issues in a state forum before proceeding with the civil rights action in federal court." *Id.* at 184. In the instant case the court noted, "the state proceedings dealt with no issue of state law that had a direct bearing on Cooper's case in district court and the court did not require him to pursue the state proceedings before returning to federal court." *Id.*

Page 439, add the following case to note 25:

Lenihan v. City of New York, 640 F. Supp. 822, 830-31 (S.D.N.Y. 1986) (disallowing time spent by plaintiff's counsel in administrative proceedings before police department Medical Board, when those proceedings "were part of the police department's discriminatory treatment" of plaintiff, and thus "were not part of the statutory *remedy* for redress of a prior wrong . . . [but rather] were part of the *wrong* complained of in plaintiff's federal civil rights action").

Page 440, add to note 26:

* Mayson v. Pierce, 806 F.2d 1556, 1558 (11th Cir. 1987) (Title VII suit). In Borunda v. Richmond, 860 F.2d 937, 942-43 (9th Cir. 1988), the court upheld an award to successful plaintiffs in a damages suit for false arrest of attorney's fees incurred in a prior criminal prosecution, not as part of § 1988 attorney's fees, but rather as an element of compensatory damages for injuries incurred as a consequence of defendants' unconstitutional conduct.

Page 440, add to cases cited in note 27:

* McDonald v. Armontrout, 860 F.2d 1456, 1461-62 (8th Cir. 1988) (upholding compensation under § 1988 for work done in habeas corpus action of prison inmate that was useful and necessary for subsequent prison conditions suit); Lebron v. Washington Metro. Area Transit Auth., 665 F. Supp. 923, 926 (D.D.C. 1987) (granting partial compensation for time spent by plaintiff's counsel in prelitigation efforts to persuade transit agency (WMATA) to accept display of his political poster, in order to "separate the compensable time spent obtaining necessary information from WMATA and building a record for future judicial review from the non-compensable time spent pleading Lebron's case before WMATA personnel"); Bovey v. City of Lafayette, 638 F. Supp. 640, 643 (N.D. Ind. 1986) (allowing compensation for hours expended on discovery in related state court suit that was to be considered discovery in the federal
* suit as well). *But cf.* Ramsey v. Chrysler First, Inc., 861 F.2d 1541, 1544-45 (11th Cir. 1988) (upholding denial of fee compensation under Age Discrimination in Employment Act, 29 U.S.C. § 626(b), for work done in preparation for mandated state administrative proceedings, since the services were duplicative of work performed in court for which compensation already was granted).

§ 17.10 Compensation for Work on the Fee Application

Page 441, update Delaware Valley citation (Third Circuit) and add to cases cited in note 30:

District of Columbia Circuit: Grano v. Barry, 783 F.2d 1104, 1113-14 (D.C. Cir. 1986) (affirming award for time spent on amended memoranda on the fee issue, noting that they were filed "to take account of the rapidly changing factual circumstances, as well as legal developments" in the fee area).

First Circuit: Jacobs v. Mancuso, 825 F.2d 559, 563 (1st Cir. 1987) (upholding reduction in plaintiffs' claimed hours spent in recovering § 1988 fees, when counsel solicited and prepared an excessive number of supporting attorney affidavits, claimed an "inordinate number of attorney hours . . . for reviewing and analyzing time records and preparing associated affidavits and memoranda" and sought compensation for time spent on unsuccessful request for a contingency multiplier).

Third Circuit: Delaware Valley, 478 U.S. 546 (1986); Black Grievance Committee v. Philadelphia Elec. Co., 802 F.2d 648, 656-57 (3d Cir. 1986) (directing district court to appropriately reduce award for partial success on fee application); Durett v. Cohen, 790 F.2d 360, 363 (3d Cir. 1986) (remanding for district court to make reasoned and appropriate reduction in award to account for partial success on fee application.)

Fourth Circuit: Daly v. Hill, 790 F.2d 1071, 1080 (4th Cir. 1986) (affirming district court's reduction of allowable hours on fee request).

Sixth Circuit: Coulter v. State of Tennessee, 805 F.2d 146, 151 (6th Cir. 1986) (affirming district court's limitation of compensable hours on fee request to approximately 3 percent of hours allowed in the main case).

Seventh Circuit: The court in *In re* Burlington Northern, Inc., 832 F.2d 430 (7th Cir. 1987), held that the lodestar reduction principles set forth in Hensley v. Eckerhart, 461 U.S. 424 (1983), apply to the determination of fees for litigating a statutory attorney's fee award, and in the instant case warranted the district court's reduction by 35% of lead counsel's award for only partial success in litigating the initial Title VII fee request. The court of appeals found that, for *Hensley* purposes, the extent of success achieved in the initial fee litigation is measured by comparing what the fee applicant sought to what he actually obtained. 832 F.2d at 435. In this case, lead counsel for the prevailing plaintiffs won a lodestar fee award of $2.2 million but failed to obtain a requested 2.5 multiplier, which would have enhanced the fee award to $5.1 million. In view of the partial success of the initial fee litigation, and particularly in light of the "great deal of time and energy" expended by lead counsel on the multiplier issue, the court of appeals found no abuse of discretion in the district court's 35% reduction of the fee requested for the fee litigation. *Id.* at 435-36.

Ninth Circuit: Harris v. McCarthy, 790 F.2d 753, 758-59 (9th Cir. 1986) (finding no abuse of discretion in district court's granting of 11.5 percent of plaintiffs' fee request for fee work, the same percentage compensation as was allowed for work on the merits phase of the litigation).

Tenth Circuit: Mares v. Credit Bureau of Raton, 801 F.2d 1197, 1205-07 (10th Cir. 1986) (Consumer Credit Protection Act, 15 U.S.C. §§ 1601 *et seq.;* stating "general rule . . . that at least some compensation is generally allowable for work reasonably expended on the fee application," but observing that "hours not spent representing the client are at best on the borderline of what Congress intended to be compensable," and concluding that "hours spent disputing a fee award," in contrast to "time necessary to prepare and submit an application for fees," are "especially suspect, and may be disallowed in their entirety").

Page 441, add following sentence ending with note 30 reference:

Several circuit courts have approved an *a priori* approach to the reduction of claimed hours on the fee request to take into account excessiveness or partial success. *See Coulter v. Tennessee,* 805 F.2d 146, 151 (6th Cir. 1986) ("In the absence of unusual circumstances, the hours allowed for preparing and litigating the attorney fee case should not exceed 3% of the hours [allowed] in the main case when the issue is submitted on the papers without a trial and should not exceed 5% of the hours in the main case when a trial is necessary."); *Harris v. McCarthy,* 790 F.2d 753, 758-59 (9th Cir. 1986) (finding no abuse of discretion in district court's " 'rather cold mathematical approach' " of allowing the same percentage award for hours claimed on the fee request as was granted for hours spent on substantive work in the case); *Durett v. Cohen,* 790 F.2d 360, 363 (3d Cir. 1986) (approving concept of reducing fee request work "by a percentage corresponding to the reduction of the fees for work on the merits," while leaving open "the possibility that in unusual circumstances it would be equitable not to make any such reduction").

Page 442, add after sentence ending with note 34 reference:

See also Hernandez v. George, 793 F.2d 264, 269 (10th Cir. 1986), in which the Tenth Circuit denied plaintiffs § 1988 fee compensation for work on their fee request, "under the unique circumstances of this case" in which plaintiffs failed to comply with the local rule requirements regarding timely filing for attorney's fees and the work on the fee issue was largely done after the time limit had expired.

Page 443, add to note 36:

However, a district court's determination of a *legal* issue, such as whether the lodestar reduction analysis of Hensley v. Eckerhart, 461 U.S. 424 (1983), applies to calculation of fees for the initial fee litigation, is subject to *de novo* review by the court of appeals. *In re* Burlington Northern, Inc., 832 F.2d 430, 433 (7th Cir. 1987).

Page 443, add to cases cited in note 37:

Thomas v. Cooper Industries, Inc., 640 F. Supp. 1374, 1379-80 (W.D.N.C. 1986) (Title VII suit); Dotson v. City of Indianola, 639 F. Supp. 1056, 1062 (N.D. Miss. 1986) (both allowing fees for work of separately-retained attorney on primary attorneys' fee request). *But cf.* Mares v. Credit Bureau of Raton, 801 F.2d 1197, 1206-07 (10th Cir. 1986) (finding that compensation for outside attorney's work on primary attorneys' fee request was not authorized under Truth-in-Lending Act, 15 U.S.C. § 1640(a) (3), Fair Credit Reporting Act, 15 U.S.C. §§ 1681n, 1681o, and Fair Debt Collection Practices Act, 15 U.S.C. § 1692k(a)).

Page 443, add to cases cited in note 38:

Rogers v. Okin, 821 F.2d 22, 30 & n.4 (1st Cir. 1987), *cert. denied,* 108 S. Ct. 709 (1988) (complex and hotly disputed fee issue warranted "engagement of specially retained fee counsel"); Alberti v. Sheriff of Harris County, 688 F. Supp. 1176, 1201 (S.D. Tex. 1987) (approving retention of special counsel to litigate plaintiffs' fee request in view of the "apparent potential for conflict of interest due to the pendency of substantial 'merits' issues" still to be litigated by plaintiffs' primary counsel); Garmong v. Montgomery County, 668 F. Supp. 1000, 1011-12 (S.D. Tex. 1987) (the "sensitive nature of the fee claim in light of unsuccessful negotiations" between plaintiff's counsel and defendant); Thomas v. Cooper Industries, Inc., 640 F. Supp. 1374, 1379-80 (W.D.N.C. 1986) (participation of outside attorney on Title VII fee request was warranted when "defendants decided to play 'hard ball' over fees").

Page 443, add at end of full paragraph:

While approving the engagement of "specially retained fee counsel" in "this unusual case," the First Circuit stated that "such a practice is inherently wasteful in many respects and should not be encouraged by the district courts in the absence of good cause." *Rogers v. Okin,* 821 F.2d 22, 30 & n.4 (1st Cir. 1987), *cert. denied,* 108 S. Ct. 709 (1988).

Page 443, add to note 40:

Cf. Rogers v. Okin, 821 F.2d 22, 30 (1st Cir. 1987), *cert. denied,* 108 S. Ct. 709 (1988) (reducing by 20% time claimed by plaintiffs' primary counsel on the fee litigation, when they spent "considerable time" reconstructing their time records and briefing the specially retained fee counsel and the fee requests included some duplicative and non-compensable effort "stemming from the ambiguity created when counsel become clients").

Page 444, add to note 41:

Cf. Ramos v. Lamm, 632 F. Supp. 376, 384 (D. Colo. 1986) (granting compensation only for attorneys who pursued the fee application and "not for all of the attorneys who are only acting as clients").

§ 17.12 The Fee Applicant's Burden of Proof

Page 444, add to note 45:

Mares v. Credit Bureau of Raton, 801 F.2d 1197, 1210 (10th Cir. 1986) (Consumer Credit Protection Act, 15 U.S.C. §§ 1601 *et seq.;* "Our instructions to district courts regarding their evaluation of tasks, hours, rates, and other matters, were never meant to cause a subtle shift in the burden of proof from counsel to court . . . . It remains counsel's burden to prove and establish the reasonableness of each dollar, each hour, above zero.").

§ 17.13 The Fee Applicant's Demonstration of Billing Judgment

Page 446, update two Palmer citations and add to cases cited in note 54:

Wagenmann v. Adams, 829 F.2d 196, 224-25 (1st Cir. 1987); Rogers v. Okin, 821 F.2d 22, 29 (1st Cir. 1987), *cert. denied,* 108 S. Ct. 709 (1988); Cooper v. Dyke,

814 F.2d 941, 950 (4th Cir. 1987) (all approving the exercise of sensible billing judgment by plaintiffs' counsel in voluntarily eliminating substantial hours from fee application that were excessive or expended on discrete unsuccessful claims); Palmer v. Shultz, *vacated & remanded on other grounds,* 478 U.S. 1015 (1986); Palmer v. City of Chicago, *rev'd on other grounds,* 806 F.2d 1316 (7th Cir. 1986); McKenzie v. Kennickell, 645 F. Supp. 437, 448-49 & n.16 (D.D.C. 1986) (Title VII suit; court generally finds reasonable the voluntary reduction of hours claimed by plaintiff's law firm counsel by 9.6 percent "in the exercise of billing judgment," although noting that counsel "does not specify which of the recorded hours have been dropped"; with respect to other attorneys for plaintiffs, court "accepts the sworn statements of these highly respected attorneys" that they "exercised billing judgment *prior* to recording their time in the proceeding," and notes that no compensation was sought for law student time); Ramos v. Lamm, 632 F. Supp. 376, 382 & nn.4,5 (D. Colo. 1986) (court generally found that time expended was reasonable, when plaintiffs' attorneys exercised "conservative and sound billing judgment" in reporting but not charging for "numerous hours which could have been included" and in "not bill[ing] defendants for time spent orienting junior lawyers, legal assistants, or law clerks" or for the "startup" time of those personnel); York v. Alabama State Bd. of Educ., 631 F. Supp. 78, 84 (M.D. Ala. 1986) (court stated that testimony that "counsel has not claimed all hours spent on this litigation and that an effort was made to bill only reasonable hours" contributed "to its conclusion that the claimed hours are reasonable"); Doss v. Long, 624 F. Supp. 1078, 1081 (N.D. Ga. 1985) (in finding claimed hours to be reasonable, court noted that plaintiffs' counsel "have not requested the total number of attorney hours spent on the case," and excluded law student and paralegal time and some of time spent on administrative functions). As the *McKenzie* decision in particular indicates, the credibility of counsel's elimination of excessive or duplicative hours from the fee request is enhanced if the discarded time is recorded and specifically indentified in the fee application. *Cf.* Orshan v. Macchiarola, 629 F. Supp. 1014, 1020 & n.4 (E.D.N.Y. 1986) (in imposing 20 percent reduction on portion of requested time, court noted that although counsel's claimed action in eliminating hours spent on an unsuccessful issue is "commendable," he "does not explain exactly how much he eliminated from his request for this issue"). See also **§ 17.14.**

Page 447, add to note 55:

Leroy v. City of Houston, 831 F.2d 576, 585 n.15 (5th Cir. 1987); N.A.A.C.P. v. City of Evergreen, 812 F.2d 1332, 1337 (11th Cir. 1987) (both criticizing plaintiffs' counsel for failing to delete from their fee requests, in the exercise of billing judgment, hours that were unsupported by adequate time records or were expended on discrete unsuccessful claims).

Page 447, add to cases cited in note 56:

Hart v. Bourque, 798 F.2d 519, 521-23 (1st Cir. 1986) (finding district court's awarding of compensation for 610 hours of claimed time to be unsupportable, particularly since counsel's contention that the fee request reflected "restraint" and "self-imposed economies" was belied by inappropriately claimed time for proofreading, delivery of papers, travel arrangements, and giving a law school lecture).

§ 17.14 The Importance of Adequate and Contemporaneous Time Records

Page 447, add to note 58:

The contemporaneous time records may be maintained on handwritten time sheets or slips or by direct entry into a computer that generates the records on computer printouts. *See* Garmong v. Montgomery County, 668 F. Supp. 1000, 1004 (S.D. Tex. 1987); Lenihan v. City of New York, 640 F. Supp. 822, 824 (S.D.N.Y. 1986) ("The Court routinely receives computerized transcriptions of contemporaneous time records from firms whose billing records are maintained in computers."); Ackerman v. Western Elec. Co., Inc., 643 F. Supp. 836, 864 (N.D. Cal. 1986) (state fee statute) (characterizing as "largely incomprehensible to the uninitiated outsider" the nonstandardized time records of plaintiff's attorney that were maintained in his day calendars and contained references not only to this case but as well to his "other professional and personal activities").

Page 448, add to note 61:

While minute-by-minute entries need not be made, the integrity of "contemporaneous" time records may be subject to question if entries are substantially rounded off, e.g., to the nearest quarter hour. *See* ECOS, Inc. v. Brinegar, 671 F. Supp. 381, 395-96 (M.D.N.C. 1987). The contemporaneous time records should closely track the time actually spent by attorneys for each entry made. Time records that are detailed to the tenth of the hour are satisfactory (Moore v. District of Columbia, 674 F. Supp. 901, 905 (D.D.C. 1987)), and entries to the nearest five minutes should be acceptable.

Page 448, add to cases cited in note 62:

Daly v. Hill, 790 F.2d 1071, 1079 & n.12 (4th Cir. 1986) (finding that counsel's time records which failed to "specify the substance or purpose of each conference" for which fee compensation was sought "do not illuminate the way in which the many hours of client conferences may have aided Street's preparation of the case"); Keith v. Volpe, 644 F. Supp. 1317, 1323-24 (C.D. Cal. 1986) (Fair Housing Act, 42 U.S.C. § 3612(c); finding inadequate "vague entries such as 'Hawthorne lawsuit,' 'Hawthorne,' 'Hawthorne documents,' and 'legal research,' " as well as the entry "conference," where "a 'conference' can legitimately cover everything from two people proofreading a document aloud to supervisory conferences between senior and junior attorneys to unavoidable strategy discussions involving all staff who have worked on the litigation"); Orshan v. Macchiarola, 629 F. Supp. 1014, 1019 (E.D.N.Y. 1986) (criticizing entries such as "review correspondence" and "prepare correspondence" which did not identify the nature of the correspondence"). *But see* Lenihan v. City of New York, 640 F. Supp. 822, 826 (S.D.N.Y. 1986) (finding that counsel's time entries, although lacking in detail, "are not so vague that the Court is unable to assess their reasonableness," when an "entry for 'general preparation' is followed immediately by an entry the next day for the preliminary injunction hearing," and "entries which read merely 'preparation,' 'preparation for trial,' and 'preparation for cross' are followed by entries for the trial").

Page 448, add to note 64:

Keith v. Volpe, 644 F. Supp. 1317, 1322 (C.D. Cal. 1986), and 644 F. Supp. 1312, 1315 (C.D. Cal. 1986) (Fair Housing Act, 42 U.S.C. § 3612(c); criticizing counsel's practice of "serial billing" by which "one time block entry will cover several related, but discrete activities making disaggregation of claimed time into various activities essentially an impossible task," or which "lumps together as a single claimed item of compensable time all work performed in the same week on the same billable matter"). The grouping of several distinct activities under the same time entry leaves the court with the "choice of estimating a portion of the time for a particular activity, or excluding the entire entry," with the court likely to opt for the second approach. *See* Claus by Claus v. Goshert, 657 F. Supp. 237, 244 (N.D. Ind. 1987).

Page 449, add to note 66:

Vaughns v. Board of Educ., 627 F. Supp. 837, 841-42 & n.5 (D. Md. 1985) (noting the "problem of identifying time spent on certain issues," in a multi-issue case, from counsel's time records which refer to activities such as "legal research" and "conference" without indicating the specific issue).

Page 449, add to note 69:

District of Columbia Circuit: Kennecott Corp. v. E.P.A., 804 F.2d 763, 766-67 (D.C. Cir. 1986) (Clean Air Act, 42 U.S.C. § 7607(f); imposing 15 percent reduction on fee award for petitioners' refusal to provide the contemporaneous time records on which their work summaries were based, and rejecting contention that "less exacting scrutiny" under the contemporaneous time record requirement of the District of Columbia Court of Appeals should be given to fee requests which "were originally submitted to a private client").

First Circuit: Rogers v. Okin, 821 F.2d 22, 29 (1st Cir. 1987), *cert. denied,* 108 S. Ct. 709 (1988) (reliability of reconstructed time records of plaintiffs' attorneys for period prior to First Circuit's requirement of contemporaneous time records); Calhoun v. Acme Cleveland Corp., 801 F.2d 558, 560-61 (1st Cir. 1986) (declining to "disallow the fees entirely nor drastically reduce them" for fee applicant's failure to submit detailed contemporaneous time records for services rendered prior to First Circuit's *Grendel's Den* decision, and instead directing district court on remand to "scrutinize carefully the hours claimed" in absence of contemporaneous time records).

Second Circuit: Soliman v. Ebasco Servs. Inc., 822 F.2d 320, 323 (2d Cir. 1987) (noting that since 1983 contemporaneous time records "have in this Circuit been a prerequisite to obtaining any court-ordered attorney's fees"); Lewis v. Coughlin, 801 F.2d 570, 577 (2d Cir. 1986) (reiterating Second Circuit rule that fee applicant's failure to maintain contemporaneous time records subsequent to issuance of *New York State Ass'n for Retarded Children* decision requires denial of fee request, and that such failure prior to that decision is properly met by denial of fees for time spent on the fee application). As discussed in **§ 17.15** of this supplement, the Second Circuit in *Lewis* announced the additional requirement that the fee applicant's contemporaneous time records must accompany the initial fee petition.

Fourth Circuit: Yohay v. City of Alexandria Employees Credit Union, 827 F.2d 967, 974 (4th Cir. 1987) (counsel's failure to submit contemporaneous time records "did not require the district court to deny an award of fees entirely if there was an adequate reconstruction of time spent on this litigation").

Fifth Circuit: *In re* Lawler, 807 F.2d 1207, 1212 (5th Cir. 1987) ("This Court has specifically rejected the . . . rule that contemporaneous, complete, and standardized time records must be kept and produced before any fee awards will be allowed."); Gipson v. Rosenberg, 797 F.2d 224, 226 (5th Cir. 1986) (noting local Fifth Circuit rule requiring maintenance of contemporaneous time records in support of appellate fee requests); Dennis v. Warren, 779 F.2d 245, 249 & n.5 (5th Cir. 1985) (noting that Fifth Circuit has "not held that contemporaneous time sheets are indispensable," but not deciding question whether local Fifth Circuit rule requiring maintenance of contemporaneous time records for appellate fee requests applies to district court
* proceedings); *cf.* Alberti v. Sheriff of Harris County, 688 F. Supp. 1176, 1184-85 (S.D. Tex. 1987) (applying Fifth Circuit local rule generally requiring maintenance of contemporaneous time records in order for plaintiff to obtain more than a minimum statutory fee award).

Seventh Circuit: Lightfoot v. Walker, 826 F.2d 516, 522 n.7 (7th Cir. 1987) (while noting that "contemporaneous time records are generally required," court approved reconstruction of hours for time expended prior to enactment of § 1988).

* *Eighth Circuit:* MacDissi v. Valmont Indus., 856 F.2d 1054, 1061 (8th Cir. 1988) (rejecting per se rule requiring automatic denial of statutory fee awards for counsel's failure to maintain contemporaneous time records, and leaving to district court's discretion the question of adequacy of reconstructed records).

Page 449, add to cases cited in note 71:

Kennecott Corp. v. E.P.A., 804 F.2d 763, 767 (D.C. Cir. 1986) (Clean Air Act, 42 U.S.C. § 7607(f); imposing 15 percent reduction in fee award because of petitioners' refusal to provide contemporaneous time records underlying fee request); *cf.* Leroy v. City of Houston, 831 F.2d 576, 585-86 & n.16 (5th Cir. 1987) (13% reduction of counsel's average hourly rate because of reconstructed and incomplete time records).

Page 449, add to cases cited in note 72:

Zabkowicz v. West Bend Co., 789 F.2d 540, 549-50 (7th Cir. 1986) (finding that the "records kept by counsel in this case were not so wholly inadequate or inaccurate as to make a total denial of fees appropriate").

§ 17.15 The Fee Applicant's Documentary and Evidentiary Support for the Claimed Hours

Page 450, add to cases cited in note 74:

Calhoun v. Acme Cleveland Corp., 801 F.2d 558, 560 (1st Cir. 1986) (concluding that district court should reject attorney's work summaries that are inadequate, because they "do not give the dates when the different tasks were performed, nor is the amount of time spent on each task specified"); Keith v. Volpe, 644 F. Supp. 1312, 1315 (C.D. Cal. 1986) (suggesting that plaintiffs' attorneys "discontinue their present practice of serial billing" and submit fee application that states "*for each person* for whom fees are claimed, the *subject matter of the claim . . . broken down by activity category*"); Tuggle v. Barksdale, 641 F. Supp. 34, 40 (W.D. Tenn. 1985) (refusing to award fees on basis of a "general and conclusory allegation" of amount earned and directing filing of "itemized time schedules").

Page 451, add to cases cited in note 75:

Gregis v. Edberg, 645 F. Supp. 1153, 1162 (W.D. Pa. 1986); Bovey v. City of Lafayette, 638 F. Supp. 640, 646 (N.D. Ind. 1986); Goetz v. Ricketts, 632 F. Supp. 926, 930 (D. Colo. 1986) (all criticizing "serial billing" in fee applicant's work summaries that include several different activities within the same time entry). See also § **17.14** n.64.

Page 451, add to cases cited in note 76:

Tomazzoli v. Sheedy, 804 F.2d 93, 97-98 (7th Cir. 1986) (criticizing work summaries in which entries included vague or overly general descriptions of services rendered). See also § **17.14** nn.62, 63.

Page 451, add the following cases to note 77:

Diver v. Goddard Memorial Hosp., 783 F.2d 6, 8 (1st Cir. 1986) (in affirming district court's allowance of only a nominal fee award, court of appeals noted that fee applicant's records failed to demonstrate allocation of time between successful and unrelated unsuccessful claims); Bovey v. City of Lafayette, 638 F. Supp. 640, 643 (N.D. Ind. 1986) (court noted that inadequate documentation made it difficult to allocate time between the instant case and other related cases for which fees were not available). On the other hand, in City of Riverside v. Rivera, 477 U.S. 561, 569 n.4 (1986) (plurality opinion), the Supreme Court concluded that the respondent fee applicant's "lapse" in failing to identify in his time records the "precise claims worked on at the time" was "unimportant, in light of the District Court's finding that all of respondents' claims were interrelated."

Page 451, update Delaware Valley citation and add the following cases to note 78:

Delaware Valley, 478 U.S. 546, 549 (1986); Norman v. Housing Auth. of Montgomery, 836 F.2d 1292, 1303 (11th Cir. 1988) (a "well-prepared fee petition also would include a summary, grouping the time entries by the nature of the activity or stage of the case"); Brewster v. Dukakis, 786 F.2d 16, 17 (1st Cir. 1986) (entries in lengthy fee application were "coded to identify six different kinds of work"); Ramos v. Lamm, 632 F. Supp. 376, 381 (D. Colo. 1986) (separate fee applications submitted for seven phases of multi-year litigation).

Page 451, delete sentence ending with note 80 reference and substitute the following at beginning of paragraph:

In *Lewis v. Coughlin,* 801 F.2d 570, 577 (2d Cir. 1986), the Second Circuit announced the rule that the contemporaneous time records that are required to be maintained must be included with the initial fee application. *Lewis* does not clarify whether a verbatim typewritten transcription of contemporaneous time sheets, instead of the original handwritten records, can be submitted with the fee application. *Cf.* Lenihan v. City of New York, 640 F. Supp. 822, 824 (S.D.N.Y. 1986) (pre-*Lewis* decision holding that plaintiff's attorneys satisfied Second Circuit's contemporaneous time records requirement by submitting typewritten transcription of the original, handwritten time sheets). Failure to comply with the *Lewis* requirement warrants the denial of any compensation for work done in preparing the fee application. *Id.* at 572. The District of Columbia Court of Appeals has articulated the same rule in a less mandatory fashion, stating that "contemporaneous time charges should be filed with the motion for attorneys' fees as a matter of course, and certainly should be provided once legitimate questions are raised by the opposing party." *Kennecott Corp. v. E.P.A.*, 804 F.2d 763, 767 (D.C. Cir. 1986). Other courts have held that the time records upon which the fee applicant's work summaries are based need not accompany the initial fee motion, but should be available to be supplied to the opposing party in discovery or at the request of the court.[80]

Page 451, delete Nat'l Ass'n of Concerned Veterans and Lyons citations from note 80 and add the following cases:

MGIC Indem. Corp. v. Weisman, 803 F.2d 500, 505 (9th Cir. 1986) (defendant Rule 11 fees; finding no reason why fee applicant's time sheets should not have been made available to fee opponent, with opportunity to challenge them); Dennis v. Warren, 779 F.2d 245, 249 & n.5 (5th Cir. 1985) (local court of appeals rule requiring that contemporaneous time records be made available for inspection by opposing counsel and by the court in the event that an issue arises concerning reasonableness of claimed hours); Moore v. District of Columbia, 674 F. Supp. 901, 904-05 (D.D.C. 1987) (Education of the Handicapped Act, 20 U.S.C. § 1415; approving defendants' request that plaintiffs' counsel provide them with the "underlying time charge-slips which were aggregated to form the computer print-outs which collect and detail the individual time-charges into one document" but refusing defendants' request for actual bills submitted to plaintiffs, because they would provide no additional relevant information).

Page 451, update Palmer citation in note 82:

478 U.S. 1015 (1986).

Page 452, add to cases cited in note 83:

Mares v. Credit Bureau of Raton, 801 F.2d 1197, 1205 (10th Cir. 1986) (Consumer Credit Protection Act, 15 U.S.C. §§ 1601 *et seq.;* noting disapprovingly that plaintiffs' primary attorney "neither filed an affidavit, nor offered any witnesses in support of the reasonableness of the time spent in preparation of plaintiffs' case"); *cf.* Calhoun v. Acme Cleveland Corp., 801 F.2d 558, 559-60 (1st Cir. 1986) (while noting that the "better practice is for each attorney filing a statement of services performed to warrant by affidavit that the submission is true and correct," court found that the absence of such affidavits in the instant case was not "fatal" because signature of plaintiff's chief counsel on the fee request "amounts to a representation that the submissions are true").

Page 452, add following sentence ending with note 86 reference:

In some jurisdictions local court rules prescribe the required documentary support for an attorney's fee request. *See Gipson v. Rosenberg,* 797 F.2d 224, 226 (5th Cir. 1986); *Dennis v. Warren,* 779 F.2d 245, 249 & n.5 (5th Cir. 1985) (Fifth Circuit rule).

Page 453, add to cases cited in note 88:

Mares v. Credit Bureau of Raton, 801 F.2d 1197, 1205 & n.15 (10th Cir. 1986) (Consumer Credit Protection Act, 15 U.S.C. §§ 1601 *et seq.;* noting failure of plaintiffs' attorney to offer "any witnesses in support of the reasonableness of the time spent in preparation of plaintiffs' case," court stated "[o]f course, the district court is not required to accept such testimony; but a credible, properly prepared witness on the subject of reasonable time or fees can provide valuable assistance").

§ 17.16 Permissible Discovery Concerning the Reasonableness of Claimed Hours

Pages 453-54, add to cases cited in note 89:

But see Hernandez v. George, 793 F.2d 264, 268 (10th Cir. 1986) (finding no abuse of discretion in district court's denial of plaintiffs' motion to compel disclosure of hours expended on case by defendants' counsel, based on finding that "under the circumstances of this case, the fees and hours of defendants' counsel were not relevant [to plaintiffs' fee request] because defendants' counsel were required to spend unnecessary time and effort due to lack of diligent prosecution on the part of plaintiffs' counsel in the early stages of the case"). See also cases cited in **§ 17.3** of this supplement.

Page 454, add the following to note 90:

Brewster v. Dukakis, 786 F.2d 16, 21-22 (1st Cir. 1986) (concluding that district court should have permitted defendants "at least a limited discovery" to determine whether some of time expended on institutional reform litigation by plaintiffs' attorneys, while under a retainer agreement with an association of state funded contractors, was noncompensable because spent "solely or principally in pursuit of Association purposes that were not coterminous with those of the plaintiff class"); Keith v. Volpe, 643 F. Supp. 37, 43 (C.D. Cal. 1985) (defendant's discovery eliciting "further breakdown of hours per task" in plaintiffs' fee request); *cf.* Lewis v. Coughlin, 801 F.2d 570, 577-78 (2d Cir. 1986) (reversing district court's reduction of allowable hours of plaintiff's counsel to compensate defendant for the expense of making a premature preclusion motion for plaintiff's failure to respond to notice for production of his counsel's contemporaneous time records).

Page 454, add the following cases to note 92:

Stewart v. County of Sonoma, 634 F. Supp. 773, 776 (N.D. Cal. 1986) (denying defendants' request for further discovery, since parties "have amassed an abundant record on this application" and court was thoroughly familiar with the case); E.E.O.C. v. Sears, Roebuck and Co., 111 F.R.D. 385, 388-91 (N.D. Ill. 1986) (defendant Title VII fees; limiting fee applicant's discovery request because (1) the information already in the record was sufficient to determine the fee issue, (2) much of the discovery request related to privileged information concerning the plaintiff's internal decision-making processes, and (3) some of the request was "overly burdensome or insufficiently relevant"); Mitroff v. Xomox Corp., 631 F. Supp. 25, 27 (S.D. Ohio 1985) (Age Discrimination in Employment Act, 29 U.S.C. § 626(b); allowing plaintiff discovery of hours expended by defendant's counsel in the case, but not permitting inquiry into "the nature of any communication by defense counsel with defendant" or into "any documents involved in other representation of defendant by defense counsel"). In Real v. Continental Group, Inc., 166 F.R.D. 211 (N.D. Cal. 1986), the court granted the plaintiff fee applicant's discovery requests for information concerning the "hours expended by the defendant on matters pertaining to this case, counsel's hourly rates, as well as total billings and costs," as "at least minimally relevant" to the fee petition. *Id.* at 213. But the court found that the "attorney-client privilege embraces attorney time records and statements to the extent that they reveal litigation strategy and the nature of the services provided." *Id.* at 213. Accordingly, the court denied plaintiff discovery of defendant's counsel's fee statements and billing computer printouts containing "highly detailed itemizations of all work performed," that "would necessarily reveal the nature of legal services provided." *Id.* at 214. However, a "simple invoice requesting payment for unspecified services rendered reveals nothing more than the amount of the fee and would not normally be privileged." *Id.*

Page 454, add the following case to note 93:

* Sablan v. Dep't of Finance, 856 F.2d 1317, 1321-22 (9th Cir. 1988) (finding that defendant could not object on appeal to district court's denial of a continuance to pursue discovery relating to the amount of fees sought by plaintiff, when defendant did not contest on appeal the amount of fees awarded); Martinez v. Schock Transfer & Warehouse Co., Inc., 789 F.2d 848, 849-50 (10th Cir. 1986) (finding no abuse of discretion in district court's denial of all discovery on fee issue, on finding that " 'further discovery would not be of any substantial assistance in resolving this issue' ").

§ 17.17 The Opposing Party's Burden of Rebuttal

Page 454, add to note 95:

The Eleventh Circuit has observed that the opposing party's failure to present evidentiary opposition to the fee application deprives the district court of "factual evidence to guide the court regarding the amount of fee or enhancement that would be reasonable, . . . as well as the clarification of issues that is a valuable part of our adversarial system." N.A.A.C.P. v. City of Evergreen, 812 F.2d 1332, 1338 (11th Cir. 1987).

Page 455, add to note 98:

For a discussion of the relevance of such evidence, see also § **17.3** in this supplement and cases cited therein.

Page 455, update Cunningham citation in note 1:

vacated & remanded on other grounds, 478 U.S. 1015 (1986), *reinstated,* 807 F.2d 49 (3d Cir. 1986), *cert. denied,* 107 S. Ct. 2179 (1987).

Page 455, add to cases cited in note 3:

Brewster v. Dukakis, 786 F.2d 16, 19 (1st Cir. 1986) (defendants, in opposing compensation for all hours claimed, "could have mounted challenges to specific claims – if not on a comprehensive basis, at least on a random one;" while "a specific challenge to every item in a 3500-item catalogue of time charges would be impracticable,. . . it is not too much to expect the Commonwealth, relying on its deep involvement in the litigation, to target significant and vulnerable areas for testing"); *cf.* Trahan v. Regan, 625 F. Supp. 1163, 1168 (D.D.C. 1985) (Equal Access to Justice Act, 28 U.S.C. § 2412; noting that government defendant "is *required* to make specific objections [to claimed hours] if it hopes to mount a successful challenge to a fee application," and that what "the applicants criticize as 'nit-picking' is no more than the government's effort to comply with the requirements of governing case law"). However, in Vaughns v. Board of Educ., 627 F. Supp. 837, 841 (D. Md. 1985), the court approved defendants' argument that was limited to the "*per se* unreasonableness" of plaintiffs' requested hours, considering it "almost impossible for defendants to be more specific since many of the time entries of plaintiffs' counsel are very general"). Of course, the defendant's failure altogether to timely object to the amount or allocation of hours claimed by plaintiff's counsel may result in the complete waiver of any objection. *See, e.g.,* In re Burlington Northern, Inc., 810 F.2d 601, 610-11 (7th Cir. 1986) (defendant union waived arguments concerning proper allocation of Title VII fee award by making arguments for first time in postjudgment Rule 59(e) motion).

Page 455, add to note 4:

In Rogers v. Okin, 821 F.2d 22, 28-30 (1st Cir. 1987), *cert. denied,* 108 S. Ct. 709 (1988), the court condemned the state defendants' excessive opposition to the fee request, that made no attempt to "prioritize" the issues presented and amounted to an "indiscriminate targeting of manifold alleged errors," with the "cumulative result" of placing a "palpable strain on our credulity." The court stated that the "realities of fee award reviews compel those who would object to such awards on appeal on the basis of time spent to select priority targets and marshal the facts as effectively as possible." *Id.* at 30. The Seventh Circuit has been particularly vocal in condemning defendant excesses in opposing statutory fee requests. Max M. v. New Trier High School Dist., 859 F.2d 1297, 1301, 1302 (7th Cir. 1988) (criticizing "yield-no-quarter strategy" pursued by defendant on fee appeal, noting that defendant's "dogged opposition to the demand for fees surely has cost more" than the fee awarded); Kurowski v. Krajewski, 848 F.2d 767, 777 (7th Cir. 1988) (urging state attorney general to "abjure the buckshot approach" to appellate fee litigation, noting that "[n]iggling objections" such as those raised by defendant's counsel, "simply increase the ultimate bill and waste judicial time"); Lenard v. Argento, 808 F.2d 1242, 1248 (7th Cir. 1987) (ordering defendants on remand "to interpose no more frivolous objections to Lenard's fee request, on pain of sanctions if they do").

Page 456, add the following case to note 6:

Toussaint v. McCarthy, 826 F.2d 901, 904 (9th Cir. 1987) (approving plaintiffs' requested lodestar fee for appellate work that "may appear to be high," noting that "defendant has not come forward with affidavits contesting the reasonableness of the rates or hours expended"); Brinker v. Guiffrida, 798 F.2d 661, 668 (3d Cir. 1986) (Equal Access to Justice Act, 28 U.S.C. § 2412; reaffirming the principle stated in *Cunningham* in the text, court of appeals directed district court on remand to make a determination of reasonable hours on the basis of the record before it where defendant had failed to submit opposing affidavits, made no request to cross-examine the fee applicant with respect to his affidavit, and merely argued in his brief that the claimed hours were excessive and duplicative).

Page 456, add to note 7:

The court concluded in Cunningham v. City of McKeesport, 807 F.2d 49, 52 (3d Cir. 1986), *cert. denied,* 107 S. Ct. 2179 (1987), that "[i]n the absence of any factual claims by defendants, the only reduction the court could properly order concerned hours about which the district judge had personal knowledge, namely, hours claimed for work at pretrial conferences and at trial."

Page 456, update Palmer citation and add to cases cited in note 8:

Palmer, 478 U.S. 1015 (1986); Leroy v. City of Houston, 831 F.2d 576, 585-86 (5th Cir. 1987) (rejecting district court's "misplaced" rationale for "wholesale acceptance" of plaintiffs' inadequately documented time, that the defendant had interposed no serious objection to the claimed hours); Curtis v. Bill Hanna Ford, Inc., 822 F.2d 549, 551 (5th Cir. 1987) ("The defendant's silence on the motion for fees cannot be equated with consent. Instead of increasing their financial burden by continued opposition, defendants may rely on the court's exercise of sound judgment as to what is reasonable. The district court may, consistent with the statute, examine the reasonableness of the fees requested, even when the request is not opposed."); Jordan v. Multnomah County, 815 F.2d 1258, 1263 n.8 (9th Cir. 1987) (district court should not "uncritically accept counsel's representations concerning the time expended"); N.A.A.C.P. v. City of Evergreen, 812 F.2d 1332, 1334 (11th Cir. 1987) ("district court does not abuse its discretion simply by reducing the amount of an unopposed fee award," because court "does not have to accept uncontradicted evidence if there is a reason for rejecting it"); Zabkowicz v. West Bend Co., 789 F.2d 540, 548-49 n.8 (7th Cir. 1986) (Title VII; court rejected plaintiff-appellant's argument that district court should not have inquired into the accuracy of her fee request because defendants failed to submit evidence challenging reasonableness of claimed hours, noting that defendant did not waive her objection to the fee request in the district court and that the district court "should award fees only to the extent the applicant establishes that the fees requested are reasonable").

CHAPTER 18

DETERMINING THE REASONABLENESS OF HOURLY RATES

§ 18.1 *Blum v. Stenson:* The Market-Value Standard

Page 460, add to note 1:

As the Eleventh Circuit has noted, the consequence of application of market-value standards to services rendered by nonprofit counsel is that a "federally funded Legal Services Corporation lawyer with the same credentials as a lawyer with a lucrative private practice is awarded the same fee under section 1988." Duncan v. Poythress, 777 F.2d 1508, 1514 (11th Cir. 1985)(en banc). The market-value standard applies as well to salaried government attorneys seeking § 1988 fees for successful representation of governmental parties in civil rights suits. *See* Hamilton v. Daley, 777 F.2d 1207, 1213 (7th Cir. 1985); Coleman v. McLaren, 635 F. Supp. 266, 267-68 (N.D. Ill. 1986)(both involving prevailing governmental defendants).

Page 460, add to note 2:

Consistent with *Stenson,* courts have rejected the applicability of a cost-based approach to the setting of appropriate hourly rates under fee-shifting statutes for law school professors with low office overhead. Coulter v. Tennessee, 805 F.2d 146, 149-50 (6th Cir. 1986), and for salaried in-house counsel, Zacharias v. Shell Oil Co., 627 F. Supp. 31, 34 (E.D.N.Y. 1984)(defendant fee award under Petroleum Marketing Practices Act, 15 U.S.C. § 2805(d)(3)). However, in the context of the Equal Access to Justice Act, 28 U.S.C. § 2412, some courts have concluded that a "nonprofit union whose charter goes beyond providing legal services and thus whose fees would inure to the benefit of a nonlegal organization is entitled to recover only its costs of litigation – overhead expenses and the costs of its attorneys." Devine v. National Treasury Employees Union, 805 F.2d 384, 389 (Fed. Cir. 1986)(distinguishing case from one in which fees are awarded directly to the attorneys, and not the union, and from one in which § 1988 fees are awarded to a nonprofit legal services organization); National Treasury Employees Union v. Department of Treasury, 656 F.2d 848 (D.C. Cir. 1981). On the other hand, the court in Curran v. Department of Treasury, 805 F.2d 1406 (9th Cir. 1986), held that there is no ethical barrier to statutory fee compensation at full market rates when the nonprofit union establishes a separate litigation fund used solely by lawyers for litigation purposes. *Id.* In that case there is "no fee splitting with a lay entity and no encouragement of the unauthorized practice of law" by a lay organization. *Id.* at 1409.

Page 460, add to note 4:

In Pennsylvania v. Delaware Valley Citizens' Council, 478 U.S. 546, 565 (1986), the Supreme Court stated that fee-shifting statutes, including § 1988, were not "intended to replicate exactly the fee an attorney could earn through a private fee arrangement with a client." The Third Circuit observed that "[a]ttorneys are not fungible" in concluding that one attorney's experience relative to another attorney's experience was "not determinative of his billing rate; rather the question is what rate . . . [the attorney] commanded in the marketplace." Black Grievance Comm. v. Philadelphia Elec. Co., 802 F.2d 648, 652 (3d Cir. 1986). In Miele v. New York State Teamsters Conference Pension & Retirement Fund, 831 F.2d 407, 409 (2d Cir. 1987), the Second Circuit concluded that " 'the lawyers of reasonably comparable skill, experience, and reputation' " referred to in *Stenson* are "those of the private bar," so that the market rates awarded to nonprofit firms must be based on the "rates charged to clients of private law firms." Otherwise, the court concluded, "the concept of 'prevailing market rates' would mean less for legal services organizations than for law firms, a position the Supreme Court has rejected." *Id.* at 409.

§ 18.2 The Standards and Proof Requirements of *Blum v. Stenson*

Page 461, add at end of first paragraph:

The Eleventh Circuit, in *Norman v. Housing Authority of Montgomery,* 836 F.2d 1292 (11th Cir. 1988), noted that, in establishing prevailing market rates for the services of nonprofit firms, the district court is "seldom presented with one figure as a prevailing market rate," and that "[m]ore typically, the fee applicant asks for rates approximating the highest charged in the community, whereas the fee opponent generally submits evidence of the lowest rate charged in any part of the community." *Id.* at 1300. The court urged the parties to provide the court with a "range of market rates for lawyers of different skill levels (perhaps as measured by quality and quantity of experience) involved in similar cases with similar clients, so that the court may interpolate the prevailing market rate based on an assessment of the skill demonstrated in the case at bar." *Id.* The court described "legal skill" as a "several faceted concept" that may be but is not necessarily a "function of experience" and incorporates elements of judgment, negotiation and tactical expertise, organization and efficiency, knowledge of trial practice and substantive law, and persuasiveness. *Id.* at 1300-01. The task of the district court in a given case is "to interpolate the reasonable rate based on an analysis of the skills enumerated above which were exhibited by the attorney in the case at bar." *Id.* at 1301. The Eleventh Circuit subsequently stated that in seeking to demonstrate that the requested rates are in fact commanded by other attorneys of "comparable skill," plaintiff's attorney may submit proof bearing on "length and type of experience, education, professional accomplishment, and professional reputation" of counsel. *Perkins v. Mobile Housing Board,* 847 F.2d 735, 737 n.1 (11th Cir. 1988). Invoking the statement in *Stenson,* 465 U.S. at 898, "the special skill and experience of counsel should be reflected in the reasonableness of the hourly rates," the Eighth

Circuit in *McDonald v. Armontrout,* 860 F.2d 1456, 1459-62 (8th Cir. 1988), expressly considered the skill, experience, and reputation of plaintiff's attorneys, the results achieved in the litigation, and the "undersirability" of the case in rejecting defendants' objections to the rates awarded by the district court.

Page 461, add to note 7:

See N.A.A.C.P. v. City of Evergreen, 812 F.2d 1332, 1338 (11th Cir. 1987)(emphasizing necessity for fee applicant to provide satisfactory evidence of prevailing market rates, even when the fee request is unopposed); Denton v. Boilermakers Local 29, 673 F. Supp. 37, 55 (D. Mass. 1987)(finding that fee applicant does not discharge its obligation to provide evidence of prevailing market rates by asking court to "take judicial notice" of the rates charged by private firms, because that is not a "matter of which the court can or will take judicial notice").

Page 462, add to note 15:

See also Texas v. New Mexico, 475 U.S. 1084 (1986)(approving requested interim fee award for special master and his staff, over dissent of Chief Justice Burger, joined by Justices Blackmun and Rehnquist, objecting to insufficiency of information submitted to support requested average hourly rate of $140/hr.).

Page 462, add after last sentence in section:

See also Texas v. New Mexico, 108 S. Ct. 1212 (1988)(approving requested interim fee award for special master and his law clerk based on current rates of $290/hr. for a partner in a major law firm in Denver, Colorado, and of $200/hr. for an associate four years out of law school and with three years of practice experience). Also significant as a calibrator of reasonable market rates is the Supreme Court's affirmance in *City of Riverside v. Rivera,* 477 U.S. 561 (1986), of a § 1988 fee award based upon a rate of $125/hr. awarded in 1981 to two attorneys who were relatively inexperienced when they instituted the suit in 1976. *Id.* at 565, 569-70 (plurality opinion), 583 (Powell, J., concurring), 587 (Burger, C.J., dissenting).

§ 18.3 The Relevant Community for Rate-Setting Purposes

Page 463, update Burlington Northern citation (Seventh Circuit) and add to note 17:

Second Circuit: In re Agent Orange Prod. Liab. Litig., 818 F.2d 226, 232 (2d Cir. 1987)(stating Second Circuit rule, originating in equitable fund case, requiring use of rates prevailing in the forum district, "whether the attorney involved was local or non-local," except that non-local rates could be used "in the rare case where the 'special expertise' of non-local counsel was essential to the case, it was clearly shown that local counsel was unwilling to take the case, or other special circumstances existed").

* *Fourth Circuit:* National Wildlife Fed'n v. Hanson, 859 F.2d 313, 317-18 (4th Cir. 1988) (Clean Water Act, 33 U.S.C. § 1365(d); approving application of higher Washington, D.C. rates to work of public interest law firm from Washington, D.C., for work done in suit litigated in Raleigh, North Carolina, since plaintiff showed that local counsel would not take the case and nearest counsel with requisite expertise and willingness to take case was located in Washington, D.C.).

Fifth Circuit: Garmong v. Montgomery County, 668 F. Supp. 1000, 1007 (S.D. Tex. 1987)(applying forum district rates, rather than rates of area where non-local attorneys resided); Dotson v. City of Indianola, 639 F. Supp. 1056, 1063 (N.D. Miss. 1986)(refusing to apply higher out-of-district rates).

Seventh Circuit: Burlington Northern, *aff'd in relevant part,* 810 F.2d 601 (7th Cir. 1986); American Booksellers Ass'n, Inc. v. Hudnut, 650 F. Supp. 324, 328-30 (S.D. Ind. 1986)(applying prevailing New York City rates, where it was reasonable for plaintiffs to engage New York City firm that was expert in the First Amendment issues involved and had long-term professional relationship with plaintiffs, and services of "*equal quality* were not *readily available*" in the local Indianapolis, Indiana area; but applying local rates to work of New York City firm's law clerk and to services of other non-local counsel from Chicago).

Eighth Circuit: McDonald v. Armontrout, 860 F.2d 1456, 1459-60 n.6 (8th Cir. 1988) (in approving rates commanded by plaintiffs' counsel in St. Louis, where they ordinarily practiced, instead of lower rates prevailing in Jefferson City, where suit was litigated, court suggested that the "argument for an expansive reading of 'community' is particularly strong in a case such as this, since Jefferson City is the capitol of the state and lawyers from throughout the state have business there"); Davis v. City of Charleston, 635 F. Supp. 197, 200 (E.D. Mo. 1986)(applying lower local rate prevailing in Southeast Missouri, when St. Louis attorney made "no showing that the same result could not have been obtained by local counsel").

Page 464, add to note 18:

Orshan v. Macchiarola, 629 F. Supp. 1014, 1021 (E.D.N.Y. 1986)(finding that New Jersey rates, and not higher New York rates, should be applied to work of New Jersey practitioners in suit filed and litigated in New York); *cf.* Tomazzoli v. Sheedy, 804 F.2d 93, 99 (7th Cir. 1986)(rejecting efforts by plaintiff's attorneys from central Illinois, in suit litigated in central Illinois destrict, to obtain rates charged in the Chicago legal community, noting that "[p]laintiffs' civil rights attorneys who practice in downstate Illinois can expect smaller fees than their counterparts in Chicago").

Page 465, update Palmer citation and add to cases cited in note 22:

Palmer, *vacated & remanded,* 478 U.S. 1015 (1986); Semar v. Platte Valley Federal S & L Ass'n, 791 F.2d 699, 706 (9th Cir. 1986)(favorably citing Eleventh Circuit precedent that market rates in Truth-in-Lending Act (15 U.S.C. § 1640(a)(3)) case should be based on rates in similarly complex litigation generally and not limited to rates "'customarily charged for Truth-in-Lending cases'" in the locality). On the other hand, it is inappropriate to set market rates that "reflect premium rates charged to substantial corporate clients for mainly commercial matters" that exceed the rates for complex federal litigation of the kind involved in the case before the court. Keith v.

* Volpe, 644 F. Supp. 1312, 1316 (C.D. Cal. 1986); *see also* Searcy v. Crim, 692 F. Supp. 1363, 1365 (N.D. Ga. 1988) (suggesting that plaintiffs' attorneys, who work in small or solo practices, "are not entitled to base their fee calculations on the rates charged by large firms with high operating expenses"). For purposes of setting market rates for nonprofit firms without market-tested rates, issues naturally arise concerning what is a
* comparable case of comparable attorneys in the private market. In Perkins v. Mobile Housing Bd., 847 F.2d 735, 737-38 (11th Cir. 1988), the Eleventh Circuit ruled that the range of market rates for federal civil litigation generally is "too over-inclusive" to be relevant to setting § 1988 market rates for a civil rights case, and that the fee applicant instead must establish the market rate for "attorneys of similar skill representing similar clients" in the community. However, as the Third Circuit has observed, it is probably erroneous to assume that an "independent public interest market" exists, since in reality that market is "largely rooted in court-generated fee shifting awards." Student Pub. Interest Research Group v. AT&T Bell Laboratories, 842 F.2d 1436, 1446 (3d Cir. 1988). In Norman v. Housing Auth. of Montgomery, 836 F.2d 1292 (11th Cir. 1988), the court considered the issue of identifying proxies in the marketplace for civil rights suits brought by nonprofit firms, in order to establish prevailing market rates for those firms. The court stated that

> [m]ajor civil rights class action matters might be akin to plaintiff's class actions in antitrust and securities matters; cohorts might be found in suits brought by professional, business or neighborhood associations against government entities. Single plaintiff civil rights cases . . . find analogies in employment discrimination cases and in other disputes where the representation is not the product of an ongoing relationship between the attorney and the client.

Id. at 1300. *See also* Palmer v. Shultz, 679 F. Supp. 68, 70 (D.D.C. 1988)(observing that "the focal point of inquiry in ascertaining relevant comparable community hourly rates concerns itself with the particular fee applicant's degree of skill in handling a particular level of litigation, as opposed to the size of the fee applicant's firm").

Page 465, delete all material after sentence with note 23 reference to end of section and replace with the following:

In upholding the utilization of national hourly rates in an equitable fund case, the Second Circuit held that "in an exceptional multiparty case such as this, where dozens of non-local counsel from all parts of the country are involved, public policy and administrative concerns call for the district court to be given the necessary flexibility to impose a national hourly rate when an adequate factual basis for calculating the rate exists." *In re Agent Orange Product Liability Litigation,* 818 F.2d 226, 232 (2d Cir. 1987). The court cautioned, however, that national hourly rates should be employed "only in the exceptional case presenting problems similar to those presented here," in which "well over one hundred fee petitions were filed by counsel throughout the country." *Id.* at 233. The court further cautioned that "even in similar cases, national hourly rates should be employed only when the district court is presented with an adequate evidentiary basis on which to fix such rates." *Id. See also Lightfoot v. Walker,* 826 F.2d 516, 524 (7th Cir. 1987)(approving district court's consideration, in fixing hourly rates for plaintiff's attorney in lengthy and complex prison conditions suit, of expert testimony "as to the national rate paid to civil rights attorneys with Flynn's experience and reputation handling a case such as this," as well as testimony regarding the rate the attorney might command for a similar case in the forum district).

§ 18.4 Affidavits of Prevailing Party's Attorneys in Support of the Requested Rates

Page 467, update Burlington Northern and Daggett citations and add to note 29:

Burlington Northern, *aff'd in relevant part,* 810 F.2d 601 (7th Cir. 1986); *Daggett, aff'd in relevant part,* 811 F.2d 793 (3d Cir. 1987); *see also* Calhoun v. Acme Cleveland Corp., 801 F.2d 558, 560 (1st Cir. 1986)(emphasizing requirement that attorneys seeking fees submit "information about fees customarily charged in the locality for similar legal services and information about the experience and billing practices of the attorneys in question").

§ 18.5 A Private Firm's Customary Billing Rates as Its Market-Value Rates

Pages 467-69, update Hart (First Circuit), Cunningham, Daggett (Third Circuit), and Burlington Northern (Seventh Circuit) citations, and add to note 32:

* *First Circuit:* United States v. Metropolitan Dist. Comm'n, 847 F.2d 12, 19 (1st Cir. 1988) ("A law firm's customary schedule of charges, though entitled to consideration, is not dispositive of the issue" of reasonable rates); Hart, *rev'd and remanded on other grounds,* 798 F.2d 519 (1st Cir. 1986).

Third Circuit: Cunningham, *vacated & remanded on other grounds,* 478 U.S. 1015 (1986), *reinstated,* 807 F.2d 49 (3d Cir. 1986), *cert. denied,* 107 S. Ct. 2179 (1987); Daggett v. Kimmelmam, 811 F.2d 793, 799-800 (3d Cir. 1987)(refusing to adopt $300 hourly rate charged by attorney to his private clients, noting that there "comes a point where a lawyer's historic rate, which private clients are willing to pay, cannot be imposed on his or her adversaries"); Black Grievance Committee v. Philadelphia Elec. Co., 802 F.2d 648, 652 (3d Cir. 1986)(market-value rate is "generally reflected in the attorney's normal billing rate").

Sixth Circuit: Birth Control Centers, Inc. v. Reizen, 652 F. Supp. 192, 197-98 (E.D. Mich. 1986)(applying customary rate of plaintiffs' lead attorney).

Seventh Circuit: Burlington Northern, *aff'd in relevant part,* 810 F.2d 601 (7th Cir. 1986); Tomazzoli v. Sheedy, 804 F.2d 93, 98 (7th Cir. 1986)("best evidence" of market rate "for private counsel with fee-paying clients" is the "hourly rate customarily charged by counsel or by her law firm").

* *Eighth Circuit:* McDonald v. Armontrout, 860 F.2d 1456, 1459 (8th Cir. 1988) (reiterating Eighth Circuit rule that an attorney's ordinary billing rate "is not conclusively 'reasonable,' but should be compared to the 'ordinary fee for similar work in the community' " as a "check on the reasonableness of the attorney's customary hourly rate").

Ninth Circuit: See also Maldonado v. Lehman, 811 F.2d 1341, 1342 (9th Cir.) (rejecting District of Columbia Circuit's *Laffey* standard, that limits an attorney's reasonable rate in a statutory fee case to his customary billing rate, finding instead that while evidence of the customary rate may be considered by the district court, it may rely on prevailing rates in the community), *cert. denied sub nom.* Webb v. Maldonado, 108 S. Ct. 480 (1987). In his dissent from the denial of certiorari in *Webb,* Justice White argued that the Supreme Court should resolve the conflict between the District of Columbia and Ninth Circuits concerning the application of a private attorney's customary rate as the reasonable rate under fee-shifting statutes; Chalmers v. City of Los Angeles, 796 F.2d 1205, 1210 (9th Cir. 1986)(stating that reasonable rate is "not made by reference to rates actually charged the prevailing party"); Harris v. McCarthy, 790 F.2d 753, 758 n.6 (9th Cir. 1986)(finding that district court "was entitled to rely upon the rates charged by the law firm" representing the plaintiffs, rather than the higher market rates claimed by the lawyers).

Tenth Circuit: Lucero v. City of Trinidad, 815 F.2d 1384, 1385-86 (10th Cir. 1987) (upholding district court's reduction of requested customary rates of plaintiff's attorneys, in absence of evidence showing that these rates were in line with prevailing market rates in the community, and noting that the "customary hourly rate of a lawyer in private practice is relevant but not conclusive in determining a reasonable rate").

Page 469, add to cases cited in note 33:

District of Columbia Circuit: Lebron v. Washington Metro. Area Transit Auth., 665 F. Supp. 923, 925-26 (D.D.C. 1987)(applying customary rates of plaintiffs' attorneys, although their principal area of expertise was public utility ratemaking, whereas the instant case involved First Amendment constitutional law, when those rates were no higher than the prevailing community rates for comparable attorneys in comparable civil rights cases).

Sixth Circuit: Coulter v. State of Tennessee, 805 F.2d 146, 149 (6th Cir. 1986)(Title VII suit; stating that "a renowned lawyer who customarily receives $250 an hour in a field in which competent and experienced lawyers in the region normally receive $85 an hour should be compensated at the lower rate").

Tenth Circuit: Ramos v. Lamm, 632 F. Supp. 376, 387-88 (D. Colo. 1986)(reducing claimed customary rates for some of plaintiffs' attorneys when they appeared to exceed market rates in the Denver area, but upholding customary rates of several other experienced attorneys upon consideration of the significance and complexity of the case).

Eleventh Circuit: Mayson v. Pierce, 806 F.2d 1556, 1557-58 (11th Cir. 1987)(district court may set a reasonable market rate for attorney's services, "even if plaintiff's attorney would normally have charged a higher rate").

Page 469, add to note 34:

Student Pub. Interest Research Group v. AT&T Bell Laboratories, 842 F.2d 1436, 1448-50 (3d Cir. 1988); Lightfoot v. Walker, 826 F.2d 516, 524 (7th Cir. 1987); Lenihan v. City of New York, 640 F. Supp. 822, 828 n.3 (S.D.N.Y. 1986)(awarding market rates above the customary billing rates of plaintiff's attorneys "in civil rights practice . . .

[who] discount the price of their services because the clients they serve cannot like large corporations pay the 'going rate' "); Bygott v. Leaseway Transp. Corp., 637 F. Supp. 1433, 1445 (E.D. Pa. 1986)(declining to limit reasonable rate to rate set in fee agreement between plaintiffs and counsel, which "is obviously set at a rate which accounted for plaintiffs' limited assets and income").

Page 469, update Rivera citation and add to cases cited in note 35:

Rivera, 477 U.S. 561 (1986); Dotson v. City of Indianola, 639 F. Supp. 1056, 1060-61 (N.D. Miss. 1986)(applying hourly rate to attorney's services that was "in line with his customary billing for work which does not depend upon a contingent outcome," rather than adopting higher claimed rate that takes account of contingency). *But see* Kennecott Corp. v. E.P.A., 804 F.2d 763, 768 n.4 (D.C. Cir. 1986)(Clean Air Act, 42 U.S.C. § 7607(f); applying customary billing rates of law firm representing plaintiff, as dictated within District of Columbia by the *Laffey* decision, even though those rates reflected the firm's normal commercial rate and not the presumably lower rates charged by "environmental lawyers who regularly handle similar issues" to those presented in the instant case).

Page 470, add to note 37:

See also Kennecott Corp. v. E.P.A., 804 F.2d 763, 768 n.4 (D.C. Cir. 1986)(discussed in note 35, *supra*).

Page 471, update Palmer citation in note 43:

vacated & remanded, 478 U.S. 1015 (1986).

Page 471, add to note 44:

In McKenzie v. Kennickell, 645 F. Supp. 437, 443-45 (D.D.C. 1986), the prevailing plaintiffs were represented in their Title VII suit by attorneys from a prominent Washington, D.C. law firm, through its *pro bono* department, and also by attorneys from two public interest organizations. The court applied the law firm's customary billing rates to the work done by the firm's lawyers, over defendant's objection that "because the work was performed by the firm's Community Services department which handles *pro bono* cases, plaintiffs must show in addition that the firm's rates are what prevails in the community for Title VII work." *Id.* at 444. The court also found that the law firm's customary rates were appropriately applied in this case to the work done by the public interest attorneys, since the plaintiffs showed that the firm rates were within the range of market rates for Title VII work (even if at the high end), and the two public interest lawyers who expended the most time on the case began their work on the litigation while employed by that firm.

Page 471, add at end of section:

In *Save Our Cumberland Mountains, Inc. v. Hodel,* 826 F.2d 43, 47-49 (D.C. Cir.),
* a divided panel of the District of Columbia Circuit limited plaintiffs' attorneys from
private firms to the $100-per-hour rates they charged some of their fee-paying clients,

although one attorney billed by the hour in only 20 to 50% of the cases he handled, and the other attorney billed most of his clients at a reduced rate based on their ability to pay. The court concluded that the fact that an attorney charges by the hour in only some of his cases or waives fees altogether for some clients "does nothing to impeach the reasonableness of the hourly rates he does charge." *Id.* at 48. The court also found that the government defendant had provided evidence corroborating that the $100-per-hour rate was "consistent" with comparable prevailing market rates. *Id.* at 49 n.3. Chief Judge Wald in dissent rebuked the majority's decision for its holding that "if an attorney has ever billed any particular type of client by the hour, then the highest rate he has in the past charged for that type of client may be used as the measure for the attorney's statutory fee compensation, regardless of whether the rate is established or merely ad hoc, and regardless of whether it accurately reflects the prevailing community market rate for the lawyer's services, as prescribed by Congress." *Id.* at 55.

In *Palmer v. Schultz,* 679 F. Supp. 68, 69-72 (D.D.C. 1988), the court held that counsel from the quasi-public interest firm representing the successful Title VII plaintiffs were entitled to be compensated at rates adjusted above the firm's actual billing rates on a showing that the actual rates were abnormally low in comparison to the prevailing market rates for equally competent counsel doing comparable litigation. Plaintiff's counsel successfully rebutted the presumptive reasonableness of their own customary billing rates by submitting affidavits from members of more than 20 Washington, D.C. law firms demonstrating that even the lowest rates charged in the community for complex federal litigation were substantially higher than the rates charged by plaintiffs' firm in the pursuit of a substantial public interest practice. *Id.* at 70. Accordingly, the court granted to plaintiffs' counsel an "upward adjustment of their below-market rates to a level commensurate with the minimum market rate at which equally competent counsel would have taken on similar litigation during the period in question." *Id.* at 72.

* On rehearing en banc in *Save Our Cumberland Mountains, Inc. v. Hodel,* 857 F.2d 1516 (D.C. Cir. 1988), the District of Columbia Court of Appeals overruled *Laffey* and held that, in awarding statutory attorney's fees to a private law firm that "customarily charges below the prevailing community rate in order to serve a particular type of client," courts must base reasonable hourly rate determinations on the "prevailing community rate for similar legal services," as opposed to the below-market rates actually charged by the particular firm. *Id.* at 1517. In his dissenting opinion Circuit Judge Starr emphasized what he called the "enablement" goal of fee-shifting statutes, to enable private parties to obtain competent counsel to litigate their meritorious civil rights claims. *Id.* at 1528-29. According to the dissent, "[e]nablement, not maximization of the range of private-party choice, is the Congressionally ordained purpose" of § 1988 and similar fee-shifting statutes. *Id.* at 1529. The dissent criticized the majority for attempting to "obliterate the manifold distinctions which abound in the legal services market and then crudely lump every practitioner of comparable experience into the same rate category." *Id.* at 1532. While acknowledging that *Laffey* created anomalies in rate setting, since quasi-public interest lawyers charging below-market rates received lower statutory fee rates than equivalently creditialed nonprofit lawyers without market-tested rates, the dissent nonetheless lauded the *Laffey* approach for its simplicity, objectivity, and fee-settlement incentives. *Id.* at 1532-34.

In *Student Public Interest Research Group v. AT&T Bell Laboratories,* 842 F.2d 1436 (3d Cir. 1988), the Third Circuit comprehensively reviewed various approaches to setting appropriate hourly rates for statutory fee awards to attorneys who "operate a for-profit law firm that handles only public interest cases and therefore bills significantly less than a traditional law firm." *Id.* at 1438. The court identified four approaches to rate-setting for such firms.

The "billing rate" rule mandates the use of the actual billing rates of the firm, even if those rates are discounted from prevailing market rates in order to accommodate the financial circumstances of the public interest firm's clients. *Id.* at 1443-45. The court rejected that approach in its application to a public interest law firm whose actual billing rates "do not approximate a fair market rate." *Id.* at 1445. The court noted that the assumption of the billing rate rule that the market value of such a firm's services are reflected in its billing rate is flawed, because it ignores the effect of a fee-shifting statute itself on the hourly rates of a public interest firm that charges a minimal fee if it loses and recovers a statutory fee if it prevails. *Id.* Similarly, the court rejected the "micro-market" rule that departs from the public interest firm's actual billing rates when they are inconsistent with a market that looks to the rates received generally by public interest lawyers. *Id.* at 1445-46. That rule is flawed because it erroneously assumes that an "independent public interest market" exists, whereas in reality that market is "largely rooted in court-generated fee shifting awards." *Id.* at 1446. The third approach would employ a "modified billing rate" that starts with the public interest firm's actual billing rate and applies to it a contingency enhancement, "to reflect the inherent risk of public interest cases that rely only on fee shifting statutes." *Id.* at 1446. The court rejected that approach because of its perception that contingency enhancements are not viewed generously by the Supreme Court and are cumbersome to calculate. *Id.* at 1447.

Finally, the Third Circuit considered the "community market rate" rule, by which the public interest attorneys would be assigned the market rates commanded by private attorneys of equivalent skill and experience for work of similar complexity. *Id.* at 1447-48. The court adopted that rule, concluding that the community market rate, rather than an artificially low actual billing rate, is the appropriate statutory fee rate for a nonprofit public interest firm. *Id.* at 1448-50.

§ 18.6 Affidavits of Other Attorneys in the Community in Support of the Requested Rates

Page 472, update Hart and Palmer citations and add to note 46:

Hart, *rev'd & remanded on other grounds,* 798 F.2d 519 (1st Cir. 1986); Palmer, *vacated & remanded,* 478 U.S. 1015 (1986). However, the First Circuit in Jacobs v. Mancuso, 825 F.2d 559, 563 (1st Cir. 1987), criticized plaintiffs' counsel for soliciting and submitting "five separate affidavits from area counsel concerning the reasonableness of plaintiffs' charges, when no more than two, barring unusual circumstances, would seem sufficient."

§ 18.6 OTHER ATTORNEYS' AFFIDAVITS

Page 472, update Burlington Northern citation and add to note 49:

Burlington Northern, *aff'd in relevant part,* 810 F.2d 601 (7th Cir. 1986); Brinker v. Guiffrida, 798 F.2d 661, 668 (3d Cir. 1986)(Equal Access to Justice Act, 28 U.S.C. § 2412); Chalmers v. City of Los Angeles, 796 F.2d 1205, 1214 (9th Cir. 1986)(all noting submission of supporting attorney affidavits indicating familiarity with work or reputation of plaintiff's counsel).

Page 473, add to note 50:

Lightfoot v. Walker, 826 F.2d 516, 524 (7th Cir. 1987)(approving consideration of expert attorney's testimony regarding national rates in complex civil rights cases).

Page 473, add the following cases to note 52:

Jordan v. Multnomah County, 815 F.2d 1258, 1263 n.9 (9th Cir. 1987)(questioning sufficiency of attorney's affidavit that conclusorily stated rates requested for plaintiffs' attorneys were reasonable and consistent with prevailing community rates without indicating that the rates sought were comparable to his rates"); Bygott v. Leaseway Transp. Corp., 637 F. Supp. 1433, 1444 n.6 (E.D. Pa. 1986)(supporting attorney affidavit "does not state a rate which she believes is reasonable in this geographic area"); Lock v. Jenkins, 634 F. Supp. 615, 626 (N.D. Ind. 1986)(attorney's supporting affidavit "does not reveal . . . where in the State he practices").

Page 473, add the following cases to note 53:

Cf. Daly v. Hill, 790 F.2d 1071, 1080 n.13 (4th Cir. 1986)(noting that supporting attorney affidavits primarily concerned market rates for in-court time, whereas most of the claimed hours in the case at hand were for out-of-court work); Keith v. Volpe, 644 F. Supp. 1312, 1316 (C.D. Cal. 1986)(citing inadequacies in supporting attorney affidavits that set forth a "unitary" billing system fixing "one hourly rate for all attorneys regardless of experience," and reflected "premium rates charged to substantial corporate clients for mainly commercial matters" rather than for complex federal litigation similar to the case at hand).

Page 473, add the following cases to note 54:

Tomazzoli v. Sheedy, 804 F.2d 93, 95 (7th Cir. 1986); Thomas v. Cooper Industries, Inc., 640 F. Supp. 1374, 1380 (W.D.N.C. 1986)(Title VII suit; both noting the detailed supporting affidavits setting forth the rates customarily charged by the attorneys for
* particular types of cases). *But see* Schirk v. Herlik, 689 F. Supp. 861, 862 (E.D. Wis. 1988) (rejecting relevance of expert attorney affidavits describing the premium rates charged by local civil rights attorneys which became the basis for their § 1988 fee requests, although their clients were not expected to be able to fully pay such rates).

Page 473, add at end of section:

In *Norman v. Housing Authority of Montgomery,* 836 F.2d 1292 (11th Cir. 1988), the Eleventh Circuit stated that satisfactory evidence that the requested rates are in line with prevailing market rates "necessarily must speak to rates actually billed and paid in similar lawsuits," so that "[t]estimony that a given fee is reasonable is therefore unsatisfactory evidence of market rate." *Id.* at 1299. The court noted that "[e]vidence of rates may be adduced through direct evidence of charges by lawyers under similar circumstances or by opinion evidence." *Id.* The court added that the "weight to be given to opinion evidence of course will be affected by the detail contained in the testimony on matters such as similarity of skill, reputation, experience, similarity of case and client, and breadth of the sample of which the expert has knowledge." *Id.* The court further urged parties to "provide the court with a range of market rates for lawyers of different skill levels (perhaps as measured by quality and quantity of experience) involved in similar cases with similar clients." *Id.* at 1300. The Fourth Circuit has stated that the "prevailing market rate may be established through affidavits reciting the precise fees that counsel with similar qualifications have received in comparable cases," as well as "information concerning recent fee awards by courts in comparable cases; and specific evidence of counsel's actual billing practice or other evidence of the actual rates which counsel can command in the market." *Spell v. McDaniel,* 824 F.2d 1380, 1402 (4th Cir. 1987).

§ 18.7 Citation of Other Relevant Fee Decisions in Support of the Requested Rates

Page 474, update Palmer (District of Columbia Circuit) and Daggett (Third Circuit) citations and add to note 57:

Palmer, *vacated & remanded,* 478 U.S. 1015 (1986); Daggett, *aff'd in relevant part,* 811 F. 2d 793 (3d Cir. 1987).

Fifth Circuit: Sellers v. Delgado Community College, 839 F.2d 1132, 1141 (5th Cir. 1988)(upholding district court's reduction of requested rates to accord with rates awarded by the court in prior similar cases).

* *Eighth Circuit:* McDonald v. Armontrout, 860 F.2d 1456, 1460-61 (8th Cir. 1988) (relying in part on rates recently awarded in other civil rights cases in the circuit, in upholding rates awarded in this case).

Page 474, add to cases cited in note 58:

Dotson v. City of Indianola, 639 F. Supp. 1056, 1063 (N.D. Miss. 1986); Davis v. City of Charleston, 635 F. Supp. 197, 200 (E.D. Mo. 1986)(both relying on prior fee decisions from within the same judicial district as in the case at hand).

Page 474, add the following case to note 59:

Cf. Orshan v. Macchiarola, 629 F. Supp. 1014, 1022 (E.D.N.Y. 1986)(rejecting citation of New York federal cases when New Jersey was found to be the relevant community for rate-setting purposes, and relying instead on New Jersey fee cases).

Page 475, Palmer v. Shultz citation in note 60 should read "594 F. Supp. at 436."

Page 475, update Burlington Northern and Black Grievance Committee citations, and add to note 61:

Burlington Northern, *aff'd in relevant part,* 810 F.2d 601 (7th Cir. 1986); Curtis v. Bill Hanna Ford, Inc., 822 F.2d 549, 552 (5th Cir. 1987)(finding that district court clearly erred in awarding rate of $100 per hour, instead of $125 per hour, to attorney in Title VII suit who customarily received $150 per hour in another employment discrimination case); Paxton v. Union Nat'l Bank, 806 F.2d 785, 786 (8th Cir. 1986)(finding "totally inadequate" $75-per-hour rate awarded by district court to two experienced civil rights litigators who had been awarded $125 per hour rate by the court of appeals in another case); Black Grievance Committee, *vacated and remanded on other grounds,* 802 F.2d 648, 651-53 (3d Cir. 1986)(upholding district court's reduction of claimed rates for a particular period based on lesser rates awarded to plaintiffs' attorneys during that period in other cases, but limiting the relevance of those prior fee decisions to the applicable time period); Coulter v. State of Tennessee, 805 F.2d 146, 149-50 (6th Cir. 1986)(Title VII suit; upholding district court's reduction of claimed rate of plaintiff's attorney on basis of rate awarded that attorney by same judge in another Title VII action, and rejecting contention of plaintiff's attorney that the prior fee decision did not adopt a market-value rate for his services); Chalmers v. City of Los Angeles, 796 F.2d 1205, 1214 (9th Cir. 1986); Semar v. Platte Valley Federal S & L Ass'n, 791 F.2d 699, 706 (9th Cir. 1986) (Truth-in-Lending Act, 15 U.S.C. § 1640(a)(3)); Thomas v. Cooper Industries, Inc., 640 F. Supp. 1374, 1378 (W.D.N.C. 1986) (Title VII suit); Lenihan v. City of New York, 640 F. Supp. 822, 828 (S.D.N.Y. 1986); Jackson v. Color Tile, Inc., 638 F. Supp. 62, 66 (N.D. Miss. 1986) (Title VII suit); York v. Alabama State Bd. of Educ., 631 F. Supp. 78, 85 (M.D. Ala. 1986); Alexander v. Hill, 625 F. Supp. 567, 569-70 (W.D.N.C. 1985) (all relying on prior fee decisions setting reasonable rates for the attorneys seeking fees in the case at hand); *cf.* Vaughns v. Board of Educ., 627 F. Supp. 837, 842-43 (D. Md. 1985) (increasing the hourly rates awarded to same attorneys at an earlier stage of the litigation by 15% "to reflect increased experience and rising fee rates in the relevant geographic area").

Page 475, add to note 63:

McKenzie v. Kennickell, 645 F. Supp. 437, 444 n.8 (D.D.C. 1986) (Title VII suit; citing approvingly rates "upheld" by Supreme Court in *Blum v. Stenson*). *See also* discussion of rates upheld in *City of Riverside v. Rivera* in **§ 18.2** of this supplement.

Page 475, add to note 64:

See also Norman v. Housing Auth. of Montgomery, 836 F.2d 1292, 1304-05 (11th Cir. 1988)(terming "irrelevant" to setting of prevailing market rates the citation of fee awards in other cases, when there was "no assurance that the attorneys in those cases possessed similar skill, experience or reputation or that the case or clients were similar to the one at bar," and no evidence that the prevailing market rates in the judicial districts where those cases arose were the same as those in the forum district of this case).

Page 476, add at end of section:

Thus, in *Black Grievance Comm. v. Philadelphia Elec. Co.,* 802 F.2d 648, 651-53 (3d Cir. 1986), the Third Circuit found that prior fee decisions setting hourly rates in other cases for the lawyers seeking fees in the case at hand established a "factual basis for . . . [their] marketplace rates" during the time period covered by the prior decisions, but were not determinative in fixing rates for subsequent time periods.

§ 18.8 Surveys of Community Rates as Evidence Supporting the Requested Rates

Page 476, update Hart citation and add to note 66:

rev'd and remanded on other grounds, 798 F.2d 519 (1st Cir. 1986). *See also* Hall v. Ochs, 817 F.2d 920, 928 (1st Cir. 1987)(upholding rate supported by survey in American Lawyer's Guide to Leading Law Firms).

Page 476, add to note 67:

Lebron v. Washington Metro. Area Transit Auth., 665 F. Supp. 923, 925 (D.D.C. 1987)(proposed fee rate schedule supported by survey in National Law Journal's Directory of the Legal Profession).

Page 476, add to note 68:

* See surveys of hourly rates of nation's largest firms, National Law Journal, November 23, 1987, and November 7, 1988.

Page 476, add the following cases to note 70:

Dameron v. Sinai Hosp. of Baltimore, 644 F. Supp. 551, 558 (D. Md. 1986)(ERISA suit; Los Angeles County area survey); McCullough v. Cady, 640 F. Supp. 1012, 1021 (E.D. Mich. 1986)(state bar survey); Starnes v. Hill, 635 F. Supp. 1270, 1272 (W.D.N.C. 1986)(*North Carolina Bar Association Economic Survey 1985*); *cf.* Save Our Cumberland Mountains, Inc. v. Hodel, 826 F.2d 43, 49 n.3 & 56 n.2 (dissent)(D.C. Cir.)(debate between majority and dissent over adequacy of hourly rate survey in District of Columbia's 1984 Lawyer Directory), *reh'g en banc granted,* 830 F.2d 1182 (D.C. Cir. 1987).

Page 477, add to note 71:

Palmer v. Shultz, 679 F. Supp. 68, 71 (D.D.C. 1988)(rejecting relevance of rate survey submitted by defendants from District of Columbia Bar Lawyer Referral and Information Service that "fails to accurately reflect relevant rates charged by community lawyers engaged in complex federal litigation"); Wiggins v. Heckler, 639 F. Supp. 126, 128 & n.3 (E.D.N.C. 1986)(Equal Access to Justice Act, 28 U.S.C. § 2412; noting that 1985 North Carolina Bar Association survey reflected rate schedules that were "simply for 'typical' work conducted by attorneys in North Carolina, based on

their geographic location, firm size and date of admission to the bar, and do not account for the type of work performed or the skill required to perform it"). An appropriate price index, such as the consumer price index for a particular area, may be used to gauge annual increases in established hourly rates due to inflation. *See, e.g.*, Wedra v. Thomas, 623 F. Supp. 272, 277 (S.D.N.Y. 1985)(Equal Access to Justice Act,
* 28 U.S.C. § 2412). The court in Pacific West Cable Co. v. City of Sacramento, 693 F. Supp. 865, 869 (E.D. Cal. 1988), concluded that the annual National Law Journal rate survey was "not competent evidence of the reasonableness of the claimed hourly rate if for no other reason than the fact that there has been no explanation provided to the court as to the basis of the survey or the method of collecting the data."

§ 18.9 Rates Charged by Counsel for the Losing Party as Evidence of Market Rates

Page 477, add to cases cited in note 72:

* United States v. Metropolitan Dist. Comm'n, 847 F.2d 12, 19 (1st Cir. 1988) (finding that district court did not act arbitrarily in its belief that rate charged by defendant's attorney in the case, for "substantially similar work," was the "best barometer" of a reasonable rate for plaintiff's counsel); Tomazzoli v. Sheedy, 804 F.2d 93, 95, 99 (7th Cir. 1986)(favorably citing rates charged by defendants' counsel); Campaign for a Progressive Bronx v. Black, 631 F. Supp. 975, 982-83 (S.D.N.Y. 1986)(Voting Rights Act, 42 U.S.C. § 19731(e); setting rate for plaintiffs' attorneys at level recently awarded in another civil rights case to defendants' attorney, whose skills and experience were similar to those of plaintiffs' lawyers).

Page 477, add to cases cited in note 74:

Thomas v. Cooper Industries, Inc., 640 F. Supp. 1374, 1381 (W.D.N.C. 1986)(Title VII suit; rejecting relevance of low rates charged by defendants' lawyers, when "their fee was not dependent on success" and they expended an exorbitant amount of time on case); *cf.* Norman v. Housing Auth. of Montgomery, 836 F.2d 1292, 1299-1300 (11th Cir. 1988)(observing that the fee charged by counsel representing a governmental defendant, when the "law firm representing a governmental entity on an ongoing basis . . . charge[s] substantially lower hourly rates than would be charged for representation in a single case," is "simply irrelevant to the establishment of a reasonable hourly rate for a plaintiff's civil rights lawyer").

§ 18.10 The Opposing Party's Burden of Rebuttal

Page 478, update Cunningham citation and add the following cases to note 77:

* McDonald v. Armontrout, 860 F.2d 1456, 1460 (8th Cir. 1988) (upholding rates awarded by district court and supported by evidence submitted by plaintiffs' attorneys, since defendants failed to make an evidentiary showing that the rates were

unreasonably high); Toussaint v. McCarthy, 826 F.2d 901, 904 (9th Cir. 1987)(in granting plaintiffs' requested lodestar, court noted defendant's failure to submit affidavits contesting requested rates or hours); Spell v. McDaniel, 824 F.2d 1380, 1402-03 (4th Cir. 1987)(upholding rates, not objected to by defendant, at high end of the range of reasonable rates); Cunningham, *vacated & remanded on other grounds,* 478 U.S. 1015 (1986), *reinstated,* 807 F.2d 49, 52-53 (3d Cir. 1986), *cert. denied,* 107 S. Ct. 2179 (1987); Black Grievance Comm. v. Philadelphia Elec. Co., 802 F.2d 648, 652-53 (3d Cir. 1986)(consistent with *Cunningham,* discussed in text, court held that district court should have accepted the rates set forth in affidavits of plaintiffs' attorneys, when defendant "filed no affidavit and offered no testimony contesting the accuracy" of * those affidavits), *on remand,* 690 F. Supp. 1393, 1396 (E.D. Pa. 1988) (finding that defendant failed to submit any evidence rebutting plaintiffs' showing of reasonableness of requested rates); Chalmers v. City of Los Angeles, 796 F.2d 1205, 1214-15 (9th Cir. 1986)(approving requested rate of plaintiff's counsel, although it "may appear to be somewhat high," when defendant filed "no contrary affidavits . . . suggesting that this rate is not in keeping with the prevailing rates in the community"); McKenzie v. Kennickell, 645 F. Supp. 437, 445 (D.D.C. 1986)(Title VII suit; applying plaintiffs' requested rates, when government defendant "has never argued, much less attempted to show, that the rates claimed for the public interest attorneys are excessive," and concluding that "[p]laintiffs' submission is simply not so weak that it can be challenged solely for being unsubstantiated"); Keith v. Volpe, 644 F. Supp. 1312, 1316 (C.D. Cal. 1986)(noting that court "has not had the benefit of any declarations from the defendants" indicating that the rates requested were not prevailing market rates, and encouraging such submissions in the future).

Page 478, update Hart citation and add to note 78:

Mayson v. Pierce, 806 F.2d 1556, 1557-58 (11th Cir. 1987)(upholding district court's 50% reduction of rate requested by plaintiff's attorney in light of record below that included affidavits solicited by defendant from three experienced local attorneys attesting to reasonableness of reduced rate); Hart, *rev'd and remanded on other grounds,* 798 F.2d 519 (1st Cir. 1986); Tomazzoli v. Sheedy, 804 F.2d 93, 95 (7th Cir. 1986); Ramos v. Lamm, 632 F. Supp. 376, 387 (D. Colo. 1986). Of course, the attorney affidavits must set forth an adequate evidentiary basis for the reduced rates suggested by the defendant. *See* Norman v. Housing Auth. of Montgomery, 836 F.2d 1292, 1305 (11th Cir. 1988)(finding "deficient" attorney affidavits, offered in opposition to requested rates, that did not attest either that the attorneys themselves charged the suggested rates or that such rates "were charged in similar cases for similar clients by lawyers of similar skill, experience and reputation"); Rogers v. Okin, 821 F.2d 22, 29-30 (1st Cir. 1987), *cert. denied,* 108 S. Ct. 709 (1988)(finding not credible the reduced rates "testified to by defendants' consulting non-lawyer expert").

Page 479, update Black Grievance Committee citation and add to note 79:

Black Grievance Committee, *vacated and remanded,* 802 F.2d 648, 652-53 (3d Cir. 1986)(upholding district court's reduction of requested rate for one period on basis of rate awarded to plaintiffs' attorneys for that period in earlier fee decisions cited by defendant, but rejecting relevance of those fee decisions to setting of market-value rates for subsequent period in the litigation); Cunningham v. City of Overland, 804 F.2d 1066, 1071 (8th Cir. 1986)(rejecting relevance of outdated fee cases cited by defendants); Tomazzoli v. Sheedy, 804 F.2d 93, 95 (7th Cir. 1986); Lenihan v. City of New York, 640 F. Supp. 822, 827 (S.D.N.Y. 1986)(noting that none of civil rights fee award cases cited by defendant reflected current rates, since the work performed in each occurred prior to the relevant time period in the case at hand).

Page 479, add to note 80:

Dameron v. Sinai Hosp. of Baltimore, 644 F. Supp. 551, 559-60 (D. Md. 1986)(ERISA suit; finding that current survey of rates charged by Baltimore law firm partners, cited by defendants, generally supported the requested rates).

Page 479, add to cases cited in note 81:

Tomazzoli v. Sheedy, 804 F.2d 93, 95, 99 (7th Cir. 1986)(upholding hourly rate awarded by district court to plaintiff's attorney, in absence of evidence that comparable rate charged by equally-experienced partners in law firm representing defendants was below-market).

Page 479, update Palmer citation in note 82:

vacated & remanded, 478 U.S. 1015 (1986).

§ 18.11 Permissible Discovery in the Litigation Over Rates

Page 480, add to note 85:

Thomas v. Cooper Industries, Inc., 640 F. Supp. 1374, 1380 (W.D.N.C. 1986)(Title VII suit; noting that rates charged by plaintiff's attorney in the past "have been the subject of extensive discovery by defendants").

Page 480, add to cases cited in note 87:

Cf. Hernandez v. George, 793 F.2d 264, 268 (10th Cir. 1986)(upholding discretion of district court to deny plaintiffs' discovery of fees and hours of defendants' counsel, when district court concluded that such information was not relevant to setting reasonable fees for plaintiffs' counsel and that court already possessed adequate information on the prevailing market rates); Mitroff v. Xomox Corp., 631 F. Supp. 25, 27 (S.D. Ohio 1985)(Age Discrimination in Employment Act, 29 U.S.C. § 626(b); in permitting plaintiff's discovery of rates charged by defendant's counsel, court prohibited inquiry into "the nature of any communication by defense counsel with defendant" and examination of "any documents involved in other representation of defendant by defense counsel").

§ 18.12 The Expertise of the District Court in Determining Market Rates

Page 480, add the following cases to note 90:

Second Circuit: Lenihan v. City of New York, 640 F. Supp. 822, 828 (S.D.N.Y. 1986)(applying "this Court's general knowledge of the prevailing rates in the New York legal community" in setting reasonable rates). In Miele v. New York State Teamsters Conference Pension & Retirement Fund, 831 F.2d 407 (2d Cir. 1987), the Second Circuit rejected the position that a district judge, in setting rates in a statutory fee case, "may not rely in part on the judge's own knowledge of private firm hourly rates in the community and instead must consider only the hourly rate data submitted into evidence." *Id.* at 409. The court further concluded that even though the nonprofit legal services organization representing the prevailing plaintiff submitted an affidavit of "hourly rates charged by numerous lawyers with a range of skills and experiences comparable to those of plaintiffs' counsel" that was "extremely detailed" and "would support the claimed hourly rate" and the opposing party "offered no evidence of a more appropriate rate," the district judge nonetheless had discretion to award a reduced rate in reliance on his knowledge of prevailing community rates, "so long as he considered rates charged by comparable lawyers at the private bar." *Id.* at 408, 409. The court of appeals remanded this case to the district court for redetermination of the appropriate rate, because the district judge, in reducing the claimed rate from $150 to $100 per hour, had not confined his inquiry to consideration of prevailing community rates charged by the private bar but also had considered rates in freedom of information, social security, and criminal cases that are subject to statutory ceilings. *Id.* at 409-10.

Fourth Circuit: Starnes v. Hill, 635 F. Supp. 1270, 1272 (W.D.N.C. 1986)(noting that court "did not accept as gospel" the affidavits of plaintiff's attorney concerning reasonable rates, but "relied on the Court's knowledge of the case, what was involved, the lack of complexity, and the fees charged in this locality in these and other matters").

Seventh Circuit: Lightfoot v. Walker, 826 F.2d 516, 524 (7th Cir. 1987)(approving district court's consideration of evidence concerning market rates "in light of its own knowledge of prevailing rates in the area").

Ninth Circuit: Keith v. Volpe, 644 F. Supp. 1312, 1316 (C.D. Cal. 1986)(in the absence of defendants' submissions controverting requested rates, court "relied on its prior orders in this case, the rates recently awarded in comparable cases, and its own experience of legal practice in Los Angeles in determining appropriate hourly rates").

Tenth Circuit: Lucero v. City of Trinidad, 815 F.2d 1384, 1385-86 (10th Cir. 1987)(when fee applicant provided no evidence of prevailing community rates, other than documentation of customary rates charged by law firm representing plaintiff, court approved district judge's consideration of its "own knowledge of prevailing market rates").

Eleventh Circuit: In Norman v. Housing Auth. of Montgomery, 836 F.2d 1292 (11th Cir. 1988), the Eleventh Circuit held that when "the affidavits submitted in support of the fee application and the affidavits submitted in opposition thereto are by and large inadequate," the district court was "correct in determining that it must rely on its own expertise in determining a reasonable hourly rate." *Id.* at 1304. However, the court of appeals remanded this case for reconsideration because the district court had selected an hourly rate allegedly based on the rates charged by "old-line" firms in the community, without demonstrating that its "standard of comparison was the prevailing market rate for lawyers similar to class counsel having similar client relationships and similar types of issues." *Id.* at 1305. On the other hand, the court of appeals did uphold the district court in taking judicial notice of the prevailing community rate for "bookkeeping" services performed by plaintiffs' attorneys. *Id.* at 1304. The court observed that it is "proper for a court to judicially notice matters outside of the record if they are generally known within the territorial jurisdiction of the trial court or capable of accurate and ready determination by resort to sources whose accuracy cannot reasonably be questioned," provided that a party is permitted on request to be heard on the matter. *Id.*

Page 481, add to cases cited in note 91:

Norman v. Housing Auth. of Montgomery, 836 F.2d 1292, 1304-05 (11th Cir. 1988); Lucero v. City of Trinidad, 815 F.2d 1384, 1385-86 (10th Cir. 1987)(both finding that district court's reliance on its own knowledge of prevailing community rates was warranted by parties' failure to submit adequate evidence of market rates); Coleman v. McLaren, 635 F. Supp. 266, 268 & n.2 (N.D. Ill. 1986)(finding that prevailing defendants had failed to adequately support their requested rate, district court judge relied on his own "knowledge of applicable rates in the higher-priced Chicago market" and, in particular, on the rates charged by his former law firm). * In Perkins v. Mobile Housing Bd., 847 F.2d 735, 738 (11th Cir. 1988), the court held that "[b]ecause the fee petition is inadequate, the district court is completely at liberty to determine the reasonable hourly rate relying on its own expertise," provided that the district court considers "what it knows of market rates for the type of litigation at bar and is not setting a fee with reference to overly generalized notions of the total range of fees for all federal civil litigaiton."

§ 18.13 The District Court's Discretion in Setting Reasonable Rates; Scope of Appellate Review

Pages 481-82, update Delaware Valley citation and add to note 94:

Delaware Valley, 478 U.S. 546 (1986); Student Pub. Interest Research Group v. AT&T Bell Laboratories, 842 F.2d 1436, 1442 (3d Cir. 1988)(characterizing question of appropriate market value rates as one of fact, subject to clearly erroneous standard of review); Greater Los Angeles Council on Deafness v. Community Television, 813 F.2d 217, 221 (9th Cir. 1987)(noting that the "abilities of an attorney appearing before the district court and the prevailing local rates are factual matters best left to the district court); Brewster v. Dukakis, 786 F.2d 16, 22 (1st Cir. 1986)(finding no abuse of discretion in setting of hourly rates, when the "legal work involved in this case was most intimately known by the district court").

Page 482, add to note 95:

Miele v. New York State Teamsters Conference Pension & Retirement Fund, 831 F.2d 407, 409-10 (2d Cir. 1987)(reversing district court's rate determination that was based not only on prevailing market rates charged by the private bar, but as well on the impermissible consideration of rates subject to statutory ceilings; Sims v. Jefferson Downs Racing Ass'n, 778 F.2d 1068, 1084-85 (5th Cir. 1985)(reversing district court's selection of a particular hourly rate for attorney's services that was not adequately supported by affidavit evidence relied on).

Page 482, add to cases cited in note 96:

Jordan v. Multnomah County, 815 F.2d 1258, 1263 & n.10 (9th Cir. 1987)(reversing district court's application of "an unsupported 'range' hourly rate" without explanation or a "finding on the sufficiency of the evidence" submitted by fee applicant in support of the claimed rates).

Page 482, update Cunningham citation and add to note 97:

N.A.A.C.P. v. City of Evergreen, 812 F.2d 1332, 1336 (11th Cir. 1987)(finding that a "trial judge cannot substitute his own judgment for uncontradicted evidence [concerning hourly rates] without record support"); Cunningham, *vacated & remanded on other grounds,* 478 U.S. 1015 (1986), *reinstated,* 807 F.2d 49, 52-53 (3d Cir. 1986), *cert. denied,* 107 S. Ct. 2179 (1987); Black Grievance Comm. v. Philadelphia Elec. Co., 802 F.2d 648, 652-53, 657 (3d Cir. 1986)(reversing district court's reduction of uncontradicted rates set forth in affidavits of plaintiffs' attorneys).

Page 482 add to note 98:

Lucero v. City of Trinidad, 815 F.2d 1384, 1385-86 (10th Cir. 1987)(finding no abuse of discretion in district court's award of § 1988 rate that coincided with maximum statutory rate under Equal Access to Justice Act, 28 U.S.C. § 2412, when fee applicant failed to submit relevant information concerning prevailing community rates and district judge viewed the EAJA rate as consonant with prevailing market rates in this case).

§ 18.14 The Choice of Uniform or Variable Rates for an Attorney's Services

Page 483, add at end of note 99:

See Keith v. Volpe, 644 F. Supp. 1312, 1316 (C.D. Cal. 1986)(rejecting, as inconsistent with the standard of prevailing market rates, a suggested "unitary billing system" that "sets one hourly rate for all attorneys regardless of experience").

Page 483, add to note 1:

In Bohen v. City of East Chicago, 666 F. Supp. 154, 157 (N.D. Ind. 1987), Judge Easterbrook observed that private firms frequently assess their clients higher rates for in-court work and brief writing, because "[w]ork in court and writing briefs makes use of the lawyer's highest skills – insight, organization, and so on," and that "[a] few hours in court or over a brief can turn a case around in a way a few days in a deposition or poring over papers is unlikely to do."

Page 484, update Delaware Valley citation in note 4:

478 U.S. 546 (1986).

Page 484, add to note 5:

* *But see* McDonald v. Armontrout, 860 F.2d 1456, 1461 (8th Cir. 1988) (upholding district court's compensation of attorney's monitoring work at full rate, where it was not merely clerical in character, while acknowledging that courts might apply "less than the full hourly rate to clerical work performed by attorneys"); Fiacco v. City of Rensselaer, 663 F. Supp. 743, 746 (N.D.N.Y. 1987)(assigning reduced attorney rates to "clerical tasks such as the photocopying, forwarding and delivering of court papers and correspondence").

Page 484, add to note 7:

* United States v. Metropolitan Dist. Comm'n, 847 F.2d 12, 18 n.6 (1st Cir. 1988) (noting that First Circuit has "regularly encouraged district courts to use lower rates" for work on the fee petition); United States v. Marengo County Comm'n, 667 F. Supp. 786, 798 (S.D. Ala. 1987)(setting rate for attorney's fee litigation at 80% of rate awarded for work on the merits).

Page 484, update Black Grievance Committee (Third Circuit) and Palmer (Seventh Circuit) citations and add to note 9:

Second Circuit: Barcia v. Sitkin, 683 F. Supp. 353, 356 (S.D.N.Y. 1988)(uniform rate for in-court and out-of-court activities).

Third Circuit: Black Grievance Comm., *vacated and remanded,* 802 F.2d 648, 651-53, 657 (3d Cir. 1986)(reversing district court's reduction of uncontested rates claimed by plaintiffs' attorneys).

Fourth Circuit: Spell v. McDaniel, 824 F.2d 1380, 1403 (4th Cir. 1987)(finding no error in district court's application of uniform rates for plaintiff's counsel, "without regard to the nature of the work performed," especially given district court's finding that counsel's "knowledge, skills and abilities were as fully engaged in their out-of-court work as they were in-court").

Seventh Circuit: Lightfoot v. Walker, 826 F.2d 516, 525 (7th Cir. 1987)(awarding uniform rate for merits and fee work to attorney who was an experienced litigator of civil rights fee petitions); *Palmer, rev'd on other grounds,* 806 F.2d 1316 (7th Cir. 1986); Tomazzoli v. Sheedy, 804 F.2d 93, 99 (7th Cir. 1986)(reaffirming that the "imposition of rate differentials for in-court and out-of-court time [is] discretionary," while noting that "courtroom work . . . usually commands a greater hourly rate").

Ninth Circuit: Schrader v. Idaho Dep't of Health and Welfare, 631 F. Supp. 1426, 1431 (D. Idaho 1986)(uniform rate applied that "represents a balance between application of a higher rate for the more exacting work and time spent that might be billed at some lower rate").

Page 486, add to note 15:

Save Our Cumberland Mountains, Inc. v. Hodel, 651 F. Supp. 1528, 1538 (D.D.C. 1986)(rejecting defendant's contention that plaintiffs' counsel should be compensated at different rates for different types of legal work, when "[n]one of the firms involved here differentiate in their billing rates between different categories of activities, and, indeed, such differentiation is extremely rare in the legal community").

Page 486, update Black Grievance Committee and Palmer citations and add to note 16:

Black Grievance Comm., *vacated and remanded,* 802 F.2d 648 (3d Cir. 1986); Palmer, *rev'd on other grounds,* 806 F.2d 1316 (7th Cir. 1986); Schrader v. Idaho Dep't of Health and Welfare, 631 F. Supp. 1426, 1431 (D. Idaho 1986)(average rate).

Page 486, update Delaware Valley, Daggett, and Black Grievance Committee citations (Third Circuit) and add to note 18:

* *First Circuit:* United States v. Metropolitan Dist. Comm'n, 847 F.2d 12, 19 (1st Cir. 1988) (citing "approved practice" of assigning "different rates to different tasks"); Jacobs v. Mancuso, 825 F.2d 559, 561 n.3 (1st Cir. 1977)(approving discretionary establishment of "multiple hourly rates to reflect differences in the types of services performed for the client").

Second Circuit: In re Agent Orange Prod. Liab. Litig., 818 F.2d 226, 238 (2d Cir. 1987)(observing, in equitable fund fee case, that "it is not unusual for hours of travel time, deposition time and other quasi-administrative items to be compensated at lower rates").

Third Circuit: Delaware Valley, 478 U.S. 546 (1986); Daggett, *vacated in relevant part,* 811 F.2d 793, 798-99 (3d Cir. 1987)(reversing district court's reduction of lodestar to adjust for assertedly excessive rates awarded for partner work that could have been handled by associates); Black Grievance Comm., *vacated and remanded,* 802 F.2d 648, 656-57 (3d Cir. 1986)(reversing district court's reduction of uncontested rates requested for work on fee petition).

Fifth Circuit: Abrams v. Baylor College of Medicine, 805 F.2d 528, 535-36 (5th Cir. 1986)(finding it appropriate to assign a reduced rate to nonlegal work such as "investigation, clerical work, compilation of facts and statistics and other work which can often be accomplished by non-lawyers but which a lawyer may do because he has no other help available").

Eighth Circuit: Cunningham v. City of Overland, 804 F.2d 1066, 1071 (8th Cir. 1986)(upholding award of different rates for in-court and out-of-court time).

Ninth Circuit: BSA, Inc. v. King County, 804 F.2d 1104, 1112 (9th Cir. 1986)(upholding award of different rates for in-court and out-of-court work).

§ 18.15 Appropriate Rates for Attorney Travel Time

Pages 488-89, update Daggett citation and add to note 26:

First Circuit: Rogers v. Motta, 655 F. Supp. 39, 48 (D. Mass. 1986)(compensating half of attorney's travel time at full hourly rate and other half at half the full rate, on assumption that no more than half of travel time could have been profitably spent conferring with co-counsel about the case).

Second Circuit: In re Agent Orange Prod. Liab. Litig., 818 F.2d 226, 238 (2d Cir 1987)(noting, in equitable fund fee case, that 'it is not unusual for hours of travel time . . . to be compensated at lower rates"); Rose v. Heintz, 671 F. Supp. 901, 905 (D. Conn. 1987)(travel time compensated at one-half normal rate).

Third Circuit: Daggett, *aff'd in relevant part,* 811 F.2d 793 (3d Cir. 1987).

Fifth Circuit: Beamon v. City of Ridgeland, 666 F. Supp. 937, 941 (S.D. Miss. 1987) (travel time compensated at half normal rate).

* *Eighth Circuit:* McDonald v. Armontrout, 860 F.2d 1456, 1462-63 (8th Cir. 1988) (upholding district court's 50 percent rate reduction for attorney travel time, stating that travel time should be compensated at full rate unless district court "determine[d] in its discretion that such a recovery would be unreasonable").

Eleventh Circuit: United States v. Marengo County Comm'n, 667 F. Supp. 786, 797-98 (S.D. Ala. 1987)(travel time compensated at half normal rate).

Page 489, add to note 27:

In Bohen v. City of East Chicago, 666 F. Supp. 154 (N.D. Ind. 1987), Judge Easterbrook explained that "[t]ravel time is an opportunity cost; while traveling, counsel cannot work on something else," and that the "private bar customarily bills for and clients pay for travel time at ordinary rates." *Id.* at 157. "Opportunity-cost billing is the norm in private practice, and therefore applies here as well." *Id.* In Rose Confections, Inc. v. Ambrosia Chocolate Co., 816 F.2d 381, 396 (8th Cir. 1987), the Eighth Circuit reaffirmed that attorney travel time should be compensated at normal rates under fee-shifting statutes, unless unreasonable because, for example, "the lawyer did not customarily charge clients for travel time, or if he did not have other work that could have been done during that time had he not been traveling."

§ 18.16 Appropriate Rates for Work Done by Nonlawyer Paraprofessionals

Page 490, update Black Grievance Committee citation and add to note 32:

Black Grievance Comm., *vacated and remanded on other grounds,* 802 F.2d 648 (3d Cir. 1986). *But see In re* Agent Orange Prod. Liab. Litig., 818 F.2d 226, 238 (2d Cir. 1987)(declining to reevaluate rule, established in equitable fund context, that paralegal time is compensable only as an expense, while conceding that it "may be appropriate not to treat paralegal time as an expense in a large class action"); Abrams v. Baylor

College of Medicine, 805 F.2d 528, 535 (5th Cir. 1986)(finding it "entirely reasonable" for district court to conclude that the "cost of the services of support personnel–such as paralegals–was encompassed within the relatively high hourly billing rate awarded for the time of the plaintiffs' attorneys"); Keith v. Volpe, 644 F. Supp. 1312, 1316 (C.D. Cal. 1986)(reimbursing plaintiffs for work of law student clerks working unpaid for class credit "at an hourly rate sufficient to defray the additional office costs that unpaid staff incur").

Page 491, update Hyatt citation in note 35:

aff'd, 807 F.2d 376 (4th Cir. 1986), *cert. denied,* 108 S. Ct. 79 (1987).

* In Jenkins. v. Missouri, 838 F.2d 260 (8th Cir.), *cert. granted,* 109 S. Ct. 218 (1988), the Supreme Court will consider the compensability under § 1988 of paralegal and law clerk services.

§ 18.17 The Choice of Current or Historic Rates

Pages 492-93, update Palmer (District of Columbia Circuit), Delaware Valley (Third Circuit), Daly (Fourth Circuit), Burlington Northern (Seventh Circuit), and Library of Congress v. Shaw citations, and add to note 40:

Second Circuit: Hillburn v. Commissioner, Conn. Dep't of Income Maintenance, 683 F. Supp. 23, 25 (D. Conn. 1987)(historic rates for first stage and current rates for second stage of multiyear litigation).

Third Circuit: Delaware Valley, 478 U.S. 546 (1986); Black Grievance Comm. v. Philadelphia Elec. Co., 802 F.2d 648, 655-56 (3d Cir. 1986)(directing district court to correctly apply delay-in-payment adjustment when historic rates were used, "to compensate the attorney for the time gap between the actual expenditure of services and the fee award").

Fourth Circuit: Daly v. Hill, 635 F. Supp. 1270, 1271-73 (W.D.N.C. 1986)(on remand from court of appeals, court reaffirmed rates awarded, characterizing them as current and not unadjusted historic rates).

Seventh Circuit: Lightfoot v. Walker, 826 F.2d 516, 523-24 (7th Cir. 1987), *aff'g* 619 F. Supp. 1481, 1489 (N.D. Ill. 1985)(upholding district court's use of current rates for current experience levels of plaintiffs' counsel, on finding that the award at current rates was "less than it would have been had the court utilized historic rates multiplied by the applicable interest rates," and rejecting defendants' argument that plaintiffs were responsible for the delay in payment by protracting the underlying litigation or the fee litigation); *Burlington Northern, aff'd in relevant part,* 810 F.2d 601, 608-09 (7th Cir. 1987)(finding that district court's refusal to award prejudgment interest to compensate for delay in payment was not an abuse of discretion, since defendants' vigorous resistance to fee application was reasonable and award of top hourly rates at end of litigation for work done throughout litigation may have partly compensated for delay in payment); Shakman v. Democratic Org. of Cook County, 634 F. Supp. 895, 902-03 (N.D. Ill. 1986)(utilizing current rates to compensate for delayed payment over 16 years of litigation); Lock v. Jenkins, 634 F. Supp. 615, 626-27 (N.D. Ind. 1986)(applying current rate for work done 5 to 10 years ago by one attorney, and for another attorney "split[ting] the difference" between historic and current rates for services spanning 4-year period).

Ninth Circuit: Jordan v. Multnomah County, 815 F.2d 1258, 1262 n.7 (9th Cir. 1987)(use of current rates "may be required if the effects of inflation would otherwise render the fee award unreasonable"); Keith v. Volpe, 644 F. Supp. 1312, 1316 (C.D. Cal. 1986)(current rates).

Tenth Circuit: Ramos v. Lamm, 632 F. Supp. 376, 388 n.8 (D. Colo. 1986)(current rates).

Eleventh Circuit: Norman v. Housing Auth. of Montgomery, 836 F.2d 1292, 1306, (11th Cir. 1988)(directing district court on remand to give "every consideration" to application of current rates "because of the delay experienced by the attorneys in receiving payment").

In the absence of other information, current rates might be conservatively estimated to account for inflation by upgrading prevailing market rates in previous years through application of consumer price index increases. United States v. State of Washington, 626 F. Supp. 1405, 1519-20 (W.D. Wash. 1985), *rev'd on other grounds,* 813 F.2d 1020 (9th Cir. 1987); *cf.* Jackson v. Heckler, 629 F. Supp. 398, 405-06 (S.D.N.Y. 1986)(Equal Access to Justice Act, 28 U.S.C. § 2412). That approach fails, however, to take account of "increased experience and rising fee rates in the relevant geographic area," thus requiring a higher percentage increase in previous years' rates in order to fully reflect current rates. Vaughns v. Board of Educ., 627 F. Supp. 837, 842-43 (D. Md. 1985)(applying 15 percent across-the-board increases to previously awarded rates as a "rough justice" approach to determining current rates for subsequent work).

Page 494, add after sentence ending with note 43 reference:

The courts are in agreement that the use of current rates, as well as the award of an upward lodestar adjustment in order to compensate for delay in payment of statutory fee awards against the *federal* government is prohibited by *Library of Congress v. Shaw,* * 106 S. Ct. 2957 (1986). *National Wildlife Federation v. Hanson,* 859 F.2d 313, 318 (4th Cir. 1988); *Thompson v. Kennickell,* 836 F.2d 616, 619 (D.C. Cir. 1988); *cf. Young v. Pierce,* 822 F.2d 1376, 1380 (5th Cir. 1987). See **§§ 20.5** and **21.9**.

In *Rogers v. Okin,* 821 F.2d 22, 27-28 (1st Cir. 1987), *cert. denied,* 108 S. Ct. 709 (1988), the First Circuit ruled that the Eleventh Amendment bars the assessment against the state, as part of a statutory fee award, of compensation for delay in payment in the form either of an upward lodestar adjustment or the use of current rates. In so ruling, the court analogized from the Supreme Court's ruling in *Library of Congress v. Shaw,* 106 S. Ct. 2957 (1986), discussed above. The *Rogers* court distinguished *Hutto v. Finney,* 437 U.S. 678 (1978), in which the Supreme Court held that the Eleventh Amendment was not a bar to an award of statutory attorney's fees against the state, pursuant to § 1988, in view of Congress' enforcement powers under § 5 of the Fourteenth Amendment, evidence in the legislative history of Congress' intent to render states liable for § 1988 fees, and § 1988's description of attorney's fees as an element of costs, traditionally not subject to Eleventh Amendment constraints. See **§ 16.8**. The *Rogers* court noted that, in contrast, there was no evidence in the legislative history of § 1988 that Congress intended to make states liable for prejudgment interest or delay compensation. 821 F.2d at 27-28.

The opposite – and better – view on this issue has been adopted by the Eighth Circuit, which in *Jenkins v. Missouri,* 838 F.2d 260, 265-66 (8th Cir. 1988), rejected the First Circuit's conclusion that states enjoy an Eleventh Amendment immunity from the application under § 1988 of current rates or an upward lodestar adjustment to compensate for delay in payment. The *Jenkins* court saw no reason to apply *Shaw*'s federal sovereign immunity holding to state Eleventh Amendment immunity analysis and preferred to follow the "generally accepted view" of the circuit courts that states are liable under fee-shifting statutes for compensation for delayed payment through * current rates or upward lodestar adjustments. *Id.* at 265-66. The Supreme Court has granted certiorari in *Jenkins,* 109 S. Ct. 218 (1988), to review this Eleventh Amendment issue.

Page 494, update Lightfoot citation in note 45:

aff'd, 826 F.2d 516, 523 (7th Cir. 1987).

Page 494, add new paragraph at end of section:

The current rates that are applied by courts generally are those in effect at the time the fee application is made, on the assumption that fee awards ordinarily are sought and "made promptly at the conclusion of the phase of the litigation to which the award relates." *Mares v. Credit Bureau of Raton,* 801 F.2d 1197, 1207 (10th Cir. 1986)(Consumer Credit Protection Act, 15 U.S.C. §§ 1601 *et seq.*). However, occasionally, as in the *Mares* case, the district court's fee determination is not made until several years after the conclusion of the litigation and the submission of the fee petition, because of the defendant's stout resistance to the application or because of delayed adjudication due to the pendency of a relevant fee appeal in a higher court. *Id.* at 1199-1200. Prevailing rates in the community may rise significantly over the substantial period between the fee request and the fee determination in such cases, and, accordingly, it might be expected that the rates finally selected by the district court would be those current at the time of the fee decision. However, the Tenth Circuit in *Mares* nonetheless upheld the district court's fixing of rates that were current at the time the main litigation was concluded and the initial fee application was made, instead of at the time, three years later, when the fee decision was finally rendered. *Id.* at 1208. The Tenth Circuit observed that while "[i]t is true that during the very substantial time between the conclusion of this case and the fee award defendants continued to enjoy, and plaintiffs' counsel was deprived of, the use of the fee award," the "same is true of awards made immediately following trials but not paid for many years because of appeals." *Id.* at 1207-08. However, delay-in-payment concerns between the time of the fee judgment and its payment are separately accommodated by the accrual of post-judgment interest under 28 U.S.C. § 1961. *See Mares,* 801 F.2d at 1208; *Black Grievance Comm. v. Philadelphia Elec. Co.,* 802 F.2d 648, 656 (3d Cir. 1986). See generally **§ 21.9**. Thus, the result in *Mares* seems somewhat harsh, especially since the delay in the adjudication of the fee request in that case was not the fault of the fee applicant. *See also In re Burlington Northern, Inc.,* 810 F.2d 601, 608-09 (7th Cir.

1986)(upholding use of rates current at time fee petition was filed in June 1984, since delay in entry of fee judgment until September 1985 "was occasioned by a legitimate dispute over several [fee] issues" and counsel "may have been compensated, at least in part, by the fact that they were paid at the top 1984 hourly rates for all of the work they performed throughout the litigation"); *Birth Control Centers, Inc. v. Reizen,* 652 F. Supp. 192, 196 (E.D. Mich. 1986)(declining to compensate for delay in fee payment by upward lodestar adjustment or use of current rates, because "[m]uch of the delay is due to plaintiffs' appeal, without which plaintiffs may not have been prevailing parties, and to the inexplicable lapse of almost two years between the appellate decision and plaintiffs' first request for attorney fees").

Courts often utilize current rates for the *current* experience levels of the prevailing party's attorneys, even though the consequence is that an attorney is compensated for services rendered during the early years of extended litigation, when she is very junior, at an elevated rate which reflects her current experience as a much more senior attorney. *See, e.g., Shakman v. Democratic Org. of Cook County,* 634 F. Supp. 895, 902-03 (N.D. Ill. 1986). Those courts do not view the use of current rates for current experience levels to be overcompensatory, since "one need only take historic rates for historic experience and account for the value of inflation and interest to realize that in present times the simplified approach . . . [of current rates for current experience] falls on the conservative side." *Lightfoot v. Walker,* 619 F. Supp. 1481, 1489 (N.D. Ill. 1985), *aff'd,* 826 F.2d 516, 523 (7th Cir. 1987).

However, courts sometimes reject the use of current rates for current experience levels of plaintiff's attorneys, as conferring an unwarranted attorney's fee windfall on counsel. *Leroy v. City of Houston,* 831 F.2d 576, 584-85 (5th Cir. 1987); *Chalmers v. City of Los Angeles,* 676 F. Supp. 1515, 1526-27 (C.D. Cal. 1987). The court in *Chalmers* observed that a current rate for current experience "more likely reflects an attorney's increased experience and skill as a lawyer than some change in the time-value of money," and that a "change in an attorney's fee schedule might reflect a change in the supply and demand of lawyers practicing in that attorney's field and community more * than the effects of inflation." 676 F. Supp. at 1526-27. *See Fleming v. County of Kane,* 686 F. Supp. 1264, 1272-73 (N.D. Ill. 1988) (characterizing use of current rates for current experience levels as "no better than a rough and ready (albeit often a highly convenient) surrogate for a more precise measure: the present value of what counsel would have collected but for the delay in billing"). On the other hand, the use of unadjusted historic rates may seriously undercompensate attorneys for the lost time value of their fees over a number of years of litigation. *See, e.g., Thompson v. Barrett,* 599 F. Supp. 806, 813-14 (D.D.C. 1984).

A delay adjustment should compensate not only for inflation, but, as well, for the loss of use of the fee money over the period of the delay in payment. The *Chalmers* court concluded that the "historic market rate of interest," which is partly linked to the inflation rate, is more relevant than current rates in measuring loss from delay. *Id.* at 1527. However, this "adjusted historic billing rate" approach presents the problem of selecting an appropriate interest rate multiplier. Absent information concerning the "cost to plaintiff's counsel of borrowing funds to support himself during the non-paying phases of the litigation," the court must select from among the market interest * rates for the relevant period. *Id.* The court in *Fleming v. County of Kane,* 686 F. Supp. 1264, 1272-74 (N.D. Ill. 1988), observing that interest rates "reflect the free market's combination of the pure cost of money and the element of inflation," adjusted historic rates to account for delayed payment by adding interest at the prime rate. *See also Lippo v. Mobil Oil Corp.,* 692 F. Supp. 826, 838-43 (N.D. Ill. 1988) (utilizing prime rate to adjust for delayed payment of fee award under Petroleum Marketing Practices Act, 15 U.S.C. § 2805(d)(1)(C)); *Black Grievance Committee v. Philadelphia Electric Co.,* 690 F. Supp. 1393, 1402-03 (E.D. Pa. 1988) (use of prime interest rates). The court in *Skelton v. General Motors Corp.,* 661 F. Supp. 1368, 1383 & n.19 (N.D. Ill. 1987), rejected the proposed approach of compensating for delay by awarding historic rates plus interest calculated at the prime rate for a given time period, as producing fees substantially higher than those determined in accordance with current rates. The *Chalmers* court utilized the interest rate on the 52-week U.S. Treasury bill, in preference to the interest rate on three- or six-month Treasury bills. The court calculated the delay adjustment by increasing the fee for each year, based on the use of historic rates, by the appropriate 52-week Treasury bill rate, under a formula described by the court. 676 F. Supp. at 1527-28. The court in *Shakman v. Democratic Organization of Cook County,* 677 F. Supp. 933, 940-42 (N.D. Ill. 1987), agreed to grant an additional delay adjustment, on top of the current rates awarded to ensure compensation for both inflation and the time value of the money, based on the average annual yield on three-month Treasury bills.

Preferable perhaps to the use in extended litigation of either adjusted historic rates or current rates for current experience is the application of current rates for the past experience levels possessed by the attorneys at the times the services were rendered. See discussion in text. On the other hand, the use of current rates for current experience levels is warranted, as not likely to be overcompensatory, when the litigation spans only a few years or arises within the Second Circuit, where current rates are permitted only for the most recent three years of multi-year litigation. See text. *Cf. Ohio-Sealy Mattress Mfg. Co. v. Sealy Inc.,* 776 F.2d 646, 663 (7th Cir. 1985).

CHAPTER 19

DOWNWARD ADJUSTMENTS TO THE LODESTAR

§ 19.1 Introduction

Page 496, update Rivera citation in note 3:

477 U.S. 561 (1986).

§ 19.2 Downward Adjustments for Limited Success: The Two-Step Analysis of *Hensley v. Eckerhart*

Page 496, update Smith citation in note 7:

468 U.S. 992, 1006-07 (1984).

Page 498, add after sentence ending with note 22 reference:

In *Spanish Action Committee v. City of Chicago,* 811 F.2d 1129 (7th Cir. 1987), the Seventh Circuit considered the particular lodestar reduction approach that should be employed in cases in which the plaintiff has obtained only partial success on related claims and, as well, has claimed hours that should be eliminated because excessive or duplicative or inadequately documented. The court concluded that district court should first eliminate all claimed hours that are not reasonably expended or are inadequately documented, and only then should "adjust the total number of 'reasonably expended' hours so that the final award is reasonable in relation to the overall results obtained by the plaintiff." *Id.* at 1137-38.

* A very confusing, and, we submit, erroneous, interpretation of *Hensley* lodestar reduction principles has recently been advanced by the Ninth Circuit in *Cunningham v. County of Los Angeles,* 859 F.2d 705, 710-13 (9th Cir. 1988). In *Cunningham,* the court read Supreme Court fee decisions to require that the "results obtained" factor generally be subsumed within the lodestar determination, instead of constituting the basis for a downward adjustment of the lodestar. *Id.* at 711-12. The court's error stems from its application to *downward* adjustments, for plaintiff's limited success, of the principle established by *Hensley* and *Stenson* that the results obtained factor only rarely should constitute the basis for an *upward* lodestar adjustment for plaintiff's exceptional success in the litigation. *Id.* at 711. The Ninth Circuit did condemn the district court's attempt to count the results obtained *twice,* to the double disadvantage of the prevailing plaintiff, by invoking it as a basis for both a diminished lodestar figure and an independent reduction of the lodestar. *Id.* at 712-13.

Page 498, update Rivera citation in note 24:

477 U.S. 561 (1986).

Page 499, update Rivera citation and add to note 32:

477 U.S. 561, 584-85 (1986) (Powell J., concurring); N.A.A.C.P. v. City of Evergreen, 812 F.2d 1332, 1335 (11th Cir. 1987) (faulting district court for reducing fee award for time purportedly spend on an unsuccessful claim, without adequate explanation).

§ 19.3 –Establishing Related Claims: Shared Facts or Legal Theories

Page 500, update Rivera citation and add to note 36:

* Rivera, 477 U.S. 561, 584-85 (1986) (Powell, J., concurring); Nash v. Chandler, 848 F.2d 567, 572-73 (5th Cir. 1988) (upholding district court's conclusion, in suit challenging constitutionality of mass picketing statute, that unsuccessful claims for monetary and injunctive relief were related to successful declaratory judgment claim); Davis v. City of Charleston, 827 F.2d 317, 323 (8th Cir. 1987) (finding related the successful and unsuccessful arguments supporting the same claim for relief involving common core of facts); Conservation Law Foundation v. Secretary of Interior, 790 F.2d 965, 968-70 (1st Cir. 1986) (carefully analyzing interrelatedness of claims under three separate federal statutes in environmental suit, by focusing on extent to which the claims basically sought to reach the same or different results in the litigation); Lenihan v. City of New York, 640 F. Supp. 822, 826-27 (S.D.N.Y. 1986) (concluding that defendant "has confused claims and remedies," court declined to reduce fee award for plaintiff's asserted lack of success on some claims in employment sex discrimination suit, since plaintiff succeeded on each of her claims although she obtained only some of the remedies she sought).

Page 500, add to note 37:

Abshire v. Walls, 830 F.2d 1277, 1282-83 (4th Cir. 1987) (finding that plaintiff's unsuccessful claims for false arrest, false imprisonment, and malicious prosecution were related to his successful strip-search claim, because, although based on different legal theories, all claims arose from a "common core of facts" that were "inextricably intertwined," and plaintiff's attorney "could not have presented the constitutional aspects of this case without developing and presenting the facts surrounding the entire sequence of events that transpired" on the morning in question); Wagenmann v. Adams, 829 F.2d 196, 225 (1st Cir. 1987) (concluding that plaintiff's successful civil rights claims for false arrest, excessive bail, and unlawful commitment were related to state law (including legal malpractice) claims, since "[a]ll of the triable issues arose out of a short, visibly linked series of events into which Wagenmann was involuntarily plunged"); Popham v. City of Kennesaw, 820 F.2d 1570, 1579 (11th Cir. 1987) (successful and unsuccessful claims concerning false arrest, excessive force, and malicious prosecution were related, because they arose out of the "same course of conduct"); Cobb v. Miller, 818 F.2d 1227, 1233 (5th Cir. 1987) (interrelated claims all stemming from unlawful use of force in regard to plaintiff's arrest and his subsequent detention); Afro-American Patrolmen's League v. Atlanta, 817 F.2d 719, 725-26 (11th

Cir. 1987) (interrelated issues of validity of promotional exam and legality of defendant's abandonment of promotion procedure in Title VII employment discrimination suit).

Page 501, add to note 38:

Toussaint v. McCarthy, 826 F.2d 901, 904-05 (9th Cir. 1987) (finding that plaintiffs' legal claims challenging prison conditions and administrative segregation procedures, some successful and some unsuccessful, involved a "common core of facts and legal theories" and were not separable); Morgan v. District of Columbia, 824 F.2d 1049, 1066 (D.C. Cir. 1987) (upholding finding of interrelatedness of successful and unsuccessful claims that all related to plaintiff prisoner's central claim that defendants had been deliberately indifferent to his rights to be free of prisoner assaults and that the indifference was rooted in defendants' longstanding overcrowding practice in the jail).

Page 501, add to cases cited in note 39:

McKenzie v. Kennickell, 645 F. Supp. 437, 446-47 (D.D.C. 1986) (finding the successful and unsuccessful claims related in case challenging a pattern and practice of race discrimination in the workplace that was treated by the parties "as one broad Title VII claim").

Page 501, add to note 42:

Garner v. Wal-Mart Stores, Inc., 807 F.2d 1536, 1539 (11th Cir. 1987) (unsuccessful constructive discharge claim was unrelated to successful employment sex discrimination claim); Bohen v. City of East Chicago, 666 F. Supp. 154, 156 (N.D. Ind. 1987) (in employment discrimination suit, successful harassment and unsuccessful discharge contentions were "separate claims for relief, not separate theories in support of a single claim;" however, difficulty in separating time spent on each claim warranted approach of 10% across-the-board reduction in total claimed hours).

Page 501, add after sentence ending with note 45 reference:

In *Lenard v. Argento,* 808 F.2d 1242 (7th Cir. 1987), the Seventh Circuit, in the context of a partially successful damages suit arising out of the plaintiff's arrest by defendant police officers, evaluated the interrelatedness of unsuccessful claims of excessive force, conspiracy to obstruct justice, and malicious prosecution, and a successful claim of conspiracy to deny plaintiff equal protection on the basis of race. The court found that the beating and equal protection claims were related to each other because they both grew out of the beating and that the malicious prosecution and conspiracy to obstruct justice claims were related to each other. *Id.* at 1246. The court further concluded that the first pair of claims essentially stated a claim of excessive force and the latter pair a claim of false arrest and that, as such, the two pairs of claims were unrelated to each other. *Id.* The court observed that false arrest and excessive force are forms of misconduct that are "independent conceptually as well as in time," and, further, that "evidence showing one form of misconduct is not relevant to establishing the other." *Id.* The court concluded that "[s]equential claims – claims that are causally related

(Lenard wouldn't have been beaten if he hadn't been arrested) but do not depend on
* the same facts–are not related for purposes of *Hensley.*" *Id.* In *Jackson v. Illinois Prisoner Review Board,* 856 F.2d 890, 894 (7th Cir. 1988), the court concluded that the plaintiff's unsuccessful ex post facto challenge to the composition of the Prisoner Review Board was unrelated to his ssuccessful due process challenge to the Board's withholding of evidence, since the two claims were based on different facts and legal theories. This was not a case, the court stated, "where the same claim was stated in two different ways, one of which fell by the wayside." *Id.* at 894. The court also ruled that hours spent on an earlier due process claim, that was mooted by the Board's rule change, were properly compensable, since the "1984 and 1986 due process claims were part of the same ultimately successful effort to force the Board to abide by its disclosure rules at Jackson's parole hearings." *Id.* at 894-95. In reviewing compensation for work done on plaintiffs' § 1988 fee request, the First Circuit in *Jacobs v. Mancuso,* 825 F.2d 559, 563 (1st Cir. 1987), deleted the time spent on plaintiffs' distinct and unsuccessful argument for a contingency enhancement of the lodestar.

Page 502, add to note 47:

Blum v. Witco Chem. Corp., 829 F.2d 367, 378 (3d Cir. 1987) (Age Discrimination in Employment Act, 29 U.S.C. § 626(b); declining to delete time spent on unsuccessful motions or depositions not used at trial); Aston v. Secretary of Health and Human Services, 808 F.2d 9, 11 (2d Cir. 1986) (Equal Access to Justice Act, 28 U.S.C. § 2412; upholding compensation for "unnecessary" summary judgment motion not separable from plaintiff's successful claim). *But see* Lebron v. Washington Mctro. Area Transit Auth., 665 F. Supp. 923, 927 (D.D.C. 1987) (denying compensation for time spent on unsuccessful sanctions motion).

Page 503, add at end of section:

In *Catlett v. Missouri Highway and Transportation Commission,* 828 F.2d 1260 (8th Cir. 1987), *cert. denied,* 108 S. Ct. 1574 (1988), the Eighth Circuit concluded that no compensation should be granted for time expended by plaintiffs' attorneys in unsuccessfully opposing defendant's motion to reduce the scope of the certified plaintiff class. *Id.* at 1270. The court found that these "extra efforts" did not in general contribute to the success of the plaintiffs' case and that the use at trial of a "few pieces of evidence" uncovered during discovery on the class size issue did not justify compensating all hours spent on the issue. *Id.*

§ 19.4 –Establishing Related Claims: Overlapping Work and Inseparable Time

Page 504, add to cases cited in note 62:

Coston v. Plitt Theatres, Inc., 831 F.2d 1321, 1337 (7th Cir. 1987) (finding unsuccessful front-pay claim related to successful back-pay claim in employment discrimination suit, noting that work involved in back-pay claim "was substantially similar to the analysis and research required to establish a basis for damages for backpay"); Dominic

v. Consolidated Edison Co., 822 F.2d 1249, 1260 (2d Cir. 1987) (Age Discrimination in Employment Act, 29 U.S.C. § 626(b); agreeing that unsuccessful age discrimination and successful retaliatory discharge claims were "inextricably intertwined," in part because of interdependence of underlying facts); Vaughns v. Board of Educ., 627 F. Supp. 837, 840-41 (D. Md. 1985) (court in school desegregation case fully excluded from fee award only so much of the time spent in preparing the unsuccessful "intent" argument as was "devoted *solely* to intent," and not the time spent developing information for that argument that also supported the successful "lack of unitary status" claim).

* In Ustrak v. Fairman, 851 F.2d 983, 988-89 (7th Cir. 1988), the court rejected defendant's contention that the plaintiff prisoner who succeeded on only one legal claim, that was legally and factually distinct from his other five claims, should recover only one-sixth of his fee request. Judge Posner noted that a "partially prevailing plaintiff should be compensated for the legal expenses he would have borne if his suit had been confined to the ground on which he prevailed plus related grounds within the meaning of *Hensley*." *Id.* at 988. Under this approach the appropriate inquiry in this case was how much time would have been expended by plaintiff's counsel if he had sued only on his successful claim. *Id.* The court noted that in litigating the one successful claim, plaintiff's counsel still would have conducted a jury trial, taken depositions, written appellate briefs, and prepared a fee petition, none of which would have taken only one-sixth of the time required to litigate the six claims. *Id.* at 988-89. The court applied a 50 percent reduction to the claimed fee, as its "best estimate" of the time needed to handle the case if confined to its single meritorious claim. *Id.* at 989. The court then declined to further reduce the fee award on account of the modest money damages recovery, emphasizing that there is an "irreducible fixed cost to litigation," and that the court's prior reduction was based, in effect, on the "minimum cost of litigating such a case." *Id.*

Page 504, add to cases cited in note 63:

Jenkins v. Missouri, 838 F.2d 260, 264 (8th Cir. 1988) (upholding only limited reduction for time spent on unsuccessful claims, because a "substantial portion of the testimony that bore upon the unsuccessful claims was closely interrelated with the remaining claims"); Rogers v. Okin, 821 F.2d 22, 25 (1st Cir. 1987) (upholding compensation for substantial hours spent on unsuccessful damage claims, when "most of the evidence relevant to damage claims was also necessary to justify injunctive relief"); United States v. Marengo County Comm'n, 667 F. Supp. 786, 795 (S.D. Ala. 1987) (granting compensation for work done on unsuccessful appellate motion that was "fully recovered in the briefing process for the [successful] appeals in chief"); Thorne v. City of El Segundo, 802 F.2d 1131, 1142 (9th Cir. 1986) (court observed that the testimony presented on plaintiff's successful Title VII claim and on her unsuccessful § 1983 claim "overlapped, and it seems unlikely that trial preparation time on the two claims could be separated").

Page 504, add to note 65:

Catlett v. Missouri Highway & Transp. Comm'n, 828 F.2d 1260, 1270 (8th Cir. 1987) (approving compensation for time spent, in successful class action suit, in pursuing unsuccessful individual claims, in light of the "relevance to the class pattern or practice claim of evidence of individual incidents of discrimination"), *cert. denied,* 108 S. Ct. 1574 (1988); Foster v. Board of School Comm'rs, 810 F.2d 1021, 1023-24 (11th Cir.) (upholding limited reduction of time spent on unsuccessful claims of some of the individual plaintiffs in class action suit, because "most of the attorney hours were spent on general research and investigation applicable to all the claims and . . . evidence adduced at hearings on unsuccessful claims contributed to the cases presented by victorious claimants"), *cert. denied,* 108 S. Ct. 99 (1987).

Page 504, add to cases cited in note 67:

Bovey v. City of Lafayette, 638 F. Supp. 640, 650 (N.D. Ind. 1986); Orshan v. Macchiarola, 629 F. Supp. 1014, 1019-20 (E.D.N.Y. 1986) (both applying percentage reduction to fee award where counsel's time records did not reflect allocation of time between successful and unsuccessful claims).

§ 19.5 —Reduction in the Fee Award in Cases of Limited Success on Interrelated Winning and Losing Claims

Page 505, update Smith citation in note 69:

468 U.S. 992, 1006 (1984).

Page 505, add to note 74:

* *See* Cunningham v. County of Los Angeles, 859 F.2d 705, 710 (9th Cir. 1988) (rejecting a "unifactor approach tying the number of hours accepted as reasonable solely to the proportion of defendants ultimately prevailed against"); Foster v. Board of School Comm'rs, 810 F.2d 1021, 1023-24 (11th Cir.) (rejecting defendants' contention that fee award for work done at second stage of class action suit, at which hearings were held for 104 individual plaintiffs, should be reduced by ratio of unsuccessful claims over total number of claims), *cert. denied,* 108 S. Ct. 99 (1987); Black Grievance Comm. v. Philadelphia Elec. Co., 802 F.2d 648, 654 (3d Cir. 1986) (court rejected defendant's contention that reduction in fee award for plaintiffs' partial success should be based on a "mechanical comparison of the claims alleged . . . to the relief obtained in the consent decree," noting that "because the claims do not bear a quantitative relationship to the result, the comparison is subjective"). *But see* Harris v. McCarthy, 790 F.2d 753, 758-59 (9th Cir. 1986) (upholding district court's percentage reduction of plaintiffs' fee request for work on the fee application, in the same percentage as was applied to their fee request for substantive work in the case, as "merely an arithmetic formulation of the extent to which the plaintiffs succeeded on their section 1988 motion").

Page 506, update Rivera citation in note 77:

Rivera, 477 U.S. 561, 584-85 (1986) (Powell, J., concurring). *See* Coston v. Plitt Theatres, Inc., 831 F.2d 1321, 1337 (7th Cir. 1987) (reduction in award not appropriate, because plaintiff achieved "substantial relief" in age discrimination suit, although front-pay relief was not obtained); Morgan v. District of Columbia, 824 F.2d 1049, 1066 (D.C. Cir. 1987) (no reduction in fee award on account of unsuccessful claims, because plaintiff achieved "outstanding" results on his central claim in prison assault case); Dominic v. Consolidated Edison Co., 822 F.2d 1249, 1260 (2d Cir. 1987) (Age Discrimination in Employment Act, 29 U.S.C. § 626(b); fully compensatory fee award warranted when plaintiff obtained same relief on his successful retaliation claim that he would have won on unsuccessful age discrimination claim); Paxton v. Union Nat'l Bank, 806 F.2d 785, 787 (8th Cir. 1986) (overturning district court's substantial reduction of fee award for plaintiffs' "limited" success in suit, because plaintiffs achieved "substantial" relief in regard to the "major thrust" of their employment discrimination suit).

Page 506, add to note 78:

* Ustrak v. Fairman, 851 F.2d 983, 988-89 (7th Cir. 1988) (applying 50 percent reduction to fee request to account for lack of success on five out of six legal claims, and as reflecting the "minimum cost" of litigating the successful claim); Toussaint v. McCarthy, 826 F.2d 901, 905 (9th Cir. 1987) (plaintiffs' limited success on appeal in complex prison conditions suit entitled them to only 37.5% of lodestar award); McCurry v. Tesch, 824 F.2d 638, 642 (8th Cir. 1987) (upholding district court's one-third reduction in fee award because plaintiffs obtained only a declaratory judgment and no injunction or money damages); Greater Los Angeles Council on Deafness v. Community Television, 813 F.2d 217, 222 (9th Cir. 1987) (plaintiffs' limited success in obtaining only partial relief against only one of several defendants entitled them to only 40% of lodestar award).

Page 507, add to cases cited in note 84:

Diaz v. Robert Ruiz, Inc., 808 F.2d 427, 429 (5th Cir. 1987) (plaintiffs entitled to compensation for time spent on non-fee claims to extent that they "interrelate and overlap" with successful fee-generating claims under Fair Labor Standards Act, 29 U.S.C. § 216(b)); Zabkowicz v. West Bend Co., 789 F.2d 540, 550-551 (7th Cir. 1986) (concluding that under *Hensley* Title VII fee compensation may be granted for work done on unsuccessful labor law and state tort claims, not themselves fee-generating in nature, if they were related to plaintiffs' successful Title VII claims).

Page 507, delete sentence ending with note 85 reference, together with note 85, and see § 15.16 of this supplement.

Page 507, add to cases cited in note 87:

Cobb v. Miller, 818 F.2d 1227, 1233-34 (5th Cir. 1987) (lodestar reduction not warranted merely because plaintiff prevailed against only one of three defendants, because claims against the three defendants were interrelated and not "easily differentiated on the basis of each defendant"); Probe v. State Teachers' Retirement System, 780 F.2d 776, 785 (9th Cir. 1986) (fully compensatory Title VII fee award granted to plaintiffs who achieved the "major relief they sought in this case," although the action was dismissed as to five out of six defendants).

Page 508, add to note 88:

Student Pub. Interest Research Group v. AT&T Bell Laboratories, 842 F.2d 1436, 1455 (3d Cir. 1988) (directing district court on remand to consider whether statutory fee for fee litigation should be reduced because of lack of success on multiplier requests); *In re* Burlington Northern, Inc., 832 F.2d 430, 433-36 (7th Cir. 1987) (applying *Hensley* reduction principles to fee award for work on fee request; upholding 35% reduction in award when $2.2 million initial fee award was only 42% of total amount sought and plaintiffs did not obtain sought-after lodestar multiplier); Durett v. Cohen, 790 F.2d 360, 363 (3d Cir. 1986) (reduced fee award for work on partially successful fee application). *But see* Greater Los Angeles Council on Deafness v. Community Television, 813 F.2d 217, 223 (9th Cir. 1987) (declining to apply *Hensley* reduction analysis to fee award for plaintiffs' work in defending initial fee award on appeal, notwithstanding that elimination of multiplier and imposition of lodestar reduction on appeal gave plaintiff only partial success, when "defending the fee award involves a single, indivisible claim");

Page 508, add after last sentence in section:

Because of the "practical desirability of having a uniform methodology," the Third Circuit has ruled that a district court should first apply the "result-obtained" adjustment to the lodestar, to account for the prevailing party's success in the litigation, and then should "add together the other (whether they be reducer or enhancer) adjustments it has found to be justified and multiply that combined factor by the result-obtained-adjusted lodestar." *Black Grievance Comm. v. Philadelphia Elec. Co.,* 802 F.2d 648, 656 (3d Cir. 1986).

§ 19.6 —Applying the *Hensley* Analysis to Partially Successful Cases Involving Money Damages Claims

Page 509, add after sentence ending with note 94 reference:

The Seventh Circuit reaffirmed these principles in *Spanish Action Committee of Chicago v. City of Chicago,* 811 F.2d 1129, 1135-36 (7th Cir. 1987). *See also Lenard v. Argento,* 808 F.2d 1242, 1248 (7th Cir. 1987). Similarly, the Eleventh Circuit has emphasized that in awarding § 1988 fees in successful damages actions, the "affirmation of constitutional principles produces an undoubted public benefit that courts must consider." *Popham v. City of Kennesaw,* 820 F.2d 1570, 1580 (11th Cir. 1987). Thus, in determining § 1988 fee awards in such cases, district courts "should not place *'undue* emphasis on the modest money damages that were found by the jury.' " *Id.* at 1580. "This is especially true," the court noted, "in the area of police misconduct where injunctive relief is generally unavailable to safeguard individual rights." *Id.*

Page 509, update Rivera citation in note 98:

477 U.S. 561 (1986).

Page 510, add to note 2:

* Quesada v. Thomason, 850 F.2d 537, 539-40 (9th Cir. 1988) (ruling that lodestar reduction was inappropriate in police brutality suit seeking only money damages, since plaintiff "managed to settle for nearly half of his original request, and a full seventy percent of the amount he sought at trial;" reduction was not warranted "simply because the damage award was small" ($17,500), when the suit also secured "important social benefits"); Aubin v. Fudala, 821 F.2d 45, 46-47 (1st Cir. 1987) (upholding district court's refusal to reduce lodestar for results obtained by plaintiff who achieved "substantial success" in recovering $300,000 on his state tort claim in police misconduct suit, although he obtained only $500 on his civil rights claim); Cooper v. Dyke, 814 F.2d 941, 951 (4th Cir. 1987) (upholding fully comensatory award for "excellent results" in obtaining $75,300 jury award on plaintiff prisoner's § 1983 claim of deliberate indifference to his serious medical needs, although he won only nominal damages on his pendent state claim on false arrest).

Page 510, delete material in note 3 and substitute the following:

In Nephew v. City of Aurora, 830 F.2d 1547 (10th Cir. 1987), *Cert. denied,* 108 S. Ct. 1269 (1988), the Tenth Circuit, sitting *en banc,* upheld the district court's refusal to reduce the § 1988 fee award for plaintiffs' limited success in winning nominal damages of $1 each in a $2 million police misconduct suit. The court approved the district court's appraisal that the "amount of monetary damages in the present case was less important than the judgment against the police officers' conduct," with its "vindication of plaintiffs' civil rights and its message to the police department." *Id.* at 1550. In Cobb v. Miller, 818 F.2d 1227, 1235 (5th Cir. 1987), the court concluded that the lodestar award should not be reduced because of the plaintiffs' relatively low damages recovery in the suit, on the somewhat cryptic reasoning that "[i]n the absence of other *Johnson* factors justifying a reduction in a fee award, a district court should not reduce the fee award solely because of a low damages award."

Page 510, delete material in note 5 and substitute the following:

Martinez v. Schock Transfer & Warehouse Co., Inc., 789 F.2d 848, 849 (10th Cir. 1986) (affirming district court's substantial reduction in requested fee award for plaintiff's limited success in failing to obtain injunctive relief and winning only $7,821 of the $350,000 sought in damages). In Popham v. City of Kennesaw, 820 F.2d 1570 (11th Cir. 1987), the Eleventh Circuit held that in determining an award of § 1988 fees in a case with a damages recovery, a district court must give consideration to the public interest served by the vindication of constitutional rights underlying the damages recovery, but that the lodestar amount nonetheless may be reduced for limited success after comparison of the amount of damages recovered with the amount of damages sought in the litigation. *Id.* at 1580-81. In this case, the court of appeals upheld a 67% reduction in the lodestar award, in view of plaintiff's limited success in winning only $30,000 in damages of the $2 million requested and because the lawsuit did not "result in specific, identifiable benefits to non-parties or challenge an institutional practice of police misconduct." *Id.* at 1581.

In Spanish Action Comm. v. City of Chicago, 811 F.2d 1129 (7th Cir. 1987), the Seventh Circuit upheld the district court's substantial reduction of the lodestar for what was characterized as plaintiff's limited success in winning $60,000 in compensatory damages (of the $70,000 sought) but no punitive damages in a police misconduct suit. The court of appeals concluded that the $60,000 recovery, although constituting substantial success with respect to the compensatory damages claims, represented only limited success in the litigation as a whole, because the plaintiff lost completely on the highly important punitive damages claims, and the requests for prospective delaratory and injunctive relief had been rendered moot by the execution of a favorable consent degree in a related class action suit. *Id.* at 1134-37. The court concluded that "[i]n light of the consent decree, this suit will not generate any 'external benefits' in civil rights enforcement, beyond the damages awarded," and "[t]o that extent, it bears close resemblance to a conventional personal injury suit." *Id.* at 1136.

In the wake of City of Riverside v. Rivera, 106 S. Ct. 2686 (1986) (see **§ 19.7**), the Seventh Circuit in *Spanish Action Committee,* the Tenth Circuit in *Nephew* (discussed in **note 3**), and the Eleventh Circuit in *Popham* all have concluded that the public interest impact of the constitutional right vindicated by a civil rights damages award must be given consideration in the *Hensley* analysis of whether the lodestar should be reduced because of a nominal or comparatively low damages recovery.

Page 511, add to cases cited in note 6:

Van Sant v. United States Postal Services, 805 F.2d 141, 142 (4th Cir. 1986) (Equal Access to Justice Act, 28 U.S.C. § 2412; sharply reducing requested fee award for plaintiff's limited success in the litigation, when "[n]ot only was his recovery small in the monetary sense, the litigation resulted in the establishment of no new significant principles of law that would be of aid to any other person except in the extraordinarily unlikely event that the facts surrounding Van Sant's claim would be duplicated").

§ 19.7 The Disproportionality of Fees to Money Damages as a Basis for a Downward Adjustment in a Fee Award

Pages 511-514, update City of Riverside v. Rivera citation throughout footnotes:

477 U.S. 561, 564-81 (plurality opinion), 581-86 (Powell, J., concurring), 587-88 (Burger, C.J., dissenting), 588-96 (Rehnquist, J., dissenting) (1986).

Page 511, add to note 9:

Jacobs v. Mancuso, 825 F.2d 559, 563-64 (1st Cir. 1987) (finding that disproportionality of fee request to damages recovery had "limited relevance" in this case, because the suit probably also induced the municipal defendant to abandon the challenged practice, thereby mooting plaintiffs' requests for injunctive relief).

Page 514, update Cunningham citation in note 30:

vacated & remanded, 478 U.S. 1015 (1986), *reinstated,* 807 F.2d 49 (3d Cir. 1986), *cert. denied,* 107 S. Ct. 2179 (1987).

§ 19.7 DISPROPORTIONALITY

Page 514, add at end of section:

The lower courts inevitably will encounter great difficulties in applying the "public interest" standard stated by Justice Powell in his concurring opinion in *Rivera,* and in determining what level of disproportionality, if any, between the § 1988 fee award and the underlying damages recovery should be tolerated in a particular case. The likely consequence is that district courts will give a broad and generous reading to the "public interest" exception to Justice Powell's dictate that § 1988 fee awards generally be proportionate to money damages recoveries in civil rights cases winning only damages relief. In turn, district court decisions awarding § 1988 fees in excess of damage recoveries in such cases are likely to be upheld on appeal, as in *Rivera* itself, provided that they rest on detailed fact findings supporting the award under a *Hensley* analysis and, as well, on an explicit finding that the "public interest" was served by the underlying findings of unconstitutionality in the case. The Third Circuit, in *Cunningham v. City of McKeesport,* 807 F.2d 49, 53-54 (3d Cir. 1986), *cert. denied,* 107 S. Ct. 2179 (1987), resists the suggestion in Justice Powell's pivotal concurring opinion in *Rivera* that only rarely can the public benefit generated by a private damages award warrant the substantial disproportionality between § 1988 fees and the damages award that was upheld in *Rivera.* The court first questioned whether Justice Powell's views on proportionality could fairly be attributed to a majority of the Supreme Court in *Rivera. Id.* at 53-54. The court further noted that the facts in *Rivera* "seem similar to those of a number of § 1983 cases that we have seen," so that if the *Rivera* facts "justify a 'disproportionate' fee award, the facts in many if not most § 1983 cases should do so as well." *Id.* at 54. Finally, the court questioned the efficacy of Justice Powell's reasoning, noting that his opinion "sets out no method or standards by which a court might calculate the public interest served by a case, evaluate that interest in light of a disproportionality between damages and fees, and eventually settle upon a particular negative multiplier." *Id.* Accordingly, the court concluded that it would not undertake the "difficult task of developing standards by which we might incorporate proportionality principles into the attorney's fee calculus." *Id.*

The Third Circuit's critique of Justice Powell's opinion, as embodying the holding in *Rivera,* is well taken and suggests that lower courts should uphold reasonable § 1988 fee awards even though they are disproportionate to damages recoveries based on findings of constitutional violations, on the theory that the vindication of even a single individual's constitutional rights almost always serves a larger public interest that warrants such disproportionality. Thus, in *Cunningham* the court disapproved a reduction in the fee award because it was disproportionate to the damages recovery for the unconstitutional demolition of a house and garage owned by the plaintiff, stating that the "mere fact that a constitutional right is singular in nature cannot be determinative." *Id.* at 54.

In *Nephew v. City of Aurora,* 830 F.2d 1547 (10th Cir. 1987), *cert. denied,* 108 S. Ct. 1269 (1988), the Tenth Circuit, sitting *en banc,* upheld a § 1988 fee award of $12,500 for plaintiff's success in recovering only $1 in nominal damages in their police misconduct suit. The court concluded that such a "widely disproportionate" fee was warranted in light of the district court's finding that the "most important aspect" of the judgment was not the money damages, but rather the "vindication of plaintiffs' civil
* rights and its message to the police department." *Id.* at 1550-51. *See also Max M.*

v. New Trier High School, 859 F.2d 1297, 1301 (7th Cir. 1988) (upholding $25,000 fee award although plaintiff recovered about $8,000 in suit under Education of the Handicapped Act, 20 U.S.C. § 1400 *et seq.*, when district court "believed that the precedential effect of its rulings produced significant intangible benefits for other handicapped children"); *Parker v. Williams,* 855 F.2d 763, 778 (11th Cir. 1988); *Ustrak v. Fairman,* 851 F.2d 983, 989 (7th Cir. 1988) (fixing a fee award 21 times greater than a plaintiff's damages recovery, and observing that a "judicial decision that finds a violation of constitutional rights and punishes the perpetrator with an award of punitive damages not only vindicates consitutional principles but is a deterrent to future violations, to the benefit not only of the plaintiff but of others in similar situations"); *Hernandez v. Hill Country Telephone Cooperative, Inc.,* 849 F.2d 139, 144 (5th Cir. 1988) (noting that fee award was "substantially less disproportionate" to the underlying damages recovery than was fee award upheld in *Rivera*); *Wadsworth v. Clindon,* 846 F.2d 265 (4th Cir. 1988) (upholding § 1988 fee award of $13,317 in civil rights case in which plaintiff recovered $1500 in damages); *Brantley v. Surles,* 804 F.2d 321, 326-27 (5th Cir. 1986) (upholding § 1988 fee award "nearly two times as large" as plaintiff's damages recovery in unconstitutional employment discharge case); *Thorne v. City of El Segundo,* 802 F.2d 1131, 1142-43 (9th Cir. 1986) (suggesting approval of Title VII fee award substantially in excess of back pay award in employment discrimination case); *Garnong v. Montgomery County,* 668 F. Supp. 1000, 1007-08 (S.D. Tex. 1987) (rejecting defendants' contention that plaintiff's fee request should be reduced because it amounted to more than three times the money damages recovery in the suit); *Gonzales v. Jillson,* 642 F. Supp. 908, 909 (D. Mass. 1986) (awarding almost $31,000 in § 1988 fees to plaintiff's counsel in police brutality case that yielded a damages award of only $1,000, on finding that "this case, like any in which police officers are found liable for exceeding their lawful authority, serves a significant public interest, well beyond those of the parties," so that the "significance of the monetary award is outweighed by the important public interests vindicated by the general jury verdict"). *Cf. Yohay v. City of Alexandria Employees Credit Union,* 827 F.2d 967, 974 (4th Cir. 1987) (finding that district court did not err in failing to reduce fee award under Fair Credit Reporting Act, 15 U.S.C. § 1681n(3), that was three times the amount of the damages recovery, especially because there "will rarely be extensive damages in an FCRA action"). *But cf. Van Sant v. United States Postal Services,* 805 F.2d 141, 142-43 (4th Cir. 1986) (Equal Access to Justice Act, 28 U.S.C. § 2412; considering the "gross disproportionality between Van Sant's recovery [approximately $5,600] and the fee requested," among other factors, in limiting fee award to $5,000, and noting that the litigation "resulted in the establishment of no new significant principles of law").

§ 19.8 Other Asserted Bases for the Downward Adjustment of the Lodestar

Pages 515 and 516, update Cunningham citations in notes 36 and 43:

vacated & remanded, 478 U.S. 1015 (1986), *reinstated,* 807 F.2d 49 (3d Cir. 1986).

Page 516, add to note 39:

Cf. Gekas v. Attorney Registration & Disciplinary Comm'n, 793 F.2d 846, 853 (7th Cir. 1986) (disapproving district court's reduction in plaintiff's fee award made in order "to discourage other attorneys from filing cases simply to obtain fees").

* *Page 516, add to cases cited in note 40:*

Cunningham v. County of Los Angeles, 859 F.2d 705, 711, 713 (9th Cir. 1988) (rejecting, as justification for reduction in the lodestar, considerations of insufficient documentation of services rendered, mediocre performance by counsel, and doubt as to whether defendant intended to deny plaintiff's civil rights in a settled action); Quesada v. Thomason, 850 F.2d 537, 539 (9th Cir. 1988) (ruling that "simplicity of the issues" may not be relied on to reduce lodestar).

§ 19.9 –Poor Quality of Representation as a Basis for a Downward Adjustment in the Fee Award

Page 518, update Delaware Valley citation in note 47:

478 U.S. 546 (1986).

Page 518, update Delaware Valley citation in note 52:

478 U.S. 546, 565-67 (1986).

Page 519, update Delaware Valley citation in note 53:

478 U.S. 546, 567-68 (1986).

Page 519, add to note 56:

Cf. Van Sant v. United States Postal Services, 805 F.2d 141, 143 (4th Cir. 1986) (Equal Access to Justice Act, 28 U.S.C. § 2412; in sharply reducing fee requested by plaintiff's counsel, court considered "his conduct which has unduly prolonged the litigation," but "disavow[ed] any attempt to be punitive"); Gekas v. Attorney Registration & Disciplinary Comm'n, 793 F.2d 846, 852 (7th Cir. 1986) (" 'If the circumstances should ever arise in which an overall penalty should be assessed [against prevailing party's fee award], the reasons for that step will have to be given with great detail and thorough justification' ").

* *Page 519, add to note 57:*

Cf. Cunningham v. County of Los Angeles, 859 F.2d 705, 711 (9th Cir. 1988) (rejecting "mediocre performance" by counsel as basis for lodestar reduction, in absence of "specific evidence" that the attorney's performance is "abysmal").

CHAPTER 20

UPWARD ADJUSTMENTS TO THE LODESTAR

Throughout this chapter, the Supreme Court's 1986 Delaware Valley Citizens' Council decision should be updated as:

478 U.S. 546 (1986).

§ 20.1 Permissible and Impermissible Bases for an Upward Adjustment to the Lodestar

Page 522, add to note 5:

Thus, the court in Shakman v. Democratic Organization of Cook County, 677 F. Supp. 933, 942-43 (N.D. Ill. 1987), properly rejected plaintiff's request for an enhancement of the lodestar for the "exceptional efficiency in which their attorneys handled this case," assertedly resulting in an "extraordinarily low number of hours charged for the work completed."

Page 522, delete three sentences ending with notes 9, 10, and 11 references, together with notes 9-11, and substitute the following:

In *Pennsylvania v. Delaware Valley Citizens' Council,* 107 S. Ct. 3078 (1987), a bare majority of the Supreme Court ruled that contingency or risk adjustments are authorized under § 1988 in some circumstances, but the badly-splintered Court set forth unclear guidelines for granting and calculating such adjustments. See § **20.4** of supplement. The *Delaware Valley* Court also appeared to approve compensation for delay in payment of § 1988 fees in extended litigation, with the majority identifying it as a factor separate from contingency as a basis for enhancement. See §§ **20.4, 20.5** of the supplement.

§ 20.3 Upward Adjustment for the Quality of Representation

Page 525, add at end of section:

Consistent with the message delivered by the Supreme Court in *Blum v. Stenson* and *Delaware Valley I,* the lower courts generally have declined to grant upward lodestar adjustments based on quality of representation. *See, e.g., Student Public Interest Research Group v. AT&T Bell Laboratories,* 842 F.2d 1436, 1453 (3d Cir. 1988)(stating that quality adjustment is available only in "very rare circumstances where the attorney's work is so superior and outstanding that it far exceeds the expectations of clients and normal levels of competence"); *Thompson v. Kennickell,* 836 F.2d 616, 621-23 (D.C. Cir. 1988)(reversing award of quality enhancement, where "fee applicant produced no specific evidence to rebut the presumption that the lodestar figure was reasonable" and rejecting notion of an "exceptional victory as an independent factor warranting enhancement *per se*"); *Save our Cumberland Mountains, Inc. v. Hodel,* 826 F.2d 43, 52-53 (D.C. Cir 1987), *reh'g en banc granted,* 830 F.2d 1182 (D.C. Cir. 1987)(reversing award of quality enhancement because fee applicant failed to show both that "exceptional" success was achieved and that the "quality of service rendered was superior to what one reasonably would expect to be compensated for by the lodestar's hourly rates"); *Catlett v. Missouri Highway and Transportation Commission,* 828 F.2d 1260, 1271 (8th Cir. 1987), *cert. denied,* 108 S. Ct. 1574 (1988); *Hall v. Ochs,* 817 F.2d 920, 929 (1st Cir. 1987)(noting that quality adjustments "are not to be given in regard for stellar performance," when counsel has not performed "disproportionately better than their quite impressive experience would suggest"); *McGee v. Hester,* 815 F.2d 1193, 1198 (8th Cir. 1987); *In re Burlington Northern, Inc.,* 810 F.2d 601, 607-08 (7th Cir. 1986)(noting that plaintiffs' counsel received a lodestar award based on "top current billing rates for every hour they expended on the litigation" and questioning whether quality enhancements are "*ever* appropriate"); *Abrams v. Baylor College of Medicine,* 805 F.2d 528, 537 (5th Cir. 1986).

One of the better reasoned contrary decisions is *Shakman v. Democratic Organization of Cook County,* 677 F. Supp. 933, 944-48 (N.D. Ill. 1987). In awarding a one-third quality enhancement in a class action suit that successfully challenged the patronage practices of the regular party organizations in the district, the district judge stated that in his 24 years on the bench, he had never presided over a case with "greater significance or more widefelt impact in the area of civil rights" than this case. *Id.* at 944. The court praised the "[i]magination and creativity" required of plaintiffs' counsel in fashioning the legal arguments that resulted in protection of the "basic functioning of the democratic system" in the district, observing that "no higher value can be ascribed to any result than the protection of a fundamentally fair electoral process." *Id.* at 945. The relief obtained in the suit "affects over 70,000 governmental employees" with a total economic benefit in excess of $250 million. *Id.* at 945, 946. *See also McKenzie v. Kennickell,* 684 F. Supp. 1097, 1105-07 (D.D.C. 1988), where the court awarded plaintiffs a quality adjustment based on a showing of the exceptional results achieved in their 15-year employment discrimination suit, coupled with a demonstration of the superior quality of counsel's services. *Cf. In re Agent Orange Product Liability Litigation,* 818 F.2d 226, 234-35 & n.2 (2d Cir. 1987)(upholding district court's award of quality adjustments to some of plaintiffs' counsel in major class action equitable fund suit, on finding that the "use of a national hourly rate skews the normal lodestar analysis enough to require consideration of quality factors in order to satisfy the requirements of just and fair compensation;" court recognized, however, that equitable fund cases "may afford courts more leeway in enhancing the lodestar" than do fee-shifting statutes). It has also been argued that a quality enhancement is appropriate if prevailing plaintiffs' counsel has been compensated at below-market rates that do not reflect counsel's high-quality representation, if the use of current rates in multi-year litigation is barred by the Eleventh Amendment, *Rogers v. Okin,* 821 F.2d 22, 28 (1st Cir. 1987), *cert. denied,* 108 S. Ct. 709 (1988), or by the federal

* government's immunity from interest awards, *McKenzie v. Kennickell,* 684 F. Supp. 1097, 1107 & n.34 (D.D.C. 1988).

§ 20.4 Upward Adjustment for Risk or Contingency

Page 528, update Palmer citation in note 45:

478 U.S. 1015 (1986).

§ 20.4A The *Delaware Valley II* Decision (New)

In *Pennsylvania v. Delaware Valley Citizens' Council,* 107 S. Ct. 3078 (1987)(*Delaware Valley II*), the Supreme Court addressed the issues whether and under what circumstances the lodestar fee under 42 U.S.C. § 1988 and similar fee-shifting statutes can be enhanced for risk or contingency. The decision in *Delaware Valley II* produced a 4-1-4 split in the Court, with Justice O'Connor's separate concurring opinion representing the swing vote between the polar extremes of the plurality and dissenting opinions. Regrettably, *Delaware Valley II* engenders as much confusion as clarification and bequeaths to the bench and bar the daunting task of translating the decision's three diverse opinions into comprehensible criteria and a methodology for awarding risk enhancements under federal fee-shifting statutes.

A bare majority of the Court agreed in *Delaware Valley II* that the lodestar fee under § 1988 and similar fee-shifting statutes may be enhanced for contingency or risk in certain cases. However, the Court failed to set forth with clarity the circumstances in which such risk adjustments or contingency enhancements (used interchangeably here) are permissible. Five justices – the four justices who joined in Justice Blackmun's dissenting opinion, together with Justice O'Connor, who joined in only part of the plurality opinion and issued a separate concurring opinion – combined to conclude that an enhancement or upward adjustment of the lodestar for contingency is authorized under certain circumstances. 107 S. Ct. at 3089 (Justice O'Connor, concurring), 3091 (dissent). This view overcame the conviction of the four justices who joined fully in Justice White's plurality opinion that Congress did not intend the "risk of losing a lawsuit to be an independent basis for increasing the amount of any otherwise reasonable fee for the time and effort expended in prevailing" under § 1988 and similar fee-shifting statutes. *Id.* at 3086.

The confusion concerning the applicable standards for awarding a risk adjustment begins with the inability of the Justices in *Delaware Valley II* to agree on the operative definition of "risk" or "contingency." While all members of the Court concurred that the risk in question is the risk of nonpayment of counsel if the suit is unsuccessful, *id.* at 3081 (plurality), 3091-92 (dissent), unanimity ended there. The plurality gave a case-specific definition to risk, which would depend on "how unsettled the applicable law is with respect to the issues posed by the case and by how likely it is that the facts could be decided against the complainant." *Id.* at 3081. The dissent, on the other hand, rejected the notion that a contingency enhancement "depend[s], in the first instance, on the *degree* of risk presented by a particular case," concluding instead that "it is the fact of contingency, not the likelihood of success in any particular case, that mandates an increase in an attorney's fee." *Id.* at 3097, 3098. On that view, contingency enhancement is "designed simply to place contingency employment *as a whole* on roughly the same economic footing as noncontingency practice." *Id.* at 3097. In her decisive concurring opinion, Justice O'Connor agreed with the dissent that "compensation for contingency must be based on the difference in market treatment of contingent fee cases *as a class,* rather than on an assessment of the 'riskiness' of any particular case." *Id.* at 3098. However, as discussed later, another majority of the Court appears to support the awarding in exceptional cases of risk adjustments based on the legal risks associated with the particular case.

The Court also divided sharply in its treatment of delay in payment in relationship to risk enhancement. The entire Court seemed in agreement that delay between the time a fee-paying client ordinarily pays his bills and the time statutory attorney's fees are paid at the end of lengthy litigation warrants compensation under § 1988 and similar fee-shifting statutes, either by the use of current rates or by an upward adjustment to the lodestar when historic rates are applied. *Id.* at 3081-82 (plurality opinion concurred in by Justice O'Connor), 3099 (dissent). However, a majority consisting of the plurality and Justice O'Connor concluded that delay in payment should be treated as an *independent* basis for enhancement of the lodestar, and may not be considered an element of the risk that justifies enhancement on the basis of contingency. *Id.* at 3082. The dissent, on the other hand, viewed delay as an "integral aspect of contingency payments for which compensation is appropriate" through an enhancement for contingency. *Id.* at 3099.

A majority of the Court concurred that certain factors are irrelevant in deciding whether to award a risk adjustment. Thus the "novelty and difficulty of the issues presented, and . . . the potential for protracted litigation" do not warrant a contingency enhancement, because those factors already are adequately reflected in the lodestar award of reasonable hours times reasonable rates. *Id.* at 3087 (plurality), 3089 (Justice O'Connor). Neither is a contingency enhancement warranted merely because "a case involves an issue of public importance, . . . the plaintiff's position is unpopular in the community, or . . . [the] defendant is difficult or obstreperous," or because of the "chance that the court will find unnecessary and not compensate some of the time and effort spent on prosecuting the case." *Id.* at 3082 (plurality opinion concurred in by Justice O'Connor). Similarly, the "tenacity of the defendant" and the " 'special skill and experience of counsel' " cannot justify a contingency enhancement, because they are reflected, respectively, in the number of hours reasonably expended and the reasonable hourly rates awarded. *Id.* at 3091 (Justice O'Connor, concurring).

A majority also concluded that "when the plaintiff has agreed to pay its attorney, win or lose, the attorney has not assumed the risk of nonpayment and there is no occasion to adjust the lodestar fee because the case was a risky one." *Id.* at 3082 (plurality opinion concurred in by Justice O'Connor). On this view, *any* guaranteed compensation paid by the plaintiff to his attorney defeats the prevailing plaintiff's eligibility for a contingency enhancement. *But see Palmer v. Shultz,* 679 F. Supp. 68, 73-74 (D.D.C. 1988)(awarding contingency enhancement notwithstanding that plaintiff was obligated to pay her counsel half their customary fee, win or lose, when plaintiff demonstrated that "the market regularly compensates quasi-contingent fee cases at a higher rate than non-contingent cases"). The dissent in *Delaware Valley II,* on the other hand, would foreclose a contingency enhancement altogether only when the client "has contracted to pay the 'lodestar' fee (i.e., reasonable hours times a reasonable hourly rate), regardless of the outcome of the case." 107 S. Ct. at 3098-99.

As noted earlier, a majority of the Court, consisting of Justice O'Connor and the dissenting Justices, agreed that a contingency enhancement generally "must be based on the difference in market treatment of contingent fee cases *as a class,* rather than on * an assessment of the 'riskiness' of any particular case." *Id.* at 3089. Justice O'Connor's decisive concurring opinion narrows the range of factors properly considered in measuring the "market treatment" of contingent fee cases for this purpose. Thus Justice O'Connor rejected the dissent's view, 107 S. Ct. at 3099-3100 & nn.14 & 15, that a contingency enhancement could rest on consideration of the economic risks created by the particular circumstances of the prevailing party's attorneys, such as the "extra economic risk endured by smaller firms . . . or by firms that take unpopular cases." *Id.* at 3090. Instead, Justice O'Connor sought a method for measuring "how the market in a community compensates for contingency" that is "objective and nonarbitrary in practice" and that does "not vary significantly from one case to the next." *Id.* Accordingly, she stated that "District Courts and Courts of Appeals should treat a determination of how a particular market compensates for contingency as controlling future cases involving the same market," and "if a fee applicant attempts to prove that the relevant market provides greater compensation for contingency than the markets involved in previous cases, the applicant should be able to point to differences in the markets that would justify the different rates of compensation." *Id.*

Unfortunately, Justice O'Connor did not offer a prescription for how fee applicants and district courts are to go about the task of proving and determining entitlement to risk enhancement based on market treatment of contingent fee cases generally. However, Justice O'Connor's broad theoretical discussion of risk enhancement is refined considerably by the principle, subscribed to by Justice O'Connor and the plurality, that "no enhancement for risk is appropriate unless the applicant can establish that without an adjustment for risk the prevailing party 'would have faced substantial difficulties in finding counsel in the local or other relevant market.' " *Id.* at 3091 (Justice O'Connor, concurring).

There appears to be a limited exception to the majority view that determination of contingency enhancements should be based on the market treatment of contingent fee cases in general, and not on the riskiness of the particular case. A combined reading of the plurality and dissenting opinions suggests that contingency enhancements for the legal risks peculiar to the particular case are authorized in very limited circumstances. As noted above, the plurality rejected altogether the concept of an adjustment for risk that depends on the legal and factual riskiness of the particular case. However, proceeding on the alternative assumption that risk enhancements are sometimes permissible, the plurality appeared to acknowledge that in rare exceptional cases an enhancement for risk would be warranted for a high degree of risk of loss in the particular case. *Id.* at 3088-89.

The dissent took the position that although "an enhancement for contingency in ordinary cases will not be based on the relative likelihood of success of a particular case," *id.* at 3097, "in exceptional cases" a contingency enhancement might be warranted when the " 'legal' risks facing a case . . . [are] so apparent and significant that they will constitute an economic disincentive independent of that created by the basic contingency in payment" and the result achieved is "significant and of broad public interest." *Id.* at 3100.

Both sets of Justices agreed that the risk in such cases should be evaluated from the perspective of the beginning of the litigation. *Id.* at 3088 (plurality), 3100 (dissent). Justice O'Connor rejected altogether the awarding of an enhancement based on legal or other risks associated with a particular case. *Id.* at 3091.

The views of the plurality and dissent thus arguably overlap to the extent of concluding that in exceptional cases an enhancement to the lodestar might be awarded, on the basis of detailed findings, for the legal risk of nonsuccess in a particular case that produced significant results in the public interest. However, that principle must be viewed with some skepticism, because it was flatly rejected by Justice O'Connor in her pivotal concurring opinion and the plurality's preference was that risk adjustments *never* be granted. Moreover, the principle is in turn qualified by the majority view, discussed above, that no risk adjustment is ever warranted except upon a showing that in its absence the prevailing party "would have faced substantial difficulties in finding counsel in the local or other relevant market." *Id.* at 3089, 3091.

The Court further held that the fee applicant bears the burden of proving "the degree to which the relevant market compensates for contingency" and establishing that, absent a contingency enhancement, the prevailing party would have encountered "substantial difficulties" in securing counsel in the relevant market. *Id.* at 3090-91 (Justice O'Connor, concurring). Correspondingly, the district court's award of a contingency enhancement must be supported by "findings of fact concerning the degree to which contingency is compensated in the relevant market." *Id.* at 3091 (Justice O'Connor, concurring). The plurality and Justice O'Connor further agreed that a court "may not enhance a fee award any more than necessary to bring the fee within the range that would attract competent counsel." *Id.* at 3089 n.12, 3090-91. The plurality's view, not endorsed by a majority of the Court, was that a risk adjustment generally should amount to "no more than 1/3 of the lodestar." *Id.* at 3089.

Justice O'Connor joined with the plurality to conclude that the substantial risk adjustments awarded in *Delaware Valley* must be reversed, because "the enhancement is not supported by any findings of fact concerning the degree to which contingency is compensated in the relevant market" and "[n]either the findings nor the evidence indicate that the large enhancements in this case were necessary to attract competent counsel in the relevant community." *Id.* at 3091.

While leaving the issue unresolved, the plurality noted that nonprofit tax-exempt law firms may not be authorized to consider the likelihood of risk enhancement or, indeed, the likelihood of a statutory fee award at all, in deciding which clients to represent, and hence might not ever qualify for a contingency enhancement of the lodestar. *Id.* at 3088 n.10. However, the dissent made clear its view that public interest firms and legal services organizations are eligible for contingency enhancements, *id.* at 3096 & n.8, and nothing in Justice O'Connor's concurring opinion suggests that such firms are disqualified from receiving contingency enhancements. Furthermore, the marketplace model selected by the majority favors the view that no distinction should be made between nonprofit and profit-making firms in the awarding of contingency enhancements, just as the Court ruled in *Blum v. Stenson,* 465 U.S. 886 (1984), that nonprofit and profit-making firms equally are entitled to compensation at market-value rates. Of doubtful validity, therefore, is the Second Circuit rule that profit-making, but not nonprofit, firms are eligible for risk adjustments. *New York State Association for Retarded Children v. Carey,* 711 F.2d 1136, 1154 (2d Cir. 1983).

§ 20.4B Difficulties in Interpreting and Implementing *Delaware Valley II* (New)

Serious problems inevitably will arise in the practical application of the disjointed and highly theoretical discussions of risk enhancement embodied in the *Delaware Valley II* decision. A synthesis of the *Delaware Valley II* opinions establishes, as discussed in § **20.4A**, a twofold requirement for granting risk adjustments to the § 1988 lodestar fee for the prevailing party whose counsel has taken his case entirely on a contingent fee basis. First, the fee applicant must establish the degree, if any, to which the relevant market compensates counsel for the risk of nonpayment in contingent fee cases as a class. Second, and wholly independent of the first requirement, the prevailing party must show that, absent the availability of a risk adjustment, he would have experienced "substantial difficulties" securing competent counsel in the relevant market to represent him in his suit. At both stages, and most seriously at the first stage, there is conspicuous omission from *Delaware Valley II* of instruction as to the methodology that should be employed to determine a fee applicant's eligibilty for a risk adjustment.

§ 20.4C –Proving Market Treatment of Contingent Fee Cases as a Class (New)

At the first stage of the analysis, a particularly vexing question is what class of contingent fee cases should be examined in order to determine whether, and to what degree, the relevant market compensates for contingency. As one circuit court has observed, there is no indication in Justice O'Connor's crucial concurring opinion that the relevant class of cases to be studied is "anything less than all contingency cases in a given geographic market, including personal injury cases, which constitute the biggest group." *Blum v. Witco Chemical Corp.,* 829 F.2d 367, 381 (3d Cir. 1987). The difficulty with such an all-inclusive approach is that the risk premium awarded in the private market to successful counsel in major damages actions, through the operation of a contingent fee arrangement, is high. Such a large risk adjustment might be excessive if applied to the great body of civil rights cases seeking primarily or exclusively injunctive relief. However, a counterweight to this tendency inheres in the Supreme Court's caveat in *Delaware II,* discussed in § **20.4A**, that a contingency enhancement should be no larger than necessary to attract competent counsel. *See Hidle v. Geneva County Board of Education,* 681 F. Supp. 752, 758 (M.D. Ala. 1988).

The alternative approach of studying only those contingency cases which are similar to the case before the court has its own problems when applied to civil rights suits seeking primarily or exclusively equitable relief. Although in some injunction cases attorneys may bill their fee-paying clients at an increased hourly rate in the event of success, it is unlikely that an attorney in the private market would undertake to represent the plaintiff in an injunction case on an *entirely* contingent fee basis (unless exclusively on a statutory fee basis) without at least some guaranteed payment for the major investment of time ordinarily required in some cases.

Beyond these issues lies the formidable question of how to conduct the required study of the relevant class of contingent fee cases, once identified, for purposes of determining whether and to what degree the market compensates for contingency. Clearly, some kind of expert testimony concerning market treatment of contingency cases will be required from a person knowledgeable about the "economics of the legal profession" and perhaps as well from an economist who could develop an "econometric model" that, for example, "determined the mathematical relationship between hourly rate and contingency." *Blum v. Witco Chemical Corp.,* 829 F.2d at 380. The importance of an initial comprehensive study is underscored by Justice O'Connor's dictate in *Delaware Valley II* that a district court's determination of how the market compensates for contingency controls all subsequent cases involving the same market, with a heavy burden falling on a subsequent fee applicant in the district to show that his case falls into a "different" market providing greater compensation for contingency. However, as the Third Circuit has noted, an authoritative study "would inevitably run into the tens of thousands of dollars, and there would thus be few cases in which the value of the multiple would justify plaintiff's lawyers in investing in such research." *Blum,* 829 F.2d at 381. *See also Student Public Interest Research Group v. AT&T Bell Laboratories,* 842 F.2d 1436, 1439, 1452 (3d Cir. 1988)(rejecting contingency enhancement in part because "computing the appropriate contingency multiplier in light of *Delaware Valley II* [would] be a most burdensome task for the district court and an expensive one for the parties"). The expense of the required study, coupled with the binding nature of the district court's initial findings, favor the commissioning by the district court of a single authoritative study in which a court-appointed special master, upon notice to potentially affected litigants and attorneys in the area, would take evidence and make findings concerning market treatment of contingency cases in the district. *Blum,* 829 F.2d at 381. The complexities of such a market study are potentially enormous, because, among other difficulties, the market-value hourly rates prevailing in the community must be carefully analyzed to ascertain the degree to which they incorporate an increment for risk as well as for delay in payment. (Correspondingly, the fee applicant who does not qualify for a risk adjustment should demonstrate that the market rates he is requesting for calculation of the lodestar fee do not incorporate a risk premium.)

Notwithstanding the potentially daunting nature of the task, plaintiffs' counsel in a number of employment discrimination suits have developed documentation of the relevant market's treatment of contingency cases as a class that has satisfied the district courts considering their requests for contingency enhancements. The Ninth Circuit, in upholding the district court's doubling of the lodestar in a Title VII suit on the basis of contingency, noted that in proof of the market's treatment of contingent cases, the plaintiff had presented the testimony of San Francisco attorneys that they undertook contingent cases only in the expectation of enhanced compensation equal to double their normal fee and had cited Ninth Circuit precedent acknowledging that "Title VII cases are especially unappealing to the private bar." *Fadhl v. City and County of San Francisco,* 859 F.2d 649 (9th Cir. 1988). In awarding a 200 percent contingency enhancement in a Title VII class action suit, the court in *Black Grievance Committee v. Philadelphia Electric Co.,* 690 F. Supp. 1393, 1399-1401 (E.D. Pa. 1988), relied on eight affidavits from experienced Philadelphia attorneys to conclude that attorneys in that community "will accept contingent cases in this type case only if their recovery would be at least double their normal billing rate." *Id.* at 1400. While acknowledging, as contended by defendants, that the affidavits submitted "do not have any statistical significance," the court concluded that the unchallenged affidavit submissions were a satisfactory alternative to the comprehensive study proposed by the Third Circuit in *Blum v. Witco Chemical Corp., supra,* to measure market treatment of contingent cases. *Id.* at 1401.

Although the particular evidence presented by plaintiffs' counsel is not made clear, the court in *Hidle v. Geneva County Board of Education,* 681 F. Supp. 752, 757 (M.D. Ala. 1988), concluded that lawyers in Alabama who take cases on a contingency basis "expect to receive anywhere from 1.5 to 8 times the traditional hourly rate for non-contingency work." Apparently, the contingency cases considered were primarily personal injury and debt collection cases, which lawyers were willing to undertake on an entirely contingent fee basis, and the court noted that "[v]ery few lawyers in Alabama are, however, willing to undertake such arrangements in employment discrimination cases." *Id.* at 757. In *Palmer v. Shultz,* 679 F. Supp. 68 (D.D.C. 1988), the court relied on plaintiffs' "thorough documentation," consisting apparently of affidavits from a number of Washington D.C. attorneys, that "attorneys in the Washington D.C. community will ordinarily not take cases on a contingency basis without an adjustment of their normal hourly rate of at least 100 percent" and "will only accept a partially contingent case if their recovery is enhanced by at least 50 percent." *Id.* at 74. In *Palmer* it is not made clear what class of contingency cases in the market was considered. In *McKenzie v. Kennickell,* 684 F. Supp. 1097, 1100-01 (D.D.C. 1988), the court relied on 21 affidavits from attorneys associated with a variety of firms in the locale, most of them with significant experience in Title VII cases, in concluding that a substantial premium was necessary to induce attorneys to undertake Title VII * representation on a contingent fee basis. In passing, the *McKenzie* court found that the relevant class of cases to be examined for this purpose was "all contingency cases, particularly other types of complex Federal litigation," and should not be confined only to Title VII cases. *Id.* at 1100. Nonetheless, the court concluded that by their affidavit submissions, the plaintiffs had made the required showing even if the relevant class were to be confined to Title VII cases. *Id.* The *McKenzie* court also ruled that the "relevant temporal focus" is on market treatment of contingent cases at the time the fee award is made, rather than at the time the suit was commenced. *Id.* at 1101-02.

Less difficult are the tasks of determining the relevant class of contingency cases and of developing an appropriate methodology for the study of such cases when the civil rights case before the court involves the recovery of substantial money damages that in the private market ordinarily is undertaken entirely on a contingent fee basis. The relevant class of cases in the private market in which representation is undertaken entirely on a contingent fee basis similarly will be composed primarily of major damages suits, even if the sample includes personal injury and mass tort suits as well as major civil rights damages actions. It would not likely prove difficult to secure expert attorneys who are familiar with the contingent fee arrangements that are structured in such cases to give testimony concerning the premium that is paid to plaintiffs' attorneys in the marketplace for the risk of loss (and hence nonpayment of fees), either as part of the fee that is based on a percentage of the damages recovery or in the form of an increased hourly billing rate above that customarily charged in noncontingent fee cases. *Cf. Delaware Valley II,* 107 S. Ct. at 3092 (dissenting opinion).

Such testimony was presented in *Garmong v. Montgomery County,* 668 F. Supp. 1000, 1007-09 (S.D. Tex. 1987), in support of the prevailing plaintiff's request for a risk enhancement of the § 1988 lodestar fee in a police brutality case that had recovered substantial money damages. The court first determined, on the basis of evidence submitted by plaintiff, the market rates charged to fee-paying clients in the Houston, Texas, locality for services rendered by comparable attorneys in comparable federal cases in which representation was undertaken on a *non*contingent fee basis. Then the court found, on the basis of the testimony of two plaintiff's witnesses, that the hourly rates charged by practitioners in the local Houston market to their fee-paying clients in contingent fee cases were significantly higher than the rates customarily assessed in noncontingency cases. The court accordingly granted plaintiff a 10 percent contingency enhancement of the hourly rates that were assigned to counsel's work on the basis of customary charges in noncontingency cases. However, the presumptively binding conclusions of the *Garmong* court concerning the local market's treatment of contingency cases inevitably will be subjected to challenge by losing defendants who are assessed risk adjustments in subsequent civil rights damages suits in that district. They legitimately will question the accuracy and validity of findings which rested on the testimony of two plaintiff-selected experts in a prior proceeding in which those defendants had no opportunity to participate.

§ 20.4D —Establishing the Need for Risk Enhancement to Attract Competent Counsel (New)

In addition to successfully proving the degree to which the relevant market grants compensation for contingent fee cases as a whole, the fee applicant seeking risk enhancement must sustain the burden of proving, by "evidence in the record," that without a risk adjustment he would have encountered "substantial difficulties" in obtaining competent counsel in the relevant market to represent him. *Delaware Valley II,* 107 S. Ct. at 3089 (plurality), 3090 (Justice O'Connor, concurring).

* One view is that only a generalized showing is required at this stage, namely, that "there exists a general dearth of counsel" willing to accept contingent cases absent risk enhancement. *McKenzie v. Kennickell,* 684 F. Supp. 1097, 1103 (D.D.C. 1988). However, that interpretation would render the second-step requirement of *Delaware Valley II* little more than a recapitulation of the first-stage showing that attorneys in the private market generally require extra compensation as a condition to accepting contingent fee cases. Furthermore, in *Delaware Valley II* Justice O'Connor expressly stated her agreement with the plurality's view of the requirement, which was that there be record evidence that "without risk-enhancement *plaintiff* would have faced substantial difficulties in finding counsel" (emphasis added), and that one relevant factor was "whether other counsel had declined to take the case." *Id.* at 3089 & n.12, 3091. These considerations strongly suggest that the showing required at this stage is *case-specific,* namely, that risk enhancement is needed to attract competent counsel to this particular case. As discussed below, most circuit courts that have addressed this

issue subscribe to this stringent interpretation of the second prong of the *Delaware Valley II* standard.

Evidence that several attorneys had declined representation in the case, because of concern about the adequacy of compensation, would be highly relevant to the required showing that risk enhancement was needed to attract competent counsel to the case. *See Delaware Valley II,* 107 S. Ct. at 3089 n.12 (plurality). Also relevant, even under a case-specific approach, would be testimony or affidavits from knowledgeable attorneys that risk enhancement is generally needed to attract competent counsel in the relevant market to the particular type of civil rights case. *See, e.g., Black Grievance Committee v. Philadelphia Electric Co.,* 690 F. Supp. 1393, 1400 (E.D. Pa. 1988); *McKenzie v. Kennickell, supra,* 684 F. Supp. at 1103. The case-specific nature of the inquiry at this stage arguably authorizes consideration of risk factors characteristic of the plaintiff's type of civil rights case, such as, for example, the unpopularity of such cases in the community, that might have made it difficult to attract competent counsel. In the final analysis, however, as discussed below, the crucial inquiry will be whether plaintiff's counsel required the lure of a contingency enhancement to induce him to represent the plaintiff in the particular case.

The fee applicant inevitably will encounter major obstacles in seeking to show that, absent risk enhancement of the § 1988 lodestar fee, he would have experienced great difficulties attracting competent counsel to his case. Civil rights cases involving large and viable damages claims ordinarily attract private attorneys through contingent fee arrangements yielding a satisfactory fee, typically based on a percentage of the damages recovery, that includes compensation for the risk of nonsuccess (and hence nonpayment of the fee). If plaintiff's attorney, in addition to seeking a statutory fee, has, or could have, entered into a contingent fee arrangement with his client that incorporates a premium for the risk of nonpayment, it is difficult to conclude that the promise of risk enhancement of the § 1988 lodestar was needed to attract counsel to the case. *Cf. id.* at 3086-87 (plurality), 3096, 3099 (dissent)(suggesting that risk enhancement of the lodestar is unnecessary when plaintiff's attorney has, or could have, entered into a contingent fee contract with his client in a case seeking substantial money damages). *See Spell v. McDaniel,* 824 F.2d 1380, 1405 (4th Cir. 1987)(finding risk enhancement unnecessary to attract competent counsel to police brutality suit recovering substantial money damages, because there is "no dearth of competent counsel willing to take this and comparable cases on a contingency basis as being 'good plaintiffs' cases' without any guarantee of special enhancement of reasonable 'lodestar' fees"); *Marsh v. Digital Equipment Corp.,* 699 F. Supp. 1411, 1416 (D. Ariz. 1988) (finding risk enhancement unnecessary to attract competent counsel to employment discrimination case in absence of showing that attorneys would not accept the case on the basis of a contingent fee arrangement such as existed between the plaintiff and his attorney in this case). The court in *Garmong v. Montgomery County,* 668 F. Supp. 1000, 1008 (S.D. Tex. 1987), incorrectly analyzed this issue, in facilely concluding that risk enhancement under § 1988 was necessary merely because competent counsel in the local market who undertake such cases on a contingent fee basis charge their clients a substantial premium for risk.

This issue becomes more complicated in cases arising in the Second and Tenth Circuits, which have ruled that when the fee yielded by a contingent fee contract in a civil rights damages action exceeds the statutory fee award under § 1988, the contingent fee must be reduced to the amount of the statutory fee award and deemed discharged by counsel's receipt of the statutory award. See § **21.3**. It is naturally in the prevailing plaintiff's interest to seek statutory fees in such cases in order to eliminate or reduce his contractual fee liability to his attorney. However, the effect is to deprive counsel of the full fruits of his contingent fee contract and, absent risk enhancement of the § 1988 lodestar fee, to deter him from taking the case on a contingent fee basis. Even under these circumstances, however, it will be the burden of the plaintiff to show that the statutory lodestar fee was not adequate to attract the attorney to the case and that counsel took the case in reliance on the awarding of a risk adjustment.

At first blush it would seem less difficult to demonstrate that risk enhancement of the § 1988 lodestar is necessary to secure competent counsel in the great majority of civil rights cases seeking primarily or exclusively injunctive relief or only nominal-to-modest money damages – cases which do not attract attorneys in the private market through contingent fee arrangements with impecunious clients. However, in these, as in all civil rights cases, the prevailing party will be required, as a practical matter, to show at this stage of the analysis that the § 1988 lodestar fee was not sufficient to attract competent counsel to the case. This burden typically will be a heavy one to sustain, given that many of the considerations that typically make a case risky, including the novelty and difficulty of the issues, the prospect of protracted litigation, and the special skills and expertise required of counsel, are factors that are to be incorporated into the base lodestar fee, which compensates successful counsel for all hours reasonably expended in the litigation at market-value rates reflecting the experience and expertise of the lawyers. *Delaware Valley II,* 107 S. Ct. at 3087 (plurality), 3091 (Justice O'Connor, concurring). *See Student Public Interest Research Group v. AT&T Bell Laboratories,* 842 F.2d 1436, 1439, 1452 (3d Cir. 1988)(disapproving contingency enhancement in part because court was "convinced that the hourly rate used by the district court in this case will be sufficient to attract competent counsel"); *Norman v. Housing Authority of Montgomery,* 836 F.2d 1292, 1306 (11th Cir. 1988)(rejecting contingency enhancement when the record is absolutely devoid of any evidence that would suggest that enhancement over the rates requested is necessary to attract competent counsel"); *Thompson v. Kennickell,* 836 F.2d 616, 621 (D.C. Cir. 1988)(finding the evidence submitted insufficient to meet the "stringent" test of *Delaware Valley II* concerning plaintiffs' difficulties in obtaining counsel absent a contingency enhancement); *ECOS, Inc. v. Brinegar,* 671 F. Supp. 381, 400 (M.D.N.C. 1987)(concluding that plaintiff in Title VI race discrimination suit "could locate competent counsel without the benefit of a contingency enhancement," because "[d]iscrimination cases are often handled on a contingency fee basis, and plaintiff did not present, nor is the court aware of, any evidence that this particular case was an 'unpopular' one in the community"). Counsel's need for risk enhancement is further diminished by the availability, in appropriate cases and independent of risk considerations, of enhancement for the delay in payment of fees over the period of protracted litigation, either by the use of current rates or by application of an upward adjustment to the lodestar when historic rates are used. See § **20.5**.

The required showing that risk enhancement is necessary to attract competent counsel will be particularly difficult when the prevailing plaintiff is represented by a nonprofit or legal services organization. While such an organization may derive substantial revenue from statutory attorney's fees, it is difficult to argue that risk enhancement, on top of the lodestar, is required to attract the organization to the case. Profit considerations motivating private attorneys do not enter into the organization's decision to take a case, and usually the organization's very purpose is to provide free legal representation through salaried counsel to impecunious plaintiffs with meritorious claims. *Delaware Valley II,* 107 S. Ct. at 3087 (plurality). This is not to say that such nonprofit and legal services organizations are not *eligible* for risk adjustments on the same terms as profit-making firms, but only that as a practical matter it may be difficult for such organizations to sustain the burden of obtaining risk enhancement. *But see McKenzie v. Kennickell,* 684 F. Supp. 1097, 1104-05 & n.28 (D.D.C. 1988) (finding that nonprofit firm that is heavily dependent on statutory fee awards would be discouraged from accepting complex Title VII class action suits absent contingency enhancement.

At a more fundamental level, the prevailing plaintiff seeking risk enhancement of the § 1988 lodestar will be confronted in every case with the burden of showing, as a practical matter, that his own counsel would not have represented him without the promise of risk enhancement. Although circular in nature, the reasoning that the fee applicant will have to refute is that, because risk adjustments are at best highly uncertain and are not to be counted on at the outset of the litigation, it follows that plaintiff's counsel must not have needed the inducement of risk enhancement in agreeing to undertake representation in the case. Put another way, the argument is that the very fact that the plaintiff managed to secure competent counsel for his case, in the highly speculative world of risk adjustments, presumptively disqualifies him from obtaining a risk adjustment. Underscoring this reasoning is the presumption embodied in both *Delaware Valley II* and *Delaware Valley I* that the § 1988 lodestar fee adequately compensates counsel in the vast majority of cases. *See Perkins v. Mobile Housing Board,* 847 F.2d 735, 738-39 (11th Cir. 1988) (upholding district court's denial of contingency enhancement, noting that "[w]hile one witness in this case testified that such an enhancement was necessary" in order to attract competent counsel, "the facts as adduced by both parties contradict that assertion"); *Friends of the Earth v. Eastman Kodak Co.,* 834 F.2d 295, 298 (2d Cir. 1987)(Federal Water Pollution Control Act, 33 U.S.C. § 1365(d); no contingency enhancement when "it does not appear that a bonus was necessary to attract competent counsel"); *Leroy v. City of Houston,* 831 F.2d 576, 587 (5th Cir. 1987)(noting, in concluding that risk enhancement was not necessary to attract competent counsel to this Voting Rights Act case, that "although . . . two public interest firms were uninterested in this litigation, the final fee award runs to a consortium of ten individual attorneys plus Hogan & Hartson, indicating a breadth of available talent"); *Spell v. McDaniel,* 824 F.2d 1380, 1405 (4th Cir. 1987)(finding, in concluding that risk enhancement was unnecessary to attract competent counsel to this police brutality damages suit, that "these counsel and others in related cases had no general reluctance to undertake contingency representation in this type case notwithstanding any general 'unpopularity' they might have among the local lay populace"), and 852 F.2d 762, 772 (4th Cir. 1988) (finding that trial counsel's "unsupported affidavits and hunches as to the possibilities of obtaining alternative or associate appellate counsel without application of a 1.5 contingency multiplier are not sufficient" to establish that a contingency enhancement of appellate fee award was necessary to secure competent appellate counsel); *Shakman v. Democratic Organization of Cook County,* 677 F. Supp. 933, 948 (N.D. Ill. 1987)("Simply put, this court believes that plaintiffs' counsel would have accepted this case without any promise of a risk enhancement."); *cf. Jenkins v. Missouri,* 838 F.2d 260, 268 (8th Cir. 1988)(concluding that testimony of several attorneys that they "would not have taken the case at all" or "would not have taken the case without regular payments" "comes short of proof that adjustment for contingency was a crucial factor in plaintiffs' ability to obtain counsel"), *cert. denied,* 109 S. Ct. 221 (1988).

However, notwithstanding these obstacles, several courts have found this branch of the *Delaware Valley II* test to be satisfied on a generalized showing that, absent the availability of a contingency enhancement, there would be a "serious shortage" or not a "sufficient number" of competent attorneys willing to handle employment discrimination cases on a contingency basis. *Black Grievance Committee v. Philadelphia Electric Co.,* 690 F. Supp. 1393, 1400-01 (E.D. Pa. 1988); *McKenzie v. Kennickell,* 684 F. Supp. 1097, 1103-04 (D.D.C. 1988) (awarding contingency enhancement although plaintiffs' attorneys conceded that they did not "explicitly consider" the possibility of a contingency enhancement when they accepted the case); *Hidle v. Geneva County Board of Education,* 681 F. Supp. 752, 758 (M.D. Ala. 1988). On the other hand, some decisions are grounded in more concrete findings that the particular plaintiffs had substantial difficulties securing counsel without the expectation of contingency enhancement. In upholding the district court's award of a 200 percent contingency enhancement in an individual Title VII suit, the Ninth Circuit relied in part on the district court's finding that "the fact that Fadhl approached 35 lawyers before she found one who would represent her was strong support for the proposition that in the absence of risk enhancement she would have faced substantial difficulties in retaining an attorney." *Fadhl v. City and County of San Francisco,* 859 F.2d 649, 651 (9th Cir. 1986). In awarding a risk enhancement in *Searcy v. Crim,* 692 F. Supp. 1363, 1366-67 (N.D. Ga. 1988), the court relied on the fact that "[a]t least one Atlanta attorney specializing in civil rights law refused to work on the case specifically because she believed that its chance of success was too slim," on the court's own experience in having to assign attorneys to civil rights cases that a number of practitioners had declined to handle, on the unpopularity of this particular case, and on the fact that the law in the circuit had upheld the principle of contingency enhancement at the time the plaintiff's counsel accepted the case.

In *Palmer v. Shultz,* 679 F. Supp. 68, 75-76 (D.D.C. 1988), the court concluded that the plaintiff would have encountered substantial difficulties obtaining counsel without the expectation of a contingency enhancement, "notwithstanding the fact that in the case at bar, Ms. Palmer encountered no particular difficulties in retaining the services of plaintiffs' firm on a quasi-contingent basis." The court reasoned that Ms. Palmer had no great difficulty obtaining her counsel because of an "ongoing attorney-client relationship" with the firm. *Id.* at 76. Furthermore, counsel had good reason to expect to receive contingency enhancement in this case because of the same court's observation, in a prior case in which this counsel had represented Ms. Palmer, that risk enhancement was appropriate. *Id.* In this regard, plaintiff's attorney represented that "the expectation of being compensated for the risk of loss was crucial to his decision to take the case, and that he would not have taken the case if he knew he could not obtain fees in excess of his normal billing rates." *Id.* Thus *Palmer* makes out a strong case for concluding that under unusual circumstances such as those present there, a contingency enhancement may be awarded even though the plaintiff managed to secure compentent counsel without the guarantee of such enhancement.

On the analysis of *Delaware Valley I* presented above, the presumption weighing against the fee applicant's request for a risk adjustment mirrors the principle enunciated in *Delaware Valley I* regarding quality of representation adjustments, that since the plaintiff "was able to obtain counsel without the promise" of lodestar enhancement, 106 S. Ct. at 3098, 3099, he presumptively was not entitled to an upward adjustment. With risk enhancement, as with quality enhancement, such a burden may well heighten "the showing required to the point where it may be virtually impossible for a plaintiff to meet." *Id.* at 3100 (Blackmun, J., dissenting).

§ 20.4E –*Chalmers v. City of Los Angeles:* A Case Study in the Complexities of *Delaware Valley II* (New)

Illustrative of the difficulties inherent in interpreting and implementing the teachings of *Delaware Valley II* is the district court's award in *Chalmers v. City of Los Angeles,* 676 F. Supp. 1515, 1519-25 (C.D. Cal. 1987), of a 33 percent contingency enhancement of the lodestar fee granted to plaintiff's counsel in a successful § 1983 damages action. The analysis of the *Chalmers* court, while representing a serious attempt to grapple with the complexities of *Delaware Valley II,* reflects a misunderstanding and misapplication of some of the basic precepts of the *Delaware Valley II* decision.

At the first stage of the inquiry, the *Chalmers* court failed to make the considered evaluation required by *Delaware Valley II* of the degree, if any, to which the relevant market compensates counsel for the risk of nonpayment in contingent fee cases as a class. Instead, the court suggested that *Delaware Valley's* concern with the "riskiness of civil rights cases overall, as opposed to that of an individual case," was satisfied by consideration of the "loss rate of cases like the one at bar." 676 F. Supp. at 1523. The court proceeded to conclude, on the basis of "the court's own experience," that the loss rate in such cases was "so marked" as to create a high risk of loss in the plaintiff's case. *Id.* at 1524.

At the second stage of the inquiry, the court observed that several public interest organizations had declined to take the plaintiff's case because it involved damages or lacked societal impact and that the plaintiff could not afford to pay an hourly fee to a private attorney. *Id.* at 1525. This buttressed the court's conclusion that "a plaintiff in the position of Julie Chalmers" faced "exceptional difficulties" in securing qualified counsel. *Id.* The relatively modest damages recovery in the suit – $28,223 – does suggest that the case might not have been attractive to a private attorney solely on the basis of a contingent fee contract. But the *Chalmers* court did not specifically consider whether the prospect of receiving the § 1988 lodestar fee – $49,558, as finally awarded – for success in the litigation, together with the independent availability of an upward adjustment for a nine-year delay in payment of the fee award, was sufficient inducement for plaintiff's attorney to take the case *without* the expectation of a risk adjustment. Indeed, the court blithely dismissed such an inquiry, stating that "[w]hile it is true that plaintiff's attorney Murdock was the first private sector lawyer offered the case, that is of little relevance in determining the market for this lawsuit." *Id.* at 1525. Finally, in awarding the risk adjustment, the court expressly considered several factors, including the defendant's "recalcitrant posture" and the economic risks assumed by a sole practitioner, that are of doubtful relevance under *Delaware Valley II. Id.* at 1524-25.

* The most astonishing deviation from the standards of *Delaware Valley II* is the Sixth Circuit's decision in *Fite v. First Tennessee Production Credit Association,* 861 F.2d 884 (6th Cir. 1988), affirming the award of a 1.75 contingency multiplier in a fee award under the Age Discrimination in Employment Act, 29 U.S.C. § 626(b). Without discussing, or even citing, *Delaware Valley II,* the majority upheld a contingency enhancement on the basis of the plaintiff's contingent fee arrangement with his attorney and the fact that plaintiff's attorney practiced in a two-person firm and had to forego a substantial amount of other business in order to undertake this case. *Id.* at 895. *Delaware Valley II* clearly does not countenance the award of a contingency enhancement in such circumstances.

§ 20.4F Conclusion: Potential Effects of the Decision (New)

Delaware Valley II is a frustratingly opaque decision, which inevitably will sow confusion in the civil rights bar and in the lower courts regarding the circumstances in which risk enhancement of the § 1988 lodestar is authorized. In determining the propriety of risk enhancement after *Delaware Valley II,* lower courts will be strongly inclined to skirt the highly theoretical and confusing requirements of the first stage of the analysis, involving market treatment of contingency cases generally, and instead proceed directly to the pragmatic inquiry of step two concerning whether risk enhancement was needed to attract competent counsel to plaintiff's case. *See, e.g., Leroy v. City of Houston,* 831 F.2d 576, 584 (5th Cir. 1987); *Spell v. McDaniel,* 824 F.2d 1380, 1405 (4th Cir. 1987). Only if the fee applicant succeeds in surmounting this threshold obstacle need the district court be concerned about the degree, if any, to which the market compensates generally for contingency.

The severity of the difficulties facing the fee applicant in meeting his burden of proof at both stages of the risk enhancement analysis suggests that the Supreme Court, and Justice O'Connor in particular, may have intended to preserve the availability of a risk adjustment only in theory, while making it impossible as a practical matter actually to obtain one. If that was the Court's message it might have been preferable to state it directly, as the Court did with regard to quality adjustments in *Delaware Valley I.* As the Third Circuit has observed, "[s]uch an approach would have been more manageable than what the Court may be asking the district courts to do, and the task of the district courts would have been simpler had it been adopted." *Blum v. Witco Chemical Corp.,* 829 F.2d 367, 380 n.13 (3d Cir. 1987).

§ 20.5 Upward Adjustment for Delay in the Payment of Fees

Page 530, add to note 60:

See also Cooper v. Dyke, 814 F.2d 941, 951 (4th Cir. 1987)(upholding 10% delay enhancement).

Page 530, add to note 61:

In Norwood v. Charlotte Memorial Hosp., 653 F. Supp. 1350, 1362 (W.D.N.C. 1987), the court granted an upward adjustment to the award of litigation expenses, as well as to the statutory fee award, to compensate for the long delay in their payment.

Page 530, add after sentence ending with note 61 reference:

The delay-in-payment adjustment "is designed to compensate the attorney for the time gap between the actual expenditure of services and the fee award," while the "period following the fee determination, on the other hand, is covered by post-judgment interest" under 28 U.S.C. § 1961. *Black Grievance Committee v. Philadelphia Electric Co.,* 802 F.2d 648, 656 (3d Cir. 1986). See § **21.9** for discussion of interest on the fee award.

Page 531, update Shaw citation in notes 62 and 66:

478 U.S. 310 (1986).

Page 531, add at end of top incomplete paragraph:

In *Pennsylvania v. Delaware Valley Citizens' Council,* 107 S. Ct. 3078 (1987), the Supreme Court appeared to approve compensation for delay in payment of § 1988 fees in protracted litigation, whether by use of current rates or the application of an upward adjustment in the lodestar when historic rates are used. A majority of the court concluded that delay in payment must be independently considered as a basis for enhancement, and may not be considered as an element of risk that justifies enhancement on the basis of contingency. *Id.* at 3081-82 (plurality opinion concurred in by Justice O'Connor). The dissent, on the other hand, viewed delay as "an integral aspect of contingency payments for which compensation is appropriate" through an enhancement for contingency. *Id.* at 3099.

Page 531, update Daggett citation and add to cases cited in note 68:

Daggett, *aff'd in part and remanded,* 811 F.2d 793 (3d Cir. 1987); Hart v. Bourque, 798 F.2d 519, 524 (1st Cir. 1986)(reversing delay-in-payment adjustment when the delay arose from time required by district court "to make the reduction in plaintiff's exceptional figures" and time expended in unsuccessful fee settlement negotiations thwarted by plaintiff); Birth Control Centers, Inc. v. Reizen, 652 F. Supp. 192, 196 (E.D. Mich. 1986)(denying delay adjustment when "[m]uch of the delay is due to plaintiffs' appeal, without which plaintiffs may not have been prevailing parties, and to the inexplicable lapse of almost two years between the appellate decision and plaintiffs' first request for attorney fees"). *See also In re* Burlington Northern, Inc., 810 F.2d 601, 608-09 (7th Cir. 1986)(affirming denial of interest award for delay in payment in Title VII suit where delay "was occasioned by a legitimate dispute over several issues" and lead counsel was compensated at top hourly rate at end of litigation for work done throughout litigation).

Page 532, add to note 69:

Cf. Barcia v. Sitkin, 683 F. Supp. 353, 358 (S.D.N.Y. 1988)(delay adjustment denied because state defendant reasonably awaited definitive Supreme Court fee decision before negotiating fee request and negotiated in good faith thereafter).

Page 532, add at end of first complete paragraph:

See § **18.17** of this supplement for a discussion of whether the Eleventh Amendment bars an award of compensation against the state for delay in payment of statutory fees in the form of current rates or an upward adjustment of historic rates.

Page 533, add to note 76:

In Chalmers v. City of Los Angeles, 676 F. Supp. 1515, 1526-28 (C.D. Cal. 1987), the court adopted an "adjusted historic billing rate" approach, utilizing the historic market rate of interest, as compensating for both inflation and the loss of use of the money over the period of delay in payment of a statutory fee. As the appropriate interest rate multiplier, the court selected the interest rate on the 52-week U.S. Treasury bill, in preference to the interest rate on three- or six-month Treasury bills. The court calculated the delay adjustment by increasing the fee for each year, based on the use of historic rates, by the appropriate 52-week Treasury bill rate, under a formula described by the court. *Id.* at 1527-28. In Shakman v. Democratic Org. of Cook County, 677 F. Supp. 933, 940-42 (N.D. Ill. 1987), the court allowed a further adjustment for delay, in addition to awarding current rates, in order to offset both inflation and the time value of money over the 17 years of the litigation. The court rejected an adjustment factor based on the cost of borrowing the earned funds from a financial institution, at a rate purportedly approximating the borrowing rate for law firms with high credit ratings. *Id.* at 941. The court found that such an approach "would result in widely disparate adjustments depending on the creditworthiness of the prevailing party's attorneys" and would be cumbersome and speculative. *Id.* at 941-42. Instead, the court concluded that an "appropriate and objective" basis for calculating a delay adjustment for both inflation and the time value of money would be the interest rate applicable to three-month Treasury bills. *Id.* at 942. *See also* Zipes v. Trans World Airlines, Inc., 846 F.2d 434, 442-43 (7th Cir. 1988)(affirming district court's award of multiplier based on interest yield from long-term treasury note, to compensate for five-year delay in payment between time Title VII fee petition was * filed and date of court's actual award); Lippo v. Mobil Oil Corp., 692 F. Supp. 826, 838-43 (N.D. Ill. 1988) (use of prime interest rate as delay enhancer); Black Grievance Comm. v. Philadelphia Elec. Co., 690 F. Supp. 1393, 1402-03 (E.D. Pa. 1988) (prime rate); Fleming v. County of Kane, 686 F. Supp. 1264, 1272-74 (N.D. Ill. 1988) (prime rate); Amico v. New Castle County, 654 F. Supp. 982, 1003-04 (D. Del. 1987)(delay in payment adjustment based on rate assessed under applicable state law for pre-judgment interest). See also § **18.17** of this supplement. In Student Pub. Interest Research Group v. AT&T Bell Laboratories, 842 F.2d 1436, 1453-54 (3d Cir. 1988), the court held that plaintiff waived its ability to seek a delay enhancement by failing to make an adequate showing in the district court of the costs it incurred because of delayed payment of the fee award.

Page 533, add at end of note 77:

But see discussion at § **18.17** in supplement of circumstances in which use of current rates at *current* experience levels is appropriate.

CHAPTER 21

OTHER FACTORS AFFECTING THE AMOUNT AND ALLOCATION OF THE § 1988 FEE AWARD

§ 21.2 Relevance of the Johnson Factors to the § 1988 Fee Calculation

Page 537, update Delaware Valley citation in notes 6 and 7:

478 U.S. 546, 564 (1986)(explaining that the lodestar adjustment approach adopted by Supreme Court represented a "hybrid approach that shared elements of both Johnson and the lodestar method of calculation").

Page 538, delete sentence with notes 12 and 13 references, together with notes 12 and 13, and substitute the following:

Debate concerning the significance of the contingency factor figured prominently in the Court's analysis in *Pennsylvania v. Delaware Valley Citizens' Council,* 107 S. Ct. 3078, 3080 (plurality), 3091 (dissent)(1987), of the availability of a risk adjustment under § 1988.

Page 538, update Rivera citation in notes 14 and 15:

477 U.S. 561 (1986).

Page 538, add to cases cited in note 15:

Fourth Circuit: Lilly v. Harris-Teeter Supermarket, 842 F.2d 1496, 1511 (4th Cir. 1988)(*Johnson* factors largely subsumed into lodestar analysis); Cooper v. Dyke, 814 F.2d 941, 950 (4th Cir. 1987)(requiring district court to explain application of *Johnson* factors in arriving at § 1988 fee award); Daly v. Hill, 790 F.2d 1071, 1077-78 (4th Cir. 1986)(observing that "*Blum* has shifted the timing of the *Johnson* analysis, as it has been applied in this circuit," so that "the lodestar fee is now the proper focus of the entire *Johnson* analysis in most cases").

Fifth Circuit: Brantley v. Surles, 804 F.2d 321, 325-26 (5th Cir. 1986); Nisby v. Commissioners Court of Jefferson County, 798 F.2d 134, 136-37 (5th Cir. 1986); Sims v. Jefferson Downs Racing Ass'n, 778 F.2d 1068, 1084 (5th Cir. 1985)(all reiterating Fifth Circuit requirement that district court indicate, however cursorily, how each of the *Johnson* factors affected its fee determination). The Fifth Circuit has recognized that the law of the Circuit on the status of *Johnson* is in "disarray," that recent statutory fee decisions of the Supreme Court have "weakened the case for strict allegiance to the *Johnson* factors," and that the "strain is beginning to show." Bhandari v. First Nat'l Bank of Commerce, 808 F.2d 1082, 1104 (5th Cir. 1987), *reh'g en banc granted,* 812 F.2d 936 (5th Cir. 1987). *See also* Cobb v. Miller, 818 F.2d 1227, 1231-32 (5th Cir. 1987)(noting that Fifth Circuit has "not always followed the framework outlined in *Johnson* consistently").

Ninth Circuit: Miller v. Los Angeles County Bd. of Educ., 827 F.2d 617, 621 (9th Cir. 1987); Jordan v. Multnomah County, 815 F.2d 1258, 1263 n.11 (9th Cir. 1987)(generally requiring consideration of *Johnson* factors); Harris v. McCarthy, 790 F.2d 753, 758 (9th Cir. 1986); (all requiring district court's consideration of *Johnson* factors, but not necessarily discussion of each of them).

Eleventh Circuit; N.A.A.C.P. v. City of Evergreen, 812 F.2d 1332, 1336 (11th Cir. 1987)(requiring district court to explain how the *Johnson* factors influenced the fee award).

§ 21.3 Interrelationship of the § 1988 Fee Award and the Fee Yielded by a Contingent Fee Arrangement

Page 539, update Cunningham citation (Third Circuit) and add to cases cited in note 18:

Second Circuit: Dominic v. Consolidated Edison Co., 822 F.2d 1249, 1259-60 (2d Cir. 1987)(reaffirming *Wheatly*).

Third Circuit: Cunningham, *vacated & remanded,* 478 U.S. 1015 (1986), *reinstated,* 807 F.2d 49 (3d Cir. 1986).

Fourth Circuit: Cooper v. Dyke, 814 F.2d 941, 951 (4th Cir. 1987)(§ 1988 fee award not limited to amount recoverable under contingency fee agreement).

Eighth Circuit: Thomas v. Booker, 784 F.2d 299, 308 (8th Cir.), *cert. denied,* 476 U.S. 1117 (1986)(reiterating that a "contingent-fee contract does not set a ceiling on the amount of attorneys' fees awardable in a section 1983 action").

* *Ninth Circuit:* Quesada v. Thomason, 850 F.2d 537, 540-43 (9th Cir. 1988) (holding that § 1988 fee award is not limited to amount recoverable under contingent fee contract; if contingent fee exceeds statutory fee award, plaintiff may be liable to his attorney for the difference, payable out of the damages recovery).

Tenth Circuit: Jones v. Wilkinson, 800 F.2d 989, 991 (10th Cir. 1986), *judgment aff'd,* _____ U.S. _____, 94 L. Ed. 2d 753 (1987)(repeating prior holding that the "presence of a contingent fee contract would not limit the amount of a fee award in a civil rights case").

Page 540, update Rivera citation in note 20:

477 U.S. 561, 574-81 (plurality), 585-86 (Powell, J., concurring), 595 (Rehnquist, J., dissenting)(1986).

Page 540, add at end of carryover paragraph:

However, notwithstanding *Rivera,* and indeed without reference to it, the Fifth Circuit reaffirmed its position that a § 1988 fee award may not exceed the fee yielded by a contingency fee agreement between the prevailing plaintiff and his counsel. *Blanchard v. Bergeron,* 831 F.2d 563, 564 (5th Cir. 1987).

* The Supreme Court has granted certiorari in *Blanchard* to consider the issue, and now has ruled that a reasonable § 1988 fee award is *not* limited to the amount provided in a contingent fee arrangement between the prevailing plaintiff and his or her counsel. *Blanchard v. Bergeron,* 57 U.S.L.W. 4191 (U.S. Feb. 21, 1989). However, while concluding that the contingent fee does not impose an "automatic" ceiling on the § 1988 fee award, the Court stated cryptically that the "presence of a pre-existing fee agreement may aid in determining reasonableness." 57 U.S.L.W. at 4192. This statement would seem to give some credence to the approach of the Seventh Circuit, discussed later in this supplement, that in certain circumstances the fee yielded by a contingent fee contract is relevant to determination of a reasonable award of § 1988 fees. The Court also stated in *Blanchard* that the "defendant is not . . . required to pay the amount called for in a contingent fee contract if it is more than a reasonable fee calculated in the usual way" under § 1988. 57 U.S.L.W. at 4192.

Page 541, add to note 25:

* The Seventh Circuit has taken the view that the amount yielded by a contigent fee arrangement may be relevant in determining reasonable fees under § 1988 in money damages cases. In Lenard v. Argento, 808 F.2d 1242, 1247-48 (7th Cir. 1987), the Seventh Circuit held that the fee yielded by a contingent fee contract is presumptively the measure of a reasonable fee award under § 1988 if the underlying civil rights suit "resembles an ordinary tort case, conventionally and satisfactorily handled on a contingent fee basis" or only "enforce[s] old precedents." The court explained that when the civil rights suit "involves substantial stakes, settled precedent, and no defense of immunity," it may sufficiently resemble a "conventional personal injury suit" to "give the terms of the contingent fee arrangement considerable evidentiary significance." *Id.* at 1248. *See also* Spanish Action Comm. v. City of Chicago, 811 F.2d 1129, 1136 (7th Cir. 1987)(contingent fee bears significantly on reasonable § 1988 fee award when civil rights suit "bears close resemblance to a conventional personal injury suit"); *cf.* Praprotnik v. City of St. Louis, 798 F.2d 1168, 1179 (8th Cir. 1986)(finding no abuse of discretion in district court's reduction of § 1988 fee award to an amount equal to one-third of the damages recovery in the case, based principally on "the absence of 'documentation evidencing a fee arrangement which would have allowed [Praprotnik's attorney] to retain more than one-third of plaintiff's award as fees for his services' "); Kirchoff v. Flynn, 786 F.2d 320, 323-28 (7th Cir. 1986)(pre-*Rivera* decision).

If, however, the civil rights damages suit is not so routine and remunerative on a contingent fee basis, the prospect of a contingent fee might not make the case sufficiently attractive to a lawyer to take without the availability of a higher § 1988 fee award. *Lenard,* 808 F.2d at 1247-48. In such cases, the *Lenard* court suggested, the § 1988 fee award is not limited to the contingent fee. *Id. See* Shorter v. Valley Bank & Trust Co., 678 F. Supp. 714, 722-23 (N.D. Ill. 1988)(concluding the contingent fee should not be used as basis for statutory fee award under Age Discrimination in Employment Act, 29 U.S.C. § 216(b), because this was not a straightforward suit with a solid claim for substantial damages); Bohen v. City of East Chicago, 666 F. Supp. 154, 156 (N.D. Ind. 1987)(declining to base § 1988 fee award on contingent fee when plaintiff's successful damages claim was "anything but an effort to 'enforce old

* precedents' "); *cf.* Rateree v. Rockett, 685 F. Supp. 670, 674-75 (N.D. Ill. 1988) (awarding § 1988 fees in excess of the amount yielded by the contingent fee contract, when plaintiffs' counsel "had to undertake entirely unanticipated efforts–separate and independent enforcement proceedings" to collect the underlying damages judgment). The *Lenard* court also indicated that the prevailing plaintiff might argue that the contingent fee arrangement, rather than a *lower* § 1988 fee lodestar amount, should be the basis for the § 1988 fee award. 808 F.2d at 1248.

In Hagge v. Bauer, 827 F.2d 101, 111-12 (7th Cir. 1987), the court affirmed the district court's § 1988 fee award that was based alternatively on a "straight contingency fee analysis or using a lodestar analysis with an upward adjustment." Although disapproving the upward adjustment to the lodestar, the court upheld the fee award as properly based on a 40% contingent fee arrangement, this being a case involving "substantial stakes, settled precedent, and no defense of immunity." *Id.* at 111-12. Significantly, the *Hagge* court concluded that the use of the contingency fee as the measure of a reasonable § 1988 fee is not inconsistent with the dictates of *Rivera,* provided that the contingent fee is not viewed as "*per se* reasonable" *and* is not less than the lodestar figure. *Id.* Thus, under *Hagge* it is arguable that the contingency fee may be utilized appropriately only to *increase* the § 1988 fee award above the lodestar figure.

Page 541, add to note 27:

Second Circuit: Lewis v. Coughlin, 801 F.2d 570, 576 (2d Cir. 1986)(reiterating Second Circuit rule that attorney's § 1988 fee award "should be offset against his claim for services provided under the contingency fee arrangement").

Fifth Circuit: Cf. Sims v. Jefferson Downs Racing Ass'n, 778 F.2d 1068, 1085 (5th Cir. 1985)(finding that if the cash and services given to his lawyer by the prevailing plaintiff adequately compensated him for his work on the case, then "at a minimum thc court should havc asscsscd that amount against thc dcfcndants, bccausc thc plaintiff himself had to pay this amount").

§ 21.4 Effect on the § 1988 Fee Award of a Rejected Rule 68 Offer of Judgment

Page 542, add the following cases to note 34 concerning technical requisites of a valid offer and acceptance under Rule 68:

Bright v. Land O'Lakes, Inc., 844 F.2d 436, 443 (7th Cir. 1988)(rejecting defendants' contention that Rule 68 cost-shifting provisions should be triggered when their rejected offer of judgment was "surprisingly close" to, though less than, plaintiff's damages recovery); Grosvenor v. Brienen, 801 F.2d 944, 948-49 (7th Cir. 1986)(holding that defendants' oral settlement offer made at a final pre-trial settlement conference did not satisfy the formal requirements for a valid written Rule 68 offer, and, similarly, that the oral settlement offer did not "extend" a previous written settlement offer that *was* valid under Rule 68 but which plaintiff had rejected); McKever v. Vondollen, 681 F. Supp. 999, 1001-02 (N.D.N.Y. 1988)(valid Rule 68 offer must be in writing); Rateree v. Rockett, 668 F. Supp. 1155 (N.D. Ill. 1987)(ruling that defendants' accepted Rule 68 offer of judgment, that made no mention of costs or attorney's fees, must be construed not to include costs or fees, so that prevailing plaintiffs were entitled to a separate court-determined award of reasonable § 1988 fees, and defendants may not attempt to vary the terms of the judgment by seeking to incorporate into the Rule 68 offer asserted pre-offer oral discussions); Rohrer v. Slatile Roofing & Sheet Metal Co., Inc., 655 F. Supp. 736 (N.D. Ind. 1987)(plaintiffs entitled to separate court award of reasonable statutory fees following acceptance of defendant's Rule 68 offer of judgment that made no mention of attorney's fees or costs); E.E.O.C. v. Hamilton Standard Div., 637 F. Supp. 1155, 1158 (D. Conn. 1986)(concluding that Rule 68 provisions are inapplicable "to cases that end in settlement and a stipulated dismissal," rather than ending in the entry of judgment after trial); Stewart v. County of Sonoma, 634 F. Supp. 773, 775-76 (N.D. Cal. 1986)(holding that a defendant's Rule 68 offer is not invalidated by his failure to serve it upon codefendants, at least when they filed a waiver of notice, and that the "judgment finally obtained" by the plaintiff under Rule 68 included "only the judgment rendered in the action in which the offer is made" and not as well judgments against any of the defendants in separate related proceedings in state court); Fisher v. Stolaruk Corp., 110 F.R.D. 74, 75-76 (E.D. Mich. 1986)(concluding that Rule 68 offer cannot be withdrawn within the 10-day period for written acceptance, but that a defendant is entitled to rescission of a Rule 68 offer that "mistakenly used the word 'costs' as a shorthand to include attorney's fees" under the Fair Labor Standards Act, 29 U.S.C. § 216(b), when plaintiff "was put on notice of defendant's subjective intent" that "costs" should include attorney's fees and "defendant's counsel acted promptly to correct his mistake before plaintiff's counsel had satisfied the technical requirements for acceptance").

* In Radecki v. Amoco Oil Co., 858 F.2d 397 (8th Cir. 1988), the court considered whether a valid Rule 68 offer and its acceptance occurred in a case in which the applicable fee-shifting provision under the Petroleum Marketing Practices Act, 15 U.S.C. § 2805(d)(1), does not define attorney's fees as part of costs. The defendant's Rule 68 offer was for a stated sum, "including costs now accrued." The following day, defendant served a second Rule 68 offer that expressly stated that the amount previously offered included attorney's fees. Subsequently, defendant's attorney orally informed plaintiff's attorney that the second offer was in clarification of the first offer. Thereafter, plaintiff accepted the initial offer and filed a motion for attorney's fees. *Id.* at 399. Applying basic contract principles concerning offer and acceptance in light of the events and circumstances surrounding the offers, the court found that defendant had intended to include attorney's fees within the amount specified in the initial offer. *Id.* at 400-02. (Note that if the case had involved § 1988, which defines attorney's fees as part of costs, the court might readily have concluded that the offer, which expressly included costs, also necessarily included attorney's fees). The court also stated its conviction that if Rule 68 offers were to be found nonrevocable, "courts should be hesitant to characterize as revocations offeror communications that clarify incomplete or ambiguous offers" *Id.* at 402. In this case the court ruled that plaintiff's purported acceptance, which assumed incorrectly that the offer did not include attorney's fees, did not sufficiently reflect the offer and hence was ineffective. *Id.* at 403. Finally, the court held that, considering the unusual circumstances and ambiguities of the case, the cost-shifting mechanism of Rule 68 should not be operative. *Id.*

Page 543, add to note 37:

Presumably, a valid Rule 68 offer made in the context of a suit involving a fee-shifting statute which, like § 1988, includes attorney's fees as part of "costs" must explicitly or implicitly make provision for attorney's fees as an element of the costs included in the offer. Thus, in that context a Rule 68 offer which expressly *excluded* attorney's fees, while including other cost elements, would not be valid. *Compare* Bentley v. Bolger, 110 F.R.D. 108, 111-14 (C.D. Ill. 1986)(invalidating Rule 68 offer which included payment of "court costs" but specifically excluded attorney's fees under Title VII fee-shifting provision which, like § 1988, defines attorney's fees as part of costs, and rejecting plaintiff's argument "that she be allowed to accept those valid portions of the Offer which meet her approval") *with* Freeman v. B & B Associates, 790 F.2d 145, 147-48 (D.C. Cir. 1986)(upholding validity of Rule 68 offer of judgment that included an offer to pay costs incurred but specifically excluded all attorney's fee liability under the Truth-in-Lending Act, 15 U.S.C. § 1640(a), which describes attorney's fees as separate from costs).

Page 543, add to note 38:

The offer of judgment, to which the plaintiff's eventual court judgment is to be compared, consists of both the amount offered to satisfy the damages caused by the challenged conduct and the costs then accrued, including attorney's fees if they are part of costs under the relevant fee-shifting statute. If costs are not included in the Rule 68 offer, the court is required to determine a reasonable amount of costs and attorney's fees that accrued up to the time of the offer. Marek v. Chesny, 473 U.S. 1, 5-6 (1985). *See* Grosvenor v. Brienen, 801 F.2d 944, 946-48 (7th Cir. 1986)(finding that the accrued amount of pre-offer attorney's fees and costs to which plaintiff is entitled must be added to plaintiff's damages award in the case to determine the total value of the judgment finally obtained by plaintiff in the litigation, for purposes of comparison with defendant's Rule 68 offer of judgment).

Page 543, add to note 39:

See Lowden v. Murphy, 664 F. Supp. 966, 969 (E.D. Pa. 1987)(defendant who is not liable for plaintiff's *post*-offer fees pursuant to Rule 68 is nonetheless liable for payment of § 1988 *pre*-offer fees to the prevailing plaintiff). The court in Stewart v. County of Sonoma, 634 F. Supp. 773, 776 (N.D. Cal. 1986), ruled that the *Marek* decision should not be applied retroactively to deny the prevailing plaintiff's recovery of post-offer § 1988 fees in a case in which defendant's Rule 68 offer was made and rejected prior to the *Marek* decision in June 1985. By recent congressional enactment, Rule 68 has been somewhat modified in its application to fee awards for plaintiff's success on claims under the Education of the Handicapped Act, 20 U.S.C. §§ 1400 *et seq.* See discussion in **§ 15.16** of this supplement.

Page 544, add to note 49:

See also Real v. Continental Group, Inc., 653 F. Supp. 736, 738-39 (N.D. Cal. 1987)(because of the "inprecision" inherent in assessing the monetary value of nonpecuniary relief offered as part of defendants' Rule 68 offer of judgment in age discrimination suit, court is persuaded to "compare monetary awards only").

Page 545, add to note 51:

To the same effect is the legislative history of the recently-enacted Handicapped Children's Protection Act, discussed in detail at **§ 15.16** of this supplement, which added a fee-shifting provision to the Education of the Handicapped Act, 20 U.S.C. §§ 1400 *et seq.*, and expressly incorporated, with some modification, the operation of Rule 68 as interpreted in *Marek.* See Statement of Rep. Pat Williams, 132 Cong. Rec. H4842 (July 24, 1986) explaining the application of Rule 68:

> First, consistent with the principles enunciated by the Supreme Court in Marek, a general offer should not be construed as being as favorable as a specific order. Second, courts should construe ambiguities in the offer against the offeror.
>
> Third, an offer which is indefinite; contains promises without necessary commitments; or contains ambiguities or contingencies, is less favorable than a judgment that is definite and specific; mandates implementation; and is clear and does not contain contingencies. Fourth, a decision by the court regarding whether an offer is more favorable than a judgment ordinarily presents a question of fact reviewable under the clearly erroneous standard.

Page 545, add to note 53:

Crossman v. Maccoccio, 806 F.2d 329, 331-33 (1st Cir. 1986)(ruling that the plaintiff who rejects defendant's Rule 68 offer that is at least as favorable as plaintiff's final judgment must pay defendant's post-offer costs, excluding attorney's fees).

Page 545, add to note 55:

The several courts that have addressed the issue agree that the prevailing civil rights plaintiff whose final judgment is not more favorable than a rejected Rule 68 offer is *not* obligated to pay the losing defendant's post-offer attorney's fees, since that result would fatally conflict with the fundamental rule that even the *winning* civil rights defendant can recover § 1988 fees only if the *losing* plaintiff's fee-generating claims were frivolous. See **ch. 23**. Crossman v. Maccoccio, 806 F.2d 329, 333-34 (1st Cir. 1986); Grosvenor v. Brienen, 801 F.2d 944, 946 n.4 (7th Cir. 1986)(dictum); Adams v. Wolff, 110 F.R.D. 291, 293-94 (D. Nev. 1986).

Page 545, add to note 58:

The Third Circuit has refused to read *Marek* broadly "to establish a uniform definition of costs that is coterminous with attorney's fees," so as to govern the definition of "costs" to include attorney's fees in a settlement agreement releasing the defendant from all "costs". Ashley v. Atlantic Richfield Co., 794 F.2d 128, 140-41 (3d Cir. 1986). The court simply found *Marek* inapplicable to that case, when the negotiated settlement that was entered into between the parties was *not* the result of a Rule 68 offer and acceptance and the parties did not intend "costs" to include attorney's fees in the settlement.

Page 545, in sentence ending with note 59 reference, change word "interaction" to interrelated".

Page 545, add following sentence ending with note 59 reference:

In *Johnston v. Penrod Drilling Co.,* 803 F.2d 867 (5th Cir. 1986)(maritime suit), the Fifth Circuit considered whether "Rule 68 applies to an unapportioned joint offer of judgment made by two defendants when (1) one of the defendants settles with the plaintiff individually after the joint offer is not accepted; and (2) the plaintiff recovers a judgment from the remaining defendant for less than the original joint offer." *Id.* at 868-69. The court held first that Rule 68 applies "to a joint offer of judgment made to a plaintiff by a number of defendants," so that if the plaintiff's final judgment had been rendered against *both* defendants who participated in the joint Rule 68 offer and was less favorable than the offer, then "Rule 68 would apply to automatically shift the costs of the action to the plaintiff." *Id.* at 869-70. But the court found Rule 68 to be inapplicable to the case in which the plaintiff settles with one of the defendants participating in the joint offer and recovers a judgment against the other defendant. The court reasoned that "Rule 68's description of the sum to be compared to the offer" does not "include amounts received by plaintiff in settlement." *Id.* at 870. The court further found that the figure represented by the unapportioned joint offer made by two defendants and the dollar judgment obtained by plaintiff against only one defendant "are not comparable figures for the purpose of shifting costs under Rule 68," and that the district court should not "undertake an apportionment of the joint offer in an attempt to obtain more comparable figures." *Id.* at 870. Finally, the court noted that the non-settling defendant could trigger the applicability of Rule 68 simply by making a new offer of judgment under Rule 68 after the other defendant settled with the plaintiff. *Id.* at 871.

* In *Corder v. Gates,* 688 F. Supp. 1418 (C.D. Cal. 1988), one plaintiff accepted and the other plaintiff rejected a Rule 68 offer, addressed jointly to both plaintiffs, for an amount in settlement of their § 1983 damages suit, including costs and attorney's fees. The court ruled that acceptance by only one plaintiff of a joint offer could not constitute a valid acceptance of the Rule 68 offer, at least when plaintiffs' ultimate judgment (including pre-offer attorney's fees and other costs) exceeded the offer. *Id.* at 1420-21 & n.3.

§ 21.5 Allocation of the Fee Award among Responsible Defendants

Page 547, update Delaware Valley citation and add to note 66:

Delaware Valley, 478 U.S. 546 (1986); Reeves v. Harrell, 791 F.2d 1481, 1483-84 (11th Cir. 1986)(court found county defendants not liable for § 1988 fees awarded to plaintiff black deputy sheriffs for plaintiffs' successful resistance to efforts by white deputy sheriffs to intervene into employment discrimination lawsuit and to dissolve or modify consent decree providing for promotion of blacks within county sheriff's office, when plaintiffs "did not 'prevail' vis-a-vis the defendants because the defendants did not join in the motion to intervene nor did they express any position on the termination of the consent decree"); Durett v. Cohen, 790 F.2d 360, 364 (3d Cir. 1986)(directing district court on remand to determine whether plaintiff prevailed against county defendant and, accordingly, whether that defendant should be assessed a portion of the plaintiff's § 1988 fee award); United States v. State of Arkansas, 787 F.2d 304, 309-10 (8th Cir. 1986)(state defendant could not be made partially liable with local school district defendants for attorney's fees assessed for school district's unsuccessful defense and appeal in school desegregation case, when school districts "made their own decisions regarding legal strategy and the vigor with which the lawsuit would be resisted," for which the State was not responsible); York v. Alabama State Bd. of Educ., 631 F. Supp. 78, 90-91 (M.D. Ala. 1986)(refusing to require state defendants to share § 1988 fee liability with municipal defendants, when municipal defendants decided to use the unconstitutional teachers' examination "despite the state defendants' warnings to the contrary" and the settlement relief obtained from the state defendants "was but necessary additional relief for the apparent wrong caused by the Mobile [municipal] defendants").

Page 547, add to note 67:

Council for Periodical Distribs. Ass'ns v. Evans, 827 F.2d 1483 (11th Cir. 1987)(adopting apportionment approach in case involving an "active instigator of a wrong and a more passive co-defendant who had a more peripheral or ministerial role in the wrong").

Page 548, update Burlington Northern citation in note 68:

aff'd in relevant part, 810 F.2d 601, 609-11 (7th Cir. 1986)(upholding allocation to union defendants of portion of Title VII fee award initially assessed exclusively against employer defendant, pursuant to employer's right under consent decree to seek contribution from unions for the fee award).

Page 548, add to note 69:

Calhoun v. Forester, 675 F. Supp. 291, 296-97 (W.D. Pa. 1987)(apportioning § 1988 fee award 70% to state defendant, as the "most culpable party" with "direct control" over the defendant City Magistrates who denied constitutional rights of indigent criminal defendants, 18.8% to the county defendant with "tangential" connection to the magistrates, and 11.12% to the city defendant with "no control" over the challenged procedures).

Page 548, add to note 70:

Council for Periodical Distribs. Ass'ns v. Evans, 827 F.2d 1483, 1487-88 (11th Cir. 1987)(discussing various principles of fee apportionment and stating that in this case district court on remand should consider mixed approach of assessing fees on one claim against only those defendants who were primarily responsible under the claim and dividing fees for other claim among all defendants "according to their legal or factual responsibility for the unconstitutional conduct").

Page 548, add to note 71:

J.G. v. Board of Educ., 830 F.2d 444, 447-48 (2d Cir. 1987)(court concluded, as a matter of "simple justice," that city defendant should not be made liable for § 1988 fees for time spent by plaintiffs' counsel on discontinued claim against state

* defendant). After reviewing the several approaches to apportionment, the court in Nash v. Chandler, 848 F.2d 567, 573-74 (5th Cir. 1988), ruled that the State of Texas could not be held jointly and severally liable with local defendants for a § 1988 fee award, in a case in which only the local officials were found liable on the merits and Texas appeared only as an intervenor, pursuant to federal statute, in defense of the constitutionality of a state statute. The court concluded that Texas could only be assessed attorney's fees directly attributable to its presence in the case. *Id.* at 574.

Page 549, add to note 77:

In Shakman v. Democratic Org. of Cook County, 634 F. Supp. 895, 903-05 (N.D. Ill. 1986), the court imposed joint and several liability for the § 1988 fee award on all the defendants, based on the finding that "a conspiracy among all defendants existed to deprive plaintiffs of their constitutional rights." However, the court made the joint and several fee liability subject to two limitations: (1) each of the defendants who consented to the final consent decree in the case was liable for fees only up until the time that particular defendant entered into the decree; and (2) the fee liability of each defendant was also limited by the amount of fees apportioned to that defendant on the basis of the number of employees that particular defendant controlled under the illegal patronage system invalidated in the case.

§ 21.6 Indemnification or Contribution for a Defendant's Fee Liability

Page 550, add after first sentence in first complete paragraph:

In *Argento v. Village of Melrose Park,* 838 F.2d 1483 (7th Cir. 1988), the Seventh Circuit affirmed district court judgments holding the village and an insurance company each liable for both underlying damages and the § 1988 attorney's fees awarded against the defendant police officers who had been found liable in their individual capacities for injuries inflicted on the plaintiff. The liability of the village for both damages and fees was based on an Illinois statute making a local public entity directly liable for the payment of a tort judgment against an employee acting within the scope of his employment. *Id.* at 1493-95. The insurance company was found liable to the plaintiff for attorney's fees in addition to the damages award under an insurance contract between the village and the insurer that covered a village employee acting within the scope of his employment and that provided for payment of "costs" under the federal fee statute, were also "costs" taxed against the insured. *Id.* at 496-99. The court found that § 1988 fees, defined as "costs" under the federal fee statute, were also "costs" under the insurance contract, a construction not contrary to Illinois law. *Id.* at 1499. *Cf. Coleman v. Smith,* 814 F.2d 1142, 1148-50 (7th Cir. 1987)(concluding that individual defendants found liable for § 1983 damages had acted within the scope of their employment, even if maliciously, and were entitled under Illinois statute to indemnification for the awards from village defendant); *Board of Education v. CNA Insurance Co.,* 839 F.2d 14 (2d Cir. 1988)(finding insurance company liable under policy for attorney's fees paid by defendant Board of Education to its counsel in racial segregation suit).

Page 551, add to cases cited in note 83:

In re Burlington Northern, Inc., 810 F.2d 601, 609-11 (7th Cir. 1986)(affirming district court's decision granting to employer defendant contribution from union defendants for a portion of Title VII fee award to plaintiffs, pursuant to employer's right under consent decree to seek such contribution).

§ 21.7 Allocation of the Fee Award among Attorneys for the Prevailing Plaintiffs

Page 551, update Black Grievance Committee citation in note 84:

vacated and remanded, 802 F.2d 648 (3d Cir. 1986).

Page 552, add to note 89:

Jordan v. City of Greenwood, 808 F.2d 1114 (5th Cir. 1987)(determining appropriate allocation of § 1988 fee award between attorney and legal services program by which he was employed for part of the litigation), *cert. denied,* 108 S. Ct. 89 (1987).

Page 552, add after sentence ending with note 89 reference:

In *In re Burlington Northern, Inc.,* 810 F.2d 601, 609 (7th Cir. 1986), the Seventh Circuit ruled that a Title VII fee award should not be distributed among the individual attorneys and paralegals in lead counsel's firm in the respective amounts awarded for the work of each of them on the case, but rather should be paid directly to the law firm. The Court noted that the statutory fee award associated with the work of an attorney on the case represented payment at an hourly rate that significantly exceeded what that attorney earned on an hourly basis at the firm, so that a "reasonable hourly rate for purposes of a fee award, therefore, is not the same as reasonable compensation for an individual attorney." *Id.* at 287.

Page 552, delete Agent Orange district court citation and add to note 91:

In *In re* Agent Orange Prod. Liab. Litig., 818 F.2d 226 (2d Cir. 1987), the Second Circuit invalidated an undisclosed fee-sharing agreement that adjusted the distribution of attorneys' fees awarded in a class action suit, under the equitable fund doctrine, in amounts representing a multiple of the sums advanced by attorneys to the class for litigation expenses. The court concluded that the arrangement "completely distorted" the allocation of fees under the lodestar approach on the basis of the services rendered by the various attorneys and placed class counsel in a position potentially in conflict with the interests of the class. *Id.* at 222-25. The court stated generally that the distribution of fees under such internal fee-sharing agreements "must bear some relationship to the services rendered" by individual counsel. *Id.* at 223. The court ruled that "in all future class actions counsel must inform the court of the existence of a fee sharing agreement at the time it is formulated." *Id.* at 226. *See generally* Stissi v. Interstate & Ocean Transp. Co., 814 F.2d 848 (2d Cir. 1987)(reversing district court's apportionment of attorneys' fees in wrongful death action on basis of relative time spent by each of two attorneys on the case, in breach of valid prelitigation agreement between the two attorneys to divide fees equally).

§ 21.8 Recovery of Litigation Expenses as § 1988 Attorney's Fees

Page 552, add to note 92:

Mennor v. Fort Hood Nat'l Bank, 829 F.2d 553, 556-57 (5th Cir. 1987)(allowing recovery of out-of-pocket expenses for postage, long-distance telephone calls, and travel as part of Title VII attorney's fees); Kuzma v. I.R.S., 821 F.2d 930, 933-34 (2d Cir. 1987)(§ 1988 attorney's fees include recovery of out-of-pocket expenses for such items as photocopying, travel, and telephone costs, as distinct from "nonrecoverable routine office overhead")(dicta); Reichman v. Bonsignore, Brignati & Mazzotta P.C., 818 F.2d 278, 283 (2d Cir. 1987)(attorney's fees under fee-shifting statutes include "reasonable out-of-pocket expenses incurred by the attorney and which are normally charged fee-paying clients"); *see also* Garmong v. Montgomery County, 668 F. Supp. 1000, 1010-11 (S.D. Tex. 1987)(recovery of investigative expenses as § 1988 fees).

Page 553, add to cases cited in note 96:

Daly v. Hill, 790 F.2d 1071, 1084 n.18 (4th Cir. 1986)("An attorney's practices in billing clients for expenses may be relevant to the question of whether compensation for litigation expenses is proper in addition to attorney's fees in a particular case.").

Page 554, add the following case to note 97:

Keith v. Volpe, 644 F. Supp. 1317, 1326 (C.D. Cal. 1986)(Fair Housing Act, 42 U.S.C. § 3612(c); awarding out-of-pocket expenses, including for transcripts, duplicating, mail, long-distance telephone calls, travel mileage, and parking, to prevailing plaintiffs represented by public-interest firm, on basis of "[u]ncontroverted declarations submitted by plaintiffs [which] indicate that it is current practice in Los Angeles to bill private clients separately for such expenses").

Pages 554-55, update Black Grievance Committee citations in notes 99, 3, 10, and 17:

vacated and remanded, 802 F.2d 648 (3d Cir. 1986).

Page 554, add to cases cited in note 7:

Terry Properties, Inc. v. Standard Oil Co., 799 F.2d 1523, 1540 (11th Cir. 1986)(upholding award to successful civil rights defendant of "reasonable costs of computerized
* research"); Alberti v. Sheriff of Harris County, 688 F. Supp. 1176, 1202 (S.D. Tex. 1987) (allowing recovery under § 1988 of expenses of Westlaw computer services).

Page 555, add the following case to note 17:

McKenzie v. Kennickell, 645 F. Supp. 437, 452 (D.D.C. 1986)(granting compensation for overtime secretarial work when private firm representing successful Title VII plaintiffs affirmed "that secretarial overtime is normally charged to fee paying clients").

Page 555, add to note 18:

* Carrero v. New York City Hous. Auth., 685 F. Supp. 904, 909 (S.D.N.Y. 1988) (denying recovery under § 1988 of expenses for word processing assistance which "falls into the secretarial subcategory under the ordinary office overhead heading"); American Booksellers Ass'n Inc. v. Hudnut, 650 F. Supp. 324, 330 (S.D. Ind. 1986)(denying recovery of expenses of New York City firm for clerks and word processing, in accordance with practice of law firms in the forum district of treating such expenses as part of overhead).

Page 555, delete sentence ending with note 19 reference, together with note 19, and add the following material to the section:

In *Crawford Fitting Co. v. J.T. Gibbons, Inc.*, 107 S. Ct. 2494 (1987), the Supreme Court ruled that a federal court is without power to tax the prevailing party's expert witness fees as costs against the losing party, as provided for in 28 U.S.C. § 1920(3), in an amount in excess of the statutory maximum set by 28 U.S.C. § 1821. The Court based its decision on the holding that "absent contract or explicit statutory authority to the contrary," 28 U.S.C. § 1920 is exhaustive of the "kinds of expenses that a federal court may tax as costs against the losing party." *Id.* at 2496. The Court specifically held that Fed. R. Civ. P. 54(d) did not supply authority for a federal court to tax as costs against the losing party expenses not explicitly authorized by § 1920, or, in the case of expert witness fees, in an amount exceeding the limit set by § 1821. *Id.* at 2497-98. The Court's conclusion in *Crawford Fitting* that "[w]e will not lightly infer that Congress has repealed §§ 1920 and 1821, either through Rule 54(d) or any other provision not referring explicitly to witness fees" (*id.* at 2499) is of a piece with the American Rule of fee-shifting announced in *Alyeska Pipeline Service Co. v. Wilderness Society,* 421 U.S. 240 (1975), that limits the prevailing party's recovery of his fees and expenses against the losing party to circumstances expressly authorized by contract, statute, or within narrow equitable exceptions.

Crawford Fitting addressed only the question whether items of litigation expense not specified in § 1920, or expert witness fees in an amount above the limit set by § 1821, could be taxed *as costs* against the losing party. In the face of the Court's categorical statement that "§ 1920 now embodies Congress's considered choice as to the kinds of expenses that a federal court may tax as costs against the losing party" (*id.* at 2496), it is unlikely that any litigation expenses other than those enumerated in § 1920 may be considered taxable *as costs* against the losing party, absent contractual or express statutory authorization. However, as the concurring and dissenting opinions take pains to emphasize, the Court did not have before it in *Crawford Fitting* the question whether litigation expenses not specified in § 1920, or expert witness fees in an amount above the § 1821 maximum, can be recovered by the prevailing party in civil rights litigation as part of the statutory *attorney's fees* assessed against the losing party under 42 U.S.C. § 1988. *Id.* at 2499 & n.1.

Pre-*Crawford Fitting* precedent in the lower courts is divided as to whether § 1988 grants authority to federal courts to award excess expert witness fees to the prevailing party as statutory attorney's fees. *Compare Heiar v. Crawford County,* 746 F.2d 1190, 1203-04 (7th Cir. 1984), *and Lenihan v. City of New York,* 640 F. Supp. 822, 830 (S.D.N.Y. 1986)(granting recovery), *with Davis v. Richmond, Fredericksburg & Potomac R. Co.,* 803 F.2d 1322, 1328 (4th Cir. 1986); *Chicago College of Osteopathic Medicine v. George A. Fuller Co.,* 801 F.2d 908, 912 (7th Cir. 1986); *Wheeler v. Durham City Bd. of Educ.,* 585 F.2d 618, 623-24 (4th Cir. 1978); *and Lyons v. Cunningham,* 583 F. Supp. 1147, 1155-56 (S.D.N.Y. 1983)(denying or questioning recovery). It is debatable whether the Court would find that § 1988 or any other fee-shifting statute not referring explicitly to witness fees authorizes the recovery as attorney's fees of expert witness fees above the limit expressly set by § 1821, even though §§ 1920 and 1821 only address the taxation of expert witness fees as "costs." Significantly, the Court expressed its disfavor for "[a]ny argument that a federal court is empowered to exceed the limitations explicitly set out in §§ 1920 and 1821 without plain evidence of congressional intent to supersede that section." *Id.* at 4822. *Compare Sevigny v. Dicksey,* 846 F.2d 953, 959 (4th Cir. 1988)(reiterating Fourth Circuit rule generally barring reimbursement under § 1988 for fees of non-legal experts); *Glenn v. General Motors Corp.,* 841 F.2d 1567, 1573-75 (11th Cir. 1988)(ruling that broad language of *Crawford Fitting* compelled conclusion that excess expert witness fees were not recoverable as attorney's fees or costs under Equal Pay Act, 29 U.S.C. § 216(b), which does not refer explicitly to witness fees); *Leroy v. City of Houston,* 831 F.2d 576, 584 (5th Cir. 1987)(concluding that the "general reasoning" of *Crawford Fitting* "leaves us no room to construe the fee-shifting provision of the Voting Rights Act, 42 U.S.C. § 19731(e), which "does not specifically allow recovery of expert witness fees," to permit recovery of excess expert witness fees as statutory attorney's fees); *International Woodworkers v. Champion International,* 790 F.2d 1174 (5th Cir. 1986) (en banc), *aff'd sub nom. Crawford Fitting Co. v. J.T. Gibbons, Inc.,* 107 S. Ct. 2494 (1987) (concluding that § 1988 and Title VII fee-shifting provision do not authorize recovery of excess
* expert withness fees), *and Pacific West Cable Co. v. City of Sacramento,* 693 F. Supp. 865, 874-76 (E.D. Cal. 1988) (§ 1988 does not authorize recovery of excess expert witness fees), *with Sapanajin v. Gunter,* 857 F.2d 463, 465 (8th Cir. 1988); *Black Grievance Committee v. Philadelphia Electric Co.,* 690 F. Supp. 1393, 1403-04 (E.D. Pa. 1988); *Hillburn v. Commissioner, Connecticut Department of Income Maintenance,* 683 F. Supp. 23, 27 (D. Conn. 1987); *and United States v. Yonkers Board of Education,* 118 F.R.D. 326, 333 (S.D.N.Y. 1987)(all concluding that excess expert witness fees are recoverable as part of § 1988 attorney's fees).

On the other hand, *Crawford Fitting* is not inconsistent with lower-court precedent that has approved the prevailing party's recovery as § 1988 attorney's fees of out-of-pocket expenses, other than those payable to a third party and taxed as costs under § 1920, that ordinarily are incurred by attorneys in the course of the litigation and normally are billed separately to fee-paying clients. See discussion and cases cited in text. The legislative history of § 1988, although sparse on this point, supports the view that Congress intended such expenses to be recoverable as part of attorney's fees under § 1988. Thus, Representative Drinan, a sponsor of § 1988, stated that "the phrase 'attorney's fees' would include . . . all incidental and necessary expenses incurred in furnishing effective and competent representation." 122 Cong. Rec. 35,123 (1976). Furthermore, one of the three cases cited approvingly in the Senate Report as having "correctly applied" the "appropriate standards" governing attorney's fees (*Swann v. Charlotte-Mecklenburg Bd. of Educ.,* 66 F.R.D. 483 (W.D.N.C. 1975)) expressly granted the recovery of litigation expenses, as well as attorney's fees, by the prevailing plaintiff. S. Rep. No. 94-1011, 94th Cong., 2d Sess. 6 (1976), *reprinted in* 5 U.S. Code Cong. & Ad. News 5913 (1976). *See Daly v. Hill,* 790 F.2d 1071, 1083 & n.17 (4th Cir. 1986).

The contrary argument is that since attorney's fees are made recoverable by § 1988 only "as part of the costs" of the suit, the rule of *Crawford Fitting* therefore applies to bar the recovery under § 1988, of any litigation expenses not enumerated in § 1920, in the absence of express authorization for their recovery in § 1988 itself. *Cf. Marek v. Chesny,* 473 U.S. 1, 9-10 (1985)(adopting " 'plain meaning' interpretation of the interplay between Rule 68 and § 1988" as the "only construction that gives meaning" to the word "costs" in both provisions). The Fifth Circuit may have implicitly adopted the extreme position that no expense not specifically authorized by 28 U.S.C. §§ 1920 and 1821 may be recovered as attorney's fees under § 1988 and similar fee-shifting statutes. *See International Woodworkers, supra,* 790 F.2d at 1188 (Rubin, J., dissenting); *cf. Shipes v. Trinity Industries, Inc.,* 685 F. Supp. 612, 614 (E.D. Tex. 1987) (denying recovery under § 1988 of expenses for out-of-court services of experts).

Page 555, add to note 21:

See also Akbar v. Fairman, 788 F.2d 1273, 1279 (7th Cir. 1986)(denying recovery, under § 1988 or Supreme Court rules, of costs incurred by plaintiffs in unsuccessfully petitioning the Supreme Court for a writ of certiorari).

Page 556, update Palmer citation in note 23:

478 U.S. 1015 (1986).

Page 556, add to note 26:

Wagenmann v. Adams, 829 F.2d 196, 225 (1st Cir. 1987)(disallowing recovery under § 1988 of "clearly segregable" expense item, which related exclusively to a state malpractice claim against another defendant and had "no conceivable relevance to the civil rights aspect of the litigation").

Page 556, add to note 27:

Culebras Enters. Corp. v. Rivera-Rios, 846 F.2d 94, 102-03 (1st Cir. 1988)(denying plaintiff recovery under § 1988 of expenses related to unsuccessful claim); Gorelangton v. City of Reno, 638 F. Supp. 1426, 1434-35 (D. Nev. 1986)(percentage reduction in recoverable expenses to reflect plaintiffs' partial success in litigation); Vaughns v. Bd. of Educ., 627 F. Supp. 837, 844 (D. Md. 1985)(percentage reduction in recoverable expenses to reflect plaintiffs' partial success in litigation and excessiveness of claimed hours); *cf.* Zabkowicz v. West Bend Co., 789 F.2d 540, 554 (7th Cir. 1986)(remanding for district court to consider reimbursement of out-of-pocket expenses arising from unsuccessful tort claims for which attorney's fees may be available because related to successful Title VII claim).

Add at end of section:

In *Norwood v. Charlotte Memorial Hosp.,* 653 F. Supp. 1350, 1362 (W.D.N.C. 1987), the court awarded interest on the recoverable litigation expenses, as well as on the statutory attorney's fees, in order to compensate for the long delay in payment.

* The Eleventh Circuit has ruled that an award of costs, whether granted under 28 U.S.C. § 1920 or as part of statutory attorney's fees, bears interest from the date of judgment. *Georgia Association of Retarded Citizens v. McDaniel,* 855 F.2d 794 (11th Cir. 1988).

Relying on *Kuzma v. IRS,* 821 F.2d 930 (2d Cir. 1987), the court in *Luna v. Harris,* 691 F. Supp. 624, 627-29 (E.D.N.Y. 1988), ruled that the successful pro se plaintiff, although not eligible for § 1988 attorney's fees, was entitled to reimbursement of out-of-pocket litigation expenses not covered by 28 U.S.C. § 1920.

§ 21.9 Interest on the Fee Award

Page 557, add to note 34:

Cf. Vaughns v. Board of Educ., 627 F. Supp. 837, 838-39 (D. Md. 1985)(acknowledging principle that district courts should have "discretion to cause interest to run on the date the [fee] judgment would have been entered but for delay," but in this case finding no delay by the parties or by the court in the entry of the fee award judgment).

Page 558, add the following after sentence ending with note 38 reference:

However, Congress has expressly provided in limited circumstances for the assessment of interest on fee awards against the federal government under the Equal Access to Justice Act (EAJA), 28 U.S.C. § 2412. Thus, 28 U.S.C. § 2412(f), added in August, 1985, provides that if the United States appeals an EAJA fee award and the award is affirmed in whole or in part, then interest is to be paid, as calculated under 28 U.S.C. § 1961(a), on the amount of the award as affirmed and is to run "from the date of the award through the day before the date of the mandate of affirmance." *See Thompson v. Kennickell,* 797 F.2d 1015, 1026 (D.C. Cir. 1986); *Haitian Refugee Center v. Meese,* 791 F.2d 1489, 1501 (11th Cir. 1986). The federal government is otherwise immune from liability for interest on a fee award under the EAJA or other fee-shifting statutes, absent an express statutory waiver. *See generally Thompson v. Kennickell, supra,* and cases cited in note 36 in text.

Page 558, update Shaw citations in notes 37 and 38:

478 U.S. 310, 319-23 (1986).

Add at end of section:

While recognizing that § 1961 does not apply to state court proceedings, the court in *Gaulin v. Commissioner of Public Welfare,* 23 Mass. App. Ct. 744, 505 N.E.2d 898

(1987), awarded post-judgment interest on a § 1988 fee award granted in state court against the state of Massachusetts, rejecting the state's contention that it was immune from an award of post-judgment interest.

* In *Georgia Association of Retarded Citizens v. McDaniel,* 855 F.2d 794 (11th Cir. 1988), the Eleventh Circuit held that awards of costs, whether granted pursuant to 28 U.S.C. § 1920 or as part of statutory attorney's fees, bear interest from the date of the original judgment.

§ 21.10 Retroactive Application of § 1988

Page 559, add to note 43:

Of course, § 1988 applies to all cases instituted after the effective date of the statute, even if the predicate acts underlying the litigation occurred prior to that date. *Wagenmann v. Adams,* 829 F.2d 196, 223-24 (1st Cir. 1987).

* *Page 560, add to cases cited in note 47:*

Alberti v. Sheriff of Harris County, 688 F. Supp. 1176, 1181-82 (S.D. Tex. 1987) (§ 1983 suit was pending on effective date of § 1988 when prior consent decree "specifically contemplated a continuing and ongoing process which would include further adjudication by the district court and which did not terminate the litigation").

CHAPTER 22

NEGOTIATING AND SETTLING § 1988 FEES

§ 22.1 The Preference for Settling the Fee Issue

Page 562, update Crest Street citation in note 5:

rev'd, 479 U.S. 6 (1986).

* *Page 563, add at end of section:*

Notwithstanding the obvious advantages to all concerned of settlement rather than litigation of the fee issue, it has been observed that frequently "lawyers litigate fee issues with greather energy and enthusiasm than they litigate any other type of issue." *Ustrak v. Fairman,* 851 F.2d 983, 988 (7th Cir. 1988). The *Ustrak* court observed that fee litigation has become a "heavy burden" on federal courts, turning a "simple civil case into two or even more cases – the case on the merits, the case for fees, the case for fees on appeal, the case for fees for proving fees, and so on ad infinitum, or at least ad nauseum." *Id.* at 987.

§ 22.5 –*Evans v. Jeff D.:* The Propriety of Simultaneous Merits/Fees Negotiations and Defendant Fee-Sacrifice Offers

Page 569, add to note 23:

Resolution of the question whether the plaintiff's lawyer is ethically bound to defer to the client's decision to accept a settlement offer, that sacrifices statutory attorney's fees to the merits of the litigation, is dependent on whether the statutory fee legally belongs to the lawyer or to the prevailing plaintiff. *See* Committee on Professional and Judicial Ethics of the New York City Bar Association, Op. No. 87-4 (*reprinted in* New York Law Journal May 22, 1987, p. 1)(compare concurring opinion and minority statement). The Supreme Court made it clear in Evans v. Jeff D., 475 U.S. 717, 730 & n.19 (1986), that entitlement to a § 1988 fee award belongs to the prevailing plaintiff, and not to his lawyer, thereby making it difficult to conclude that the lawyer has an ethical right to oppose the plaintiff's choice, in a non-class action suit, to accept a fee-sacrifice settlement offer. See complete discussion at **§ 22.8**.

Page 569-70, add to note 24:

In the wake of the *Jeff D.* decision, the Committee on Professional and Judicial Ethics of the New York City Bar Association, in Op. No. 87-4 (*reprinted in* New York Law

Journal, May 22, 1987, p. 1), has withdrawn its prior Opinions 80-94 and 82-80, concluding that *Jeff D.* removed the "principal underpinning" of those opinions by interpreting § 1988 to authorize the simultaneous negotiation of merits and fee issues in civil rights litigation and the making of at least some kinds of fee-sacrifice offers. See further discussion at § **22.8** of this supplement.

Page 573, add to note 44:

See also Freeman v. B&B Associates, 790 F.2d 145, 151-52 (D.C. Cir. 1986)(Truth-in-Lending Act, 15 U.S.C. § 1640(a); finding that *Jeff D.*'s proscription against district court's revision of settlement agreement, by voiding fee waiver provision while enforcing merits portion, applies with especial force to accepted settlement offer made pursuant to Fed. R. Civ. P. 68). In Huertas v. East River Housing Corp., 813 F.2d 580 (2d Cir. 1987), the Second Circuit reversed the district court's decision to enforce a settlement agreement that resolved all issues in a class action housing discrimination suit except for the issue of statutory attorney's fees and to award a reasonable amount of fees to the plaintiffs, over defendants' objections. The court concluded that, under *Jeff D.*, the district judge "acted without authority when he ordered defendants to be bound by the proposed stipulation of settlement when they had not yet agreed with respect to the attorneys' fees to be awarded to plaintiffs." *Id.* at 582.

§ 22.6 —Evaluating Whether a Defendant's Fee-Sacrifice Offer is Valid after *Jeff D.*

Page 573, in fourth line in section, change "waiver of limitation" to "waiver or limitation."

Page 575, in third line from top of page, change "undermining of the fundamental objective" to "undermining the fundamental objective."

§ 22.8 —Plaintiffs' Options after *Jeff D.*

Page 580, add to note 74:

It has been suggested, however, that it is not unethical for plaintiff's attorney to seek, even over the client's objection in a non-class action suit, judicial resolution of the question whether a particular fee-sacrifice offer made by the civil rights defendant is unlawful under the *Jeff D.* guidelines. Goldstein, "Settlement Offers Contingent upon Waiver of Attorney Fees: A Continuing Dilemma after *Evans v. Jeff D.*," 20 *Clearinghouse Review* 693, 698 (Oct. 1986). However, the Eleventh Circuit, in Panola Land Buying Ass'n v. Clark, 844 F.2d 1506 (11th Cir. 1988), upheld the district court's refusal of the request of plaintiff's attorney that it resolve the question of the propriety of a fee waiver provision (of fees under the Equal Access to Justice Act, 28 U.S.C. § 2412) in a settlement agreement that the plaintiff wished to accept but which his attorney asserted was improperly coercive under the principles of Evans v. Jeff D., 475 U.S. 717 (1986). In dissent, Judge Clark persuasively argued that the district court should have acceded to the request of the plaintiff's attorney "for some form of judicial participation in the settlement process to determine the reasons for the government's desire to settle and whether its demand that settlement exclude payment of attorney's fees was coercive." *Id.* at 1525.

Page 580, add at end of complete paragraph containing note 76 reference:

Cf. Willard v. City of Los Angeles, 803 F.2d 526, 528 (9th Cir. 1986)(court affirmed denial of plaintiffs' § 1988 fee request following settlement of a non-class action civil rights suit for a lump-sum amount that included § 1988 fees, finding that "the record does not indicate that the City of Long Beach has adopted a statute, policy, or practice requiring waiver of fees as a condition of settlement or that it has vindictively sought to deter attorneys from bringing civil rights suits").

Page 580, add to note 79:

Subsequent to the *Jeff D.* decision, the Committee on Professional and Judicial Ethics of the New York City Bar Association issued Opinion No. 87-4 (*reprinted in* New York Law Journal, May 22, 1987, p. 1), by which it withdrew its earlier Opinions 80-94 and 82-80 that had forbidden a defendant's simultaneous negotiation of merits and fee issues in civil rights cases and had barred defendant settlement offers conditioning merits relief on plaintiff's waiver of statutory attorney's fees. The Committee opinion acknowledged that its prior ethics opinions had been principally based on an understanding of the underlying purposes of § 1988 that had been undercut by the Supreme Court's interpretation of that provision in *Jeff D.* to authorize simultaneous merits/fees negotiations and some kinds of fee-sacrifice offers. Accordingly, the Committee was compelled to conclude that "it is not unethical *per se* for defense counsel to propose settlements conditioned on the waiver by plaintiffs of an award of attorneys' fees authorized by statutes in civil rights and civil liberties cases." Recognizing, however, that *Jeff D.* did not validate all defendant fee-sacrifice offers, the Committee in its recent opinion chose to determine the ethical propriety of particular variants of the fee-sacrifice offer "on a case-by-case basis," in "concrete factual settings" presented by "concrete inquiries" made to the Committee. In its opinion the Committee also left open the issue of the ethical propriety of a lawyer's including a no-fee-sacrifice provision in the retainer agreement entered into with a civil rights plaintiff, by which the plaintiff would obligate herself to reject settlement offers that sacrifice statutory fees to the merits of the litigation.

A substantial minority of the Committee issued a separate statement seeking to provide guidance to the Bar concerning the ethical propriety of fee-sacrifice offers and their rejection and regarding the propriety of no-fee-sacrifice provisions in retainer agreements. The minority concluded that, to the extent that entitlement to a statutory attorney's fee award is found to vest in the lawyer and not the prevailing plaintiff in civil rights litigation, then "the lawyer has no [ethical] duty to relinquish or waive any right he may possess to seek such an award and payment [of statutory fees], even if it would be in the client's best interest to do so or the client were to so direct, and even assuming it were ethical for the adverse attorney to propose settlement conditioned on such relinquishment or waiver." However, the underlying assumption of the minority statement's conclusion is at odds with the Supreme Court's statement in *Jeff D.* that the right to statutory attorney's fees belongs to the prevailing plaintiff and not to the plaintiff's lawyer. *See* separate concurring opinion to Committee Opinion No. 87-4, and §§ **22.5** and **24.1** of this book. The minority statement goes on to state its conclusion that, in any event, there is no ethical proscription against the structuring of a lawyer-client retainer agreement to forbid the plaintiff's acceptance of a defendant fee-sacrifice offer in an individual or class action civil rights suit. See further discussion later in this section. However, the majority opinion for the Committee specifically cautioned the Bar against reliance on the minority statement as *sub silentio* evidencing the views of the Committee on issues that the Committee preferred to leave to case-by-case determination.

Page 583, add to note 90:

In its recent Opinion No. 87-4, discussed in note 79, *supra,* the Committee on Professional and Judicial Ethics of the New York City Bar Association has left open the question of the ethical propriety of no-fee-sacrifice provisions in retainer agreements entered into between lawyers and their plaintiff clients in individual or class action civil rights suits. In a separate statement, a substantial minority of that Committee endorsed the ethical propriety of such a provision, provided that disclosure and consent requirements were fulfilled and any additional legal requirements in the class action context were satisfied.

Page 583, add new paragraph at end of section:

Even where the civil rights plaintiff has obligated herself by the terms of a formal retainer agreement with her lawyer to reject a fee-sacrifice offer, it is arguable that the plaintiff nonetheless may properly decide to accept the fee-sacrifice offer consonant with the client's exclusive right under prevailing ethical norms to make settlement decisions. ABA Model Code of Professional Responsibility EC 7-7; ABA Model Rules of Professional Conduct 1.2(a). The plaintiff's lawyer then would be relegated, as a practical matter, to the unsatisfactory remedy of withdrawal from the representation, unless he could persuade the district court that the fee-sacrifice offer was independently invalid under the *Jeff D.* guidelines discussed in §§ **22.6** and **22.8** of the text.

* An alternative strategy for deflecting a defendant fee-compromise settlement offer is for plaintiff's attorney to take a contractual assignment, in the client retainer agreement, of the plaintiff's § 1988 fee claim. Since the statutory attorney's fee is a contingent fee, it comes within the exception to the ethical prohibition against the attorney's acquisition of a "proprietary interest" in the litigation. ABA Model Code of Professional Responsibility DR5-103(A); ABA Model Rules of Professional Conduct 1.8(j). Having assigned her statutory fee claim to her lawyer, the plaintiff is no longer in a position to compromise that claim in exchange for favorable merits relief. Furthermore, it is arguably unethical for the defendant even to make a fee-compromise settlement offer, since it now creates a direct conflict of interest between the client's concern for merits relief and the attorney's concern for statutory

fees which, by reason of the assignment provision, now belong to him. However, there remains the question whether the fee assignment provision runs afoul of Model Rule 1.7(b), which prohibits a lawyer from representing a client if the representation "may be materially limited . . . by the lawyer's own interests."

§ 22.9 Reserving the Attorney's Fee Issue in a Settlement Agreement; Silence and Waiver

Page 584, add to note 92:

See also Keith v. Volpe, 833 F.2d 850, 858-59 (9th Cir. 1987)(finding that in its initial § 1988 fee award, district court's reservation of jurisdiction to make additional fee awards authorized its award of supplemental fees for plaintiffs' monitoring of the consent judgment).

Page 584, add to note 93:

District of Columbia Circuit: In Elmore v. Shuler, 787 F.2d 601 (D.C. Cir. 1986), the court held that plaintiffs waived their right to seek § 1988 fees by entering into a settlement agreement that included a release discharging defendants from all "claims and demands" in the suit, including "all . . . claims for damages, costs and expenses." Finding that "costs" should be construed to include attorney's fees, since attorney's fees are an element of costs under § 1988, the court concluded that the burden rested on the fee-eligible party to preserve her statutory fee claim by expressly reserving the issue in the settlement agreement. *Id.* at 603.

* *Eighth Circuit:* Pilliard v. Meyer, 689 F. Supp. 979 (E.D. Mo. 1988) (concluding that settlement agreement providing for defendants' payment of the costs of the action did not include an agreement to pay attorney's fees).

* *Ninth Circuit:* In Wakefield v. Mathews, 852 F.2d 482 (9th Cir. 1988), the Ninth Circuit, while agreeing generally that "[w]aiver of attorneys' fees should not be presumed from a silent record," upheld the district court's ruling that plaintiffs in this case had waived their right to § 1988 fees by signing a settlement agreement that sweepingly released defendants from "costs or expenses of any nature whatsoever, known or unknown, fixed or contingent," in the absence of evidence that plaintiffs meant to exempt attorney's fees from the waiver.

Page 585, add to note 94:

Third Circuit: In Ashley v. Atlantic Richfield Co., 794 F.2d 128, 136-41 (3d Cir. 1986), the court reaffirmed, following the *Jeff D.* decision, the Third Circuit rule that the prevailing plaintiff's waiver of her right to seek § 1988 fees is not to be inferred from silence on the fee issue in a settlement agreement in the case, and that the burden rests on the losing party in the suit to secure such a waiver by express provision to that effect in the settlement agreement. The Court refused to find the required express waiver of § 1988 fees in the settlement provision releasing defendant from all "costs," where it was clear that the parties, by first including and then excluding settlement language that would have waived fees, did not consider "costs" to include § 1988 attorney's fees. *Id.* at 140-41. *See also* Amico v. New Castle County, 654 F. Supp. 982, 990-91 (D. Del. 1987)(rejecting defendant's contention that judgment barring further litigation on the question of damages also barred additional litigation concerning plaintiff's request for § 1988 fees).

Page 586, add at end of section:

In *Blackwell v. Department of Offender,* 807 F.2d 914 (11th Cir. 1987), the court upheld the awarding of Rule 11 sanctions against plaintiff's attorney for his "lack of factual candor" in making a motion for § 1988 fees without mentioning to the district court that the plaintiff had executed a release from defendants' liability which included attorney's fees. The court reasoned that plaintiff's attorney "had the affirmative obligation in his initial filings .... to apprise the trial judge that although the settlement agreement foreclosed claims for attorney's fees as well as everything else, he nevertheless felt that he was entitled to attorney's fees under section 1988." *Id.* at 915.

§ 22.10 Judicial Supervision over Attorney's Fee Agreements

Page 588, add to note 5:

See Huertas v. East River Housing Corp., 813 F.2d 580 (2d Cir. 1987)(reversing district court's judgment that enforced settlement stipulation reflecting agreement on all issues except § 1988 attorney's fees and, over defendants' objections, made an award of fees to plaintiffs).

CHAPTER 23

AWARDING § 1988 FEES TO THE SUCCESSFUL CIVIL RIGHTS DEFENDANT –A HIGHER STANDARD

§ 23.1 Standards of Eligibility: Supreme Court Decisions

Page 591, add to note 14:

See also Popham v. City of Kennesaw, 820 F.2d 1570, 1583 (11th Cir. 1987)("If a plaintiff brings a lawsuit for a vexatious purpose or in bad faith, i.e., not in the hope of winning but solely in order to put the defendant to the burden off defending himself, the prevailing defendant arguably is entitled to attorneys' fees regardless of whether the plaintiff's claims technically were frivolous.")

Page 591, add to cases cited in note 15:

Bacon v. American Federation of State, County, 795 F.2d 33 (7th Cir. 1986)(assessing Title VII attorney's fees against pro se plaintiff for frivolous appeal, when "the pro se litigant's brief is not merely inartful and does not merely reflect a lack of firm grasp over the relevant principles of law ... [but] is essentially incoherent and makes no colorable effort to point out legal or factual errors in the district judge's patient opinion").

§ 23.2 –Application by the Lower Courts

Page 591, add to note 20:

Fellowship Baptist Church v. Benton, 815 F.2d 485, 499 (8th Cir. 1987)("Litigation which presents only claims which have been previously rejected and which is brought against a party in no position to change the law short of an 'informal accommodation' is, in our view, vexatious and unreasonable.' ").

Page 592, add after sentence ending with note 21 reference:

In *Hamer v. Lake County,* 819 F.2d 1362, 1367-68 (7th Cir. 1987), the court held that § 1988 fees may be assessed against plaintiffs who persist in their suit, which was reasonably instituted in light of the state of the law as it existed at the outset of the litigation, after intervening developments in the law rendered the suit groundless.

Page 592, add to cases cited in note 25:

Soffer v. City of Costa Mesa, 798 F.2d 361, 363-64 (9th Cir. 1986); Vandenplas v. City of Muskego, 797 F.2d 425, 430-32 (7th Cir. 1986); Holloway v. Walker, 784 F.2d 1294, 1296 (5th Cir. 1986)(all finding civil rights claims of losing plaintiffs not to be frivolous, for purposes of awarding § 1988 fees to successful defendants, since relevant law was in a "state of flux" at the time the suits were filed and while they were pending); *see also* Thomas v. Metroflight, Inc., 814 F.2d 1506, 1512 (10th Cir. 1987)(reversing award of Title VII fees against plaintiff whose nonfrivolous claim was "one of first impression at the circuit level").

Page 592, add to note 26:

Coates v. Bechtel, 811 F.2d 1045, 1052 (7th Cir. 1987)(rejecting proposed standard for defendant fee award based on whether there was "any admissible evidence to support the plaintiff's claim when he filed the complaint and thereafter," because "factual uncertainty may exist at the outset of litigation and . . . decisive facts may not emerge until discovery or trial").

Page 592, add to note 27:

E.E.O.C. v. Kenneth Balk & Assoc., Inc., 813 F.2d 197, 198 (8th Cir. 1987)(Title VII suit not frivolous when district court gave it careful consideration and based decision on "resolution of conflicting evidence and testimony"). *But see* Hicks v. Southern Md. Health Sys. Agency, 805 F.2d 1165, 1167-68 (4th Cir. 1986)(upholding fee award against plaintiffs, although district court engaged in "extensive consideration of legal problems before the baselessness of all the claims was fully exposed," because "it was first necessary to blow away the smoke screens the plaintiffs had thrown up").

Page 592, add to cases cited in note 29:

Vaughner v. Pulito, 804 F.2d 873, 878 (5th Cir. 1986); LeBeau v. Libbey-Owens-Ford Co., 799 F.2d 1152, 1156-61 (7th Cir. 1986); Berry v. E.I. duPont de Nemours and Co., 635 F. Supp. 262, 266 (D. Del. 1986)(all denying § 1988 fees to successful defendants in substantial part because plaintiffs' claims survived a defendant motion for dismissal, directed verdict, or summary judgment); *see also* Coates v. Bechtel, 811 F.2d 1045, 1050 (7th Cir. 1987)(holding that "plaintiff's failure to adduce factual evidence to survive a motion for summary judgment or a motion to dismiss for failure to state a claim does not alone render the action frivolous justifying an award of fees to the defendant").

Page 593, add after sentence ending with note 31 reference:

In *Fidelity Guarantee Mortgage Corp. v. Reben,* 809 F.2d 931, 936 (1st Cir. 1987), the court rejected plaintiff's contention that § 1988 fees should not be assessed against it because the ultimate recipient of the fee award is defendant's insurance carrier.

Page 593, add to note 32:

Coates v. Bechtel, 811 F.2d 1045, 1053 (7th Cir. 1987)(stating that plaintiff risks being assessed § 1988 fees if he "insists on continuing the litigation" in spite of warnings from district judge that plaintiff's discovery has failed to "uncover any evidence to substantiate his claims").

Page 594, add after sentence ending with note 38 reference:

The Seventh Circuit, in *Szabo Food Service, Inc. v. Canteen Corp.,* 823 F.2d 1073 (7th Cir. 1987), agreed with the result in *Santiago* but did not endorse its reasoning. The Seventh Circuit concluded that a Rule 41(a)(i) voluntary dismissal without prejudice by the plaintiff does not entitle the defendant to § 1988 fees because such a dismissal does not decide the case on the merits and, hence, the defendant has not prevailed under § 1988. *Id.* at 1076-77. Further, because "costs" may not be awarded against the plaintiff who takes such a voluntary dismissal, *see* Fed. R. Civ. P. 41(d), neither may § 1988 fees, which are authorized "as part of the costs" of the action. *Id.* at 1077.

Page 594, add to note 40:

In Wrenn v. Gould, 808 F.2d 493, 504-05 (6th Cir. 1986), the court declined to assess fees against the plaintiff-appellant on appeal, finding that although plaintiff had filed a number of groundless civil rights suits, "*this particular appeal* was not frivolous."

Page 594, add at end of section:

In *East-Bibb Twiggs Neighborhood Association v. Macon-Bibb Planning and Zoning Commission,* 674 F. Supp. 1475 (M.D. Ga. 1987), the court ruled that a state-law counterclaim for abusive litigation could not be asserted by the successful defendant in a § 1983 action in federal court, where § 1988 set the applicable standard for * defendant's recovery of fees for groundless § 1983 litigation. In *Hidahl v. Gilpin County Department of Social Services,* 699 F. Supp. 846, 849 (D. Colo. 1988), the court suggested that § 1988 fees could not be awarded to the defendant who gained dismissal of plaintiff's § 1983 suit on jurisdictional (here Eleventh Amendment) grounds, since defendant had not thereby prevailed on the merits of the litigation.

§ 23.3 —The Partially Prevailing Defendant

Page 594, add to note 43:

See Popham v. City of Kennesaw, 820 F.2d 1570, 1582 (11th Cir. 1987)(noting that defendants may not be denied § 1988 fees for successfully defending against frivolous claims on an "equitable approach" of reducing the § 1988 fees awarded plaintiff for his successful claims).

Page 595, add at end of carryover paragraph:

In *Trevino v. Holly Sugar Corp.,* 811 F.2d 896, 907 (5th Cir. 1987), the Fifth Circuit upheld the denial of Title VII and § 1988 fees to the winning defendant because of defendant's failure to undertake or to request the district court to perform a claim-by-claim analysis of plaintiffs' suit in order to segregate particular related claims that were frivolous and hence warranted the assessment of statutory fees against plaintiffs.

Page 595, update Vandenplas citation and add to cases cited in note 48:

Vandenplas, *rev'd,* 797 F.2d 425 (7th Cir. 1986); Quiros v. Hernandez Colon, 800 F.2d 1, 2 (1st Cir. 1986)(refusing to assess statutory fees against losing plaintiff whose civil rights complaint contained both nonfrivolous and frivolous claims).

Page 596, add to note 49:

But see Hamer v. Lake County, 819 F.2d 1362, 1369 (7th Cir. 1987)(finding this case to be an exception to the "general rule" against assessing § 1988 fees against plaintiffs in cases with a mix of frivolous and nonfrivolous claims, "because of the largely disproportionate time and expense the defendants have had to devote to defending against the frivolous aspects of the plaintiffs' claims").

§ 23.4 –Other Bases for Defendant Fee Awards

Page 596, add to cases cited in note 51:

Oliveri v. Thompson, 803 F.2d 1265, 1274-81 (2d Cir. 1986)(standards for imposition of * attorney's fee sanctions pursuant to Fed. R. Civ. P. 11). In Paul v. Federal Nat'l Mfg. Ass'n, 697 F. Supp. 547, 551 (D.D.C. 1988), the court observed that while Rule 11 "expressly gives the court flexibility to sanction *particular* pleadings or motions that it finds wantonly or vexatiously asserted," the suit itself must be frivolous in order for a defendant to recover fees under a fee-shifting statute such as § 1988.

Page 596, add to cases cited in note 52:

Oliveri v. Thompson, 803 F.2d 1265, 1273-81 (2d Cir. 1986); Ford v. Temple Hosp., 790 F.2d 342, 346-50 (3d Cir. 1986); Jones v. Continental Corp., 789 F.2d 1225, 1229-33 (6th Cir. 1986)(all discussing standards for imposition of attorney's fee sanctions pursuant to 28 U.S.C. § 1927).

§ 23.5 Determining the Amount of § 1988 Fees to Be Awarded to the Prevailing Defendant

Page 597, add to cases cited in note 55:

Hamilton v. Daley, 777 F.2d 1207, 1213-16 (7th Cir. 1985)(vacating § 1988 fee award to successful defendant and remanding for redetermination of amount of award, with elimination of claimed hours that were inappropriately expended or excessive).

Page 597, update Vandenplas citation in note 56:

rev'd, 797 F.2d 425 (7th Cir. 1986).

§ 23.5 AMOUNT OF AWARD

Page 598, add to note 59:

Johnson v. New York City Transit Auth., 823 F.2d 31, 33 (2d Cir. 1987)(recognizing plaintiff's ability to pay as relevant consideration in determining size of statutory fee award to prevailing defendant).

* *Page 598, add at end of section:*

In *Patton v. County of Kings,* 857 F.2d 1379, 1382 (9th Cir. 1988), the Ninth Circuit rejected plaintiff's contention that he was entitled to a separate hearing on his ability to pay the § 1988 fee award to be assessed against him.

CHAPTER 24

PROCEDURAL ASPECTS OF REQUESTING, LITIGATING, AND COLLECTING § 1988 FEES

§ 24.1 Standing to Seek Fees

Pages 599-600, add at end of note 2:

Soliman v. Ebasco Servs. Inc., 822 F.2d 320, 322-23 (2d Cir. 1987); Keesee v. Orr, 816 F.2d 545, 547-48 (10th Cir. 1987)(right to seek statutory fees vests in prevailing party, not his attorney). In Evans v. Jeff D., 475 U.S. 717, 730 & n.19, 731-32 (1986), the Supreme Court made clear that "Congress bestowed on the 'prevailing *party*' (generally plaintiffs) a statutory eligibility" for § 1988 attorney's fees and, correspondingly, that Congress did not intend to vest the right to statutory fees in the prevailing party's attorney. The conclusion that entitlement to a § 1988 fee award belongs to the prevailing plaintiff, and not to his lawyer, figures significantly in the Supreme Court's analysis in *Jeff D.* of the ethical and statutory propriety of the making and acceptance of fee-sacrifice settlement offers. See discussion at §§ **22.5, 22.6,** and **22.8** of text and supplement.

Page 600, add to note 4:

In re Burlington Northern, Inc., 832 F.2d 422, 424 n.2 (7th Cir. 1987)(law firms representing successful plaintiffs in Title VII employment discrimination suit sought increased recovery of statutory fees, although the named plaintiffs were "technically the parties bringing this appeal").

Page 600, add to note 5:

The Seventh Circuit has ruled that a Title VII fee award should be paid to the law firms that represented the prevailing plaintiffs in the litigation, instead of directly to the individual attorneys and paralegals in the firm in the amounts represented by the separately calculated sums for their services in the case. *In re* Burlington Northern, Inc., 810 F.2d 601, 609 (7th Cir. 1986). The court observed that the market rates at which the attorney's services were valued for statutory fee purposes exceeded "what the attorney earns on an hourly basis," so that a "reasonable hourly rate for purposes of a fee award . . . is not the same as reasonable compensation for an individual attorney." *Id.*

Page 600, add to note 6:

In Evans v. Jeff D., 475 U.S. 717, 730-31 (1986), the Supreme Court interpreted § 1988 to authorize the prevailing party's assignment of her statutory right to attorney's fees
* to her attorney. See § **22.8**.

Page 601, add to note 9:

However, after *Jeff D.,* it is apparent that the prevailing plaintiff's attorney generally lacks standing to seek court-awarded statutory attorney's fees following the plaintiff's entry into a settlement agreement with defendants that waives the plaintiff's statutory fee claim. Willard v. City of Los Angeles, 803 F.2d 526, 527 (9th Cir. 1986)(§ 1988 fees); Freeman v. B & B Associates, 790 F.2d 145, 147-150 (D.C. Cir. 1986)(Truth-in-Lending Act, 15 U.S.C. § 1640(a)(3)). In *Jeff D.,* 89 L. Ed. 2d at 760 n.19, the Supreme Court suggested its disapproval of the contrary ruling in James v. Home Constr. Co., cited in note 9 in the text. *Cf.* Freeman v. B & B Associates, 790 F.2d at 149 (suggesting that *James* was incorrectly decided in light of *Jeff D.*).

§ 24.2 Timeliness of the Fee Motion

Page 601, update Palmer citation and add to note 14:

vacated & remanded on other grounds, 478 U.S. 1015 (1986). Similarly, in Buckanan v. Stanships, Inc., 108 S. Ct. 1130 (1988), the Supreme Court held that a motion for costs raises issues wholly collateral to the judgment in the main cause of action and, hence, does not constitute a rule 59(e) motion.

Pages 602-03, update Daggett (Third Circuit) and Crest Street (Fourth Circuit) citations and add to note 18:

First Circuit: Fidelity Guarantee Mortgage Corp. v. Reben, 809 F.2d 931, 937 (1st Cir. 1987)(construing local rule of Maine District Court consistent with Fed. R. Civ. P. 6(a) concerning computation of time, to find that plaintiff timely filed § 1988 fee motion).

Third Circuit: Daggett, *aff'd in relevant part,* 811 F.2d 793 (3d Cir. 1987); Amico v. New Castle County, 654 F. Supp. 982, 991-95 (D. Del. 1987)(exercising discretion to decide plaintiff's § 1988 fee motion although not filed in compliance with the timeliness requirement of local court rule, when motion did not unfairly surprise or prejudice defendant).

Fourth Circuit: Crest Street, *rev'd,* 479 U.S. 6 (1986); Jackson v. Beard, 828 F.2d 1077 (4th Cir. 1987)(upholding district court's interpretation of local Maryland District Court rule that period within which § 1988 fee motion must be filed after entry of judgment was not tolled by pendency of post-verdict motions); Hicks v. Southern Md. Health Sys. Agency, 805 F.2d 1165, 1167 (4th Cir. 1986)(concluding that district court had "jurisdictional power" to consider and grant defendants' motion for statutory fees despite possible noncompliance with local timeliness rule of the Maryland District Court, characterized as a "housekeeping rule").

Fifth Circuit: Jackson v. U.S. Postal Service, 799 F.2d 1018, 1023 (5th Cir. 1986)(affirming dismissal of plaintiffs' fee request under Equal Access to Justice Act, 28 U.S.C. § 2412(b), as untimely under local rule of Northern District of Texas requiring fee applications to be filed within 30 days after entry of judgment).

* *Seventh Circuit:* Max M. v. New Trier High School Dist., 859 F.2d 1297, 1300 (7th Cir. 1988) (upholding district court's decision that local rule prescribing time after final judgment within which fee motion must be made was inapplicable to fee application under Education of the Handicapped Act, 20 U.S.C. § 1415(e), which was not amended to authorize a fee award until time to file had lapsed); Buggs v. Elgin, Joliet & E. Ry. Co., 852 F.2d 318, 322-23 (7th Cir. 1988) (finding that magistrate's allowance of fee petition filed after deadline set by the judgment "effectively constituted a grant of enlargement of time in which to file").

Eighth Circuit: McKee v. Bi-State Development Agency, 801 F.2d 1014, 1016-18 (8th Cir. 1986)(invalidating local rule of Eastern District of Missouri insofar as it provided that a fee request made within 21 days after entry of judgment on the merits suspended the finality of the merits judgment until district court ruled on the fee request); Williams v. Omodt, 640 F. Supp. 120, 124 (D. Minn. 1986)(local district court rule requiring fee application to be filed within 30 days after merits judgment).

Ninth Circuit: Visa Int'l Serv. Assoc. v. Bankcard Holders, 784 F.2d 1472, 1476 (9th Cir. 1986)(affirming denial of fee request as untimely under California Northern District rule requiring fee applications to be filed within 60 days of entry of final judgment). Ninth Circuit Rule 39-1.6 requires that all requests for appellate attorney's fees be filed in the court of appeals "within 30 days after the entry of the court's decision," absent a timely filed rehearing petition in the case.

* *Tenth Circuit:* Willner v. Budig, 848 F.2d 1032, 1035 (10th Cir. 1988) (finding that guidelines established by chief judge of district court for the filing of fee applications in his cases "are not binding on other district judges"); Hernandez v. George, 793 F.2d 264, 266-69 (10th Cir. 1986)(court upheld district court's waiver of requirement of New Mexico local court rule that fee request be filed within 21 days after entry of final judgment, where plaintiffs' fee claim was not stale and "[o]pposing counsel knew of the claim months before the final judgment" and continued to engage the plaintiffs in fee negotiations beyond the time limit for filing of the fee request; however, court denied compensation for plaintiffs' fee work performed after time limit expired).

* *Eleventh Circuit:* Davidson v. City of Avon Park, 848 F.2d 172 (11th Cir. 1988) (reversing district court's denial of plaintiff's § 1988 fee motion as untimely filed under local court rule, since district court led plaintiff to reasonably believe that rule would be interpreted to permit fee motion to be filed following disposition of appeal from merits judgment); Watkins v. McMillan, 779 F.2d 1465 (11th Cir. 1985)(affirming denial of plaintiff's fee motion as untimely under requirement of Middle District of Alabama local rule that statutory fee application be filed within 30 days from the "date of judgment," and rejecting plaintiff's contention that for this purpose the finality of the district court judgment was suspended by the pendency of an appeal).

Page 603, add to note 19:

Grusendorf v. City of Oklahoma City, 816 F.2d 539, 544-45 (10th Cir. 1987)(plaintiff's failure to timely respond under local Oklahoma District Court rule to prevailing defendants' § 1988 fee motion); Jordan v. Mark IV Hair Styles, Inc., 806 F.2d 695, 697-98 (6th Cir. 1986)(reversing district court's § 1988 fee award, for its "exclusive reliance" on defendant's failure to timely file, under local Ohio District Court rule, response to plaintiff's § 1988 fee motion).

Page 603, add to note 20:

But see Montgomery & Assocs., Inc. v. C.F.T.C., 816 F.2d 783 (D.C. Cir. 1987)(dismissing prevailing appellee's appellate fee motion, under fee-shifting statute that defined attorney's fees as a part of costs, as untimely because filed after the 14-day period from entry of judgment established by Fed. R. App. P. 39(d) for the filing of requests for costs).

Page 604, add the following case to note 21:

Watkins v. McMillan, 779 F.2d 1465, 1466 (11th Cir. 1985)(see discussion in note 18, *supra*).

Page 605, add to cases cited in note 28:

Second Circuit: Orshan v. Macchiarola, 629 F. Supp. 1014, 1018 (E.D.N.Y. 1986)(noting that although 17-month delay in filing of § 1988 fee application following entry of judgment "may permit defendants to claim prejudice," defendants "have not raised or addressed the issue").

Third Circuit: Sellers v. Local 1598, 638 F. Supp. 507, 510-11 (E.D. Pa. 1986)(finding that plaintiff's § 1988 fee request filed more than a year after judgment was entered in the case should be dismissed as untimely, where the delay made it difficult for the court to "assess the intricacies of the case" and thereby prejudiced both parties)(alternative holding).

* *Seventh Circuit:* Max M. v. New Trier High School Dist., 859 F.2d 1297, 1301 (7th Cir. 1988) (finding no abuse of discretion in district court's decision that fee motion filed a year after effective date of fee amendments to Education of the Handicapped Act, 20 U.S.C. § 1415(e), was not untimely, when district court concluded that delay-causing dispute between plaintiff's lawyer and ex-partner about the division of fees was resolved within a reasonable time, defendant was on early notice that fees would be sought, and defendant was not prejudiced in its ability to defend against the fee request).

Page 605, add at end of section:

In *Keith v. Volpe,* 833 F.2d 850, 860 n.6 (9th Cir. 1987), the Ninth Circuit noted the "perplexing task which a district court faces when it is called upon to consider a fee request which spans a period of years" and approved the district court's approach, in the context of § 1988 fee requests for post-judgment monitoring, of requiring quarterly fee applications from plaintiffs' counsel.

§ 24.3 The Need for an Evidentiary Hearing on the Fee Request

Page 607, update Cunningham citation (Third Circuit) and add to note 33:

First Circuit: Calhoun v. Acme Cleveland Corp., 801 F.2d 558, 561 (1st Cir. 1986)(upholding district court's refusal to hold evidentiary hearing on plaintiff's fee request when defendants initially opposed it and district court explained its fee decision in detail).

Third Circuit: Cunningham, *vacated & remanded on other grounds,* 478 U.S. 1015 (1986), *reinstated,* 807 F.2d 49 (3d Cir. 1986), *cert. denied,* 107 S. Ct. 2179 (1987); Blum v. Witco Chem. Corp., 829 F.2d 367, 377-78 (3d Cir. 1987)(evidentiary hearing required when defendant failed to "identify for the court any factual dispute or pinpoint any specific area where a hearing would have been helpful").

Fifth Circuit: Curtis v. Bill Hanna Ford, Inc., 822 F.2d 549, 551 (5th Cir. 1987)(evidentiary hearing not required when opposing party failed to request one); Sorola v. City of Lamesa, 808 F.2d 435, 437 (5th Cir. 1987)(evidentiary hearing not required when neither party requested one and opposing party presented no evidence creating fact dispute).

Tenth Circuit: Mares v. Credit Bureau of Raton, 801 F.2d 1197, 1205 n.16 (10th Cir. 1986)(Consumer Credit Protection Act, 15 U.S.C. §§ 1601 *et seq.*; finding that although "[n]ormally we would expect the district court to hold a hearing," in this case "plaintiffs' counsel expressly waived their right to a hearing" on the fee issue).

Page 608, add to note 35:

* *Ninth Circuit:* After noting that the defendant had waived its right to challenge the absence of an evidentiary hearing on the prevailing party issue by not requesting one in the district court, the court of appeals stated generally that an evidentiary hearing is not required "if the record and supporting affidavits are sufficiently detailed to provide an adequate basis for calculating an award . . . and if the material facts necessary to calculate the award are not generally in dispute." Sablan v. Department of Fin., 856 F.2d 1317, 1322 (9th Cir. 1988).

Eleventh Circuit: Norman v. Housing Auth. of Montgomery, 836 F.2d 1292, 1304 (11th Cir. 1988)(evidentiary hearing not required merely because the "written pleadings present a dispute of opinions on matters as to which the courts possess expertise," such as "the reasonableness of the fee, the reasonableness of the hours and the significance of the outcome").

Page 609, add to note 38:

Norman v. Housing Auth. of Montgomery, 836 F.2d 1292, 1304 (11th Cir. 1988)(evidentiary hearing required "where there is a dispute of material historical fact such as whether or not a case could have been settled without litigation or whether attorneys were duplicating each other's work"); Savidge v. Fincannon, 836 F.2d 898, 905 (5th Cir. 1988)(district court "erred in deciding the 'intensely factual' issue of causation [for defendants' cessation of challenged conduct] without an evidentiary hearing").

Page 610, add to note 46:

Cf. Norman v. Housing Auth. of Montgomery, 836 F.2d 1292 (11th Cir. 1988)(under Federal Rules of Evidence, district court may take judicial notice of "matters outside of the record if they are generally known within the territorial jurisdiction of the trial court or capable of accurate and ready determination by resort to sources whose accuracy cannot reasonably be questioned," provided that a party has a right to be heard on the matter upon seasonable request).

* *Page 610, add at end of section:*

In *Sablan v. Department of Finance,* 856 F.2d 1317, 1323 (9th Cir. 1988), the court rejected the government's objection to the consideration by the district court of several government documents bearing on the issue of whether the suit prompted the governmental defendant to abandon the constitutionally challenged practice. The court concluded that two of the documents were admissible evidence on the basis of the government's admissions made in producing them in discovery, and that the other document, a presumably privileged interoffice memo from counsel to client, was admissible as merely cumulative of other evidence and, in any event, was nonprejudicial to the defendant. In *Searcy v. Crim,* 692 F. Supp. 1363, 1364 (N.D. Ga. 1988), the court took judicial notice, unopposed by defendants, of affidavits relating to other fee requests in the district that were relevant to establishment of market rates and the award of a contingency enhancement in this case.

§ 24.4 The Appealability of Attorney's Fee Orders

Page 611, add to note 50:

Consistent with *White's* identification of the attorney's fee issue as collateral to and independent of the merits judgment in a case, the Supreme Court has ruled that a party's liability for § 1988 attorney's fees does not by itself confer standing on that party to appeal from the underlying merits judgment. Diamond v. Charles, 476 U.S. 54, 69-71 (1986)("The fee award is wholly unrelated to the subject matter of the litigation, and bears no relation to the statute whose constitutionality is at issue here," even though "were the Court to resolve the case on the merits against appellees, appellees would no longer be 'prevailing parties' entitled to an award of fees [against the purported appellant] under 42 U.S.C. § 1988").

Page 611, add to cases cited in first paragraph of note 52:

Shultz v. Crowley, 802 F.2d 498, 501-05 (D.C. Cir. 1986)(Equal Access to Justice Act, 28 U.S.C. § 2412; holding that "a judgment finally disposing of the merits of a suit is final and appealable notwithstanding the pendency of a request for statutory attorney's fees, whether the pending request was made in the complaint, by prejudgment motion, or by postjudgment motion"); Crossman v. Maccoccio, 792 F.2d 1, 3 (1st Cir. 1986); Ellender v. Schweiker, 781 F.2d 314, 317-18 (2d Cir. 1986)(both agreeing that a final merits judgment is appealable notwithstanding that statutory fee issue is not yet resolved).

Page 611, delete second and third paragraphs from note 52, and substitute the following:

In Budinich v. Becton Dickinson & Co., 108 S. Ct. 1717 (1988), the Supreme Court, resolving a conflict among the courts of appeals, established the bright-line rule that *all* claims for attorney's fees, whether based on statute or contract, are collateral to and separate from the underlying merits of the actions. Consequently, a judgment on the merits in any federal court suit is final and appealable, pursuant to 28 U.S.C. § 1291, even though an attorney's fee issue remains unresolved as to recoverability or amount. Finding that federal law governs the question of appealability in federal court, even in a diversity action, the Court adopted a "practical approach" that uniformly treats fees as collateral to the merits of the action, thereby making merits and fee orders independently appealable, even if applicable statute or decisional law might characterize fees as an integral part of the merits of the case. *Id.* at 1720-21. Such an approach furthers interests in "operational consistency and predictability in the overall application of § 1291." *Id.* at 1721. In *Budinich* the Court upheld the Tenth Circuit's ruling that the merits judgment in a diversity action involving a claim under Colorado state law was final and appealable, notwithstanding that the merits judgment did not resolve the integral issue of attorney's fees under Colorado law.

Page 612, add to cases cited in note 53:

Crossman v. Maccoccio, 792 F.2d 1 (1st Cir. 1986)(holding that plaintiffs' notice of appeal filed more than 30 days after entry of final judgment on the merits of the litigation, but within 30 days after the subsequent order granting defendants costs and § 1988 attorney's fees under Fed. R. Civ. P. 68, was timely as to the fee award order but untimely as to the merits judgment, which became final notwithstanding that the statutory attorney's fee issue remained unresolved); Beaudry Motor Co. v. ABKO Properties, Inc., 780 F.2d 751, 753-56 (9th Cir. 1986)(finding that minute order finally disposing of merits of action, that was prepared at district judge's direction, entered in civil docket, and mailed to plaintiff's counsel, satisfied "separate document" requirement of Fed. R. Civ. P. 58, so that plaintiff's notice of appeal filed more than 30 days after entry of minute entry, but within 30 days of entry of order awarding attorney's fees to defendant, was untimely as to the merits appeal); *cf.* Ellender v. Schweiker, 781 F.2d 314, 317-18 (2d Cir. 1986)(discussing "separate document" requirement of Rule 58).

Page 612, add to note 55:

* *See also* Roberts v. College of the Desert, 861 F.2d 1163, 1170 (9th Cir. 1988) (court had no jurisdiction over fee issue since plaintiff specifically limited her notice of appeal to merits order and did not include order denying fees); *In re* Burlington Northern, Inc., 810 F.2d 601, 605-06 (7th Cir. 1986)(finding notices of appeal by private parties on Title VII fee issues to be timely, although filed more than 30 days after entry of final fee orders, since presence of the EEOC, an agency of the United States, in the litigation triggered the applicability of the 60-day appeal time limit under Fed. R. Civ. P. 4(a)(1), even though the EEOC was not directly interested in the fee appeals); Harris v. McCarthy, 790 F.2d 753, 756-57 (9th Cir. 1986)(ruling that lack of formal compliance with "separate document" requirement of Fed. R. Civ. P. 58 did not defeat plaintiffs' § 1988 fee appeal, when plaintiffs' appeal was timely and defendants-

appellees made no claim of prejudice); Freeman v. B&B Associates, 790 F.2d 145, 150-53 (D.C. Cir. 1986)(declining to consider issue of validity of plaintiffs' waiver of statutory attorney's fees through accepted Rule 68 offer of judgment, since plaintiffs and their counsel failed to take a cross-appeal from district court's judgment, when the effect of invalidation of the fee-sacrifice provision of the judgment would be to "vacate rather than reform the offer of judgment"). Paddack v. Morris, 783 F.2d 844, 846 (9th Cir. 1986)(ERISA suit; finding that plaintiffs' notice of appeal filed within 30 days of supplemental fee judgment, but more than 30 days after district court's original fee order, was timely, since only supplemental judgment satisfied separate document requirement).

Pursuant to Fed. R. App. P. 4(a)(4), a timely motion under Fed. R. Civ. P. 59(e) to alter or amend an attorney's fee order suspends the finality of that order and acts to toll the running of the 30 days to appeal from the fee order. *See* Autorama Corp. v. Stewart, 802 F.2d 1284, 1286-87 (10th Cir. 1986)(securities action); Charles v. Daley, 799 F.2d 343 (7th Cir. 1986)(extensive analysis); Wort v. Vierling, 778 F.2d 1233 (7th Cir. 1985)(holding that defendant's untimely Rule 59(e) motion did not toll the 30-day time within which to appeal from district court's § 1988 fee order, and hence dismissing defendants' untimely fee appeal). In Acosta v. Louisiana Dep't of Health and Human Resources, 478 U.S. 251 (1986), the Supreme Court ruled that pursuant to Fed. R. App. P. 4(a)(4), a notice of appeal filed following the district court's denial of a timely Rule 59(e) motion to alter or amend a statutory fee order is effective only if filed after entry of judgment on the Rule 59(e) motion, and not if filed after announcement of the Rule 59 decision but before entry of the order on the Rule 59 motion. In Cox v. American Cast Iron Pipe Co., 784 F.2d 1546, 1549-51 (11th Cir. 1986), *cert. denied,* 479 U.S. 883 (1986), the court concluded that a notice of appeal from the merits judgment was not rendered ineffectual because it was filed during the pendency of a motion for Title VII attorney's fees that was incorrectly styled as a Rule 59 motion.

Page 612, change sentence in fourth line of complete paragraph to read:

However, not all attorney's fees orders are final and appealable.

Page 612, delete Palmer citation in note 56 and add following the sentence in text ending with note 56 reference:

In *Palmer v. City of Chicago,* 806 F.2d 1316, 1317-20 (7th Cir. 1986)(Posner, J.), the Seventh Circuit held that the district court's order directing the defendant to pay an interim award of § 1988 attorney's fees was appealable in the particular circumstances of that case. The court found the interim fee order appealable as a collateral order on the reasoning that the appeal would not interfere with the litigation in the district court and, further, that postponement of appellate review would work irreparable harm on the City defendant. The court emphasized that the irreparable harm branch of the collateral order doctrine could not be satisfied if the order sought to be appealed merely determined the interim fee liability of the defendant without directing, as in *Palmer,* payment of the fee award. *Id.* at 1320. The irreparable harm inherent in the fee payment order appealed in *Palmer* arose from the substantial risk that the paid-out interim fees would not be recoverable by the City, after a successful appeal at the conclusion of the litigation, from the plaintiff class of prisoners and criminal defendants, many of whom might no longer be parties, might be insolvent, or might have disappeared by the time repayment was sought. *Id.* at 1319. Although the danger "that the fees would disappear into insolvent hands" would be minimized if the interim fee payment were to be made to plaintiffs' lawyers, rather than to class members, the City could not be expected to make the requisite investigation of "the fee arrangements between the plaintiffs and their attorneys" within the 30-day grace period for taking the appeal. *Id.* Finally, the court noted that there was nothing tentative about the interim fee order in this case, which in the mind of the district judge "was not . . . * subject to any further revision." *Id.* at 1320. *See also* Dardar v. Lafourche Realty Co., Inc., 849 F.2d 955 (5th Cir. 1988) (order denying interim fee motion was not appealable since, under collateral order doctrine, it was not conclusive or unreviewable); Webster v. Sowders, 846 F.2d 1032, 1035 (6th Cir. 1988)(appealability of interim fee award order that imposed prospective burden on state to pay substantial attorney's fees without assurance of their recoverability in event of appellate reversal on the merits); Lac Courte Oreilles Band v. Wisconsin, 829 F.2d 601, 602 (7th Cir. 1987)(interim fee awards are not appealable, unless they come within the "narrow scope of the collateral-order doctrine," such as when appellant can show that he "will suffer irreparable harm if appeal is postponed to the end of the litigation"); Ray v. Florida Cabinet, 845 F.2d 311 (11th Cir. 1988)(ruling that an interim § 1988 fee award is not immediately appealable unless the plaintiff has attained prevailing party status by finally establishing a right to relief on the merits of a legal claim); Haitian Refugee Center v. Meese, 791 F.2d 1489, 1493-94 (11th Cir. 1986)(finding appealable the district court order awarding fees under Equal Access to Justice Act, 28 U.S.C. § 2412, for services of plaintiffs' counsel up to the point of district court's order, affirmed on appeal with some modifications, in favor of plaintiffs on liability issues, although final judgment had not yet been entered and further proceedings were contemplated for approval of governmental defendant's remedial plans).

* In Rosenfeld v. United States, 859 F.2d 717 (9th Cir. 1988), the court ruled that an order awarding interim attorney's fees to the plaintiff under the Freedom of Information Act, 5 U.S.C. § 552(a)(4)(E), was not immediately appealable, since under the collateral order doctrine it was not conclusive or unreviewable and, as distinct from *Palmer, supra,* the government could not show that ultimately it could not obtain repayment of the fees, and the order was not appealable as an interlocutory injunction since the government could not show irreparable harm. *Id.* at 720-22. However, the court did find the order to be subject to mandamus review on the basis of the government's contention, ultimately rejected on the appeal, that it was immune from interim fee awards under FOIA. *Id.* at 722-23.

Page 612, add to cases cited in note 57:

Phelps v. Washburn Univ., 807 F.2d 153 (10th Cir. 1986); Rodriguez v. Hardy, 802 F.2d 817, 820-21 (5th Cir. 1986); May v. Cooperman, 780 F.2d 240, 243 & n.1, 253 (3d Cir. 1985)(all finding that court of appeals had no jurisdiction over purported appeals from district court orders establishing defendants' liability for § 1988 attorney's fees without yet fixing the amount of fees); *see also* Lac Courte Oreilles Band v. Wisconsin, 829 F.2d 601, 603 (7th Cir. 1987)(nonappealability of order which awards fees but does not "fix the amount of the award or specify a formula allowing the amount to be computed mechanically," except for case when "the order awarding fees in an amount not yet determined can be consolidated on appeal with a final order").

Page 612, add to note 59:

Rodriguez v. Hardy, 802 F.2d 817, 821 (5th Cir. 1986); Vandenplas v. City of Muskego, 797 F.2d 425, 427-28 (7th Cir. 1986)(both finding that a party could properly obtain appellate review over both fee liability and fee amount issues by appealing in timely fashion from district court's order awarding a specific amount of § 1988 fees against that party, rather than from earlier nonappealable order merely establishing the party's fee liability).

* In United States v. Metropolitan Dist. Comm'n, 847 F.2d 12, 14 (1st Cir. 1988), the court concluded that the district court's order determining a total award of attorney's fees under the Clean Water Act, 33 U.S.C. § 1365(d), was not final and appealable, since it contemplated a future entry apportioning the award between two defendants. The court also noted that the applicable appeal period was 60 days, since a federal agency was a defendant, although not a party to the appeal. *Id.* at 14. In Burr v. Ambach, 863 F.2d 1071, 1074-75 (2d Cir. 1988), the court ruled that a Rule 54(b) certification of an appeal from an order denying a fee award, under the Education of the Handicapped Act, § 1415(e), against the state defendant was improvidently granted, since the full fee request still could be made against another party.

Page 613, add to note 60:

See also Loudermill v. Cleveland Bd. of Educ., 844 F.2d 304, 308 (6th Cir. 1988)(consolidating merits appeal with appeal from determination of § 1988 fee liability when amount of fees has not been set); Palmer v. City of Chicago, 806 F.2d 1316, 1318 (7th Cir. 1986)(noting principle that an interim fee award may be reviewable as pendent to a preliminary injunction on appeal, provided that the fee appeal could be taken in time to be consolidated with the preliminary injunction appeal) *cert. denied,* 107 S. Ct. 2180 (1987); Vandenplas v. City of Muskego, 797 F.2d 425, 428 n.1 (7th Cir. 1986)(noting cases in which an otherwise nonappealable order establishing fee liability but leaving amount of fees undetermined "was reviewed in conjunction with an appeal from a final judgment on the merits").

Page 613, delete Taylor and Wright citations and add to cases cited at end of note 61:

Langham-Hill Petroleum Inc. v. Southern Fuels Co., 813 F.2d 1327, 1330-31 (4th Cir. 1987); Thomas v. Capital Sec. Servs., Inc., 812 F.2d 984, 987 (5th Cir. 1987)(stating that district court retains jurisdiction, during pendency of merits appeal to court of appeals, to entertain and resolve attorney's fee motion).

Page 613, add to Seventh Circuit cases in note 62:

Argento v. Village of Melrose Park, 838 F.2d 1483, 1500 (7th Cir. 1988)(approving use of Rule 60(b)(5) motion in district court to vacate fee order that is dependent on another order reserved on appeal).

Page 614, add to cases cited in note 63:

First Circuit: Crossman v. Maccoccio, 792 F.2d 1, 4 (1st Cir. 1986)(recommending that prevailing party's counsel "ask the district court to refrain from entering a final [merits] judgment until attorney's fees have been resolved (and then, in the event the district court grants the request, to ensure that the record clearly reflects that entry of final judgment has been deferred)," in order to insure a single appeal combining merits and fee issues); *cf.* McKee v. Bi-State Development Agency, 801 F.2d 1014, 1017-18 (8th Cir. 1986)(invalidating local court rule that suspended the finality of a merits judgment already entered in a case whenever a party timely filed an attorney's fee motion).

Page 614, add to note 65:

Cf. In re Ruben, 825 F.2d 977, 981-82 (6th Cir. 1987); Hicks v. Southern Md. Health Sys. Agency, 805 F.2d 1165, 1166-67 (4th Cir. 1986); Howard v. International Molders & Allied Workers Union, 779 F.2d 1546, 1553 (11th Cir. 1986)(upholding district court's decision to postpone determination of plaintiffs' motion for an interim fee award during pendency of a merits appeal). In S-1 v. Spangler, 832 F.2d 294, 297 n.1 (4th Cir. 1987), the Fourth Circuit stated that the district court possesses "continuing equitable jurisdiction" to determine a statutory attorney's fee issue on remand from a court of appeals determination of mootness of the action on the merits.

§ 24.5 Scope of Appellate Review of Attorney's Fee Decisions

Pages 614-15, update Shaw citation (District of Columbia Circuit) and add case at end of note 68 following Cinevision Corp. case:

Shaw, *rev'd on other grounds,* 478 U.S. 310 (1986). *See also* McQuiston v. Marsh, 790 F.2d 798, 801 (9th Cir. 1986)(Equal Access to Justice Act, 28 U.S.C. § 2412; while reviewing court should give "special scrutiny to proposed findings adopted verbatim by the district court," no justification was thereby provided for departure from clearly erroneous standard of review of fact findings underlying statutory fee determinations).

Fourth Circuit: Spell v. McDaniel, 824 F.2d 1380, 1401 (4th Cir. 1987)(district court's fee award should not be overturned unless "clearly wrong").

* *Seventh Circuit:* Tonya K. v. Board of Educ., 847 F.2d 1243, 1248-49 (7th Cir. 1988) ("Fact-bound appraisals of questions such as the allocation of fees between city and state, and the identification of special circumstances that might make an award of fees unjust, are therefore entrusted to district courts, with deferential review."); Lightfoot v. Walker, 826 F.2d 516, 520 (7th Cir. 1987)(district court fee award should be upheld "[i]f reasonable persons could differ from the trial court's view").

In Pierce v. Underwood, 108 S. Ct. 2541, 2546, 2553 (1988), the Supreme Court described the abuse-of-discretion standard as applicable to appelate review of § 1988 fee decisions.

Page 616, add to cases cited in note 80:

Norman v. Housing Auth. of Montgomery, 836 F.2d 1292, 1304 (11th Cir. 1988)("If the court disallows hours, it must explain which hours are disallowed and show why an award of these hours would be improper."); Hart v. Bourque, 798 F.2d 519, 522 (1st Cir. 1986); Sims v. Jefferson Downs Racing Ass'n, 778 F.2d 1068, 1084-85 (5th Cir. 1985)(both vacating district courts' § 1988 fee determinations partly for inadequate explanations for imposed reductions in claimed hours).

Page 616, add to cases cited in note 81:

Jordan v. Multnomah County, 815 F.2d 1258, 1263 & n.10 (9th Cir. 1987)(vacating § 1988 fee determination partly because of district court's failure to justify selection of hourly rates).

Page 616, add to cases cited in note 82:

BSA, Inc. v. King County, 804 F.2d 1104, 1112-13 (9th Cir. 1986); Gekas v. Attorney Registration & Discipline Comm'n, 793 F.2d 846, 852-53 (7th Cir. 1986)(both vacating § 1988 fee determinations for district courts' failure to evaluate appropriateness of downward adjustment to lodestar awards).

Page 616, change phrase following note 82 reference to read "or granted or denied fees."

Page 616, add to note 83:

Davis v. Mills, 777 F.2d 1524 (11th Cir. 1985)(vacating § 1988 defendant fee award for district court's failure to make required findings underlying award).

Page 617, update Rivera citation in note 84:

477 U.S. 561, 584 (1986)(Powell, J., concurring).

Page 617, change phrase in last line of note 85 to read "Fed. R. Civ. P. 52(a)."

Page 617, add to cases cited in note 86:

* Sablan v. Department of Fin., 856 F.2d 1317, 1324 (9th Cir. 1988) (stating that district court's factual determinations underlying finding that plaintiff's suit provoked defendant's corrective action are reversible only for "clear error"); *In re* Burlington Northern, 832 F.2d 422, 425 (7th Cir. 1987)("clearly erroneous" standard of review applied to determination of "whether plaintiff's lawsuit was causally linked to relief provided by defendant"); Heath v. Brown, 807 F.2d 1229, 1234 (5th Cir. 1987)(vacating fee award and remanding for a factual determination of whether lawsuit caused defendants' remedial action); Supre v. Ricketts, 792 F.2d 958, 961-62 (10th Cir. 1986)(discussing applicable standards of appellate review of statutory fee determinations, and concluding that with regard to prevailing party issue the clearly erroneous standard of review applies to factual determination of whether lawsuit prompted defendant's corrective action, and *de novo* review applies to legal determination of whether plaintiff's legal claims met required standard of substantiality); Braafladt v.

Board of Governors, 778 F.2d 1442, 1444 (9th Cir. 1985)(deferring to district court's factual determination of whether plaintiff's lawsuit caused defendant's corrective action).

Page 617, add to note 87:

See also Coulter v. State of Tennessee, 805 F.2d 146, 151 (6th Cir. 1986)(treating as a mixed question of law and fact the issue of whether the attorney exercised proper billing judgment with regard to hours claimed).

Page 617, add to note 88:

Student Pub. Interest Research Group v. AT&T Bell Laboratories, 842 F.2d 1436, 1442 (3d Cir. 1988).

Page 617, add to note 91:

Jacobs v. Mancuso, 825 F.2d 559, 562-64 (1st Cir. 1987); Rogers v. Okin, 821 F.2d 22, 31 (1st Cir. 1987)(court of appeals determines reasonable fee award after vacating
* district court's award). In Ustrak v. Fairman, 851 F.2d 983, 989 (7th Cir. 1988), the court observed that, while there is "great theoretical appeal" to the approach of permitting the district court to redetermine a vacated fee award on remand from the court of appeals, the "practical difficulty is that such as approach would prolong litigation on what to begin with is a collateral matter, and might generate additional appeals." Accordingly, the court stated, "[p]ractice has trumped theory; for in many cases in this and other circuits the court of appeals has made the adjustment in the fee award that it thought necessary, without bothering to remand the case." *Id.* at 989.

* *Page 617, add at end of section:*

In *National Wildlife Federation v. Hanson,* 859 F.2d 313, 318 (4th Cir. 1988), the court reviewed an issue concerning the federal government's immunity from an award of current rates, although raised for the first time on appeal, on the ground that the error was "plain" and that refusal to consider it would result in a "miscarriage of justice."

§ 24.6 Fee Motions for Appellate Work: Which Court to File In

Page 618, add to cases cited in note 94:

First Circuit: Wagenmann v. Adams, 829 F.2d 196, 226-27 (1st Cir. 1987); Aubin v. Fudala, 821 F.2d 45, 47-48 (1st Cir. 1987).

Fourth Circuit: Cooper v. Dyke, 814 F.2d 941, 951 (4th Cir. 1987); Ganey v. Garrison, 813 F.2d 650, 652 (4th Cir. 1987); Mammano v. Pittston Co., 792 F.2d 1242, 1246 (4th Cir. 1986)(directing district court to award reasonable Title VII fees for appellate work). However, Fourth Circuit Internal Operating Procedure 46.4 provides that the court of appeals "may award attorney's fees and expenses whenever authorized by statute."

Fifth Circuit: Fontenot v. Louisiana Bd. of Elementary & Secondary Educ., 835 F.2d 117, 121 (5th Cir. 1988).

* *Seventh Circuit:* Jackson v. Illinois Prisoner Review Bd., 856 F.2d 890, 896 (7th Cir. 1988) (directing successful plaintiff-appellee to submit his appellate fee request to court of appeals); Ustrak v. Fairman, 851 F.2d 983, 990 (7th Cir. 1988) (court of appeals makes appellate fee determination); Ekanem v. Health & Hosp. Corp., 778 F.2d 1254, 1257 (7th Cir. 1985)(concluding that a "petition on entitlement to appellate attorneys fees may be filed in either the district court or the court of appeals").

Page 618, delete last paragraph in note 94 and substitute the following:

The Second Circuit has ruled that only the appellate court, and not the district court, can decide whether an appeal is frivolous or in bad faith so as to warrant the assessment of appellate attorney's fees against the appellant. Sierra Club v. United States Army Corps of Eng'rs, 776 F.2d 383, 392 (2d Cir. 1985), *cert. denied,* 475 U.S. 1084 (1986).

Pages 618-19, add to cases cited in note 95:

Third Circuit: But see Brinker v. Guiffrida, 798 F.2d 661, 669 (3d Cir. 1986)(Equal Access to Justice Act, 28 U.S.C. § 2412; directing district court to determine appellate fees); Disabled in Action v. Pierce, 789 F.2d 1016, 1021 (3d Cir. 1986)(Rehabilitation Act, 29 U.S.C. § 794a(b); determining plaintiff's entitlement to fees and directing district court to calculate a reasonable fee, "with no multipliers").

Eighth Circuit: McGee v. Hester, 815 F.2d 1193, 1198 (8th Cir. 1987); Patteson v. Johnson, 790 F.2d 712 (8th Cir. 1986); Little Rock School Dist. v. Pulaski County Special School Dist., 787 F.2d 372 (8th Cir. 1986)(all determining awards of appellate attorney's fees).

Ninth Circuit: The Ninth Circuit has provided in Rule 39-1.6 that an appellate attorney's fee request should be filed in the court of appeals, but also has authorized the fee applicant, by Rule 39-1.8, to move to transfer the appellate fee issue to the district court. *See* Toussaint v. McCarthy, 826 F.2d 901, 903 n.2 (9th Cir. 1987)(declining to remand appellate fee application to district court); Jordan v. Multnomah County, 815 F.2d 1258, 1264 (9th Cir. 1987)(remanding appellate fee issue to district court); Greater L.A. Council on Deafness v. Community TV of So. Cal., 813 F.2d 217, 223 (9th Cir. 1987)(directing plaintiffs to file appellate fee request in court of appeals).

§ 24.7 Enforcing and Collecting the Attorney's Fee Award

Page 621, add at end of first complete paragraph:

In *Argento v. Village of Melrose Park,* 838 F.2d 1483 (7th Cir. 1988), the Seventh Circuit held that the district court possessed inherent jurisdiction over proceedings supplementary to the initial civil rights money judgment for the collection, pursuant to Fed.

R. Civ. P. 69(a), of the prevailing plaintiff's § 1988 attorney's fee award. *Id.* at 1487-90. In particular, the court upheld the district court's ancillary jurisdiction over the non-party village to determine its direct liability under state law to the plaintiffs for the attorney's fee award issued against the defendant police officers. *Id.* at 1488-89. Alternatively, the court held, the district court had pendent jurisdiction over the state law claim against the village for direct liability to the plaintiffs for the § 1988 fee award. *Id.* at 1490-92. The court further held that the district court had jurisdiction over the plaintiffs' garnishment or indemnity proceeding, whether considered a separate action or a post-judgment motion in the original action, against the village's insurer for recovery of the § 1988 fee award that was covered by the insurance policy. *Id.* at 1492-93.

Page 622, add to note 10:

See also Vaughns v. Board of Ed., 627 F. Supp. 837, 838 (D. Md. 1985)(establishing a schedule for payment of § 1988 fee award).

Page 622, update Palmer citation in note 11:

rev'd, 806 F.2d 1316 (7th Cir. 1986).

APPENDIX B

SIGNIFICANT DECISIONS EXAMINING CLAIMED HOURS FOR EXCESSIVENESS

Pages 628-33, update Hart (First Circuit) and Black Grievance Committee (Third Circuit) citations and add the following cases:

District of Columbia Circuit

Save Our Cumberland Mountains, Inc. v. Hodel, 826 F.2d 43, 51-52 (D.C. Cir. 1987)(Surface Mining Control and Reclamation Act, 30 U.S.C. § 1270(d); agreeing that hours spent on plaintiffs' rehearing petition were not redundant merely because plaintiffs also sought rehearing on same issue in a parallel, but unconsolidated, case), *reh'g en banc granted,* 830 F.2d 1182 (D.C. Cir. 1987);

Morgan v. District of Columbia, 824 F.2d 1049, 1066-67 (D.C. Cir. 1987)(approving time spent by plaintiff's attorney reasonably preparing an expert witness who ultimately did not testify, and time spent by counsel's paralegal in taking notes and otherwise assisting counsel at trial);

McKenzie v. Kennickell, 645 F. Supp. 437, 44851 (D.D.C. 1986)(Title VII suit; court generally found that the number of hours eliminated through plaintiff's counsel's voluntary 6 percent reduction of expended hours, in the exercise of billing judgment, was reasonable, and that with the exclusion of some additional hours from lead counsel's time to bring the overall reduction to 9 percent, excessive hours had been eliminated).

First Circuit

Hart v. Bourque, 798 F.2d 519, 52123 (1st Cir. 1986), *rev'g and remanding* 608 F. Supp. 1091 (D. Mass. 1985)(finding 610 hours allowed by district court to be "[o]n its face . . . far too much," noting particularly that "the turnover among Mr. Owens's associates, or, at least, transfers of duties, was highly extravagant from the standpoint of time" and that time charged for telephone calls was excessive);

Brewster v. Dukakis, 786 F.2d 16, 1819 (1st Cir. 1986)(affirming district court's compensation for substantial time expended by plaintiffs' counsel in post-judgment monitoring, reflecting forty-four percent reduction of time claimed).

Second Circuit

Orshan v. Macchiarola, 629 F. Supp. 1014, 1020 (E.D.N.Y. 1986)(reducing by approximately 20 percent the hours requested for trial and trial preparation, when 19 and 20 hours per day were claimed and the documentation by plaintiff's counsel was not sufficiently detailed to determine whether the time was excessive).

APPENDIX B

Third Circuit

Student Public Interest Research Group v. AT&T Bell Laboratories, 842 F.2d 1436, 1454-55 (3d Cir. 1988)(suggesting that some of hours spent in litigating statutory fee issue in case possibly should be allocated to other similar cases in which plaintiff's counsel already had prevailed, because counsel "should have anticipated employing the fee litigation research of this case in litigating other fees cases");

Black Grievance Committee v. Philadelphia Elec. Co., vacated and remanded on other grounds, 802 F.2d 648 (3d Cir. 1986).

* **Fourth Circuit**

Spell v. McDaniel, 852 F.2d 762, 767-70 (4th Cir. 1988)(because appellate fee petition "claims such an inflated expenditure of time in so many particulars and overall that it is impossible for this court to cull in detail the justified from the unjustified," court makes its own determination of the "reasonable number of hours assignable to counsel's appeal-related endeavors").

Sixth Circuit

Coulter v. State of Tennessee, 805 F.2d 146, 15052 (6th Cir. 1986)(Title VII suit; affirming district court's elimination as excessive of one-half of hours claimed for preparing stipulations and pretrial brief and in trial preparation, and the limitation of compensable hours in preparing and litigating fee request to 3 percent of hours allowed in the main case, but reversing district court's elimination of time spent on summary judgment motion that advanced plaintiff's successful case).

Seventh Circuit

* *Ustrak v. Fairman,* 851 F.2d 983, 988 (7th Cir. 1988)(disallowing two-thirds of time claimed for preparation of fee petitions, observing that the fee petitions are "marvels of misplaced ingenuity and thoroughness, rehearsing in great detail basic principles well known to the district court"); *Charles v. Daley,* 846 F.2d 1057, 1075-77 (7th Cir. 1988)(eliminating excessive hours devoted by plaintiffs' counsel to "reviewing and re-reviewing, revising and re-revising their briefs and other submissions" to U.S. Supreme Court, and excessive expenses associated with holding three in-person mock oral arguments in diverse locations, in preparation for Supreme Court argument);

Tomazzoli v. Sheedy, 804 F.2d 93, 9798 (7th Cir. 1986)(affirming district court's reduction of claimed hours by a lump sum to adjust for inflated fee request);

Zabkowicz v. West Bend Co., 789 F.2d 540, 553 (7th Cir. 1986)(Title VII suit; upholding district court's finding that expenditure of 800 hours on plaintiff's back pay claim was unreasonable);

Bohen v. City of East Chicago, 666 F. Supp. 154, 158 (N.D. Ind. 1987)(in approving time spent by plaintiff's counsel with expert witnesses who were not called to testify, court observed that it "is an essential function of lawyers" to "track down leads that do not pan out," and that "[b]lind alleys are an ordinary part of litigation, as are standby witnesses");
Easter House v. State of Illinois Department of Children, 663 F. Supp. 456, 461 (N.D. Ill. 1987)(finding it reasonable for plaintiff's attorneys to "occasionally bill 15- and 16-hour days during trial," when "such long hours were almost inevitable in light of this court's lengthy trial days and the high level of preparation that this court demands of counsel").

Eighth Circuit

Steele v. Van Buren Public School District, 845 F.2d 1492, 1496 (8th Cir. 1988) (disallowing hours spent by plaintiff's attorney seeking extensions of time, because of failure to meet court deadlines);
Cole v. Williams, 624 F. Supp. 712, 71820 (W.D. Ark. 1985)(finding excessive the spending of "more than 19 eight-hour days doing nothing more than work on this case," which was "not a particularly difficult case to prepare and try," and, accordingly, reducing claimed hours for depositions, attorney discussions, legal research, complaint drafting, interrogatories, and trial preparation).

Ninth Circuit

Harris v. McCarthy, 790 F.2d 753, 758 & n.7 (9th Cir. 1986)(affirming district court's approximately two-third reduction in claimed hours for preliminary injunction work to adjust for excessiveness);
Stewart v. County of Sonoma, 634 F. Supp. 773, 77980 (N.D. Cal. 1986)(substantially reducing fee request after finding that case "did not warrant ten lawyers from two law offices representing plaintiff, generating an aggregate of over 5,400 hours, the equivalent of two lawyers working full time through the entire period from the day counsel was retained to the return of the verdict").

Tenth Circuit

Mares v. Credit Bureau of Raton, 801 F.2d 1197, 120207 (10th Cir. 1986)(Consumer Credit Protection Act, 15 U.S.C. §§ 1601 *et seq.*; affirming district court's 77 percent reduction of inflated trial preparation time of inexperienced lead counsel but restoring some of hours eliminated from his post-trial work, and approving complete disallowance of compensable time to second attorney for work on the merits and fee request).

APPENDIX C

SIGNIFICANT DECISIONS EXAMINING CLAIMED HOURS FOR DUPLICATION OF EFFORT BY MULTIPLE ATTORNEYS

Pages 634-39, update Delaware Valley and Daggett citations (Third Circuit,) and add the following cases:

District of Columbia Circuit

McKenzie v. Kennickell, 645 F. Supp. 437, 450 (D.D.C. 1986)(Title VII suit; finding "duplicative time charged for attending status calls, hearings, and other proceedings before this Court," and permitting compensation only for the attorney who appeared for routine status calls and for the most senior additional attorney for major oral arguments or hearings).

First Circuit

Hart v. Bourque, 798 F.2d 519, 523 (1st Cir. 1986)(finding that claimed hours must be discounted for "dual attendance at motion hearings" that "did not advance the case");
Denton v. Boilermakers Local 29, 673 F. Supp. 37, 56 (D. Mass. 1987)(reducing claimed hours of two plaintiff's attorneys in Title VII suit who "chose to handle this case in tandem when one able and experienced attorney would have been adequate to the task, particularly if supported by a less expensive attorney to assist with legal research").

Second Circuit

Lenihan v. City of New York, 640 F. Supp. 822, 82526 (S.D.N.Y. 1986)(finding no unnecessary duplication of effort in joint participation of plaintiff's two attorneys at pretrial conferences, preliminary injunction hearing, and trial, in researching and preparing preliminary injunction brief, in preparing and revising post-trial brief, and in conferring together).

Third Circuit

Delaware Valley Citizens' Council v. Commonwealth of Pennsylvania, aff'd in part, rev'd in part on other grounds, 478 U.S. 546 (1986);
Daggett v. Kimmelman, aff'd in relevant part, 811 F.2d 793, 79798 (3d Cir. 1987)(see text).

Fifth Circuit

Curtis v. Bill Hanna Ford, Inc., 822 F.2d 549, 552 (5th Cir. 1987)(affirming district court's exclusion of redundant time spent by counsel other than plaintiff's lead

counsel and by consultant law professor in Title VII suit that was not complex or protracted, consistent with the "policy of rewarding efficient litigators");
Garmong v. Montgomery County, 668 F. Supp. 1000, 1005 (S.D. Tex. 1987)(finding reasonable the "forty-five to fifty hours claimed by plaintiff's co-counsel for conferences with each other and third parties," considering the difficulty of the plaintiff's burden of proving an unconstitutional county policy and securing supporting testimony);
Beamon v. City of Ridgeland, 666 F. Supp. 937, 942 n.3 (S.D. Miss. 1987)(finding reasonable the presence of two attorneys at the numerous depositions conducted by plaintiffs in voting rights case, considering "the close proximity to trial, the importance of the depositions, and the fact that three defense counsel were present at each of the depositions in question").

Sixth Circuit

Coulter v. State of Tennessee, 805 F.2d 146, 152 (6th Cir. 1986)(affirming district court's 50 percent reduction of time "[w]here duplication of effort is a serious problem");
McCullough v. Cady, 640 F. Supp. 1012, 1027 (E.D. Mich. 1986)(reducing by 50 percent claimed hours for attorney conferences between senior and junior attorneys because of duplication and excessiveness).

Seventh Circuit

Tolliver v. Amici, 800 F.2d 149, 15253 (7th Cir. 1986)(affirming district court's 30 percent reduction of claimed hours of two of plaintiff's attorneys and a paralegal "in order to compensate for unjustified double staffing");
Shakman v. Democratic Org. of Cook County, 634 F. Supp. 895, 902 (N.D. Ill. 1986)(finding no duplication of effort in time spent in telephone conferences between attorneys, where the "size and complexity of the case certainly would require conferences between plaintiffs' attorneys for coordination and strategy");
Lock v. Jenkins, 634 F. Supp. 615, 62123 (N.D. Ind. 1986)(disallowing time spent by plaintiffs' attorneys that, without adequate documentation, appeared to be redundant or otherwise unnecessary and "can only be attributable to overstaffing," including time spent by inexperienced attorney in meetings with co-counsel, consulting and reviewing time spent by senior attorney who "did not play an active part in this litigation," and time spent by lead counsel in meetings or conferences with law students who did not appear to have contributed to the litigation).

Ninth Circuit

Probe v. State Teachers' Retirement System, 780 F.2d 776, 785 (9th Cir. 1986)(Title VII suit; finding no unnecessary duplication in the assignment of more than one attorney to an important class action suit and in sending more than one attorney to hearings);

Keith v. Volpe, 644 F. Supp. 1317, 1323 (C.D. Cal. 1986)(allowing time spent in hearing by principal plaintiffs' attorneys, whether alone or together, and time spent at hearings by the supervisory attorney with either principal attorney alone, but disallowing "as unnecessarily duplicative time claimed by attorneys, paralegals, and legal clerks to attend hearings for which the court has allowed expenses for two attorneys;);

Vance v. Hegstrom, 629 F. Supp. 747, 750 (D. Or. 1985)(finding it "reasonable for plaintiffs to have two lawyers with different expertise," one "familiar with practice in federal court but on related type claims," and the other an "expert on medicaid regulations").

Tenth Circuit

Mares v. Credit Bureau of Raton, 801 F.2d 1197, 120506 (10th Cir. 1986)(Consumer Credit Protection Act, 15 U.S.C. § 1601 *et seq.;* upholding district court's denial of fee compensation for services of second attorney that were "unnecessary to a proper presentation of plaintiffs' case");

Ramos v. Lamm, 632 F. Supp. 376, 38384 (D. Colo. 1986)(generally no duplication of services in complex litigation where the many attorneys involved "worked on different aspects of the case and made special efforts to coordinate their work to avoid any duplication," so that "[e]ach attorney's presence and input was necessary at the various hearings, depositions, negotiations, and trial proceedings");

City Consumer Services, Inc. v. Horne, 631 F. Supp. 1050, 1060 (D. Utah 1986)(Truth-in-Lending Act, 15 U.S.C. § 1640(a)(3); finding it "reasonable that three or four lawyers per day were involved in actual trial," but reducing claimed hours for certain inefficiencies, including the assignment of about twelve attorneys to work on jury instructions and trial brief, where, although the "work was split up among many associates according to the claims for relief, and each associate performed a great deal of research on each issue," nonetheless "the work seems to have been spread a little thin").

Eleventh Circuit

Afro-American Patrolmen's League v. City of Atlanta, 817 F.2d 719, 726 (11th Cir. 1987)(rejecting defendants' argument, made without evidence of actual duplication, that because two attorneys in Title VII suit "had distinct areas of expertise (one in validation, one in trial work) any time spent by one on the other's area was duplicative").

APPENDIX D

SIGNIFICANT DECISIONS EVALUATING CLAIMED HOURS IN LIGHT OF ADEQUACY OF ATTORNEY TIME RECORDS

Pages 640-644, update Delaware Valley citation and add the following cases:

District of Columbia Circuit

Kennecott Corp. v. E.P.A., 804 F.2d 763, 76667 (D.C. Cir. 1986)(Clean Air Act, 42 U.S.C. § 7607(f); 15 percent reduction in fee award for poor documentation of hours expended and for refusal to submit contemporaneous time records).

First Circuit

Calhoun v. Acme Cleveland Corp., 801 F.2d 558, 56061 (1st Cir. 1986)(no disallowance or drastic reduction of claimed hours not based on detailed contemporaneous time records where services were rendered prior to decision requiring such records).

Second Circuit

Lewis v. Coughlin, 801 F.2d 570, 577 (2d Cir. 1986)(affirming district court's refusal of fee award for time spent on fee application, when applicant failed to submit contemporaneous time records with original fee petition);
Orshan v. Macchiarola, 629 F. Supp. 1014, 101820 (E.D.N.Y. 1986)(finding that noncompliance with contemporaneous time records requirement warrants a more than 30 percent reduction in claimed hours, including time spent in preparing fee application).

Third Circuit

Delaware Valley, 478 U.S. 546 (1986).

Fourth Circuit

Daly v. Hill, 790 F.2d 1071, 107980 & n.12 (4th Cir. 1986)(affirming reduction in claimed hours for conferences where time records failed to "specify the substance or purpose of each conference").

Fifth Circuit

Dennis v. Warren, 779 F.2d 245, 249 (5th Cir. 1985)(rejecting defendants' contention that maintenance of contemporaneous time records is a prerequisite to fee award).

APPENDIX D

Seventh Circuit

Zabkowicz v. West Bend Co., 789 F.2d 540, 54950 (7th Cir. 1986)(Title VII suit; reversing district court's denial of fee award when counsel's time records were "not so wholly inadequate or inaccurate as to make a total denial of fees appropriate").

Eleventh Circuit

Haitian Refugee Center, Inc. v. Smith, 644 F. Supp. 382, 391 (S.D. Fla. 1984), *aff'd,* 791 F.2d 1489 (11th Cir.), *as amended,* 804 F.2d 1573 (11th Cir. 1986)(reducing claimed hours by 40 percent for "poor record keeping").

APPENDIX E

DECISIONS SETTING PREVAILING MARKET RATES FOR ATTORNEYS AND PARAPROFESSIONALS UNDER § 1988 AND SIMILAR FEE-SHIFTING STATUTES*

Pages 645-53, update Hart (First Circuit), Daggett, Delaware Valley, Cunningham, Black Grievance Comm. (Third Circuit), Hyatt (Fourth Circuit), and Burlington Northern (Seventh Circuit) cases, and add the following cases:

U.S. Supreme Court

Texas v. New Mexico, 108 S. Ct. 1212 (1988)(average rates of $275.12 for partner-level master and $191.30 for associate-level clerk).

District of Columbia Circuit

Lebron v. Washington Metropolitan Area Transit Authority, 665 F. Supp. 923, 930-31 (D.D.C. 1987)($57-115 for attorneys, $35 for law clerks, and $32 for paralegal, on underlying litigation; $65-130 for attorneys for fee litigation);
McKenzie v. Kennickell, 645 F. Supp. 437, 445, (D.D.C. 1986)(Title VII)($35-120 for attorneys for work from 1973-1980; $25 and $30 for paralegals and law clerks).

First Circuit

Maine

Broussard v. CACI, Inc.-Federal, 634 F. Supp. 155, 157 (D. Me. 1986)(defendant Title VII fee award)($50-125 for attorneys; $25 for travel time).

Massachusetts

Hall v. Ochs, 817 F.2d 920, 928-29 (1st Cir. 1987)($125 and $175 for attorneys);
Hart, rev'd and remanded, 798 F.2d 519, 523 (1st Cir. 1986)(accepting rates set by district court);
Brewster v. Dukakis, 786 F.2d 16, 21 (1st Cir. 1986)(Springfield)(1982 attorney rates of $80 for court activities and $70 for decree implementation; 1984 attorney rates of $95 for court work and $85 for implementation);
Rogers v. Motta, 655 F. Supp. 39, 52 (D. Mass. 1986)(attorney rates of $60 and $100 for legal work, $30 and $50 for nonproductive travel time);
Gonzales v. Jillson, 642 F. Supp. 908, 909 (D. Mass. 1986)($125 for primary attorney, $75 for associate attorney, and $40 for student assistant);
Rogers v. Okin, 638 F. Supp. 934, 939 (D. Mass. 1986)(Boston) (attorney rates of $140 and $162.50 for primary legal work, and $127.50 for fee petition).

---

* All stated figures represent hourly rates.

APPENDIX E

Second Circuit

Connecticut

Hillburn v. Commissioner, Connecticut Department of Income Maintenance, F. Supp. 23, 25-26 (D. Conn. 1987)($100 and $110 current attorney rates);

Clark v. Stach, 674 F. Supp. 969, 972 (D. Conn. 1987)($100 attorney rate);

Rose v. Heintz, 671 F. Supp. 901, 908 (D. Conn. 1987)(historic attorney rates of $75-125 for 1982 work, and current attorney rates of $100 and $150 for 1985-87 work; travel rates at one-half regular rates);

Barbara R. v. Tirozzi, 665 F. Supp. 141, 147 (D. Conn. 1987)($110 attorney rate).

New York State

In re Agent Orange Product Liability Litigation, 818 F.2d 226, 234 (2d Cir. 1987)(equitable fund case; national rates of $150 for partners, $100 for associates, and $125 for law professors);

Lewis v. Coughlin, 801 F.2d 570, 572 (2d Cir. 1986)(New York City)($160 for experienced attorney);

Carrero v. New York City Housing Authority, 685 F. Supp. 904, 908 (S.D.N.Y. 1988) (New York City) ($150 and $175 for attorneys);

Barcia v. Sitkin, 683 F. Supp. 353, 357 (S.D.N.Y. 1988)(New York City)(historic attorney rates of $140 and $185 for work done during period 1979-1983 by 1968 law graduates; court concluded that 1969 law graduate could command $200+ for work done in 1984 and thereafter);

McKever v. Vondollen, 681 F. Supp. 999, 1004 (N.D.N.Y. 1988)(upstate New York)($70 and $75 for attorneys);

Rickman v. Dole, 671 F. Supp. 982, 990 (S.D.N.Y. 1987)(New York City)($94.52-150 for attorneys; $25 for paralegals);

Kappenberger v. Oates, 663 F. Supp. 991, 994 (S.D.N.Y. 1987)($140 and $150 for prevailing defendants' attorneys);

Fiacco v. City of Rensselaer, 663 F. Supp. 743, 746 (N.D.N.Y. 1987)(attorney rates of $75 for legal work, $40 for travel time, and $20 for clerical tasks);

United States v. Yonkers Board of Education, 118 F.R.D. 326, 329 (S.D.N.Y. 1987)($150 attorney rate for 1981-87 work);

Martin v. Supreme Court of State of N.Y., 644 F. Supp. 1537, 1545 (N.D.N.Y. 1986)(defendant fee award)(Syracuse)($80 for attorney);

Lenihan v. City of New York, 640 F. Supp. 822, 831 (S.D.N.Y. 1986)(New York City) $250 and $180 for experienced attorneys, $125 and $75 for associate attorneys, and $50 for law student clerk);

Campaign for a Progressive Bronx v. Black, 631 F. Supp. 975, 983 (S.D.N.Y. 1986) (Voting Rights Act, 42 U.S.C. § 1973l(e))(New York City)($100 for attorneys);

Orshan v. Macchiarola, 629 F. Supp. 1014, 1023 (E.D.N.Y. 1986)(New Jersey rates)($125 for primary attorneys, and $45 for associates).

APPENDIX E

Third Circuit

Delaware

Brown v. Eichler, 680 F. Supp. 138, 143 (D. Del. 1988)($125 and $150 for attorneys);
Amico v. New Castle County, 654 F. Supp. 982, 1001 (D. Del. 1987)($65-125 for attorneys; $25 for paralegal).

New Jersey

Daggett v. Kimmelman, 811 F.2d 793, 799 (3d Cir. 1987)($150 and $200 for attorneys);
Frank's Chicken House, Inc. v. Mayor and Council, 208 N.J. Super. 542, 506 A.2d 751, 754 (1986)($95 for primary attorney and $65 for associate);
Bung's Bar & Grille, Inc. v. Township Council, 206 N.J. Super. 432, 502 A.2d 1198, 1223 (1985)($90 for attorney).

Pennsylvania

Delaware Valley Citizens' Council, 478 U.S. 546 (1986);
Cunningham, vacated and remanded on other grounds, 478 U.S. 1015 (1986), *reinstated,* 807 F.2d 49 (3d Cir. 1986);
Black Grievance Committee, vacated and remanded, 802 F.2d 648, 651-53 (3d Cir. 1986)(directing district court to apply uncontested rates requested by plaintiffs' attorneys of $125, $150, and $225 for 1984-85 work, but upholding rates set for 1975-1983);
Calhoun v. Forester, 675 F. Supp. 291, 295 (W.D. Pa. 1987)($125 for attorneys);
Gregis v. Edberg, 645 F. Supp. 1153, 1162-64 (W.D. Pa. 1986)(attorney rates of $85-125 for work done from 1982-86);
Bygott v. Leaseway Transp. Corp., 637 F. Supp. 1433, 1444-45 (E.D. Pa. 1986)(Philadelphia)($90 for trial time and $80 for other time of experienced attorneys; $20 for paralegal);
Ad World, Inc. v. Township of Doylestown, 634 F. Supp. 4, 11 (E.D. Pa. 1985)($150 for attorney).

Fourth Circuit

Maryland

N.A.A.C.P. v. Thompson, 671 F. Supp. 1051, 1053 n.4 (D. Md. 1987)($85 and $125 for attorneys);
Vaughns v. Board of Educ., 627 F. Supp. 837, 843, 847 (D. Md. 1985)(attorney rates of $74.50-172.50, and paralegal/law clerk rates of $30-60).

APPENDIX E

North Carolina

* *Spell v. McDaniel,* 852 F.2d 762, 771 (4th Cir. 1988) ($125 for attorneys and $35 for paralegals, for appellate services), and 824 F.2d 1380, 1402-03 (4th Cir. 1987)(attorney rates of $100-125 for trial work);

Hyatt, aff'd, 807 F.2d 376 (4th Cir. 1986);

Jones v. Board of Governors, 790 F.2d 1120 (4th Cir. 1986)($100 for attorney);

ECOS, Inc. v. Brinegar, 671 F. Supp. 381, 398 (M.D.N.C. 1987)($85 for attorneys, $45 for law graduates, $25 for paralegals, and $20 for law clerks);

Norwood v. Charlotte Memorial Hospital and Medical Center, 653 F. Supp. 1350, 1358 (W.D.N.C. 1987)($90-175 for attorneys, $40 for law clerks, and $35 for paralegals);

Thomas v. Cooper Industries, Inc., 640 F. Supp. 1374, 1381 (W.D.N.C. 1986)(Title VII)(Charlotte)($150 and $125 for attorneys);

Starnes v. Hill, 635 F. Supp. 1270, 1273 (W.D.N.C. 1986)(Charlotte and Gastonia)($90 and $70 for out-of-court work by attorneys in 1982-83);

Alexander v. Hill, 625 F. Supp. 567, 570 (W.D.N.Y. 1985)(attorney rates of $60-95, and paralegal rates of $25-60).

Virginia

Blizzard v. Newport News Redevelopment, 635 F. Supp. 23, 27 (E.D. Va. 1985)(Title VII)(attorney rate of $75 for work prior to 1982 and $100 for work from 1982-84).

Fifth Circuit

Louisiana

Curtis v. Bill Hanna Ford, Inc., 822 F.2d 549, 552 (5th Cir. 1987)($125 for attorney);

Prejean v. Ochsner Clinic, 669 F. Supp. 146, 148 (E.D. La. 1987)($75-150 for attorneys; $35 for paralegal);

Danielson v. Winnfield Funeral Home, 634 F. Supp. 1110, 1119 (E.D. La. 1986)(defendant fee award)(attorney rates of $50-100).

Mississippi

Brantley v. Surles, 804 F.2d 321, 327 (5th Cir. 1986)($75 attorney rate);

Beamon v. City of Ridgeland, 666 F. Supp. 937, 945 (S.D. Miss. 1987)($65-100 for attorneys);

Dotson v. City of Indianola, 639 F. Supp. 1056, 1060-61 (N.D. Miss. 1986)(attorney rates of $50-100);

Catchings v. City of Crystal Springs, 626 F. Supp. 987, 989-90 (S.D. Miss. 1986)(attorney rate of $75 for legal work and $37.50 for travel time).

APPENDIX E

Texas

Garmong v. Montgomery County, 668 F. Supp. 1000, 1012 (S.D. Tex. 1987) (attorney rates of $150 and $200 for legal work and $160 and $225 for fee request).

Sixth Circuit

Michigan

Birth Control Centers, Inc. v. Reizen, 652 F. Supp. 192, 195, 198 (E.D. Mich. 1986)($75 and $175 for attorneys).

Ohio

Horne v. Clemens, 25 Ohio App. 3d 44, 495 N.E.2d 441, 443 (1985)($85 attorney rate).

Tennessee

Coulter v. State of Tennessee, 805 F.2d 146, 149-50 (6th Cir. 1986)(Title VII)(Nashville)($85 for 1982 work and $110 for 1983-84 work of one attorney, and $85 for 1982-84 work of other attorney);
Brandon v. Allen, 645 F. Supp. 1261, 1272 (W.D. Tenn. 1986)(attorney rates of $100-250).

Seventh Circuit

Illinois

Lightfoot v. Walker, 826 F.2d 516, 524-25 (7th Cir. 1987)($85 and $115 for attorneys);
Burlington Northern, aff'd in relevant part, 810 F.2d 601 (7th Cir. 1986);
Tomazzoli v. Sheedy, 804 F.2d 93, 99 (7th Cir. 1986)(Springfield)($75 for attorney);
Hamilton v. Daley, 777 F.2d 1207, 1213 (7th Cir. 1985)(defendant fee award) (Cook County)($65 for attorneys);
* *Rateree v. Rockett,* 685 F. Supp. 670, 677-74 (N.D. Ill. 1988) ($125 for attorneys);
Easter House v. State of Illinois Department of Children, 663 F. Supp. 456, 461 (N.D. Ill. 1987)($75-150 for attorneys; $30 and $35 for paralegals);
Shakman v. Democratic Org., 634 F. Supp. 895, 909 (N.D. Ill. 1986)(attorney rates of $50-185, and paralegal rate of $45).

APPENDIX E

Indiana

* *Kurowski v. Krajewski,* 848 F.2d 767, 776 (7th Cir. 1988) ($100 for attorneys);
Bohen v. City of East Chicago, 666 F. Supp. 154, 157 (N.D. Ind. 1987)($100 and $125 for attorneys);
Claus v. Goshert, 657 F. Supp. 237, 247 (N.D. Ind. 1987)($50-95 for attorneys);
American Booksellers Association, Inc. v. Hudnut, 650 F. Supp. 324, 328-30 (S.D. Ind. 1987)($105-225 for attorneys; $50 for law student);
Bovey v. City of Lafayette, 638 F. Supp. 640, 648 (N.D. Ind. 1986)($80 for attorneys);
Felts v. Radio Distributing Co., 637 F. Supp. 234, 239 (N.D. Ind. 1985)(Title VII)($60 attorney rate);
Lock v. Jenkins, 634 F. Supp. 615, 627 (N.D. Ind. 1986)(attorney rates of $95 and $50 for work done over 10-year period);
Robinson v. City of Lake Station, 630 F. Supp. 1052, 1064 (N.D. Ind. 1986)(Title VII)(attorney rates of $100 for trial and trial preparation work and $80 for out-of-court work);
Indiana Hosp. Licensing v. Women's Pavilion, 486 N.E.2d 1070, 1073-75 (Ind. Ct. App. 1985)(historic attorney rates ranging from $50-125).

Wisconsin

* *Schirk v. Herlik,* 689 F. Supp. 861, 864 (E.D. Wis. 1988) ($75 and $90 for attorneys).

Eighth Circuit

Arkansas

* *Hill v. Southside Public Schools,* 688 F. Supp. 493, 500 (E.D. Ark. 1988) ($70 and $75 for attorneys, and $25 for law clerks);
Rogers v. Kelly, 674 F. Supp. 1372, 1378 (E.D. Ark 1987)($85 for attorney);
Cole v. Williams, 624 F. Supp. 712, 718 (W.D. Ark. 1985)($75 attorney rate).

Minnesota

Swart v. Scott County, 650 F. Supp. 888, 895 (D. Minn. 1987)($100 for attorneys).

Missouri

* *McDonald v. Armontrout,* 860 F.2d 1456, 1458-61 (8th Cir. 1988) ($150 for experienced attorneys);
Jenkins v. Missouri, 838 F.2d 260, 266 (8th Cir. 1988)($40 for paralegals, $35 for law clerks);
Davis v. City of Charleston, 827 F.2d 317, 323 (8th Cir. 1987)($75 for attorneys).

Cunningham v. City of Overland, 804 F.2d 1066, 1071 (8th Cir. 1986)($90 attorney rate for trial work, and $60 for post-trial work);

* *Griffin v. Ozark County,* 688 F. Supp. 1372, 1375 (W.D. Mo. 1988) ($55-70 for attorney);

Woodard v. Hardee's Restaurant, 643 F. Supp. 691, 693 (W.D. Mo. 1986)($100 attorney rate);

Davis v. City of Charleston, 635 F. Supp. 197, 200 (E.D. Mo. 1986)(Southeast Missouri)($60 attorney rate).

Ninth Circuit

California

City of Riverside v. Rivera, 477 U.S. 561, 565, 570, 582-83 (1986)($125 attorney rate and $25 law clerk rate, awarded in 1981 for work begun in 1976);

Chalmers v. City of Los Angeles, 796 F.2d 1205, 1214-15 (9th Cir. 1986)(Los Angeles)($175 attorney rate);

Semar v. Platte Valley Federal S. & L. Ass'n, 791 F.2d 699, 70607 (9th Cir. 1986)(Truth-in-Lending Act, 15 U.S.C. § 1640(a)(3))($135 attorney rate);

* *Pacific West Cable Co. v. City of Sacramento,* 693 F. Supp. 865, 870 (E.D. Cal. 1988) ($85-150 for attorneys);

* *Corder v. Gates,* 688 F. Supp. 1418, 1422-23 (C.D. Cal. 1988) ($180 for 1984-85 work and $200 for 1986-87 work of experienced attorney);

Chalmers v. City of Los Angeles, 676 F. Supp. 1515, 1519 (C.D. Cal. 1987)(historical attorney rates of $95-175 for 1978-83 work);

Keith v. Volpe, 644 F. Supp. 1312, 1316 (C.D. Cal. 1986)(attorney rates of $50-180, and law student rate of $30);

Stewart v. County of Sonoma, 634 F. Supp. 773, 780 (N.D. Cal. 1986)($210 for partners, $120 for associates, and $50 for paralegals).

Idaho

Schrader v. Idaho Dep't of Health and Welfare, 631 F. Supp. 1426, 1431 (D. Idaho 1986)($75 and $65 attorney rates).

Nevada

Gorelangton v. City of Reno, 638 F. Supp. 1426, 1437, 1440 (D. Nev. 1986)(for work done from 1982-86, attorney rates of $100-175 for in-court time and $85-150 for out-of-court time, and paralegal rates of $40 and $50).

Oregon

Vance v. Hegstrom, 629 F. Supp. 747, 750 (D. Or. 1985)($125 attorney rate).

APPENDIX E

Washington

BSA, Inc. v. King County, 804 F.2d 1104, 1112 (9th Cir. 1986)(attorney rates of $100 for in-court work and $75 for out-of-court work).

Tenth Circuit

Colorado

Nephew v. City of Aurora, 830 F.2d 1547, 1550 (10th Cir. 1987)(*en banc*)($125 for attorneys), *cert. denied,* 108 S. Ct. 1269 (1988);
Goetz v. Ricketts, 632 F. Supp. 926, 930 (D. Colo. 1986)(Denver)($90 attorney rate);
Ramos v. Lamm, 632 F. Supp. 376, 387-88 (D. Colo. 1986)(Denver)($70-150 for attorneys, and $25-40 for legal assistants and law clerks).

Kansas

Ortega v. City of Kansas City, 659 F. Supp. 1201, 1216 (D. Kan. 1987)($75 and $100 for attorneys).

New Mexico

Mares v. Credit Bureau of Raton, 801 F.2d 1197, 1207-08 (10th Cir. 1986)(Consumer Credit Protection Act, 15 U.S.C. §§ 1601 *et seq.*)($60 attorney rate for work done in 1980-81).

Utah

Blake v. Yackovich, 683 F. Supp. 240, 245 (D. Utah 1988)($70-125 for attorneys);
Bee v. Greaves, 669 F. Supp. 372, 378 n.14 (D. Utah 1987)($60-125 for attorneys, $40 for paralegals and law clerks);
City Consumer Services, Inc. v. Horne, 631 F. Supp. 1050, 1061-62 (D. Utah 1986)(Truth-in-Lending Act, 15 U.S.C. § 1640(a)(3))(attorney rates of $44-98 for work done in 1982-84).

Wyoming

MacLaird v. Werger, 633 F. Supp. 286 (D. Wyo. 1986)(Cheyenne)($75 attorney rate).

APPENDIX E

Eleventh Circuit

Alabama

Hidle v. Geneva County Board of Education, 681 F. Supp. 752, 756 (M.D. Ala. 1988)(Title VII suit)($75-125 for attorneys);

Georgia Association of Realtors v. Alabama Real Estate Commission, 678 F. Supp. 854, 857 (M.D. Ala. 1987)($45-200 for attorneys);

United States v. Marengo County Commission, 667 F. Supp. 786, 797 (S.D. Ala. 1987)($100 and $120 for attorneys);

Birl v. Wallis, 649 F. Supp. 868, 872 (M.D. Ala. 1986)($85-120 for attorneys);

York v. Alabama State Bd. of Educ., 631 F. Supp. 78, 86 (M.D. Ala. 1986)(attorney rates of $75-115).

* **Florida**

* *Allen v. Freeman,* 694 F. Supp. 1554, 1556 (S.D. Fla. 1988) (attorney rates of $200 for partner and $125 for associate).

Georgia

Walters v. City of Atlanta, 803 F.2d 1135, 1151 (11th Cir. 1986)($85 attorney rate and $30 paralegal rate);

* *Searcy v. Crim,* 692 F. Supp. 1363, 1365 (N.D. Ga. 1988) ($150 for attorneys);

Segars v. Fulton County, 654 F. Supp. 42, 43-44 (N.D. Ga. 1986)($30-120 for attorneys);

Doss v. Long, 624 F. Supp. 1078, 1082 (W.D. Ga. 1985)($125 and $100 attorney rates);

Hubby v. Historic Savannah Foundation, Inc., 623 F. Supp. 637, 644 (S.D. Ga. 1985)(defendant fee award)(Savannah)($85 maximum attorney rate).

APPENDIX F

SIGNIFICANT DECISIONS CONSIDERING DOWNWARD ADJUSTMENT OF THE LODESTAR FOR PARTIAL LITIGATION SUCCESS

Pages 654-63, update Hart (First Circuit), Durett, Black Grievance Committee (Third Circuit), Hyatt (Fourth Circuit), and Rivera (Ninth Circuit) citations, and add to cases cited:

District of Columbia Circuit

Kennecott Corp. v. E.P.A., 804 F.2d 763, 765-66 (D.C. Cir. 1986)(Clean Air Act, 42 U.S.C. § 7607(f)); (one-third reduction in fee award for lack of success on one of plaintiffs' three primary arguments, if counsel's time records fail to reflect time spent on that issue, but no reduction for lack of success on another argument that was merely an alternative contention to another successful claim);

McKenzie v. Kennickell, 645 F. Supp. 437, 446-47 (D.D.C. 1986)(no reduction in Title VII fee award for plaintiffs' lack of success on one of three aspects of their employment discrimination claim, when that claim was related to successful claims in the suit because all claims were aspects of "one broad Title VII claim" and shared overlapping research and briefing, and plaintiffs achieved excellent results).

First Circuit

Hart, rev'd and remanded, 798 F.2d 519, 520-21 (1st Cir. 1986)(finding that individual defendants were freed from § 1988 fee liability by settlement agreement which "released and discharged" them "in every respect");

Conservation Law Foundation v. Secretary of Interior, 790 F.2d 965, 968-70 (1st Cir. 1986)(concluding that plaintiff was not entitled to fee compensation for work done on one unsuccessful environmental claim that was unrelated to other environmental claims in case, but that other two claims were "so interrelated that success on one supports an award of fees for both");

Diver v. Goddard Memorial Hosp., 783 F.2d 6 (1st Cir. 1986)(Fair Labor Standards Act, 29 U.S.C. § 216(b))(affirming sharp reduction in fee request for plaintiff's "partial and nominal victory" in her employment discharge case in prevailing on only one claim that was "factually and legally distinct" from her losing claims and in winning only small overtime payment award).

Second Circuit

* *Carrero v. New York City Housing Authority,* 685 F. Supp. 904, 907 (S.D.N.Y. 1988) (35 percent reduction in fee award for limited success in Title VII sex discrimination suit involving claims that were "to some degree interrelated" because of overlapping proof);

Lenihan v. City of New York, 640 F. Supp. 822, 826-27 (S.D.N.Y. 1986) (refusing to reduce fee award for plaintiff's success in obtaining only some of the remedies sought in her employment discrimination suit, when she prevailed on all legal claims asserted and obtained excellent results);

Campaign for a Progressive Bronx v. Black, 631 F. Supp. 975, 982 (S.D.N.Y. 1986) (Voting Rights Act, 42 U.S.C. § 1973l(e)) (50 percent reduction in fee award for plaintiffs' success on only two out of five interrelated claims and in obtaining relief addressing two out of four problems challenged in suit).

Third Circuit

Black Grievance Committee, vacated and remanded, 802 F.2d 648, 653-54 (3d
* Cir. 1986) (but upholding 25 percent reduction in lodestar for partial success), *on remand,* 690 F. Supp. 1393, 1397-98 (E.D. Pa. 1988) (25 percent lodestar reduction based on comparison of relief requested and relief achieved in consent decree settling employment discrimination suit);

Durett, aff'd in relevant part, 790 F.2d 360, 362-63 (3d Cir. 1986).

Fourth Circuit

Hyatt, aff'd in relevant part, 807 F.2d 376, 381-83 (4th Cir. 1986);

Van Sant v. United States Postal Services, 805 F.2d 141 (4th Cir. 1986) (Equal Access to Justice Act, 28 U.S.C. § 2412) (sharply reduced fee award in light of small damages recovery and relative insignificance of legal right vindicated).

* Fifth Circuit

* *Nash v. Chandler,* 848 F.2d 567, 572-73 (5th Cir. 1988) (no lodestar reduction for lack of success on claims for monetary and injunctive relief in § 1983 suit when those claims were related to successful claim for declaratory judgment).

* Sixth Circuit

* *Fite v. First Tennessee Production Credit Association,* 861 F.2d 884, 894 (6th Cir. 1988) (no reduction in fee award under Age Discrimination in Employment Act, 29 U.S.C. § 626(b), because plaintiff, who received complete relief, did not succeed on all issues raised or against all defendants.

Seventh Circuit

* *Jackson v. Illinois Prisoner Review Board,* 856 F.2d 890, 894-95 (7th Cir. 1988) (reduction of award for partial success in prisoner's suit involving unrelated claims concerning composition of parole review board and adequacy of procedural safeguards in review board proceedings);

Zabkowicz v. West Bend Co., 789 F.2d 540, 550-52 (7th Cir. 1986) (finding that time spent on unsuccessful tort and labor claims was not totally excludable since those claims were related to plaintiff's successful Title VII claim, but that plaintiff's husband's tort claims were unrelated to Title VII claim and hence noncompensable);

* *Fleming v. County of Kane,* 686 F. Supp. 1264, 1274-75 (N.D. Ill. 1988) (exclusion of time expended on defamation counterclaim and unsuccessful pendent state law claim unrelated to successful § 1983 employment discharge claim).

Eighth Circuit

Williams v. Mensey, 785 F.2d 631, 639-40 (8th Cir. 1986) (affirming substantial reduction in fee award when plaintiff succeeded on only one claim against one defendant and recovered only nominal damages).

Ninth Circuit

Rivera, aff'd, 477 U.S. 561 (1986);

Clark v. City of Los Angeles, 803 F.2d 987, 990 (9th Cir. 1986) (upholding district court's refusal to reduce fee award because plaintiffs did not succeed on their damages claim, when they obtained injunctive relief in which defendants acquiesced and which gave plaintiffs the "practical result they sought");

Planned Parenthood v. State of Arizona, 789 F.2d 1348, 1352-53 (9th Cir. 1986) (concluding that fee award should not be reduced for time spent on unsuccessful motions and activities, when they amounted only to "ancillary efforts" that were not "discrete claims" and they all aimed at the successful result achieved by plaintiffs in the litigation);

Probe v. State Teachers' Retirement System, 780 F.2d 776, 785 (9th Cir. 1986) (concluding that no reduction was warranted in Title VII fee award because action was dismissed as to five out of six defendants, when plaintiffs achieved the major class-wide relief they sought in the case);

* *Corder v. Gates,* 688 F. Supp. 1418, 1423-24 (C.D. Cal. 1988) (20 percent lodestar reduction based on plaintiff's relatively small damages recovery, which was substantially less than rejected Rule 68 offer of judgment).

Tenth Circuit

Hernandez v. George, 793 F.2d 264, 268 (10th Cir. 1986) (affirming district court's imposition of 50 percent reduction in fee award for plaintiffs' success in gaining some improvements in six out of ten general areas addressed by constitutional challenge to jail conditions);

Martinez v. Schock Transfer & Warehouse Co., Inc., 789 F.2d 848, 849 (10th Cir. 1986) (upholding district court's substantial reduction in fee request in case in which plaintiff "seeks both injunctive relief and substantial damages but wins only nominal damages");

Ramos v. Lamm, 632 F. Supp. 376, 385-86 (D. Colo. 1986) (imposing five percent reduction in claimed hours to reflect plaintiffs' partial success in prison conditions suit, when plaintiffs' lack of success on several minor claims rendered the results obtained less than "excellent").

Eleventh Circuit

* *Avila v. Coca-Cola Co.,* 849 F.2d 511, 514-15 (11th Cir. 1988) (upholding district court's elimination of all time expended in Title VII suit on unsuccessful national origins claim that was related to successful retaliation claim);

* *Perkins v. Mobile Housing Board,* 847 F.2d 735, 739 (11th Cir. 1988) (upholding 15 percent reduction in lodestar award in public housing class action suit since, although the central objective of suit was accomplished, not all claims were sustained, the monetary recovery was small compared to the recovery sought, and the state law claims were not compensable);

York v. Alabama State Bd. of Educ., 631 F. Supp. 78, 84 (M.D. Ala. 1986) (declining to disallow time spent on claims of class members "who were ultimately found not to be entitled to relief under the consent decree," when the work relating to those claims was closely intertwined with work on the successful claims to enjoin the use of a racially discriminatory teachers' examination).

APPENDIX G

DECISIONS CONCERNING UPWARD ADJUSTMENTS TO THE LODESTAR FOR QUALITY OF REPRESENTATION

* *Pages 664-667, update Palmer (District of Columbia Circuit), Daggett, Black Grievance Committee (Third Circuit), Burlington Northern (Seventh Circuit), and Rivera (Ninth Circuit) citations, and add to cases cited (see also cases cited at* **§ 20.3***):*

District of Columbia Circuit

Palmer, 478 U.S. 1015 (1986).

First Circuit

Conservation Law Foundation v. Secretary of Interior, 790 F.2d 965, 970-71 (1st Cir. 1986) (reversing award of quality adjustment under environmental fee-shifting statutes for district court's inadequate explanation).

Third Circuit

Daggett, aff'd in part and remanded, 811 F.2d 793 (3d Cir. 1987);
Black Grievance Committee, vacated on other grounds, 802 F.2d 648 (3d Cir. 1986);
Durett v. Cohen, 790 F.2d 360, 363-64 (3d Cir. 1986) (vacating upward adjustment based on "complexity of the legal claims").

Seventh Circuit

Burlington Northern, aff'd in relevant part, 810 F.2d 601, 606-08 (7th Cir. 1986).

Ninth Circuit

Rivera, 477 U.S. 561 (1986);
Planned Parenthood v. State of Arizona, 789 F.2d 1348, 1353 (9th Cir. 1986) (finding upward adjustment not justified by plaintiff's success in case).

Eleventh Circuit

Lattimore v. Oman Construction, 795 F.2d 930, 931-33 (11th Cir. 1986) (reversing quality adjustment in Title VII suit that was erroneously based on "past success ratios" reflecting past success rate for Title VII suits in particular judicial district and on equating of complete success in case with "exceptional" results).

APPENDIX H

DECISIONS CONCERNING UPWARD ADJUSTMENTS TO THE LODESTAR FOR RISK

All risk adjustment decisions cited in Appendix H of the main text must be re-evaluated in light of *Delaware Valley II,* as discussed in §§ **20.4A** through **20.4F** of this
* supplement. See §§ **20.4A** through **20.4F** for post-*Delaware Valley II* decisions.

APPENDIX I

DECISIONS CONCERNING UPWARD ADJUSTMENTS TO THE LODESTAR FOR DELAY IN PAYMENT OF FEES

Pages 674-76, update Daggett, Black Grievance Committee (Third Circuit), and Burlington Northern (Seventh Circuit) citations, and add to cases cited:

District of Columbia Circuit

McKenzie v. Kennickell, 645 F. Supp. 437, 442-43 (D.D.C. 1986) (denying delay adjustment in Title VII fee award against federal government, on authority of Supreme Court's *Shaw* decision, but suggesting that award of current rates in fee awards against federal government might be permissible to compensate for delayed payment).

First Circuit

Hart v. Bourque, 798 F.2d 519, 524 (1st Cir. 1986) (reversing district court's award of prejudgment interest to account for delay in payment, when 13-month delay resulted from time spent by court "to make the reduction in plaintiff's exceptional figures" and from time expended in unsuccessful fee settlement negotiations thwarted by plaintiff, so that the "delay in payment is chargeable to plaintiff, not defendant").

Third Circuit

Daggett, aff'd in part and remanded, 811 F.2d 793 (3d Cir. 1987);
Black Grievance Committee, vacated, 802 F.2d 648, 655-56 (3d Cir. 1986) (requiring redetermination of delay-in-payment adjustment when district court failed to consider the full time period "between the actual expenditure of services and the fee award" for which the delay-in-payment adjustment is designed to provide compensation).

Seventh Circuit

Burlington Northern, aff'd in relevant part, 810 F.2d 601, 608-09 (7th Cir. 1986) (delay in payment adjustment unwarranted when delay "was occasioned by a legitimate dispute over several issues" and lead counsel was compensated at top hourly rates).

APPENDIX J

DECISIONS ALLOCATING THE § 1988 FEE AWARD AMONG SEVERAL DEFENDANTS

Pages 677-80, update Burlington Northern citation (Seventh Circuit) and add to cases cited:

Apportionment Approach

Seventh Circuit

Burlington Northern, aff'd in relevant part, 810 F.2d 601, 60911 (7th Cir. 1986) (upholding district court's allocation to union defendants of a portion of plaintiffs' Title VII fee award, by way of contribution from unions to employer defendant, when consent decree authorized such contribution, union defendants were not immune from fee liability, and unions waived objections by failing to make them in the underlying contribution proceeding instead of waiting until they filed a post-judgment Rule 59(e) motion).

Eighth Circuit

Little Rock School Dist. v. Pulaski County Special School Dist., 787 F.2d 372, 374 (8th Cir. 1986) (apportioning plaintiff-intervenors' § 1988 fee award for appeal in school desegregation case among state, county school district, and local school districts).

Ninth Circuit

Stewart v. County of Sonoma, 634 F. Supp. 773, 780 (N.D. Cal. 1986) (in allocating § 1988 fee award between County and Junior College defendants in sexual harassment case, court attributed 13 percent of award to Junior College defendants, as representing the mean between the approximately 4 percent of the total hours that was spent on the claim against the College and the approximately 22 percent of the total damages award that was recovered from the College);

Schrader v. Idaho Dep't of Health and Welfare, 631 F. Supp. 1426, 1430-31 (D. Idaho 1986) (allocating to state defendant alone the § 1988 fees incurred prior to federal defendant's joinder in the suit, and apportioning remainder of fee award 10 percent against state defendant and 90 percent against federal defendant, where the "federal defendant, through its policies and mandates, was a moving force in the promulgation of the state regulations declared invalid in this case").

APPENDIX J

Joint and Several Liability

Seventh Circuit

Shakman v. Democratic Org. of Cook County, 634 F. Supp. 895, 903-05 (N.D. Ill. 1986) (imposing joint and several liability on all defendants, based on finding that "a conspiracy among all defendants existed to deprive plaintiffs of their constitutional rights," subject to apportionment and liability limits).

Eighth Circuit

Woodard v. Hardee's Restaurant, 643 F. Supp. 691, 69395 (W.D. Mo. 1986) (assessing § 1988 fee award jointly and severally against defendant security guard who falsely arrested plaintiffs and against defendant restaurant whose official policy security guard was executing in making the false arrest);

Cole v. Williams, 624 F. Supp. 712, 720 (W.D. Ark. 1985) (imposing joint and several liability for § 1988 fees on several defendants in § 1983 action for false arrest and failure to take plaintiffs before a magistrate, where "it would be impossible to equitably divide the fees and expenses among them").

APPENDIX K

DECISIONS CONCERNING RECOVERY OF LITIGATION EXPENSES AS STATUTORY ATTORNEY'S FEES

Pages 681-85, update Palmer (District of Columbia Circuit), Daggett, Black Grievance Committee (Third Circuit), International Woodworkers (Fifth Circuit) citations, and add to cases cited:

District of Columbia Circuit

Palmer, vacated and remanded, 478 U.S. 1015 (1986).

Second Circuit

* *Carrero v. New York City Housing Authority,* 685 F. Supp. 904, 909 (S.D.N.Y. 1988) (allowing recovery of expenses for postage, photocopying, delivery and service of papers, supplies for court papers, court filing fee, Federal Express, witness fees, trial transcript, investigator, and depositions; denying recovery of expenses for transportation to office in morning or to court in lieu of going to office, local telephone calls, word processing assistance, and meals);
Campaign for a Progressive Bronx v. Black, 631 F. Supp. 975, 983 (S.D.N.Y. 1986) (Voting Rights Act, 42 U.S.C. § 1973l(e)); finding that paralegal time is reimbursable only as an expense, but denying compensation in this case because of plaintiffs' failure to submit information concerning wages paid to paralegal.

Third Circuit

Daggett, aff'd in part & remanded, 811 F.2d 793 (3d Cir. 1987);
Black Grievance Committee, vacated & remanded, 802 F.2d 648, 657 (3d Cir. 1986) (vacating recovery of expert witness expenses in excess of statutory maximum).

Fourth Circuit

Starnes v. Hill, 635 F. Supp. 1270, 1273 (W.D.N.C. 1986) (declining to rule on compensability of claimed litigation expenses until plaintiff's attorneys provide more detailed information concerning expenses);
Vaughns v. Bd. of Educ., 627 F. Supp. 837, 843-44 (D. Md. 1985) (allowing recovery of claimed transportation and messenger service claims, except for extra expenses incurred because law firm representing plaintiffs was located outside forum district).

Fifth Circuit

International Woodworkers, aff'd, 107 S. Ct. 2494 (1987).

Ninth Circuit

Chalmers v. City of Los Angeles, 796 F.2d 1205, 1216 (9th Cir. 1986) (granting recovery of transportation expenses incurred by plaintiff's counsel in appearing for oral argument in court of appeals);
Stewart v. County of Sonoma, 634 F. Supp. 773, 781 (N.D. Cal. 1986) (allowing recovery of $5,000 in word processing expenses).

Tenth Circuit

Mares v. Credit Bureau of Raton, 801 F.2d 1197, 1208-09 (10th Cir. 1986) (Consumer Credit Protection Act, 15 U.S.C. § 1601 *et seq.*, awarding additional long-distance telephone and travel expenses disallowed by district court).

APPENDIX L

DECISIONS AWARDING AND DENYING FEES TO CIVIL RIGHTS DEFENDANTS

Decisions Granting Fees, or Reversing Denial of Fees to Successful Defendants

Pages 686-92, update Vandenplas (Seventh Circuit) and Hardin (Ninth Circuit) citations and add to cases cited:

* Fourth Circuit

* *Introcaso v. Cunningham,* 857 F.2d 965, 967-68 (4th Cir. 1988) (upholding § 1988 fee award against plaintiff although defendant's motion to dismiss was denied, finding this to be a case in which plaintiff established a "prima facie case which is weak but which is sufficient to survive a directed verdict, but which is nonetheless groundless in light of a defense readily apparent to the plaintiff from the outset of the litigation").

Fifth Circuit

Jackson v. Color Tile, Inc., 803 F.2d 201 (5th Cir. 1986) (affirming Title VII fee award against plaintiff who presented no relevant evidence to support her race discrimination claim).

Seventh Circuit

Vandenplas, rev'd, 797 F.2d 425, 428-32 (7th Cir. 1986) (reversing § 1988 fee award to successful defendants, where relevant law was in state of flux and plaintiffs were justified in proceeding with their claims);
Bacon v. American Fed. of State, County, 795 F.2d 33 (7th Cir. 1986) (assessing Title VII fees against pro se plaintiff-appellant for frivolous appeal);
Williams v. Kobel, 789 F.2d 463, 472 (7th Cir. 1986) (affirming §!5 1988 fee award against plaintiff who continued to litigate his police misconduct suit "after the meritless nature of his case became clear");
Hamilton v. Daley, 777 F.2d 1207, 1211-16 (7th Cir. 1985) (upholding plaintiff's liability for § 1988 fees for frivolous prosecutorial misconduct suit, but remanding for redetermination of amount of award in light of inappropriateness and excessiveness of some of hours claimed by defendants' counsel);
Hershinow v. Bonamarte, 772 F.2d 394 (7th Cir. 1985) (affirming § 1988 fee award against plaintiff for meritless suit challenging suspension from police force);
Coleman v. McLaren, 631 F. Supp. 763 (N.D. Ill. 1986) (awarding § 1988 fees to prevailing defendants from point at which plaintiffs continued to litigate their § 1983 action after they were put on notice of its frivolousness by an adverse

decision in a related action and by the district judge's warning that their claims were dubious).

Ninth Circuit

Hardin, amended, 779 F.2d 476, 480 (9th Cir. 1985) (affirming § 1988 fee award against losing plaintiff).

Decisions Denying Fees, or Reversing Awards of Fees, to Successful Defendants

Pages 692-97, add to cases cited:

First Circuit

Quiros v. Hernandez Colon, 800 F.2d 1 (1st Cir. 1986) (upholding denial of § 1988 fee award to successful defendant when plaintiff's complaint "contained both nonfrivolous and frivolous claims" and district court imposed Rule 11 fees on plaintiff's counsel who was primarily at fault for pursuing frivolous claims).

Fourth Circuit

Glymph v. Spartanburg Gen. Hosp., 783 F.2d 476, 479-80 (4th Cir. 1986) (reversing assessment of Title VII fees against losing plaintiff when district court denied defendant's motions for summary judgment and dismissal and plaintiff presented significant evidence in support of her race discrimination claim).

Fifth Circuit

Vaughner v. Pulito, 804 F.2d 873, 879 (5th Cir. 1986) (upholding denial of § 1988 fees against unsuccessful plaintiffs whose claims survived motions for dismissal and directed verdict and who "presented some credible evidence on their claims during their trial");

Holloway v. Walker, 784 F.2d 1294, 1296 (5th Cir. 1986) (affirming denial of § 1988 fee award to successful defendant when the relevant caselaw "was in a state of flux at the time the suit was filed and while the suit was pending").

Sixth Circuit

Jones v. Continental Corp., 789 F.2d 1225, 1232-33 (6th Cir. 1986) (reversing fee award against losing plaintiff whose claim of racially discriminatory employment discharge was "tenable" and supported by some evidence).

APPENDIX L

Seventh Circuit

LeBeau v. Libbey-Owens-Ford Co., 799 F.2d 1152, 1156-64 (7th Cir. 1986) (reversing Title VII fee award against unsuccessful plaintiffs in district court and on appeal, where plaintiffs defeated a summary judgment motion and established a *prima facie* case of employment sex discrimination at trial and plaintiff's position on appeal was not foreclosed by prior precedent).

Ninth Circuit

United States ex. rel. Chunie v. Ringrose, 788 F.2d 638, 647-48 (9th Cir. 1986) (denying award of § 1988 fees against losing plaintiffs on appeal who raised "issues not previously addressed by the courts").

Eleventh Circuit

* *O'Neal v. DeKalb County,* 850 F.2d 653, 658 (11th Cir. 1988) (upholding denial of § 1988 fees against losing defendant, noting that "[s]imply because the district court granted the defendants' motion for summary judgment does not mean that the plaintiffs' action was frivolous");

Terry Properties, Inc. v. Standard Oil Co., 799 F.2d 1523, 1538-40 (11th Cir. 1986) (reversing § 1988 fee award to several winning defendants in race discrimination suit when plaintiffs' legal claims were supported by some evidence and were "fully tried" before being rejected);

Davis v. Mills, 777 F.2d 1524 (11th Cir. 1985) (vacating § 1988 fee award to successful defendant when district court failed to make required specific findings concerning frivolousness of plaintiff's claims).

APPENDIX M (NEW)

RECENT SIGNIFICANT § 1988 FEE DECISIONS BY STATE COURTS

Alabama

Alabama State Personnel Board v. Hubbard, 508 So. 2d 230, 235 (Ala. 1987)(state official found immune from § 1983 damages claim is not liable for § 1988 fees);

Federation of City Employees v. City of Birmingham, 492 So. 2d 1304 (Ala. 1986)(plaintiffs who succeeded on state law claim but whose constitutional due process claim was found to be "premature" and not yet justiciable were not entitled to § 1988 fees, because the constitutional claim was, in effect, affirmatively denied).

Arizona

* *Barrow v. Arizona Board of Regents,* 158 Ariz. 71, 761 P.2d 145, 153-54 (1988) (upholding § 1988 fee award to several defendants for plaintiff's frivolous § 1983 claims against them, but reversing § 1988 fee award to another defendant against whom plaintiff asserted a "colorable" due process claim);

Central Machinery Co. v. State, 152 Ariz. 134, 730 P.2d 843 (1986)(*en banc*)(successful claim that state sales tax on Indian enterprise was preempted by federal Indian trader statutes, and hence was invalid under Supremacy Clause, was not actionable under § 1983 and did not qualify successful plaintiff for § 1988 fees);

Gilbert v. Board of Medical Examiners, 155 Ariz. 169, 745 P.2d 617, 630 (Ariz. Ct. App. 1987)(§ 1988 fee award against plaintiff for groundless § 1983 claim);

Tiffany v. Arizona Interscholastic Association, Inc., 151 Ariz. 134, 726 P.2d 231, 236 (Ariz. Ct. App. 1986)(plaintiff who succeeded on state law claim was not entitled to § 1988 fees on basis of related constitutional claim that was rejected by the court).

California

* *Best v. California Apprenticeship Council,* 193 Cal. App. 3d 1448, 240 Cal. Rptr. 1 (1987) (plaintiff who succeeded on state law grounds in his religious accommodation claim is entitled to § 1988 fees since state law claim was entwined with a federal constitutional claim actionable under § 1983; plaintiff is entitled to § 1988 compensation for work done in administrative proceedings which were part of the single course of legal redress he successfully pursued; defendant's asserted good faith rejected as basis for denying § 1988 fees; § 1988 compensation may be based on adequately reconstructed time records).

APPENDIX M

Colorado

Brown v. City of Colorado Springs, 749 P.2d 475, 477 (Colo. Ct. App. 1987)(plaintiff was not entitled to § 1988 fees for work done in administrative disciplinary proceeding that occurred prior to § 1983 court suit);
Oten v. Colorado Board of Social Services, 738 P.2d 37 (Colo. Ct. App. 1987)(§ 1988 fees were properly awarded against defendant state official, sued in official capacity, and were recoverable from the state, when defendant director was charged with responsibility for implementing state agency rules concerning distribution of federal energy assistance benefits that were found violative of federal statute; no reduction imposed in § 1988 fee award because of unsuccessful claim that was of relatively minor significance, was a bargaining chip in gaining greater settlement benefits, and involved only a minor part of counsel's work; time spent by plaintiffs' attorneys in counseling beneficiaries of settlement agreement was compensable, at paralegal rates).

Georgia

* *State v. Private Truck Council,* 258 Ga. 531, 371 S.E.2d 378 (1988) (concluding that plaintiff's success on claim that state statute violated commerce clause of United States Constitution did not entitle them to § 1988 fees).

Idaho

Hale v. Walsh, 113 Idaho 759, 747 P.2d 1288, 1300-01 (Idaho Ct. App. 1987)(prevailing plaintiff need not show that defendant resisted § 1983 claim in bad faith in order to recover § 1988 fees).

Kansas

Allison v. Johnson County Board of County Commissioners, 241 Kan. 266, 737 P.2d 6, 13-16 (1987)(plaintiff landowners were entitled to § 1988 fees for obtaining significant benefits from settlement of suit challenging levy of assessments based on claims that included a substantial constitutional "taking" claim).

Maine

* *Burr v. Town of Rangeley,* 549 A.2d 733, 735 (Me. 1988) (affirming § 1988 fee award against plaintiff for including frivolous constitutional claim in his land use suit).

Maryland

Shapiro v. Chapman, 70 Md. App. 307, 520 A.2d 1330, 1333-34 (1987)(reversing trial court's dismissal of plaintiffs' § 1983 constitutional claim, although it amounted to no more than an alternative theory to the common law tort claim on which plaintiffs succeeded, because erroneous dismissal of § 1983 claim would improperly render plaintiffs ineligible for § 1988 fees).

Massachusetts

Crane v. Commissioner of Public Welfare, 400 Mass. 46, 507 N.E.2d 751 (1987)(plaintiffs whose § 1983 federal statutory/regulatory claim was not decided, because they succeeded on state law grounds in gaining recovery of retroactive benefits that had been wrongly denied under federal statute (as determined in a predecessor federal suit), were entitled to § 1988 fees);
Gaulin v. Commissioner of Public Welfare, 23 Mass. App. Ct. 744, 505 N.E.2d 898 (1987)(upholding imposition of post-judgment interest past due on § 1988 fee award against state, while acknowledging that in appropriate cases the court might allow an "interest-free interval" to permit administrative processing of the fee payment).

Michigan

Young v. Barker, 158 Mich. App. 709, 405 N.W.2d 395, 403-04 (1987)(prevailing defendants' § 1988 fee motion need not comply with time requirements of local court rule governing recovery of costs);
Guider v. Smith, 157 Mich. App. 92, 403 N.W.2d 505, 515 (1987)(upholding denial of § 1988 fees, on "bright prospects" principle, to plaintiff who recovered substantial money damages in police misconduct case based on § 1983 claim that was sufficiently strong to attract private counsel on contingent fee basis);
Varney v. Genesee County Sheriff, 156 Mich. App. 539, 402 N.W.2d 57 (1986)(holding that local court rule, authorizing defendant's recovery of attorney's fees against plaintiff who rejected a mediation evaluation more than 10 percent above the judgment ultimately recovered by plaintiff, was applicable, along with § 1988, in determining fees recoverable by plaintiff who succeeded on his § 1983 claim);
Dorfman v. Department of Transportation, 155 Mich. App. 57, 399 N.W.2d 437 (1986)(plaintiffs were not entitled to § 1988 fees when they voluntarily dismissed their § 1983 claim before the court granted them equitable relief on state law grounds, and thereafter sought to reassert their § 1983 claim).

Minnesota

* *L.K. v. Gregg,* 425 N.W.2d 813 (Minn. 1988) (concluding that since plaintiffs adequately pled fourteenth amendment due process claim, they were eligible for § 1988 fees, although they did not specifically cite § 1983, and that plaintiffs were entitled to § 1988 fees for their success on their federal due process claim).

APPENDIX M

Mississippi

* *Marx v. Truck Renting & Leasing Association,* 520 So. 2d 1333, 1346 (Miss. 1987) (plaintiffs who successfully challenged constitutionality of state sales tax stated § 1983 claim and were entitled to § 1988 fees);

Nevada

Tarkanian v. National Collegiate Athletic Association, 741 P.2d 1345, 1351-52 (Nev. 1987)(plaintiff who succeeded on constitutional claim was entitled to § 1988 fees although he did not specifically plead § 1983; fees were not recoverable for distinct phase of litigation in which plaintiff did not prevail against defendant or for time not supported by billing records; fees were recoverable for time spent on undecided constitutional claim which was related to successful constitutional claim which afforded complete relief).

New Hampshire

Daigle v. City of Portsmouth, 534 A.2d 689, 705 (N.H. 1987)(plaintiff who succeeded on common law tort claim, but whose § 1983 constitutional claim was specifically rejected, was not entitled to § 1988 fees).

New Jersey

Urban League v. Township Committee, 222 N.J. Super. 131, 536 A.2d 287 (App. Div. 1987)(plaintiffs who succeeded on their state constitutional claims, joined with an unresolved fee claim under the Federal Fair Housing Act, 42 U.S.C. § 3612(c), were entitled to statutory fees upon a ruling that the record also establishes a violation of the federal statute)(for discussion of questionableness of this approach, see **§ 15.17);**

Carlstadt Education Association v. Mayor & Council, 219 N.J. Super. 164, 530 A.2d 34 (App. Div. 1987)(§ 1988 fees may not be denied to prevailing plaintiff based on relative worth of the constitutional rights vindicated by the suit).

New Mexico

Rubio v. Carlsbad Municipal School District, 106 N.M. 446, 744 P.2d 919, 923-24 (N.M. Ct. App. 1987)(upholding § 1988 fee award to prevailing defendant for plaintiffs' groundless § 1983 claim).

New York

* *Campain v. Marlboro Cent. School District Board of Education,* 138 A.D.2d 914, 526 N.Y.S.2d 658 (1988) (defendants' good faith reliance on state statutory provision that was construed favorably to plaintiff to avoid constitutional conflict,

and reliance on prior decisions of state court, were not special circumstances preventing award of § 1988 fees to prevailing plaintiff);

* *Martinez v. Perales,* 135 A.D.2d 818, 522 N.Y.S.2d 922 (1987) (plaintiff was prevailing party entitled to § 1988 fees in suit, asserting both fee-generating and non-fee-generating claims, that was favorably concluded by settlement stipulation that was silent as to the legal grounds upon which it was based; court ruled that State Social Services Commissioner was solely liable for fees);

* *Humphrey v. Gross,* 135 A.D.2d 634, 522 N.Y.S.2d 213 (1987) (nonprofit organizations representing prevailing plaintiffs are entitled to prevailing market rates under § 1988; state commissioner is solely liable for fees in social services cases);

* *Loretto v. Group W. Cable,* 135 A.D.2d 444, 522 N.Y.S.2d 543 (1987) (plaintiff property owner did not establish that defendant cable company's taking of its property was without just compensation, since it had not yet applied to the appropriate state agency to obtain compensation; accordingly, plaintiff had not succeeded on its § 1983 constitutional claim and was not eligible for § 1988 fees), *cert. denied,* 109 S. Ct. 78 (1988);

Matter of Goodwin v. D'Elia, 132 Misc. 2d 527 (Sup. Ct. Nassau County, 1986)(plaintiff who successfully negotiated and settled his public assistance case on the basis of a state law claim was entitled to § 1988 fees, because his § 1983 constitutional claim was not meritless).

Oregon

Lofft v. State Board of Higher Education, 89 Or. App. 614, 750 P.2d 515 (1988)(plaintiff was entitled to § 1988 fees when his undecided constitutional claim was nonfrivolous and arose out of the same core of facts as the successful state law claim);

* *Rogers v. Saylor,* 306 Or. 267, 760 P.2d 232 (1988)(concluding that state statute could not effectively prohibit the award of punitive damages or limit the amount of recoverable compensatory damages in a § 1983 suit in state court, and did not bar the recovery of § 1988 fees for a successful § 1983 claim).

Vermont

* *Packard v. Gordon,* 537 A.2d 140, 144 (Vt. 1987) (plaintiff's failure to state explicitly in his complaint that he was proceeding under § 1983 did not preclude § 1988 fee award for success on constitutional claim);

Furno v. Pignona, 522 A.2d 746, 752 (S. Ct. Vt. 1987)(plaintiff who succeeded on § 1983 constitutional claim was entitled to § 1988 fees in trial court and on appeal, with trial court to determine fee award for both courts).

Washington

Levinson v. Washington Horse Racing Commission, 48 Wash. App. 822, 740 P.2d 898, 903 (1987)(plaintiff who succeeded on constitutional claim, but did not make claim pursuant to § 1983, is not entitled to § 1988 fees);

Hale v. City of Seattle, 48 Wash. App. 451, 739 P.2d 723 (1987)(plaintiffs were not entitled to § 1988 fees, when they succeeded on a state constitutional claim but received an adverse decision on their § 1983 federal constitutional claim when they requested that it be decided).

Wisconsin

Dowd v. City of New Richmond, 137 Wis. 2d 539, 405 N.W.2d 66, 78 (1987)(defendant city was entitled to § 1988 fees for defending successfully against groundless § 1983 claim).

TABLE OF AUTHORITIES

Case	*Book §*
Albenga v. Ward, 635 F. Supp. 660 (S.D.N.Y. 1986)	§ 9.4
Albert v. Carovano, 851 F.2d 561 (2d Cir. 1988)	§§ 1.3A, 5.12, 5.14
Alberti v. Sheriff of Harris County, 688 F. Supp. 1176 (S.D. Tex. 1987)	§§ 17.9, 17.14, 21.8, 21.10
Alcan Aluminum Corp. v. Lyntel Prods., 656 F. Supp. 1138 (N.D. Ill. 1987)	§ 7.4
Alder v. Columbia Historical Soc'y, 690 F. Supp. 9 (D.D.C. 1988)	§§ 9.10, 10.6
Alexander v. Hill, 625 F. Supp. 567 (W.D.N.C. 1985)	§§ 15.8, 17.6, 17.8, 18.7, App. E
Alfaro Motors v. Ward, 814 F.2d 883 (2d Cir. 1987)	§§ 1.3A, 3.8
Alioto v. City of Shively, 835 F.2d 1173 (6th Cir. 1987)	§ 7.9
Allen v. Board of Dentistry, 835 F.2d 100 (5th Cir. 1988)	§§ 12.8, 12.11
Allen v. District of Columbia, 503 A.2d 1233 (D.C. App. 1986)	§§ 15.7, 16.9
Allen v. Freeman, 694 F. Supp. 1554 (S.D. Fla. 1988)	App. E
Allen v. Thompson, 815 F.2d 1433 (11th Cir. 1987)	§ 7.8
Alliance to End Repression v. City of Chicago, 820 F.2d 873 (7th Cir. 1987)	§§ 13.3, 15.4
Allingham v. Seattle, 109 Wash. 2d 947, 749 P.2d 160 (1988)	§ 3.10
Allison v. Johnson County Bd. of County Comm'rs, 241 Kan. 266, 737 P.2d 6 (1987)	§ 12.13, App. M
Almodovar v. Reiner, 832 F.2d 1138 (9th Cir. 1987)	§§ 12.4, 12.9
Alvarado v. Chicago, 648 F. Supp. 994 (N.D. Ill. 1986)	§ 4.12
Alvarado v. Picur, 859 F.2d 448 (7th Cir. 1988)	§ 7.18
Alvarez v. Chicago, 649 F. Supp. 43 (N.D. Ill. 1986)	§ 2.5
Alyeska Pipeline Serv. Co. v. Wilderness Soc'y, 421 U.S. 240 (1975)	§ 21.8
American Booksellers Ass'n v. Commonwealth of Va., 792 F.2d 1261 (4th Cir. 1986)	§§ 16.3, 16.12
American Booksellers Ass'n, Inc. v. Hudnut, 650 F. Supp. 324 (S.D. Ind. 1986)	§§ 15.2, 15.10, 18.3, 21.8, App. E
American Disposal Servs. v. O'Brien, 839 F.2d 84 (2d Cir. 1988)	§ 12.11
Americans United for Separation of Church & State v. School Dist., 835 F.2d 627 (6th Cir. 1987)	§§ 1.3A, 15.1
Amico v. New Castle County, 654 F. Supp. 982 (D. Del. 1987)	§§ 20.5, 22.9, 24.2, App. E
Anaya Serbia v. Lavsell, 646 F. Supp. 1236 (D.P.R. 1986)	§ 2.3
Anderson v. Atlanta, 778 F.2d 678 (11th Cir. 1985)	§§ 4.6, 4.8
Anderson v. City of Hopkins, 393 N.W.2d 363 (Minn. 1986)	§ 7.18
Anderson v. Creighton, 107 S. Ct. 3034 (1987)	§§ 7.11-7.14, 7.16, 7.18
Anderson v. Gutschenritter, 836 F.2d 346 (7th Cir. 1988)	§§ 3.4B, 4.7
Anderson v. Lyng, 652 F. Supp. 1237 (M.D. Ala. 1987)	§ 6.9
Anderson v. Roberts, 823 F.2d 235 (8th Cir. 1987)	§§ 4.11, 7.18
Andree v. Ashland County, 818 F.2d 1306 (7th Cir. 1987)	§ 3.6
Anela v. City of Wildwood, 790 F.2d 1063 (3d Cir.), *cert. denied,* 107 S. Ct. 434 (1986)	§ 4.8
Angell v. Leslie, 832 F.2d 817 (4th Cir. 1987)	§ 14.13
Anton v. Lehpamer, 787 F.2d 1141 (7th Cir. 1986)	§§ 10.6, 10.7
Archie v. City of Racine, 847 F.2d 1211 (7th Cir. 1988)	§§ 3.2, 3.5, 4.3

AUTHORITIES

Case	*Book §*
Banks v. City of Emeryville, 109 F.R.D. 535 (N.D. Cal. 1985)	§ 14.14
Barbara R. v. Tirozzi, 665 F. Supp. 141 (D. Conn. 1987)	App. E
Barbera v. Smith, 836 F.2d 96 (2d Cir. 1987)	§ 7.8
Barcia v. Sitkin, 683 F. Supp. 353 (S.D.N.Y. 1988)	§§ 18.14, 20.5, App. E
Barnes v. Bosley, 828 F.2d 1253 (8th Cir. 1987)	§ 6.5
Barnes v. Bosley, 625 F. Supp. 81 (E.D. Mo. 1985), *appeal dismissed,* 790 F.2d 718 (8th Cir. 1986)	§ 6.12
Barnes v. McDowell, 647 F. Supp. 1307 (E.D. Ky. 1986), *aff'd in part, rev'd & remanded in part,* 848 F.2d 725 (6th Cir. 1988), *cert. denied,* 109 S. Ct. 789 (1989)	§§ 9.10, 12.5
Barnes v. Smith, 654 F. Supp. 1244 (E.D. Mo. 1987)	§ 7.5
Barr v. Abrams, 810 F.2d 358 (2d Cir. 1987)	§§ 1.3A, 7.8, 7.16
Barr v. Mateo, 360 U.S. 564 (1959)	§ 7.12
Barrett v. Thomas, 809 F.2d 1151 (5th Cir. 1987)	§ 16.8
Barrett v. United States, 798 F.2d 565 (2d Cir. 1986)	§ 7.8
Barrow v. Arizona Bd. of Regents, 158 Ariz. 71, 761 P.2d 145 (1988)	App. M
Bartalone v. County of Berrien, 643 F. Supp. 574 (W.D. Mich. 1986)	§§ 3.2, 4.12
Bartel Dental Books v. Schultz, 786 F.2d 486 (2d Cir.), *cert. denied,* 106 S. Ct. 3298 (1986)	§§ 9.4, 9.8
Bartholomew v. Fischl, 782 F.2d 1148 (3d Cir. 1986)	§§ 10.6, 10.7
Barton v. Gulf States Entertainment, 655 F. Supp. 782 (M.D. La. 1987)	§ 1.5
Bass v. NKC, 644 F. Supp. 24 (W.D. Ky. 1985)	§ 10.6
Bass v. Wallenstein, 769 F.2d 1173 (7th Cir. 1985)	§§ 11.2, 11.3
Bates v. McKeon, 650 F. Supp. 476 (D. Conn. 1986)	§ 3.3
Bateson v. Geisse, 857 F.2d 1300 (9th Cir. 1988)	§§ 3.2, 3.10, 4.7, 7.10, 16.6
Bath Memorial Hosp. v. Maine Health Care Fin. Comm'n, 853 F.2d 1007 (1st Cir. 1988)	§§ 12.11, 12.12
Bay Ridge Util. Dist. v. 4M Laundry, 717 S.W.2d 92 (Tex. Ct. App. 1986)	§ 1.3
Beamon v. City of Ridgeland, 666 F. Supp. 937 (S.D. Miss. 1987)	§§ 17.5, 18.15, App. C, App. E
Beaudry Motor Co. v. ABKO Properties, Inc., 780 F.2d 751 (9th Cir. 1986)	§ 24.4
Beck v. Kansas Adult Auth., 241 Kan. 13, 735 P.2d 222 (1987)	§ 5.2
Bee v. Greaves, 669 F. Supp. 372 (D. Utah 1987)	App. E
Behre v. Thomas, 665 F. Supp. 89 (D.N.H. 1987), *aff'd,* 843 F.2d 1385 (1st Cir. 1988)	§ 7.9
Bell v. City of Milwaukee, 746 F.2d 1205 (7th Cir. 1984)	§§ 11.2, 11.3
Bello v. Walker, 840 F.2d 1124 (3d Cir.), *cert. denied,* 109 S. Ct. 176 (1988)	§ 3.2
Beltran v. California, 857 F.2d 542 (9th Cir. 1988)	§§ 12.7, 12.8
Benavidez v. Gunnell, 722 F.2d 615 (10th Cir. 1983)	§§ 5.13, 7.8
Bender v. Williamsport Area School Dist., 475 U.S. 534 (1986)	§§ 2.4, 16.9
Bendiburg v. Dempsey, 692 F. Supp. 1354 (N.D. Ga. 1988)	§ 4.7
Bendt v. Tennessee, 796 F.2d 879 (6th Cir. 1986)	§ 10.6
Benigni v. City of Hemet, 853 F.2d 1519 (9th Cir. 1988)	§ 7.18

AUTHORITIES

Case	*Book §*
Blanchard v. Bergeron, 57 U.S.L.W. 4191 (U.S. Feb. 21, 1989)	§§ 16.14, 21.3
Blanchard v. Bergeron, 831 F.2d 563 (5th Cir. 1987), *cert. granted,* 108 S. Ct. 2869 (1988)	§ 21.3
Blaylock v. Schwinden, 862 F.2d 1352 (9th Cir. 1988)	§ 6.11
Blizzard v. Newport News Redevelopment, 635 F. Supp. 23 (E.D. Va. 1985)	App. E
Blount v. Redmond, 649 F. Supp. 319 (D. Me. 1986)	§ 12.8
Blum v. Stenson, 465 U.S. 886 (1984)	§§ 18.1, 18.7, 20.4A
Blum v. Witco Chem. Corp., 829 F.2d 367 (3d Cir. 1987)	§§ 17.6, 19.3, 20.4C, 20.4F, 24.3
Board of Educ. v. CNA Ins. Co., 839 F.2d 14 (2d Cir. 1988)	§ 21.6
Board of Educ. v. Diamond, 808 F.2d 987 (3d Cir. 1986)	§§ 3.2, 15.16
Board of Pardons v. Allen, 107 S. Ct. 2415 (1987)	§ 13.3
Board of School Directors v. Wisconsin, 649 F. Supp. 82 (E.D. Wis. 1985)	§ 6.6
Board of Trustees v. Mississippi Publishers Corp., 478 So. 2d 269 (Miss. 1985)	§ 15.17
Bodine v. Elkhart County Election Bd., 788 F.2d 1270 (7th Cir. 1986)	§§ 3.2, 3.5
Bohen v. City of East Chicago, 666 F. Supp. 154 (N.D. Ind. 1987)	§§ 18.14, 18.15, 19.3, 21.3, App. B, App. E
Bohen v. East Chicago, 799 F.2d 1180 (7th Cir. 1986)	§ 4.8
Bolden v. Alston, 810 F.2d 353 (2d Cir.), *cert. denied,* 108 S. Ct. 229 (1987)	§ 7.18
Bond v. Stanton, 630 F.2d 1231 (7th Cir. 1980)	§ 15.8
Bonitz v. Fair, 804 F.2d 164 (1st Cir. 1986)	§ 7.18
Bonnes v. Long, 599 F.2d 1316 (4th Cir. 1979)	§§ 15.13, 15.14
Borek v. Town of McLeansboro, 629 F. Supp. 657 (S.D. Ill. 1986)	§§ 3.2, 4.11
Borunda v. Richmond, 860 F.2d 937 (9th Cir. 1988)	§§ 3.4, 3.5, 3.7, 17.9
Bostick v. Rappleyea, 629 F. Supp. 1328 (N.D.N.Y. 1985)	§ 7.10
Boston Environmental Sanitation Inspections Ass'n v. Boston, 794 F.2d 12 (1st Cir. 1986)	§ 8.1
Boswell v. Sherburne County, 849 F.2d 1117 (8th Cir. 1988)	§§ 4.11, 7.13A
Bovey v. City of Lafayette, 638 F. Supp. 640 (N.D. Ind. 1986)	§§ 17.9, 17.15, 19.4, App. E
Braafladt v. Board of Governors, 778 F.2d 1442 (9th Cir. 1985)	§§ 15.13, 24.5
Bradberry v. Pinellas County, 789 F.2d 1513 (11th Cir. 1986)	§§ 3.2, 4.3
Bradley v. Fisher, 80 U.S. (13 Wall.) 335, 20 L. Ed. 646 (1871)	§ 7.3
Bradley v. Heckler, 785 F.2d 954 (11th Cir. 1986)	§ 15.14
Brady v. Gebbie, 859 F.2d 1543 (9th Cir. 1988)	§§ 7.18, 14.1
Brandman v. North Shore Guidance Center, 636 F. Supp. 877 (E.D.N.Y. 1986)	§ 8.2
Brandon v. Allen, 645 F. Supp. 1261 (W.D. Tenn. 1986)	§ 4.8, App. E
Brandon v. Holt, 469 U.S. 464 (1985)	§ 2.4
Brantley v. Surles, 804 F.2d 321 (5th Cir. 1986)	§§ 17.3, 17.9, 19.7, 21.2, App. E
Bray v. New York Life Ins., 851 F.2d 60 (2d Cir. 1988)	§§ 9.4, 9.5
Breault v. Chairman, 401 Mass. 26, 513 N.E.2d 1277 (1987), *cert. denied,* 108 S. Ct. 1078 (1988)	§§ 7.12, 7.18
Brennan v. Cunningham, 813 F.2d 1 (1st Cir. 1987)	§ 8.6

AUTHORITIES

Case	*Book §*
Bretz v. Kelmon, 773 F.2d 1026 (9th Cir. 1985)	§§ 3.6, 3.8
Brewster v. Dukakis, 786 F.2d 16 (1st Cir. 1986)	§§ 15.8, 16.3, 17.2, 17.3, 17.8, 17.15, 17.16, 17.17, 18.13, App. B, App. E
Bridgeman v. Nebraska State Penn, 849 F.2d 1076 (8th Cir. 1988)	§§ 10.6, 10.7
Bright v. Land O' Lakes, Inc., 844 F.2d 436 (7th Cir. 1988)	§ 21.4
Brinker v. Guiffrida, 798 F.2d 661 (3d Cir. 1986)	§§ 17.17, 18.6, 24.6
Brock v. Roadway Express, 107 S. Ct. 1740 (1987)	§ 13.5
Brookins v. General Motors, 843 F.2d 879 (6th Cir. 1987)	§ 9.8
Brooks v. Nance, 801 F.2d 1237 (10th Cir. 1986)	§ 12.13
Brotzler v. County of Scott, 427 N.W.2d 685 (Minn. Ct. App. 1988)	§ 6.2
Broussard v. CACI, Inc.-Federal, 634 F. Supp. 155 (D. Me. 1986)	App. E
Brower v. Inyo County, 817 F.2d 540 (9th Cir. 1987), *cert. granted,* 108 S. Ct. 2869 (1988)	§§ 3.3, 3.4, 3.8
Brown v. Allenstown, 648 F. Supp. 831 (D.N.H. 1986)	§ 6.2
Brown v. City of Clewiston, 848 F.2d 1534 (11th Cir. 1988)	§§ 3.4, 4.8
Brown v. City of Colorado Springs, 749 P.2d 475 (Colo. Ct. App. 1987)	App. M
Brown v. Eichler, 680 F. Supp. 138 (D. Del. 1988)	App. E
Brown v. Fauver, 819 F.2d 395 (3d Cir. 1987)	§§ 2.5, 8.6
Brown v. Foley, 810 F.2d 55 (3d Cir. 1987)	§ 10.7
Brown v. Freedman Baking Co., 810 F.2d 6 (1st Cir. 1987)	§§ 14.13, 15.6
Brown v. Hotel & Restaurant Employees Local 54, 468 U.S. 491 (1984)	§ 12.10
Brown v. Patterson, 823 F.2d 167 (7th Cir.), *cert. denied,* 108 S. Ct. 162 (1987)	§ 3.7
Brown v. Smith, 813 F.2d 1187 (11th Cir. 1987)	§ 3.4A
Brown v. Texas A&M Univ., 804 F.2d 327 (5th Cir. 1986)	§ 7.18
Brown v. Trench, 787 F.2d 167 (3d Cir. 1986)	§ 3.8
Brown v. Triche, 660 F. Supp. 281 (N.D. Ill. 1987)	§ 14.10
Brown v. United States, 851 F.2d 615 (3d Cir. 1988)	§ 7.18
Brown v. United States, 742 F.2d 1498 (D.C. Cir. 1984), *cert. denied,* 471 U.S. 1073 (1985)	§ 10.9
Browning v. Clerk, United States House of Representatives, 789 F.2d 923 (D.C. Cir.), *cert. denied,* 107 S. Ct. 601 (1986)	§ 7.10
Brumfield v. Jones, 849 F.2d 152 (5th Cir. 1988)	§ 3.7
Brunet v. City of Columbus, 642 F. Supp. 1214 (S.D. Ohio 1986)	§ 15.18
Brunken v. Lance, 807 F.2d 1325 (7th Cir. 1986)	§§ 3.5, 6.1, 6.5, 12.8
Bryant Ave. Tenants' Ass'n v. Koch, 511 N.Y.S.2d 279 (1st Dep't 1987), *aff'd,* 71 N.Y.2d 856, 527 N.Y.S.2d 743 (1988)	§ 1.3A
BSA, Inc. v. King County, 804 F.2d 1104 (9th Cir. 1986)	§§ 15.9, 15.10, 18.14, 24.5, App. E
Buckanan v. Stanships, Inc., 108 S. Ct. 1130 (1988)	§ 24.2
Buckhalter v. Pepsi-Cola Gen. Bottlers, 820 F.2d 892 (7th Cir. 1987)	§ 9.10
Budinich v. Becton Dickinson & Co., 108 S. Ct. 1717 (1988)	§ 24.4
Buggs v. Elgin, Joliet & E. Ry. Co., 852 F.2d 318 (7th Cir. 1988)	§ 24.2
Buise v. Hudkins, 584 F.2d 223 (7th Cir. 1978), *cert. denied,* 440 U.S. 916 (1979)	§ 3.2A

Case	*Book §*
Bung's Bar & Grille, Inc. v. Township Council of Florence, 206 N.J. Super. 432, 502 A.2d 1198 (1985)	§§ 15.17, 16.7, App. E
Burch v. Apalachee Community Mental Health Servs., 804 F.2d 1549 (11th Cir. 1986), *rev'd on other grounds,* 840 F.2d 797 (11th Cir. 1988)	§ 3.8
Burlington N., Inc., *In re,* 832 F.2d 422 (7th Cir. 1987)	§§ 15.8, 15.10, 15.13, 24.1, 24.5
Burlington N., Inc., *In re,* 832 F.2d 430 (7th Cir. 1987)	§§ 17.10, 19.5
Burlington N., Inc., *In re,* 618 F. Supp. 1046, *later opinion,* 810 F.2d 601 (7th Cir. 1986)	§§ 17.17, 18.17, 20.3, 20.5, 21.6, 24.1, 24.4, App. E, App. G, App. J
Burlington N. R.R. v. Brotherhood of Maintenance of Way Employees, 107 S. Ct. 1841 (1987)	§ 13.5
Burnett v. Grattan, 468 U.S.42 (1984)	§ 10.6
Burpee v. Manchester School Dist., 661 F. Supp. 731 (D.N.H. 1987)	§ 15.16
Burr v. Ambach, 683 F. Supp. 46 (S.D.N.Y.), *appeal dismissed for lack of jurisdiction,* 863 F.2d 1071 (2d Cir. 1988)	§§ 15.16, 24.4
Burr v. Town of Rangeley, 549 F.2d 733 (Me. 1988)	App. M
Burton v. Livingston, 791 F.2d 97 (8th Cir. 1986)	§ 3.3
Burton v. Wilmington Parking Auth., 365 U.S. 715 (1961)	§ 5.10
Busch v. Viterna, 795 F.2d 1203 (5th Cir. 1986)	§ 4.6
Buthy v. Commissioner of Office of Mental Health, 818 F.2d 1046 (2d Cir. 1987)	§ 8.6
Byers v. City of Reno, 663 F. Supp. 94 (D. Nev. 1987)	§ 4.6
Bygott v. Leaseway Transp. Corp., 637 F. Supp. 1433 (E.D. Pa. 1986)	§§ 18.5, 18.6, App. E
Byrd v. Clark, 783 F.2d 1002 (11th Cir. 1986)	§§ 3.2, 4.11
Byrd v. Stewart, 803 F.2d 1168 (11th Cir. 1986)	§ 3.8
Calhoun v. Acme Cleveland Corp., 801 F.2d 558 (1st Cir. 1986)	§§ 17.14, 17.15, 18.4, 24.3, App. D
Calhoun v. Forester, 675 F. Supp. 291 (W.D. Pa. 1987)	§ 21.5, App. E
California Ass'n of Physically Handicapped v. F.C.C., 721 F.2d 667 (9th Cir. 1983)	§ 15.13
Callaway v. Hafeman, 628 F. Supp. 1478 (W.D. Wis. 1986)	§ 7.10
Camarano v. City of N.Y., 624 F. Supp. 1144 (S.D.N.Y. 1986)	§ 4.12
Cameron v. City of Pontiac, 813 F.2d 782 (6th Cir. 1987)	§ 3.4
Cameron v. Fogarty, 806 F.2d 380 (2d Cir. 1986), *cert. denied,* 107 S. Ct. 1894 (1987)	§§ 3.7, 9.3
Campaign for a Progressive Bronx v. Black, 631 F. Supp. 975 (S.D.N.Y. 1986)	§§ 16.12, 16.13, 17.6, 18.9, App. E, App. F, App. K
Campain v. Marlboro Cent. School Dist. Bd. of Educ., 138 A.D.2d 914, 526 N.Y.S.2d 658 (1988)	App. M
Campbell v. City of Allen Park, 829 F.2d 576 (6th Cir. 1987)	§ 9.5
Campbell v. Maine, 787 F.2d 776 (1st Cir. 1986)	§ 7.8

Case	*Book §*
Campo v. Employees Retirement Sys., 843 F.2d 96 (2d Cir.), *cert. denied,* 109 S. Ct. 220 (1988)	§§ 3.8, 8.2
Cannady v. Valentin, 768 F.2d 501 (2d Cir. 1985)	§§ 12.11, 12.12
Cannon v. Taylor, 782 F.2d 947 (11th Cir. 1986)	§§ 3.5, 4.9
Canton, City of v. Harris, 109 S. Ct. _____, 57 U.S.L.W. 4270 (U.S. Feb. 28, 1989) (No. 86-1088)	§ 4.9
Capello v. District of Columbia Bd. of Educ., 669 F. Supp. 14 (D.D.C. 1987)	§ 15.16
Carey v. Continental Airlines, 823 F.2d 1402 (10th Cir. 1987)	§ 5.13
Carey v. Piphus, 435 U.S. 247 (1978)	§§ 14.5, 14.10
Carlin Communication v. Mountain States Tel. & Tel. Co., 827 F.2d 1291 (9th Cir. 1987), *cert. denied,* 108 S. Ct. 1586 (1988)	§§ 5.11, 5.12, 5.14
Carlin Communication v. Southern Bell Tel. & Tel. Co., 802 F.2d 1352 (11th Cir. 1986)	§§ 5.11, 5.14, 12.14
Carlson v. Conklin, 813 F.2d 769 (6th Cir. 1987)	§§ 3.2, 4.3, 7.18
Carlstadt Educ. Ass'n v. Mayor & Council, 219 N.J. Super. 164, 530 A.2d 34 (App. Div. 1987)	App. M
Carnegie-Mellon Univ. v. Cohill, 108 S. Ct. 614 (1988)	§§ 1.5, 1.8
Carras v. Williams, 807 F.2d 1286 (6th Cir. 1986)	§§ 7.4, 12.7
Carrero v. New York City Hous. Auth., 685 F. Supp. 904 (S.D.N.Y. 1988)	§ 21.8, App. E, App. F, App. K
Carroll v. Wilkerson, 782 F.2d 44 (6th Cir.), *cert. denied,* 107 S. Ct. 330 (1986)	§ 10.6
Carter v. City of Chattanooga, 850 F.2d 1119 (6th Cir. 1988), *cert. denied,* 109 S. Ct. 795 (1989)	§ 3.4
Carter v. District of Columbia, 795 F.2d 116 (D.C. Cir. 1986)	§§ 4.8, 14.10
Carter v. Three Unknown Police Officers, 112 F.R.D. 48 (D. Del. 1986)	§ 10.6
Cassettari v. Nevada County, 824 F.2d 735 (9th Cir. 1987)	§§ 3.10, 8.2
Cassiano v. Amigos Del Valle, 776 F.2d 1300 (5th Cir. 1985)	§ 5.14
Catchings v. City of Crystal Springs, 626 F. Supp. 987 (S.D. Miss. 1986)	§ 17.6, App. E
Catlett v. Missouri Highway & Transp. Comm'n, 828 F.2d 1260 (8th Cir. 1987), *cert. denied,* 108 S. Ct. 1574 (1988)	§§ 19.3, 19.4, 20.3
Central Mach. Co. v. State, 152 Ariz. 134, 730 P.2d 843 (1986)	§§ 3.2, 3.11, App. M
Cepulonis v. Registrars of Voters, 396 Mass. 808, 488 N.E.2d 1166 (1986)	§§ 15.7, 16.7
Cerbone v. Conway, 107 S. Ct. 390 (1986)	§ 3.6
Chalmers v. City of Los Angeles, 676 F. Supp. 1515 (C.D. Cal. 1987)	§§ 18.17, 20.4E, 20.5, App. E
Chalmers v. City of Los Angeles, 796 F.2d 1205 (9th Cir. 1986)	§§ 15.6, 17.3, 18.5, 18.6, 18.7, 18.10, App. E, App. K
Chamberlain v. Brown, 223 Tenn. 25, 442 S.W.2d 248 (1969), *overruled,* Poling v. Goins, 713 S.W.2d 305 (Tenn. 1986)	§ 1.6
Champion Int'l Corp. v. Brown, 731 F.2d 1406 (9th Cir. 1984)	§ 12.6
Chandler v. Presiding Judge, 838 F.2d 977 (8th Cir. 1988)	§ 10.6
Chapman v. Detroit, 808 F.2d 459 (6th Cir. 1986)	§ 1.3A
Chapoose v. Hodel, 831 F.2d 931 (10th Cir. 1987)	§ 5.6

Case	*Book §*
Chappell v. Wallace, 462 U.S. 296 (1983)	§§ 6.1, 7.17A
Charles v. Daley, 846 F.2d 1057 (7th Cir. 1988)	§§ 15.6, 16.11, App. B
Charles v. Daley, 799 F.2d 343 (7th Cir. 1986)	§ 24.4
Charlestown, Town of v. United States, 696 F. Supp. 800 (D.R.I. 1988)	§ 2.3
Checki v. Webb, 785 F.2d 534 (5th Cir. 1986)	§§ 3.3, 10.4
Chernin v. Welchans, 844 F.2d 322 (6th Cir. 1988)	§ 15.11
Chevron Oil Co. v. Huson, 404 U.S. 97 (1971)	§ 10.7
Chicago & N. Transp. Co. v. Ulery, 787 F.2d 1239 (8th Cir. 1986)	§ 7.18
Chicago College of Osteopathic Medicine v. George A. Fuller Co., 801 F.2d 908 (7th Cir. 1986)	§ 21.8
Chicipee Lions Club v. District Attorney, 396 Mass. 244, 485 N.E.2d 673 (1985)	§ 7.8
Childs v. Reynoldson, 777 F.2d 1305 (8th Cir. 1985)	§ 7.3
Chitty v. Walton, 680 F. Supp. 683 (D. Vt. 1987)	§ 7.6
Christ the King Regional High School v. Culvert, 815 F.2d 219 (2d Cir.), *cert. denied,* 108 S. Ct. 102 (1987)	§ 12.8
Church of Human Potential v. Vorsky, 636 F. Supp. 93 (D.N.J. 1986)	§ 5.6
Citizens for John W. Moore v. Board of Election Comm'rs, 781 F.2d 581 (7th Cir. 1986)	§ 6.6
City Consumer Servs., Inc. v. Horne, 631 F. Supp. 1050 (D. Utah 1986)	App. C, App. E
Clallam County v. Department of Transp., 849 F.2d 424 (9th Cir. 1988), *cert. denied,* 109 S. Ct. 790 (1989)	§ 3.11
Clark v. City of Los Angeles, 803 F.2d 987 (9th Cir. 1986)	§§ 15.6, 15.13, App. F
Clark v. Cohen, 794 F.2d 79 (3d Cir.), *cert. denied,* 107 S. Ct. 459 (1986)	§ 6.5
Clark v. Evans, 840 F.2d 876 (11th Cir. 1988)	§§ 7.13A, 7.16
Clark v. Link, 855 F.2d 156 (4th Cir. 1988)	§ 3.7
Clark v. Stach, 674 F. Supp. 969 (D. Conn. 1987)	App. E
Clark v. Tarvant County, 798 F.2d 736 (5th Cir. 1986)	§ 6.11
Clark v. Yosemite Community College Dist., 785 F.2d 781 (9th Cir. 1986)	§ 9.5
Clarke v. Washington Metro. Area Transit Auth., 654 F. Supp. 712 (D.D.C. 1985)	§ 6.11
Claus by Claus v. Goshert, 657 F. Supp. 237 (N.D. Ind. 1987)	§ 17.14, App. E
Clay v. Conlee, 815 F.2d 1164 (8th Cir. 1987)	§ 4.11
Cleary v. Commissioner of Pub. Welfare, 21 Mass. App. 140, 485 N.E.2d 955 (1985)	§ 15.13
Cleavinger v. Saxner, 106 S. Ct. 496 (1985)	§ 7.7
Cleveland Bd. of Educ. v. Loudermill, 470 U.S. 532 (1985)	§ 3.2
Client's Council v. Pierce, 778 F.2d 518 (8th Cir. 1985)	§§ 15.1, 15.15
Coates v. Bechtel, 811 F.2d 1045 (7th Cir. 1987)	§ 23.2
Coats v. Woods, 819 F.2d 236 (9th Cir.), *appeal dismissed & cert. denied,* 108 S. Ct. 46 (1987)	§ 12.15
Cobb v. Miller, 818 F.2d 1227 (5th Cir. 1987)	§§ 19.3, 19.5, 19.6, 21.2
Coe v. Ziegler, 817 F.2d 29 (6th Cir. 1987)	§ 7.18

Case	*Book §*
Coe v. Ziegler, 657 F. Supp. 182 (S.D. Ohio 1987)	§ 9.5
Coen v. Runner, 854 F.2d 374 (10th Cir. 1988)	§§ 7.12, 7.18
Coin Call v. Southern Bell Tel. & Tel. Co., 636 F. Supp. 608 (N.D. Ga. 1986)	§ 12.12
Colaizzi v. Walker, 812 F.2d 304 (7th Cir. 1987)	§ 7.13
Colburn v. Upper Darby Township, 838 F.2d 663 (3d Cir. 1988)	§§ 1.3A, 3.4B, 3.5
Cole v. Williams, 624 F. Supp. 712 (W.D. Ark. 1985)	App. B, App. E, App. J
Coleman v. McLaren, 635 F. Supp. 266 (N.D. Ill. 1986)	§§ 17.4, 17.6, 18.1, 18.12
Coleman v. McLaren, 631 F. Supp. 763 (N.D. Ill. 1986)	App. L
Coleman v. McLaren, 631 F. Supp. 749 (N.D. Ill. 1985)	§ 12.13
Coleman v. Smith, 814 F.2d 1142 (7th Cir. 1987)	§§ 4.13, 21.6
Coleman v. Turner, 838 F.2d 1004 (8th Cir. 1988)	§ 15.3
Collins v. Kendall County, 807 F.2d 95 (7th Cir. 1986), *cert. denied,* 107 S. Ct. 3228 (1987)	§§ 12.7, 12.9
Committee of United States Citizens Living in Nicaragua v. Reagan, 859 F.2d 929 (D.C. Cir. 1988)	§ 3.5
Commonwealth Bank & Trust Co. v. Russell, 825 F.2d 12 (3d Cir. 1987)	§ 4.3
Concerned Tenants Ass'n v. Pierce, 685 F. Supp. 316 (D. Conn. 1988)	§ 3.11
Conlon v. Long Beach, 676 F. Supp. 1289 (E.D.N.Y. 1987)	§ 3.11
Connecticut Legal Sources v. Heintz, 689 F. Supp. 82 (D. Conn. 1988)	§ 3.11
Conners, Estate of v. O'Connor, 846 F.2d 1205 (9th Cir. 1988)	§§ 3.5, 7.17
Connor v. Reinhard, 847 F.2d 384 (7th Cir.), *cert. denied,* 109 S. Ct. 147 (1988)	§§ 7.18, 9.12
Conservation Law Found. v. Secretary of Interior, 790 F.2d 965 (1st Cir. 1986)	§§ 15.20, 19.3, App. F, App. G
Consolidated Freightways Corp. v. Kassel, 730 F.2d 1139 (8th Cir.), *cert. denied,* 469 U.S. 834 (1984)	§ 15.15
Continental Life Ins. Co. v. Pierce County, 690 F. Supp. 930 (W.D. Wash. 1987)	§ 10.6
Coogon v. City of Wixom, 820 F.2d 170 (6th Cir. 1987)	§§ 9.3, 9.8
Cook v. Board of Educ., 671 F. Supp. 1110 (S.D. W. Va. 1987)	§ 9.10
Coollick v. Town of Windham, 7 Conn. 142, 508 A.2d 46 (Ct. App. 1986)	§ 3.8
Coon v. Ledbetter, 780 F.2d 1158 (5th Cir. 1986)	§ 4.10
Cooper v. Aaron, 358 U.S. 1 (1958)	§ 14.1
Cooper v. Dyke, 814 F.2d 941 (4th Cir. 1987)	§§ 14.13, 17.13, 19.6, 20.5, 21.2, 21.3, 24.6
Cooper v. Williamson County Bd. of Educ., 820 F.2d 180 (6th Cir. 1987), *cert. denied,* 108 S. Ct. 699 (1988)	§§ 15.8, 17.8, 17.9
Cooperman v. University Surgical Assocs., 32 Ohio St. 3d 191, 513 N.E.2d 288 (1987)	§ 6.1
Coos Bay Care Center v. Oregon Dep't of Human Resources, 803 F.2d 1060 (9th Cir. 1986), *vacated,* 108 S. Ct. 52 (1987)	§§ 3.11, 3.12
Corder v. Gates, 688 F. Supp. 1418 (C.D. Cal. 1988)	§§ 17.3, 21.4, App. E, App. F

Case	*Book §*
Cordero-Martinez v. Aponte-Roque, 685 F. Supp. 314 (D.P.R. 1988)	§ 3.11
Corn v. City of Lauderdale Lakes, 816 F.2d 1514 (11th Cir. 1987)	§ 3.10
Corselli v. Coughlin, 842 F.2d 23 (2d Cir. 1988)	§ 3.4A
Costello v. Town of Fairfield, 811 F.2d 782 (2d Cir. 1987)	§ 3.8
Coston v. Plitt Theatres, Inc., 831 F.2d 1321 (7th Cir. 1987)	§§ 19.4, 19.5
Cotton v. Mansour, 634 F. Supp. 1094 (E.D. Mich. 1986)	§§ 6.9, 6.11
Cougan v. City of Wixon, 820 F.2d 170 (5th Cir. 1987)	§ 3.6
Coulter v. State of Tennessee, 805 F.2d 146 (6th Cir. 1986)	§§ 17.1, 17.2, 17.10, 18.1, 18.5, 18.7, 24.5, App. B, App. C, App. E
Council for Periodical Distribs. Ass'ns v. Evans, 827 F.2d 1483 (11th Cir. 1987)	§§ 16.6, 16.13, 21.5
Counsel v. Dow, 849 F.2d 731 (2d Cir. 1988)	§§ 15.10, 15.16
Courtemanche v. Enlarged City School Dist., 686 F. Supp. 1025 (S.D.N.Y. 1988)	§ 10.9
Coverdell v. Department of Social & Health Servs., 834 F.2d 758 (9th Cir. 1987)	§§ 7.5, 7.8
Cowles v. Brownell, 127 A.D.2d 325, 515 N.Y.S.2d 131 (3d Dep't 1987)	§ 14.15
Cox v. American Cast Iron Pipe Co., 784 F.2d 1546 (11th Cir. 1986), *cert. denied,* 479 U.S. 883 (1986)	§ 24.4
Craft v. Wipf, 836 F.2d 412 (8th Cir. 1987)	§ 7.18
Craft v. Wipf, 810 F.2d 170 (8th Cir. 1987)	§ 7.18
Craig v. Ewing Township, 678 F. Supp. 1106 (D.N.J. 1988)	§ 10.6
Crane v. Commissioner of Pub. Welfare, 400 Mass. 46, 507 N.E.2d 751 (Sup. Jud. Ct. 1987)	§ 15.17, App. M
Crane v. Texas, 766 F.2d 193 (5th Cir.), *cert. denied,* 474 U.S. 1020 (1985)	§ 4.7
Crawford v. Texas Army Nat'l Guard, 794 F.2d 1034 (5th Cir. 1986)	§§ 7.17A, 8.3
Crawford Fitting Co. v. J.T. Gibbons, Inc., 107 S. Ct. 2494 (1987)	§ 21.8
Crawley v. Hamilton County Comm'rs, 744 F.2d 28 (6th Cir. 1984)	§ 12.11
Crazy Eddie v. Cotter, 666 F. Supp. 503 (S.D.N.Y. 1987)	§ 12.8
Creekside Assocs. v. City of Wood Dale, 684 F. Supp. 201 (N.D. Ill. 1988)	§ 7.10
Crest St. Community Council, Inc. v. North Carolina Dep't of Transp., 598 F. Supp. 258 (M.D.N.C. 1984), 769 F.2d 1025 (4th Cir. 1985), *rev'd,* 479 U.S. 6 (1986)	§§ 16.10, 17.9, 22.1, 24.2
Cronson v. Clark, 645 F. Supp. 793 (C.D. Ill. 1986), *aff'd,* 810 F.2d 662 (7th Cir.), *cert. denied,* 108 S. Ct. 199 (1987)	§ 12.8
Crooker v. Mulligan, 788 F.2d 809 (1st Cir. 1986)	§ 7.16
Crooks v. Maynard, 851 F.2d 1562 (9th Cir. 1988)	§ 7.3
Crooks v. Maynard, 820 F.2d 329 (9th Cir. 1987), *vacated,* 108 S. Ct. 744 (1988)	§ 7.3
Crossman v. Maccoccio, 806 F.2d 329 (1st Cir. 1986)	§ 21.4
Crossman v. Maccoccio, 792 F.2d 1 (1st Cir. 1986)	§ 24.4
Crot v. Byrne, 646 F. Supp. 1245 (N.D. Ill. 1986)	§ 9.10
Crump v. Lane, 807 F.2d 1394 (7th Cir. 1986)	§ 8.6

Case	***Book §***
Cuesnongle v. Ramos, 835 F.2d 1486 (1st Cir. 1987)	§§ 6.6, 12.3, 12.4
Culebras Enters. v. Rivera-Rios, 846 F.2d 94 (1st Cir. 1988)	§§ 16.6, 21.8
Culebras Enters. v. Rivera Rios, 813 F.2d 506 (1st Cir. 1987)	§§ 3.10, 5.13
Cullen v. Margiotta, 811 F.2d 698 (2d Cir.), *cert. denied,* 107 S. Ct. 3226 (1987)	§ 10.8
Cunningham v. City of McKeesport, 753 F.2d 262 (3d Cir. 1985), *vacated & remanded,* 478 U.S. 1015 (1986), *reinstated,* 807 F.2d 49 (3d Cir. 1986), *cert. denied,* 107 S. Ct. 2179 (1987)	§§ 16.3, 16.5, 16.14, 17.2, 17.17, 18.5, 18.10, 18.13, 19.7, 19.8, 21.3, 24.3, App. E
Cunningham v. City of Overland, 804 F.2d 1066 (8th Cir. 1986)	§§ 18.10, 18.14, App. E
Cunningham v. County of Los Angeles, 859 F.2d 705 (9th Cir. 1988)	§§ 15.13, 19.2, 19.5, 19.9
Curran v. Department of Treasury, 805 F.2d 1406 (9th Cir. 1986)	§ 18.1
Curry v. Baker, 802 F.2d 1302 (11th Cir.), *cert. dismissed,* 479 U.S. 1023 (1986)	§ 3.2
Curtis v. Bill Hanna Ford, Inc., 822 F.2d 549 (5th Cir. 1987)	§§ 17.17, 18.7, 24.3, App. C, App. E
Czikalla v. Malloy, 649 F. Supp. 1212 (D. Colo. 1986)	§ 7.8
Czura v. Supreme Court of Carolina, 632 F. Supp. 267 (D.S.C. 1986), *aff'd,* 813 F.2d 644 (4th Cir. 1987)	§ 1.4
Daggett v. Kimmelman, 617 F. Supp. 1269 (D.N.J. 1985), *modified,* 811 F.2d 793 (3d Cir. 1987)	§§ 15.6, 15.8, 15.15, 16.7, 16.13, 17.2, 17.4, 17.5, 17.6, 17.8, 18.4, 18.5, 18.7, 18.14, 18.15, 20.5, 24.2, App. B, App. C, App. E, App. G, App. I, App. K
Daigle v. City of Portsmouth, 534 A.2d 689 (N.H. 1987)	§ 15.17, App. M
Dale v. Janklow, 828 F.2d 481 (8th Cir. 1987), *cert. denied,* 108 S. Ct. 1486 (1988)	§ 3.3
Daloia v. Rose, 849 F.2d 74 (2d Cir.), *cert. denied,* 109 S. Ct. 242 (1989)	§ 7.9
Daly v. Hill, 790 F.2d 1071 (4th Cir. 1986)	§§ 17.2, 17.5, 17.10, 17.14, 18.6, 21.2, 21.8, App. D
Daly v. Hill, 635 F. Supp. 1270 (W.D.N.C. 1986)	§ 18.17
D'Amario v. Providence Civic Center Auth., 783 F.2d 1 (1st Cir. 1986)	§ 5.12
Dameron v. Sinai Hosp. of Baltimore, 644 F. Supp. 551 (D. Md. 1986)	§§ 18.8, 18.10
Daniel v. Ferguson, 839 F.2d 1124 (5th Cir. 1988)	§ 5.14
Daniels v. Stovall, 660 F. Supp. 301 (S.D. Tex. 1987)	§ 12.15

Case	*Book §*
Daniels v. Williams, 474 U.S. 327 (1986)	§ 3.4
Danielson v. Winnfield Funeral Home, 634 F. Supp. 1110 (E.D. La. 1986)	App. E
Dardar v. Lafourche Realty Co., Inc., 849 F.2d 955 (5th Cir. 1988)	§ 24.4
Darlak v. Bobear, 814 F.2d 1055 (5th Cir. 1987)	§ 6.11
Daryl H. v. Coler, 801 F.2d 893 (7th Cir. 1986)	§ 2.5
Dautremont v. Broadlawns Hosp., 827 F.2d 291 (8th Cir. 1987)	§§ 7.17, 10.6, 10.7
Davenport v. Saint Mary Hosp., 633 F. Supp. 1228 (E.D. Pa. 1986)	§§ 5.11, 5.14
Davey v. Tomlinson, 627 F. Supp. 1458 (E.D. Mich. 1986)	§ 3.8
David D. v. Dartmouth School Comm., 775 F.2d 411 (1st Cir. 1985), *cert. denied sub nom.* Massachusetts Dep't of Educ. v. David D., 475 U.S. 1140 (1986)	§ 15.16
Davidson v. Capuano, 792 F.2d 275 (2d Cir. 1986)	§ 9.4
Davidson v. City of Avon Park, 848 F.2d 172 (11th Cir. 1988)	§ 24.2
Davis v. City of Camden, 657 F. Supp. 396 (D.N.J. 1987)	§ 4.6
Davis v. City of Charleston, 827 F.2d 317 (8th Cir. 1987)	§§ 3.7, 9.3, 19.3, App. E
Davis v. City of Charleston, 635 F. Supp. 197 (E.D. Mo. 1986)	§§ 16.7, 18.3, 18.7, App. E
Davis v. Halpern, 813 F.2d 37 (2d Cir. 1987)	§ 9.4
Davis v. Harvey, 789 F.2d 1332 (9th Cir. 1986)	§§ 10.4, 10.6
Davis v. Herring, 800 F.2d 513 (5th Cir. 1986)	§ 12.9
Davis v. Holly, 835 F.2d 1175 (6th Cir. 1987)	§§ 7.12, 7.13A
Davis v. Lansing, 851 F.2d 72 (2d Cir. 1988)	§ 12.7
Davis v. Little, 851 F.2d 605 (2d Cir. 1988)	§§ 3.3, 3.4
Davis v. Mills, 777 F.2d 1524 (11th Cir. 1985)	§ 24.5, App. L
Davis v. Mobile Consortium of CETA, 857 F.2d 737 (11th Cir. 1988)	§ 3.11
Davis v. Richmond, Fredericksburg & Potomac R. Co., 803 F.2d 1322 (4th Cir. 1986)	§ 21.8
De Abadia v. Izquierdo Mora, 792 F.2d 1187 (1st Cir. 1986)	§ 7.18
Deakins v. Monoghan, 108 S. Ct. 523 (1988)	§ 12.7
Deane v. Dunbar, 777 F.2d 871 (2d Cir. 1985)	§ 7.15
Deary v. Guardian Loan Co., Inc., 623 F. Supp. 630 (S.D.N.Y. 1985)	§ 16.7
De Botton v. Marple Township, 689 F. Supp. 477 (E.D. Pa. 1988)	§ 7.10
DeCintio v. Westchester County Medical Center, 821 F.2d 111 (2d Cir.), *cert. denied,* 108 S. Ct. 455 (1987)	§ 9.10
Decker v. United States Dep't of Labor, 564 F. Supp. 1273 (E.D. Wis. 1983)	§ 16.11
Del A. v. Edwards, 855 F.2d 1148 (5th Cir.), *reh'g granted,* 862 F.2d 1107 (5th Cir. 1988)	§ 7.13A
Delahunty v. Hawaii, 677 F. Supp. 1052 (D. Haw. 1987)	§ 1.4

Case	*Book §*
Diver v. Goddard Memorial Hosp., 783 F.2d 6 (1st Cir. 1986)	§§ 17.3, 17.15, App. E
Dodd v. City of Norwich, 827 F.2d 1 (2d Cir. 1987), *cert. denied,* 108 S. Ct. 701 (1988)	§§ 3.4, 3.5, 4.6
Dodd v. Fort Smith Special School Dist., 666 F. Supp. 1278 (W.D. Ark. 1987)	§ 3.11
Dodds v. Simpson, 676 F. Supp. 1045 (D. Or. 1987)	§ 15.16
Doe v. Bobbitt, 682 F. Supp. 388 (N.D. Ill. 1988)	§ 1.5
Doe v. Bobitt, 665 F. Supp. 691 (N.D. Ill. 1987)	§ 5.5
Doe v. Cuddy, 21 Ohio App. 3d 270, 487 N.E.2d 914 (1985)	§ 15.17
Doe v. Department of Social Servs., 649 F.2d 134 (2d Cir. 1981), *cert. denied,* 464 U.S. 864 (1983)	§§ 3.2, 4.3
Doe v. Duling, 782 F.2d 1202 (4th Cir. 1986)	§ 2.5
Doe v. United Social & Mental Health Servs., 670 F. Supp. 1121 (D. Conn. 1987)	§ 7.6
Dominic v. Consolidated Edison Co., 822 F.2d 1249 (2d Cir. 1987)	§§ 19.4, 19.5, 21.3
Dominque v. Telb, 831 F.2d 673 (6th Cir. 1987)	§ 7.18
Donahey v. Wellman, 687 F. Supp. 194 (W.D. Pa. 1988)	§ 1.5
Donald M. v. Matava, 668 F. Supp. 714 (D. Mass. 1987)	§ 6.5
Donivan v. Dallastown Borough, 835 F.2d 486 (3d Cir. 1987), *cert. denied,* 108 S. Ct. 1596 (1988)	§ 7.10
Dorfman v. Department of Transp., 155 Mich. App. 57, 399 N.W.2d 437 (1986)	App. M
Dorman v. Higgins, 821 F.2d 133 (2d Cir. 1987)	§ 7.6
Dorsey v. City of Detroit, 858 F.2d 338 (6th Cir. 1988)	§ 1.8
Doss v. Long, 624 F. Supp. 1078 (N.D. Ga. 1985)	§§ 16.7, 16.8, 16.12, 17.13, App. E
Dotson v. City of Indianola, 639 F. Supp. 1056 (N.D. Miss. 1986)	§§ 17.4, 17.9, 17.10, 18.5, 18.7, App. E
Doty v. Carey, 626 F. Supp. 359 (N.D. Ill. 1986)	§ 3.9
Dowd v. City of New Richmond, 137 Wis. 2d 539, 405 N.W.2d 66 (1987)	App. M
Doyle v. Dukakis, 634 F. Supp. 1441 (D. Mass. 1986)	§ 6.5
Drake v. Pierce, 691 F. Supp. 264 (W.D. Wash. 1988)	§ 3.11
Drake v. Scott, 812 F.2d 395 (8th Cir.), *cert. denied,* 108 S. Ct. 455 (1987)	§ 7.18
Draper v. Coombs, 792 F.2d 915 (9th Cir. 1986)	§ 3.11
Drayton v. Hayes, 589 F.2d 117 (2d Cir. 1979)	§ 12.9
Duane M. v. Orleans Parish School Bd., 861 F.2d 115 (5th Cir. 1988)	§ 15.16
Duchesne v. Williams, 849 F.2d 1004 (6th Cir. 1988)	§ 3.2
Duckworth v. Franzen, 780 F.2d 645 (7th Cir. 1985), *cert. denied,* 107 S. Ct. 71 (1986)	§§ 6.1, 6.11
Duersherl v. Foley, 681 F. Supp. 1364 (D. Minn. 1987), *aff'd,* 845 F.2d 1027 (8th Cir. 1988)	§ 7.8
Dugan v. Ball State Univ., 815 F.2d 1132 (7th Cir. 1987)	§§ 10.6, 10.7
Dugan v. Brooks, 818 F.2d 513 (6th Cir. 1987)	§ 3.9
Duncan v. Peck. 844 F.2d 1261 (6th Cir. 1988)	§ 7.11
Duncan v. Poythress, 777 F.2d 1508 (11th Cir. 1985)	§§ 16.3, 18.1
Dunton v. Suffolk County, 729 F.2d 903 (2d Cir.), *amended on other grounds,* 748 F.2d 69 (2d Cir. 1984)	§ 4.13

Case	*Book §*
Duran v. Carruthers, 678 F. Supp. 839 (D.N.M. 1988)	§ 6.6
Durett v. Cohen, 790 F.2d 360 (3d Cir. 1986)	§§ 15.14, 16.7, 16.12, 16.13, 17.10, 19.5, 21.5, App. F, App. G
Dwyer v. Regan, 777 F.2d 825 (2d Cir. 1985), *modified,* 793 F.2d 457 (2d Cir. 1986)	§§ 3.8, 6.5, 16.8
Eades v. Sterlinske, 810 F.2d 723 (7th Cir.), *cert. denied,* 108 S. Ct. 143 (1987)	§§ 7.3, 7.5
Eades v. Thompson, 823 F.2d 1055 (7th Cir. 1987)	§ 10.7
East-Bibb Twiggs Neighborhood Ass'n v. Macon-Bibb Planning & Zoning Comm'n, 674 F. Supp. 1475 (M.D. Ga. 1987)	§ 23.2
East-Bibb Twiggs Neighborhood Ass'n v. Macon-Bibb Planning & Zoning Comm'n, 662 F. Supp. 1465 (M.D. Ga. 1987)	§ 3.10
Easter House v. Felder, 852 F.2d 901 (7th Cir.), *reh'g granted,* 861 F.2d 494 (7th Cir. 1988)	§§ 3.1, 3.6, 3.8, 5.13, 7.12, 7.13A
Easter House v. State of Ill. Dep't of Children, 663 F. Supp. 456 (N.D. Ill. 1987)	App. B, App. E
Eastwood v. Department of Corrections, 846 F.2d 627 (10th Cir. 1988)	§§ 7.13, 7.18
Economic Dev. Corp. v. Stierheim, 782 F.2d 952 (11th Cir. 1986)	§ 3.8
ECOS, Inc. v. Brinegar, 671 F. Supp. 381 (M.D.N.C. 1987)	§§ 15.2, 17.9, 17.14, 20.4D, App. E
Edmondson v. Leesville Concrete Co., 860 F.2d 1308 (5th Cir. 1988)	§ 5.14
Edward B. v. Brunelle, 662 F. Supp. 1025 (D.N.H. 1986)	§ 15.16
Edwards v. District of Columbia, 821 F.2d 651 (D.C. Cir. 1987)	§ 3.11
Edwards v. Jewish Hosp., 855 F.2d 1345 (8th Cir. 1988)	§ 14.13
Edwards v. Philadelphia, 860 F.2d 568 (3d Cir. 1988)	§ 3.3
E.E.O.C. v. Burlington N., Inc., 618 F. Supp. 1046 (N.D. Ill. 1985), *aff'd in relevant part,* 810 F.2d 601 (7th Cir. 1986)	§§ 17.7, 18.3, 18.4, 18.5, 18.6, 18.7, 21.5, App. G, App. I
E.E.O.C. v. Hamilton Standard Div., 637 F. Supp. 1155 (D. Conn. 1986)	§ 21.4
E.E.O.C. v. Kenneth Balk & Assocs., Inc., 813 F.2d 197 (8th Cir. 1987)	§ 23.2
E.E.O.C. v. Sears, Roebuck & Co., 111 F.R.D. 385 (N.D. Ill. 1986)	§ 17.16
Eggers v. Bullitt County School Dist., 854 F.2d 892 (6th Cir. 1988)	§§ 15.16, 16.3
Eilrich v. Remas, 839 F.2d 630 (9th Cir.), *cert. denied,* 109 S. Ct. 60 (1988)	§ 9.10
Eitel v. Holland, 798 F.2d 815 (5th Cir. 1986)	§ 12.11
Eitel v. Holland, 787 F.2d 995 (5th Cir. 1986)	§ 7.4
Ekanem v. Health & Hosp. Corp., 778 F.2d 1254 (7th Cir. 1985)	§§ 15.4, 15.6, 15.7, 15.10, 15.13, 15.20, 24.6
Elbe v. Yankton Indep. School Dist., 640 F. Supp. 1234 (D.S.D. 1986)	§ 15.17

Case	*Book §*
Eling v. Jones, 797 F.2d 797 (8th Cir. 1986), *cert. denied,* 107 S. Ct. 1371 (1987)	§ 5.5
Ellender v. Schweiker, 781 F.2d 314 (2d Cir. 1986)	§ 24.4
Elliott v. Hinds, 786 F.2d 298 (7th Cir. 1986)	§ 6.5
Elmore v. Shuler, 787 F.2d 601 (D.C. Cir. 1986)	§ 22.9
Elwood v. Rice, 423 N.W.2d 671 (Minn. 1988)	§ 7.16
Emery v. Holmes, 824 F.2d 143 (1st Cir. 1987)	§ 7.18
Emswiler v. McCoy, 622 F. Supp. 786 (S.D. W. Va. 1985)	§ 5.14
Eng v. Coughlin, 858 F.2d 889 (2d Cir. 1988)	§§ 6.3, 7.18
England v. Board of Medical Examiners, 375 U.S. 411 (1964)	§ 9.7
England v. Rockefeller, 739 F.2d 140 (4th Cir. 1984)	§ 7.18
Enright v. School Directors Bd., 118 Wis. 2d 236, 346 N.W.2d 771 (1984)	§ 3.8
Epstein v. Township of Whitehall, 693 F. Supp. 309 (E.D. Pa. 1988)	§§ 7.10, 12.12
Escamilla v. City of Santa Ana, 796 F.2d 266 (9th Cir. 1986)	§§ 3.2, 4.3
Esquivel v. Village of McCullom Lake, 633 F. Supp. 1199 (N.D. Ill. 1986)	§ 3.8
Estelle v. Gamble, 429 U.S. 97 (1976)	§ 5.5
Evans v. Jeff D., 475 U.S. 717 (1986)	§§ 22.5, 22.8, 24.1
Evans v. Little Bird, 656 F. Supp. 872 (D. Mont. 1987)	§ 5.6
Everett v. Schramm, 772 F.2d 1114 (3d Cir. 1985)	§ 6.6
EWAP, Inc. v. City of Ontario, 177 Cal. App. 3d 1108, 223 Cal. Rptr. 422 (1986)	§§ 15.4, 15.6, 16.12, 16.13
Exeter-West Greenwich Regional School Dist. v. Pontarelli, 788 F.2d 47 (1st Cir. 1986)	§§ 15.13, 15.17, 16.8, 17.9
Ezpeleta v. Sisters of Mercy Health Corp., 800 F.2d 119 (7th Cir. 1986)	§§ 5.8, 5.14
Ezzell v. Board of Regents, 838 F.2d 1569 (11th Cir. 1988)	§ 6.5
Fadhl v. City & County of San Francisco, 859 F.2d 649 (9th Cir. 1988)	§§ 20.4C, 20.4D
Fadhl v. City & County of San Francisco, 804 F.2d 1097 (9th Cir. 1986)	§§ 15.19, 20.4C, 20.4D
Fair Assessment in Real Estate Ass'n v. McNary, 454 U.S. 100 (1981)	§ 12.13
Fairley v. Jones, 824 F.2d 440 (5th Cir. 1987)	§ 14.13
Fallett v. United States Postal Serv., 644 F. Supp. 625 (N.D. Tex. 1986)	§ 3.11
Fargo v. San Juan Bautista, 857 F.2d 638 (9th Cir. 1988)	§ 3.5
Farid v. Smith, 850 F.2d 917 (2d Cir. 1988)	§§ 6.1, 6.11
Farmer v. Cook, 782 F.2d 780 (8th Cir. 1986)	§ 10.7
Farrish v. State Parole Bd., 836 F.2d 969 (5th Cir. 1988)	§ 7.6
Fay v. South Colonie Cent. School Dist., 802 F.2d 21 (2d Cir. 1986)	§§ 3.11, 3.12, 6.11, 9.4, 9.10
Feagin v. Broglin, 693 F. Supp. 741 (N.D. Ind. 1988)	§ 14.1
Feaster v. Miksch, 846 F.2d 21 (6th Cir. 1988)	§§ 7.18, 12.7

Case	*Book §*
Federal Home Loan Bank Bd. v. Empie, 778 F.2d 1447 (10th Cir. 1985)	§ 12.2
Federation of City Employees v. City of Birmingham, 492 So. 2d 1304 (Ala. 1986)	§ 15.17, App. M
Feeney v. Auger, 808 F.2d 1279 (8th Cir. 1986)	§ 8.6
Felder v. Casey, 108 S. Ct. 2302 (1988)	§§ 1.6, 6.1, 8.3, 10.2, 10.6, 10.9, 11.3, 16.8
Feliciano-Angulo v. Rivera-Cruz, 858 F.2d 40 (1st Cir. 1988)	§§ 7.12, 7.18
Fellowship Baptist Church v. Benton, 815 F.2d 485 (8th Cir. 1987)	§ 23.2
Felmeister v. Office of Attorney Ethics, 856 F.2d 529 (3d Cir. 1988)	§§ 8.3A, 12.12
Felts v. Radio Distrib. Co., 637 F. Supp. 234 (N.D. Ind. 1985)	App. E
Feres v. United States, 340 U.S. 135 (1950)	§§ 6.1, 7.17A
Fernandez v. Leonard, 784 F.2d 1209 (1st Cir. 1986)	§§ 3.3, 3.4, 7.13A
Fiacco v. City of Rensselaer, 783 F.2d 319 (2d Cir. 1986), *cert. denied,* 107 S. Ct. 1384 (1987)	§§ 4.9, 4.10
Fiacco v. City of Rensselaer, 663 F. Supp. 743 (N.D.N.Y. 1987)	§§ 17.6, 18.14, App. E
Fialkowski v. Greenwich Home for Children, 683 F. Supp. 103 (E.D. Pa. 1987)	§§ 5.11, 5.14
Fidelity Guar. Mortgage Corp. v. Reben, 809 F.2d 931 (1st Cir. 1987)	§§ 23.2, 24.2
Fields v. Durham, 856 F.2d 655 (4th Cir. 1988)	§ 3.8
Fields v. Rockdale County, 785 F.2d 1558 (11th Cir.), *cert. denied,* 107 S. Ct. 571 (1987)	§ 12.1
Fincher v. Department of Labor, 798 F.2d 1371 (11th Cir. 1986), *cert. denied,* 107 S. Ct. 1262 (1987)	§ 6.11
Firman v. Abreu, 691 F. Supp. 811 (S.D.N.Y. 1988)	§ 5.4
First Ala. Bank v. Parsons Steel, 825 F.2d 1475 (11th Cir. 1987), *cert. denied,* 108 S. Ct. 1015 (1988)	§ 12.8
First English Evangelical Lutheran Church v. Los Angeles County, 107 S. Ct. 2378 (1987)	§ 3.10
Fisher v. Stolaruk Corp., 110 F.R.D. 74 (E.D. Mich. 1986)	§ 21.4
Fite v. First Tenn. Prod. Credit Ass'n, 861 F.2d 884 (6th Cir. 1988)	§ 20.4E
Fitzgerald v. Larson, 769 F.2d 160 (3d Cir. 1985)	§ 10.6
Fitzgerald v. McDaniel, 833 F.2d 1516 (11th Cir. 1987)	§ 6.1
Fitzgerald v. Mountain Laurel Racing, 607 F.2d 589 (3d Cir. 1979), *cert. denied,* 446 U.S. 956 (1980)	§ 5.14
Fitzgerald v. Williamson, 787 F.2d 403 (8th Cir. 1986)	§ 3.3
Fleming v. County of Kane, 686 F. Supp. 1264 (N.D. Ill. 1988)	§§ 18.17, 20.5, App. F
Fleming v. Department of Pub. Safety, 837 F.2d 401 (9th Cir.), *cert. denied,* 109 S. Ct. 222 (1988)	§§ 5.2, 6.12
Fleming v. Moore, 780 F.2d 438 (4th Cir. 1985), *cert. denied,* 475 U.S. 1123 (1986)	§ 5.14
Flores v. Chicago, 682 F. Supp. 950 (N.D. Ill. 1988)	§ 10.8
Follette v. Vitanza, 658 F. Supp. 492 (N.D.N.Y.), *modified,* 658 F. Supp. 514 (N.D.N.Y.), *vacated in part,* 671 F. Supp. 1362 (N.D.N.Y. 1987)	§ 3.11
Folsom Inv. Co. v. Moore, 681 F.2d 1032 (5th Cir. 1982)	§ 7.11

Case	*Book §*
Fonte v. Board of Managers, 848 F.2d 24 (2d Cir. 1988)	§ 1.3A
Fontenot v. Louisiana Bd. of Elementary & Secondary Educ., 835 F.2d 117 (5th Cir. 1988)	§§ 15.16, 24.6
Fontenot v. Louisiana Bd. of Elementary & Secondary Educ., 805 F.2d 1222 (5th Cir. 1986)	§ 15.16
Ford v. Childers, 855 F.2d 1271 (7th Cir. 1988)	§§ 3.4, 4.6, 4.11
Ford v. Temple Hosp., 790 F.2d 342 (3d Cir. 1986)	§ 23.4
Forrester v. White, 108 S. Ct. 538 (1988)	§§ 7.2, 7.3, 7.8, 7.10
Foster v. Board of School Comm'rs, 810 F.2d 1021 (11th Cir.), *cert. denied,* 108 S. Ct. 99 (1987)	§§ 15.8, 19.4, 19.5
Foster v. Murphy, 686 F. Supp. 471 (S.D.N.Y. 1988)	§ 12.9
Foster v. Wyrick, 823 F.2d 218 (8th Cir. 1987)	§ 3.11
Foulds v. Coiley, 833 F.2d 52 (5th Cir. 1987)	§ 3.4A
Fountain v. Metropolitan Atlanta Rapid Transit, 849 F.2d 1412 (11th Cir. 1988)	§§ 3.10, 9.5
423 South Salina St., Inc. v. Syracuse, 68 N.Y.2d 474, 503 N.E.2d 63, 510 N.Y.S.2d 507, *appeal dismissed,* 107 S. Ct. 1880 (1987)	§ 10.6
Fowler v. Carrollton Pub. Library, 799 F.2d 976 (5th Cir. 1986)	§ 14.5
Fox v. Custis, 712 F.2d 84 (4th Cir. 1983)	§ 4.3
Francis v. Coughlin, 849 F.2d 778 (2d Cir. 1988)	§ 7.18
Franco v. Kelly, 854 F.2d 584 (2d Cir. 1988)	§§ 3.2A, 3.6
Franklin v. Aycock, 795 F.2d 1253 (6th Cir. 1986)	§ 3.5
Frank's Chicken House, Inc. v. Mayor & Council, 208 N.J. Super. 542, 506 A.2d 751 (1986)	App. E
Frantz v. United States Powerlifting Fed'n, 836 F.2d 1063 (7th Cir. 1987)	§ 16.15
Franza v. Abrams, 695 F. Supp. 747 (S.D.N.Y. 1988)	§§ 12.1, 12.8
Fraser v. Schultze, 663 F. Supp. 512 (N.D. Ill. 1987)	§ 4.4
Free v. Briody, 793 F.2d 807 (7th Cir. 1986)	§ 17.8
Freeman v. B&B Assocs., 790 F.2d 145 (D.C Cir. 1986)	§§ 21.4, 22.5, 24.1, 24.4
Freeman v. Blair, 793 F.2d 166 (8th Cir. 1986), *vacated,* 107 S. Ct. 3254 (1987)	§ 7.8
Freeman v. Rideout, 808 F.2d 949 (2d Cir. 1986), *reh'g denied,* 826 F.2d 194 (2d Cir. 1987), *cert. denied,* 108 S. Ct. 1273 (1988)	§ 3.6
Freeze v. Griffith, 849 F.2d 172 (5th Cir. 1988)	§§ 7.6, 7.9, 10.6
Frett v. Virgin Islands, 839 F.2d 968 (3d Cir. 1988)	§§ 4.4, 6.1
Friends of the Earth v. Eastman Kodak Co., 834 F.2d 295 (2d Cir. 1987)	§ 20.4D
Frisby v. Board of Educ., 707 S.W.2d 359 (Ky. Ct. App. 1986)	§ 10.6
Frost v. Hawkins County Bd. of Educ., 851 F.2d 822 (6th Cir.), *cert. denied,* 109 S. Ct. 529 (1988)	§ 4.6
Fuller v. State Bd. of Pardons & Paroles, 851 F.2d 1307 (11th Cir. 1988)	§ 7.6
Fuller Co. v. Ramon I. Gil, Inc., 782 F.2d 306 (1st Cir. 1986)	§§ 9.7, 12.5, 12.11
Fultz v. Neighborhood Legal Servs., 654 F. Supp. 881 (W.D. Pa. 1987)	§§ 3.11, 5.14
Fundiller v. Cooper City, 777 F.2d 1436 (11th Cir. 1985)	§§ 1.5, 3.2, 3.3, 3.9, 4.11
Furman v. Edwards, 657 F. Supp. 1243 (D. Vt. 1987)	§ 8.3
Furno v. Pignona, 522 A.2d 746 (Vt. 1986)	App. M

Case	*Book §*
Geter v. Fortenberry, 849 F.2d 1550 (5th Cir. 1988)	§§ 3.2, 7.13A, 7.18
Ghandi v. Police Dep't, 823 F.2d 959 (6th Cir. 1987), *cert. denied,* 108 S. Ct. 774 (1988)	§ 5.14
Giacolone v. Abrams, 850 F.2d 79 (2d Cir. 1988)	§ 7.18
Giannattasio v. Stamford Youth Hockey Ass'n, 621 F. Supp. 825 (D. Conn. 1985)	§§ 5.11, 5.14
Giano v. Flood, 803 F.2d 769 (2d Cir. 1986)	§ 9.4
Gibson v. Merced County Dep't of Human Resources, 799 F.2d 582 (9th Cir. 1986)	§ 7.17
Gibson v. United States, 781 F.2d 1334 (9th Cir. 1986), *cert. denied,* 107 S. Ct. 928 (1987)	§§ 3.2, 10.4, 10.6, 10.7
Gieseking v. Schafer, 672 F. Supp. 1249 (W.D. Mo. 1987)	§ 3.11
Gilbert v. Board of Medical Examiners, 155 Ariz. 169, 745 P.2d 617 (Ariz. Ct. App. 1987)	App. M
Giles v. Garwood, 853 F.2d 876 (11th Cir. 1988)	§ 10.6
Gillespie v. Crawford, 833 F.2d 47 (5th Cir. 1987)	§ 3.4A
Gillis, *In re,* 836 F.2d 1001 (6th Cir. 1988)	§ 12.13
Gilmore, Estate of v. Buckley, 787 F.2d 714 (1st Cir.), *cert. denied,* 107 S. Ct. 270 (1986)	§§ 3.2, 4.3
Gipson v. Rosenberg, 797 F.2d 224 (5th Cir. 1986)	§§ 17.14, 17.15
Gittens v. New York, 132 Misc. 2d 399, 504 N.Y.S.2d 969 (Ct. Cl. 1986)	§ 1.6
Gjellum v. City of Birmingham, 829 F.2d 1056 (11th Cir. 1987)	§ 9.10
Glenn v. General Motors Corp., 841 F.2d 1567 (11th Cir. 1988)	§ 21.8
Glover v. Johnson, 831 F.2d 99 (5th Cir. 1987)	§§ 10.4, 10.6
Glover v. City of Portland, 675 F. Supp. 398 (M.D. Tenn. 1987)	§§ 1.6, 12.11
Glymph v. Spartanburg Gen. Hosp., 783 F.2d 476 (4th Cir. 1986)	App. L
Goddard v. Urrea, 847 F.2d 765 (11th Cir. 1988)	§ 7.18
Goetz v. Ricketts, 632 F. Supp. 926 (D. Colo. 1986)	§§ 17.3, 17.5, 17.6, 17.15, App. E
Goff v. Nix, 803 F.2d 358 (8th Cir. 1986), *cert. denied,* 108 S. Ct. 115 (1987)	§ 2.5
Goichman v. City of Aspen, 859 F.2d 1466 (10th Cir. 1988)	§ 15.13
Golden State Transit Corp. v. Los Angeles, 857 F.2d 631 (9th Cir. 1988)	§§ 3.2, 3.11
Golemis v. Kirby, 632 F. Supp. 159 (D.R.I. 1985)	§ 3.10
Golkin v. Abrams, 803 F.2d 55 (2d Cir. 1986)	§ 9.5
Gonzales v. Jillson, 642 F. Supp. 908 (D. Mass. 1986)	§ 19.7, App. E
Gonzales v. Kangas, 814 F.2d 1411 (9th Cir. 1987)	§ 15.3
Gonzalez v. Pingree, 821 F.2d 1526 (11th Cir. 1987)	§ 3.11
Gonzalez Martinez v. Autoridad de Energia Electrica, 644 F. Supp. 364 (D.P.R. 1986), *vacated,* 831 F.2d 280 (1st Cir. 1987)	§ 8.1
Goodman v. Burris, 695 F. Supp. 973 (N.D. Ill. 1988)	§ 12.13
Goodman v. Lukens Steel Co., 107 S. Ct. 2617 (1987)	§ 10.7
Goodwin v. D'Elia, Matter of, 132 Misc. 2d 527 (Sup. Ct. Nassau County 1986)	App. M
Goolsby v. City of Montgomery, 805 F.2d 1008 (11th Cir. 1987)	§ 3.8
Gordon v. Norman, 788 F.2d 1194 (6th Cir. 1986)	§§ 4.13, 14.13
Gorelangton v. City of Reno, 638 F. Supp. 1426 (D. Nev. 1986)	§ 21.8, App. E
Graham v. City of Charlotte, 827 F.2d 945 (4th Cir. 1987), *cert. granted,* 109 S. Ct. 54 (1988)	§ 3.3

Case	*Book §*
Guider v. Smith, 157 Mich. App. 92, 403 N.W.2d 505 (Mich. Ct. App. 1987)	§ 3.4, App. M
Guiney v. Roache, 833 F.2d 1079 (1st Cir. 1987)	§ 12.3
Gulfstream Aerospace Corp. v. Mayacamas Corp., 108 S. Ct. 1133 (1988)	§ 12.11
Gumz v. Morrissette, 772 F.2d 1395 (7th Cir. 1985), *cert. denied,* 106 S. Ct. 1644 (1986)	§ 3.3
Gunby v. Pennsylvania Elec. Co., 840 F.2d 1108 (3d Cir. 1988)	§ 14.9
Gutierrez v. Coughlin, 841 F.2d 484 (2d Cir. 1988)	§§ 9.3, 9.8, 9.12
Gutierrez v. Municipal Court, 838 F.2d 1031 (9th Cir. 1988)	§§ 7.10, 7.12
Gutzwiller v. Fenik, 860 F.2d 1317 (6th Cir. 1988)	§§ 14.1, 14.2
G. Waltney of Smithfield v. Chesapeake Bay Found., 108 S. Ct. 376 (1987)	§ 13.4
Hadi v. Horn, 830 F.2d 779 (7th Cir. 1987)	§ 6.1
Hagee v. City of Evanston, 729 F.2d 510 (7th Cir. 1984)	§ 9.5
Hagge v. Bauer, 827 F.2d 101 (7th Cir. 1987)	§§ 14.10, 21.3
Haile v. Village of Sag Harbor, 639 F. Supp. 718 (E.D.N.Y. 1986)	§§ 4.12, 6.2, 14.13
Haitian Refugee Center v. Meese, 644 F. Supp. 382 (S.D. Fla. 1984), *aff'd,* 791 F.2d 1489 (11th Cir.), *as amended,* 804 F.2d 1573 (11th Cir. 1986)	§§ 15.18, 21.9, 24.4, App. D
Hale v. City of Seattle, 48 Wash. App. 451, 739 P.2d 723 (1987)	App. M
Hale v. Harney, 786 F.2d 688 (5th Cir. 1986)	§ 1.4
Hale v. Walsh, 113 Idaho 759, 747 P.2d 1288 (Ct. App. 1987)	App. M
Hall v. Ochs, 817 F.2d 920 (lst Cir. 1987)	§§ 7.13, 14.10, 14.13, 14.14, 14.15, 15.6, 18.8, 20.3, App. E
Hall v. Six Unknown Named Agents, 647 F. Supp. 136 (N.D.N.Y. 1986), *rev'd in part, aff'd in part,* 825 F.2d 642 (2d Cir. 1987)	§ 14.1
Hamer v. Lake County, 819 F.2d 1362 (7th Cir. 1987)	§§ 12.13, 23.2, 23.3
Hamilton v. Daley, 777 F.2d 1207 (7th Cir. 1985)	§§ 18.1, 23.5, App. E, App. L
Hamilton v. Rodgers, 791 F.2d 439 (5th Cir. 1986)	§ 4.8
Hamilton v. Smith, 808 F.2d 36 (10th Cir. 1986)	§ 14.18
Hamman v. Southwestern Gas Pipeline, Inc., 832 F.2d 55 (5th Cir. 1987)	§§ 15.6, 15.17
Hammond v. Bales, 843 F.2d 1320 (10th Cir. 1988)	§ 14.15
Hammond v. County of Madera, 859 F.2d 797 (9th Cir. 1988)	§ 3.5
Hand v. Gary, 838 F.2d 1420 (5th Cir. 1988)	§§ 3.6, 3.7
Hanner v. Mississippi, 833 F.2d 55 (5th Cir. 1987)	§ 10.7
Hanrahan v. Hampton, 446 U.S. 754 (1980)	§ 15.4
Hanrahan v. Lane, 747 F.2d 1137 (7th Cir. 1984)	§ 3.6
Hanson v. Heckel, 791 F.2d 93 (7th Cir. 1986)	§ 8.6
Hanson v. Madison Serv. Corp., 125 Wis. 2d 138, 370 N.W.2d 586 (Ct. App. 1985)	§ 10.6
Hardin v. Straub, 836 F.2d 549 (6th Cir. 1987), *cert. granted,* 109 S. Ct. 217 (1988)	§ 10.8
Hardin v. White Mountain Apache Tribe, 761 F.2d 1285 (9th Cir. 1985), *amended,* 799 F.2d 476 (9th Cir. 1985)	App. L
Harlow v. Fitzgerald, 457 U.S. 800 (1982)	§§ 7.12, 7.18

Case	*Book §*
Harper v. Jeffries, 808 F.2d 281 (3d Cir. 1986)	§§ 7.6, 8.6
Harper v. Washington, 110 Wash. 2d 873, 759 P.2d 358 (1988)	§ 7.12
Harpole v. Arkansas Dep't of Human Servs., 820 F.2d 923 (8th Cir. 1987)	§§ 4.3, 11.3
Harris v. Arkansas Book Co., 794 F.2d 358 (8th Cir. 1986)	§ 5.11
Harris v. Birmingham Bd. of Educ., 817 F.2d 1525 (11th Cir. 1987)	§ 1.8
Harris v. City of Canton, 798 F.2d 1414 (6th Cir. 1986), *cert. granted,* 108 S. Ct. 1105 (1988)	§ 4.9
Harris v. City of Pagedale, 821 F.2d 499 (8th Cir.), *cert. denied,* 108 S. Ct. 504 (1987)	§§ 4.8, 4.10, 14.6
Harris v. Deveaux, 780 F.2d 911 (11th Cir. 1986)	§ 7.3
Harris v. Maynard, 843 F.2d 414 (10th Cir. 1988)	§§ 3.4A, 3.5
Harris v. McCarthy, 790 F.2d 753 (9th Cir. 1986)	§§ 15.13, 15.17, 15.20, 17.9, 17.10, 18.5, 19.5, 21.2, 24.4, App. B
Harris v. Missouri Conservation Comm'n, 790 F.2d 678 (8th Cir. 1986)	§§ 3.8, 3.10
Harris v. Missouri Court of Appeals, 787 F.2d 427 (8th Cir.), *cert. denied,* 107 S. Ct. 179 (1986)	§§ 5.2, 6.3
Harrison v. Texas Dep't of Corrections, 694 F. Supp. 226 (E.D. Tex. 1988)	§ 1.8
Hart v. Bourque, 608 F. Supp. 1091 (D. Mass. 1985), *rev'd & remanded on other grounds,* 798 F.2d 519 (1st Cir. 1986)	§§ 17.2, 17.3, 17.4, 17.5, 17.6, 17.13, 18.5, 18.6, 18.8, 18.10, 20.5, 24.5, App. B, App. C, App. E, App. F, App. I
Hartley v. Fine, 780 F.2d 1383 (8th Cir. 1985)	§§ 7.11, 7.18
Hartshorn v. Heydinger, 647 F. Supp. 73 (S.D. W. Va. 1986)	§ 12.12
Harvey v. Little Rock, 787 F.2d 1223 (8th Cir. 1986)	§ 3.2
Haskins v. City of Boaz, 822 F.2d 1014 (11th Cir. 1987)	§ 14.1
Haskins v. Stanton, 794 F.2d 1273 (7th Cir. 1986)	§ 3.12
Haskins v. United States Dep't of Army, 808 F.2d 1192 (6th Cir. 1987)	§ 15.11
Hassett v. Lemay Bank & Trust Co., 851 F.2d 1127 (8th Cir. 1988)	§ 5.14
Hawaii Tel. Co. v. Public Utils. Comm'n, 827 F.2d 1264 (9th Cir. 1987), *cert. denied,* 108 S. Ct. 2870 (1988)	§ 12.14
Hawk v. Perillo, 642 F. Supp. 380 (N.D. Ill. 1985)	§ 3.2
Hawkins v. Steingut, 829 F.2d 317 (2d Cir. 1987)	§ 7.13
Hayes v. Vessey, 777 F.2d 1149 (6th Cir. 1985)	§§ 3.8, 3.9, 4.3
Haynesworth v. Miller, 820 F.2d 1245 (D.C. Cir. 1987)	§§ 3.6, 4.11, 7.8, 14.15
Hays v. Jefferson County, 668 F.2d 869 (6th Cir.), *cert. denied,* 459 U.S. 833 (1982)	§ 4.9
Headley v. Bacon, 828 F.2d 1272 (8th Cir. 1987)	§§ 9.8, 9.12
Healy v. Town of Pembroke Park, 831 F.2d 989 (11th Cir. 1987)	§§ 7.10, 9.10, 15.4
Healy v. Town of Pembroke Park, 643 F. Supp. 1208 (S.D. Fla. 1986)	§ 15.11
Heath v. Brown, 858 F.2d 1092 (5th Cir. 1988)	§ 15.13
Heath v. Brown, 807 F.2d 1229 (5th Cir. 1987)	§§ 15.13, 15.17, 24.5

Case	*Book §*
Heath v. Henning, 854 F.2d 6 (2d Cir. 1988)	§§ 3.3, 3.4
Hefner v. Alexander, 779 F.2d 277 (5th Cir. 1985)	§ 1.4
Heiar v. Crawford County, 746 F.2d 1190 (7th Cir. 1984)	§ 21.8
Heine v. Connelly, 644 F. Supp. 1508 (D. Del. 1986)	§ 7.16
Helms v. Hewitt, 780 F.2d 367 (3d Cir. 1986), *rev'd on other grounds,* 107 S. Ct. 2672 (1987)	§§ 15.4, 15.6, 15.9, 15.12, 15.14, 15.18
Helton v. Clements, 832 F.2d 332 (5th Cir. 1987)	§§ 10.4, 10.6
Helton v. Clements, 787 F.2d 1026 (5th Cir. 1986)	§ 7.18
Henderson v. Idaho, 110 Idaho 318, 715 P.2d 978, *cert. denied,* 106 S. Ct. 3282 (1986)	§ 10.6
Henderson v. Lopez, 790 F.2d 44 (7th Cir. 1986)	§ 7.8
Henry v. Farmer City State Bank, 808 F.2d 1228 (7th Cir. 1986)	§ 7.5
Henry v. Gross, 803 F.2d 757 (2d Cir. 1986)	§ 15.9
Hensley v. Carey, 633 F. Supp. 1251 (N.D. Ill. 1986)	§ 3.2
Hensley v. Corey, 818 F.2d 646 (7th Cir.), *cert. denied,* 108 S. Ct. 456 (1987)	§ 3.2
Hensley v. Eckerhart, 461 U.S. 424 (1983)	§§ 15.11, 17.10, 19.2, 19.5
Hensley v. Wilson, 850 F.2d 269 (6th Cir. 1988)	§ 7.13
Hernandez v. Estelle, 788 F.2d 1154 (5th Cir. 1986)	§ 7.18
Hernandez v. George, 793 F.2d 264 (10th Cir. 1986)	§§ 17.10, 17.16, 18.11, 24.2, App. F
Hernandez v. Hill Country Tel. Coop., Inc., 849 F.2d 139 (5th Cir. 1988)	§ 19.7
Hernandez v. Spencer, 780 F.2d 504 (5th Cir. 1986)	§ 8.6
Herren v. Bowyer, 850 F.2d 1543 (11th Cir. 1988)	§ 7.16
Herrera v. Valentine, 653 F.2d 1220 (8th Cir. 1981)	§ 14.6
Herrington v. Sonoma County, 834 F.2d 1488 (9th Cir. 1987)	§ 3.10
Herrington v. Sonoma County, 655 F. Supp. 1111 (N.D. Cal. 1987)	§ 16.3
Hershinow v. Bonamarte, 772 F.2d 394 (7th Cir. 1985)	App. L
Hewitt v. Helms, 107 S. Ct. 2672 (1987)	§§ 15.4, 15.6, 15.9, 15.10, 15.12, 15.14, 15.18
Hickey v. Duffy, 827 F.2d 234 (7th Cir. 1987)	§ 12.6
Hicks v. Southern Md. Health Sys. Agency, 805 F.2d 1165 (4th Cir. 1986)	§§ 23.2, 24.2, 24.4
Hidahl v. Gilpin County Dep't of Social Servs., 699 F. Supp. 846 (D. Colo. 1988)	§ 23.2
Hidle v. Geneva County Bd. of Educ., 681 F. Supp. 752 (M.D. Ala. 1988)	§§ 20.4C, 20.4D, App. E
Higgs v. District Court, 713 P.2d 840 (Colo. 1985)	§ 7.8
Hight v. Burden, 180 Ga. 716, 350 S.E.2d 471 (Ct. App. 1986)	§ 3.8
Higley v. Michigan Dep't of Corrections, 835 F.2d 623 (6th Cir. 1987)	§ 10.8
Hikel v. King, 659 F. Supp. 337 (E.D.N.Y. 1987)	§ 3.8
Hill v. Coca Cola Bottling Co., 786 F.2d 550 (2d Cir. 1986)	§§ 9.4, 9.8
Hill v. Department of Corrections, 513 So. 2d 129 (Fla. 1987), *cert. denied,* 108 S. Ct. 1024 (1988)	§ 6.1
Hill v. Ogburn, 812 F.2d 679 (11th Cir. 1987)	§ 3.11

Case	*Book §*
Hill v. Southside Pub. Schools, 688 F. Supp. 493 (E.D. Ark. 1988)	App. E
Hillburn v. Commissioner, Conn. Dep't of Income Maintenance, 683 F. Supp. 23 (D. Conn. 1987)	§§ 18.17, 21.8, App. E
Hillman Flying Serv. v. City of Roanoke, 652 F. Supp. 1142 (W.D. Va. 1987)	§ 3.11
Himple v. Moore, 673 F. Supp. 758 (E.D. Va. 1987)	§ 3.4
Hinojosa v. City of Terrell, 834 F.2d 1223 (5th Cir. 1988)	§ 3.3
Hinshaw v. Doffer, 785 F.2d 1260 (5th Cir. 1986)	§§ 3.7, 14.10, 14.14
Hobson v. Wilson, 737 F.2d 1 (D.C. Cir. 1984), *cert. denied,* 470 U.S. 1084 (1985)	§§ 1.3A, 7.12
Hodorowski v. Ray, 844 F.2d 1210 (5th Cir. 1988)	§ 7.8
Hoffman v. McNamara, 688 F. Supp. 830 (D. Conn. 1988)	§ 14.14
Hogue v. Clinton, 791 F.2d 1318 (8th Cir.), *cert. denied,* 107 S. Ct. 648 (1986)	§ 14.5
Holdeman v. Consolidated Rail Corp., 649 F. Supp. 1188 (N.D. Ind. 1986), *aff'd,* 840 F.2d 20 (7th Cir. 1988)	§ 4.4
Holdiness v. Stroud, 808 F.2d 417 (5th Cir. 1987)	§§ 5.6, 6.1, 7.17A
Hollins v. Powell, 773 F.2d 191 (8th Cir. 1985), *cert. denied,* 106 S. Ct. 1635 (1986)	§§ 4.7, 14.13
Hollins v. Wessel, 819 F.2d 1073 (11th Cir. 1987)	§ 7.4
Holloway v. Lockhart, 813 F.2d 874 (8th Cir. 1987)	§ 9.12
Holloway v. Walker, 790 F.2d 1170 (5th Cir.), *cert. denied,* 107 S. Ct. 571 (1986)	§ 3.8
Holloway v. Walker, 784 F.2d 1294 (5th Cir. 1986)	§ 23.2, App. L
Holly v. Housing Auth., 684 F. Supp. 1363 (E.D. La. 1988)	§ 3.11
Holman v. Walls, 648 F. Supp. 947 (D. Del. 1986)	§§ 1.5, 6.3, 6.6, 14.14
Holt v. Castaneda, 832 F.2d 123 (9th Cir. 1987), *cert. denied,* 108 S. Ct. 1275 (1988)	§ 7.9
Honig v. Doe, 108 S. Ct. 592 (1988)	§ 13.5
Hontz v. State, 105 Wash. 2d 302, 714 P.2d 1176 (1986)	§ 5.2
Horne v. Clemens, 25 Ohio App. 3d 44, 495 N.E.2d 441 (1985)	App. E
Hornung v. Village of Park Forrest, 634 F. Supp. 540 (N.D. Ill. 1986)	§§ 4.12, 9.3
Horwitz v. State Bd. of Medical Examiners, 822 F.2d 1508 (10th Cir. 1987), *cert. denied,* 108 S. Ct. 453 (1988)	§ 7.8
Hossman v. Spradlin, 812 F.2d 1019 (7th Cir. 1987)	§ 3.8
Housatonic Cable Vision v. Department of Pub. Util. Control, 622 F. Supp. 798 (D. Conn. 1985)	§ 12.2
Houston, City of v. Hill, 107 S. Ct. 2502 (1987)	§§ 2.5, 12.3, 12.4
Howard v. City of Greenwood, 783 F.2d 1311 (5th Cir. 1986)	§ 2.5
Howard v. International Molders & Allied Workers Union, 779 F.2d 1546 (11th Cir. 1986)	§§ 15.18, 24.4
Howard v. Regional Transit Auth., 667 F. Supp. 540 (N.D. Ohio 1987)	§ 3.7
Howard Gault Co. v. Texas Rural Legal Aid, 848 F.2d 544 (5th Cir. 1988)	§§ 5.12-5.14, 7.8, 7.11
Howe v. Baker, 796 F.2d 1355 (11th Cir. 1986)	§ 15.11
Howerton v. Gabica, 708 F.2d 380 (9th Cir. 1983)	§ 7.11

Case	*Book §*
Howland v. Kilquist, 833 F.2d 639 (7th Cir. 1987)	§ 3.2A
Hubby v. Historic Savannah Found., Inc., 623 F. Supp. 637 (S.D. Ga. 1985)	App. E
Hudak v. D'Elia, 120 A.D.2d 667, 502 N.Y.S.2d 261 (2d Dep't 1986)	§ 2.2
Hudson v. S.D. Warren Co., 665 F. Supp. 937 (D. Me. 1987)	§ 5.13
Huertas v. East River Hous. Corp., 813 F.2d 580 (2d Cir. 1987)	§§ 22.5, 22.10
Huggins v. Isenbarger, 798 F.2d 203 (7th Cir. 1986)	§ 8.6
Hughes v. Halifax County School Bd., 855 F.2d 183 (4th Cir. 1988), *cert. denied,* 109 S. Ct. 867 (1989)	§§ 3.2A, 4.7
Hughes v. Sheriff, 814 F.2d 532 (8th Cir.), *appeal dismissed & cert. denied,* 108 S. Ct. 46 (1987)	§§ 10.6, 10.8
Humphrey v. Gross, 135 A.D.2d 634, 522 N.Y.S.2d 213 (1987)	App. M
Hunt v. Robeson County Dep't of Social Servs., 816 F.2d 150 (4th Cir. 1987)	§ 3.11
Hunt v. Washington Apple Advertising Comm'n, 432 U.S. 333 (1977)	§ 2.6
Hunter v. Allis-Chalmers Corp., 797 F.2d 1417 (7th Cir. 1986)	§ 14.16
Hurley, Guardianship of, 394 Mass. 554, 476 N.E.2d 941 (1985)	§ 1.3A
Huron Valley Hosp. v. City of Pontiac, 686 F. Supp. 608 (E.D. Mich. 1988)	§ 3.8
Hurt v. G.C. Murphy, 624 F. Supp. 512 (S.D. W. Va. 1986)	§ 5.13
Hussein v. Oshkosh Motor Truck Co., 816 F.2d 348 (7th Cir. 1987)	§ 14.2
Hutchinson v. Miller, 797 F.2d 1279 (4th Cir. 1986), *cert. denied,* 107 S. Ct. 1295 (1987)	§ 3.2
Hutto v. Finney, 437 U.S. 678 (1978)	§§ 15.16, 18.17
Hyatt v. Heckler, 618 F. Supp. 227 (W.D.N.C. 1985), *aff'd,* 807 F.2d 376 (4th Cir. 1986), *cert. denied,* 108 S. Ct. 79 (1987)	§§ 15.14, 18.16, App. E, App. F
Hynson v. City of Chester, 684 F. Supp. 1294 (E.D. Pa. 1988)	§ 1.5
Hynson v. City of Chester, 827 F.2d 932 (3d Cir. 1987), *cert. denied,* 108 S. Ct. 702 (1988)	§ 7.18
I.A. Durbin, Inc. v. Jefferson Nat'l Bank, 793 F.2d 1541 (11th Cir. 1986)	§§ 7.12, 12.11
Ibarra v. Texas Employment Comm'n, 823 F.2d 873 (5th Cir. 1987)	§ 6.6
Imbler v. Pachtman, 424 U.S. 409 (1976)	§ 14.15
Indiana Hosp. Licensing v. Women's Pavilion, 486 N.E.2d 1070 (Ind. Ct. App. 1985)	App. E
Inmates v. Barry, 844 F.2d 828 (D.C. Cir. 1988)	§ 14.1
International Ass'n of Machinists v. Affleck, 504 A.2d 468 (R.I. 1986)	§ 15.17
International Olympic Comm. v. San Francisco Arts & Athletics, Inc., 781 F.2d 733 (9th Cir.), *aff'd on other grounds,* 107 S. Ct. 2971 (1987)	§ 5.14
International Org. of Masters, Mates & Pilots v. Andrews, 831 F.2d 843 (9th Cir. 1987), *cert. denied,* 108 S. Ct. 1228 (1988)	§ 3.2

Case	*Book §*
J.G. v. Board of Educ., 830 F.2d 444 (2d Cir. 1987)	§§ 8.3, 15.16, 21.5
J.L. v. Massinga, 838 F.2d 118 (4th Cir. 1988), *cert. denied,* 109 S. Ct. 816 (1989)	§§ 3.11, 7.13A
Jodeco v. Hahn, 674 F. Supp. 488 (D.N.J. 1987)	§ 7.10
John Does 1-100 v. Ninneman, 634 F. Supp. 341 (D. Minn. 1986)	§§ 15.18, 15.19
John H. v. Brunelle, 631 F. Supp. 208 (D.N.H. 1986)	§ 15.16
Johnson v. Barker, 799 F.2d 1396 (9th Cir. 1986)	§ 3.6
Johnson v. Carroll, 694 F. Supp. 500 (N.D. Ill. 1988)	§ 3.2
Johnson v. Chapel Hill Indep. School Dist., 853 F.2d 375 (5th Cir. 1988)	§ 14.1
Johnson v. Glick, 481 F.2d 1028 (2d Cir.), *cert. denied,* 414 U.S. 2033 (1973)	§ 3.4A
Johnson v. Moral, 843 F.2d 846 (5th Cir. 1988)	§ 3.3
Johnson v. New York City Transit Auth., 823 F.2d 31 (2d Cir. 1987)	§ 23.5
Johnson v. Orr, 780 F.2d 386 (3d Cir.), *cert. denied,* 107 S. Ct. 107 (1986)	§ 5.6
Johnson v. Pfeiffer, 821 F.2d 1120 (5th Cir. 1987)	§ 8.6
Johnson v. Rhode Island Parole Bd. Members, 815 F.2d 5 (1st Cir. 1987)	§ 7.6
Johnson, Estate of v. Village of Libertyville, 819 F.2d 174 (7th Cir. 1987)	§ 11.3
Johnston v. Penrod Drilling Co., 803 F.2d 867 (5th Cir. 1986)	§ 21.4
Jones v. American State Bank, 857 F.2d 494 (8th Cir. 1988)	§ 17.9
Jones v. Board of Governors, 790 F.2d 1120 (4th Cir. 1986)	App. E
Jones v. Bowman, 664 F. Supp. 433 (N.D. Ind. 1987)	§ 2.5
Jones v. Chicago, 856 F.2d 985 (7th Cir. 1988)	§§ 3.6, 3.7, 4.11, 7.16
Jones v. Chicago, 787 F.2d 200 (7th Cir. 1986)	§ 4.10
Jones v. Continental Corp., 789 F.2d 1225 (6th Cir. 1986)	§ 23.4, App. L
Jones v. Coughlin, 665 F. Supp. 1040 (S.D.N.Y. 1987)	§ 10.4
Jones v. Denver, 854 F.2d 1206 (10th Cir. 1988)	§§ 7.16, 7.18
Jones v. Duncan, 840 F.2d 359 (6th Cir. 1988)	§ 5.14
Jones v. Frederick County Bd. of Educ., 689 F. Supp. 535 (D. Md. 1988)	§ 10.6
Jones v. Grunewarld, 644 F. Supp. 256 (S.D.N.Y. 1986)	§ 5.14
Jones v. Key W., 679 F. Supp. 1547 (S.D. Fla. 1988)	§ 14.13
Jones v. Preuit & Mauldin, 851 F.2d 1321 (11th Cir. 1988)	§§ 1.2, 4.4, 7.11, 8.1
Jones v. Preuit & Mauldin, 763 F.2d 1250 (11th Cir. 1985), *cert. denied,* 106 S. Ct. 893 (1986)	§ 10.6
Jones v. Shankland, 800 F.2d 77 (6th Cir. 1986), *cert. denied,* 107 S. Ct. 2177 (1987)	§§ 10.6, 10.7
Jones v. Sherrill, 827 F.2d 1102 (6th Cir. 1987)	§§ 3.4, 3.5, 4.3
Jones v. Smith, 784 F.2d 149 (2d Cir. 1986)	§§ 6.1, 6.5
Jones v. Wilkinson, 800 F.2d 989 (10th Cir. 1986), *judgment aff'd,* ____ U.S. ____, 94 L. Ed. 2d 753 (1987)	§§ 15.2, 16.3, 16.12, 16.14, 21.3
Jordan v. City of Greenwood, 808 F.2d 1114 (5th Cir.), *cert. denied,* 108 S. Ct. 89 (1987)	§§ 16.4, 21.7
Jordan v. Mark IV Hair Styles, Inc., 806 F.2d 695 (6th Cir. 1986)	§ 24.2

Case	*Book §*
Jordan v. Multnomah County, 815 F.2d 1258 (9th Cir. 1987)	§§ 15.6, 17.2, 17.17, 18.6, 18.13, 18.17, 21.2, 24.6
Jorden v. National Guard Bureau, 799 F.2d 99 (3d Cir. 1986), *cert. denied,* 108 S. Ct. 66 (1987)	§§ 6.1, 7.17A
Jordi v. Sauk Prairie School Bd., 651 F. Supp. 1566 (W.D. Wis. 1987)	§ 12.12
Joseph v. Patterson, 795 F.2d 549 (6th Cir. 1986), *cert. denied,* 107 S. Ct. 1910 (1987)	§§ 7.7, 7.8
Joseph L. v. Office of Judicial Support, 638 F. Supp. 833 (E.D. Pa. 1986)	§§ 15.10, 16.6, 16.13
Juidice v. Vail, 430 U.S. 327 (1977)	§ 12.8
Juluke v. Hodel, 811 F.2d 1553 (D.C. Cir. 1987)	§ 12.6
Jungels v. Pierce, 825 F.2d 1127 (7th Cir. 1987)	§ 6.1
Jurgens v. E.E.O.C., 660 F. Supp. 1097 (N.D. Tex. 1987)	§ 15.19
Justice v. Dennis, 834 F.2d 380 (4th Cir. 1987)	§ 3.3
Justice v. Town of Blackwell, 820 F.2d 238 (7th Cir. 1987)	§§ 1.5, 7.18
Kaiter v. Town of Boxford, 836 F.2d 704 (1st Cir. 1988)	§ 7.18
Kappenberger v. Oates, 663 F. Supp. 991 (S.D.N.Y. 1987)	App. E
Karcher v. May, 108 S. Ct. 388 (1987)	§§ 2.4, 6.1, 11.4, 13.2
Karim-Panahi v. Los Angeles Police Dep't, 839 F.2d 621 (9th Cir. 1988)	§§ 3.6, 4.12, 10.7
Karmanos v. Baker, 816 F.2d 258 (6th Cir. 1987)	§ 5.14
Kashani v. Purdue Univ., 813 F.2d 843 (7th Cir.), *cert. denied,* 108 S. Ct. 141 (1987)	§§ 6.5, 6.11
Kauth v. Hartford Ins., 852 F.2d 951 (7th Cir. 1988)	§ 8.1
Kay v. David Douglas School Dist., 79 Or. App. 384, 719 P.2d 875 (1986), *cert. denied,* 108 S. Ct. 740 (1988)	§§ 15.1, 15.20
Keenan v. Washington Metro. Area Transit Auth., 643 F. Supp. 324 (D.D.C. 1986)	§ 6.12
Keesee v. Orr, 816 F.2d 545 (10th Cir. 1987)	§ 24.1
Keith v. Volpe, 833 F.2d 850 (9th Cir. 1987)	§§ 15.8, 16.8, 17.8, 22.9, 24.2
Keith v. Volpe, 644 F. Supp. 1317 (C.D. Cal. 1986)	§§ 15.17, 17.4, 17.6, 17.8, 17.14, 21.8, App. C
Keith v. Volpe, 644 F. Supp. 1312 (C.D. Cal. 1986)	§§ 17.3, 17.6, 17.8, 17.14, 17.15, 18.3, 18.6, 18.10, 18.12, 18.14, 18.16, 18.17, App. E
Keith v. Volpe, 643 F. Supp. 37 (C.D. Cal. 1985)	§§ 17.5, 17.8, 17.16
Keller v. Prince George's County, 827 F.2d 952 (4th Cir. 1987)	§ 3.2
Kelley v. Metropolitan County Bd. of Educ., 836 F.2d 986 (6th Cir. 1987), *cert. denied,* 108 S. Ct. 2844 (1988)	§§ 6.3, 6.5
Kemp v. Ervin, 651 F. Supp. 495 (N.D. Ga. 1986)	§ 14.13
Kennecott Corp. v. E.P.A., 804 F.2d 763 (D.C. Cir. 1986)	§§ 17.14, 17.15, 18.5, App. D, App. F
Kennedy v. City of Cleveland, 797 F.2d 297 (6th Cir. 1986), *cert. denied,* 107 S. Ct. 1334 (1987)	§ 7.18

Case	*Book §*
Kennedy v. Hardiman, 684 F. Supp. 540 (N.D. Ill. 1988)	§ 6.1
Kentucky v. Graham, 473 U.S. 159, 105 S. Ct. 3099 (1985)	§§ 2.4, 16.9
Kentucky W. Va. Gas Co. v. Public Util. Comm'n, 791 F.2d 1111 (3d Cir. 1986)	§§ 12.6, 12.12
Kercado Melendez v. Aponte-Roque, 829 F.2d 255 (1st Cir.), *cert. denied,* 108 S. Ct. 2037 (1987)	§ 12.8
Kerr Center Parents Ass'n v. Charles, 842 F.2d 1052 (9th Cir. 1988)	§§ 6.12, 8.3, 15.16
Kessel v. Schaff, 697 F. Supp. 1102 (D.N.D. 1987)	§ 10.6
Ketchum v. Alameda County, 811 F.2d 1243 (9th Cir. 1987)	§§ 3.2, 4.3
Keystone Bituminous Coal Co. v. DeBenedictis, 107 S. Ct. 1232 (1987)	§ 3.10
Kibbe v. Springfield, 777 F.2d 801 (1st Cir. 1985), *cert. granted,* 106 S. Ct. 1374 (1986)	§ 4.9
King v. Jones, 824 F.2d 324 (4th Cir. 1987)	§ 14.13
King v. Massarweh, 782 F.2d 825 (9th Cir. 1986)	§§ 3.7, 3.9, 5.13
King v. Palmer, 641 F. Supp. 186 (D.D.C. 1986)	§§ 15.18, 15.19
Kinzli v. Santa Cruz, 818 F.2d 1449 (9th Cir.), *amended,* 830 F.2d 968 (9th Cir. 1987), *cert. denied,* 108 S. Ct. 775 (1988)	§ 3.10
Kirby v. Dutton, 794 F.2d 245 (6th Cir. 1986)	§ 8.6
Kirchoff v. Flynn, 786 F.2d 320 (7th Cir. 1986)	§ 21.3
Kirkland v. New York State Dep't of Correctional Servs., 524 F. Supp. 1214 (S.D.N.Y. 1981)	§ 16.11
Kirkland v. City of Peekskill, 828 F.2d 104 (2d Cir. 1987)	§§ 9.4, 9.5, 9.10
Kirkpatrick v. Los Angeles, 803 F.2d 485 (9th Cir. 1986)	§ 7.13
Kitchens v. Bowen, 825 F.2d 1337 (9th Cir. 1987), *cert. denied,* 108 S. Ct. 1109 (1988)	§ 12.8
Klein v. Ryan, 847 F.2d 368 (7th Cir. 1988)	§ 7.18
Knight v. Mills, 836 F.2d 659 (lst Cir. 1987)	§§ 7.13, 7.13A
Knoll v. Springfield Township School Dist., 763 F.2d 584 (3d Cir. 1985)	§ 10.6
Knoll v. Webster, 838 F.2d 450 (10th Cir. 1988)	§ 7.6
Kompare v. Stein, 801 F.2d 883 (7th Cir. 1986)	§§ 7.9, 7.11
Kopunec v. Nelson, 801 F.2d 1226 (10th Cir. 1986)	§ 15.18
Kovats v. Rutgers, the State Univ., 822 F.2d 1303 (3d Cir. 1987)	§§ 6.11, 7.18
Kristi W. v. Graham Indep. School Dist., 663 F. Supp. 86 (N.D. Tex. 1987)	§ 15.16
Kuchka v. Kile, 634 F. Supp. 502 (M.D. Pa. 1985)	§ 7.10
Kukla v. Village of Antioch, 647 F. Supp. 799 (N.D. Ill. 1986)	§§ 7.9, 7.10
Kulick v. Pocono Downs Racing Ass'n, 816 F.2d 895 (3d Cir. 1987)	§ 5.9
Kunzelman v. Thompson, 799 F.2d 1172 (7th Cir. 1986)	§§ 9.3, 9.8, 9.12
Kurowski v. Krajewski, 848 F.2d 767 (7th Cir.), *cert. denied,* 109 S. Ct. 309 (1988)	§§ 7.3, 7.18, 17.3, 17.4, 17.17, App. E
Kuzma v. Internal Revenue Serv., 821 F.2d 930 (2d Cir. 1987)	§ 21.8
Labov v. Lalley, 809 F.2d 220 (3d Cir. 1987)	§ 3.8
Lac Courte Oreilles Band v. Wisconsin, 663 F. Supp. 682 (W.D. Wis.), *appeal dismissed,* 829 F.2d 601 (7th Cir. 1987)	§§ 2.3, 3.11, 24.4
Lach v. Robb, 679 F. Supp. 508 (W.D. Pa. 1988)	§ 6.6

Case	*Book §*
LaCroix v. Board of Educ., 844 F.2d 88 (2d Cir. 1988)	§ 10.6
LaFrance v. Rampone, 678 F. Supp. 72 (D. Vt. 1988)	§ 7.6
Lagon v. Barry, 658 F. Supp. 55 (D.D.C. 1987)	§ 10.8
Lai v. Honolulu, 841 F.2d 301 (9th Cir.), *cert. denied,* 109 S. Ct. ____ (1988)	§ 3.10
Laird v. Tatum, 408 U.S. 1, *reh'g denied,* 409 U.S. 901 (1972)	§ 3.2
Lake Nacimiento Ranch Co. v. San Luis Obispo County, 830 F.2d 977 (9th Cir.), *opinion amended,* 841 F.2d 872 (9th Cir. 1987)	§§ 3.8, 3.10, 4.7
Lakewood, City of v. Plain Dealer Publishing Co., 108 S. Ct. 2138 (1988)	§ 2.4
Langham-Hill Petroleum Inc. v. Southern Fuels Co., 813 F.2d 1327 (4th Cir. 1987)	§ 24.4
Lappe v. Loeffelholz, 815 F.2d 1173 (8th Cir. 1987)	§ 7.13
Lasa v. Colberg, 622 F. Supp. 557 (D.P.R. 1985)	§ 7.10
La Salle Nat'l Bank v. County of DuPage, 856 F.2d 925 (7th Cir. 1988)	§ 8.5
Lattimore v. Oman Constr., 795 F.2d 930 (11th Cir. 1986)	App. G
Lavelle v. Quinones, 679 F. Supp. 253 (E.D.N.Y. 1988)	§ 8.1
Law v. Cullen, 613 F. Supp. 259 (S.D.N.Y. 1985)	§ 3.3
Lawler v. Eugene Wuesthoff Memorial Hosp. Ass'n, 497 So. 2d 1261 (Fla. Dist. Ct. App. 1986)	§ 9.12
Lawler, *In re,* 807 F.2d 1207 (5th Cir. 1987)	§ 17.14
Lawrence v. McGuire, 651 F. Supp. 312 (S.D.N.Y. 1987)	§ 9.5
Lawrence v. Staats, 586 F. Supp. 1375 (D.D.C. 1984)	§ 15.3
Leaman v. Ohio Dep't of Mental Retardation & Developmental Disabilities, 825 F.2d 946 (6th Cir. 1987), *cert. denied,* 108 S. Ct. 2844 (1988)	§ 14.15
LeBeau v. Libbey-Owens-Ford Co., 799 F.2d 1152 (7th Cir. 1986)	§ 23.2, App. L
Leber v. Smith, 773 F.2d 101 (6th Cir. 1985), *cert. denied,* 475 U.S. 1084 (1986)	§ 3.4
Lebron v. Washington Metro. Area Transit Auth., 665 F. Supp. 923 (D.D.C. 1987)	§§ 17.3, 17.6, 17.9, 18.5, 18.8, 19.3, App. E
Lee v. Hutson, 810 F.2d 1030 (11th Cir. 1987)	§§ 3.8, 3.9, 8.2
Lee v. Mihalich, 847 F.2d 66 (3d Cir. 1988)	§§ 3.6, 7.12
Lee v. Town of Estes Park, 820 F.2d 1112 (10th Cir. 1987)	§ 5.13
Leggett v. Badger, 798 F. 2d 1387 (11th Cir. 1986)	§ 16.9
Lelsz v. Kavanagh, 807 F.2d 1243 (5th Cir.), *cert. denied,* 108 S. Ct. 44 (1987)	§§ 6.6, 6.12
Lemke v. Cass County, 846 F.2d 469 (8th Cir. 1987)	§ 3.2
Lenard v. Argento, 808 F.2d 1242 (7th Cir. 1987)	§§ 17.4, 17.17, 19.3, 19.6, 21.3
Lendo v. Garret County Bd. of Educ., 820 F.2d 1365 (4th Cir. 1987)	§ 10.4
Lenihan v. City of N.Y., 640 F. Supp. 822 (S.D.N.Y. 1986)	§§ 17.4, 17.6, 17.9, 17.14, 17.15, 18.5, 18.7, 18.10, 18.12, 19.3, 21.8, App. C, App. E, App. F

Case	*Book §*
Leonard v. Hammond, 804 F.2d 838 (4th Cir. 1986)	§§ 8.6, 13.5
Lepley v. Dresser, 681 F. Supp. 418 (W.D. Mich. 1988)	§ 7.9
Leroy v. City of Houston, 831 F.2d 576 (5th Cir. 1987)	§§ 15.13, 17.9, 17.13, 17.14, 17.17, 18.17, 20.4D, 20.4F, 21.8
Lesher v. Lavrich, 784 F.2d 193 (6th Cir. 1986)	§ 3.11
Leslie v. Ingram, 786 F.2d 1533 (11th Cir. 1986)	§§ 3.3, 3.9
Lester v. Chicago, 830 F.2d 706 (7th Cir. 1987)	§§ 3.3, 3.4
Levee Comm'rs, Bd. of v. Huls, 852 F.2d 140 (5th Cir. 1988)	§ 2.3
Levine v. Heffernan, 691 F. Supp. 173 (W.D. Wis. 1988)	§ 15.3
Levine v. Supreme Court of Wis., 679 F. Supp. 1478 (W.D. Wis. 1988)	§ 12.13
Levinson v. Washington Horse Racing Comm'n, 48 Wash. App. 822, 740 P.2d 898 (1987)	App. M
Lewellen v. Raff, 843 F.2d 1103 (8th Cir. 1988)	§§ 7.8, 12.9
Lewis v. Coughlin, 801 F.2d 570 (2d Cir. 1986)	§§ 17.14, 17.15, 17.16, 21.3, App. D, App. E
Lewis v. Harrison School Dist., 805 F.2d 310 (8th Cir. 1986), *cert. denied,* 107 S. Ct. 2481 (1987)	§ 14.8
Lewis v. Meyer, 815 F.2d 43 (7th Cir. 1987)	§ 8.3
Lewis v. O'Grady, 853 F.2d 1366 (7th Cir. 1988)	§ 3.7
Lewis v. School Bd., 820 F.2d 143 (5th Cir. 1987)	§ 1.4
Lewis v. State Bar Ass'n, 792 F.2d 493 (5th Cir. 1986)	§ 6.11
Libby v. Marshall, 653 F. Supp. 359 (D. Mass. 1986), *appeal dismissed,* 833 F.2d 402 (1st Cir. 1987)	§§ 6.3, 6.5, 6.6
Libin v. Town of Greenwich, 625 F. Supp. 393 (D. Conn. 1985)	§ 5.11
Library of Congress v. Shaw, 106 S. Ct. 2957 (1986)	§§ 15.19, 18.17
Lieberman v. Reisman, 857 F.2d 896 (2d Cir. 1988)	§ 3.2A
Lightfoot v. Walker, 619 F. Supp. 1481 (N.D. Ill. 1985), *aff'd,* 826 F.2d 516 (7th Cir. 1987)	§§ 17.3, 17.14, 18.3, 18.5, 18.6, 18.12, 18.14, 18.17, 24.5, App. E
Lile v. University of Iowa Hosps. & Clinics, 674 F. Supp. 288 (S.D. Iowa 1987)	§ 3.11
Liles v. Reagan, 804 F.2d 493 (8th Cir. 1986)	§ 7.3
Lilly v. Harris-Teeter Supermarket, 842 F.2d 1496 (4th Cir. 1988)	§ 21.2
Linderkamp v. Bismarck School Dist., 397 N.W.2d 76 (N.D. 1986)	§ 12.13
Lion Boulos v. Wilson, 834 F.2d 504 (5th Cir. 1987)	§ 7.18
Lippo v. Mobil Oil Corp., 692 F. Supp. 826 (N.D. Ill. 1988)	§§ 18.17, 20.5
Littlefield v. City of Afton, 785 F.2d 596 (8th Cir. 1986)	§ 3.9
Little Rock School Dist. v. Pulaski County Special School Dist., 787 F.2d 372 (8th Cir. 1986)	§ 24.6, App. J
Liverman-Melton v. British Aerospace, Inc., 628 F. Supp. 102 (D.D.C. 1986)	§ 17.3
L.K. v. Gregg, 425 N.W.2d 813 (Minn. 1988)	§ 1.3A, App. M
L.K. v. Gregg, 413 N.W.2d 833 (Minn. Ct. App. 1987)	§ 1.3A
Local 17, Int'l Ass'n v. Young, 775 F.2d 870 (7th Cir. 1985)	§ 15.6
Lock v. Jenkins, 634 F. Supp. 615 (N.D. Ind. 1986)	§§ 17.4, 17.5, 17.9, 18.6, 18.17, App. C, App. E

Case	*Book §*
Lodestar Co. v. County of Mono, 639 F. Supp. 1439 (E.D. Cal. 1986)	§ 11.4
Loeffler v. Frank, 108 S. Ct. 1965 (1988)	§ 14.16
Lofft v. State Bd. of Higher Educ., 89 Or. App. 614, 750 P.2d 515 (1988)	App. M
Long Island Lighting Co. v. Cuomo, 666 F. Supp. 370 (N.D.N.Y. 1987)	§ 12.12
Lopez v. Houston Indep. School Dist., 817 F.2d 351 (5th Cir. 1987)	§§ 3.2, 3.5, 4.3, 4.7
Loretto v. Group W. Cable, 135 A.D.2d 444, 522 N.Y.S.2d 543 (1987), *cert. denied,* 109 S. Ct. 78 (1988)	App. M
Los Angeles v. Heller, 106 S. Ct. 1571 (1986)	§ 4.6
Los Angeles, City of v. Lyons, 461 U.S. 95 (1983)	§ 2.5
Loudermill v. Cleveland Bd. of Educ., 844 F.2d 304 (6th Cir. 1988)	§§ 15.11, 24.4
Love v. Sheffield, 777 F.2d 1453 (11th Cir. 1985)	§ 3.9
Lovell v. City of Kankakee, 783 F.2d 95 (7th Cir. 1986)	§ 15.13
Lowden v. Murphy, 664 F. Supp. 966 (E.D. Pa. 1987)	§ 21.4
Loy v. Clamme, 804 F.2d 405 (7th Cir. 1986)	§§ 10.6, 10.7
Loza v. Lynch, 625 F. Supp. 850 (D. Conn. 1986)	§ 4.12
Lucas v. O'Loughlin, 831 F.2d 232 (11th Cir. 1987), *cert. denied,* 108 S. Ct. 1595 (1988)	§§ 4.7, 14.1
Lucero v. City of Trinidad, 815 F.2d 1384 (10th Cir. 1987)	§§ 18.5, 18.12, 18.13
Lugar v. Edmondson Oil Co., 457 U.S. 922 (1982)	§ 5.13
Lumbermen's Mut. Cas. Co. v. Connecticut Bank & Trust Co., 806 F.2d 411 (2d Cir. 1986)	§ 12.11
Lumen Constr. v. Brant Constr. Co., 780 F.2d 691 (7th Cir. 1986)	§ 12.11
Luna v. Harris, 691 F. Supp. 624 (E.D.N.Y. 1988)	§ 21.8
Lunde v. Oldi, 808 F.2d 219 (2d Cir. 1986)	§ 3.5
Lundgren v. McDaniel, 814 F.2d 600 (11th Cir. 1987)	§§ 6.1, 7.13A
Lusby v. T.G.&Y. Stores, 796 F.2d 1307 (10th Cir.), *cert. denied,* 107 S. Ct. 275 (1986)	§ 4.9
Lutz v. Weld County School Dist., 784 F.2d 340 (10th Cir. 1986)	§ 7.18
Lynch v. Cannatella, 810 F.2d 1363 (5th Cir. 1987)	§ 3.3
Lynk v. La Porte Superior Court, 789 F.2d 554 (7th Cir. 1986)	§ 12.9
Lyons v. Barrett, 851 F.2d 406 (D.C. Cir. 1988)	§ 14.5
Lyons v. Cunningham, 583 F. Supp. 1147 (S.D.N.Y. 1983)	§ 21.8
Mabe v. Galveston Park Bd., 635 F. Supp. 105 (S.D. Tex. 1986)	§ 5.14
MacDissi v. Valmont Indus., Inc., 856 F.2d 1054 (8th Cir. 1988)	§ 17.14
Mack v. Varelas, 835 F.2d 995 (2d Cir. 1987)	§ 8.6
MacLaird v. Werger, 633 F. Supp. 286 (D. Wyo. 1986)	App. E
Maddocks v. Salt Lake City Corp., 740 P.2d 1337 (Utah 1987)	§ 10.6
Maddox v. Los Angeles, 792 F.2d 1408 (9th Cir. 1986)	§ 3.3
Maestri v. Jutkofsky, 860 F.2d 50 (2d Cir. 1988)	§ 7.3
Maher v. Gagne, 448 U.S. 122 (1980)	§ 15.16
Mahoney v. Hankin, 844 F.2d 64 (2d Cir. 1988)	§ 7.18
Maine v. Thiboutot, 448 U.S. 1 (1980)	§ 15.15

Case	*Book §*
Maine Ass'n of Interdependent Neighborhoods v. Petit, 659 F. Supp. 1309 (D. Me. 1987)	§ 6.12
Mairena v. Foti, 816 F.2d 1061 (5th Cir. 1987), *cert. denied,* 108 S. Ct. 697 (1988)	§§ 3.7, 14.14
Malachowski v. City of Keene, 787 F.2d 704 (1st Cir.), *cert. denied,* 107 S. Ct. 107 (1986)	§§ 5.11, 5.14, 7.8, 12.8, 12.9
Malak v. Associated Physicians, 784 F.2d 277 (7th Cir. 1986)	§ 4.7
Maldonado v. Lehman, 811 F.2d 1341 (9th Cir.), *cert. denied sub nom.* Webb v. Maldonado, 108 S. Ct. 480 (1987)	§ 18.5
Maldonado v. Department of Pub. Welfare, 223 Neb. 485, 391 N.W.2d 105 (1986)	§§ 1.3A, 15.1, 15.15, 16.8, 17.9
Malley v. Briggs, 106 S. Ct. 1092 (1986)	§§ 3.7, 7.1, 7.13, 7.16
Maloney v. City of Marietta, 822 F.2d 1023 (11th Cir. 1987)	§§ 15.10, 15.14, 16.5
Mammano v. Pittston Co., 792 F.2d 1242 (4th Cir. 1986)	§§ 16.3, 16.6, 16.15, 24.6
Manax v. McNamara, 842 F.2d 808 (5th Cir. 1988)	§ 5.14
Mangels v. City of Orange, 678 F. Supp. 1452 (C.D. Cal. 1988)	§ 10.8
Mann v. Jett, 781 F.2d 1448 (9th Cir. 1986)	§ 12.7
Mann v. Tuscon, 782 F.2d 790 (9th Cir. 1986)	§ 3.9
Manning v. Jones, 696 F. Supp. 1231 (S.D. Ind. 1988)	§ 5.4
Mantolete v. Bolger, 791 F.2d 784 (9th Cir. 1986)	§ 15.4
Marek v. Chesny, 473 U.S. 1 (1985)	§§ 15.16, 21.4, 21.8
Mares v. Credit Bureau of Raton, 801 F.2d 1197 (10th Cir. 1986)	§§ 17.2, 17.3, 17.10, 17.12, 17.15, 18.17, 24.3, App. B, App. C, App. E, App. K
Marino v. Ameruso, 837 F.2d 45 (2d Cir. 1988)	§§ 3.8, 8.2
Marks v. Parla, 785 F.2d 1419 (9th Cir. 1986)	§ 10.6
Marrical v. Detroit News, 805 F.2d 169 (6th Cir. 1986)	§ 7.18
Marsh v. Digital Equip. Corp., 699 F. Supp. 1411 (D. Ariz. 1988)	§ 20.4D
Martin v. City of Eastlake, 686 F. Supp. 620 (N.D. Ohio 1988)	§§ 7.16, 7.18
Martin v. Dallas County, 822 F.2d 553 (5th Cir. 1987)	§§ 3.8, 3.9
Martin v. Demma, 831 F.2d 69 (5th Cir. 1987)	§ 10.4
Martin v. District of Columbia, 824 F.2d 1049 (D.C. Cir. 1987)	§ 3.4A
Martin v. District of Columbia Metro. Police Dep't, 812 F.2d 1425 (D.C. Cir.), *reh'g denied,* 824 F.2d 1240 (D.C. Cir. 1987)	§ 7.18
Martin v. Gentile, 849 F.2d 863 (4th Cir. 1988)	§§ 3.3, 3.4
Martin v. Heckler, 773 F.2d 1145 (11th Cir. 1985)	§ 16.5
Martin v. Malhoyt, 830 F.2d 237 (D.C. Cir. 1987)	§§ 3.3, 3.4, 7.18
Martin v. Metropolitan Police Dep't, 812 F.2d 1425 (D.C. Cir.), *reh'g denied,* 824 F.2d 1240 (D.C. 1987)	§§ 7.12, 7.18
Martin v. Salem, 801 F.2d 324 (8th Cir. 1986)	§ 3.9
Martin v. Sargent, 780 F.2d 1334 (8th Cir. 1985)	§ 13.3
Martin v. Supreme Court of State of N.Y., 644 F. Supp. 1537 (N.D.N.Y. 1986)	App. E
Martinez v. California, 444 U.S. 277 (1980)	§ 4.3

Case	*Book §*
Martinez v. El Paso County, 673 F. Supp. 1030 (D. Colo. 1987)	§ 6.1
Martinez v. Perales, 135 A.D.2d 818, 522 N.Y.S.2d 922 (1987)	App. M
Martinez v. Schock Transfer & Warehouse Co., Inc., 789 F.2d 848 (10th Cir. 1986)	§§ 17.16, 19.6, App. F
Martinez v. Winner, 771 F.2d 424 (10th Cir.), *modified,* 778 F.2d 553 (10th Cir. 1985), *action found moot,* 800 F.2d 230 (10th Cir. 1986)	§ 7.8
Martori Bros. Distribs. v. Massengale, 781 F.2d 1349 (9th Cir.), *amended,* 791 F.2d 799 (9th Cir.), *cert. denied,* 107 S. Ct. 435 (1986)	§ 12.8
Marx v. Gumbinner, 855 F.2d 783 (11th Cir. 1988)	§§ 7.8, 11.18
Marx v. Truck Rental & Leasing Ass'n, 520 So. 2d 1333 (Miss. 1987)	§ 12.13, App. M
Massengil v. Scott, 738 S.W.2d 629 (Tenn. 1987)	§ 9.12
Massey v. Shepack, 12 Kan. App. 2d 770, 757 P.2d 329 (1988)	§ 1.3A
Mathern v. Campbell Country Children's Center, 674 F. Supp. 816 (D. Wyo. 1987)	§ 15.16
Matherne v. Wilson, 851 F.2d 752 (5th Cir. 1988)	§§ 7.18, 14.12
Matthew v. Eldridge, 424 U.S. 319 (1976)	§ 3.2
Matthiesen v. North Chicago School Dist., 857 F.2d 404 (7th Cir. 1988)	§ 3.8
Maulick v. Central Classification Bd., 659 F. Supp. 24 (E.D. Va. 1986)	§ 8.3
Max M. v. Illinois State Bd. of Educ., 684 F. Supp. 514 (N.D. Ill. 1988)	§ 15.16
Max M. v. New Trier High School Dist., 859 F.2d 1297 (7th Cir. 1988)	§§ 15.16, 17.17, 19.7, 24.2
May v. Cooperman, 780 F.2d 240 (3d Cir. 1985)	§ 24.4
Mayson v. Pierce, 806 F.2d 1556 (11th Cir. 1987)	§§ 17.9, 18.5, 18.10
Mazanec v. North Judson-San Pierre School Corp., 798 F.2d 230 (7th Cir. 1986)	§§ 4.7, 15.10, 15.17
McCarthy v. Mayo, 827 F.2d 1310 (9th Cir. 1987)	§§ 3.6, 7.8
McClary v. O'Hare, 786 F.2d 83 (2d Cir. 1986)	§§ 3.2, 3.8, 3.9, 4.3, 6.1, 6.3
McCormack v. National Collegiate Athletic Ass'n, 845 F.2d 1338 (5th Cir. 1988)	§§ 5.11, 5.14
McCrory v. Johnson, 296 Ark. 231, 755 S.W.2d 566 (1988)	§ 7.5
McCullough v. Cady, 640 F. Supp. 1012 (E.D. Mich. 1986)	§§ 17.4, 17.6, 17.9, 18.8, App. C
McCune v. Grand Rapids, 842 F.2d 903 (6th Cir. 1988)	§§ 10.4, 10.6
McCurry v. Tesch, 824 F.2d 638 (8th Cir. 1987)	§ 19.5
McDonald v. Armontrout, 860 F.2d 1456 (8th Cir. 1988)	§§ 17.8, 18.2, 18.3, 18.5, 18.7, 18.10, 18.14, 18.15, App. E
McDonald v. Board of Miss. Levee Comm'rs, 832 F.2d 901 (5th Cir. 1987)	§ 6.11
McDonald v. City of West Branch, 466 U.S. 284 (1984)	§ 9.9
McDonald v. Krajewski, 649 F. Supp. 370 (N.D. Ill. 1986)	§ 7.3

Case	*Book §*
McDonald, Somer & Frates v. Yolo County, 477 U.S. 340 (1986)	§ 3.10
McDougald v. Jenson, 786 F.2d 1465 (11th Cir.), *cert. denied,* 107 S. Ct. 207 (1986)	§ 5.14
McDowell v. Moore, 635 F. Supp. 280 (W.D.N.C. 1986)	§ 17.6
McGaughey v. Chicago, 664 F. Supp. 1131 (N.D. Ill. 1987), *vacated in part,* 690 F. Supp. 707 (N.D. Ill. 1988)	§ 7.16
McGee v. Hester, 815 F.2d 1193 (8th Cir. 1987)	§§ 20.3, 24.6
McGhee v. Foltz, 852 F.2d 876 (6th Cir. 1988)	§ 3.4A
McGlumphy v. Fraternal Order of Police, 633 F. Supp. 1074 (N.D. Ohio 1986)	§ 5.13
McGowan v. Riley, 628 F. Supp. 1087 (N.D. Miss. 1985)	§ 3.8
McIntosh v. Arkansas Republican Party, 856 F.2d 1185 (8th Cir. 1988)	§ 7.16
McIntosh v. Arkansas Republican Party, 816 F.2d 409 (8th Cir. 1987)	§ 3.9
McIntosh v. Weinberger, 810 F.2d 1411 (8th Cir. 1987), *vacated,* 108 S. Ct. 2870 (1988)	§§ 7.12, 7.18
McKee v. Bi-State Dev. Agency, 801 F.2d 1014 (8th Cir. 1986)	§§ 24.2, 24.4
McKenna v. Clayton County, 657 F. Supp. 221 (N.D. Ga. 1987)	§§ 3.4, 3.5
McKenna v. Memphis, 785 F.2d 560 (6th Cir. 1986)	§ 4.9
McKenzie v. Kennickell, 684 F. Supp. 1097 (D.D.C. 1988)	§§ 20.3, 20.4C, 20.4D
McKenzie v. Kennickell, 669 F. Supp. 529 (D.D.C. 1987)	§ 15.19
McKenzie v. Kennickell, 645 F. Supp. 437 (D.D.C. 1986)	§§ 15.18, 15.19, 17.2, 17.4, 17.5, 17.13, 18.5, 18.7, 18.10, 19.3, 21.8, App. B, App. C, App. E, App. F, App. I
McKever v. Vondollen, 681 F. Supp. 999 (N.D.N.Y. 1988)	§ 21.4, App. E
McMaster v. Cabinet for Human Resources, 824 F.2d 518 (6th Cir. 1987)	§ 3.6
McMillan v. Goleta Water Dist., 792 F.2d 1453 (9th Cir. 1986), *cert. denied,* 107 S. Ct. 1348 (1987)	§§ 10.4, 10.6
McQuillen v. Wisconsin Educ. Ass'n Council, 830 F.2d 659 (7th Cir. 1987)	§ 15.4
McQuiston v. Marsh, 790 F.2d 798 (9th Cir. 1986)	§ 24.5
McRorie v. Shimoda, 795 F.2d 780 (9th Cir. 1986)	§§ 3.3, 3.4A, 3.9, 4.10
McSurely v. Hutchison, 823 F.2d 1002 (6th Cir. 1987), *cert. denied,* 108 S. Ct. 1107 (1988)	§ 10.6
Meade v. Grubbs, 841 F.2d 1512 (10th Cir. 1988)	§§ 3.3, 3.4, 4.11, 7.8, 10.6
Meadows v. Indiana, 854 F.2d 1068 (7th Cir. 1988)	§§ 6.1, 6.3
Medical Inst. v. National Ass'n of Trade & Technical Schools, 817 F.2d 1310 (8th Cir. 1987)	§§ 5.11, 5.14
Medical Laundry Serv. v. Board of Trustees, 840 F.2d 840 (11th Cir.), *cert. denied,* 109 S. Ct. 77 (1988)	§ 3.2
Medina County Agricultural Soc'y v. Swagler, 34 Ohio App. 3d 336, 518 N.E.2d 589 (1987)	§ 14.14
Meeker v. Kercher, 782 F.2d 153 (10th Cir. 1986)	§ 5.5
Memphis Community School Dist. v. Stachura, 106 S. Ct. 2537 (1986)	§§ 14.6, 14.8, 14.10

Case	*Book §*
Mennor v. Fort Hood Nat'l Bank, 829 F.2d 553 (5th Cir. 1987)	§ 21.8
Merkel v. Scovill, Inc., 787 F.2d 174 (6th Cir. 1986)	§ 15.6
Merola v. National R.R. Passenger Corp., 683 F. Supp. 935 (S.D.N.Y. 1988)	§ 5.13
Merredith v. Talbot County, 828 F.2d 228 (4th Cir. 1987)	§ 12.12
Merrell v. Block, 797 F.2d 740 (9th Cir. 1986)	§ 15.3
Merrell Dow Pharmaceuticals v. Thompson, 106 S. Ct. 3229 (1986)	§ 3.12
Merritt v. Faulkner, 823 F.2d 1150 (7th Cir. 1987)	§ 14.15
Merritt v. Mackey, 827 F.2d 1368 (9th Cir. 1987)	§ 3.8
Messick v. Leavins, 811 F.2d 1439 (11th Cir. 1987)	§ 4.7
Metropolitan Hosp. v. Thornburgh, 667 F. Supp. 208 (E.D. Pa. 1987)	§ 12.8
Metzger v. Osbeck, 841 F.2d 518 (3d Cir. 1988)	§§ 3.3, 3.5
Meyers v. Contra Costa County Dep't of Social Servs., 812 F.2d 1154 (9th Cir.), *cert. denied,* 108 S. Ct. 98 (1987)	§§ 7.5, 7.8
MGIC Indem. Corp. v. Weisman, 803 F.2d 500 (9th Cir. 1986)	§ 17.15
Michael M. v. Board of Educ., 686 F. Supp. 995 (E.D.N.Y. 1988)	§ 15.16
Michigan Injured Workers v. Blanchard, 647 F. Supp. 571 (W.D. Mich. 1986)	§ 12.12
Middle S. Energy v. Public Serv. Comm'n, 772 F.2d 404 (8th Cir. 1985), *cert. denied,* 106 S. Ct. 884 (1986)	§ 12.6
Middlesex County Sewerage Auth. v. National Sea Clammers Ass'n, 453 U.S. 1 (1981)	§ 3.11
Miele v. New York State Teamsters Conference Pension & Retirement Fund, 831 F.2d 407 (2d Cir. 1987)	§§ 18.1, 18.12, 18.13
Miga v. City of Holyoke, 398 Mass. 343, 497 N.E.2d 1 (1986)	§ 3.8
Migra v. Warren City School Dist., 465 U.S. 75 (1984)	§ 9.5
Miletich v. Raley's, 593 F. Supp. 124 (D. Nev. 1984)	§ 1.5
Miller v. Carson, 628 F.2d 346 (5th Cir. 1980)	§ 15.8
Miller v. Garrett, 695 F. Supp. 740 (S.D.N.Y. 1988)	§ 7.6
Miller v. Los Angeles County Bd. of Educ., 827 F.2d 617 (9th Cir. 1987)	§ 21.2
Miller v. NYS Pub. Serv. Comm'n, 807 F.2d 28 (2d Cir. 1986)	§ 12.14
Milliken v. Bradley, 433 U.S. 267 (1977)	§ 6.5
Miltier v. Beorn, 696 F. Supp. 1086 (E.D. Va. 1988)	§ 11.3
Mindes v. Seaman, 453 F.2d 197 (5th Cir. 1971), *cert. denied,* 109 S. Ct. 402 (1988)	§§ 5.6, 6.1, 7.17A
Mineo v. Transportation Management of Tenn., 694 F. Supp. 417 (M.D. Tenn. 1988)	§ 5.11
Minne v. Indiana, 627 F. Supp. 1189 (N.D. Ind. 1986)	§ 2.5
Minotti v. Lensink, 798 F.2d 607 (2d Cir. 1986), *cert. denied,* 107 S. Ct. 2484 (1987)	§ 6.3
Minton v. St. Bernard Parish School Bd., 803 F.2d 129 (5th Cir. 1986)	§ 7.10
Mirshak v. Joyce, 652 F. Supp. 359 (N.D. Ill. 1987)	§ 7.10
Missouri v. Jenkins, 109 S. Ct. 218 (1988), *granting cert. to* 838 F.2d 260 (8th Cir. 1988)	§§ 17.6, 18.16

Case	*Book §*
Misuraca v. Perales, 120 A.D.2d 592, 501 N.Y.S.2d 907 (2d Dep't 1986)	§ 15.17
Mitchel v. City of Hartford, 674 F. Supp. 60 (D. Conn. 1986)	§ 3.7
Mitchell v. City of Sapulpa, 857 F.2d 713 (10th Cir. 1988)	§ 3.4
Mitchell v. Forsyth, 472 U.S. 511 (1985)	§§ 6.3, 7.18
Mitchell v. Mills County, 673 F. Supp. 332 (S.D. Iowa 1987), *aff'd,* 847 F.2d 486 (8th Cir. 1988)	§§ 3.10, 9.5
Mitchum v. Foster, 407 U.S. 225 (1972)	§ 12.6
Mitroff v. Xomox Corp., 631 F. Supp. 25 (S.D. Ohio 1985)	§§ 17.16, 18.11
Mitson v. Coler, 670 F. Supp. 1568 (S.D. Fla. 1987)	§ 5.6
Molten v. Cleveland, 839 F.2d 240 (6th Cir. 1987)	§ 3.4B
Monaghan v. Deakins, 798 F.2d 632 (3d Cir. 1986)	§ 12.7
Monell v. Department of Social Servs., 436 U.S. 658 (1978)	§ 2.3
Monitor v. Chicago, 653 F. Supp. 1294 (N.D. Ill. 1987)	§ 4.12
Mont v. Heintz, 849 F.2d 704 (2d Cir. 1988)	§ 6.6
Montauk-Caribbean Airways v. Hope, 784 F.2d 91 (2d Cir.), *cert. denied,* 107 S. Ct. 248 (1986)	§ 3.11
Montgomery v. Chicago, 670 F. Supp. 230 (N.D. Ill. 1987)	§ 1.5
Montgomery & Assocs., Inc. v. C.F.T.C., 816 F.2d 783 (D.C. Cir. 1987)	§ 24.2
Moore v. Costa Mesa, 678 F. Supp. 1448 (C.D. Cal. 1987)	§§ 3.10, 9.5
Moore v. District of Columbia, 674 F. Supp. 901 (D.D.C. 1987)	§§ 15.16, 17.6, 17.14, 17.15
Moore v. District of Columbia, 666 F. Supp. 263 (D.D.C. 1987)	§ 15.16
Morales v. Department of Corrections, 842 F.2d 27 (2d Cir. 1988)	§ 3.5
Morales v. Turman, 820 F.2d 728 (5th Cir. 1987)	§§ 15.2, 16.4
Morell v. Stone, 638 F. Supp. 163 (W.D. Va. 1986)	§ 1.3
Morello v. James, 810 F.2d 344 (2d Cir. 1987)	§ 3.9
Morgan v. District of Columbia, 824 F.2d 1049 (D.C. Cir.), *reh'g denied,* 824 F.2d 1240 (D.C. Cir. 1987)	§§ 1.2, 19.3, 19.5, App. B
Morgan v. Humboldt County School Dist., 623 F. Supp. 440 (D. Nev. 1985)	§ 3.11
Morrash v. Strobel, 842 F.2d 64 (4th Cir. 1987)	§ 4.7
Morris v. County of Tehama, 795 F.2d 791 (9th Cir. 1986)	§ 7.16
Morrison v. LeFever, 592 F. Supp. 1052 (S.D.N.Y. 1984)	§ 3.6
Moses v. Parwatikar, 813 F.2d 891 (8th Cir.), *cert. denied,* 108 S. Ct. 97 (1987)	§ 7.5
Mount Healthy School Dist. v. Doyle, 429 U.S. 274 (1977)	§§ 3.2A, 7.12
Mow v. Cheeseborough, 696 F. Supp. 1360 (D. Haw. 1988)	§ 1.5
Mrs. W. v. Tirozzi, 832 F.2d 748 (2d Cir. 1987)	§§ 3.2, 8.3, 15.16
Muhammad v. Wainwright, 839 F.2d 1422 (11th Cir. 1987)	§ 7.13
Mulligan v. Hazard, 777 F.2d 340 (6th Cir. 1985), *cert. denied,* 106 S. Ct 2902 (1986)	§§ 10.6, 10.7
Mullinax v. McElhenney, 817 F.2d 711 (11th Cir. 1987)	§§ 7.8, 10.4, 10.6, 10.7
Mullinax v. McElhenney, 672 F. Supp. 1449 (N.D. Ga. 1987)	§ 3.2

Case	*Book §*
New York State Ass'n for Retarded Children v. Carey, 711 F.2d 1136 (2d Cir. 1983)	§ 20.4A
New York State Ass'n for Retarded Children v. Carey, 596 F.2d 27 (2d Cir.), *cert. denied,* 444 U.S. 836 (1979)	§ 17.14
New York State Club Ass'n v. City of N.Y., 108 S. Ct. 2225 (1988)	§ 2.6
Ngiraingas v. Sanchez, 858 F.2d 1368 (9th Cir. 1988)	§§ 5.2, 10.6
Nichols v. Rysavy, 809 F.2d 1317 (8th Cir.), *cert. denied,* 108 S. Ct. 147 (1987)	§ 10.6
Niehaus v. Kansas Bar Ass'n, 793 F.2d 1159 (10th Cir. 1986)	§ 5.14
Nisby v. Commissioners Court of Jefferson County, 798 F.2d 134 (5th Cir. 1986)	§ 21.2
Nishiyama v. Dickson County, 814 F.2d 277 (6th Cir. 1987)	§§ 3.5, 4.3
Nollan v. California Coastal Comm'n, 107 S. Ct. 3141 (1987)	§ 3.10
Norco Constr. v. King County, 801 F.2d 1143 (9th Cir. 1986)	§§ 3.10, 10.4
Nordgreen v. Hafter, 789 F.2d 334 (5th Cir.), *cert. denied,* 107 S. Ct. 177 (1986)	§ 1.4
Norman v. Housing Auth. of Montgomery, 836 F.2d 1292 (11th Cir. 1988)	§§ 17.1, 17.3, 17.6, 17.8, 17.15, 18.2, 18.3, 18.6, 18.7, 18.9, 18.10, 18.12, 18.17, 20.4D, 24.3, 24.5
Norris v. Turner, 637 F. Supp. 1116 (N.D. Ala. 1986)	§ 15.10
North Carolina Dep't of Transp. v. Crest St. Community Council, Inc., 479 U.S. 6 (1986)	§§ 15.1, 15.14, 15.16, 17.9
Northcross v. Board of Educ., 611 F.2d 624 (6th Cir. 1979), *cert. denied,* 447 U.S. 911 (1980)	§ 15.8
Northern Va. Law School v. City of Alexandria, 680 F. Supp. 222 (E.D. Va. 1988)	§ 12.12
Norwood v. Charlotte Memorial Hosp., 653 F. Supp. 1350 (W.D.N.C. 1987)	§§ 20.5, 21.8, App. E
Noyola v. Flores, 740 S.W.2d 493 (Tex. Ct. App. 1987)	§ 7.18
Noyola v. Texas Dep't of Human Resources, 846 F.2d 1021 (5th Cir. 1988)	§ 7.13A
Nunnelley v. Douglas County, 622 F. Supp. 124 (D. Nev. 1985)	§ 1.5
Nygren v. Predovich, 637 F. Supp. 1083 (D. Colo. 1986)	§§ 5.11, 5.14
O'Brien v. Town of Westerly Hous. Auth., 626 F. Supp. 1065 (D.R.I. 1986)	§ 16.7
Odgen v. District of Columbia, 676 F. Supp. 324 (D.D.C. 1987)	§ 7.16
Offet v. Solem, 823 F.2d 1256 (8th Cir. 1987)	§ 8.6
Ohio Civil Rights Comm'n v. Dayton Christian Schools, 106 S. Ct. 1718 (1986)	§ 12.8
Ohio Civil Serv. Employees Ass'n v. Seiter, 858 F.2d 1171 (6th Cir. 1988)	§ 7.13
Ohio-Sealy Mattress Mfg. Co. v. Sealy Inc., 776 F.2d 646 (7th Cir. 1985)	§ 18.17
Ohse v. Hughes, 816 F.2d 1144 (7th Cir. 1987), *vacated,* 108 S. Ct. 1070 (1988)	§ 7.3

Case	*Book §*
Oklahoma City v. Tuttle, 471 U.S. 808, 105 S. Ct. 2427 (1985)	§§ 4.7, 4.9
O'Leary v. Luongo, 692 F. Supp. 893 (N.D. Ill. 1988)	§ 9.3
Oliva v. Heller, 839 F.2d 37 (2d Cir. 1988)	§ 7.5
Oliver v. Fort Wayne Educ. Ass'n, 820 F.2d 913 (7th Cir. 1987)	§ 12.11
Oliveri v. Thompson, 803 F.2d 1265 (2d Cir. 1986), *cert. denied,* 107 S. Ct. 1373 (1987)	§§ 4.12, 23.4
Ollie v. Riggin, 848 F.2d 1016 (9th Cir. 1988)	§ 12.11
Olson v. Tyler, 825 F.2d 1116 (7th Cir. 1987)	§ 7.16
O'Neal v. DeKalb County, 850 F.2d 653 (11th Cir. 1988)	App. L
O'Neil v. Krzeminski, 839 F.2d 9 (2d Cir. 1988)	§§ 3.2, 4.11, 14.13
Oregon v. Coos Bay Care Center, ____ U.S. ____, 95 L. Ed. 2d 811 (1987), *granting cert. to* 803 F.2d 1060 (9th Cir. 1986)	§ 15.15
Orshan v. Macchiarola, 629 F. Supp. 1014 (E.D.N.Y. 1986)	§§ 17.6, 17.13, 17.14, 18.3, 18.7, 19.4, 24.2, App. B, App. D, App. E
Ortega v. City of Kansas City, 659 F. Supp. 1201 (D. Kan. 1987)	App. E
Ortiz v. Burgos, 807 F.2d 6 (1st Cir. 1986)	§ 11.3
Osabutey v. Welch, 857 F.2d 220 (4th Cir. 1988)	§ 7.16
O'Shea v. Littleton, 414 U.S. 488 (1974)	§ 12.7
Ostlund v. Bobb, 825 F.2d 1371 (9th Cir. 1987), *cert. denied,* 108 S. Ct. 2016 (1988)	§ 7.13
Oten v. Colorado Bd. of Social Servs., 738 P.2d 37 (Colo. Ct. App. 1987)	App. M
Owens v. Atlanta, 780 F.2d 1564 (11th Cir. 1986)	§ 3.3
Owens v. Fulton County, 690 F. Supp. 1024 (N.D. Ga. 1988)	§ 4.7
Owens v. Okure, 109 S. Ct. 573 (1989)	§ 10.6
Pace Resources v. Shrewsbury Township, 808 F.2d 1023 (3d Cir.), *cert. denied,* 107 S. Ct. 2482 (1987)	§ 1.3A
Pachaly v. City of Lynchburg, 696 F. Supp. 180 (W.D. Va. 1988)	§ 9.3
Pacific W. Cable Co. v. City of Sacramento, 693 F. Supp. 865 (E.D. Cal. 1988)	§§ 18.8, 21.8, App. E
Packard v. Gordon, 148 Vt. 579, 537 A.2d 140 (1987)	§ 1.3A, App. M
Paddack v. Morris, 783 F.2d 844 (9th Cir. 1986)	§ 24.4
Paisey v. Vitale, 807 F.2d 889 (11th Cir. 1986)	§§ 5.14, 7.4
Palmer v. City of Chicago, 576 F. Supp. 252 (N.D. Ill. 1983), *enforced,* 596 F. Supp. 1060 (N.D. Ill. 1984), *rev'd,* 806 F.2d 1316 (7th Cir. 1986), *cert. denied,* 107 S. Ct. 2180 (1987)	§§ 15.4, 15.6, 15.13, 15.18, 15.19, 15.20, 17.13, 18.14, 24.4, 24.7
Palmer v. Schultz, 679 F. Supp. 68 (D.D.C. 1988)	§§ 18.3, 18.5, 18.8, 20.3, 20.4A, 20.4C, 20.4D
Palmer v. Schultz, 594 F. Supp. 433 (D.D.C.), *modified on reconsideration,* 598 F. Supp. 382 (D.D.C. 1984), *aff'd in part, remanded in part,* 38 FEP Cas (BNA) 672 (D.C. Cir. 1985), *vacated & remanded on other grounds,* 478 U.S. 1015 (1986)	§§ 17.13, 17.15, 17.17, 18.3, 18.5, 18.6, 18.7, 18.10, 20.4, 21.8, 24.2, App. G, App. K

Case	*Book §*
Palmerin v. City of Riverside, 794 F.2d 1409 (9th Cir. 1986)	§ 4.6
Panola Land Buying Ass'n v. Clark, 844 F.2d 1506 (11th Cir. 1988)	§ 22.8
Papapetropoulous v. Milwaukee Transp. Servs., 795 F.2d 591 (7th Cir. 1986)	§ 9.9
Papasan v. Allain, 106 S. Ct. 2932 (1986)	§ 6.5
Paradise v. Prescott, 626 F. Supp. 117 (M.D. Ala. 1985)	§§ 16.11, 16.13
Pariser v. Christian Health Care Sys., 816 F.2d 1248 (8th Cir. 1987)	§ 5.14
Parker v. Board of Dentistry, 818 F.2d 504 (6th Cir. 1987)	§ 12.8
Parker v. Department of Pub. Welfare, 811 F.2d 925 (5th Cir. 1987)	§ 3.2
Parker v. District of Columbia, 850 F.2d 708 (D.C. Cir. 1988)	§ 4.9
Parker v. Williams, 862 F.2d 1471 (11th Cir. 1988)	§§ 4.7, 19.7
Parkerson v. Carrouth, 782 F.2d 1449 (8th Cir. 1986)	§ 11.2
Parratt v. Taylor, 451 U.S. 527 (1981)	§ 1.5
Parrett v. City of Connersville, 737 F.2d 690 (7th Cir. 1984), *cert. dismissed,* 469 U.S. 1145 (1985)	§ 8.1
Parrish v. Johnson, 800 F.2d 600 (6th Cir. 1986)	§§ 14.1, 14.6, 14.8, 14.11
Pasterczyk v. Fair, 819 F.2d 12 (1st Cir. 1987)	§ 9.5
Patsy v. Board of Regents, 457 U.S. 496 (1982)	§§ 3.11, 8.3, 10.9, 12.8
Patterson v. Aiken, 628 F. Supp. 1068 (N.D. Ga. 1985), *aff'd,* 784 F.2d 403 (11th Cir. 1986)	§ 7.3
Patterson v. Fuller, 654 F. Supp. 418 (N.D. Ga. 1987)	§§ 3.4, 3.5
Patterson v. Portch, 853 F.2d 1399 (7th Cir. 1988)	§ 3.2
Patteson v. Johnson, 790 F.2d 712 (8th Cir. 1986)	§§ 15.6, 24.6
Patteson v. Johnson, 787 F.2d 1245 (8th Cir.), *cert. denied,* 107 S. Ct. 109 (1986)	§ 6.5
Patton v. County of Kings, 857 F.2d 1379 (9th Cir. 1988)	§ 23.5
Patton v. Przybylski, 822 F.2d 697 (7th Cir. 1987)	§§ 3.7, 4.12
Patzner v. Burkett, 779 F.2d 1363 (8th Cir. 1985)	§§ 3.3, 7.12
Paul v. Federal Nat'l Mfg. Ass'n, 697 F. Supp. 547 (D.D.C. 1988)	§ 23.4
Paulucci v. Duluth, 826 F.2d 780 (8th Cir. 1987)	§§ 3.10, 9.5
Paxton v. Union Nat'l Bank, 806 F.2d 785 (8th Cir. 1986)	§§ 18.7, 19.5
Peduto v. North Wildwood, 696 F. Supp. 1004 (D.N.J. 1988)	§§ 3.10, 9.5
P. Edward A. v. Williams, 696 F. Supp. 1432 (D. Utah 1988)	§ 12.8
Peery v. Department of Agriculture, 402 N.W.2d 695 (S.D. 1987)	§ 9.12
Pembaur v. City of Cincinnati, 746 F.2d 337 (6th Cir. 1984), *rev'd,* 106 S. Ct. 1292 (1986)	§§ 4.4, 4.7
Pendleton Constr. Corp. v. Rockbridge County, 652 F. Supp. 312 (W.D. Va. 1987), *aff'd,* 837 F.2d 178 (4th Cir. 1988)	§ 7.10
Pennell v. San Jose, 108 S. Ct. 849 (1988)	§ 3.10
Pennhurst State School & Hosp. v. Halderman, 465 U.S. 89 (1984)	§ 16.8
Pennsylvania v. Delaware Valley Citizens' Council, 107 S. Ct. 3078 (1987)	§§ 20.4A-20.4F, 20.5, 21.2
Pennsylvania Coal Co. v. Mahon, 260 U.S. 393 (1922)	§ 3.10

Case	*Book §*
Pennzoil Co. v. Texaco, 107 S. Ct. 1519 (1987)	§§ 5.13, 5.14, 12.1, 12.8, 12.9
People's Nat'l Util. Co. v. Houston, 837 F.2d 1366 (5th Cir. 1988)	§ 12.14
Perez v. Ortiz, 849 F.2d 793 (2d Cir. 1988)	§§ 1.5, 4.12
Perkins v. Mobile Hous. Bd., 847 F.2d 735 (11th Cir. 1988)	§§ 17.3, 18.2, 18.3, 18.12, 20.4D, App. F
Perlman v. City of Chicago, 801 F.2d 262 (7th Cir. 1986)	§ 15.13
Pernell v. San Jose, 108 S. Ct. 849 (1988)	§ 2.4
Perotti v. Carty, 647 F. Supp. 39 (S.D. Ohio 1986), *aff'd,* 848 F.2d 193 (6th Cir. 1988)	§ 10.8
Perry v. Brakke, 826 F.2d 740 (8th Cir. 1987), *cert. denied,* 108 S. Ct. 722 (1988)	§§ 9.10, 12.8, 14.1
Perry v. Larson, 794 F.2d 279 (7th Cir. 1986)	§ 14.17
Pesticide Pub. Policy v. Village of Wauconda, 622 F. Supp. 423 (N.D. Ill. 1985), *aff'd,* 826 F.2d 1068 (7th Cir. 1987)	§ 3.2
Petition for Review of Opinion 552, *In re,* 102 N.J. 194, 507 A.2d 233 (1986)	§ 4.13
Phelps v. Washburn Univ., 807 F.2d 153 (10th Cir. 1986)	§ 24.4
Picozzi v. Sandalow, 623 F. Supp. 1571 (E.D. Mich. 1986), *aff'd,* 827 F.2d 770 (6th Cir. 1987), *cert. denied,* 108 S. Ct. 777 (1988)	§ 6.6
Pierce v. Underwood, 108 S. Ct. 2541 (1988)	§ 24.5
Piesco v. City of N.Y., 693 F. Supp. 96 (S.D.N.Y. 1988)	§ 10.9
Pietroniro v. Borough of Oceanport, 764 F.2d 976 (3d Cir.), *cert. denied,* 474 U.S. 1020 (1985)	§ 3.11
Pillette v. Detroit Police Dep't, 661 F. Supp. 1145 (E.D. Mich. 1987)	§ 6.1
Pilliard v. Meyer, 689 F. Supp. 979 (E.D. Mo. 1988)	§ 22.9
Pincham v. Judicial Inquiry Bd., 681 F. Supp. 1309 (N.D. Ill. 1988)	§ 12.8
Pinehurst Enters. v. Town of S. Pines, 690 F. Supp. 444 (M.D.N.C. 1988)	§ 3.2
Pitt v. Pine Valley Golf Club, 695 F. Supp. 778 (D.N.J. 1988)	§ 5.11
Pizzato's v. City of Berwyn, 168 Ill. App. 3d 796, 523 N.E.2d 51 (1988)	§ 7.18
Plain v. Flicker, 645 F. Supp. 898 (D.N.J. 1986)	§§ 5.11, 5.14, 10.6
Planned Parenthood v. Arizona, 789 F.2d 1348 (9th Cir. 1985)	§ 17.8, App. F, App. G
Planned Parenthood v. Montana, 648 F. Supp. 47 (D. Mont. 1986)	§ 3.11
Pliska v. City of Stevens Point, 823 F.2d 1168 (7th Cir. 1987)	§ 9.5
P.L.S. Partners v. City of Cranston, 696 F. Supp. 788 (D.R.I. 1988)	§ 3.10
Poe v. Haydon, 853 F.2d 418 (6th Cir. 1988), *cert. denied,* 109 S. Ct. 788 (1989)	§§ 4.11, 7.12, 7.18
Polenz v. Parrott, 694 F. Supp. 599 (E.D. Wis. 1988)	§ 7.10
Poling v. Goins, 713 S.W.2d 305 (Tenn. 1986)	§ 1.6
Polk v. Montgomery County, 782 F.2d 1196 (4th Cir. 1986)	§ 9.12
Polk County v. Dodson, 454 U.S. 312 (1981)	§§ 5.4, 5.5
Polykoff v. Collins, 816 F.2d 1326 (9th Cir. 1987)	§§ 12.7, 12.8, 12.11

Case	*Book §*
Popham v. City of Kennesaw, 820 F.2d 1570 (11th Cir. 1987)	§§ 3.3, 15.11, 16.9, 19.3, 19.6, 23.1, 23.3
Port Auth. Police Benevolent Ass'n v. Port Auth. of N.Y. & N.J., 819 F.2d 413 (3d Cir.), *cert. denied,* 108 S. Ct. 344 (1987)	§ 6.11
Potomac Elec. Power Co. v. Sachs, 802 F.2d 1527 (4th Cir. 1986), *vacated,* 108 S. Ct. 743 (1988)	§§ 12.6, 12.7
Praprotnik v. St. Louis, 798 F.2d 1168 (8th Cir. 1986), *rev'd on other grounds,* 108 S. Ct. 915 (1988)	§§ 4.6, 4.7, 4.8, 4.9, 21.3
Pratt v. Thornburgh, 807 F.2d 355 (3d Cir. 1986), *cert. denied,* 108 S. Ct. 125 (1987)	§ 10.7
Prejean v. Ochsner Clinic, 669 F. Supp. 146 (E.D. La. 1987)	App. E
Presco v. City of N.Y., 650 F. Supp. 896 (S.D.N.Y. 1987)	§ 10.9
Prescott v. Palos Verdes Peninsula Unified School Dist., 659 F. Supp. 921 (C.D. Cal. 1987)	§ 15.16
Preuit & Mauldin v. Jones, 763 F.2d 1250 (11th Cir. 1985), *cert. denied,* 106 S. Ct. 893 (1986)	§ 10.6
Price v. County of Erie, 654 F. Supp. 1206 (W.D.N.Y. 1987)	§§ 3.2, 3.11
Price v. Digital Equip. Corp., 846 F.2d 1026 (5th Cir. 1988)	§ 10.6
Prisco v. Department of Justice, 851 F.2d 93 (3d Cir. 1988)	§§ 7.11, 7.18
Private Truck Council v. Secretary of State, 503 A.2d 214 (Me.), *cert. denied,* 476 U.S. 1129 (1986)	§§ 3.2, 15.15
Probe v. State Teachers' Retirement Sys., 780 F.2d 776 (9th Cir. 1986)	§§ 17.4, 19.5, App. C, App. F
Proctor v. Consolidated Freightways Corp., 795 F.2d 1472 (9th Cir. 1986)	§§ 15.4, 15.6
Pryzina v. Levy, 813 F.2d 821 (7th Cir. 1987)	§§ 7.7, 7.8
Public Serv. Co. v. Town of W. Newbury, 835 F.2d 380 (1st Cir. 1987)	§ 14.1
Puckett v. City of Emmelt, 113 Idaho 639, 747 P.2d 48 (1987)	§ 9.12
Pueblo Neighborhood Health Centers v. Losavio, 847 F.2d 642 (10th Cir. 1988)	§§ 7.12, 7.18
Pulliam v. Allen, 466 U.S. 522, 80 L. Ed. 2d 565 (1984)	§ 16.7
Punton v. City of Seattle, 805 F.2d 1378 (9th Cir. 1986), *cert. denied,* 107 S. Ct. 1954 (1987)	§§ 9.5, 15.17
Quesada v. Thomason, 850 F.2d 537 (9th Cir. 1988)	§§ 19.6, 19.8, 21.3
Quinones v. Coler, 651 F. Supp. 1028 (N.D. Ill. 1987)	§ 2.5
Quiros v. Hernandez Colon, 800 F.2d 1 (1st Cir. 1986)	§ 23.3, App. L
Radecki v. Amoco Oil Co., 858 F.2d 397 (8th Cir. 1988)	§ 21.4
Raffucci Alvarado v. Sonia Zayas, 816 F.2d 818 (1st Cir. 1987)	§ 7.12
Railroad Comm'n v. Pullman Co., 312 U.S. 496 (1941)	§ 15.7
Rakovich v. Wade, 850 F.2d 1180 (7th Cir.), *cert. denied,* 109 S. Ct. 497 (1988)	§§ 3.2A, 7.12, 7.13, 7.18
Ramah Navajo School Bd. v. Bureau of Revenue, 104 N.M. 302, 720 P.2d 1243 (Ct. App.), *cert. denied,* 479 U.S. 940 (1986)	§§ 3.2, 3.11, 6.1, 15.1, 15.15, 16.8
Ram Ditta v. Maryland Nat'l Capital Park & Planning Comm'n, 822 F.2d 456 (4th Cir. 1987)	§ 6.11

Case	*Book §*
Ramos v. Lamm, 632 F. Supp. 376 (D. Colo. 1986)	§§ 15.19, 17.3, 17.4, 17.5, 17.6, 17.10, 17.13, 17.15, 18.5, 18.10, 18.17, App. C, App. E, App. F
Ramsey v. Board of Educ., 844 F.2d 1268 (6th Cir. 1988)	§ 3.2
Ramsey v. Chrysler First, Inc., 861 F.2d 1541 (11th Cir. 1988)	§ 17.9
Randolph County v. Alabama Power Co., 784 F.2d 1067 (11th Cir.), *modified,* 798 F.2d 425 (11th Cir. 1986), *cert. denied,* 107 S. Ct. 878 (1987)	§ 2.3
Ransom v. Marrazzo, 848 F.2d 398 (3d Cir. 1988)	§ 13.4
Rascon v. Hardiman, 803 F.2d 269 (7th Cir. 1986)	§§ 3.2, 4.11
Rateree v. Rockett, 852 F.2d 946 (7th Cir. 1988)	§ 7.10
Rateree v. Rockett, 685 F. Supp. 670 (N.D. Ill. 1988)	§ 21.3, App. E
Rateree v. Rockett, 668 F. Supp. 1155 (N.D. Ill. 1987)	§ 21.4
Rateree v. Rockett, 630 F. Supp. 763 (N.D. Ill. 1986)	§ 7.10
Ratliff v. Board of Educ., 820 F.2d 792 (6th Cir. 1987)	§§ 14.6, 14.8
Ratliff v. Milwaukee, 795 F.2d 612 (7th Cir. 1986)	§ 3.2
Ratzel v. Marinette County, 694 F. Supp. 606 (E.D. Wis. 1988)	§ 10.6
Ray v. Florida Cabinet, 845 F.2d 311 (11th Cir. 1988)	§ 24.4
Real v. Continental Group, Inc., 653 F. Supp. 736 (N.D. Cal. 1987)	§ 21.4
Real v. Continental Group, Inc., 116 F.R.D. 211 (N.D. Cal. 1986)	§ 17.16
Reeves v. Harrell, 791 F.2d 1481 (11th Cir. 1986)	§§ 16.11, 16.13, 21.5
Reichman v. Bonsignore, Brignati & Mazzotta P.C., 818 F.2d 278 (2d Cir. 1987)	§ 21.8
Reigh v. Schleigh, 829 F.2d 1334 (4th Cir. 1987), *cert. denied,* 108 S. Ct. 1247 (1988)	§ 15.14
Rhodes v. Stewart, 109 S. Ct. 202 (1988)	§ 15.4
Richardson v. Bonds, 860 F.2d 1427 (7th Cir. 1988)	§ 7.16
Rich v. Dollar, 841 F.2d 1558 (11th Cir. 1988)	§§ 7.8, 7.16
Rickman v. Dole, 671 F. Supp. 982 (S.D.N.Y. 1987)	App. E
Ridgway v. Wapello County, 795 F.2d 646 (8th Cir. 1986)	§§ 10.6, 10.7
Ring v. Crisp County Hosp. Auth., 652 F. Supp. 477 (M.D. Ga. 1987)	§§ 3.2, 3.11
Rinker v. Napa County, 831 F.2d 829 (9th Cir. 1987)	§ 3.3
Rinker v. Napa County, 820 F.2d 295 (9th Cir. 1987)	§ 3.5
Ritter v. Mount St. Mary's College, 814 F.2d 986 (4th Cir.), *cert. denied,* 108 S. Ct. 260 (1987)	§ 14.2
Ritter, Estate of v. University of Mich., 851 F.2d 846 (6th Cir. 1988)	§§ 6.11, 6.12
Rivera v. City of Riverside, 763 F.2d 1580 (9th Cir.), *aff'd,* 477 U.S. 561 (1986)	Chap. 15 Intro., §§ 16.3, 16.14, 17.2, 17.3, 17.5, 17.15, 18.2, 18.5, 18.7, 19.1, 19.2, 19.3, 19.5, 19.6, 19.7, 21.2, 21.3, 24.5, App. E, App. F, App. G

Case	*Book §*
Rivera v. Coler, 629 F. Supp. 366 (N.D. Ill. 1986)	§§ 15.13, 15.20
Rivera v. Green, 775 F.2d 1381 (9th Cir. 1985), *cert. denied,* 475 U.S. 1128 (1986)	§ 10.6
Riverside, City of v. Rivera, 106 S. Ct. 2686 (1986)	§ 19.6
Robert D. v. Sobel, 688 F. Supp. 861 (S.D.N.Y. 1988)	§ 15.16
Roberts v. College of the Desert, 861 F.2d 1163 (9th Cir. 1988)	§ 24.4
Roberts v. Louisiana Downs, 742 F.2d 221 (5th Cir. 1984)	§ 5.14
Roberts v. Murphy, 684 F. Supp. 759 (D. Mass. 1988)	§ 10.6
Robertson v. Wegmann, 436 U.S. 584 (1978)	§ 11.2
Robinette v. Barnes, 854 F.2d 909 (6th Cir. 1988)	§ 3.4
Robinson v. Beaumont, 291 Ark. 477, 725 S.W.2d 839 (1987)	§ 7.18
Robinson v. Bibb, 840 F.2d 349 (6th Cir. 1988)	§ 7.13
Robinson v. Boyer, 825 F.2d 64 (5th Cir. 1987)	§ 9.5
Robinson v. Chicago, 638 F. Supp. 186 (N.D. Ill. 1986)	§ 2.5
Robinson v. City of Lake Station, 630 F. Supp. 1052 (N.D. Ind. 1986)	App. E
Robinson v. Young, 674 F. Supp. 1356 (W.D. Wis. 1987)	§ 8.3
Robison v. Canterbury Village, 848 F.2d 424 (3d Cir. 1988)	§ 5.11
Robison v. Via, 821 F.2d 913 (2d Cir. 1987)	§§ 1.5, 3.3, 3.9, 7.8
Rocky v. Vittorie, 813 F.2d 734 (5th Cir. 1987)	§ 8.3
Rocky Mountain Airways v. Pitkin County, 674 F. Supp. 312 (D. Colo. 1987)	§ 3.11
Rode v. Dellarciprete, 845 F.2d 1195 (3d Cir. 1988)	§ 4.11
Rodgers v. Corporation of Harpers Ferry, 371 S.E.2d 358 (W. Va. 1988)	§ 10.6
Rodriguez v. Hardy, 802 F.2d 817 (5th Cir. 1986)	§ 24.4
Rodriguez v. Schweiger, 796 F.2d 930 (7th Cir. 1986), *cert. denied,* 107 S. Ct. 1899 (1987)	§ 9.3
Rodriguez Hernandez v. Almodovar, 631 F. Supp. 960 (D.P.R. 1986)	§ 2.3
Roe v. Drexel Univ., 852 F.2d 715 (3d Cir. 1988)	§ 14.2
Rogers v. Bruntrager, 841 F.2d 853 (8th Cir. 1988)	§ 7.5
Rogers v. Kelly, 674 F. Supp. 1372 (E.D. Ark. 1987)	App. E
Rogers v. Motta, 655 F. Supp. 39 (D. Mass. 1986)	§ 18.15, App. E
Rogers v. Okin, 821 F.2d 22 (1st Cir. 1987), *cert. denied,* 108 S. Ct. 709 (1988)	§§ 16.8, 17.10, 17.13, 17.14, 17.17, 18.10, 18.17, 19.4, 20.3, 24.5
Rogers v. Okin, 638 F. Supp. 934 (D. Mass. 1986)	§ 17.4, App. E
Rogers v. Saylor, 306 Or. 267, 760 P.2d 232 (1988)	§ 6.1, App. M
Rohena Encarnacion v. Department of Treasury, 665 F. Supp. 102 (D.P.R. 1987)	§ 10.4
Rohrer v. Slatile Roofing & Sheet Metal Co., Inc., 655 F. Supp. 736 (N.D. Ind. 1987)	§ 21.4
Rojas v. Alexander's Dep't Store, 654 F. Supp. 856 (E.D.N.Y. 1986)	§§ 1.5, 5.13
Roland v. Johnson, 856 F.2d 764 (6th Cir. 1988)	§ 3.4A
Rollison v. Biggs, 656 F. Supp. 1204 (D. Del.), *reargument denied,* 660 F. Supp. 875 (D. Del. 1987)	§ 15.16

AUTHORITIES

Case	*Book §*
Sanok v. Grimes, 306 Or. 259, 760 P.2d 228 (1988)	§ 10.6
Santella v. Grishaber, 672 F. Supp. 321 (N.D. Ill. 1987)	§ 1.5
Sapanajin v. Gunter, 857 F.2d 463 (8th Cir. 1988)	§ 21.8
Sattler v. Johnson, 857 F.2d 224 (4th Cir. 1988)	§ 10.6
Savage v. Toan, 636 F. Supp. 156 (W.D. Mo. 1986)	§§ 5.6, 16.7, 16.10, 16.12, 16.13
Save Our Cumberland Mountains, Inc. v. Hodel, 857 F.2d 1516 (D.C. Cir. 1988)	§ 18.5
Save Our Cumberland Mountains, Inc. v. Hodel, 826 F.2d 43 (D.C. Cir.), *reh'g en banc granted,* 830 F.2d 1182 (D.C. Cir. 1987)	§§ 18.5, 18.8, 20.3, App. B
Save Our Cumberland Mountains, Inc. v. Hodel, 651 F. Supp. 1528 (D.D.C. 1986)	§ 18.14
Save Our Cumberland Mountains, Inc. v. Hodel, 622 F. Supp. 1160 (D.D.C. 1985)	§ 17.6
Savidge v. Fincannon, 836 F.2d 898 (5th Cir. 1988)	§§ 7.13, 7.13A, 15.13
Savin v. Samaritan Health Center, 813 F.2d 755 (6th Cir. 1987)	§ 5.14
Saye v. St. Vrain Valley School Dist., 650 F. Supp. 716 (D. Colo. 1986)	§ 4.7
Schaefer v. Wilcock, 676 F. Supp. 1092 (D. Utah 1987)	§§ 2.5, 5.11
Schafer v. Waupaca, 637 F. Supp. 176 (E.D. Wis. 1986)	§ 3.10
Schaper v. City of Huntsville, 813 F.2d 709 (5th Cir. 1987)	§§ 3.2, 3.8, 7.18
Scherer v. Balkema, 840 F.2d 437 (7th Cir.), *cert. denied,* 108 S. Ct. 1035 (1988)	§ 10.4
Schiavone Constr. Co. v. Merola, 678 F. Supp. 64 (S.D.N.Y.), *aff'd,* 848 F.2d 43 (2d Cir.), *cert. denied,* 109 S. Ct. 144 (1988)	§ 3.2
Schirk v. Herlik, 689 F. Supp. 861 (E.D. Wis. 1988)	§ 18.6, App. E
Schlegel v. Bebout, 841 F.2d 937 (9th Cir. 1988)	§§ 7.7, 7.8, 7.18
School Bd. of Prince William County v. Malone, 662 F. Supp. 999 (E.D. Va. 1987)	§ 15.16
Schrader v. Idaho Dep't of Health & Welfare, 631 F. Supp. 1426 (D. Idaho 1986)	§§ 5.6, 15.15, 16.10, 16.12, 16.13, 18.14, App. E, App. J
Schulte v. Dodge City, 630 F. Supp. 327 (D. Kan. 1986)	§ 7.16
Schultz v. Crowley, 802 F.2d 498 (D.C. Cir. 1986)	§ 24.4
Schwartzman v. Valenzuela, 846 F.2d 1209 (9th Cir. 1988)	§§ 7.8, 7.18
Schwarz v. Board of Trustees, 31 Ohio St. 3d 267, 510 N.E.2d 808 (1987)	§ 6.1
Scott v. Lacy, 811 F.2d 1153 (7th Cir. 1987)	§ 7.18
Scott v. Rieht, 690 F. Supp. 368 (E.D. Pa. 1988)	§ 1.5
Scott v. Schmidt, 773 F.2d 160 (7th Cir. 1985)	§ 7.3
Scott County Master Docket, *In re,* 672 F. Supp. 1152 (D. Minn. 1987)	§ 6.2
Scrivner v. Andrews, 816 F.2d 261 (6th Cir. 1987)	§ 3.11
Scroggins v. Kansas, 802 F.2d 1289 (10th Cir. 1986)	§§ 9.8, 9.10
Scurlock v. City of Lynn Haven, 858 F.2d 1521 (11th Cir. 1988)	§§ 15.15, 15.17
Scutieri v. Estate of Revitz, 683 F. Supp. 795 (S.D. Fla. 1988)	§§ 4.4, 5.14

Case	*Book §*
S&D Maintenance Co. v. Goldin, 844 F.2d 962 (2d Cir. 1988)	§ 3.2
Searcy v. Crim, 692 F. Supp. 1363 (N.D. Ga. 1988)	§§ 18.3, 20.4D, 24.3, App. E
Seaway Drive-In, Inc. v. Township of Clay, 791 F.2d 447 (6th Cir.), *cert. denied,* 479 U.S. 884 (1986)	§§ 15.15, 15.17, 15.20
Sebra v. Neville, 801 F.2d 1135 (9th Cir. 1986)	§§ 6.1, 7.17A
Segars v. Fulton County, 654 F. Supp. 42 (N.D. Ga. 1986)	App. E
Segundo v. City of Rancho Mirage, 813 F.2d 1387 (9th Cir. 1987)	§§ 3.2, 15.15
Seibring v. Parcell's, Inc., 159 Ill. App. 3d 376, 512 N.E.2d 394 (1987)	§ 1.6
Sellers v. Delgado Community College, 839 F.2d 1132 (5th Cir. 1988)	§ 18.7
Sellers v. Local 1598, 638 F. Supp. 507 (E.D. Pa. 1986)	§ 24.2
Selzer v. Board of Educ., 113 F.R.D. 165 (S.D.N.Y. 1986)	§ 10.4
Semar v. Platte Valley Fed. S&L Ass'n, 791 F.2d 699 (9th Cir. 1986)	§§ 18.3, 18.7, App. E
Serio v. Members of State Bd. of Pardons, 821 F.2d 1112 (5th Cir. 1987)	§§ 7.6, 8.6
Sevigny v. Dicksey, 846 F.2d 953 (4th Cir. 1988)	§§ 7.16, 21.8
Sexton v. Ryan, 804 F.2d 26 (2d Cir. 1986)	§ 14.15
Shabazz v. Coughlin, 852 F.2d 697 (2d Cir. 1988)	§ 6.1
Shaddy v. Gunter, 690 F. Supp. 860 (D. Neb. 1988)	§ 7.7
Shah v. County of Los Angeles, 797 F.2d 743 (9th Cir. 1986)	§§ 1.3, 3.9, 4.12, 15.4, 15.6
Shakman v. Democratic Org. of Cook County, 677 F. Supp. 933 (N.D. Ill. 1987)	§§ 18.17, 20.1, 20.3, 20.4D, 20.5
Shakman v. Democratic Org. of Cook County, 634 F. Supp. 895 (N.D. Ill. 1986)	§§ 15.3, 17.4, 17.5, 17.9, 18.17, 21.5, App. C, App. E, App. J
Shannon v. Bepko, 684 F. Supp. 1465 (S.D. Ind. 1988)	§ 6.11
Shannon v. Recording Indus. Ass'n, 661 F. Supp. 205 (S.D. Ohio 1987)	§ 10.4
Shannon v. Telco Communications, 824 F.2d 150 (1st Cir. 1987)	§ 12.10
Shapiro v. Chapman, 70 Md. App. 307, 520 A.2d 1330 (Ct. Spec. App. 1987)	§ 15.17, App. M
Sharma v. Stevas, 790 F.2d 1486 (9th Cir. 1986)	§ 7.5
Sharpe v. City of Lewisburg, 677 F. Supp. 1362 (M.D. Tenn. 1988)	§§ 11.3, 14.10
Sharpley v. Davis, 786 F.2d 1109 (11th Cir. 1986)	§ 9.4
Shaw v. Department of Alcoholic Beverage Control, 788 F.2d 600 (9th Cir. 1986)	§§ 4.7, 4.12
Shaw v. Library of Congress, 747 F.2d 1469 (D.C. Cir. 1984), *rev'd on other grounds,* 478 U.S. 310 (1986)	§§ 20.5, 21.9, 24.5
Sheets v. Department of Corrections, 656 F. Supp. 733 (S.D. Ind. 1986)	§ 3.8
Shelby v. McAdory, 781 F.2d 1053 (5th Cir. 1986)	§ 10.6
Shelly v. Johnson, 849 F.2d 228 (6th Cir. 1988)	§ 7.7

Case	*Book §*
Shelter Creed Dev. Corp. v. City of Oxnard, 838 F.2d 375 (9th Cir.), *cert. denied,* 159 S. Ct. 134 (1988)	§ 3.10
Sherrell v. Longview, 683 F. Supp. 1108 (E.D. Tex. 1987)	§ 3.2
Sherrod v. Berry, 827 F.2d 195 (7th Cir. 1987), *reh'g granted,* 835 F.2d 1222 (7th Cir.), *rev'd,* 856 F.2d 802 (7th Cir. 1988)	§§ 3.4, 11.2, 11.3, 14.10
Shertz v. Waupaca County, 683 F. Supp. 1551 (E.D. Wis. 1988)	§ 7.16
Shields v. Martin, 109 Idaho 32, 706 P.2d 21 (1985)	§§ 14.13, 14.14
Shipes v. Trinity Indus., Inc., 685 F. Supp. 612 (E.D. Tex. 1987)	§ 21.8
Shockley v. Jones, 823 F.2d 1068 (7th Cir. 1987)	§ 6.1
Shorter v. Valley Bank & Trust Co., 678 F. Supp. 714 (N.D. Ill. 1988)	§ 21.3
Showery v. Samaniego, 814 F.2d 200 (5th Cir. 1987)	§ 12.9
Sierra Club v. United States Army Corps of Eng'rs, 776 F.2d 383 (2d Cir. 1985), *cert. denied,* 475 U.S. 1084 (1986)	§ 24.6
Silano v. Tirozzi, 651 F. Supp. 1021 (D. Conn. 1987)	§ 15.16
Silver v. Baggiano, 804 F.2d 1211 (11th Cir. 1986)	§§ 3.11, 6.6, 6.12
Simien v. City of San Antonio, 809 F.2d 255 (5th Cir. 1987)	§ 15.11
Simmons v. Dickhaut, 804 F.2d 182 (1st Cir. 1986)	§ 3.9
Sims v. Jefferson Downs Racing Ass'n, 778 F.2d 1068 (5th Cir. 1985)	§§ 5.12, 5.14, 14.14, 18.13, 21.2, 21.3, 24.5
Sinn v. The Daily Nebraskan, 829 F.2d 662 (8th Cir. 1987)	§ 5.14
Skehan v. State Sys. of Higher Educ., 815 F.2d 244 (3d Cir. 1987)	§ 6.11
Skelton v. General Motors Corp., 661 F. Supp. 1368 (N.D. Ill. 1987)	§ 18.17
Skevofilax v. Quigley, 810 F.2d 378 (3d Cir.), *cert. denied,* 107 S. Ct. 1956 (1987)	§ 14.18
Skinner v. Total Petroleum, 859 F.2d 1439 (10th Cir. 1988)	§ 14.2
Small v. Inhabitants of Belfast, 796 F.2d 544 (1st Cir. 1986)	§§ 4.7, 10.6, 10.7
Smiddy v. Varney, 803 F.2d 1469 (9th Cir. 1986), *modified,* 811 F.2d 504 (9th Cir. 1987)	§ 3.7
Smiddy v. Varney, 665 F.2d 261 (9th Cir. 1981), *cert. denied,* 459 U.S. 829 (1982)	§ 3.7
Smith v. Chicago, 820 F.2d 916 (7th Cir. 1987)	§ 9.12
Smith v. City of Fontana, 818 F.2d 1411 (9th Cir.), *cert. denied,* 108 S. Ct. 1311 (1987)	§§ 2.5, 3.3, 3.4, 3.9, 11.3
Smith v. City of N.Y., 611 F. Supp. 1080 (S.D.N.Y. 1985)	§ 3.3
Smith v. Department of Pub. Health, 428 Mich. 540, 410 N.W.2d 749 (1987), *cert. granted sub nom.* Will v. Department of State Police, 108 S. Ct. 1466 (1988)	§ 5.2
Smith v. Kirk, 821 F.2d 980 (4th Cir. 1987)	§ 3.11
Smith v. Montgomery County, 643 F. Supp. 435 (D. Md. 1986)	§ 14.11
Smith v. Pittsburgh, 764 F.2d 188 (3d Cir.), *cert. denied,* 106 S. Ct. 349 (1985)	§ 10.6
Smith v. Reagan, 841 F.2d 28 (2d Cir. 1988)	§ 6.3
Smith v. Robinson, 468 U.S. 992 (1984)	§§ 3.2, 3.11, 15.12, 15.13, 15.14, 15.15, 15.16, 15.17, 16.1

Case	*Book §*
Smith v. Springer, 859 F.2d 31 (7th Cir. 1988)	§ 8.6
Smith v. Wade, 461 U.S. 30 (1983)	§ 14.13
Smith v. Winter, 782 F.2d 508 (5th Cir. 1986)	§ 5.4
Smith v. Wood, 649 F. Supp. 901 (E.D. Pa. 1986)	§ 7.4
Smith, Estate of v. Heckler, 622 F. Supp. 403 (D. Colo. 1985)	§§ 5.6, 16.10
Smothers v. Gibson, 778 F.2d 470 (8th Cir. 1985)	§ 7.16
Society for Good Will to Retarded Children v. Cuomo, 652 F. Supp. 515 (E.D.N.Y. 1987)	§ 6.6
Soderbeck v. Burnett County, 821 F.2d 446 (7th Cir. 1987)	§ 4.7
Soffer v. City of Costa Mesa, 798 F.2d 361 (9th Cir. 1986)	§ 23.2
Soliman v. Ebasco Servs. Inc., 822 F.2d 320 (2d Cir. 1987)	§§ 17.14, 24.1
Solomon v. City of Gainesville, 796 F.2d 1464 (11th Cir. 1986)	§§ 15.1, 15.11
S-1 v. Spangler, 832 F.2d 294 (4th Cir. 1987)	§ 24.4
Sorey v. Kellett, 849 F.2d 960 (5th Cir. 1988)	§ 7.18
Sorola v. City of Lamesa, 808 F.2d 435 (5th Cir. 1987)	§§ 15.13, 24.3
Sosna v. Iowa, 419 U.S. 393 (1975)	§ 6.12
Soto v. Lord, 693 F. Supp. 8 (S.D.N.Y. 1988)	§§ 3.8, 14.11
Soto-Gomez v. Lopez-Feliciano, 698 F. Supp. 28 (D.P.R. 1988)	§ 2.3
Soto-Lopez v. Civil Serv. Comm'n, 840 F.2d 162 (2d Cir. 1988)	§ 14.1
Soules v. Kauaians for Nukolii Campaign Comm., 849 F.2d 1176 (9th Cir. 1988)	§ 3.2
Sourbeer v. Robinson, 791 F.2d 1094 (3d Cir. 1986), *cert. denied sub nom.* Patton v. Sourbeer, 107 S. Ct. 3276 (1987)	§§ 3.5, 7.13, 14.11
Southerland v. International Longshoremen's Local 8, 845 F.2d 796 (9th Cir. 1987)	§ 16.15
South Macomb Disposal Auth. v. Township, 790 F.2d 500 (6th Cir. 1986)	§ 2.3
Sowers v. Bradford Area School Dist., 694 F. Supp. 125 (W.D. Pa. 1988)	§ 10.4
Spanish Action Comm. v. City of Chicago, 811 F.2d 1129 (7th Cir. 1987)	§§ 17.3, 17.6, 19.2, 19.6, 21.3
Sparks v. Kentucky Character & Fitness Comm., 859 F.2d 428 (6th Cir. 1988)	§§ 7.3, 7.7
Specht v. Jensen, 832 F.2d 1516 (10th Cir. 1987)	§§ 3.4, 3.5
Spell v. McDaniel, 852 F.2d 762 (4th Cir. 1988)	§§ 17.5, 17.6, 20.4D, App. B
Spell v. McDaniel, 824 F.2d 1380 (4th Cir. 1987), *cert. denied,* 108 S. Ct. 752 (1988)	§§ 4.9, 4.10, 17.6, 18.6, 18.10, 18.14, 20.4D, 20.4F, 24.5, App. E
Spence v. Board of Educ., 806 F.2d 1198 (3d Cir. 1986)	§ 14.8
Spencer v. South Fla. Water Mgmt. Dist., 657 F. Supp. 66 (S.D. Fla. 1986)	§ 1.8
Springfield, City of v. Kibbe, 107 S. Ct. 1114 (1987)	§ 4.9
Sproul v. City of Wooster, 840 F.2d 1267 (6th Cir. 1988)	§ 3.8
St. Amant v. Benoit, 806 F.2d 1294 (5th Cir. 1987)	§ 10.6
Stanulonis v. Marzec, 649 F. Supp 1536 (D. Conn. 1986)	§ 3.5
Starnes v. Hill, 635 F. Supp. 1270 (W.D.N.C. 1986)	§§ 18.8, 18.12, App. E, App. K

Case	*Book §*
State v. Private Truck Council, 258 Ga. 531, 371 S.E.2d 378 (1988)	App. M
Steele v. Stephan, 633 F. Supp. 950 (D. Kan. 1986)	§ 1.5
Steele v. Van Buren Pub. School Dist., 845 F.2d 1492 (8th Cir. 1988)	§ 13.4, App. B
Stefan v. Laurenitis, 695 F. Supp. 1330 (D. Mass. 1988)	§ 1.2
Stein v. Board of Educ., 792 F.2d 13 (2d Cir.), *cert. denied,* 107 S. Ct. 572 (1986)	§ 7.18
Stensvad v. Towe, 759 P.2d 138 (Mont. 1988)	§ 7.11
Stephans v. Nevada, 685 F. Supp. 217 (D. Nev. 1988)	§ 6.12
Sterling v. Calvin, 694 F. Supp. 1382 (E.D. Mo. 1988)	§ 7.4
Stern v. Nix, 840 F.2d 208 (3d Cir.), *cert. denied,* 109 S. Ct. 77 (1988)	§ 1.4
Stevens v. Corbell, 832 F.2d 884 (5th Cir. 1987), *cert. denied,* 108 S. Ct. 2018 (1988)	§§ 3.3, 7.13A
Stevens v. Gay, 792 F.2d 1000 (11th Cir. 1986)	§ 16.9
Stewart v. County of Sonoma, 634 F. Supp. 773 (N.D. Cal. 1986)	§§ 17.16, 21.4, App. B, App. E, App. J, App. K
Stewart v. General Motors Corp., 756 F.2d 1285 (7th Cir. 1985)	§§ 15.6, 15.8
Stewart v. Lattanzi, 832 F.2d 12 (2d Cir. 1987)	§ 7.6
Stinson v. Hornsby, 821 F.2d 1537 (11th Cir. 1987), *cert. denied,* 109 S. Ct. 402 (1988)	§§ 5.6, 6.1, 7.17A, 8.3
Stissi v. Interstate & Ocean Transp. Co., 814 F.2d 848 (2d Cir. 1987)	§ 21.7
Stock v. Forbes Health Sys., 697 F. Supp. 1399 (W.D. Pa. 1988)	§ 6.1
Stokes v. Bullins, 844 F.2d 269 (5th Cir. 1988)	§ 4.9
Stokes v. Chicago, 660 F. Supp. 1459 (N.D. Ill. 1987)	§ 4.7
Stokes v. Village of Wurtsboro, 818 F.2d 4 (2d Cir. 1987)	§ 13.3
Stone v. Powell, 428 U.S. 465 (1976)	§ 12.7
Stoneking v. Bradford Area School Dist., 856 F.2d 594 (3d Cir. 1988)	§§ 3.2, 4.3, 71.3A
Storey v. United States, 629 F. Supp. 1174 (N.D. Miss. 1986)	§§ 3.8, 10.4
Strandell v. Jackson County, 634 F. Supp. 824 (S.D. Ill. 1986)	§§ 2.5, 3.9, 14.16
Strength v. Hubert, 854 F.2d 421 (11th Cir. 1988)	§§ 3.6, 7.9
Strength v. Hubert, 660 F. Supp. 878 (M.D. Ala.), *adhered to,* 670 F. Supp. 322 (M.D. Ala. 1987)	§ 7.9
Stubbs v. Dudley, 849 F.2d 83 (2d Cir. 1988)	§ 3.4A
Student Pub. Interest Research Group v. AT&T Bell Laboratories, 842 F.2d 1436 (3d Cir. 1988)	§§ 18.3, 18.5, 18.13, 19.5, 20.3, 20.4C, 20.4D, 20.5, 24.5, App. B
Suarez v. Illinois Valley Community College, 688 F. Supp. 376 (N.D. Ill. 1988)	§ 8.1
Suggs v. Brannon, 804 F.2d 274 (2d Cir. 1986)	§ 12.7
Sullivan v. Marshall, 628 F. Supp. 1080 (D. Mass. 1985)	§ 1.5
Sullivan v. Pittsburgh, 811 F.2d 171 (3d Cir.), *cert. denied,* 108 S. Ct. 148 (1987)	§ 12.8

Case	*Book §*
Sullivan v. Town of Salem, 805 F.2d 81 (2d Cir. 1986)	§§ 3.2, 3.8, 12.12
Sun Publishing Co. v. Mecklenburg News, Inc., 823 F.2d 818 (4th Cir. 1987)	§ 16.15
Supre v. Ricketts, 792 F.2d 958 (10th Cir. 1986)	§§ 15.13, 24.5
Swank v. Charlotte-Mecklenburg Bd. of Educ., 66 F.R.D. 483 (W.D.N.C. 1975)	§ 21.8
Swart v. Scott County, 650 F. Supp. 888 (D. Minn. 1987)	App. E
Swayne v. L.D.S. Social Servs., 670 F. Supp. 1537 (D. Utah 1987)	§ 5.14
Swentek v. USAFR, 830 F.2d 532 (4th Cir. 1987)	§ 14.2
Swink v. City of Pagedale, 810 F.2d 791 (8th Cir.), *cert. denied,* 107 S. Ct. 3274 (1987)	§ 4.6
Sykes v. McDowell, 786 F.2d 1098 (11th Cir. 1986)	§ 14.8
Szabo Food Serv., Inc. v. Canteen Corp., 823 F.2d 1073 (7th Cir. 1987)	§ 23.2
Takahashi v. Board of Trustees, 783 F.2d 848 (9th Cir.), *cert. denied,* 106 S. Ct. 2916 (1986)	§ 9.5
Talbert v. Kelly, 799 F.2d 62 (3d Cir. 1986)	§ 4.9
Tallman v. Reagan, 846 F.2d 494 (8th Cir. 1988)	§ 3.5
Tarabishi v. McAlester Regional Hosp., 827 F.2d 648 (10th Cir. 1987)	§ 5.14
Tarantino v. Baker, 825 F.2d 772 (4th Cir. 1987)	§ 7.16
Tarkanian v. National Collegiate Athletic Ass'n, 741 P.2d 1345 (Nev. 1987), *cert. granted,* 108 S. Ct. 1011 (1988)	§§ 5.11, 5.14, App. M
Tarpley v. Salerno, 803 F.2d 57 (2d Cir. 1986)	§§ 9.7, 12.5
Tavarez v. O'Malley, 826 F.2d 671 (7th Cir. 1987)	§ 8.1
Taylor v. City of Fort Lauderdale, 810 F.2d 1551 (11th Cir. 1987)	§§ 15.11, 15.14, 15.20
Taylor v. Ledbetter, 818 F.2d 791 (11th Cir. 1987)	§§ 3.2, 3.5, 4.3
Taylor v. Ledbetter, 791 F.2d 881 (11th Cir. 1986)	§ 3.8
Taylor v. Watters, 636 F. Supp. 181 (E.D. Mich. 1986)	§ 3.8
Tennessee v. Garner, 471 U.S. 1 (1985)	§§ 3.4, 4.9, 7.16
Terry Properties, Inc. v. Standard Oil Co., 799 F.2d 1523 (11th Cir. 1986)	§ 21.8, App. L
Texaco v. Short, 454 U.S. 516 (1982)	§ 5.14
Texas v. New Mexico, 108 S. Ct. 1212 (1988)	App. E
Texas v. New Mexico, 475 U.S. 1084 (1986)	§ 18.2
Texas State Teachers v. Garland Indep. School Dist., 837 F.2d 190 (5th Cir.), *cert. granted,* 109 S. Ct. 51 (1988)	§ 15.11
Theis v. Smith, 827 F.2d 260 (7th Cir. 1987)	§ 7.18
Thomas v. Booker, 784 F.2d 299 (8th Cir.), *cert. denied,* 476 U.S. 1117 (1986)	§ 21.3
Thomas v. Capital Sec. Servs., Inc., 812 F.2d 984 (5th Cir. 1987)	§ 24.4
Thomas v. Cooper Indus., Inc., 640 F. Supp. 1374 (W.D.N.C. 1986)	§§ 17.3, 17.5, 17.6, 17.10, 18.6, 18.7, 18.9, 18.11, App. E

Case	*Book §*
Thomas v. Kippermann, 846 F.2d 1009 (5th Cir. 1988)	§ 3.6
Thomas v. Metroflight, Inc., 814 F.2d 1506 (10th Cir. 1987)	§ 23.2
Thomas v. Shipka, 818 F.2d 496 (6th Cir.), *modified,* 829 F.2d 570 (6th Cir. 1987)	§§ 1.3, 4.4, 10.6, 10.7
Thomas v. State Bd. of Medical Examiners, 807 F.2d 453 (5th Cir. 1987)	§ 12.7
Thomas S. v. Morrow, 781 F.2d 367 (4th Cir.), *cert. denied,* 107 S. Ct. 235 (1986)	§§ 5.5, 5.13, 7.17
Thompkins v. Belt, 828 F.2d 298 (5th Cir. 1987)	§ 14.11
Thompkins v. Stuttgart School Dist., 787 F.2d 439 (8th Cir. 1986)	§ 1.5
Thompson v. Barrett, 599 F. Supp. 806 (D.D.C. 1984)	§ 18.17
Thompson v. County of Rock, 648 F. Supp. 861 (W.D. Wis. 1986)	§ 4.6
Thompson v. Kennickell, 836 F.2d 616 (D.C. Cir. 1988)	§§ 18.17, 20.3, 20.4D
Thompson v. Kennickell, 797 F.2d 1015 (D.C. Cir. 1986)	§ 21.9
Thompson v. Thompson, 108 S. Ct. 513 (1988)	§ 3.12
Thompson v. Woodall, 819 F.2d 1052 (11th Cir. 1987)	§ 3.2
Thornburgh v. American College of Obstetricians, 106 S. Ct. 2169 (1986)	§ 12.3
Thorne v. City of El Segundo, 802 F.2d 1131 (9th Cir. 1986)	§§ 15.10, 16.9, 19.4, 19.7
Thourner v. Meyer, 803 F.2d 1093 (10th Cir. 1986)	§ 9.8
Thurman v. City of Torrington, 595 F. Supp. 1521 (D. Conn. 1984)	§ 3.2
Thurston v. United States, 810 F.2d 438 (4th Cir. 1987)	§§ 7.18, 9.8, 9.12
Tiffany v. Arizona Interscholastic Ass'n, Inc., 151 Ariz. 134, 726 P.2d 231 (Ct. App. 1986)	§ 15.17, App. M
Tolliver v. Amici, 800 F.2d 149 (7th Cir. 1986)	§ 16.3, App. C
Tomazzoli v. Sheedy, 804 F.2d 93 (7th Cir. 1986)	§§ 17.2, 17.5, 17.15, 18.3, 18.5, 18.6, 18.9, 18.10, 18.14, App. B, App. E
Tomer v. Gates, 811 F.2d 1240 (9th Cir. 1987)	§ 7.18
Tonya K. v. Board of Educ., 847 F.2d 1243 (7th Cir. 1988)	§§ 15.16, 16.8, 24.5
Torres v. Perales, 121 A.D.2d 386, 503 N.Y.S.2d 96 (2d Dep't 1986)	§§ 15.15, 15.17
Toussaint v. McCarthy, 826 F.2d 901 (9th Cir. 1987)	§§ 15.6, 17.17, 18.10, 19.3, 19.5, 24.6
Toussaint v. McCarthy, 801 F.2d 1080 (9th Cir. 1986), *cert. denied,* 107 S. Ct. 2462 (1987)	§ 8.6
Trahan v. Regan, 625 F. Supp. 1163 (D.D.C. 1985)	§§ 15.4, 17.5, 17.6, 17.17
Transport Careers v. National Home Study Council, 646 F. Supp. 1474 (N.D. Ind. 1986)	§§ 5.11, 5.14
Trans Sterling v. Bible, 804 F.2d 525 (9th Cir. 1986)	§ 14.15
Trapnell v. Ralston, 819 F.2d 182 (8th Cir. 1987)	§ 7.18
Travelers Social Club v. Pittsburgh, 685 F. Supp. 929 (W.D. Pa. 1988)	§ 2.5
Trevino v. Holly Sugar Corp., 811 F.2d 896 (5th Cir. 1987)	§§ 15.11, 23.3

Case	*Book §*
Tribble v. Gardner, 860 F.2d 321 (9th Cir. 1988)	§ 15.4
Tripati v. United States Immigration & Naturalization Serv., 784 F.2d 345 (10th Cir. 1986), *cert. denied,* 108 S. Ct. 755 (1988)	§ 7.6
Trujillo v. Board of County Comm'rs, 768 F.2d 1186 (10th Cir. 1985)	§ 11.3
Trujillo v. County of Santa Clara, 775 F.2d 1359 (9th Cir. 1985)	§ 15.17
Trujillo v. Goodman, 825 F.2d 1453 (10th Cir. 1987)	§ 3.3
Tubbesing v. Arnold, 742 F.2d 401 (8th Cir. 1984)	§ 7.18
Tucker v. Callahan, 663 F. Supp. 375 (M.D. Tenn. 1987)	§ 12.11
Tucker v. Phyfer, 819 F.2d 1030 (11th Cir. 1987)	§§ 2.5, 13.6
Tucker v. Summers, 784 F.2d 654 (5th Cir. 1986)	§§ 15.4, 15.13, 15.20
Tuggle v. Barksdale, 641 F. Supp. 34 (W.D. Tenn. 1985)	§ 17.15
Tull v. United States, 107 S. Ct. 1831 (1987)	§ 14.2
Tulsa Professional Collection Servs. v. Pope, 108 S. Ct. 1340 (1988)	§ 5.14
Tunca v. Lutheran Gen. Hosp., 844 F.2d 411 (7th Cir. 1988)	§ 5.14
Tunstall v. Office of Judicial Support, 820 F.2d 631 (3d Cir. 1987)	§ 5.14
Turk v. McCarthy, 661 F. Supp. 1526 (E.D.N.Y. 1987)	§ 1.5
Turner v. Barry, 856 F.2d 1539 (D.C. Cir. 1988)	§ 7.6
Turner v. Dammon, 848 F.2d 440 (4th Cir. 1988)	§§ 7.16, 7.18
Turner v. Orr, 785 F.2d 1498 (11th Cir. 1986)	§§ 15.8, 17.8
Uberoi v. University of Colo., 713 P.2d 894 (Colo. 1986)	§§ 3.4, 3.5, 5.2
Umphlet v. Connick, 815 F.2d 1061 (5th Cir. 1987)	§ 12.10
Unger v. Blum, 117 A.D.2d 607, 498 N.Y.S.2d 154 (2d Dep't 1986)	§ 16.8
Unified School Dist. v. Newton, 673 F. Supp. 418 (D. Kan. 1987)	§ 15.16
United Books v. Conte, 739 F.2d 30 (1st Cir. 1984)	§ 12.7
United Mine Workers v. Gibbs, 383 U.S. 715 (1966)	§ 1.5
United Servs. Auto. Ass'n v. Muir, 792 F.2d 356 (3d Cir. 1986), *cert. denied,* 107 S. Ct. 875 (1987)	§§ 12.2, 12.3
United States v. Alabama, 791 F.2d 1450 (11th Cir. 1986), *cert. denied sub nom.* Board of Trustees v. State Bd., 107 S. Ct. 1287 (1987)	§ 2.3
United States v. Arkansas, 787 F.2d 304 (8th Cir. 1986)	§ 21.5
United States v. City of Yonkers, 856 F.2d 444 (2d Cir. 1988)	§ 7.10
United States v. Concentrated Phosphate Export Ass'n, 393 U.S. 199 (1968)	§ 13.4
United States v. Marengo County Comm'n, 667 F. Supp. 786 (S.D. Ala. 1987)	§§ 18.14, 18.15, 19.4, App. E
United States v. Metropolitan Dist. Comm'n, 847 F.2d 12 (1st Cir. 1988)	§§ 17.2, 18.5, 18.9, 18.14, 24.4
United States v. Munsingwear, 340 U.S. 36 (1950)	§ 13.2
United States v. Salerno, 107 S. Ct. 2095 (1987)	§ 3.3

Case	*Book §*
United States v. State of Wash., 626 F. Supp. 1405 (W.D. Wash. 1985), *rev'd,* 813 F.2d 1020 (9th Cir. 1987), *cert. denied,* 108 S. Ct. 1593 (1988)	§§ 1.3A, 3.11, 15.15, 18.17
United States v. Wallace, 673 F. Supp. 205 (S.D. Tex. 1987)	§ 3.6
United States v. Yonkers Bd. of Educ., 118 F.R.D. 326 (S.D.N.Y. 1987)	§ 21.8, App. E
United States *ex. rel.* Chunie v. Ringrose, 788 F.2d 638 (9th Cir. 1986)	App. L
United States Dep't of Treasury v. Galioto, 106 S. Ct. 2683 (1986)	§ 13.4
United Steelworkers v. Phelps Dodge, 833 F.2d 804 (9th Cir. 1987)	§ 5.13
University Club v. City of N.Y., 842 F.2d 37 (2d Cir. 1988)	§ 12.8
University of Tenn. v. Elliott, 106 S. Ct. 3220 (1986)	§ 9.10
Unwin v. Campbell, 863 F.2d 124 (1st Cir. 1988)	§ 7.18
Urban v. Henley, 654 F. Supp. 870 (D. Kan. 1987)	§§ 9.3, 9.8, 9.12
Urban League v. Township Comm., 222 N.J. Super. 131, 536 A.2d 287 (App. Div. 1987)	App. M
Usher v. Los Angeles, 828 F.2d 556 (9th Cir. 1987)	§§ 3.6, 10.6, 10.7
Ustrak v. Fairman, 851 F.2d 983 (7th Cir. 1988)	§§ 15.6, 19.4, 19.5, 19.7, 22.1, 24.5, 24.6, App. B
Ustrak v. Fairman, 781 F.2d 573 (7th Cir.), *cert. denied,* 107 S. Ct. 95 (1986)	§ 14.11
Valasquez v. Senko, 813 F.2d 1509 (9th Cir. 1987)	§ 7.18
Valley Wood Preserving v. Paul, 785 F.2d 751 (9th Cir. 1986)	§ 9.10
Valliere v. Kaplan, 694 F. Supp. 517 (N.D. Ill. 1988)	§ 1.5
Vanaman v. Palmer, 506 A.2d 190 (Del. 1986)	§ 10.6
Van Cauwenberghe v. Biard, 108 S. Ct. 1945 (1988)	§ 7.18
Vance v. Hegstrom, 629 F. Supp. 747 (D. Or. 1985)	§ 17.4, App. C, App. E
Vandenplas v. City of Muskego, 612 F. Supp. 342 (E.D. Wis. 1985), *rev'd,* 797 F.2d 425 (7th Cir. 1986)	§§ 23.2, 23.3, 23.5, 24.4, App. L
Van Meter v. Township of Maplewood, 696 F. Supp. 1024 (D.N.J. 1988)	§ 3.11
Vann v. Board of Tax Assessors, 186 Ga. App. 208, 367 S.E.2d 43 (1988)	§ 12.13
Van Sant v. United States Postal Serv., 805 F.2d 141 (4th Cir. 1986)	§§ 15.10, 19.6, 19.7, 19.9, App. F
Vantage Healthcare Corp. v. Virginia Bd. of Medical Assistance Servs., 684 F. Supp. 1329 (E.D. Va. 1988)	§ 3.11
Vargas v. Salvation Army, 649 F. Supp. 763 (N.D. Ill. 1986)	§§ 5.11, 5.14
Varney v. Genesee County Sheriff, 156 Mich. App. 539, 402 N.W.2d 57 (1986)	App. M
Vaughan v. Ricketts, 859 F.2d 736 (9th Cir. 1988)	§ 7.13A
Vaughner v. Pulito, 804 F.2d 873 (5th Cir. 1986)	§ 23.2, App. L

Case	*Book §*
Vaughns v. Board of Educ., 627 F. Supp. 837 (D. Md. 1985)	§§ 17.14, 17.17, 18.7, 18.17, 19.4, 21.8, 21.9, 24.7, App. E, App. K
Vazquez Rios v. Hernandez Colon, 819 F.2d 319 (1st Cir. 1987)	§ 7.18
Venetie, Native Village of v. Alaska, 687 F. Supp. 1380 (D. Alaska 1988)	§ 6.3
Victorian v. Miller, 813 F.2d 718 (5th Cir. 1987)	§§ 3.11, 3.12, 15.15
Video Int'l Prod. v. Warner-Amex Cable Co., 858 F.2d 1075 (5th Cir. 1988)	§§ 4.7, 5.8, 5.13
Vinson v. Campbell County Fiscal Court, 820 F.2d 194 (6th Cir. 1987)	§§ 3.3, 3.5, 3.8, 3.9, 4.9
Virginia v. American Booksellers Ass'n, 108 S. Ct. 636 (1988)	§§ 2.5, 2.6, 12.3
Visa Int'l Serv. Assoc. v. Bankcard Holders, 784 F.2d 1472 (9th Cir. 1986)	§ 24.2
Vitalone v. Curran, 665 F. Supp. 964 (D. Me. 1987)	§ 7.16
Vodila v. Clelland, 836 F.2d 231 (6th Cir. 1987)	§§ 10.6, 10.7
Volk v. Coler, 845 F.2d 1422 (7th Cir. 1988)	§ 14.2
Vosburg v. Solem, 845 F.2d 763 (8th Cir. 1988)	§§ 14.6, 14.11
Wade v. Hegner, 804 F.2d 67 (7th Cir. 1986)	§ 7.12
Wade v. Orange County Sheriff's Office, 844 F.2d 951 (2d Cir. 1988)	§ 14.2
Wadsworth v. Clindon, 846 F.2d 265 (4th Cir. 1988)	§ 19.7
Wagenmann v. Adams, 829 F.2d 196 (1st Cir. 1987)	§§ 5.13, 15.6, 17.13, 19.3, 21.8, 21.10, 24.6
Wakefield v. Mathews, 852 F.2d 482 (9th Cir. 1988)	§ 22.9
Waldron v. Collins, 788 F.2d 736 (11th Cir.), *cert. denied,* 107 S. Ct. 274 (1986)	§ 12.13
Walje v. City of Winchester, 827 F.2d 10 (6th Cir. 1987)	§§ 14.6, 14.8
Walker v. Dugger, 860 F.2d 1010 (11th Cir. 1988)	§ 6.5
Walker v. Maruffi, 106 N.M. 763, 737 P.2d 544 (Ct. App. 1987)	§ 10.6
Walker v. Rowe, 791 F.2d 507 (7th Cir.), *cert. denied,* 107 S. Ct. 597 (1986)	§§ 3.2, 4.3
Walker v. Schaeffer, 854 F.2d 138 (6th Cir. 1988)	§ 3.7
Wall v. Heath, 622 F. Supp. 105 (S.D. Miss. 1985)	§ 9.3
Walsh v. Franco, 849 F.2d 66 (2d Cir. 1988)	§ 7.13A
Walsh v. Mellas, 837 F.2d 789 (7th Cir.), *cert. denied,* 108 S. Ct. 2832 (1988)	§ 3.4A
Walters v. City of Atlanta, 803 F.2d 1135 (11th Cir. 1986)	App. E
Ward v. Hunt, 667 F. Supp. 782 (N.D. Ala. 1987)	§ 6.9
Ward v. Portland, 857 F.2d 1373 (9th Cir. 1988)	§ 2.5
Ward v. San Diego County, 791 F.2d 1329 (9th Cir. 1986), *cert. denied,* 107 S. Ct. 3263 (1987)	§§ 7.13, 15.4, 15.13, 15.20
Ward v. Texas Employment Comm'n, 823 F.2d 907 (5th Cir. 1987)	§ 14.2
Warner v. Graham, 845 F.2d 179 (8th Cir. 1988)	§ 7.13
Washco v. Darby Borough Police Dep't, 688 F. Supp. 1026 (E.D. Pa. 1988)	§ 1.5

Case	*Book §*
Washington v. Breaux, 782 F.2d 553 (5th Cir. 1986)	§ 10.6
Washington v. District of Columbia, 802 F.2d 1478 (D.C. Cir. 1986)	§§ 3.2, 3.5, 4.3
Washington v. Kirksey, 811 F.2d 561 (11th Cir.), *cert. denied,* 108 S. Ct. 96 (1987)	§ 14.13
Waste Management of Wis. v. Fokakis, 614 F.2d 138 (7th Cir.), *cert. denied,* 449 U.S. 1060 (1980), *reh'g denied,* 450 U.S. 960 (1981)	§ 8.6
Watertown Equip. Co. v. Norwest Bank, 830 F.2d 1487 (8th Cir. 1987), *cert. denied,* 108 S. Ct. 1723 (1988)	§§ 5.13, 7.12
Watseka, City of v. Illinois Pub. Action Council, 796 F.2d 1547 (7th Cir. 1986), *aff'd,* 107 S. Ct. 919 (1987)	§§ 14.8, 14.12
Watkins v. Blinzinger, 789 F.2d 474 (7th Cir. 1986), *cert. denied,* 107 S. Ct. 1976 (1987)	§ 6.5
Watkins v. McMillan, 779 F.2d 1465 (11th Cir. 1985)	§ 24.2
Watson v. Buck, 313 U.S. 387 (1941)	§ 12.9
Watson v. Kansas City, 857 F.2d 690 (10th Cir. 1988)	§§ 3.2, 4.6, 4.8
Watts v. Burkhart, 854 F.2d 839 (6th Cir. 1988)	§ 12.8
Webb v. City of Chester, 813 F.2d 824 (7th Cir. 1987)	§§ 4.7, 14.9A
Weber v. Dell, 804 F.2d 796 (2d Cir. 1986)	§§ 4.7, 7.13A
Webster v. Houston, 735 F.2d 838 (5th Cir. 1984)	§ 4.7
Webster v. Sowders, 846 F.2d 1032 (6th Cir. 1988)	§§ 7.18, 15.20, 24.4
Wedra v. Thomas, 623 F. Supp. 272 (S.D.N.Y. 1985)	§ 18.8
Weiser v. Koch, 632 F. Supp. 1369 (S.D.N.Y. 1986)	§§ 2.5, 12.11
Welch v. State Dep't of Highways & Pub. Transp., 107 S. Ct. 2941 (1987)	§ 6.3
Wells v. Franzen, 777 F.2d 1258 (7th Cir. 1985)	§ 7.17
Wells v. Walker, 852 F.2d 368 (8th Cir. 1988)	§§ 3.2, 4.3
Weseman v. Meeker County, 659 F. Supp. 1571 (D. Minn. 1987)	§ 7.6
West v. Atkins, 108 S. Ct. 2250 (1988)	§§ 5.4, 5.5, 5.11, 5.14
West v. Conrail, 107 S. Ct. 1538 (1987)	§ 10.4
Westborough Mall v. City of Cape Girardeau, 794 F.2d 330 (8th Cir. 1986), *cert. denied,* 107 S. Ct. 1373 (1987)	§§ 3.8, 4.6
Westfall v. Erwin, 108 S. Ct. 580 (1988)	§ 7.12
Western Air Lines, Inc. v. Port Auth., 817 F.2d 222 (2d Cir. 1987)	§§ 3.11, 15.15
West Va. v. United States, 479 U.S. 305 (1987)	§ 14.16
Whalen v. Roe, 429 U.S. 589 (1977)	§ 7.13A
Wharton v. Knefel, 562 F.2d 550 (8th Cir. 1977)	§ 15.4
Whatley v. Philo, 817 F.2d 19 (5th Cir. 1987)	§§ 3.6, 7.18
Wheeler v. Durham City Bd. of Educ., 585 F.2d 618 (4th Cir. 1978)	§ 21.8
White v. Frank, 855 F.2d 956 (2d Cir. 1988)	§§ 3.6, 7.9
White v. Frank, 680 F. Supp. 629 (S.D.N.Y. 1988)	§ 7.9
White v. Gerbitz, 860 F.2d 661 (6th Cir. 1988)	§ 14.15
White v. New Hampshire Dep't of Employment Sec., 455 U.S. 445 (1982)	§ 24.4
White v. Pierce County, 797 F.2d 812 (9th Cir. 1986)	§ 7.18
Whiteley v. Warden, 401 U.S. 560 (1971)	§ 7.16

Case	*Book §*
White Mountain Apache Tribe v. Williams, 798 F.2d 1205 (9th Cir. 1984), *opinion amended,* 810 F.2d 844 (9th Cir.), *cert. denied,* 479 U.S. 1060 (1987)	§§ 3.2, 12.5, 15.15, 15.17
Whitley v. Albers, 106 S. Ct. 1078 (1986)	§ 3.4A
Wichert v. Walter, 606 F. Supp. 1516 (D.N.J. 1985)	§ 12.9
Wicker v. Board of Educ., 826 F.2d 442 (6th Cir. 1987)	§§ 9.7, 12.5
Wickwire v. State, 725 P.2d 695 (Alaska 1986)	§ 5.2
Wideman v. Shallowford Community Hosp., 826 F.2d 1030 (11th Cir. 1987)	§§ 3.2, 4.3
Wierstak v. Heffernan, 789 F.2d 968 (1st Cir. 1986)	§ 4.9
Wiggins v. Heckler, 639 F. Supp. 126 (E.D.N.C. 1986)	§ 18.8
Wilbanks v. Smith County, 661 F. Supp. 212 (E.D. Tex. 1987)	§ 14.5
Wilder v. Bernstein, 645 F. Supp. 1292 (S.D.N.Y. 1986)	§§ 5.11, 5.14
Wilkinson v. Forst, 832 F.2d 1330 (2d Cir. 1987), *cert. denied,* 108 S. Ct. 1593 (1988)	§ 2.2
Willard v. City of Los Angeles, 803 F.2d 526 (9th Cir. 1986)	§§ 22.8, 24.1
Williams v. Atlanta, 794 F.2d 624 (11th Cir. 1986)	§§ 10.6, 10.7
Williams v. Boles, 841 F.2d 181 (7th Cir. 1987)	§ 3.4A
Williams v. Butler, 802 F.2d 296 (8th Cir. 1986), *vacated,* 108 S. Ct. 1102 (1988)	§ 4.7
Williams v. D'Elia, 119 A.D.2d 678, 501 N.Y.S.2d 365 (2d Dep't 1986)	§ 15.17
Williams v. Hartje, 827 F.2d 1203 (8th Cir. 1987)	§§ 7.8, 10.6
Williams v. Hepting, 844 F.2d 138 (3d Cir.), *cert. denied,* 109 S. Ct. 135 (1988)	§§ 7.9, 8.6
Williams v. Kobel, 789 F.2d 463 (7th Cir. 1986)	§§ 9.3, 9.8, 9.12, App. L
Williams v. Lane, 851 F.2d 867 (7th Cir. 1988)	§§ 7.18, 14.1
Williams v. Mensey, 785 F.2d 631 (8th Cir. 1986)	App. F
Williams v. North, 685 F. Supp. 502 (D. Md. 1988)	§ 7.4
Williams v. Omodt, 640 F. Supp. 120 (D. Minn. 1986)	§ 24.2
Williams v. St. Louis, 783 F.2d 114 (8th Cir. 1986)	§ 5.11
Williams v. St. Louis County, 812 F.2d 1079 (8th Cir. 1987)	§ 3.8
Williams v. St. Louis County, 643 F. Supp. 1150 (E.D. Mo.), *aff'd,* 785 F.2d 631 (8th Cir. 1986)	§ 15.10
Williams v. Smith, 781 F.2d 319 (2d Cir. 1986)	§§ 4.11, 7.13
Williamson v. Handy Button Mach. Co., 817 F.2d 1290 (7th Cir. 1987)	§ 14.16
Williamson County Regional Planning Comm'n v. Hamilton Bank, 473 U.S. 172 (1985)	§§ 8.2, 8.3A
Willner v. Budig, 848 F.2d 1032 (10th Cir. 1988)	§ 24.2
Willocks v. Dodenhoff, 110 F.R.D. 652 (D. Conn.), *aff'd,* 805 F.2d 392 (2d Cir. 1986)	§§ 3.5, 7.16
Wilson v. Civil Town of Clayton, 839 F.2d 375 (7th Cir. 1988)	§ 3.8
Wilson v. Garcia, 471 U.S. 261 (1985)	§§ 10.6, 10.7
Wilson v. Lyng, 662 F. Supp. 1391 (E.D.N.C. 1987)	§§ 6.9, 6.11
Wilson v. Stocker, 819 F.2d 943 (10th Cir. 1987)	§§ 16.6, 16.13
Wing v. Britton, 748 F.2d 494 (8th Cir. 1984)	§ 3.3
Winicki v. Mallard, 783 F.2d 1567 (11th Cir.), *cert. denied,* 107 S. Ct. 70 (1986)	§ 12.13

Case	*Book §*
Wise v. Pea Ridge School Dist., 855 F.2d 560 (8th Cir. 1988)	§ 3.3
Woe by Woe v. Cuomo, 638 F. Supp. 1506 (E.D.N.Y. 1986)	§ 15.13
Wolfenbarger v. Williams, 826 F.2d 930 (10th Cir. 1987)	§ 7.8
Wood v. Ostrander, 851 F.2d 1212 (9th Cir. 1988)	§§ 3.3, 3.5, 3.9, 7.13A
Woodard v. Hardee's Restaurant, 643 F. Supp. 691 (W.D. Mo. 1986)	§§ 15.17, 16.6, 16.9, App. E, App. J
Woods v. Michigan City, 694 F. Supp. 1344 (N.D. Ind. 1988)	§ 4.7
Woods v. White, 689 F. Supp. 874 (W.D. Wis. 1988)	§ 7.13A
Wool v. Maryland Nat'l Capital Park & Planning Comm'n, 664 F. Supp. 225 (D. Md. 1987)	§ 9.10
World Famous Drinking Emporium v. City of Tempe, 820 F.2d 1079 (9th Cir. 1987)	§ 12.8
Wort v. Vierling, 778 F.2d 1233 (7th Cir. 1985)	§ 24.4
Wozniak v. DuPage County, 845 F.2d 677 (7th Cir. 1988)	§§ 9.4, 9.5
Wrenn v. Gould, 808 F.2d 493 (6th Cir. 1986)	§ 23.2
Wright v. McClain, 835 F.2d 143 (6th Cir. 1987)	§ 12.12
Wright v. McClain, 626 F. Supp. 1073 (W.D. Tenn. 1986)	§ 7.6
Wright v. Newsome, 795 F.2d 964 (11th Cir. 1986)	§§ 1.5, 4.8
Wright v. Roanoke Redevelopment & Hous. Auth., 479 U.S. 418 (1987)	§§ 3.11, 15.15
Wright v. South Ark. Regional Health Center, 800 F.2d 199 (8th Cir. 1986)	§ 7.18
Wulf v. City of Wichita, 644 F. Supp. 1211 (D. Kan. 1986)	§ 14.8
Wycoff v. Menke, 773 F.2d 983 (8th Cir. 1985)	§ 10.6
Yancy v. McDevitt, 802 F.2d 1025 (8th Cir. 1986)	§ 9.10
Yates v. Jamison, 782 F.2d 1182 (4th Cir. 1986)	§ 3.8
Yates v. Philip Morris, 690 F. Supp. 180 (S.D.N.Y. 1988)	§ 9.10
Yohay v. City of Alexandria Employees Credit Union, 827 F.2d 967 (4th Cir. 1987)	§§ 17.14, 19.7
York v. Alabama State Bd. of Educ., 631 F. Supp. 78 (M.D. Ala. 1986)	§§ 16.13, 17.4, 17.5, 17.13, 18.7, 21.5, App. E, App. F
Young v. Barker, 158 Mich. App. 709, 405 N.W.2d 395 (1987)	App. M
Young v. Biggers, 820 F.2d 727 (5th Cir. 1987)	§ 10.7
Young v. Lynch, 846 F.2d 960 (4th Cir. 1988)	§ 7.18
Young v. Pierce, 822 F.2d 1376 (5th Cir. 1987)	§ 18.17
Young v. Sedgwick, 660 F. Supp. 918 (D. Kan. 1987)	§ 4.8
Youngberg v. Romeo, 457 U.S. 307 (1982)	§§ 3.5, 7.13, 7.17
Zabkowicz v. West Bend Co., 789 F.2d 540 (7th Cir. 1986)	§§ 15.10, 17.14, 17.17, 19.5, 21.8, App. B, App. D, App. F
Zacharias v. Shell Oil Co., 627 F. Supp. 31 (E.D.N.Y. 1984)	§ 18.1
Zalman v. Armstrong, 802 F.2d 199 (6th Cir. 1986)	§§ 12.7, 12.9
Zamlen v. City of Cleveland, 655 F. Supp. 1451 (N.D. Ohio 1987)	§ 15.18
Zemsky v. New York City, 821 F.2d 148 (2d Cir.), *cert. denied,* 108 S. Ct. 456 (1987)	§ 12.11

Case	*Book §*
Zipes v. Trans World Airlines, Inc., 846 F.2d 434 (7th Cir. 1988), *cert. granted,* 57 U.S.L.W. 3466 (U.S. Jan. 17, 1989)	§§ 16.6, 16.11, 20.5
Zizka v. Water Pollution Control Auth., 195 Conn. 682, 490 A.2d 509 (1985)	§ 12.13
Zwarton v. Chicago, 625 F. Supp. 1211 (N.D. Ill. 1985)	§ 4.12

United States Code Section	*Book §*
5 U.S.C. § 552(a)(4)(E)	§§ 15.19, 24.4
7 U.S.C. § 2011 *et seq.* (Food Stamp Act)	§§ 3.11, 15.15
15 U.S.C. §§ 1601 *et seq.* (Consumer Credit Protection Act)	§§ 17.2, 17.3, 17.10, 17.12, 17.15, 18.17, 24.3, App. C, App. E, App. K
15 U.S.C. § 1640(a) (Truth-in-Lending Act)	§§ 21.4, 22.5
15 U.S.C. § 1640(a)(3) (Truth-in-Lending Act)	§§ 17.10, 18.3, 18.7, 24.1, App. C, App. E
15 U.S.C. § 1673 (Consumer Credit Protection Act)	§ 3.11
15 U.S.C. § 1681n (Fair Credit Reporting Act)	§ 17.10
15 U.S.C. § 1681n(3) (Fair Credit Reporting Act)	§ 19.7
15 U.S.C. § 1681o (Fair Credit Reporting Act)	§ 17.10
15 U.S.C. § 1692k(a) (Fair Debt Collection Practices Act)	§ 17.10
15 U.S.C. § 2805(d)(1)	§ 21.4
15 U.S.C. § 2805(d)(1)(C)	§ 18.17
15 U.S.C. § 2805(d)(3) (Petroleum Marketing Practices Act)	§§ 16.4, 18.1
18 U.S.C. § 3182 (Extradition Statute)	§ 3.11
20 U.S.C. § 1232g (Family Education Rights and Privacy Act)	§ 3.11
20 U.S.C. § 1400 *et seq.* (Education of the Handicapped Act)	§§ 8.3, 15.6, 15.14, 16.8, 19.7, 21.4
20 U.S.C. § 1415	§§ 15.16, 17.6, 17.15
20 U.S.C. § 1415(e)	§§ 15.10, 16.3, 16.8, 24.1, 24.2, 24.4
20 U.S.C. § 1415(e)(4)(B)	§ 15.16
20 U.S.C. § 1415(e)(4)(C)	§ 15.16
20 U.S.C. § 1415(e)(4)(D)	§ 15.16
20 U.S.C. § 1415(e)(4)(E)	§ 15.16
20 U.S.C. § 1415(e)(4)(F)	§ 15.16
20 U.S.C. § 1415(e)(4)(G)	§ 15.16
20 U.S.C. § 1415(f)	§§ 8.3, 15.16
23 U.S.C. § 101	§ 3.11
25 U.S.C. §§ 261-264 (Indian Trader Act)	§ 3.11
25 U.S.C. §§ 450a-450n (Indian Self-Determination & Educational Assistance Act)	§§ 3.2, 3.11, 15.14, 15.15

United States Code Section	*Book §*
25 U.S.C. §§ 1301-1303 (Indian Civil Rights Act)	§ 5.6
26 U.S.C. §§ 3402-3407	§ 3.11
28 U.S.C. § 1291	§ 24.4
28 U.S.C. § 1343	§ 5.6
28 U.S.C. § 1343(a)(3)	§ 15.1
28 U.S.C. § 1415 (Handicapped Children's Protection Act of 1986)	§ 3.2
28 U.S.C. § 1821	§ 21.8
28 U.S.C. § 1920	§§ 21.8, 21.9
28 U.S.C. § 1920(3)	§ 21.8
28 U.S.C. § 1927	§ 23.4
28 U.S.C. § 1961(a)	§ 21.9
28 U.S.C. §§ 2201-02	§ 15.1
28 U.S.C. § 2412 (Equal Access to Justice Act)	§§ 15.3, 15.9, 15.13, 15.14, 15.18, 17.5, 17.6, 17.17, 18.1, 18.6, 18.8, 18.13, 18.17, 19.3, 19.6, 19.7, 19.9, 21.8, 22.8, 24.4, 24.5, 24.6, App. E
28 U.S.C. § 2412(b) (Equal Access to Justice Act)	§§ 15.15, 16.10, 24.2
28 U.S.C. § 2412(d) (Equal Access to Justice Act)	§ 15.13
28 U.S.C. § 2412(f) (Equal Access to Justice Act)	§ 21.9
28 U.S.C. § 2671 (Federal Tort Claims Act)	§ 16.10
29 U.S.C. § 151 *et seq.* (National Labor Relations Act)	§ 3.11
29 U.S.C. § 216(b) (Fair Labor Standards Act)	§§ 17.3, 19.5, 21.3, 21.4, 21.8, App. F
29 U.S.C. § 412 (Labor-Management Reporting & Disclosure Act)	§ 16.15
29 U.S.C. § 623 *et seq.* (Age Discrimination in Employment Act)	§ 3.11
29 U.S.C. § 626(b) (Age Discrimination in Employment Act)	§§ 17.6, 17.9, 17.16, 18.11, 19.3, 19.4, 19.5, 20.4E, App. F
29 U.S.C. § 791 *et seq.* (Rehabilitation Act)	§ 3.11
29 U.S.C. § 794a (Rehabilitation Act)	§§ 3.11, 15.4
29 U.S.C. § 794a(b) (Rehabilitation Act)	§§ 15.4, 15.13, 15.14
29 U.S.C. § 801	§ 3.11
29 U.S.C. § 1415(e)	§ 15.13
30 U.S.C. § 1270(d) (Surface Mining Control & Reclamation Act)	§ 17.6, App. B
33 U.S.C. § 1365(d) (Federal Water Pollution Control Act)	§§ 17.2, 18.5, 20.4D, 24.4
42 U.S.C. § 291 *et seq.* (Hill-Burton Act)	§ 3.11
42 U.S.C. § 291c(e)	§ 15.15
42 U.S.C. § 300 (Public Health Service Act)	§ 3.11

AUTHORITIES

United States Code Section	*Book §*
42 U.S.C. § 300a *et seq.* (Public Health Service Act)	§ 3.11
42 U.S.C. § 422 (pt. Social Security Act)	§ 3.11
42 U.S.C. §§ 620-628 (Adoption Assistance Act)	§ 3.11
42 U.S.C. § 671	§ 3.11
42 U.S.C. § 675	§ 3.11
42 U.S.C. §§ 1401 *et seq.* (United States Housing Act of 1937)	§§ 15.14, 15.15
42 U.S.C. § 1437 (United States Housing Act)	§ 3.11
42 U.S.C. § 1437f	§ 3.11
42 U.S.C. § 1738	§§ 9.3, 9.5
42 U.S.C. § 1973c (Voting Rights Act)	§ 16.5
42 U.S.C. § 1973l(e) (Voting Rights Act)	§§ 15.13, 15.14, 17.6, 18.9, 21.8, App. F, App. K
42 U.S.C. § 1981	§§ 1.3A, 9.4, 9.10, 10.6, 15.1, 15.15
42 U.S.C. § 1982	§§ 15.1, 15.15
42 U.S.C. § 1986	§ 16.10
42 U.S.C. § 1997e (Civil Rights of Institutionalized Persons Act)	§ 8.3
42 U.S.C. § 2000d *et seq.*	§ 15.1
42 U.S.C. § 2000e *et seq.* (Civil Rights Act of 1964)	§ 3.11
42 U.S.C. § 2000e-5(k)	§ 15.19
42 U.S.C. § 2996 *et seq.* (Legal Services Corporation Act)	§ 3.11
42 U.S.C. § 3612(c) (Fair Housing Act)	§§ 17.14, 21.8, App. M
42 U.S.C. § 4635	§ 3.11
42 U.S.C. §§ 6022-6023 (Developmental Disability Act)	§ 3.11
42 U.S.C. § 7607(f) (Clean Air Act)	§§ 17.14, 18.5, App. D, App. F
42 U.S.C. § 8261 *et seq.* (Low Income Home Energy Assistance Energy Act)	§ 3.11
43 U.S.C. § 1349(a)(5) (Outer Continental Shelf Act)	§ 15.20
47 U.S.C. § 605	§ 3.11
48 U.S.C. § 7604(d) (Clean Air Act)	§ 15.8
49 U.S.C. § 1305(a) (Aviation Act)	§ 3.11
49 U.S.C. § 1349(a) (Aviation Act)	§ 3.11
49 U.S.C. § 2210 (Airport & Airway Development Act)	§ 3.11
Pub. L. No. 89-152, § 213, 83 Stat. 389 (1969)	§ 15.15
Pub. L. No. 97-35, § 322, 95 Stat. 400 (1978)	§ 15.15
Pub. L. No. 99-372, 100 Stat. 796 (1986) (Handicapped Children's Protection Act of 1986)	§§ 3.2, 15.15, 15.16, 16.8
Pub. L. No. 99-506, 100 Stat. ____ (1986) (Rehabilitation Act Amendments of 1986)	§ 15.16

INDEX